T0291208

Central Bank Independence and the Legacy of the German Past

The 2008 financial crisis led to an increasing number of political attacks on central banks. The recent spotlight on central bank independence is reminiscent of the fiery debates amongst Germany's political elites in 1949 on the same issue, debates that were sparked by the establishment of West Germany in that year. Simon Mee shows how, with the establishment of West Germany's central bank – today's Deutsche Bundesbank – the country's monetary history became a political football, as central bankers, politicians, industrialists and trade unionists all vied for influence over the legal provisions that set out the remit of the future monetary authority. The author reveals how a specific version of inter-war history, one that stresses the lessons learned from Germany's periods of inflation, was weaponised and attached to a political, contemporary argument for an independent central bank. The book challenges assumptions around the evolution of central bank independence, a topic of continued relevance today.

SIMON MEE is a former Theodor Heuss Research Fellow of the University of Oxford and Alexander von Humboldt-Stiftung. He studied at the universities of Dublin, Cambridge and Oxford. His Oxford doctoral research on the Bundesbank went on to win the 2017 PhD Prize of the German Historical Institute London.

Central Bank Independence and the Legacy of the German Past

Simon Mee

CAMBRIDGE
UNIVERSITY PRESS

CAMBRIDGE
UNIVERSITY PRESS

University Printing House, Cambridge CB2 8BS, United Kingdom

One Liberty Plaza, 20th Floor, New York, NY 10006, USA

477 Williamstown Road, Port Melbourne, VIC 3207, Australia

314–321, 3rd Floor, Plot 3, Splendor Forum, Jasola District Centre,
New Delhi – 110025, India

79 Anson Road, #06–04/06, Singapore 079906

Cambridge University Press is part of the University of Cambridge.

It furthers the University's mission by disseminating knowledge in the pursuit of
education, learning, and research at the highest international levels of excellence.

www.cambridge.org
Information on this title: www.cambridge.org/9781108499781
DOI: 10.1017/9781108759601

First published 2019

Printed in the United Kingdom by TJ International Ltd, Padstow Cornwall

A catalogue record for this publication is available from the British Library.

Library of Congress Cataloging-in-Publication Data
Names: Mee, Simon, 1986– author.
Title: Central bank independence and the legacy of the German past /
    Simon Mee.
Description: Cambridge, United Kingdom ; New York, NY : Cambridge
    University Press, 2019. | Includes bibliographical references and index.
Identifiers: LCCN 2019019442 | ISBN 9781108499781 (hardback) |
    ISBN 9781108731300 (pbk.)
Subjects: LCSH: Banks and banking, Central–Germany–History. |
    Monetary policy–Germany–History. | Germany–Economic policy. |
    Germany–Economic conditions.
Classification: LCC HG3054 .M44 2019 | DDC 332.1/10943–dc23
LC record available at https://lccn.loc.gov/2019019442

ISBN 978-1-108-49978-1 Hardback

For my father, Frank

Contents

List of Figures	*page* viii
List of Tables	ix
Acknowledgements	x
List of Abbreviations	xiii
Introduction	1
1 In Search of the Reichsbank	33
2 The Bank deutscher Länder and the Foundation of West Germany, 1948–1951	90
3 Adenauer's Challenge: The 'Gürzenich Affair' and the Bank deutscher Länder, 1956–1957	149
4 The Shadow of National Socialism: Karl Blessing and the Bundesbank in 1965	192
5 The Bundesbank, Social Democracy and the Era of the 'Great Inflation', 1970–1978	252
Conclusion	314
Bibliography	333
Index	346

Figures

1.1 A reichsmark banknote dated 6 February 1920. *page* 51
1.2 A reichsmark banknote dated 1 September 1923. 51
1.3 Hjalmar Schacht. 58
1.4 Wilhelm Vocke. 60
1.5 A cartoon with the title 'Independence of the Reichsbank', published in *Kladderadatsch*, 2 February 1930. 64
1.6 The signatures found on the Reichsbank memorandum sent to Adolf Hitler on 7 January 1939. 74
2.1 The Bank deutscher Länder building in Frankfurt in 1950. 106
3.1 Wilhem Vocke portrayed as the 'chancellor of the deutschmark' on the front page of *Der Spiegel*, 6 June 1956. 178
3.2 An advertisement for *Gesundes Geld*, a collection of Vocke's speeches published in 1956. 182
4.1 Karl Blessing, the first president of the Bundesbank, on the front cover of *Der Spiegel*, 17 August 1960. 200
4.2 Viktor von der Lippe, head of the Bundesbank's press department and personal advisor to Vocke and Blessing. 206
5.1 Karl Klasen, president of the Bundesbank, 1970–7. 260
5.2 Otmar Emminger, vice president of the Bundesbank, 1970–7, and later president 1977–9. 266

Tables

4.1 Nazi party membership of leading West German central
   bank officials.   *page* 210
4.2 Public opinion survey: 'Fears of daily life' in January 1971.   235
4.3 Breakdown of those surveyed in the 'Fears of daily life'
   poll, depicted in Table 4.2, who believed 'that it will come
   to an inflation' in January 1971.   236

Acknowledgements

This book's development can be measured in years of my life – years of research at the University of Oxford and in historical archives scattered across Germany. But the book's own story is, in part, also related to the history of Europe in recent times. I first stumbled upon the idea for the project while on the Nico Colchester Fellowship of the *Financial Times* back in 2011. From the perch of the newspaper's Brussels bureau, one could observe the eurozone crisis engulfing the continent. I kept noticing politically charged narratives in the media about how Germans were psychologically scarred by the trauma of the 1922–3 hyperinflation, and how it was inevitable that such an experience underlined their country's need for *Stabilitätspolitik* – or politics of stability – to be applied not only at home, but across the European continent. I was sceptical about the use of such narratives. I wanted to trace their roots. When did they first take shape, and who shaped them? Gently encouraged at the time by the *Financial Times* journalists Peter Spiegel and Stanley Pignal, I submitted a DPhil application to Oxford. To my surprise, I was not only accepted but received a full scholarship package from the university and the UK-based Economic and Social Research Council. Without such funding, this book would not be here today.

The book stands at the crossroads of economic and cultural history. And in this sense, it is very much a development from my doctoral thesis at Oxford. Under the fruitful joint supervision of the economic historian Kevin O'Rourke (All Souls College, Oxford) and the cultural historian Paul Betts (St Antony's College, Oxford), I sought to build a bridge between the two literatures, one that approached Germany's monetary history from a cultural angle. I remain deeply thankful to both Kevin and Paul for their sound advice and encouragement across the years.

I am indebted, too, to the German Historical Institute London, German Academic Exchange Service (Deutscher Akademischer Austauschdienst) and German History Society for research grants that allowed me to travel across Germany to archives based in Frankfurt, Koblenz, Bonn, Berlin and Munich. During those research trips, I have been very fortunate to receive the support and advice from a number of archivists. Hands down, the Bundesbank historical archive staff has been the most open and supportive among them. I visited the Bundesbank historical archive across a five-year period; and with Rolf Herget, Karin Fitzner, Gerd-Christian Wannovius and Carmen Partes, I could not have had better help and advice for my project. I am also grateful for the support of staff at the federal archives in Berlin and Koblenz, the Archiv der sozialen Demokratie in Bonn, the Institut für Zeitgeschichte in Munich, and the historical archive of the Bundesverband der Deutschen Industrie in Germany's capital.

That I was able to visit these archives was also due to another development: I am particularly thankful to the University of Oxford for awarding me the Theodor Heuss Research Fellowship, a two-year research fellowship attached to the Alexander von Humboldt-Stiftung. This allowed me the time and resources not only to finish the DPhil, but to expand the scope of the analysis and transform it into a book. I was based at the Humboldt-Universität zu Berlin for the duration of the fellowship, as a guest researcher under the helpful support and guidance of the historian Alexander Nützenadel. My time at the Humboldt-Universität zu Berlin sharpened the focus of my work; I benefited enormously from the constructive critiques of Alexander and others whom I encountered at the history faculty.

I am grateful as well for the crystal-clear advice given to me throughout the years by Kim Christian Priemel, whom I first met at the University of Cambridge when I was an MPhil student there. Kim, like all good academics, has the very good habit of asking the right questions, leaving his conversation partner to join the dots on their own terms. Other historians, such as Dieter Lindenlaub, provided hard-hitting and valuable pointers on how to improve various points in the manuscript. The same applies for the detailed comments provided by the two anonymous readers for Cambridge University Press. The book is all the better for them. After spending five years researching central banks, there seemed only one logical thing to do. Following my time on the Theodor Heuss Research Fellowship, I moved to Frankfurt to work at the European Central Bank (ECB). This book, however, does not represent the views of the ECB. It is an independent, academic work.

I remain very grateful to Michael Watson at Cambridge University Press for the faith he placed in this book project, and for the excellent support and help provided along the way by Lisa Carter, Julie Hrischeva, Vinithan Sethumadhavan and Elizabeth Stone. The book could not have had a better team. And with that, I should add, any mistakes found in the text – be they of fact, analysis or emphasis – are and remain my own.

Most of all, however, I am thankful to my parents, Maureen and Frank, for their love and support over the years, and for the value they placed in their son receiving a good education. On their shoulders, I stood; and on their shoulders, I continue to stand.

Abbreviations

ABC	Allied Banking Commission
AdsD	Archiv der sozialen Demokratie, Friedrich-Ebert-Stiftung, Bonn
ARC	Allied Reparation Commission
BAB	Bundesarchiv, Berlin-Lichterfelde
BAK	Bundesarchiv, Koblenz
BDI	Bundesverband der Deutschen Industrie
BdL	Bank deutscher Länder
BIS	Bank for International Settlements
CDU	Christian Democratic Union
CSU	Christian Social Union
DBHA	Deutsche Bundesbank Historisches Archiv, Frankfurt
DBP	Deutscher Bundestag Parlamentsarchiv, Berlin
DBPA	Deutsche Bundesbank Pressearchiv, Frankfurt
DGB	Deutscher Gewerkschaftsbund
ECB	European Central Bank
EMS	European Monetary System
EPU	European Payments Union
FDP	Free Democratic Party
IfZ	Institut für Zeitgeschichte, Munich
OMT	Outright Monetary Transactions
SPD	Social Democratic Party
SS	*Schutzstaffel*

Introduction

When two journalists of *Bild*, Germany's best-selling tabloid, arrived in March 2012 at the European Central Bank (ECB) to interview its president, they brought with them a special gift. It was a *Pickelhaube*, or Prussian military helmet, dating from the time of the Franco-Prussian War.[1] The present, the journalists explained, was to remind Mario Draghi, an Italian, that the newspaper had deemed him back in 2011 as the 'most Germanic' of candidates in the race for the ECB's top position. According to *Bild*, the manner in which Draghi pursued his career demonstrated that he was imbued with what the tabloid saw as 'Prussian virtues'.[2] This fact overcame his problematic nationality – at least in the eyes of *Bild* – and made him the ideal man for the job.[3]

In the photograph published alongside the interview, Draghi appeared to be delighted with the gift. It signalled to him the approval of one of Germany's most powerful media outlets – and at a time when the euro-zone was reeling from an economic crisis. Commenting on the present, the central banker noted that 'the Prussian is a good symbol for the most important task of the ECB: maintaining price stability and protecting European savers'. Furthermore, Germany served as a 'model' for both Europe and its central bank. In part, this exemplary role stemmed from how the country took lessons from its troubled monetary past and applied them towards the goal of economic stability.[4]

---

[1] 'Interview mit EZB-Chef Mario Draghi zur Euro-Krise: "Deutschland ist ein Vorbild"', *Bild*, 22 Mar. 2012. See www.bild.de/politik/ausland/mario-draghi/deutschland-ist-ein-vorbild-23270668.bild.html. Last accessed on 20 December 2018.

[2] Quoted in 'Chancen für "Super-Mario" steigen', *Bild*, 11 May 2011. See www.bild.de/politik/ausland/mario-draghi/mario-draghi-neuer-ezb-chef-17844972.bild.html. Last accessed on 20 December 2018.

[3] The tabloid's endorsement came only after Germany's candidate, the Bundesbank president Axel Weber, had let it be known that he was withdrawing from the race. Refer to 'So deutsch ist der neue EZB-Chef', *Bild*, 29 Apr. 2011. See www.bild.de/geld/wirtschaft/mario-draghi/ist-neuer-ezb-chef-17630794.bild.html. Last accessed on 20 December 2018.

[4] 'Interview mit EZB-Chef Mario Draghi zur Euro-Krise', *Bild*, 22 Mar. 2012.

'The Germans had terrible experiences with inflation in the twentieth century', Draghi said. 'It does away with value and makes forecasting impossible. More still – inflation can downright destroy the society of a country.'[5] To be dead set against inflation, to be for a strong currency, and above all, to be independent of politics – these were indeed 'German virtues', he observed, and they were virtues that every European central banker should strive towards.[6]

The symbolism of the encounter provokes interest. And indeed, some questions come to mind. Why did the journalists of a German newspaper deem it fitting to give an Italian central banker a Prussian military helmet, something that is usually associated with militarism? Why was such a gift taken as a compliment? Why is it important today that one appears 'Germanic' as a central banker? And why was Draghi himself keen to evoke the lessons of Germany's experience with inflation?

These questions give rise to three brief points. First, to an extent at least, the ECB president's comments demonstrated that he was quite aware of his target audience. By evoking German history, Draghi was appealing to the readership of the tabloid newspaper, explaining the ECB's duties in terms an average German would understand. Second, though, and perhaps more indirectly, the central banker was paying tribute to the intellectual debt that the ECB owes the Deutsche Bundesbank, the central bank of West Germany, and later, a reunified Germany. Amid heated political debates surrounding the steps towards economic and monetary union during the 1980s and early 1990s, the structure and institutions of the Bundesbank emerged triumphant as providing the model for a European monetary authority.[7]

Yet it is perhaps the third point that is the most intriguing. Simply put, to be seen today in financial circles as a 'Germanic' central banker is treated as a very good thing indeed. We have reached the point where such an image has almost become a caricature in the media. The German central banker: conservative, independent and not a smile to be seen. If there was a punch bowl at a party, the German central banker would be the first to take it away. No doubt, today's reputation stems in large part from the performance of the Bundesbank. West German central bankers were among the most successful in tackling inflation in the decades that

---

[5] Ibid.   [6] Ibid.

[7] See, among others, John Singleton, *Central banking in the twentieth century* (Cambridge, 2011), pp. 262–4; David Marsh, *The euro: the battle for the new global currency* (Southampton, 2011), pp. 138–9; and Carl-Ludwig Holtfrerich, 'Monetary policy in Germany since 1948: national tradition, international best practice or ideology?', in Jean-Philippe Touffut (ed.), *Central banks as economic institutions* (Cheltenham, 2008), pp. 36–46.

followed the end of the Second World War.[8] To be seen as a 'Germanic' central banker, then, is to be seen as being good at your job. No wonder Draghi took the compliment.

But is that all? The appearance of the *Pickelhaube* hints at an image that is more deeply rooted, an image that draws upon a past pre-dating the achievements hard won during the post-war era. Taking a step back, one can see the Prussian military helmet as something entwined with the story of the German nation, and its people, since the foundation of the Second Reich back in 1871.[9] What story did the *Pickelhaube* tell, however?

Germany experienced two inflations in the first half of the twentieth century, both triggered by exorbitant government spending.[10] The first episode was the hyperinflation of 1922–3, which occurred during the Weimar Republic.[11] Wheelbarrows filled to the brim with cash; little children standing on the pavement, building small castles with thick wads of banknotes. We have all seen these photographs. Indeed, the hyperinflation still commands interest to this day, with popular works emerging (and re-emerging) on bookshop shelves in recent years.[12]

[8] Refer, for instance, to Andreas Beyer, Vitor Gaspar, Christina Gerberding and Otmar Issing, 'Opting out of the Great Inflation: German monetary policy after the break down of Bretton Woods', *European Central Bank: Working Paper Series*, No. 1020 (2009), pp. 6–8.

[9] For more on the cultural considerations of the *Pickelhaube*, and its place in German history, see Jakob Vogel, 'Die Pickelhaube', in Etienne François and Hagen Schulze (eds.), *Deutsche Erinnerungsorte, Band II* (Munich, 2001), pp. 299–314.

[10] Christoph Buchheim offers a succinct overview of Germany's monetary history in the twentieth century. See Christoph Buchheim, 'Von altem Geld zu neuem Geld. Währungsreformen im 20. Jahrhundert', in Reinhard Spree (ed.), *Geschichte der deutschen Wirtschaft im 20. Jahrhundert* (Munich, 2001); see also Otto Pfleiderer, 'Die beiden großen Inflationen unseres Jahrhunderts und ihre Beendigung', in Peter Hampe (ed.), *Währungsreform und Soziale Marktwirtschaft: Rückblicke und Ausblicke* (Munich, 1989).

[11] The best accounts of the German hyperinflation remain Constantino Bresciani-Turroni, *The economics of inflation: a study of currency depreciation in post-war Germany* (London, 1937), Gerald D. Feldman, *The great disorder: politics, economics, and society in the German inflation 1914–1924* (Oxford, 1996), and Carl-Ludwig Holtfrerich, *The German inflation, 1914–1923: causes and effects in international perspective* (Berlin, 1986). The classic references in the economics field are Thomas J. Sargent and Neil Wallace, 'Expectations and the dynamics of hyperinflation', *International Economic Review*, Vol. 14, No. 2 (1973); and Thomas J. Sargent, 'The demand for money during hyperinflations under rational expectations: 1', *International Economic Review*, Vol. 18, No. 1 (1977).

[12] See Frederick Taylor, *The downfall of money: Germany's hyperinflation and the destruction of the middle class* (London, 2013). Adam Fergusson's 1975 study, *When money dies*, was republished again in 2010. Refer to Adam Fergusson, *When money dies: the nightmare of the Weimar collapse* (London, 1975); and Adam Fergusson, *When money dies: the nightmare of deficit spending, devaluation, and hyperinflation in Weimar Germany* (New York, 2010).

The lesser-known second inflation, however, was a more gradual one, occurring before and during the Second World War. It was a 'repressed' inflation, characterised by price controls, empty shelves and a flourishing black market.[13] Though they were different creatures, both inflations ended with the same result: the currency had become worthless as a medium of exchange, unit of account and store of value.

The post-war lessons that emerged from these two monetary catastrophes were apparently clear – and indeed, Draghi had already outlined them in his interview with *Bild*: one should be dead set against inflation; one should be for a strong currency; and one should support the independence of the central bank – a central bank that would never again allow its printing presses to be abused by political interference. It is in this context, then, that we should view the *Pickelhaube*. With respect to money, the Prussian military helmet symbolises a cultural mindset: headstrong, independent and all too informed by the painful lessons of German history.

Of course, Draghi was not alone in expressing these remarks. The central banker was merely repeating a historical narrative that has persisted for decades in the media. Indeed, this narrative has experienced a revival since the outbreak of the eurozone crisis. In 2010, for example, *The Economist* argued that,

Germany's interwar experience with hyperinflation famously created a political climate amenable to [the] rise of Adolph [*sic*] Hitler and generated sufficient national trauma that the German central bank (and its descendent, the ECB) has ever since focused first, second and last on keeping inflation well in check.[14]

In 2011, *Spiegel Online*, Germany's leading online media outlet, widened this point to encompass the German population. 'For the Bundesbank', the news website observed, 'it has always been taboo to finance the state by purchasing its sovereign bonds'. It continued:

[13] Historians often disagree as to the timing and sequence of the second inflation. Some observers describe it as the 'Hitler' inflation, with its roots in the Third Reich and ending in 1945; while others define it as continuing into the post-war period – in other words, also occurring under the watch of the Allied military authorities. This book views the origins of the second inflation as dating back to 1936, noting the currency's gradual and then absolute demise by 1945. After this year, the reichsmark was replaced by a barter exchange economy, in which the prices of goods largely remained stable. The historian Alan Kramer flatly rejects the notion of a 'post-war' inflation. See Alan Kramer, *The West German economy, 1945–1955* (Oxford, 1991), p. 2.

[14] 'Inflation hawks: once bitten, twice hawkish', *The Economist*, 4 Mar. 2010. See www.economist.com/blogs/freeexchange/2010/03/inflation_hawks. Last accessed on 20 December 2018.

Behind this belief was the terrifying example of its predecessor, the Reichsbank, which had printed money with abandon in the 1920s in order to support the budget of the Weimar Republic. The result was a hyperinflation that has become deeply entrenched in the collective memory of Germans.[15]

Such lines of argument are often found in the academic literature too – particularly with reference to the Bundesbank Law of 1957, a piece of legislation that enshrined the independence of the West German central bank. 'Inflation destroyed the value of money in Germany twice during this century', observed Ellen Kennedy at the turn of the millennium.

The national traumas associated with the great inflation of the 1920s and with the years immediately following Germany's defeat in 1945 created a powerful political culture in favor of monetary stability that informed the spirit of the Bundesbank Act and can still function today as a reservoir of support for the Bank's policies.[16]

Perhaps it is Otmar Issing, though, the former chief economist of the Bundesbank, and later chief economist of the ECB, who is most associated with this argument. The central bank's task of safeguarding the currency 'reflects twentieth century German experience of hyperinflation, which twice within a generation destroyed the value of the currency', he notes. 'The same experience motivated the institution of strict independence from government.'[17]

Inflation, 'trauma', and the 'spirit' of the Bundesbank Law. The four extracts cited above hint at the extent to which the post-war central bank's independence is closely associated with the experiences of the inter-war era; the argument being that West Germans transformed the turbulent events prior to 1945 into edifying lessons for a post-war republic, ensuring that their central bankers would have the power to say 'no' to government demands for financing. The lessons stemming from Germany's troubled inter-war era, as embodied in the Bundesbank Law, and as expressed by Draghi, seem obvious today. They are rarely challenged. But an air of inevitability hangs over such arguments – and they ignore some important points.

---

[15] 'Breaking taboos: concerns mount in Germany over ECB bond buys. Part 2: we cannot give way to panic', *Spiegel Online*, 15 Aug. 2011. See www.spiegel.de/international/spiegel/breaking-taboos-concerns-mount-in-germany-over-ecb-bond-buys-a-780258-2.html. Last accessed on 20 December 2018.

[16] Contrast this statement concerning the timing of the second inflation to the viewpoint of Kramer in footnote 13. See Ellen Kennedy, 'The Bundesbank', *German Issues*, Vol. 19 (1998), p. 2.

[17] Otmar Issing, 'Central bank independence and monetary stability', *Institute of Economic Affairs Occasional Paper*, No. 89 (1993), p. 67.

For starters, the Reichsbank was actually independent of government instruction during the hyperinflation.[18] The central bank became independent in May 1922 at the behest of foreign pressure, and as part of a wider deal concerning the alleviation of German reparations payments that were imposed after the First World War. And following the hyperinflation, the Reichsbank, under its new president Hjalmar Schacht, became an overtly political actor, and a continual thorn in the side of various Weimar governments for the remainder of the 1920s.

The central bank was independent, too, during the twilight years of the Weimar Republic, when it embarked on deflationary measures amid efforts to stay on the gold standard – efforts that helped to accelerate Germany's descent into depression.[19] Deflation aggravated mass unemployment in the economy, which in turn radicalised an electorate and propelled the Weimar Republic to its fateful end with Hitler's ascent to the chancellery.[20]

Of course, this is not to suggest that the independent Reichsbank, by dint of its own decisions, *caused* the hyperinflation and deflation. Far from it, and indeed, to make such an argument would be both misleading and naively simplistic. The causes behind the events of 1922–3 can be lain squarely at the government's door, as well as the socio-economic consequences arising from the First World War. And with respect to the Great Depression, the factors sparking this global phenomenon are as complex as they are international in nature.[21] It should also be noted that, during both the hyperinflation and deflation, the independent

---

[18] This is a point repeatedly acknowledged in the literature. But it remains overlooked in the more popular accounts of the hyperinflation. The Reichsbank's policy during the hyperinflation is a 'classic counter-example' to the idea that an independent central bank is automatically stability orientated, as the historian Dieter Lindenlaub notes. For the emergence and evolution of the Reichsbank's independence during the Weimar Republic, see Simone Reinhardt, *Die Reichsbank in der Weimarer Republik. Eine Analyse der formalen und faktischen Unabhängigkeit* (Frankfurt am Main, 2000). See also Dieter Lindenlaub, 'Die Errichtung der Bank deutscher Länder und die Währungsreform von 1948: Die Begründung einer stabilitätsorientierten Geldpolitik', in Dieter Lindenlaub, Carsten Burhop and Joachim Scholtyseck (eds.), *Schlüsselereignisse der deutschen Bankengeschichte* (Stuttgart, 2013), p. 310.

[19] Harold James, 'The Reichsbank 1876–1945', in Deutsche Bundesbank (ed.), *Fifty years of the Deutsche Mark: central bank and the currency in Germany since 1948* (Oxford, 1999), pp. 29–31. See also Harold James, *The German slump: politics and economics 1924–1936* (Oxford, 1986).

[20] The topic of mass unemployment during the Weimar Republic has been left relatively unexamined. An exception, however is the volume edited by Richard J. Evans and Dick Geary. See Richard J. Evans and Dick Geary (eds.), *The German unemployed: experiences and consequences of mass unemployment from the Weimar Republic to the Third Reich* (London, 1987).

[21] The standard account of the Great Depression remains Barry Eichengreen, *Golden fetters: the gold standard and the Great Depression* (Oxford, 1992). A more recent

Reichsbank was, by and large, co-operating with the general direction of government policy.

In 1949, however, the year in which the Federal Republic was established, West Germans could look back on three chaotic decades of monetary history. The population had endured two inflations and one deflation. And during much of this time, the Reichsbank was legally independent from government instruction. In 1949, then, the record of central bank independence *could* be interpreted as a mixed one.[22] It could be challenged. And that is the key point to be made here; for as we will see, it *was* challenged.

Monetary Mythology

'History is the realm of choice and contingency', notes the historian Jeffrey Herf. 'Writing history is a matter of reconstructing the openness of past moments before choices congealed into seemingly inevitable structures.'[23] Today, we often view central bank independence in West Germany as an almost inevitable lesson stemming from the inter-war period. But this was not the case back in 1949. Back then, central bank independence was not synonymous with economic stability. There was no West German consensus for central bank independence at the dawn of the new republic. Rather, the topic was a controversial one, sparking a fiery public debate that lasted for seven long years. Over the decades, however, one version of history has trampled over another, and we have forgotten that 'openness of past moments'.

Why is this important? In short, the rise of this particular interpretation of history, one that stresses the lessons of the two inflations, has lent a sheen of historical legitimacy to the arguments of central bankers and politicians who advocate *Stabilitätspolitik* – that is, monetary and economic policies geared in support of price stability. And, as we have seen in *Bild*'s interview with Draghi, it is a version of history that has found an expression in the form of the ECB. The lessons of two inflations, once German, have now become European. But how did the dominance of these lessons come about in the first place? That is the guiding research question underlying the book at hand.

---

perspective is offered in Barry Eichengreen, *Hall of mirrors: the Great Depression, the Great Recession, and the uses – and misuses – of history* (New York, 2016).

[22] For more on the mixed record of central bank independence during the inter-war era, see Herbert Giersch and Harmen Lehment, 'Monetary policy: does independence make a difference? – the German experience', *ORDO*, Vol. 32 (1981).

[23] Jeffrey Herf, *Divided memory: the Nazi past in the two Germanys* (Cambridge, MA, 1997), preface.

This study examines the emergence and development of what I call 'monetary mythology', a carefully constructed historical narrative about the inter-war period of Germany that flourished in the West German public sphere following the Second World War.[24] It explores this myth-making by analysing how the lessons of Germany's experience of inflation, namely the 1922–3 hyperinflation and 1936–45 inflation, became politicised in the post-war era and transformed into political weapons in support of central bank independence. In the debate surrounding the establishment of West Germany's central bank, the country's monetary history became a political football as central bankers, politicians, industrialists and trade unionists all vied for influence over the legal provisions grounding the future monetary authority. The debate centred on power. Who should control the lever of monetary policy in a country that suffered two inflations and one deflation within the span of a single generation? In 1949, this question provoked a variety of passionate answers.

This is not the first academic study to examine the West German central bank; nor is it the first to analyse the circumstances surrounding the emergence of its independence.[25] Historians such as Volker Hentschel, Christoph Buchheim and Dieter Lindenlaub, in addition to the economist Jörg Bibow, have all documented, with varying degrees of emphasis, the controversies during the early years of the West German monetary authority's existence and the debates concerning the Bundesbank Law.[26] But this book is the first to stress the sheer extent to which

---

[24] This work is not the first to use the term 'mythology' in the sphere of central banking. For an unrelated case study on the Canadian central bank, analysed in terms of public policy, see Keith Acheson and John F. Chant, 'Mythology and central banking', *Kyklos*, Vol. 26, No. 2 (1973). See also Jeremy Leaman, *The Bundesbank myth: towards a critique of central bank independence* (London, 2001).

[25] The concept of central bank independence can be broken down into a number of smaller fields, too, from personnel independence, to functional independence, as well as financial independence. See Reinhardt, *Die Reichsbank in der Weimarer Republik*, pp. 23–9.

[26] Volker Hentschel, 'Die Entstehung des Bundesbankgesetzes 1949–1957. Politische Kontroversen und Konflikte: Teil I', *Bankhistorisches Archiv*, Vol. 14 (1988); and his second contribution, Volker Hentschel, 'Die Entstehung des Bundesbankgesetzes 1949–1957. Politische Kontroversen und Konflikte: Teil II', *Bankhistorisches Archiv*, Vol. 14 (1988); Christoph Buchheim, 'The establishment of the Bank deutscher Länder and the West German currency reform', in Deutsche Bundesbank (ed.), *Fifty years of the Deutsche Mark: central bank and the currency in Germany since 1948* (Oxford, 1999); and Christoph Buchheim, 'Die Unabhängigkeit der Bundesbank. Folge eines amerikanischen Oktrois?', *Vierteljahrshefte für Zeitgeschichte*, Vol. 49, No. 1 (2001); Jörg Bibow, 'On the origin and rise of central bank independence in West Germany', *European Journal of the History of Economic Thought*, Vol. 16, No. 1 (2009); and Jörg Bibow, 'Zur (Re-)Etablierung zentralbankpolitischer Institutionen und Traditionen in Westdeutschland: Theoretische Grundlagen und politisches Kalkül (1946–1967)', in

the disputed record of the Reichsbank formed the troubled background to such discussions.[27]

The Bundesbank Law, a 'foundational law of the social market economy', to use the words of Hentschel, set the stage for this power struggle over the monetary authority.[28] According to the West German constitution, the Bundesbank Law was to establish a federal central bank, one that could ideally provide for a more prosperous and stable future. So why, then, were West German elites so fixated on the past? In short, the record of the inter-war Reichsbank constituted the overwhelming reference point for the public debate surrounding the Bundesbank Law. Of course, contemporary examples, such as the Federal Reserve System of America, were also important. But they made for a distant second place in terms of how frequently they were evoked during these discussions. Where did the Reichsbank go wrong? What did it get right?

References to the Reichsbank's history, both positive and negative, grounded political arguments aimed at influencing both the institutions and structure of the future monetary authority. On the one hand, supporters of central bank independence pointed to the lessons of Germany's two inflations. These suggested that the Bundesbank should retain a sizeable degree of independence from government influence. After all, could the Federal Republic really risk letting the state exert control over the central bank after two disastrous inflations? The somewhat inconvenient fact that the Reichsbank was independent during the hyperinflation was almost always overlooked.

Political opponents of monetary autonomy, on the other hand, fell back upon their own lessons of the inter-war era. They focused on the

---

Christian Scheer (ed.), *Die deutschsprachige Wirtschaftswissenschaft in den ersten Jahrzehnten nach 1945: Studien zur Entwicklung der Ökonomischen Theorie, Band XXV* (Berlin, 2010). For the works of Dieter Lindenlaub, see Dieter Lindenlaub, 'Deutsches Stabilitätsbewußtsein: Wie kann man es fassen, Wie kann man es erklären, welche Bedeutung hat es für die Geldpolitik', in Bernhard Löffler (ed.), *Die kulturelle Seite der Währung. Europäische Währungskulturen, Geldwerterfahrungen und Notenbanksysteme im 20. Jahrhundert* (Munich, 2010); and Lindenlaub, 'Die Errichtung der Bank deutscher Länder und die Währungsreform von 1948'. Lindenlaub also wrote 'Der Zentralbankrat vor fünfzig Jahren', *Monatsbericht der Deutschen Bundesbank*, Mar. 1998.

[27] By focusing on the elements of continuity that remained in the post-war era, however, Theo Horstmann also touches on the legacy of the Reichsbank. See Theo Horstmann, 'Kontinuität und Wandel im deutschen Notenbanksystem. Die Bank deutscher Länder als Ergebnis alliierter Besatzungspolitik nach dem Zweiten Weltkrieg', in Theo Pirker (ed.), *Autonomie und Kontrolle. Beiträge zur Soziologie des Finanz- und Steuerstaats* (Berlin, 1989).

[28] Hentschel, 'Die Entstehung des Bundesbankgesetzes 1949–1957. Politische Kontroversen und Konflikte: Teil I', p. 5.

record of the Reichsbank during the Great Depression, linking its deflationary policies to the emergence of mass unemployment and, consequently, the rise of National Socialism. Could the West German state once again allow unelected officials to control a powerful lever of economic policy? And was it not the case, too, that the independent Reichsbank had become a controversial political player under the leadership of Schacht in the 1920s? With these kinds of lessons in mind, economic stability was not just about safeguarding the currency, but about promoting policies of full employment too. Both supporters and opponents of central bank independence presented skewed historical arguments geared along the lines of political interest.

Similarly, West German elites approached the question of the future central bank's structure in historical terms. Should the Bundesbank be a decentralised institution, one that reflected the federalised structure of the young republic? Or should it adopt a more centralised form, akin to the inter-war Reichsbank?

The public debate surrounding the Bundesbank Law was complicated by the fact that West Germany already *had* a central bank in the form of the Bank deutscher Länder (BdL).[29] This monetary authority pre-dated the foundation of the West German state by well over a year, having been established in early 1948. The BdL, based in Frankfurt, was a by-product of its era. It was a creature of the occupation authorities – more specifically, the American and British ones. Indeed, this fact has led the literature concerning the early years of the post-war central bank to become somewhat lopsided in emphasis. Numerous studies have concentrated on the foreign origins of the West German central bank system, and in doing so, they underplay the subsequent, domestic discussions centring on the German monetary past, as well as their sizeable impact on the

---

[29] For more studies concerning the BdL, see Monika Dickhaus, *Die Bundesbank im westeuropäischen Wiederaufbau: die internationale Währungspolitik der Bundesrepublik Deutschland 1948 bis 1958* (Munich, 1996); Monika Dickhaus, 'The foster-mother of "The bank that rules Europe": the Bank deutscher Länder, the Bank of England and the Allied Banking Commission', in Alan Bance (ed.), *The cultural legacy of the British occupation in Germany* (Stuttgart, 1997); Helge Berger, *Konjunkturpolitik im Wirtschaftswunder: Handlungsspielräume und Verhaltensmuster von Bundesbank und Regierung in den 1950er Jahren* (Tübingen, 1997); Theo Horstmann, 'Die Entstehung der Bank deutscher Länder als geldpolitische Lenkungsinstanz in der Bundesrepublik Deutschland', in Hajo Riese and Heinz-Peter Spahn (eds.), *Geldpolitik und ökonomische Entwicklung. Ein Symposion* (Regensburg, 1990); and Deutsche Bundesbank (ed.), *Geheimrat Wilhelm Vocke, Hüter der Währung, Zum hundertsten Geburtstag am 9. Februar 1986* (Frankfurt am Main, 1986).

Bundesbank Law.[30] This book seeks to redirect that focus towards the record of the Reichsbank.

The BdL was subject to the instructions and influence of the Western Allied powers. But the Allies made it independent of German political instruction. Only the German states could exert an indirect form of influence in so far as each one could appoint the president of its own state central bank. The presidents of the state central banks formed the central bank council, the decision-making body of the BdL. The central bank council convened every fortnight in Frankfurt and decided policy by majority vote.

The BdL, then, was established at a time when there was no federal state of which to speak. As a result, the Bundesbank Law was viewed by some political circles in Bonn, the new political capital of West Germany, as an ideal opportunity to assert federal influence over the future central bank. Among these men were Konrad Adenauer, the first chancellor of West Germany, and his influential finance minister, Fritz Schäffer. And they were not alone. According to Hentschel, '[p]oliticians of all parties were of the view that the complete independence of the Bank deutscher Länder was a mistake of occupation policy in need of correcting'.[31] Where they disagreed, however, was over the manner in which, and the extent to which, Bonn should be able to influence the decisions taken in Frankfurt.

But such federal ambitions were met with fierce resistance from both the BdL and the individual states. The BdL wanted to protect its independence when it was to be transformed into the Bundesbank; and the state governments jealously sought to guard what little influence they had over the monetary authority. As Bibow convincingly argues, the Bundesbank Law became an arena in which a three-way power struggle emerged.[32] In this respect, the Allies played an indirect but important role in creating the circumstances that led to this tripartite tug of war. There are two points to note here. First, they created a central bank that predated the Federal Republic. As such, the monetary authority

---

[30] See, for instance, Buchheim, 'The establishment of the Bank deutscher Länder and the West German currency reform'; see also Karl Häuser, 'Gründung der Bank deutscher Länder und Währungsreform', in Hans Pohl (ed.), *Geschichte der deutschen Kreditwirtschaft seit 1945* (Frankfurt am Main, 1998); and Eckhard Wandel, *Die Entstehung der Bank deutscher Länder und die deutsche Währungsreform 1948* (Frankfurt, 1980).

[31] Hentschel, 'Die Entstehung des Bundesbankgesetzes 1949–1957. Politische Kontroversen und Konflikte: Teil I', p. 10.

[32] As best outlined in Bibow, 'On the origin and rise of central bank independence in West Germany'; and, in more extensive detail, Bibow, 'Zur (Re-)Etablierung zentralbankpolitischer Institutionen und Traditionen in Westdeutschland'.

remained independent of any federal influence when West Germany was established. And second, West German elites knew that, at some point in the near future, the Allies would transfer monetary sovereignty back to them, giving the West German state the opportunity to decide what form that sovereignty took. The BdL, the federal government and the various state governments all vied to influence the provisions of the Bundesbank Law in a manner that best reflected their own respective interests.

What the literature overlooks, however, is the manner in which historical narratives of Germany's monetary past were forged amid this political power struggle. While the Federal Republic has been the subject of a rich wealth of cultural studies since the 1990s, few if any cultural historians have turned their sights towards the central bank or the wider question of Germany's historical experience of inflation.[33] This is somewhat surprising, given that both the BdL and Bundesbank presided over the West German deutschmark, a currency that went on to assume an important, symbolic role in a society where political forms of nationalism remained taboo.[34] Instead, the field of cultural history has been dominated by themes of genocide, remembrance, politics and gender.[35]

Nevertheless, with the help of some important findings in the field of cultural history, we can discern how West Germans came to understand and interpret their troubled experiences during the Third Reich and the Second World War.[36] In the late 1940s and 1950s, West Germans did

---

[33] This is not the case, however, for East Germany. Jonathan Zatlin has written eloquently about the ostmark and its role in the East German economy and society. See Jonathan R. Zatlin, *The currency of socialism: money and political culture in East Germany* (New York, 2007).

[34] Though not a cultural historian, Harold James has written about the role of the deutschmark in West German society. See Harald James, 'Die D-Mark', in Etienne François and Hagen Schulze (eds.), *Deutsche Erinnerungsorte, Band II* (Munich, 2001). More recently, the deutschmark has been examined, however briefly, by Neil MacGregor in his work on Germany. See Neil MacGregor, *Germany: memories of a nation* (London, 2014), pp. 499–506.

[35] An exception is S. Jonathan Wiesen, who focuses on West German industry and documents its efforts to disassociate itself from the Nazi past. See, for example, Herf, *Divided memory*; Norbert Frei, *Vergangenheitspolitik: Die Anfänge der Bundesrepublik und die NS Vergangenheit* (Munich, 1996); Axel Schildt, *Moderne Zeiten: Freizeit, Massenmedien und 'Zeitgeist' in der Bundesrepublik der 50er Jahre* (Hamburg, 1995); Ulrich Brochhagen, *Nach Nürnberg: Vergangenheitsbewältigung und Westintegration in der Ära Adenauer* (Hamburg, 1994); and Robert Moeller, *Protecting motherhood: women and the family in the politics of postwar West Germany* (Berkeley, 1993). For Wiesen's work, see S. Jonathan Wiesen, *West German industry and the challenge of the Nazi past, 1945–1955* (London, 2001).

[36] See Hanna Schissler (ed.), *The miracle years: a cultural history of West Germany, 1949–1968* (Princeton, 2001); Richard Bessel and Dirk Schumann (eds.), *Life after death: approaches to a cultural and social history of Europe during the 1940s and 1950s* (Cambridge, 2003); Robert Moeller (ed.), *West Germany under construction: politics,*

not shy away from their past; far from it, they embraced their experiences. But they did so on their own selective terms, and in manners that emphasised their own suffering.[37]

But if West Germans did not turn their backs on recent events, and instead sought to discern meaning from them, where did contemporary conceptions of Germany's monetary history, and their implications for the Bundesbank Law, fit within this wider perspective? The cultural historian Robert Moeller has written of 'war stories'; in other words, the emergence in West Germany of historical narratives concerning the Germans' collective suffering during the Second World War.[38] This book argues that West German elites did something quite similar in the monetary realm; one can even write of 'inflation stories' and 'deflation stories'. Central bankers, politicians, industrialists, trade unionists and other post-war elites all reverted to the troubled and contradictory lessons of the inter-war period and put them to political use along grounds of self-interest. And in 1949 there was no certainty as to which version of the past would triumph with respect to the Bundesbank Law.

To trace the roots of the central bank's monetary mythology, we journey back to Nuremberg in 1946; for it was at the Nuremberg trials that the first outline of what later came to be monetary mythology was forged. There are two points to note here. First, the former president of the Reichsbank, Schacht, stood trial as a war criminal. He had become a leading personality in the Third Reich following the collapse of the Weimar Republic. At the helm of the Reichsbank, Schacht was known as 'Hitler's magician', conjuring financial instruments that allowed the dictator to finance his rearmament ambitions.[39] But in the dock at Nuremberg, Schacht was accused of helping to prepare the financing behind a disastrous war that destroyed the European continent. It was not just the record of Schacht that stood on trial, however. It was at Nuremberg, too, that the record of the inter-war Reichsbank was first scrutinised in detail.

This is where the second point comes in. Schacht, his lawyer and defence witnesses constructed a version of the past that portrayed the

society, and culture in the Adenauer era (Ann Arbor, 1997); and Uta G. Poiger, Jazz, rock, and rebels: Cold War politics and American culture in a divided Germany (London, 2000), among other works.

[37] As best outlined in Robert Moeller, War stories: the search for a usable past in the Federal Republic of Germany (Berkeley, 2001).

[38] Ibid.

[39] The nickname was a contemporary one. See Norbert Mühlen, Hitler's magician: Schacht. The life and loans of Dr. Hjalmar Schacht, trans. E. W. Dickes (London, 1938).

finance man in the finest light. At the centre of these efforts lay the Reichsbank memorandum of 7 January 1939, which had been sent to Hitler. This document, signed by Schacht and the entire directorate, protested against Hitler's inflationary spending on rearmament in unusually strong terms. It sparked the circumstances in which most members of the directorate departed from the central bank, either being sacked by the dictator, or choosing to resign. The former Reichsbank president used this document to argue that he was a monetary martyr, one who sacrificed himself for the ideals of sound money. He also contended that his departure effectively spelled the end of the Reichsbank's independence, after which the central bank became a cog in the Nazi war machine. By acquitting Schacht of all charges, the Nuremberg military tribunal gave the green light to his defence team's arguments.

This episode is important. And it is important because personalities matter. Among Schacht's defence witnesses at Nuremberg was one Wilhelm Vocke, the future chairman of the BdL's directorate. The signature of Vocke, a long-time member of the Reichsbank directorate, could also be found on the January 1939 memorandum; and he was among those members of the directorate who left the central bank, having chosen to resign. The Reichsbank memorandum, which protested against the inflation in strictly financial terms, became a *moral* document at Nuremberg. And it remained a moral one thereafter in the Federal Republic. The signature of Vocke could be found on the Reichsbank memorandum; now it could be found on deutschmark banknotes, guaranteeing the credibility of each and every one.

The West German monetary authority remains one of the few institutions of German public life around which lingers a thin veneer of a *Stunde Null*, the idea of a fresh break from the past.[40] The BdL and Bundesbank always stressed, quite rightly too, that they were not the legal successors to the Reichsbank. As this study argues, however, there was a strong link of continuity between the inter-war Reichsbank and the BdL in the media. This is because the BdL's leadership became personified with both the central bank and the West German currency. Vocke, in particular, became the public face of the monetary authority. Politicians in parliamentary debates would come to use 'Vocke' as a byword for the BdL, while other political figures referred to the central bank as 'Vocke's tower'. By 1956, *Der Spiegel* had crowned Vocke 'chancellor of the

---

[40] The writer David Marsh, however, has also stressed levels of continuity between the inter-war and post-war central banks. See David Marsh, *The Bundesbank: the bank that rules Europe* (London, 1992).

deutschmark' on its front page.[41] Of course, this was despite the fact that the man had but one vote on the central bank council.

Yet twenty years before *Der Spiegel* took to calling him 'chancellor of the deutschmark', newspapers in the Third Reich were labelling Vocke 'foreign minister of the Reichsbank'. This man had a history. He was at the Reichsbank directorate table at the height of the hyperinflation and the depths of deflation. His signature helped to co-guarantee the 'value' of banknotes issued by the Reichsbank throughout the hyperinflation. Vocke was also present at the directorate meeting during which Schacht pushed through the passage of the 'Mefo' bills, the infamous financial instruments that allowed Hitler to covertly finance rearmament.[42]

As we will see, however, the BdL embraced Vocke's past. Indeed, the monetary authority had to. If the central bank did not, it knew that its political opponents would attack Vocke's record regardless. The Reichsbank memorandum became a corner stone in the West German central bank's monetary mythology. Vocke derived his credibility, in part, from his signature on the memorandum. It allowed the central bank and journalists to portray contemporary political struggles between Frankfurt and Bonn in historical terms. The Reichsbank memorandum went on to be published alongside a collection of Vocke's speeches; and its inclusion in the volume was even highlighted in advertisements for the book. Thus, as time progressed, Vocke was not portrayed a central banker implicated in the mistakes of the past; instead, he increasingly emerged as a monetary martyr, one of the few men who had said 'no' to Hitler. And if he could say no once, he could say no again. The central bank transformed Vocke's controversial inter-war record into an edifying lesson, embodied by his very person.

Recall, however, *Der Spiegel*'s use of the term 'chancellor of the deutschmark'. When we think of the era of Adenauer, we think of the word 'sovereignty', and its gradual reclamation on the part of the West German state.[43] Indeed, the economic historian Werner Abelshauser, in his discussion of the 'long 1950s', characterises the era 1949–55 in part as the 'recovery of economic sovereignty'.[44] And certainly, under

---

[41] See Chapter 3 for more details.

[42] For more on Vocke's role at the Reichsbank, see Chapter 1.

[43] Hans-Peter Schwarz's study remains one of the best accounts of this era. See Hans-Peter Schwarz, *Die Ära Adenauer. Gründerjahre der Republik 1949 1957 (Geschichte der Bundesrepublik Deutschland, Band 2)* (Stuttgart, 1981). More recent works include Anthony J. Nicholls, *Freedom with responsibility: the social market economy in Germany, 1918–1963* (Oxford, 1994); and James C. van Hook, *Rebuilding Germany: the creation of the social market economy, 1945–1957* (Cambridge, 2004).

[44] Werner Abelshauser, *Die langen Fünfziger Jahre: Wirtschaft und Gesellschaft der Bundesrepublik Deutschland 1949–1966* (Düsseldorf, 1987), p. 25.

Adenauer, the federal state made steady gains in the fields of political and economic independence during this time. But the expression 'chancellor of the deutschmark', and its attachment to Vocke, implied a mental boundary, a threshold of sorts. Adenauer might have been the chancellor of the West Germans, but he was not the chancellor of their currency.

Adenauer opposed the principle of central bank independence on the grounds that the constitution granted the ultimate responsibility of economic policy to parliament – not to an autonomous central bank. Yet the lessons of the two inflations worked directly against the interests of the chancellor, who, throughout his tenure in office, demonstrated a keen, wily awareness of power, and more importantly, the accumulation and maintenance of it. Political historians have yet to fully incorporate the implications of the Bundesbank Law debate in the wider context of Adenauer's *Kanzlerdemokratie*, a form of democratic government in which the office of the chancellor played a powerful, even authoritarian role.[45] This study hopes, in part, to address this gap, detailing the uses of inter-war monetary history, and the construction of historical narratives that could be set against the ambitions of *Der Alte*, or 'the old one', as Adenauer was popularly known among West Germans. As will be shown, though, Adenauer was not the only chancellor to face this problem. The historical narratives concerning Germany's two inflations were anti-statist by nature, and helped to fuel a suspicion of democratic governance that remained strong up until the turbulent era of the 1970s and beyond.[46]

While the 1970s were years of economic uncertainty, the same cannot be said for much of the 1950s and 1960s, the decades during which *Der 'Rheinische Kapitalismus'*, or the 'capitalism of the Rhine', more commonly known as the German economic model, assumed much of its form.[47] Where does the West German central bank, and its independence, fit in the economic historiography of the so-called *Wirtschaftswunder*, or 'economic miracle', which saw West German living standards rise markedly throughout Abelshauser's 'long 1950s'? More often than not, economic historians have followed suit to Ludwig Erhard, the famous economics minister, who penned one of the first accounts of West Germany's economic resurgence in his 1957 book, *Wohlstand für*

---

[45] For more on the *Kanzlerdemokratie*, see Arnulf Baring, *Im Anfang war Adenauer. Die Entstehung der Kanzlerdemokratie*, 2nd ed. (Munich, 1989).

[46] See Chapter 5 for more details.

[47] A detailed discussion concerning the 'capitalism of the Rhine' can be found in Hans Günter Hockerts and Günther Schulz (eds.), *Der 'Rheinische Kapitalismus' in der Ära Adenauer* (Paderborn, 2016).

Alle, or *Prosperity for all*.[48] In describing and discussing the 'economic miracle', a term he had always loathed, Erhard devoted relatively little attention to the central bank.

In Abelshauser's classic accounts of the West German economy, too, the BdL plays a secondary, if still somewhat important role in the outplay of events.[49] In part, this is because Abelshauser's argument stresses the long-run trends that propelled the growth of the West German economy, which experienced a 'catch-up' relative to other industrialised economies during the early post-war era.[50] But even in the more recent literature, which gives relatively more credit to the importance of decisions undertaken by Allied officials and West German elites, the BdL remains in the shadows, appearing briefly during the Korean crisis, but soon after fading away in the narrative.[51] This focus, or lack thereof, has left the central bank's independence being treated as a 'given' in the more general, overarching accounts of the West German economy.

By re-examining the political debate surrounding the Bundesbank Law, and linking it to the central bank's wider role in the economy, we begin to further understand the fragile foundations upon which the West German economic recovery initially rested. Such insights are important considering the crucial and, it should be stressed, positive role that central bank independence played throughout the economic reconstruction of the 1950s. Given that the capital market was non-existent, financing for infrastructural projects came from either the government or the BdL. And the central bank, for its part, faced significant pressure to provide deficit financing during this period. Deficit financing could have shaken the budding confidence attached to the new deutschmark.[52] Central bank independence bolstered confidence in the deutschmark at

---

[48] See Ludwig Erhard, *Wohlstand für Alle* (Düsseldorf, 1957). Erhard was beaten to the finish line, however, by Henry Wallich, who published an influential account some years earlier. See Henry C. Wallich, *Mainsprings of the German revival* (New Haven, 1955).

[49] A good example here is Werner Abelshauser, *Deutsche Wirtschaftsgeschichte seit 1945* (Bonn, 2004).

[50] Abelshauser's original argument can be found in Werner Abelshauser, *Wirtschaft in Westdeutschland 1945–1948: Rekonstruktion und Wachstumsbedingungen in der amerikanischen und britischen Zone* (Stuttgart, 1975).

[51] See Christoph Buchheim, *Die Wiedereingliederung Westdeutschlands in die Weltwirtschaft, 1945–1958* (Munich, 1990). For more on the Korean crisis, refer to Ludwig-Erhard-Stiftung, *Die Korea-Krise als ordnungspolitische Herausforderung der deutschen Wirtschaftspolitik. Texte und Dokumente* (Stuttgart, 1986).

[52] As underlined by Knut Borchardt and Buchheim. See Knut Borchardt and Christoph Buchheim, 'The Marshall Plan and key economic sectors: a microeconomic perspective', in Charles S. Maier and Günter Bischof (eds.), *The Marshall Plan and Germany: West German development within the framework of the European Recovery Program* (New York, 1991), pp. 447–9.

the crucial moment, and the institution emerged to become an asset to the economic recovery.

Such an outcome was not immediately apparent, however. In late 1950, Schäffer, the cabinet minister responsible for drafting the Bundesbank Law, stressed the controversial policies of the independent Reichsbank during the Great Depression amid efforts to justify legal provisions that would eliminate any such autonomy for the future Bundesbank. Such views were common during the early years of the Federal Republic – though they were arguably in the minority.

Schäffer's proposals helped to spark a public debate about the Bundesbank Law. The BdL sought to influence the legislation, both behind the scenes and in the media. A number of historians, political scientists and central bankers have already made this observation.[53] Lindenlaub has gone so far as to recognise that the BdL used in speeches the example of the two inflations as a historical justification for central bank independence – though he mentions this point in passing, devoting a single sentence to it.[54] The economic historian Carl-Ludwig Holtfrerich, for his part, suggests that the West German central bank benefitted from the fact that the population was 'traumatized' by inflation when embarking on its hard-edged, export-orientated policies.[55] But in each and every case, such remarks have been made in brief. Only Bibow has examined the BdL's efforts in some detail, and he devotes just ten pages to the central bank's interaction with the press as part of his wider examination of the emergence of central bank independence in West Germany.[56] No systematic effort to date has been made to examine the central bank's use of historical narratives concerning inflation, be it behind closed curtains or in the wider media.

And indeed, any detailed discussion of the media needs an operating construct through which it can be examined. This is where the term 'public sphere' comes in, an expression that dates well beyond Jürgen

---

[53] John B. Goodman, 'Monetary politics in France, Italy, and Germany', in Paolo Guerrieri and Pier Carlo Padoan (eds.), *The political economy of European integration: states, markets and institutions* (London, 1989), pp. 196–7; Peter A. Johnson, *The government of money: monetarism in Germany and the United States* (Ithaca, 1998), p. 199; Bibow, 'On the origin and rise of central bank independence in West Germany', p. 158 (footnote); and Otmar Emminger, *D-Mark, Dollar, Währungskrisen: Erinnerungen eines ehemaligen Bundesbankpräsidenten* (Stuttgart, 1986), p. 27.

[54] Lindenlaub, 'Die Errichtung der Bank deutscher Länder und die Währungsreform von 1948', p. 309.

[55] Holtfrerich, 'Monetary policy in Germany since 1948: national tradition, international best practice or ideology?', pp. 33–4.

[56] Bibow, 'Zur (Re-)Etablierung zentralbankpolitischer Institutionen und Traditionen in Westdeutschland', pp. 565–76.

Habermas's influential study in 1962.[57] The study uses the definition of the public sphere that has been carefully outlined by Christina von Hodenberg in her work on the West German media. She defines it 'broadly as a structure of many co-existing forums in which a society selects topics for debate and negotiates patterns of interpretation, values and conflicting interests'.[58] Newspapers, books, radio and, later, television; platforms such as these formed the channels through which West Germany's monetary past was debated. Von Hodenberg's research has also documented in detail the shift from a consensus-based journalism, prevalent in the early 1950s, to a more critical public sphere that came to dominate the 1960s. This shift was driven by generational change – and actually pre-dates the famous '*Spiegel* affair' of 1962, a political scandal that saw editors of *Der Spiegel* arrested, and during which Franz Josef Strauß, an influential minister, was forced to resign.[59]

A working definition of the public sphere is important when we examine the Bundesbank in the 1960s. The study documents three episodes in and around the year 1965, occurring during the tenure of Karl Blessing, the first president of the Bundesbank.[60] Blessing was Schacht's protégé at the Reichsbank, and a contemporary of Vocke. His signature, too, could be found on the Reichsbank memorandum sent to Hitler in 1939, sparking the circumstances in which he resigned from the central bank. Under Blessing, then, the West German central bank leadership continued to be closely identified with the Reichsbank in the public sphere.

First, the study examines how Schacht, a tarnished figure in West Germany, emerged once again in the 1960s. The former Reichsbank

---

[57] Jürgen Habermas, *The structural transformation of the public sphere: an inquiry into a category of bourgeois society*, trans. Thomas Burger and Frederick Lawrence (Cambridge, 1993).

[58] See Christina von Hodenberg, 'Mass media and the generation of conflict: West Germany's long sixties and the formation of a critical public sphere', *Contemporary European History*, Vol. 15, No. 3 (2006), p. 369 (footnote); the collection of essays in Bernd Weisbrod (ed.), *Die Politik der Öffentlichkeit – die Öffentlichkeit der Politik: politische Medialisierung in der Geschichte der Bundesrepublik* (Göttingen, 2003); and the essays in Axel Schildt and Arnold Sywottek (eds.), *Modernisierung im Wiederaufbau: Die westdeutsche Gesellschaft der 50er Jahre* (Bonn, 1993).

[59] Christina von Hodenberg, *Konsens und Krise: eine Geschichte der westdeutschen Medienöffentlichkeit 1945–1973* (Göttingen, 2006). See also Matthias Weiß, 'Journalisten: Worte als Taten', in Norbert Frei (ed.), *Karrieren im Zwielicht. Hitlers Eliten nach 1945* (Frankfurt, 2001); and Horst Pöttker, 'Zwischen Politik und publizistischer Professionalität', in Jürgen Wilke (ed.), *Massenmedien und Zeitgeschichte* (Konstanz, 1999).

[60] The historian Christopher Kopper devotes a chapter to Karl Blessing's inter-war career in Christopher Kopper, *Bankiers unterm Hakenkreuz* (Munich, 2008), pp. 183–205. For Blessing's post-war stint at the Bundesbank, see Dieter Lindenlaub, 'Karl Blessing', in Hans Pohl (ed.), *Deutsche Bankiers des 20. Jahrhunderts* (Stuttgart, 2008).

president launched a campaign in the public sphere attacking the policies of the Bundesbank and the character of its president, Blessing. In particular, Schacht accused Blessing of partaking in the second inflation that destroyed the reichsmark.[61] Second, the former Reichsbank president also argued that the Bundesbank was embarking on a 'third inflation', helping to give popularity to a term that had been used only sporadically in the past.[62] Such accusations proved enormously embarrassing for Blessing, and highlighted how the past was never that far behind. The emergence of the 'third inflation' as a point of public discussion – a debate that the Bundesbank sought to discredit, given that the term suggested the central bank was presiding over another inflation – also illustrated how historical narratives of inflations could be used *against* the West German central bank.

The third instance of when the shadow of the inter-war era loomed over the Bundesbank can be found in the appearance of news stories in the mainstream press detailing Blessing's former membership of Heinrich Himmler's 'circle of friends', or *Freundeskreis*. The *Freundeskreis* was an elite group of *Schutzstaffel* (SS) officials and industrialists that served as a platform for networking, as well as a channel of additional funding for the SS. These news reports originally emerged from East Germany, spearheaded by a propaganda campaign on the part of the East German ministry for state security, more commonly known as the Stasi. The Stasi was determined the blacken the reputation of the 'president of the deutschmark', as Blessing was popularly known in the West German media.[63]

Both Blessing and the Bundesbank, then, became a political football in Cold War Europe, a continent riven by an ideological divide. But this East German propaganda campaign soon found an echo in West Germany both with the publication of *Deutschland Report*, a left-wing book that sought to highlight an alleged continuity between the Third Reich and Federal Republic, as well as coverage in mainstream magazines such as *Der Spiegel*. The Bundesbank president's murky past even became the subject of a scene in a cabaret show that toured around the country, and which was broadcast on national television in 1965.

---

[61] Lindenlaub has been the first to note Schacht's accusation, albeit he does so with a single sentence. See Lindenlaub, 'Karl Blessing', p. 13.

[62] Similarly, Lindenlaub is also the first to mention the emergence of the 'third inflation' as a topic of discussion in the 1960s. See Lindenlaub, 'Deutsches Stabilitätsbewußtsein', p. 77.

[63] See, for instance, the front-page cover of *Der Spiegel* (Figure 4.1, Chapter 4), in which Blessing is depicted as 'president of the deutschmark'.

Such reports, however, clashed with Blessing's image as a man of sound moral principles, a man who safeguarded the deutschmark. This study, then, examines how the Bundesbank's press department entered crisis mode, creating an alternate version of Blessing's past in the form of a document called the 'short comprehensive summary'. This document portrayed his inter-war actions in the best light possible. The Bundesbank press department sent it to the journalists and editors of the publications that published the negative stories about Blessing. In doing so, the Bundesbank compiled a small army of supporting documents to be included alongside the 'short comprehensive summary', many of which stemmed from the Nuremberg trials. These included the court testimonies of Vocke, Schacht and Blessing at Nuremberg – and, of course, the Reichsbank memorandum of January 1939. The *Freundeskreis* episode revealed how the Bundesbank's monetary mythology could be challenged – and indeed was challenged – by using the very same Nuremberg documents upon which the central bank's version of the past was based.

Himmler, cabaret shows, the Stasi – and the Bundesbank. Such linkages are not common fare when it comes to the study of central bank independence, a concept that has spread like wildfire since the late 1980s and early 1990s.[64] Several influential economic studies have demonstrated a negative correlation between the degree of central bank independence, on the one hand, and the inflation rate of a given country, on the other.[65] In other words, the higher the degree to which the central bank is independent of government influence, the lower the country's rate of inflation. Now, as any good economist will tell you, correlation is not the same as causation. But one possible argument to take from this is that the independent central banker, not beholden to democratic pressure, will be able to embark on politically unpopular, but economically necessary policies at a time when politicians, with their eyes on the next election, cannot.

But economic studies surrounding the autonomy of central banks are often statistical by nature, with little historical analysis provided. Of

---

[64] See Carlo Tognato, *Central bank independence: cultural codes and symbolic performance* (New York, 2012), pp. 5, 21; and Singleton, *Central banking in the twentieth century*, p. 204.

[65] See the influential article by Alberto Alesina and Lawrence H. Summers, 'Central bank independence and macroeconomic performance: some comparative evidence', *Journal of Money, Credit and Banking*, Vol. 25, No. 2 (1993). The literature is also documented in Bernd Hayo, 'Inflationseinstellungen, Zentralbankunabhängigkeit und Inflation', in Bernhard Löffler (ed.), *Die kulturelle Seite der Währung. Europäische Währungskulturen, Geldwertefahrungen und Notenbanksysteme im 20. Jahrhundert* (Munich, 2010).

course, parallels can be made with the economist Kenneth Rogoff's idea of a 'conservative central banker' and the image of a German central banker pained by the lessons of Germany's monetary history, a role that Hans Tietmeyer, the president of the Bundesbank from 1993 to 1999, played rather effectively.[66] And indeed, we have also seen how Draghi was keen to tap into this narrative during his interview with *Bild*. Yet the statistical literature has remained dominant when it comes to examining monetary autonomy. The need to subject central bank independence to historical analysis has never been more important.

Why is this the case, however? Since the global financial crisis of 2007–8, the consensus surrounding the benefits of central bank independence has begun to fracture. During 2016, for instance, right-wing populist forces on both sides of the Atlantic increased their attacks on the institution of central bank independence, criticising, in their words, the actions of unelected technocratic experts.[67] In October 2018, the American president, Donald Trump, attacked the American central bank as 'crazy' and 'loco' for the latter's decision to increase interest rates amid efforts to ward off inflation.[68] In doing so, Trump broke a presidential taboo. Two weeks later, Italy's deputy prime minister Luigi Di Maio accused Draghi of 'poisoning the atmosphere' following the latter's remarks that government officials in Rome should tone down their conflict with the European Commission over Italy's budget plans and stop calling into question the 'existential framework' of the euro.[69] Regardless of where you look, the political climate is

---

[66] Kenneth Rogoff, 'The optimal degree of commitment to an intermediate monetary target', *Quarterly Journal of Economics*, Vol. 100, No. 4 (1985); Hans Tietmeyer, 'The role of an independent central bank in Europe', in Patrick Downes and Reza Vaez-Zadeh (eds.), *The evolving role of central banks* (Washington DC, 1991), pp. 182–3; and Hans Tietmeyer, 'The Bundesbank: committed to stability', in Stephen F. Frowen and Robert Pringle (eds.), *Inside the Bundesbank* (Basingstoke, 1998), pp. 1–2.

[67] For more on central bank independence in an era of rising populism, see Charles Goodhart and Rosa Lastra, 'Populism and central bank independence', *Open Economies Review*, Vol. 29, No. 1 (2018). In addition, refer also to 'Carney says politicians "deflect blame" by attacking central banks', *Financial Times*, 15 Nov. 2016. See www.ft.com/content/8de147b6-ab31-11e6-9cb3-bb8207902122. Last accessed on 20 December 2018. See also 'Ed Balls calls for curbs on BoE independence', *Financial Times*, 17 Nov. 2016. See www.ft.com/content/2616611e-a665-11e6-8b69-02899e8bd9d1. Last accessed on 20 December 2018.

[68] 'Trump calls "loco" Federal Reserve "too aggressive"', *Reuters*, 11 Oct. 2018. See www.reuters.com/article/us-usa-trump-fed/trump-calls-federal-reserve-too-aggressive-fox-interview-idUSKCN1ML1TA. Last accessed on 20 December 2018.

[69] 'Italy's Di Maio says ECB's Draghi poisoning atmosphere: news agency', *Reuters*, 26 Oct. 2018. See www.reuters.com/article/us-italy-budget-dimaio-ecb/italys-di-maio-says-ecbs-draghi-poisoning-atmosphere-news-agency-idUSKCN1N01M1. Last accessed on 20 December 2018.

getting uglier and uglier. Wolfgang Münchau, the influential *Financial Times* columnist, has argued that recent events could signal 'the end of the era of central bank independence'.[70] It is too early to tell if events will prove Münchau right. But it is nevertheless telling that the titles of two notable publications on central banking, published in 2014 and 2016 respectively, refer to central banks standing at a 'crossroads'.[71] Paul Tucker, the former deputy governor of the Bank of England, has written of 'unelected power' in the wake of a crisis that saw independent central banks assuming the additional task of banking supervision.[72] Today, just like in 1949, the question of monetary autonomy is firmly back on the agenda.

Where does monetary mythology fit into all this? In short, it played a powerful role in constructing a veneer of historical legitimacy surrounding what academics and commentators have come to call the German *Stabilitätskultur*, or stability culture.[73] Proponents of a *Stabilitätskultur* stress the central importance of price stability, achieved through fiscal consolidation.[74] More generally, a stability culture can be defined as a population's willingness to tolerate difficult economic and monetary policies that could entail economic losses in the short-run, but lead to larger economic gains in the long-run.[75]

---

[70] Wolfgang Münchau, 'The end of the era of central bank independence', *Financial Times*, 13 Nov. 2016. See www.ft.com/content/8d52615e-a82a-11e6-8898-79a99e2a4de6. Last accessed on 20 December 2018.

[71] See Charles Goodhart, Daniela Gabor, Jakob Vestergaard and Ismail Ertürk (eds.), *Central banking at a crossroads: Europe and beyond* (London, 2014); and Michael D. Bordo, Øyvind Eitrheim, Marc Flandreau and Jan F. Qvigstad (eds.), *Central banks at a crossroads: what can we learn from history?* (Cambridge, 2016).

[72] Paul Tucker, *Unelected power: the quest for legitimacy in central banking and the regulatory state* (Princeton, 2018).

[73] Indeed, the coining of the phrase *Stabilitätskultur* has at times been traced to either Tietmeyer or Helmut Schlesinger, another Bundesbank president. See Bernard Löffler, 'Währungsgeschichte als Kulturgeschichte? Konzeptionelle Leitlinien und analytische Probleme kulturhistorischer Ansätze auf wirtschafts- und währungsgeschichtlichem Feld', in Bernhard Löffler (ed.), *Die kulturelle Seite der Währung. Europäische Währungskulturen, Geldwerterfahrungen und Notenbanksysteme im 20. Jahrhundert* (Munich, 2010), p. 34 (footnote).

[74] David Howarth and Charlotte Rommerskirchen, 'Inflation aversion in the European Union: exploring the myth of a North–South divide', *Socio-Economic Review*, Vol. 15, No. 2 (2017), pp. 386–8.

[75] See, for instance, Rudolf Richter, 'Stabilitätskultur als Problem der Institutionen-Ökonomik', in Helmut Hesse and Otmar Issing (eds.), *Geld und Moral* (Munich, 1994); Peter Bofinger, Kai Pfleger and Carsten Hefeker, 'Stabilitätskultur in Europa', in Hans-Hermann Francke, Eberhart Ketzel and Hans-Helmut Kotz (eds.), *Europäische Währungsunion. Von der Konzeption zur Gestaltung* (Berlin, 1998); Bernhard Löffler, 'Währungsrecht, Bundesbank und deutsche "Stabilitätskultur" nach 1945. Überlegungen zu mentalitätsgeschichtlichen Dimensionen normativ-institutioneller Regelungen', in Manfred Seifert and Winfried Helm (eds.), *Recht und Religion im*

Since the eurozone crisis, the term *Stabilitätskultur* has experienced a revival in use. Indeed, according to the political scientists David Howarth and Charlotte Rommerskirchen, the term has even become a 'strategic political resource' used by German elites to defend their country's economic success and, more recently, explain the failures of their profligate, debt-laden neighbours in southern Europe.[76] In 2010, the German finance minister, Wolfgang Schäuble, attacked American suggestions that Germany should embark on a 'more expansionary fiscal course' to help pull neighbouring eurozone economies out of their doldrums. Germans, Schäuble countered, are 'more preoccupied with the implications of excessive debts and the dangers of high inflation' than Americans. This 'aversion to deficits and inflationary fears', the finance minister continued, 'have their roots in German history in the past century'.[77] In the same year, Angela Merkel, the German chancellor, declared that the solution to the continent's economic woes was not debt relief, but rather 'that the whole of Europe commits herself to a new stability culture'.[78] In other words, Italy, Spain and Portugal needed to learn how to tighten their belts. Forget Rome and the Romans: when in Europe, do as the Germans do.

But the German *Stabilitätskultur* is based on a very specific version of the country's history, one that emerged from the debates surrounding the Bundesbank Law. In this sense, it is no accident that in 2016 the Bundesbank declared its thirteen-storey, brutalist headquarters the 'symbol of the stability culture'.[79] The West German central bank was central to its emergence. As this book demonstrates, the monetary authority played a key role in transforming the complex experiences of the inter-war era in such a manner that made the concept of central bank independence synonymous with economic stability. It successfully

Alltagsleben. Perspektiven der Kulturforschung. Festschrift für Walter Hartinger zum 65. Geburtstag (Passau, 2005); and, more recently, the detailed and enlightening discussion found in Lindenlaub, 'Deutsches Stabilitätsbewußtsein'. For a discussion in English, see Bernd Hayo, 'Inflation culture, central bank independence and price stability', *European Journal of Political Economy*, Vol. 14 (1998).

[76] See David Howarth and Charlotte Rommerskirchen, 'A panacea for all times? The German stability culture as strategic political resource', *West European Politics*, Vol. 36 (2013).

[77] Wolfgang Schäuble, 'Maligned Germany is right to cut spending', *Financial Times*, 24 Jun. 2010. See www.ft.com/content/216daeba-7f0c-11df-84a3-00144feabdc0. Last accessed on 20 December 2018.

[78] Howarth and Rommerskirchen, 'Inflation aversion in the European Union: exploring the myth of a North–South divide', p. 386.

[79] See 'Symbol der Stabilitätskultur', www.bundesbank.de/de/aufgaben/themen/symbol-der-stabilitaetskultur-664760. Last accessed on 20 December 2018.

argued that an independent central bank was crucial for price stability, which was in turn instrumental for social peace and thus a flourishing democracy. And it did so despite the fact that such an argument is not at all apparent from the record of the inter-war Reichsbank. Therein lay what this book labels the 'paradox' of West German democracy: the popular belief, carefully crafted in the post-war era, that an independent central bank was a crucial pillar of a successful democratic state.[80]

The lessons of the two inflations, tied to the need for an independent Bundesbank, lay at the heart of the German *Stabilitätskultur*. In 1949, these lessons were merely one among several historical narratives in the public sphere. But they soon emerged in the ascendant, aided by the central bank's efforts in the media. Numerous historians have shown how the 1956 'Gürzenich affair' – during which Adenauer attacked the BdL's independence, comparing its restrictive monetary policy to a 'guillotine' falling upon the West German people – solidified popular support for central bank independence and boosted the monetary authority's reputation.[81]

This book, however, also argues that the 'Gürzenich affair' proved to be a crucial moment in terms of how West Germans interpreted their monetary history. The media scandal that followed Adenauer's remarks, unprecedented in scale, proved to be a publicity coup for the central bank, and it marked the ascendance, and dominance, of the BdL's version of history, in turn narrowing and ossifying the parameters through which West Germans analysed their past in the public sphere.[82] Indeed, it was shortly after the 'Gürzenich affair' when Erhard, the economics minister, reduced the experiences of the inter-war era to a simple (if not outright simplistic) equation: 'The formula "dependent central bank = inflation" is valid at all times and everywhere. Historical experience proves that to us with crystal clarity.' Such a statement, and the sheer confidence with which it was expressed, would have been unlikely six years earlier. Back then, the 'crystal clarity' of which Erhard spoke was distinctly absent in the political realm.

The BdL's conception of monetary history found an expression in the provisions outlined in the Bundesbank Law. By allowing for a monetary authority independent of political instruction, this piece of legislation

---

[80] This is discussed in greater detail in Chapter 5.
[81] Daniel Koerfer, *Kampf ums Kanzleramt: Adenauer und Erhard* (Stuttgart, 1987); Berger, *Konjunkturpolitik im Wirtschaftswunder*; and Christian N. Wolz, *Konflikte zwischen der Notenbank und der Regierung in der Bundesrepublik Deutschland 1956–1961* (Stuttgart, 2009).
[82] This is discussed in detail in Chapter 3.

spoke to one version of the past, but not to another.[83] The lessons stemming from the two inflations were prioritised over those arising from the experience of mass unemployment.

Indeed, the study shows how the Bundesbank Law itself entrenched the power struggle so evident in previous years. By not providing for a formal resolution process through which disputes over monetary policy between Frankfurt and Bonn could be solved, the Bundesbank Law encouraged such disputes to become 'dramatised' and spill into the public sphere, as already demonstrated by the 'Gürzenich affair' the year prior to its passage through parliament.[84] These future controversies would centre on the central bank's independence, in turn creating further instances in which the lessons of Germany's two inflations could suddenly *become* relevant again, and applied in defence of the Bundesbank's independence.

An institutional struggle, one evident from the Federal Republic's establishment in 1949, but later embedded into its legislative framework from 1957 onwards, perpetuated a cultural preoccupation with Germany's inflationary episodes. To emphasise this point, the study examines an episode that occurred in 1973, during which a debate surrounding a *Novellierung*, or amendment, to the Bundesbank Law provoked a media storm evoking the lessons of the two inflations. A generation might have

---

[83] The Bundesbank's independence, as outlined in the Bundesbank Law, has since been the subject of numerous studies over the decades, the more notable of which are as follows: Carl-Ludwig Holtfrerich, 'Relations between monetary authorities and governmental institutions: the case of Germany from the 19th century to the present', in Gianni Toniolo (ed.), *Central banks' independence in historical perspective* (Berlin, 1988); John B. Goodman, *The politics of central banking in Western Europe* (London, 1992), pp. 58–102; Rolf H. Kaiser, *Bundesbankautonomie – Möglichkeiten und Grenzen einer unabhängigen Politik* (Frankfurt, 1980); Rolf Caesar, *Der Handlungsspielraum von Notenbanken: Theoretische Analyse und internationaler Vergleich* (Baden-Baden, 1981), pp. 167–214; Ellen Kennedy, *The Bundesbank: Germany's central bank in the international monetary system* (London, 1991); Rüdiger Robert, *Die Unabhängigkeit der Bundesbank: Analyse und Materialien* (Kronberg im Taunus, 1978); Helge Berger, 'The Bundesbank's path to independence: evidence from the 1950s', *Public Choice*, Vol. 93, Nos. 3–4 (1997); Helge Berger and Jakob de Haan, 'A state within the state? An event study on the Bundesbank (1948–1973)', *Scottish Journal of Political Economy*, Vol. 46, No. 1 (1999); and the essays in Dieter Duwendag (ed.), *Macht und Ohnmacht der Bundesbank* (Frankfurt, 1973).

[84] The 'dramatisation' potential of the Bundesbank Law has already been highlighted by a number of central bankers and historians. See Bertold Wahlig, 'Relations between the Bundesbank and the Federal Government', in Stephen F. Frowen and Robert Pringle (eds.), *Inside the Bundesbank* (Basingstoke, 1998), p. 52; Lindenlaub, 'Deutsches Stabilitätsbewußtsein', pp. 82–3; Bibow, 'Zur (Re-)Etablierung zentralbankpolitischer Institutionen und Traditionen in Westdeutschland', p. 569; and the comments of Hugo Scharnberg, a politician with the Christian Democratic Union, in Deutsche Bundesbank (ed.), *30 Jahre Deutsche Bundesbank. Die Entstehung des Bundesbankgesetzes vom 26. Juli 1957* (Frankfurt am Main, 1988), p. 148.

separated the eras of Adenauer and Helmut Schmidt, the chancellor of West Germany from the mid-1970s to early 1980s, but the references and examples they used remained eerily the same.

A cultural preoccupation with inflation. But haven't we been here before? This introduction began by documenting how central bankers, journalists and historians have commented upon a 'national trauma' that has arisen from the experience of the Weimar hyperinflation. But this event occurred almost a century ago. Few if any Germans alive remember it. By 1972, for instance, the economic historian Knut Borchardt noted that less than 13 per cent of the West German population was above the age of 65 – that is, the age that would have allowed them to consciously remember the hyperinflation.[85]

Of course, this is not to claim that a German 'trauma' concerning inflation never existed. Historians have documented in detail an aversion to inflationary policies in the latter years of the Weimar Republic, and the political implications that such popular attitudes had for the economic policies of the chancellor at the time, Heinrich Brüning.[86] But the real question is why such historical narratives have persisted so steadily in the public sphere. The common assertion that these experiences were passed down through German families is often based on flimsy, anecdotal evidence.[87] There is research that suggests memories of high inflation fade as time progresses.[88]

Moreover, Germany was not the only European country to have experienced a hyperinflation during the twentieth century. Austria, Poland, Russia

---

[85] Knut Borchardt, 'Die Erfahrung mit Inflationen in Deutschland', in Johannes Schlemmer (ed.), *Enteignung durch Inflation? Fragen der Geldwertstabilität* (Munich 1972), p. 9.

[86] See, for instance, Jürgen von Kruedener, 'Die Entstehung des Inflationstraumas. Zur Sozialpsychologie der deutschen Hyperinflation 1922/23', in Gerald D. Feldman (ed.), *Konsequenzen der Inflation* (Berlin, 1989); and Knut Borchardt, 'Das Gewicht der Inflationsangst in den wirtschaftspolitischen Entscheidungsprozessen während der Weltwirtschaftskrise', in Gerald D. Feldman (ed.), *Die Nachwirkungen der Inflation auf die deutsche Geschichte 1924–1933* (Munich, 1985). The works of Harold James, Theo Balderston and Patricia Clavin also support the argument of an inflation aversion evident during the latter years of the Weimar Republic. See James, *The German slump*; Theo Balderston, *The origins and course of the German economic crisis: November 1923 to May 1932* (Berlin, 1993); and Patricia Clavin, *The Great Depression in Europe, 1929–1939* (London, 2000).

[87] An example of this argument can be found in Elisabeth Noelle-Neumann, 'Geldwert und öffentliche Meinung: Anmerkungen zur "Psychologie der Inflation"', in Clemens-August Andreae, Karl-Heinrich Hansmeyer, Gerhard Scherhorn (eds.), *Geldtheorie und Geldpolitik: Günter Schmölders zum 65. Geburtstag* (Berlin, 1968), pp. 37–40.

[88] Michael Ehrmann and Panagiota Tzamourani, 'Memories of high inflation', *European Journal of Political Economy*, Vol. 28 (2012), pp. 174–5, 190.

and Hungary have also experienced hyperinflations.[89] But these countries –
or, expressed more specifically, their political cultures – fail to place price
stability on the same vaunted pedestal of economic policy priorities.

Perhaps the rise of Hitler explains the Germany's subsequent fixation
on inflation? Well, no. The National Socialists remained a marginal
party until well into the late 1920s. It was arguably mass unemployment,
not inflation, which radicalised the electorate in the twilight years of
the Weimar Republic, propelling the National Socialists to power. But
why has the German hyperinflation remained so relevant, when other
European inflations have not? To date, no one has adequately explained
the apparent inter-generational transmission of the experiences of the
German hyperinflation.

Is it really the case that 'the ninety-year-old national sense of trauma
has not yet been fully overcome', as the writer Frederick Taylor suggests
in his popular account of the Weimar hyperinflation?[90] This book suggests otherwise. And in doing so, it eschews terms such as 'collective
memory', a concept pioneered by the French sociologist Maurice
Halbwachs.[91] Using collective memory as an operational construct
invites more problems than it solves, partly because it is so hard to define.

Instead, the study centres on the question of power. It shows how a
clash of interests, one given continual life in the Bundesbank Law,
compelled new generations of West Germans to understand contemporary political disputes in historical terms. The origins of this cultural
'aversion' to inflation might well have been psychological, and derived
from personal experience. But the reasons as to why it has persisted so
well in the public sphere are institutional. The preoccupation of
Germany's political culture with inflation today has little to do with the
actual events of 1922–3; rather, we can find its roots in an institutional
divide that the Allied military authorities had set in place in 1948.

Sources

In making its argument, the study uses a variety of sources from a total of
eight archives based in Germany. The sources are of a qualitative nature

---

[89] As noted in Patricia Clavin, 'Review: the impact of inflation and depression on
democracy. New writing on the inter-war economy', *The Historical Journal*, Vol. 38,
No. 3 (1995), p. 749. Refer also to Mark Blyth, *Austerity: the history of a dangerous idea*
(Oxford, 2013), p. 48.
[90] Taylor, *The downfall of money*, p. 359.
[91] See Maurice Halbwachs, *On collective memory*, trans. and ed. Lewis A. Coser (Chicago,
1992); and Maurice Halbwachs, *The collective memory*, trans. Francis J. Ditter and Vida
Y. Ditter (New York, 1980).

for the most part. This reflects the nature of the topic at hand: the book approaches economic history from a cultural perspective and examines the construction of historical narratives that centre on the inter-war era. But this reliance on qualitative sources is also indicative of the fact that quantitative sources are hard to come by. There were no public opinion surveys commissioned in West Germany that examined attitudes to central bank independence until 1986.[92] Where relevant data are available, however, as in the case of media consumption during the 1950s, as well as general attitudes to inflation, the study makes ready use of them.

The majority of sources used, then, are personal correspondence, internal reports, court transcripts, minutes of meetings, speeches, newspaper articles and books. It was important to examine the emergence and development of monetary mythology from several angles and, indeed, eras. This meant travelling to the federal archives in Berlin, to examine Reichsbank files of the pre-1945 period, as well as journeying to Koblenz, where the files for the post-war economics and finance ministries can be found, in addition to those of the federal chancellery. At the centre of my research efforts, however, were the historical and press archives of the Bundesbank, both of which reside in the central bank's compound in Frankfurt.

The archives consulted during the research of the book are as follows: the historical and press archives of the Bundesbank; the federal archives in Koblenz; the other branch of the federal archives in Berlin; the Archiv der sozialen Demokratie in Bonn, in which Social Democratic Party (SPD) sources are held; the Institut für Zeitgeschichte in Munich, which holds a number of useful sources from the United States' Office of Military Government, crucial for understanding the early post-war years; das Historische Archiv des Bundesverbandes der Deutschen Industrie, which holds files pertaining to the influential industrialist lobbying organisation, and which is situated in Berlin; and the German Bundestag parliamentary archive, also located in the capital city. The Zeitungsabteilung, or newspaper branch, of the Staatsbibliothek zu Berlin was also consulted.

Chapter Outline

Chapter 1: In Search of the Reichsbank

Chapter 1 is a background chapter. As such, it relies on secondary sources, though a small number of primary sources are used to reinforce certain points. The chapter examines the evolution of the Reichsbank,

---

[92] And even then, the survey was not commissioned by the government, but rather the Bundesbank. See Lindenlaub, 'Deutsches Stabilitätsbewußtsein', p. 77.

from its establishment in 1876 until the departure of key figures of the directorate in 1939. It devotes particular attention to the record of central bank independence during the inter-war era, and the careers of those Reichsbankers who went on to lead the post-war central bank. The chapter argues that the origins of monetary mythology can be traced back to the Nuremberg trials, where a form of it was first applied in defence of Schacht amid efforts to sanitise both his record and the conduct of the Reichsbank under his tenure.

Chapter 2: The Bank deutscher Länder and the Foundation of West Germany, 1948–1951

Chapter 2 examines the world in which the BdL was established. It centres on the period 1948–51, the latter being the year when monetary sovereignty was transferred by the Allies to the West Germans. The chapter documents the opinions of West German elites in the lead-up to the creation of the BdL, noting that they were split on the question of central bank independence. It argues that a political struggle surrounding the future of the central bank incentivised a variety of West German elites to confront their inter-war monetary history. The chapter then shows how the BdL adopted an active press policy in the effort to influence the Bundesbank Law. Such efforts failed to prove effective during this period, however. Other events, such as the Allied decision to transfer monetary sovereignty to West Germany in 1951, proved more decisive. But it was in this very period that the central bank established a workable framework of historical narratives that could be applied for political ends.

Chapter 3: Adenauer's Challenge: The 'Gürzenich Affair' and the Bank deutscher Länder, 1956–1957

Chapter 3 examines the final years of the Bundesbank Law debate. It documents the extent to which the West German central bank's reputation improved since 1951, and devotes particular attention to a 1956 public attack launched by the chancellor, Adenauer, on the central bank. The controversy that erupted resulted in a publicity coup for the BdL and its independence. The chapter argues that the crucial consequence of the 'Gürzenich affair' was the narrowing of the parameters of monetary debate through which West Germans interpreted the inter-war era.

Moreover, it argues that the provisions outlined in the Bundesbank Law reconfirmed an institutional conflict between Bonn and Frankfurt, one that was originally left behind by the Allied authorities. In providing

no formal process through which conflicts between the federal government and the central bank could be solved quietly, the Bundesbank
Law increased the likelihood that such disagreements would become
'dramatised' and spill into the public sphere. These disagreements, then,
gave rise to public controversies surrounding central bank independence,
and in turn, provided further instances in which inflation narratives could
be geared in support of the Bundesbank. It explains West Germany's
cultural preoccupation with inflation in institutional terms.

Chapter 4: The Shadow of National Socialism: Karl Blessing and the Bundesbank in 1965

Chapter 4 argues that the shadows of the Reichsbank and National
Socialism troubled the Bundesbank well into the 1960s. This was in
large part because of the central bank's president, Blessing. After years
of using the president's inter-war record as a source of credibility, the
central bank began to see these historical narratives being challenged.
Chapter 4, then, examines three case studies that centred on Blessing's
questionable past. The chapter documents the re-emergence in the
public sphere of Schacht, Blessing's mentor during the Reichsbank years.
The former Reichsbank president used his notoriety to popularise the
term 'third inflation', while accusing Blessing of having a role to play in
the second one.

In 1965, too, news reports emerged in West Germany of the central
banker's past membership in Himmler's *Freundeskreis*. These revelations
forced the central bank to intervene covertly in the public sphere, with
the aim of killing these stories as quickly as possible. Proxies of the
Bundesbank sent historical documents, compiled by Blessing's personal
advisor and press chief, to the journalists and editors of the publications
that published the damning allegations. These accusations, and the
Bundesbank's difficulty in addressing them, highlight how the legacy of
the inter-war era continued to trouble the West German central bank
even two decades after the end of the war.

Chapter 5: The Bundesbank, Social Democracy and the Era of the 'Great Inflation', 1970–1978

Chapter 5 examines the independence of the central bank in a decade
riven by economic crises. In 1973, the Bundesbank faced a challenge to
its independence – a challenge that emerged from within the SPD, which
shared power in a coalition government. The argument of Chapter 5
underlines Chapter 3's concluding argument. It highlights how the

Bundesbank Law provided the impetus for conflicts between Bonn and Frankfurt, in turn prompting the use of historical narratives concerning the two inflations applied in support of central bank independence. Furthermore, the chapter goes on to note the extent to which the 1970s were littered with monetary anniversaries. It argues that these occasions, coupled with the economic crises at hand, served as moments of reflection that allowed the Bundesbank to bolster its reputation and reinforce the parameters through which West Germans interpreted the monetary past. The chapter concludes by examining a ceremony that marked the thirtieth anniversary of the deutschmark in 1978. It was a ceremony described by *Time* magazine as a 'monetary memorial'. It is a fitting conclusion to three decades of monetary mythology.

1   In Search of the Reichsbank

Introduction

In June 1945, six weeks after Germany's unconditional surrender to
the Allies, an officer from the Allied military authorities was instructed
to track down missing records and leading officials of the Reichsbank,
an institution that had been the central bank of Germany since 1876. It
was an arduous task, for much of the country lay in ruins. The officer
summarised his findings in a report that captured the uncertainty
and disarray prevailing at the time. It was titled 'In search of the
Reichsbank'.[1] The central bank's headquarters in Berlin was destroyed,
the officer noted. That much was certain. But rumours abounded amid
the rubble. Some Reichsbank officials may have fled to the French zone
of occupation, he heard. Others, like the former Reichsbank president
Hjalmar Schacht, were already caught. Others were missing still.

The minor Reichsbank officials that he could find were in a sorry
state. 'An atmosphere of depression' and resignation reigned among
them.[2] Given the war and the subsequent destruction of the economy,
the country's banking system was now 'pure Alice in Wonderland'.[3]
Frustratingly, much of the information the military officer could gather
was contradictory and led to dead ends. But some common themes did
emerge. 'All Reichsbank men speak with reverence of Schacht', he wrote.
'His portrait still adorned the otherwise empty wall of the manager's
parlour at Meiningen', a town in central Germany.[4]

At the time of the report's submission, American military authorities
were transporting the real Schacht to a small castle near liberated Versailles in France.[5] Only the previous week they decided to try the former
central banker as a war criminal, alongside other leading officials of the

---

[1] E. S. G. Bach, 'In search of the Reichsbank', 30 Jun. 1945, Institut für Zeitgeschichte
[IfZ], 2/206/4 FINAD.
[2] Ibid., pp. 1–2.   [3] Ibid., p. 5.   [4] Ibid., p. 3.
[5] Christopher Kopper, *Hjalmar Schacht. Aufstieg und Fall von Hitlers mächtigstem Bankier*
(Munich, 2010), p. 360.

Third Reich.[6] This news came as a 'great surprise' to Schacht when it reached him.[7] Hitler might have sacked Schacht from his post as president of the Reichsbank in January 1939 – after he and the Reichsbank's directorate sent a memorandum protesting against the inflationary policies of the regime – but that did not stop Schacht being accused of helping to prepare the financing of a war that devastated the European continent.

The Allies set about collecting and compiling information in preparation for the trials. The proceedings came to be known as the Nuremberg trials, which took place from late 1945 onwards. What role did Schacht play in allowing Hitler to come to power back in 1933? What happened in the years leading up to the outbreak of hostilities? How did the Reichsbank, which once looked back on a prestigious history, end up as just another cog in Hitler's war machine? As Schacht sat in the dock at Nuremberg, these questions, among others, came to the fore for the first time.

The first serious, post-war attempt to make sense of Germany's monetary past took place in the courtrooms at Nuremberg. In this respect, the Allied military authorities played a crucial, if somewhat indirect role in laying out the initial parameters of what later became monetary mythology. Schacht was eventually acquitted at Nuremberg. And during his trial, certain historical narratives – or spins on the past – emerged triumphant in the courtroom at the expense of other competing interpretations. These narratives would later be adopted by the leadership of the West German central bank amid efforts to portray their inter-war past in a credible, edifying light. To what extent, however, did the narratives that helped Schacht escape the hangman reflect the actual record of the Reichsbank and the performance of its leading officials?

Like that Allied military officer back in June 1945, this chapter, too, goes in search of the Reichsbank. In doing so, however, it will focus on certain themes. First, it will examine the origins and evolution of central bank independence in Germany. The chapter notes that the Reichsbank was independent of government instruction during both the hyperinflation and Great Depression. Moreover, it will examine how the German central bank, under Schacht, became an overtly political actor in the public sphere for the first time, using its independence to force the hand of democratically elected governments. The chapter highlights the mixed record of inter-war central bank independence, offering context as to why central bank independence would go on to

---

[6] Ibid., pp. 359–60.
[7] Hjalmar Schacht, *76 Jahre meines Lebens* (Bad Wörishofen, 1953), p. 568.

be a subject of controversy in the immediate post-war period, when legislators and politicians tussled over the Bundesbank Law, a piece of legislation that would create the future Bundesbank. The performance of the inter-war Reichsbank was one of the main reference points during these debates.

Second, the chapter will document the respective careers of three Reichsbankers: Schacht, Wilhelm Vocke and Karl Blessing. It does so for several reasons. In Germany, Schacht was the first to pioneer an active press policy in the realm of central banking, thereby establishing a precedent and example for the post-war era. More importantly, however, the first outline of monetary mythology at Nuremberg centred on defending Schacht's record. To have a deeper understanding of these historical narratives, then, we will need to understand what happened to Schacht and the Reichsbank leading up to his departure in 1939. Vocke and Blessing, for their part, later went on to assume the public face of the West German central bank in the media between 1948 and 1969 – that is, a period spanning two decades. Both men, who appeared at the Nuremberg trials as witnesses, would later use monetary mythology to defend their credibility and reputations in the post-war era.

Finally, the chapter will conclude by examining how the record of the Reichsbank first came to be debated during the Nuremberg trials. True, the origins of central banking in Germany were statist. Entwined with questions of nation and empire in the late nineteenth century, the rise and fall of the Reichsbank mirrored the fortunes of the state itself. But the origins of monetary mythology, this chapter argues, are far more recent. All roads lead back to Nuremberg.

The Reichsbank in Wilhelmine Germany

The Reichsbank was a product of a newly unified Germany. From its inception, the central bank oversaw the gold mark, a currency that could be used across the nation. But the gold mark itself was only a recent creation. Before the establishment of the Second Reich, a plethora of states and currencies littered the German landscape. Even as late as the early 1870s, over thirty private note-issuing banks issued paper currency, and twenty-two different states issued treasury notes, all of which could be used as legal tender.[8] The metal, value and denomination of the currency used often differed from one region to the next, creating serious

---

[8] Statistische Abteilung der Reichsbank, 'Reichsbank. Geschichte und Organisation', 30 Dec. 1930, Bundesarchiv, Berlin-Lichterfelde [BAB], R2501/6346, p. 1.

obstacles for trade across the states.[9] Crucially, it would take political
unification to create the momentum for a single currency – which
emerged in its own right as 'a symbol of national unity' – and, moreover,
an institution to oversee that currency.[10] As one Reichsbank report in
1930 noted, '[t]he establishment of the Reichsbank stemmed from the
acknowledgement that the political unification of Germany required a
unified regulation of monetary affairs and, in particular, the centralisation of the central bank system'.[11]

The birth of the German gold mark was streaked with blood and iron,
however, much like the nation itself. A series of small wars in the 1860s,
engineered by Otto von Bismarck, the Prussian statesman, created political conditions suitable for a unified Germany to emerge onto the world
stage. But it was the outcome of Franco-Prussian War of 1870–1, in
particular, that proved particularly conducive to the establishment of the
German gold mark. Following its decisive defeat in the conflict, France
was obliged to pay reparations to the victor, and to the Germans' surprise, these payments arrived in quick fashion. Five billion gold francs
flowed into Germany. This inflow allowed for the amassing of sufficient
gold reserves to create a unified currency and place the country on the
gold standard.[12] France's disintegration on the battlefield contributed
decisively to Germany's monetary integration.

But the Reichsbank had yet to be established. A centralised monetary
authority, in other words, did not regulate the issuance of gold, silver and
fractional money for the first few years of the mark's life. This task was
left to politicians and private banks. Two parliamentary assemblies, the
Reichstag and Bundesrat, passed a series of legislative acts – in 1871,
1873 and 1874 – which took to regulating the supply of money in the
wider economy.[13] And as the historian Harold James notes, private banks
often took on central banking functions during this crucial period;
Deutsche Bank, for instance, assumed the task of selling the country's

[9] Knut Borchardt, 'Währung und Wirtschaft', in Deutsche Bundesbank (ed.), *Währung und Wirtschaft in Deutschland 1876–1975* (Frankfurt am Main, 1976), pp. 3–4.
[10] Christoph Buchheim, 'Von altem Geld zu neuem Geld. Währungsreformen im 20. Jahrhundert', in Reinhard Spree (ed.), *Geschichte der deutschen Wirtschaft im 20. Jahrhundert* (Munich, 2001), pp. 141–2.
[11] Statistische Abteilung der Reichsbank, 'Reichsbank. Geschichte und Organisation', p. 1.
[12] Marc Flandreau, 'The French crime of 1873: an essay on the emergence of the international gold standard, 1870–1880', *Journal of Economic History*, Vol. 56, No. 4 (1996), p. 873.
[13] Carl-Ludwig Holtfrerich, 'Relations between monetary authorities and governmental institutions: the case of Germany from the 19th century to the present', in Gianni Toniolo (ed.), *Central banks' independence in historical perspective* (Berlin, 1988), p. 107.

silver on the world market amid Germany's transition to gold.[14] Yet private banks in Germany were rocked by financial instability during the early 1870s. A sustained outflow of gold only served to aggravate this instability, placing the country's commitment to the gold standard under intense scrutiny.[15] These dangers emphasised the need for a centralised institution capable of tackling Germany's monetary problems and stabilising the financial system.

The Bank Law – the piece of legislation that established the Reichsbank – was passed on 14 March 1875, and the new central bank opened its doors in Berlin on 1 January 1876.[16] The Reichsbank was closely modelled on, and indeed it largely assumed the functions of, the Prussian Bank, a leading private bank that had been founded in the 1840s to help foster and stabilise the industrialisation of the Prussian state.[17] Though the Prussian Bank was explicitly statist, serving the interests of Prussia and its elites, it also had a private character. The bank's share capital was held largely by private shareholders – by and large, the big banks – with the state allotted a minority share. The Prussian Bank served as the German states' de facto central bank, circulating as much as two-thirds of banknotes across the numerous territories.[18] Despite its private ownership, however, the Prussian Bank was treated as a 'juridical person under public law'. The importance of this legal definition lay in the fact that the bank's policies could be formally controlled by the Prussian state.

Enter the Reichsbank. The new central bank was once again treated as a 'juridical person under public law', and again it was largely owned by private capital. The monetary authority was established to promote the interests of the Reich: to regulate the circulation of money; to facilitate the settlement of payments; and to promote the use of available capital in the economy.[19] Under the Bank Law of 1875, the chancellor of the Reich became the head of the new monetary authority.[20] Members of the

---

[14] Harold James, 'The Reichsbank 1876–1945', in Deutsche Bundesbank (ed.), *Fifty years of the Deutsche Mark: central bank and the currency in Germany since 1948* (Oxford, 1999), p. 6.

[15] 'It was in the context of protecting German gold from flowing out that the phrase "guardian of the currency" was first used [for the Reichsbank]'. Ibid., pp. 7–8.

[16] Simone Reinhardt, *Die Reichsbank in der Weimarer Republik. Eine Analyse der formalen und faktischen Unabhängigkeit* (Frankfurt am Main, 2000), p. 69.

[17] Dieter Ziegler, 'Die Entstehung der Reichsbank 1875', in Dieter Lindenlaub, Carsten Burhop and Joachim Scholtyseck (eds.), *Schlüsselereignisse der deutschen Bankengeschichte* (Stuttgart, 2013), pp. 168–70.

[18] The details concerning the Prussian Bank here are found in Holtfrerich, 'Relations between monetary authorities and governmental', pp. 108–9.

[19] Ibid., p. 109.   [20] Reinhardt, *Die Reichsbank in der Weimarer Republik*, p. 69.

central bank's executive body, the directorate, were nominated by
Germany's upper parliament and in turn appointed by the Kaiser. When
it came to cases of conflict with the government, the Reichsbank had to
follow the instructions of the chancellor.[21] The government exercised
another form of influence over the central bank in the form of the
Kuratorium, an oversight body of which the Reich's chancellor was
chairman. The *Generalversammlung*, or general assembly, represented
the interests of private shareholders. It elected a central committee, or
Zentralausschuß, to offer advisory functions for the benefit of the directorate.[22] Taken as a whole, it can be seen that the Reichsbank was placed
under the thumb of the government – indeed, 'much more so than the
central banks in other European states, like France and Great Britain', as
Carl-Ludwig Holtfrerich observes.[23]

The provisions in the Bank Law could be changed. The government
retained the right to terminate the central bank itself or purchase its share
capital at face value, the latter a move that would in effect nationalise the
Reichsbank. There were checks and balances against this procedure, of
course. For instance, the Kaiser had to receive the agreement of the
Bundesrat before the government could follow through with the action.
And the state could only exercise this option fifteen years after the
establishment of the Reichsbank – the first debate kicked off in 1889 –
and only then every ten years thereafter; for example, in 1899 and
1909.[24]

Crucially, this legal provision sparked a regular debate every decade
about whether the Reichsbank should be nationalised. And these
debates, for their part, revealed the political appetite concerning the
central bank's relative autonomy vis-à-vis the state. On one side of the
fence stood right-wing organisations and political parties that favoured
the nationalisation of the central bank, a step that would allow the state to
further serve the interests of industry and agriculture. On the other side,
however, stood liberals and figures on the left, who pushed for the
maintenance of a private–public framework that could act as a bulwark,
or counterweight, against what they saw as an unduly authoritarian
state.[25] The German political left, in other words, originally supported
the autonomy of the central bank. In the end, the Reichsbank was never
nationalised. Arguments contending that a nationalised central bank

---

[21] Ibid., pp. 70–1.   [22] Ibid., p. 72.
[23] Holtfrerich, 'Relations between monetary authorities and governmental institutions',
p. 108.
[24] Ibid., pp. 110, 112.   [25] James, 'The Reichsbank 1876–1945', p. 10.

would easily become the tool of the government's fiscal ambitions won the day.

On paper, the mixed status of the Reichsbank suggested a sizeable degree of government influence. But, in practice, the Reichsbank enjoyed a considerable amount of autonomy. There were just two occasions when the chancellor ordered its directorate to undertake specific actions. The first occurred in late 1880, when the chancellor instructed the central bank to increase the discount rate and restrict Lombard credit – the latter decision essentially making it more difficult for banks to use security deposits against loans. The second episode was more overtly political and fused with considerations of foreign policy; in November 1887, Bismarck ordered the Reichsbank to disallow the use of Russian securities as collateral for loans.[26]

These were isolated incidents, though. The main constraints were to be found elsewhere. And they were not political, but economic in nature. The Reichsbank was required to cover one-third of its note circulation with German 'legal tender'. This term primarily meant gold reserves, but it also included Reich treasury notes, which were strictly limited in size, as well as silver coins minted by German states. The remainder of the Reichsbank's note circulation had to be covered by qualified commercial bills and cheques.[27] Unlike the Bank of England, the Reichsbank was given the ability to issue banknotes in accordance to the needs of its business; this flexibility allowed it to issue notes beyond the one-third coverage requirement, but at the expense of the central bank having to pay a small tax.[28] As a result, an incentive structure was in place to ensure that the Reichsbank's note issue was kept within the approved limit. The level of note circulation, then, depended primarily on the Reichsbank's gold reserves.[29]

Today, central banks are interventionist institutions. But under the international gold standard, they were largely seen as passive actors. The idea of an interventionist central bank had not yet come about during this period, something that Blessing often remarked upon in a wistful fashion

---

[26] Holtfrerich documents both occasions in Holtfrerich, 'Relations between monetary authorities and governmental institutions', p. 112.

[27] Reinhardt, *Die Reichsbank in der Weimarer Republik*, pp. 76–7.

[28] James, 'The Reichsbank 1876–1945', pp. 8–9.

[29] For more on the gold standard, and its relevance for inter-war policymakers, see Barry Eichengreen's chapter, 'The classical gold standard in interwar perspective', in Barry Eichengreen, *Golden fetters: the gold standard and the Great Depression* (Oxford, 1992), pp. 29–66. In terms of a purely historical treatment, see John Singleton, *Central banking in the twentieth century* (Cambridge, 2011), pp. 46–9. Refer also to Patricia Clavin, *The Great Depression in Europe, 1929–1939* (London, 2000), p. 43.

as Bundesbank president during the post-war era.[30] An adherence to the gold standard meant, at times, a weary toleration of recessions amid efforts to maintain the gold parity. This was entirely possible in an era when suffrage was relatively limited, as was the case in imperial Germany. People could not yet oust the governments that asked for too much economic sacrifice on the part of their citizens. It was arguably the gold standard, and not the German government, that acted as the major constraint on the Reichsbank's room for manoeuvre before 1914.

Between 1876 and the lead-up to the First World War, the Reichsbank oversaw rising prosperity among large segments of the population. Industrial production rose sixfold in Germany between 1871 and 1914, whereas industrial production in England merely doubled. German steel production shot up tenfold in the same period.[31] Germany had transformed itself into a largely industrialised state. During this time, the Reichsbank won itself a sizeable degree of credibility, particularly on the international circuit. 'This bank organization, which strikes the mean between a purely state bank and a purely private one, has proved to be the best system according to the experiences of most European countries', observed one American study in 1910.[32]

War

In 1914, European commerce and trade came to a sudden halt with the outbreak of war. Many Germans, though not the military leadership, expected the war to be a relatively short one – like the Franco-Prussian War, which had erupted some forty years earlier.[33] This expectation of a short war was important when it comes to explaining Germany's war financing strategies at the start of the conflict. A crucial decision was made: Germans were not to be taxed for the war effort. The government set about pursuing other methods of financing the conflict. Sizeable attempts were made to win over the support of the population. Numerous,

---

[30] See, for instance, Karl Blessing, 'Vortrag des Präsidenten der Deutschen Bundesbank Karl Blessing', 10 Nov. 1961, Deutsche Bundesbank Historisches Archiv [DBHA], B330/7528, pp. 2–3.

[31] Hans-Joachim Braun, *The German economy in the twentieth century* (London, 1990), p. 19.

[32] National Monetary Commission, United States Senate, *The Reichsbank, 1876–1900* (Washington, 1910), p. 29.

[33] Braun, *The German economy in the twentieth century*, p. 25. The historian Annika Mombauer details how Helmuth von Moltke, the chief of the general staff, expected a long war. See Annika Mombauer, *Helmuth von Moltke and the origins of the First World War* (Cambridge, 2001), p. 95.

and, during the first two years at least, successful war bonds were issued by the German government.[34] The initial success of these bonds was, in effect, a sign of support and confidence on the part of the German people.[35] But their confidence did not last and deprivations took their toll on the morale of the population.[36] Widespread hardship became evident during the 'turnip winter' of 1916–17.[37] Indeed, by 1916, the government was unable to sell all its war bonds to the German people, a development suggesting that the population was tiring of the war.

The German government had to look elsewhere for financing. In short, the state borrowed the resources to pay for the war effort. This was a political calculation. And it was a gamble. The decision was dependent on the implicit assumption that future generations of Germans would be expected to foot the bill, and the somewhat more explicitly stated aim that the war's losers would be expected to pay reparations. And Germany had no intention of being among the losers. In a famous and oft-cited address before the German Reichstag in 1915, Karl Helfferich, the secretary of state for the treasury, announced that it would be Germany's opponents that would have to pay for the suffering and costs entailed during the fighting.[38]

Where did the Reichsbank fit into all this? The German mark's convertibility into gold was effectively suspended with the outbreak of war.[39] Technically, the Reichsbank was still obliged to maintain its one-third coverage requirement. But as the historian Gerald Feldman notes, new measures were put in place by the government that allowed the central bank to circumvent this constraint.[40] The Reichsbank was now allowed to use 'loan bureau' notes as an optional substitute for its gold reserves. Loan bureaus were newly created subsidiaries of the Reichsbank itself. They issued notes that were to be backed by collateral such as commodities or bonds. Conveniently, this collateral included war bonds issued by

[34] Indeed, Gerald Feldman writes of the Reichsbank's 'verve, skill and imagination' in 'promoting' these war bonds. See Gerald D. Feldman, *The great disorder: politics, economics, and society in the German inflation 1914–1924* (Oxford, 1996), p. 654. Also quoted in James, 'The Reichsbank 1876–1945', p. 18.
[35] James, 'The Reichsbank 1876–1945', pp. 18–19.
[36] This morale, too, should be placed in its proper context. The narrative concerning the jubilant 'spirit of 1914' has been challenged by more recent research. The outbreak of the First World War was greeted in a variety of fashions, ranging from enthusiasm to resignation. See Roger Chickering, *Imperial Germany and the Great War, 1914–1918*, 3rd edn (Cambridge, 2014), pp. 14–18.
[37] Braun, *The German economy in the twentieth century*, p. 30.
[38] David Marsh, *The Bundesbank: the bank that rules Europe* (London, 1992), p. 91.
[39] Volkswirtschaftliche und Statistische Abteilung der Reichsbank, 'Entwicklung, Aufbau und Aufgaben der Reichsbank', Nov. 1933, BAB, R2501/6355, p. 2.
[40] Feldman, *The great disorder*, pp. 32–3.

the government. As a result, war bonds issued by the government allowed the central bank to expand credit.[41] The rudiments of a credit-creating mechanism had been put in place.

Germany had become a war economy. As government expenditure soared, the amount and quality of goods in the economy began to dwindle. By the war's end, some 10.1 billion marks' worth of loan bureau notes and 22.2 billion marks' worth of Reichsbank notes were in circulation.[42] The money supply had increased fivefold since the start of the war, and price and exchange rate controls were put in place during the hostilities to counter the inflationary pressure stemming from such an increase.[43] Indeed, the government banned the media's very use of the word 'inflation'.[44] Nevertheless, despite these measures, wholesale prices roughly doubled in the four-year period.[45]

The German government saw rising prices as preferable to the alternative of increasing taxes and imposing a direct burden upon the population – a move that had the potential of triggering social unrest across the country. Inflation was seen as a tolerable by-product of state policies that were geared towards winning the war. Indeed, as Christoph Buchheim notes, many Germans at the time viewed this '*Teuerung*', or rise in prices, as a largely reversible one come the end of hostilities.[46] This was not to be, however. In 1914, the arbitrary will of the government had replaced the level of gold reserves as the main determinant of credit supply in the economy. As such, it was in that year that the seeds of the 1922–3 hyperinflation were first sown.

Revolution

The war came to a bloody end in November 1918. And instead of victory, Germans were greeted with defeat. Revolution broke out on the streets of Berlin.[47] A democratic republic was declared and an armistice signed. The Kaiser fled, seeking refuge in the Netherlands. All the while, hundreds of thousands of soldiers returned from the front – but to what jobs? The economy, stricken with economic, social and political disruption, was paralysed. Days turned into months. The

---

[41] Ibid., pp. 34–7.   [42] James, 'The Reichsbank 1876–1945', p. 17.
[43] Braun, *The German economy in the twentieth century*, p. 37.
[44] Singleton, *Central banking in the twentieth century*, p. 71.
[45] Theo Balderston, *Economics and politics of the Weimar Republic* (Cambridge, 2002), p. 34.
[46] Buchheim, 'Von altem Geld zu neuem Geld. Währungsreformen im 20. Jahrhundert', p. 143. See also Clavin, *The Great Depression*, p. 17.
[47] The classic overview is detailed in Eberhard Kolb, *The Weimar Republic* (London, 1988), pp. 3–23.

political power of labour increased markedly. Government spending began to swell amid efforts to cope with the economic situation. Employers agreed to unprecedented wage increases in the effort to stave off the revolutionary fervour.[48]

On top of these domestic developments, the terms of the punitive post-war settlement, the Versailles Treaty, were announced in June 1919. Article 231 of the treaty held Germany responsible for the outbreak of war, thereby establishing legal ground for German reparations, the figure of which had yet to be determined.[49] Even before this total had been announced, the terms of the settlement were met with disgust within and, indeed, outside Germany.[50] Eventually, in May 1921, the Allied powers settled on a reparations figure of 132 billion gold marks, an amount greeted with outrage in the Weimar Republic.[51]

All these factors, and more, contributed towards ballooning state budget deficits. Government spending served as the primary motor for the inflation that followed. Onlookers were not impressed. 'The public finances are in that desperate state which must necessarily follow on four years of gambling [financing the war] followed by two years during which revenue could not meet expenditure', wrote one British observer with respect to the situation in Germany in 1920.

The root of the evil is beyond doubt the incessant flow of paper money which ever swells the note circulation. The possibility of putting a stop to this fatal increase has been the subject of much discussion without any really positive result being reached.[52]

It is in this troubled context that we must approach the Reichsbank. Any prospect of returning to the gold standard, now seen as a 'Paradise Lost', was ruled out considering Germany's debt and the government's spending woes.[53] As before the First World War, the central bank remained beholden to government instructions. The directorate could have resigned in protest of the state's spending ambitions. But such a protest would have been, at best, of moral value. It would have served little practical use. Its hands tied, the Reichsbank took to issuing

---

[48] Harold James, 'Economic reasons for the collapse of Weimar', in Ian Kershaw (ed.), *Weimar: why did German democracy fail?* (London, 1990), p. 38.

[49] Charles Feinstein, Peter Temin and Gianni Toniolo, *The European economy between the wars* (Oxford, 1997), p. 35.

[50] See, for instance, Keynes's famous work, John M. Keynes, *The economic consequences of the peace* (London, 1919).

[51] Balderston, *Economics and politics of the Weimar Republic*, p. 20.

[52] J.W.F. Thelwall, *General report on the industrial and economic situation in Germany in December, 1920 (Department of Overseas Trade)* (London, 1921), p. 3.

[53] Feldman, *The great disorder*, p. 29.

confidential letters and annual reports to the government, warning of the dire consequences of such inflationary spending.[54] At one point, in 1919, the Reichsbank even threatened to cut off the credit line to the government.[55] This threat, however, did not materialise. In late 1921 the Reichsbank president, Rudolf Havenstein, lamented to his friend Montagu Norman, the governor of the Bank of England, that to stop the printing press was to send a cash-strapped government over the brink.[56] Nevertheless, as the historian Simone Reinhardt notes, during the inflation years the central bank explicitly 'avoided criticising the government in the public sphere and presented itself as loyal to the Reich'.[57] With Havenstein at the helm of the Reichsbank, tension between the central bank and government was kept hidden from the public eye.

The Weimar state used inflationary financing as a coping mechanism of sorts. In this sense, the republic pursued a policy that was common across Europe in the years immediately following the First World War. 'Allowing inflation to rise, enabled governments to sidestep awkward political choices and helped to ease the distributional conflict in society', argues Patricia Clavin.[58] There were other advantages for the German government, too. The inflation, for example, reduced the real burden of its very sizeable domestic debts. Furthermore, between 1920 and 1921, the mark depreciated to such an extent that Germany could 'enjoy relatively high employment and strong export advantages in comparison to the victor nations, which [were] undergoing a severe depression induced by their deflationary policies'.[59] Rising prices assisted industrial production and allowed for various economic groups to be bought off temporarily, allowing the state to buy itself much-needed time to get its house in order.[60]

It was during these heady times that Vocke and Blessing arrived at the central bank. Born in 1886 to a pastor's family in northern Bavaria, Vocke entered the Reichsbank as a young man in 1918, having spent the years during the war working in government ministries. He became a member of the directorate just one year later, an ascent that caused some

---

[54] Reinhardt, *Die Reichsbank in der Weimarer Republik*, pp. 136–9.
[55] Marsh, *The Bundesbank*, p. 98.   [56] Ibid., p. 287 (footnote).
[57] Reinhardt, *Die Reichsbank in der Weimarer Republik*, p. 136.
[58] Clavin, *The Great Depression*, p. 31.
[59] Gerald D. Feldman, 'The historian and the German inflation', in Nathan Schmukler and Edward Marcus (eds.), *Inflation through the ages: economic, social, psychological, and historical aspects* (New York, 1983), p. 390.
[60] Otto Pfleiderer, 'Die Reichsbank in der Zeit der großen Inflation, die Stabilisierung der Mark und die Aufwertung von Kapitalforderungen', in Deutsche Bundesbank (ed.), *Währung und Wirtschaft in Deutschland 1876–1975* (Frankfurt am Main, 1976), p. 176.

discomfort among other potential candidates for the position.[61] Vocke remained in the directorate until his departure from the central bank in February 1939, some two decades later. The Reichsbank had another new recruit during this period. Born in Württemberg in 1900, Blessing joined the central bank in 1920. He worked in the foreign exchange and economics departments of the central bank, delving into the reparations and transfer problems that troubled the young republic. Despite the lack of a third level education, a sharp intelligence ensured Blessing's rapid ascent within the Reichsbank, as well as earning the confidence of a future Reichsbank president: a man by the name of Schacht.[62]

Central Bank Independence

In May 1922, the Reichsbank became independent of German government instruction. A few factors led to this development. In her study of the Reichsbank, Reinhardt highlights three in particular.[63] First, she stresses the crucial role played by the Allied powers, forcing the hand of the German government to implement central bank independence.[64] Second, Reinhardt highlights the international Zeitgeist of the inter-war era. A number of international conferences concerning the economic reconstruction of Europe, such as the Brussels conference in 1920, as well as the Geneva conference in 1922, called for the establishment of independent central banks as one means towards rectifying the mistakes of economically illiterate politicians.[65] The finance committee of the newly established League of Nations, too, was an active supporter of central bank independence in the 1920s, organising the imposition of independent monetary authorities in Austria and Hungary during the decade.[66]

And third, Reinhardt notes how the collapse of the gold standard transformed central banks from largely passive institutions, which

---

[61] Wilhelm Vocke, *Memoiren* (Stuttgart, 1973), pp. 75–6.

[62] Christopher Kopper, *Bankiers unterm Hakenkreuz* (Munich, 2008), p. 184.

[63] Reinhardt summarises these three points in her conclusion. See Reinhardt, *Die Reichsbank in der Weimarer Republik*, pp. 273–4.

[64] Ibid., pp. 85–92.

[65] Ibid., pp. 44–9. Refer also to Singleton, *Central banking in the twentieth century*, pp. 58–9.

[66] Germany, however, was not yet a member of the League of Nations. See Patricia Clavin, *Securing the world economy: the reinvention of the League of Nations, 1920–1946* (Oxford, 2013), pp. 25–6. At any rate, the Allied powers chose to intervene directly. Reinhardt, *Die Reichsbank in der Weimarer Republik*, pp. 51–5. For more on the finance committee of the League of Nations, see Patricia Clavin, '"Money talks." Competition and cooperation with the League of Nations, 1929–40', in Marc Flandreau (ed.), *Money doctors: the experience of international financial advising, 1850–2000* (London, 2003), pp. 219–24.

oversaw inflows and outflows of the balance of payments, to active players that could manipulate the value of their respective currencies.[67] Central banks now controlled the important lever that was monetary policy. In a new democratic environment, inter-war elites viewed it important that central banks be independent of these new, worrisome political pressures.

With the wider European context in mind, we can now approach the case of the Reichsbank. How did the Allies exert pressure upon Germany to make the Reichsbank independent vis-à-vis the Weimar state? It centred on reparations. In order that Germany should receive a moratorium on reparations payments, the Allied powers demanded that the Reichsbank be made autonomous.[68] The international pressure placed upon Germany was enormous; and the British played a significant role in pushing for a Reichsbank that was independent of government influence.[69] The Autonomy Law was passed on 21 May 1922.[70] The central bank's directorate could now decide monetary policy on its own; it was not beholden to government instruction. The chancellor was no longer the head of the Reichsbank, but he remained the chairman of the *Kuratorium*, a board that merely exercised supervisory functions.[71] The Reichsbank appointment procedure also changed. The second parliament, the Reichsrat, nominated members of the directorate, who were then formally appointed by the Reich president – but only after the expert opinion of both the directorate and central committee had been heard.[72]

'This is not the voluntary act of the German legislation, but rather the implementation of an Allied dictate', argued Helfferich, who remained an influential conservative figure.[73] It would be the first of two occasions that foreign governments imposed central bank independence upon Germany, as Buchheim wryly notes, the second time occurring in 1948 with the establishment of the Bank deutscher Länder (BdL).[74] Helfferich, however, grudgingly supported the legislation. He was not

---

[67] Reinhardt, *Die Reichsbank in der Weimarer Republik*, pp. 273–4.   [68] Ibid., pp. 85–92.
[69] Liaquat Ahamed, *Lords of finance: the bankers who broke the world* (New York, 2009), p. 188.
[70] Helmut Müller has written of the 'foreign policy origins of autonomy' of the Reichsbank. See Helmut Müller, *Die Zentralbank – Eine Nebenregierung: Reichsbankpräsident Hjalmar Schacht als Politiker der Weimarer Republik* (Opladen, 1973), p. 38.
[71] Reinhardt, *Die Reichsbank in der Weimarer Republik*, pp. 93–4.
[72] See Salomon Flink, *The German Reichsbank and economic Germany* (New York, 1930), pp. 63–4.
[73] Karl Helfferich, 'Die Autonomie der Reichsbank', *Bank-Archiv*, 1. Apr. 1922, BAB, R2501/6405, p. 215.
[74] Buchheim, 'Von altem Geld zu neuem Geld. Währungsreformen im 20. Jahrhundert', pp. 151–2.

alone. Though disillusioned by the manner in which central bank independence was forced upon the German central bank, broad swathes of the German political elite supported the move. Representatives of the Social Democratic Party (SPD), too, were in favour of the Autonomy Law.[75] This position was largely in line with the left's favourable opinion of central bank autonomy during the Wilhelmine era.

But trouble soon emerged. In June 1922, shortly after the law's passage, the Allied Reparation Commission (ARC) complained to the German government about the Autonomy Law. The commission highlighted the manners in which the Autonomy Law failed to safeguard the Reichsbank's independence. There were two concerns. First, the German government still had a say in the appointment of leading central bank officials. And second, the Autonomy Law failed to outline a set, fixed limit as to the amount the Reichsbank could lend the government.[76] The independent Reichsbank, the ARC noted, could still finance the government should it *choose* to do so. These fears soon turned out to be justified.

The Reichsbank had become independent, but little changed. The central bank still continued to discount government paper, thereby allowing the inflation to continue. In a letter to Norman, the Reichsbank president outlined his views as to the actual value of the Reichsbank's new-found independence. Havenstein saw 'limited possibilities' for any change of course in the Reichsbank's financing.[77] His reasons were largely political ones. The Reichsbank president was convinced that the roots of the inflation lay in Germany's balance of payments problems, which, in his mind, stemmed from the reparations payments to the Allied powers. Without removing this obstacle, the Reichsbank had little choice but to finance the government's growing deficits. '[T]he conditions forced upon us are stronger than human beings', he confessed.[78] Indeed, Havenstein argued later that, were the Reichsbank to refuse the government the latter's requests for credits, the consequences would have been catastrophic for the economy; and that was a responsibility that the Reichsbank could not assume.[79]

---

[75] Statistische Abteilung der Reichsbank, 'Stellung der Sozialdemokratie zur Autonomie der Reichsbank', 11 Jan. 1928, BAB, R2501/6405.

[76] Reparation Commission, 'Material (Ergänzungsnote der Repko), wonach der Reparationskommission die Regelung der Autonomic nicht "volle" Umfange genugt (English version)', 14 Jun. 1922, BAB, R2501/6405, pp. 9–10.

[77] Rudolf Havenstein to Montagu Norman (English version), 4 Mar. 1922, BAB, R2501/6308, p. 9.

[78] Ibid.

[79] Havenstein made this point in an angry response to *The Daily Telegraph*, a British newspaper, after it published a report blaming the Reichsbank for the inflation. See

Born in turmoil, the Weimar Republic enjoyed little support among large segments of the population. The republic continued to be rocked by political and economic unrest, and the memory of the 1918 revolution was still vivid. Inflation was seen as a lesser evil to that of revolution. Crucially, Havenstein saw himself as a 'dutiful *Beamter*', or civil servant, to the Reich first and foremost.[80] The Reichsbank leadership saw its first duty as being loyal to the state, a consideration all too informed by the fact that its recent independence came from foreign pressure.[81] 'From May 1922 on, the Reichsbank was dependent not on the government, but on the national interest, as the bank's leaders judged it to be', notes Holtfrerich.[82] And although he became increasingly desperate behind the scenes, Havenstein still refused to criticise the government in public.[83]

Events accelerated. Burdened by reparations and rampant speculation on international markets, the German currency continued its descent in exchange markets. The onset of hyperinflation began in June 1922, shortly after the central bank became independent.[84] Some months later, in January 1923, France and Belgium occupied the Ruhr, Germany's major industrial region, after the country fell behind on its reparations payments. The German government sided with the Ruhr people and supported – that is, funded – an open-ended policy of passive resistance, assisting workers and firms alike.[85] Considerations of foreign policy trumped economic reason, in turn aggravating the inflation.

A young Sebastian Haffner, who later became a leading journalist in the post-war era, recalled how the values and order of the old world seemed to dissolve.[86] His father, an austere Prussian civil servant, floundered helplessly amid what the old man saw as a 'monstrous scandal'. Only the astute efforts of Haffner's mother saved the family from ruin; for

---

'Übersetzung aus "The Daily Telegraph" vom 6. September 1922: "Die deutsche Reichsbank"', 6 Sep. 1922, BAB, R2501/6308, p. 3.

[80] Kopper, *Hjalmar Schacht*, pp. 62–3.

[81] Reinhardt, *Die Reichsbank in der Weimarer Republik*, p. 142.

[82] Holtfrerich, 'Relations between monetary authorities and governmental institutions', p. 116.

[83] Müller, *Die Zentralbank – Eine Nebenregierung*, p. 38.

[84] The chapter adopts the conventional definition of hyperinflation: '[c]onventionally defined as a rate of price increase exceeding 50% per month'. See Balderston, *Economics and politics of the Weimar Republic*, pp. 35, 104 (glossary definition). A similar definition is also used in Singleton, *Central banking in the twentieth century*, p. 179.

[85] Feldman, *The great disorder*, pp. 576–7, 704, 706.

[86] Sebastian Haffner, *Defying Hitler: a memoir* (London, 2002), pp. 41–54. See also the experiences detailed in Thomas A. Kohut, *A German generation: an experiential history of the twentieth century* (London, 2012), pp. 72–6.

instance, the family descended on the wholesale market as soon as the father's wages arrived, towing one month's supply of non-perishable foodstuffs back to the house before breakfast time. The next day, his father's wages would have been worthless.[87]

Economic incentives were skewed. The inflation benefited those without scruples. Borrowers won out, while creditors were punished. 'The old and unworldly had the worst of it', wrote Haffner.[88] People on fixed incomes, such as pensioners, saw what little wealth they had disappear. There was a flight into real assets, such as property; and a barter exchange system developed in place of the mark. By November 1923, over 300 paper mills and roughly 2,000 printing presses worked around the clock to distribute Reichsbank notes. On 11 November, a 1 kg loaf of bread cost 428 thousand million marks.[89]

The events of 1922–3 marked the culmination of Germany's ten-year inflation. The hyperinflation came to an end in November 1923. For months prior to this, however, the government had sought the resignation of Havenstein. The Reichsbank president had become vilified in the media.[90] Indeed, one news report at the time dubbed Havenstein as the 'father of the inflation'.[91] Gustav Stresemann, the chancellor from August to November of that year, saw Havenstein as being inextricably associated with the inflation. A new currency required confidence – and that confidence was hard to win if Havenstein remained as the figurehead of the Reichsbank.

Yet Havenstein pointed to the central bank's recent independence: Berlin was no longer able to remove Reichsbank officials from their positions. The Reichsbank president informed the government that he intended to step down in 1924 – and not any sooner.[92] The provisions of the Autonomy Law thus inadvertently prolonged the length of the crisis by allowing Havenstein, a 'tragic personality', as Vocke later noted, to remain in office.[93] At the height of the hyperinflation, there were numerous calls in the public sphere to have the Autonomy Law altered so as to enable the removal of Havenstein and stop the Reichsbank from acting like, in the words of chancellor Stresemann, a 'state within a state'.[94] The argument surrounding Havenstein's departure soon solved itself,

[87] Haffner, *Defying Hitler*, pp. 46–7.   [88] Ibid., p. 45.
[89] Braun, *The German economy in the twentieth century*, p. 39.
[90] Reinhardt, *Die Reichsbank in der Weimarer Republik*, p. 158.
[91] 'Hugo Stinnes möchte den Leiter der Reichsbank entfernen (German translation of article published in *The Commercial and Financial Chronicle*)', 13 Nov. 1922, BAB, R2501/6339, p. 1.
[92] Müller, *Die Zentralbank – Eine Nebenregierung*, p. 27.   [93] Vocke, *Memoiren*, p. 76.
[94] Reinhardt, *Die Reichsbank in der Weimarer Republik*, pp. 158–9.

however. After months of tussling, the beleaguered Reichsbank president died of a heart attack on 20 November 1923.[95] In the end, regardless of whether the central bank was independent or not, the hyperinflation had 'seriously damaged its credibility' as a guardian of the German currency.[96] As Figures 1.1 and 1.2 demonstrate, by the end of the hyperinflation, the signatures of the Reichsbank directorate guaranteeing the value of their banknotes meant very little indeed.

Stabilisation

How did monetary stabilisation come about? Germany required a complete currency and banking reform. This would only emerge in 1924. Until then, two institutions were set up to tide the economy over: the Rentenbank and the Gold Discount Bank. These banks operated alongside the Reichsbank in the crucial period leading up to the currency reform. The Rentenbank issued the rentenmark. This new currency was an altogether different creature to that of the mark. Its value stemmed from collateral of debentures on German industrial and agricultural real estate – that is, from private property, not gold.[97] The Rentenbank was treated as a 'juridical person under private law', its operations run by private officials.[98] The Rentenbank, then, was entirely independent of government influence amid efforts to establish confidence in the new unit of exchange. Yet the creation of the Rentenbank was just one step towards stopping the inflation. Another related to the Reichsbank's printing presses: in November, the deficit-financing of state expenditures came to an end, removing the primary mechanism behind the inflation.[99] The Reichsbank's own banknotes continued to circulate alongside the rentenmarks – albeit, now at a stabilised rate.

A second institution was created to complement the activities of the Rentenbank. The Gold Discount Bank began its operations in early April 1924. The monetary authority's central goal was to alleviate Germany's capital shortage by attracting foreign credit; few investors wished to invest in a country scarred by a recent history of inflation. So the Gold

---

[95] See Holtfrerich, 'Relations between monetary authorities and governmental institutions', p. 117.

[96] Quoted in Clavin, *The Great Depression*, p. 23; see also Reinhardt, *Die Reichsbank in der Weimarer Republik*, pp. 98–9; and, in particular, Giersch and Lehment, 'Monetary policy: does independence make a difference? – the German experience'.

[97] Holtfrerich, 'Relations between monetary authorities and governmental institutions', p. 118.

[98] Reinhardt, *Die Reichsbank in der Weimarer Republik*, pp. 98–9.

[99] James, 'The Reichsbank 1876–1945', p. 23.

Figures 1.1 and 1.2 A point of contrast. Two Reichsbank banknotes, with the signatures of the Reichsbank directorate guaranteeing their respective values. The first amounts to 10 marks and is dated 6 February 1920; the second amounts to 50 million marks and is dated 1 September 1923, at the height of the hyperinflation. The signature of Wilhelm Vocke, the future directorate chairman of the Bank deutscher Länder, can be seen on both.

Note: The two Reichsbank banknotes pictured above belong to the present author.

Discount Bank stepped in with the aim of providing loans to German businesses. Using credits supplied in large part by the Bank of England, the Reichsbank provided half of the Gold Discount Bank's capital. Private banks in Germany bestowed the other half.[100] Both the Renten-bank and Gold Discount Bank operated until the currency and banking reform, with the Reichsbank assuming their duties thereafter.

That reform eventually arrived in August 1924, and with it the new reichsmark was introduced. The legislation was entwined with the Dawes Plan, an agreement hammered out by the Allied powers and Germany, and one that helped to alleviate the real burden of Germany's annual reparations payments, boosting international confidence in the economy. After years of antagonistic relations, too, the agreement underlying the Dawes Plan demonstrated Germany's growing commitment to inter-national co-operation.[101]

A part of this commitment entailed the overhauling of the central bank. The new Bank Act of 1924 closely resembled the 1875 law estab-lishing the Reichsbank.[102] But there were important differences. At the insistence of the Allies, the Reichsbank would remain independent from the German government.[103] 'The Reichsbank is a bank independent of the Reich government', the law stated, in no uncertain terms.[104] The autonomy granted to the central bank back in the heady days of 1922 had now been reaffirmed. But what is more, this independence vis-à-vis the German government was strengthened.

The new Bank Act ensured that a strict credit limit was now imposed. Even if the Reichsbank wanted to finance the government's deficits, it was legally blocked from lending above a certain, small amount.[105] This, as the banking historian Christopher Kopper notes, was a lesson hard won from the experiences of having an independent Reichsbank during the hyperinflation.[106] The German government's influence with regard to the appointment of directorate members, including the president, was sharply curtailed. A new body, called the *Generalrat*, or general council, would appoint these men. The general council was made up of seven German officials, appointed by the Reichsbank's private

---

[100] Ibid.; Holtfrerich, 'Relations between monetary authorities and governmental institutions', p. 118.

[101] Karl Hardach, *The political economy of Germany in the twentieth century* (Berkeley, 1980), p. 29.

[102] Reinhardt, *Die Reichsbank in der Weimarer Republik*, pp. 106–7.

[103] Flink, *The German Reichsbank and economic Germany*, pp. 137–8.

[104] Reinhardt, *Die Reichsbank in der Weimarer Republik*, p. 107.   [105] Ibid., p. 111.

[106] Kopper, *Hjalmar Schacht*, p. 95.

shareholders, and seven foreign officials.[107] It replaced the *Kuratorium*, the government-dominated board that had offered supervisory functions.

And yet the general council was more powerful than the erstwhile *Kuratorium*. Directorate appointments were now decided by vote in the general council. As such, the foreign officials, providing they took a united stand, could exercise a veto on candidates they deemed unsuitable for the central bank.[108] The general council could also dismiss the Reichsbank president, or, with his agreement, members of the directorate.[109] 'This right of dismissal was a first for the new Bank Law', writes Reinhardt, 'for neither the Bank Law of 1875 nor the Autonomy Law of 1922 provided for such possibilities'.[110] Moreover, in contrast to the post-war law establishing the Bundesbank, the Reichsbank was not obliged to support the general economic policy of the government. All the central bank had to do was report its decisions to Berlin.

Did the German government have any influence on the appointment procedure at all? The answer is yes, but not that much. Under the new legislation, the Reich president was entitled to veto the appointment of the Reichsbank president twice. But should the Reichsbank president be elected by the general council for a third time, the Reich president had no choice but to accept the appointment.[111] Two further positions were created at the expense of the German government's influence. First, there was the commissioner for the note issue. The task of this new officer, who also happened to be one of the foreign officials on the general council, was to ensure that banknote circulation corresponded to the regulations outlined in the Bank Act. The commissioner for the note issue could stop the printing presses should he deem the decision necessary. The agent-general for reparations payments was the second position created. His duty, broadly defined, was to oversee the collection and transfer of Germany's reparations.[112]

What about the new reichsmark? The Reichsbank was beholden to the rules of the newly constructed gold-exchange standard.[113] The central bank was obliged to cover 40 per cent of its note circulation with gold or foreign exchange – a requirement that was more restrictive than the

---

[107] One of each of the following nationalities were represented: British, French, Italian, Belgian, American, Dutch and, finally, Swiss. See Flink, *The German Reichsbank and economic Germany*, p. 141.

[108] Reinhardt, *Die Reichsbank in der Weimarer Republik*, p. 118.   [109] Ibid., p. 119.

[110] Ibid.

[111] Holtfrerich, 'Relations between monetary authorities and governmental institutions', p. 119.

[112] James, 'The Reichsbank 1876–1945', p. 25.

[113] For more on the gold-exchange standard, see Singleton, *Central banking in the twentieth century*, p. 59.

one-third coverage requirement at work before the outbreak of the First World War. The remaining 60 per cent of the note circulation was to be covered by qualified commercial bills and cheques. Like the rentenmark that came before it, the reichsmark was fixed at the symbolic pre-war rate. The exchange rate vis-à-vis the American dollar was set at 4.2 reichsmarks.[114]

Schacht

Schacht became president of the Reichsbank following Havenstein's sudden death. A director at the Darmstädter and National Bank, one of the leading private banks in Germany, he was known for his political connections.[115] Schacht was the favourite candidate of Stresemann, the chancellor in late 1923, and later the Weimar Republic's influential foreign minister, to replace Havenstein. But Schacht's appointment to the Reichsbank was met with fierce resistance on the part of the central bank's directorate and the central committee, the latter representing the views of the Reichsbank's private shareholders.[116]

His candidacy was mired by allegations of misconduct during the First World War when he was a government official in occupied Belgium. Back then, Schacht had been accused of corruption in Belgium. It was asserted that he had given preferential treatment to Dresdner Bank, an institution for which he had worked prior to the war.[117] Vocke, a member of the directorate at the time, recalled that, in light of this accusation, the directorate strongly preferred Helfferich, the former state secretary for the treasury during the war.[118] The government, however, had different ideas. Aided by the second parliament, the Reichsrat, it ignored the objections of the directorate and central committee and pushed through Schacht's appointment as president of the central bank in December 1923.[119]

It would prove to be a fateful decision. During the 1920s, the central bank emerged as a powerful political actor in its own right. Much of this development can be credited to the personal figure of Schacht. He was 'one of the great men of our time, one of the most important and remarkable personalities', Vocke later recalled in his memoirs. But Vocke

[114] Holtfrerich, 'Relations between monetary authorities and governmental institutions', p. 120.
[115] Joachim Scholtyseck, 'Hjalmar Schacht', in Hans Pohl (ed.), *Deutsche Bankiers des 20. Jahrhunderts* (Stuttgart, 2008), p. 358.
[116] Müller, *Die Zentralbank – Eine Nebenregierung*, pp. 35–6.
[117] Vocke, *Memoiren*, p. 92; Kopper, *Hjalmar Schacht*, pp. 70–2; see also Scholtyseck, 'Hjalmar Schacht', p. 358.
[118] Vocke, *Memoiren*, p. 92.   [119] Müller, *Die Zentralbank – Eine Nebenregierung*, p. 36.

also noted that Schacht could be inspired by 'ruthless selfishness'.[120] With his arrival at the Reichsbank, the directorate became less collegial and more authoritarian. The so-called golden era of the Weimar Republic had begun. This period, however, was marked by stagnant economic growth and social conflict.[121] Schacht, in his speeches throughout the decade, took direct issue with the government on a number of areas. These ranged from controversies related to the centralisation of public funds, on the one hand, to foreign loans for municipality administrations, on the other. Schacht also honed in on issues relating to reparations policy and fiscal policy.[122]

If a new era had begun for the Weimar Republic, the same could be said for the Reichsbank. Aided by its independence from government instruction, the German central bank began to develop a distinct voice – even a personality – in the public sphere for the first time. This development can be attributed to its new president. As Kopper observes,

[i]n his public appearance, too, Schacht brought with him a new style to the Reichsbank. While his predecessor, Havenstein, seldom stepped into the public sphere, Schacht gladly accepted invitations from associations. Schacht took advantage of these opportunities amid efforts to put the Reichsbank's policy and his own economic ideas before a wider audience. His pronounced vanity reinforced his desire to adopt an active public relations activity, one that even went on the offensive.[123]

The new Reichsbank president had an eye for publicity. Indeed, one writer has written of the Reichsbank's 'expansion of power through publicity' during the Weimar Republic.[124] Schacht himself exhibited a strong 'journalistic streak', cultivated from an early age through various stints of employment in newspapers and journals.[125] Moreover, before the outbreak of the First World War, he had helped conduct (what we would now call) public relations for both an interest group and a private bank.[126] 'He wrote well and often for various minor journals; indeed his

---

[120] Vocke, *Memoiren*, p. 92.
[121] A succinct overview of this period is offered in Kolb, *The Weimar Republic*, pp. 53–100. See also James, 'Economic reasons for the collapse of Weimar', pp. 31–45.
[122] Holtfrerich offers a brief outline of these debates in Holtfrerich, 'Relations between monetary authorities and governmental institutions', pp. 124–7.
[123] Kopper, *Hjalmar Schacht*, pp. 90–1.
[124] Muller, *Die Zentralbank – Eine Nebenregierung*, p. 44.
[125] Scholtyseck, 'Hjalmar Schacht', p. 357. Indeed, as a young man, Schacht's first job in journalism was an internship with a disreputable tabloid newspaper, the *Kleines Journal*, which catered to scandal and high society gossip. See Kopper, *Hjalmar Schacht*, p. 18.
[126] Schacht worked in the press offices of the *Handelsvertragsverein*, an interest group for the export industry and, later, Dresdner Bank. See Kopper, *Hjalmar Schacht*, pp. 19, 26–7, 31.

introduction to banking came from his ability as a writer', notes the historian Edward Peterson. 'Far from being a handicap, his ability as a phrase maker was a vital one; his ability to express himself sharply and concisely or in vague generalities as he chose was a key talent.'[127]

Schacht cultivated relationships with several newspapers in the Weimar Republic, which in turn often supported his cause – most notably the *Vossische Zeitung, Berliner Börsen-Courier, Der Deutsche Volkswirt* and *Berliner Tageblatt*. By the end of the Weimar Republic, the Reichsbank had taken to using the nationalist *Berliner Börsen Zeitung* almost as a 'mouthpiece' for its arguments.[128] The new Reichsbank president made an impression in the public sphere. 'Who would have been able to say before the war what Reichsbank president Havenstein looked like?' asked one contemporary in 1930. He continued:

Leaving aside readers of the business section, whom would have been interested in Havenstein's resignation or even be bothered about it? The image of the tall, flaxen-haired Hjalmar Schacht with a pince-nez on that narrow, fresh daredevil face is known to every German. How has it come about that the Germans, and even the international community, prick their ears in recent years whenever the name of this man is mentioned? Why do the tabloids always paint his name in a manner that takes up half the newspaper page whenever he speaks or does something?[129]

The answer is simple: Schacht actively intervened in the public sphere to influence the parameters of public debate as well as boost his own profile. He also published books on economic affairs during the 1920s and early 1930s.[130] But the man was at his best delivering speeches; they were Schacht's preferred form of communication with the wider public. The writer Helmut Müller estimates that Schacht delivered some 165 speeches and interviews during his years as president of the Reichsbank in the Weimar Republic (1923–30).[131] During the Third Reich, this number almost doubled.[132] In 1937, the Reichsbank would go on to publish a volume of Schacht's speeches.[133] The central bank

---

[127] Edward N. Peterson, *Hjalmar Schacht for and against Hitler: a political-economic study of Germany 1923–1945* (Boston, 1954), p. 20. Also quoted in Müller, *Die Zentralbank – Eine Nebenregierung*, p. 45.

[128] Schacht soon fell out with the *Berliner Tageblatt*, however. See Müller, *Die Zentralbank – Eine Nebenregierung*, pp. 44–5.

[129] Ibid., p. 44.

[130] See, for example, Hjalmar Schacht, *Die Stabilisierung der Mark* (Stuttgart, 1926); and Hjalmar Schacht, *Das Ende der Reparationen* (Oldenburg, 1931). The latter was written shortly after Schacht's (temporary) departure from the Reichsbank in 1930.

[131] Müller, *Die Zentralbank – Eine Nebenregierung*, p. 46.   [132] Ibid., pp. 46–7.

[133] For Schacht's collection of speeches, see Reichsbank, *Schacht in seinen Äusserungen: Im Auftrage des Reichsbankdirektoriums zusammengestellt in der Volkswirtschaftlichen und Statistischen Abt. der Reichsbank. Zum Januar 1937* (Berlin, 1937).

also published that same year a collection of newspaper caricatures of the Reichsbank president, in celebration of his sixtieth birthday.[134] These two publications indicate the extent to which the central bank had come to be seen as a one-man show in the public sphere. They also point to the seemingly approving stance the Reichsbank had taken of such a development. Indeed, the publication of Schacht's speeches in 1937 established a precedent in German central banking, one that enhanced the link between personality and currency, and one that was later mimicked by Vocke and Blessing in the post-war era.

Very quickly, then, Schacht (Figure 1.3) became the spokesperson for the reichsmark itself, a persona that he himself actively fostered. All this was a pioneering example of public relations, and in the realm of central banking no less. Such an example could not have been lost on directorate members Vocke and Blessing, the latter in particular known as Schacht's protégé in the media.[135] But perhaps this development should be placed in its wider context, too. During the 1920s, the heads of central banks emerged to become powerful political actors in their own right – for example the Bank of England's Norman, or Benjamin Strong Jr., the governor of the Federal Reserve Bank of New York.[136] Schacht, like Norman, became an international personality, enjoying respect from abroad. Yet it was the *degree* to which Schacht promoted himself in the public sphere that separated him from his British and American counterparts.

Under Schacht, the Reichsbank gradually strengthened its position against various weak and unstable coalition governments. As the 1920s progressed, however, Schacht became disillusioned with politics and gradually lurched to the right. In 1926, he left the Deutsche Demokratische Partei, a left liberal party that he had helped to establish years before.[137] There was one issue in particular, though, that led to Schacht's

---

[134] See Reichsbank, *Schacht in der Karikatur: Im Auftrage des Reichsbankdirektoriums zusammengestellt in der Volkswirtschaftlichen und Statistischen Abt. der Reichsbank. Zum 22 Januar 1937* (Berlin, 1937).
[135] Newspapers during the inter-war period commented upon Blessing's attachment to Schacht. See 'Reichsbank's new directors: Dr. Schacht's choice', *Financial Times*, 4 Jun. 1937, BAB, R2501/3413; and 'Ergänzung des Reichsbankdirektoriums', *Basler Nachrichten*, Jun. 1937, BAB, R2501/3413. A number of post-war newspapers and magazines also noted that Blessing was the protégé of Schacht, as will be detailed in Chapter 4. See, for instance, 'Der neue Hüter der Deutschen Mark', *Frankfurter Rundschau*, 12 Jul. 1957, Deutsche Bundesbank Pressearchiv [DBPA], no. 1363; 'Die goldenen Fünfziger', *Die Welt*, 29. Apr. 1959, DBHA, BSG 1/12; and 'Karl Blessing. Ein unbequemer Mann zwar – aber ein ehrlicher Makler', *Aktuell*, 5 May 1962, BSG 1/12.
[136] Reinhardt, *Die Reichsbank in der Weimarer Republik*, pp. 273–4.
[137] Scholtyseck, 'Hjalmar Schacht', p. 359.

Figure 1.3 Hjalmar Schacht.
(DBHA, BSG 3/3019 – © Deutsche Bundesbank – Historisches Archiv)

emergence as a spokesperson for the right. That issue was reparations. The Dawes Plan of 1924 had always been a temporary solution to Germany's reparations troubles.[138] A final reparations plan was in the offing. This eventually culminated in the Young Plan of 1929, which lightened the real burden of Germany's reparations payments, as well as extending the reparations payment schedule to 1988.[139] The Young Plan was hammered out between the Allied powers and Germany at a conference in Paris. Schacht, along with industrialist Albert Vögler, represented the German delegation at the negotiation table.

Both Vocke and Blessing accompanied the Reichsbank president to Paris, acting as advisors.[140] Indeed, Vocke made for an ideal advisor. He was an expert on monetary matters and fluent in English to boot. The central banker had already earned the respect of foreign officials, such as the Bank of England's Norman, and would go on to represent the Reichsbank at international conferences and the Bank for International Settlements (BIS), as well as conduct a number of diplomatic trips for the central bank.[141] By 1936, German newspapers referred to him as the 'foreign minister of the Reichsbank'.[142] This moniker originally stemmed from a Reichsbank press release, too, suggesting that the central bank approved of the term.[143]

Unlike Schacht, however, Vocke (Figure 1.4) avoided the public lime-light during his time at the Reichsbank – if he was a representative of the central bank, such representation remained within elite circles. There is little, if any, evidence suggesting that he delivered speeches or even wrote articles on behalf of the central bank – an interesting point, given his subsequent appearance in the public sphere in West Germany. This was not the case for Blessing, however, who was a prolific writer during his time with the central bank in the Third Reich, already demonstrating the media-friendly attitude he would later adopt at the Bundesbank.[144]

---

[138] Holtfrerich, 'Relations between monetary authorities and governmental institutions', p. 126.

[139] Braun, *The German economy in the twentieth century*, p. 46.

[140] Vocke, *Memoiren*, pp. 95, 97–8; Volkmar Muthesius, 'Vorwort', in Karl Blessing, *Die Verteidigung des Geldwertes* (Frankfurt am Main, 1960), p. 10.

[141] Hans Luther, *Vor dem Abgrund, 1930–33. Reichsbankpräsident in Krisenzeiten* (Berlin, 1964), pp. 85–6, 326; Vocke, *Memoiren*, pp. 93–8, 113–18; and Wilhelm Vocke, 'Der 13. Juli 1931', *Die Zeitschrift für das gesamte Kreditwesen*, Jul. 1971, DBPA, no. 1244.

[142] For the articles, see 'Geheimrat Dr. Vocke 50 Jahre', *Berliner Tageblatt*, 7 Feb. 1936, BAB, R2501/3416 II; 'Dr. Vocke 50 Jahre alt', *Deutsche Allgemeine Zeitung*, 7 Feb. 1936, BAB, R2501/3416 II.

[143] For the press release, see 'Material für die Presse', 6 Feb. 1936, BAB, R2501/3416 II.

[144] See for instance, Karl Blessing, 'Deutschlands Stellung zum Clearing', *Berliner Börsen-Zeitung*, 24 Aug. 1937, BAB, R2501/3413; and Karl Blessing, 'Gegenwartsaufgaben der Reichsbank', *Die Staatsbank*, 27 Aug. 1937, BAB, R2501/3413.

Figure 1.4 Wilhelm Vocke.
(DBHA, BSG 3/745 – © Deutsche Bundesbank – Historisches Archiv)

Yet, at the Paris conference in 1929, Schacht overplayed his hand of cards, making seemingly independent political demands that infuriated both the Allied powers and German politicians back home. Schacht demanded, for instance, the return of the 'Polish corridor', a strip of land taken from Germany and given to Poland in the aftermath of the First World War.[145] These political demands caused an outcry at the conference and were eventually dropped after the German government disowned them, leaving Schacht feeling cheated and humiliated.[146] Nevertheless, weary and resigned, the Reichsbank president signed the Young Plan agreement. The Young Plan was a compromise, leaving both the Allied powers and Germans dissatisfied. It stated that Germany should pay an average annuity of two billion reichsmarks, a figure that still constituted a sizeable reduction of the real burden of reparations.[147] The participants agreed that a supranational institution, the aforementioned BIS, would be created in order to co-ordinate and facilitate the reparations payments.

Significantly, the Young Plan also signalled a shift in the independence of the Reichsbank. Two measures were taken to eliminate foreign control of the Reichsbank. First, the position of commissioner for the note issue was removed. And second, foreign officials of the general council – that is, the body, established in 1924, which appointed members of the directorate – were replaced by German ones. This meant that the Reichsbank's private shareholders now appointed the entire general council. The Young Plan increased the influence of the German government, too. The Reich president, pending the support of the chancellor or responsible cabinet member, could now veto the appointment or revocation of directorate members, including the central bank's president.[148] Despite these changes, though, the Reichsbank directorate could still pursue an independent monetary policy, free from government instruction.

Schacht was bitterly disappointed with the Young Plan – particularly its provisions relating to Germany's annual reparations burden. In his eyes, reparations payments were still far too high. But Schacht had put his signature to the agreement, so the Reichsbank president found himself in an awkward position. After returning to Germany, Schacht defended the Young Plan alongside the government for a number of months. But this support gradually withered over time. By December 1929, Schacht emerged as an opponent of the deal, ostensibly on the

[145] Reinhardt, *Die Reichsbank in der Weimarer Republik*, pp. 201–3.   [146] Ibid., p. 204.
[147] Holtfrerich, 'Relations between monetary authorities and governmental institutions', p. 127.
[148] Ibid., p. 121.

grounds that the government continued to pursue a reckless financial policy, in turn destroying the conditions under which the Young Plan could have succeeded. The Reichsbank president penned an open letter attacking the government's financial policy, sending it to both the chancellor and the media. Indeed, by the time the letter arrived on the chancellor's desk, its contents were already published in the newspapers.[149]

The memorandum, an overtly political act by the central bank president, poured fire on growing political unrest concerning the Young Plan. Schacht's move was greeted with enthusiasm among nationalist circles, including Hitler's National Socialists.[150] Further public spats with the government followed. In particular, at the insistence of Schacht, the government forced through parliament a controversial piece of legislation that worked towards the consolidation of its budget. The government did so lest the central bank president refuse his co-operation in helping the former to secure crucial financing needed for its political survival. In light of the open fighting between the government and central bank, this law became popularly known as 'Lex Schacht'.[151] The political affair resulted in the resignation of the finance minister, the Social Democrat Rudolf Hilferding, who was outraged by what he saw as Schacht's dictation of government policy.[152]

The episode also resulted in several political attacks on the character of the Reichsbank president, and the way Schacht was viewed as abusing the central bank's independence. These attacks came from the left. The Social Democratic politicians in the Reichstag, for example, accused Schacht of 'abusive exploitation', condemning how he used the central bank's independence to transform it into a '*Nebensregierung*', or additional government.[153] Indeed, it was during the late 1920s that the SPD, for the first time, became disillusioned with the idea of an autonomous central bank, a development observed in an internal Reichsbank report that was commissioned on the topic.[154] In parliament, Social Democratic politicians called for a change in the law so as to enable the government to remove Schacht – a demand soon rejected by their chancellor on the grounds that it would infuriate public opinion.[155] But that

---

[149] Kopper, *Hjalmar Schacht*, p. 162.
[150] Adam J. Tooze, *The wages of destruction: the making and breaking of the Nazi economy* (London, 2007), p. 16; and Marsh, *The Bundesbank*, pp. 106–8.
[151] Reinhardt, *Die Reichsbank in der Weimarer Republik*, pp. 213–21.
[152] Ibid., pp. 218, 225.   [153] Ibid., p. 226.
[154] Statistische Abteilung der Reichsbank, 'Stellung der Sozialdemokratie zur Autonomie der Reichsbank'. Schacht would later trace the hostility of the left-wing press back to the year 1926, when he left the *Deutsche Demokratische Partei*. See Schacht, *76 Jahre meines Lebens*, p. 321.
[155] Reinhardt, *Die Reichsbank in der Weimarer Republik*, p. 226.

was as far as it went. A clear majority of the press, including the SPD's organ, *Vorwärts*, remained cautiously supportive of the idea of an independent central bank so long as it served the interests of a stable currency.[156]

In part, such a development can be attributed to the way Schacht presented the Reichsbank in the public sphere. The Reichsbank president continually criticised the government's profligate spending policies, portraying the central bank as a bedrock of fiscal common sense, one that supported the interests of the currency's stability, which the government and other spendthrift forces were so intent on ruining. Figure 1.5 demonstrates the sheer extent to which the personality of Schacht was associated with the central bank's independence: the Reichsbank president is portrayed as the sole pillar supporting the monetary authority's autonomy.

Yet, as Clavin notes, such favourable attitudes concerning central bank independence can also be linked to the Zeitgeist of the era. Following the inflationary years of the early 1920s, continental European economies – that is, not only Germany's – placed tremendous importance upon 'currency stabilization [which] became the dominant, sometimes the sole, preoccupation of government policy' in the mid- to late 1920s.[157] Schacht, in other words, could avail of a ready audience for his arguments.

In March 1930, Schacht resigned from office. He was no longer central bank president. It was during this time that Schacht had aligned himself with the extreme right – namely, with the National Socialist party, which had emerged as a strong electoral force in a population radicalised by mass unemployment and apparent government inaction.[158] Winning just 2.5 per cent of the national vote in the elections of May 1928, the National Socialists shot to 18.3 per cent of the vote when the next elections came round in September 1930.[159] Schacht used his influence to introduce Hitler to industrial circles; his reputation and renown lent a veneer of credibility to Hitler at a crucial point in the Nazis' rise to power.[160]

Hans Luther, a former finance minister, became the new Reichsbank president. But where Schacht was abrasive and brash in the public

---

[156] Ibid., p. 225.

[157] Clavin, *The Great Depression*, p. 3; see also pp. 58–9, and, for Germany in particular, pp. 117–19.

[158] Tooze, *The wages of destruction*, p. 23; and Richard J. Evans, 'Introduction: the experience of unemployment in the Weimar Republic' in Richard J. Evans and Dick Geary (eds.), *The German unemployed: experiences and consequences of mass unemployment from the Weimar Republic to the Third Reich* (London, 1987), pp. 18–19.

[159] Tooze, *The wages of destruction*, pp. 12, 17.

[160] Johnson, *The government of money*, p. 35.

Figure 1.5 'Independence of the Reichsbank'. The cartoon portrays
Schacht as the sole pillar supporting the central bank's independence.
Red forces, symbolising the political left, attack the pillar. If Schacht
falls, the Reichsbank's independence falls. Like the Bank deutscher
Länder, and later the Bundesbank, the Reichsbank's independence was
closely associated with its leadership in the public sphere. Published by
Kladderadatsch, a right-wing satirical publication, on 2 February 1930.
Source: Reichsbank, *Schacht in der Karikatur*, p. 57.

sphere, Luther struck a more conciliatory note. The new Reichsbank president sought to foster ties with the government.[161] This attitude, Luther later confided, was a direct response to Schacht's antagonistic relations with previous governments.[162] Luther shied away from taking a public position on political matters. In this respect, he adopted a similar attitude to Havenstein during the hyperinflation. The Weimar Republic thus offers two examples of independent central bank presidents who were publicity shy, offering a counterfoil to the conduct of Schacht.

Members of the Reichsbank's directorate, however, did not think much of their new president. By his own account, Luther was often met with opposition and resistance in the directorate.[163] 'Luther really did not understand anything about banking and credit', Vocke later recalled, somewhat scathingly.[164] These troubles aside, Luther sought to co-operate with the government where he felt the Reichsbank was able to do so. Keep in mind that Germany remained on the gold standard, though; this fact restricted the Reichsbank's room for monetary manoeuvre.[165] In general, however, Luther supported the aims and policies of the new government led by Heinrich Brüning, a chancellor who ruled largely by emergency decree.[166] The new chancellor pursued a restrictive economic policy, one that intentionally aggravated deflationary forces amid efforts to win concessions on German reparations at the international level.

Though the relationship between the Reichsbank and government was largely co-operative under Luther, there were some clashes behind the scenes. These disputes centred on two areas: the central bank's credit policy and the provision of credit for the government's use. When Europe's banking crisis began in July 1931, Brüning's administration came to judge the Reichsbank's credit policy as being far too restrictive, placing unnecessary pressure on banks considering the dire circumstances prevalent in the economy. But the government received a rebuff from the central bank.[167] The Reichsbank, for its part, viewed its tight measures as a means towards halting the depletion of its exchange reserves, which were alarmingly low, meaning that Reichsbank was verging on the 40 per cent minimum coverage requirement that it was obliged to keep.

---

[161] For an overview of Luther, see Albert Fischer, 'Hans Luther [1879–1962]', in Hans Pohl (ed.), *Deutsche Bankiers des 20. Jahrhunderts* (Stuttgart, 2008).
[162] Luther, *Vor dem Abgrund, 1930–33*, pp. 128–9.   [163] Ibid., pp. 85–6.
[164] See Vocke, 'Der 13. Juli 1931'. Luther, by contrast, rated Vocke's ability in central banking matters quite highly, though he admitted he never became close with the man. See Luther, *Vor dem Abgrund, 1930–33*, pp. 85–6.
[165] Tooze, *The wages of destruction*, p. 17; James, 'The Reichsbank 1876–1945', p. 30.
[166] Reinhardt, *Die Reichsbank in der Weimarer Republik*, p. 262.   [167] Ibid., pp. 242–3.

Brüning and Luther had a dramatic argument in December 1931, during which Luther allegedly threatened to resign if the chancellor pushed for a substantial reduction in the discount rate. At his own end, the Reichsbank president had been facing intense pressure from Britain and the United States to keep the discount rate high in light of considerations concerning the international economy. In the event, the discount rate was reduced by 1 percentage point, giving both men enough reason to remain seething.[168]

Further strains in the relationship between the central bank and the government emerged when the Reichsbank president rejected the request by the economics minister, Hermann Warmbold, for the provision of a 'clandestine expansion of credit'.[169] According to Warmbold, the additional finance would be applied towards steering the economy out of the depression. Luther rejected these plans on the grounds that such credit could lead to another inflation, prompting the economics minister to push for legal change in the Bank Act with respect to the Reichsbank's independence. Brüning, the chancellor, rejected this call.[170]

In July 1930, too, Luther opposed the financing of a work creation scheme. The programme, put forward by Brüning's government, was to be financed in part by a foreign loan, the attainment of which required the central bank's approval. The scheme, though a minor one, could have worked towards reducing mass unemployment. But the Reichsbank rejected the idea, leaving the project to flounder on the drawing board. The Reichsbank turned down another request for a loan to finance a work creation programme in May 1932.[171] Luther grounded these two refusals with the argument that reparations first had to come to an end before Germany could commit itself to such spending ambitions. The Reichsbank president's stubborn position exasperated the chancellor.[172]

A fear of another inflation underlay the Reichsbank's caution. Certainly, in his memoirs, Luther documented that an angst concerning inflation was prevalent at the time.[173] Numerous historians, among them Knut Borchardt and Jürgen von Kruedener, have argued that reflationary policies – that is, ones aimed at kick-starting economic activity by means of increased government spending – were politically difficult ones in the

---

[168] Holtfrerich, 'Relations between monetary authorities and governmental institutions', p. 133.

[169] Reinhardt, *Die Reichsbank in der Weimarer Republik*, p. 246.   [170] Ibid.

[171] Holtfrerich, 'Relations between monetary authorities and governmental institutions', p. 132.

[172] Heinrich Brüning, *Memoiren 1918–1934* (Stuttgart, 1970), pp. 573–5.

[173] Luther, *Vor dem Abgrund, 1930–33*, p. 102.

twilight years of the Weimar Republic.[174] Reflation meant rising prices, and Germans, scarred by the experiences of 1922–3, perceived rising prices as synonymous with inflation.

This argument has remained a dominant one in the literature. 'The German public, a once-burned child, had developed a mortal fear of inflation that militated against any expansion of money supply or budget deficits', notes Karl Hardach in his classic account of the German economy.[175] 'In the midst of the deepest deflationary crisis in modern history, the German people continued to worry about inflation!' observes Clavin.[176] As noted above, however, government officials did attempt to embark on minor work creation schemes to be financed by the Reichsbank, indicating that such fears, though palpable, were not all pervasive. And once reparations had come to an end in mid-1932, the Reichsbank under Luther co-operated with the government with respect to the financing of work creation programmes.[177] Indeed, as the historian Adam Tooze observes, the National Socialists' employment creation schemes were modelled on designs stemming from the late Weimar era.[178]

These disputes, however, were the exception to the rule. Both Brüning's government and the Reichsbank were in general agreement that a deflationary economic policy was the right course to pursue. There were other factors at work as well, constraining the chancellor's room for manoeuvre. With a lack of a domestic capital market on which to fall back, and tight legal limitations with respect to central bank lending, Brüning's government scrambled for funding amid efforts to avoid bankruptcy. The administration felt it had little choice but to actively embark on a deflationary path.[179] Such a path, however, aggravated mass unemployment, in turn fuelling social unrest and helping to radicalise a German electorate already tired with the apparent failures of democracy. The Reichsbank played an indirect, but no less important role in this development.

---

[174] Borchardt, 'Das Gewicht der Inflationsangst in den wirtschaftspolitischen Entscheidungsprozessen während der Weltwirtschaftskrise'; and von Kruedener, 'Die Entstehung des Inflationstraumas. Zur Sozialpsychologie der deutschen Hyperinflation 1922/23'; and Gerhard Schulz, 'Inflationstrauma, Finanzpolitik und Krisenbekämpfung in den Jahren der Wirtschaftskrise, 1930–33', in Gerald D. Feldman (ed.), *Die Nachwirkungen der Inflation auf die deutsche Geschichte 1924–1933* (Munich, 1985)
[175] Hardach, *The political economy of Germany in the twentieth century*, p. 45.
[176] Clavin, *The Great Depression in Europe, 1929–1939*, p. 126.
[177] Holtfrerich, 'Relations between monetary authorities and governmental institutions', p. 132.
[178] Tooze, *The wages of destruction*, pp. 27, 39, 43–4.
[179] Clavin, *The Great Depression*, p. 118.

The Third Reich

In January 1933 Hitler came to power, and within months, new legislation was passed revising the Bank Act of 1924. The legislation, coming into effect in October 1933, helped to restore the state's grip on the central bank's personnel. The general council was abolished. In its place, the country's president could now appoint the Reichsbank's president, after hearing the expert opinion of the directorate. The central bank president, for his part, could in turn nominate directorate members who were then appointed by the Reich's president.[180] Legally speaking, however, the Reichsbank was still independent of government instruction – although such legal independence soon meant little in what emerged to be a totalitarian dictatorship.[181]

Other changes were afoot, too. Schacht returned as president of the central bank. Hitler sought credibility in the economic sphere; and Schacht, who enjoyed an excellent working relationship with his British counterpart, had the advantage of having an international reputation. But this time the Reichsbank president struck a markedly different tone in the public sphere. Instead of collision with the government, the Reichsbank president now stressed a course of co-operation.[182]

This change of attitude constituted a remarkable volte-face. According to Reinhardt, Schacht's conception of central bank independence was such that he felt it was necessary in a democracy crowded with irresponsible politicians who were clamouring for finance, but not wholly necessary in a dictatorship that could be guided along the lines of sound economic reasoning.[183] This argument fits with Vocke's observations of Schacht from within the walls of the Reichsbank. The Reichsbank president marvelled at Hitler's dynamism, Vocke later recalled, and yet Schacht assumed he could also control the dictator. 'I am the brains', Vocke portrayed Schacht as saying. 'I will steer him!'[184]

Schacht had been appointed Reichsbank president with the expectation that, under his leadership, the central bank would support the

---

[180] Holtfrerich, 'Relations between monetary authorities and governmental institutions', p. 133.
[181] As coyly noted by the Reichsbank vice president Friedrich Dreyse in 1937. See Friedrich W. Dreyse, 'Die Reichsbank im Dritten Reich', 27 Jan. 1937, BAB, R2501/3414, pp. 127–8. See also Rudolf Eicke, 'Die Befreiung der Reichsbank von internationalen Bindungen', 21 Feb. 1937, BAB, R2501/6860.
[182] Kopper, *Hjalmar Schacht*, p. 203.
[183] Reinhardt, *Die Reichsbank in der Weimarer Republik*, p. 271.
[184] 'A catastrophic mistake arising from his conceitedness, his ambition', Vocke later observed. See Vocke, *Memoiren*, p. 100.

Nazis' work creation ambitions and rearmament plans. When asked by Hitler what the Reichsbank could contribute towards these two causes, Schacht responded, 'Any amount, my Führer'.[185] There were few conflicts in the early years of the Third Reich. In short, Schacht's immediate goals did not clash with those of Hitler. Both men, for instance, sought to bring the economy to full employment.

In August 1934, the Reichsbank president was appointed 'commissary' minister for the economy, whilst maintaining his position as head of the central bank.[186] Schacht was also appointed as the government's general commissioner for the war economy, a position he held for over two years.[187] Such appointments collided head on with the notion that the central bank remained independent in practice. The Reichsbank president, once so critical of the Weimar Republic's various governments, was now an active member of Hitler's cabinet.

The central bank's problems began in 1936. It was the year in which the country achieved full employment. Inflationary forces, spurred by rapid rearmament since 1934, had now become more pronounced.[188] The government's rearmament ambitions started to clash with the Reichsbank's task of safeguarding the currency. Schacht, though he continued to enjoy the confidence of Hitler, earned the ire and jealously of other officials in light of his 'outsider' credentials and unaccommodating attitude.[189] He gradually became embroiled in a power struggle with Hermann Göring, a leading Nazi official who succeeded in removing Schacht as 'commissary' minister for the economy in 1937.[190] Göring, for his part, soon emerged as an 'economic dictator', instructed by Hitler to spearhead the regime's Four Year Plan, itself a concerted effort to make Germany self-sufficient in key raw materials that were instrumental for war purposes.[191] Given Schacht's international reputation, however,

---

[185] Kopper, *Hjalmar Schacht*, p. 211. See also pp. 208–10.

[186] This 'commissary' position, which was initially a temporary appointment, but soon emerged to be permanent one, was created in light of the Bank for International Settlements guideline that stated that no central bank head could be a minister of a government cabinet. See 'Intelligence report no. EF-FB-2. Interrogation of Hjalmar Horace Greeley Schacht, July 11, 1945, 1050 hours', 25 Jul. 1945, IfZ, 2/206/4 FINAD, p. 6.

[187] Karl-Heinrich Hansmeyer and Rolf Caesar, 'Kriegswirtschaft und Inflation (1936–1948)', in Deutsche Bundesbank (ed.), *Währung und Wirtschaft in Deutschland 1876–1975* (Frankfurt am Main, 1976), p. 375.

[188] Richard J. Overy, *War and economy in the Third Reich* (Oxford, 1994), p. 184.

[189] Scholtyseck, 'Hjalmar Schacht', pp. 361–2.

[190] Marsh, *The Bundesbank*, pp. 109, 113; Kopper, *Hjalmar Schacht*, pp. 308–9.

[191] Overy, *War and economy in the Third Reich*, pp. 186–7; see also Tooze, *The wages of destruction*, pp. 219–22.

Hitler insisted on keeping the Reichsbank president in his cabinet as a minister without portfolio.[192]

Schacht's acrimonious departure from the Reichsbank in 1939, an event that went on to play an important role at the Nuremberg trials, can be traced back to the pivotal role he played in the early rearmament of the Third Reich. In particular, 'Hitler's magician' conjured the 'Mefo' bill, a financial instrument named after the Metallurgische Forschungs-gesellschaft, or Society for Metallurgical Research, a company that served as a front for state interests.[193] The 'Mefo' bill was a promissory note formulated in such a manner that circumvented the restrictions of banking law: it allowed the government to pay private firms for goods and services using the Reichsbank's credit.

The financial instruments were used for employment programmes as well as for funding rearmament in the Third Reich. But their origins actually go back to the last years of the Weimar Republic, when the Reichsbank used a similar instrument to covertly fund public construc-tion programmes after the ending of German reparations.[194] How did the 'Mefo' bill work in practice? There were three steps. First, private firms delivered armaments to the state. Second, these firms could then draw bills accepted and signed by the Metallurgische Forschungsge-sellschaft, which were to serve as payment. And third, since these bills were guaranteed by the state, the Reichsbank was allowed to discount them, letting the money arrive in the private firms' accounts. As a result, Hitler's government could buy today and pay tomorrow. But when exactly was that tomorrow? Ostensibly, 'Mefo' bills were short-term paper representing obligations that were to be paid within three months. But they could in fact be renewed for up to five years. As such, they really acted as medium- to long-term paper.[195] It was the creation of the 'Mefo' bills, among other factors, that helped the economy reach full employ-ment and finance the first stages of rearmament.

In the 1960s, Schacht claimed in the public sphere that the Reichsbank directorate passed these 'Mefo' bills 'unanimously'.[196] This statement implied that Vocke, who was a member of the directorate at the time,

[192] 'Intelligence report no. EF-FB-2. Interrogation of Hjalmar Horace Greeley Schacht, July 11, 1945, 1050 hours', p. 11.
[193] Tooze, *The wages of destruction*, pp. 54–5.
[194] James, 'The Reichsbank 1876–1945', p. 31.
[195] Holtfrerich, 'Relations between monetary authorities and governmental institutions', p. 137.
[196] This episode is documented in more detail in Chapter 4. See Hjalmar Schacht, *The magic of money*, trans. Paul Erskine (London, 1967), p. 119.

voted in favour of the 'Mefo' bills.[197] Vocke hotly denied such a claim, asserting that he alone in the directorate had opposed the creation of the financial instruments.[198] The minutes of the meeting concerning the passage of the 'Mefo' bills do not survive. Nevertheless, in the post-war era, the BdL chairman defended the 'Mefo' bills' legality at least three times, noting that they complied with the legal provisions of the time, however distasteful they were in his mind to the practice of sound central banking.[199] Faced with mass unemployment, the Reichsbank could 'not just sit there with hands in its lap', Vocke was reported to have said regarding the 'Mefo' bills' creation.[200]

With inflationary pressures on the rise, Schacht pushed for the government to stop the issuance of 'Mefo' bills and start repaying the existing ones that were outstanding. After much fluster, Schacht threatened to resign as Reichsbank president if his wishes were not heeded. The government, in response, began to repay the promissory notes – though on a small scale.[201] Armaments spending and credit requirements continued to increase to what Schacht considered dangerous levels.

The regime had already implemented price controls from 1936 onwards amid efforts to stop another inflation in its tracks.[202] All the same, another inflation was under way. Indeed, Buchheim traces the roots of the second inflation to the fateful decision back in 1931 to suspend the reichsmark's convertibility with other currencies. Such a move later opened the gateway for the Third Reich's abuse of the currency, allowing the regime to completely manipulate the value of the reichsmark.[203] This time, however, it was a 'repressed' inflation. Prices remained ostensibly stable via state control, but the quality and supply of goods at such prices deteriorated. As time went on, this encouraged the emergence of a black market, which flourished by the war's end.

---

[197] In *The magic of money*, Schacht also accused Blessing of having supported the 'Mefo' bills. But Blessing was not even a member of the directorate at this time, and would only join in May 1937. See Kopper, *Bankiers unterm Hakenkreuz*, pp. 189–90.

[198] Vocke, *Memoiren*, p. 101. See also Vocke's fiery letter to Schacht in 1966: Wilhelm Vocke to Hjalmar Schacht, 6 Apr. 1966, DBHA, B330/294.

[199] For more details, refer to Chapters 3 and 4.

[200] 'Vocke: Mefo-Wechsel zulässig', *Frankfurter Allgemeine Zeitung*, 22 Nov. 1952.

[201] Hansmeyer and Caesar, 'Kriegswirtschaft und Inflation (1936–1948)', p. 393 (footnote).

[202] Buchheim, 'Von altem Geld zu neuem Geld. Währungsreformen im 20. Jahrhundert', p. 149.

[203] Ibid., p. 150. See also p. 148.

While the second inflation was emerging, Schacht continued to speak of an aversion to rising prices and outright opposition to currency experiments in the Third Reich's public sphere. In doing so, he used language that bared an uncanny echo to Vocke's later speeches. 'Since the German people had to endure to the bitter end the horrors of an inflation', Schacht noted in 1936, 'it has become extremely chary of currency experiments. A stable currency is the first and most necessary condition for the financing of the great work-creating programme which has given new life to German industry, and employment and bread to many of our compatriots'.[204] Indeed, even after Schacht's expulsion from the Reichsbank in 1939, and the elimination of its legal autonomy, some central bank officials continued to speak of the importance of a stable currency and an independent central bank.[205] But such messages were inconsistent; numerous Reichsbank reports during the Third Reich also praised the close relationship between the central bank and state.[206]

By 1938, however, relations between the central bank and government had deteriorated. Hitler's regime soon began to circumvent the central bank and directly tap the capital market for funding.[207] Soon, however, the capital market could not supply the credit the government required, its means having become exhausted. The Third Reich urgently needed financing. And in its hour of need, the state turned its eyes once more towards Schacht and the central bank.

Reichsbank Memorandum of January 1939

Hitler approached Schacht on 2 January 1939 with the idea of using Reichsbank credits to finance the gap in receipts and expenditures.[208] The Reichsbank president, who was now exasperated with the economy's situation, responded in a harmless fashion by noting the central bank would send a memorandum, offering its opinion with respect to Hitler's suggestions.[209] In fact, such a document had been in preparation for some time within the walls of the Reichsbank. The monetary overhang

---

[204] As quoted in 'Dr. Schacht rejects mark devaluation', *The Daily Telegraph*, 18 Apr. 1936, BAB, R2501/3412.
[205] James, 'The Reichsbank 1876–1945', p. 40; Marsh, *The Bundesbank*, p. 129.
[206] See, for example, Eicke, 'Die Befreiung der Reichsbank von internationalen Bindungen'; and Rudolf Brinkmann, 'Stabile Währung', 10 Feb. 1939, BAB, R2501/6521.
[207] Hjalmar Schacht, *My first seventy-six years*, trans. Diana Pyke (London, 1955), p. 364.
[208] Ibid.
[209] 'Intelligence report no. EF-FB-2. Interrogation of Hjalmar Horace Greeley Schacht, July 11, 1945, 1050 hours', p. 10.

prevalent in the economy – and particularly the pace at which it developed in the course of 1938 – had alarmed the directorate.[210]

On 7 January 1939, five days after Hitler's meeting with Schacht, the entire directorate – Schacht, Vocke, Blessing and the other members – put their names to a memorandum addressed to Hitler. In doing so, they established one of the central tenets of what would later become monetary mythology in the post-war public sphere. The memorandum, some seven pages long, protested against the government's inflationary policies in unusually strong terms.[211] In the document, the directorate grounded its opposition to further rearmament spending specifically on *financial* grounds: the reichsmark's stability was in danger. No moral opposition was expressed. 'The currency is threatened to a critical extent by the reckless policy of expenditure on the part of public authorities', the memorandum began. It continued:

> The unlimited increase in government expenditure defeats every attempt to balance the budget, brings the national finances to the verge of bankruptcy despite an immense tightening of the taxation screw, and as a result is ruining the central bank and the currency. There exists no recipe, no system of financial or monetary techniques – however ingenious or well thought-out – there is no organisation or measure of control sufficiently powerful to check the devastating effects on the currency of a policy of unrestricted spending. No central bank is capable of maintaining the currency against an inflationary spending policy on the part of the state.[212]

These were strong words. And as the historian Kopper rightfully notes, they were brave ones too.[213] That all members of the directorate signed the document was somewhat unusual; normally, only the president and vice president would have been required to sign correspondence on behalf of the directorate. A complete set of signatures (Figure 1.6) was intended as a signal to Hitler.[214]

But they were also carefully prepared words. The memorandum had been in preparation for some months. Most accounts, but not all, trace the document back to early October 1938.[215] International events forced the directorate to act. Some years later, in 1946, Ernst Hülse,

---

[210] *Trials of the major war criminals before the International Military Tribunal, vol. XIII* (Nuremberg, 1948), p. 63.

[211] Reichsbank directorate to Adolf Hitler, 7 Jan. 1939, DBHA, B330/574.

[212] Ibid., p. 4. See also Vocke, *Memoiren*, p. 106.

[213] Kopper, *Bankiers unterm Hakenkreuz*, p. 191.

[214] Schacht, *My first seventy-six years*, p. 392.

[215] Vocke claimed in his memoirs that the memorandum dated back as early as July 1938. But this claim contradicts his testimony at Nuremberg in 1946, where he said it dated to early October 1938. See Vocke, *Memoiren*, p. 103; and refer also to Vocke's testimony in *Trials of the major war criminals before the International Military Tribunal, vol. XIII*, p. 69.

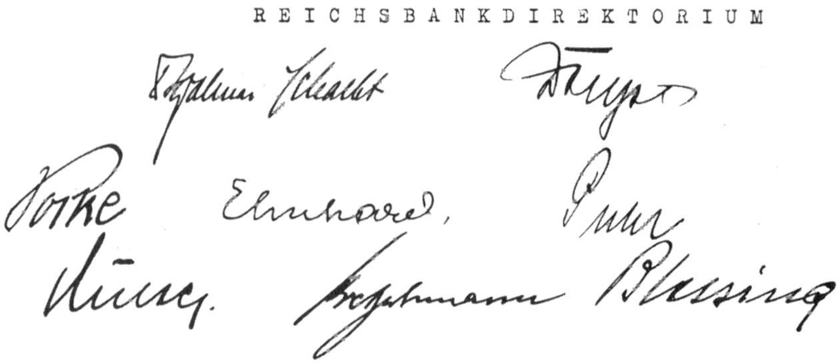

R E I C H S B A N K D I R E K T O R I U M

Figure 1.6 Signatures found on the Reichsbank memorandum sent on
7 January 1939. Vocke's signature is in the middle row on the left,
Blessing's to the bottom right, Schacht's to the top left.
(Reichskanzlei R43 – Bundesarchiv, Berlin-Lichterfelde)

a directorate member who had also signed the memorandum, recalled that
it was specifically the Munich Agreement in late September 1938, which
saw Germany annex parts of Czechoslovakia, that confirmed the fears of
both Schacht and the directorate that another war seemed inevitable.
According to Hülse, Schacht then stated in a directorate meeting that they
were left with little choice but to force their own departure from the central
bank.[216] Schacht confirmed this rationale at his trial in Nuremberg in
1946.[217] At Nuremberg, too, Schacht stressed the importance of the
Munich Agreement in dispelling any illusion of future peace in Europe,
and propelling the Reichsbank directorate to write its position with regard
to Hitler's financial policies.[218] Why, then, was it only sent in January? It
was a question of timing. Vocke attributed the delay of its dispatch to the
hesitations of Schacht, who wanted to wait for the opportune moment.[219]

Who wrote the memorandum? Years later, in West Germany, Vocke
claimed sole authorship of the memorandum.[220] But at the Nuremberg

[216] *Trials of the major war criminals before the International Military Tribunal, vol. XLI*
(Nuremberg, 1949), pp. 290–1.
[217] In his otherwise excellent biography of Schacht, Kopper states that Schacht never
confessed the memorandum was aimed at ridding him of his office at the central
bank. But at the Nuremberg trials Schacht stated quite clearly that this was indeed
the case. See *Trials of the major war criminals before the International Military Tribunal, vol.
XII* (Nuremberg, 1947), p. 533. Contrast with Kopper, *Hjalmar Schacht*, p. 325.
[218] *Trials of the major war criminals before the International Military Tribunal, vol. XIII*, p. 29.
[219] Ibid., p. 69.
[220] See Wilhelm Vocke, *Gesundes Geld* (Frankfurt, 1956), for example; and Vocke,
Memoiren, p. 102.

trials in 1946, Vocke, who was acting as a defence witness for Schacht, never stated this. Instead, he described how a draft of the memorandum was sent to members of the directorate who made their own corrections to the document.[221] Archival evidence complicates the picture further. The earliest trace of what eventually became the memorandum among surviving Reichsbank files can be traced to a report written on 3 October 1938 by the economics and statistics department of the central bank.[222] The timing of this report, too, supports the statements of Hülse and Schacht as the memorandum being a response to the events of Munich, which had occurred just days before. Yet the economics and statistics department was not Vocke's domain, and the writer David Marsh traces the authorship of the partial draft in question to Rudolf Eicke, a Reichsbank official.[223] Nevertheless, in 1986, the Bundesbank published typed extracts of two drafts, one dating from October 1938, and attributed the authorship of both to Vocke.[224] What seems clear is that Vocke played a sizeable role in the drafting of the document, but others played a hand in determining the final wording.

But why are these questions of authorship important? In the end, the memorandum sparked off events that led to the almost complete departure of the directorate and the outright elimination of whatever legal remnants of central bank independence that had remained up to 1939. This event would go on to have significant political advantages in the post-war sphere for all those involved. Hitler, who was usually an 'extraordinarily lazy reader of documents', read the memorandum in detail on 19 January.[225] In doing so, he fell into a rage. The next day, the directorate received a short, curt message, informing the men that Schacht, his vice president Ernst Dreyse, and Hülse were sacked from the central bank with immediate effect.[226] However, the other directorate members,

---

[221] According to Vocke's own words, at least. See *Trials of the major war criminals before the International Military Tribunal, vol. XIII*, p. 69.

[222] Volkswirtschaftliche und Statistische Abteilung der Reichsbank, 'Teilentwurf einer Denkschrift über die künftige Währungspolitik', 3 Oct. 1938, BAB, R2501/6521. The historian Adam Tooze also comes to this conclusion. See Tooze, *The wages of destruction*, pp. 287, 297.

[223] The 3 October 1938 draft, however, is not signed by Eicke – nor by any one person for that matter. At the same time, Marsh does not challenge Vocke's claim of authorship of what eventually emerged to be the Reichsbank memorandum of 7 January 1939. See Marsh, *The Bundesbank*, p. 296 (footnote).

[224] These drafts were published in a Bundesbank volume celebrating the 100th birthday of Vocke. See Deutsche Bundesbank, *Geheimrat Wilhelm Vocke*, pp. 83–4, 85–6.

[225] Kopper, *Hjalmar Schacht*, p. 327.

[226] Chancellor's office to the Reichsbank directorate, 20 Jan. 1939, BAB, R43 II / 234; see also Chancellor's office to Hjalmar Schacht, 19 Jan. 1939, BAB, R43 II / 234.

Blessing and Vocke among them, were not mentioned.[227] As such, both men remained in the directorate. Only after much persistence did Vocke and Blessing secure their resignations in February 1939.[228] In the words of one American official after the war, 'He [Vocke] resigned in 1939 according to a provision which permitted leading members of the Reichsbank to retire on past pay if they disagree with policy etc. His retirement had nothing to do with the dismissal of Schacht. The reason can be found in his opposition to the Nazi party'.[229] Vocke had finally called an end to his time in the directorate, a stint that lasted twenty years, ten of which under the leadership of Schacht.[230] By the time of his departure in 1939, he was by far the longest-serving member of the directorate.[231]

The 'End' of Central Bank Independence

In his memoirs, Vocke portrayed his resignation as a direct, moral response to the legal changes afoot in the Reichsbank.[232] The January 1939 memorandum triggered these changes. Furious that the Reichsbank's directorate could be so impudent, Hitler resolved to place the Reichsbank completely under his control. Back in January 1937, Hitler announced in the Reichstag that the Reich had assumed unlimited sovereignty over the Reichsbank. This announcement created the political impetus by which a law was passed on 10 February of that year which stated the central bank was subordinated to the Reich's president and chancellor – namely, Hitler.[233] The directorate was no longer able to conduct monetary policy independently. This 1937 law, however, merely affirmed in legal terms a development that had gradually taken place since 1933.[234]

The 1939 legislation, which had been secretly passed in the weeks following the memorandum, but only announced publicly in June in light of concerns surrounding public opinion, reaffirmed the bank's

[227] 'And me? They had forgotten about me', Vocke later recalled. See Vocke, *Memoiren*, p. 110.
[228] Ibid.   [229] The letter is undated. See Marsh, *The Bundesbank*, p. 313 (footnote).
[230] *Trials of the major war criminals before the International Military Tribunal, vol. XIII*, p. 49.
[231] Reinhardt provides a useful table that charts the length of tenure of various Reichsbank directorate members. See Reinhardt, *Die Reichsbank in der Weimarer Republik*, p. 277.
[232] Vocke, *Memoiren*, p. 110.
[233] 'Gesetz zur Neuregelung der Verhältnisse der Reichsbank und der Deutsche Reichsbahn. Vom 10. Februar 1937', 12 Feb. 1937, BAB, R2501/6860. See also 'Begründung [Gesetz vom 10. Februar 1937]', 10 Feb. 1937, BAB, R2501/6860.
[234] As pointed out in a sycophantic piece written by a Reichsbank official at the time. See Eicke, 'Die Befreiung der Reichsbank von internationalen Bindungen'.

subordination to the government.[235] It stated that the Reichsbank was obliged to support the policies of the government while safeguarding the stability of the currency; in other words, the directorate was subject to instructions and supervision by the 'Führer', who could appoint and fire them at will. And the directorate, for its part, no longer decided policy by majority vote. Instead, this would be decided by the Reichsbank president alone. In other words, the *Führerprinzip*, or Führer principle, was introduced to the central bank itself.[236]

Both in 1937 and 1939, newspapers and Reichsbank reports portrayed these laws as National Socialist triumphs against foreign intrusions of German sovereignty. The symbiotic relationship now enjoyed by the state and central bank was a natural one, these articles claimed, and marked a return to the relationship found in the glory years of Second Reich.[237] 'In National Socialist Germany, we have overthrown the idols of a grimy economic and monetary ideology in the most irreverent fashion', exclaimed the new Reichsbank vice president, Rudolf Brinkmann.[238] That such lines were found in an article entitled 'Stable money' marked the extent to which rhetoric and monetary practice diverged in the Third Reich.

Reckoning with National Socialism

Reichsbank officials greeted the gradual encroachment of National Socialism in different ways. Vocke, for his part, had become increasingly aloof following 1933. He avoided politics where possible, and eschewed membership of the National Socialist party. The future BdL chairman later documented how he would stroll into the central bank at 10 a.m. after a morning of horse riding, before departing again shortly after lunch time.[239] Indeed, according to one contemporary, Vocke had a reputation of 'exceptional laziness' during these years.[240] All the same, Vocke

[235] 'Gesetz über die Deutsche Reichsbank. Vom 15 Juni 1939 (Reichsgesetz I S. 1015)', BAB, R2501/7573. An English translation can be found here: 'Law Concerning the German Reichsbank, June 15, 1939. Aus: Federal Reserve Bulletin, Washington, vom September 1939, s. 737/742', Sep. 1939, BAB, R2501/6861, pp. 1–2. Vocke notes the passage of the 'Geheimgesetz' as well as the reason why its announcement was delayed. See Vocke, *Memoiren*, p. 110.
[236] 'Die neue Reichsbank', *Die Staatsbank*, 25 Jun. 1939, BAB, R2501/3415.
[237] See, for instance, 'Befreite Reichsbank', *Völkischer Beobachter*, 2 Feb. 1937, BAB, R2501/6860; Eicke, 'Die Befreiung der Reichsbank von internationalen Bindungen'; Frede, 'Die neue Reichsbank', 25 Jun. 1939, BAB, R2501/6861, p. 1; 'Reichsbank unter Staatshoheit', *Südost-Echo*, 23 Jun. 1939, BAB, R2501/3415.
[238] Brinkmann, 'Stabile Währung', p. 1.   [239] Vocke, *Memoiren*, p. 102.
[240] Marsh, *The Bundesbank*, p. 272 (footnote).

actively partook in directorate meetings during this period and, like Blessing, signed routine notices that upheld the financial persecution of Jews up until his departure.[241]

Other Reichsbank officials, such as the younger Blessing, took a slightly different path. When Schacht resigned from the Reichsbank in 1930 amid political turmoil that engulfed the Weimar Republic, Blessing spent the years 1930–4 in Switzerland as a department head at the BIS. Then, the Württemberger was recalled in 1934 to the Reichsbank, while also acting as an advisor for Schacht at the economics ministry. In May of 1937, at the age of just 37, Blessing was appointed to the Reichsbank's directorate, assigned with questions of monetary policy, foreign exchange and external debt problems.[242]

Blessing joined the National Socialist party in May 1937 – the same month in which he joined the Reichsbank directorate.[243] It was known, however, that the man had little taste for Nationalism Socialism.[244] Nevertheless, representing the Reichsbank, Blessing participated in a 1938 conference working towards measures that persecuted the Jewish population in Germany. The conference took place three days after *Kristallnacht*, a pogrom in which dozens of Jews were murdered, thousands arrested, Jewish stores looted and synagogues burned.[245] Among those present were Joseph Goebbels, Reinhard Heydrich and other leading officials of the Third Reich. The conference, according to the American official in 1948, 'was concerned with formulating specific steps to be taken to insure [*sic*] the complete elimination of Jewish participation in the economic and social life of Germany'.[246] Among other punitive measures, it was agreed that a fine of one billion reichsmarks was to be imposed on Germany's Jewish population. Blessing, on behalf of the

[241] Ibid., pp. 119–20.
[242] 'Curriculum Vitae (Karl Blessing)', no date, DBHA, BSG 1/12. See also Willi A. Boelcke, 'Karl Blessing (1900–1971). Der Großbankier aus Enzweihingen', *Vaihinger Köpfe: Biographische Porträts aus fünf Jahrhunderten* (Vaihingen an der Enz, 1993), p. 250.
[243] The date 1 May 1937 is listed by Blessing in 'Parteistatistische Erhebung 1939 – Karl Blessing', Jul. 1939, BAB, R9361-1 261; see also 'Militaergerichtshof Nr. IV, Fall V, Nuernberg, Deutschland 18. August 1947. Sitzung von 9.30 – 12.30 Uhr (Karl Blessing's testimony)', 18 Aug. 1947, DBHA, B330/3506, p. 5572.
[244] 'The Reichsbank and its relations with other institutions. Appendix: – personalities', Aug. 1944, IfZ, 2/206/4 FINAD, pp. xvi–xvii. See also 'Statement by Friedrich Ernst. OMGUS VII', 23 Aug. 1945, DBHA, BSG 1/12, p. 1.
[245] Tooze, *The wages of destruction*, pp. 278–9. A detailed account of the conference, as well as its intimidating atmosphere, is provided in Gerald D. Feldman, *Allianz and the German Insurance Business, 1933–1945* (Cambridge, 2001), pp. 197–205.
[246] Claus Notulsky to Saul Kagan, 26 Mar. 1948, DBHA, BSG 1/12, p. 2.

Reichsbank, participated in the discussion leading to the decision to impose the fine.[247]

After the Reichsbank

Following his departure from the central bank, Vocke retired to private life and saw out the war's end from his house in Berlin, when Russian soldiers arrived at his doorstep.[248] Blessing, however, was still a young man with a future. He accepted a position in a newly established advisory council at the Reichsbank, a role with little practical importance, but, according to one Allied official, was 'the only member of this body who has really discharged his duty to the bank seriously'.[249] In the 1960s, Schacht would misleadingly use this fact to ground a claim in the public sphere that Blessing actively partook in the second inflation, provoking the Bundesbank president's quiet fury.[250]

Two months after leaving the Reichsbank, in April 1939, Blessing began to work for the Margarine-Union, which was attached to Unilever, a Dutch corporate.[251] It was during this time that Blessing sought to protect himself politically where possible. A chance appeared. The future Bundesbank president sought out, joined and actively participated in Heinrich Himmler's 'circle of friends', or *Freundeskreis*, a group of elite industrialists and SS officials who met on a regular basis to discuss matters of economic importance.[252] 'Karl Blessing was one of the most faithful members of the Circle of Friends of [the] Reichsführer SS', wrote one American military official in 1948.[253] 'Among the activities of the Circle of Friends were two visits to concentration camps by a group of members of the Circle, personally conducted by Heinrich Himmler.' The first visit took place in 1937 when a party of twenty members

---

[247] Ibid. This claim is supported in other documents, including copies of Stasi reports found in the Bundesbank historical archive. See 'Karl Blessing (Stasi report)', no date, DBHA, BSG 1/12.

[248] Vocke, *Memoiren*, pp. 133–5, 137–8.

[249] For evidence of Blessing's membership, see 'Beirat der Deutschen Reichsbank [list of members]', 1939, BAB, R2501/6861, p. 1; and 'The Reichsbank and its relations with other institutions. Appendix: – personalities', p. xvii.

[250] This episode is detailed in Chapter 4.

[251] 'Synopsis of career (Karl Blessing)', no date, DBHA, BSG 1/12.

[252] An overview of Himmler's 'circle of friends', along with various documentary evidence, can be found in *Trials of war criminals before the Nuernberg Military Tribunal under Control Council Law No. 10, vol. VI* (Washington, 1952), pp. 226–87. Blessing's name can be found in a list offered by the group's founder at Nuremberg, 'Eidesstattliche Erklärung des Wilhelm Keppler', no date, DBHA, B330/3506.

[253] Notulsky to Kagan, 26. Mar. 1948, p. 1.

inspected the Dachau camp; the second, in 1939, when a similar number visited the Oranienburg camp. 'Karl Blessing took part in both visits.'[254]

At Nuremberg, however, it emerged that Blessing's membership of the 'circle of friends' dated from early 1939 onwards – that is, following his departure from the Reichsbank – which casts at least some doubt on the American official's claims.[255] Blessing downplayed his ties to Himmler's *Freundeskreis* in the Nuremberg courtroom, but admitted that he had attended 30 out of 38 such gatherings over the years.[256] The forum of industrialists and SS officials also served as a source of cash for the SS. Blessing, on behalf of his new employer, provided two payments. Each amounted to 15,000 reichsmarks, the first delivered in 1939, the second in 1940. Unilever supported Blessing in these endeavours, believing the payments would be seen as a gesture of goodwill should the company's fortunes take a turn for the worse in future.[257]

And indeed they did. In 1941, the Third Reich targeted Unilever, a foreign firm, accusing the company of treasonous activities.[258] Unilever's head offices in occupied Rotterdam were raided, and Blessing ended up in an interrogation room with the Geheime Staatspolizei, more commonly known as the Gestapo, Himmler's secret police.[259] He was arrested because his attendance was listed in minutes of meetings deemed worthy of confiscation. In the end, the Gestapo released Blessing without charge, but the event highlighted the extent to which Blessing was now politically suspect. Shortly afterwards, the former central banker was offered an olive branch that he quickly grabbed. The former Reichsbanker accepted an offer from Göring's state secretary to join the board of Kontinentale Öl-Aktiengesellschaft, or Continental Oil, a new enterprise established with the aim of plundering the oil fields of conquered territory in south-east Europe.[260] As one Allied war official noted, however, Continental Oil 'never got far past the planning stage, owing to war developments in Russia and Roumania'.[261] Germany's defeat at

---

[254] Ibid. The subject of concentration camp trips was not broached at Blessing's testimony. See 'Militaergerichtshof Nr. IV, Fall V, Nuernberg, Deutschland 18. August 1947. Sitzung von 9.30 – 12.30 Uhr (Karl Blessing's testimony)', pp. 5563–4.

[255] 'Militaergerichtshof Nr. IV, Fall V, Nuernberg, Deutschland 18. August 1947. Sitzung von 9.30 – 12.30 Uhr (Karl Blessing's testimony)', p. 5564. Lindenlaub also dates Blessing's membership of the 'circle of friends' from 1939. See Lindenlaub, 'Karl Blessing', p. 15.

[256] 'Militaergerichtshof Nr. IV, Fall V, Nuernberg, Deutschland 18. August 1947. Sitzung von 9.30 – 12.30 Uhr (Karl Blessing's testimony)', p. 5580.

[257] Kopper, *Bankiers unterm Hakenkreuz*, p. 194.   [258] Ibid., p. 195.

[259] Ibid., pp. 195–6.   [260] Ibid., p. 196.

[261] 'The Reichsbank and its relations with other institutions. Appendix: – personalities', p. xvi.

Stalingrad in early 1943 signalled an end to Hitler's ambitions in the east. Blessing would remain with the Continental Oil until the war's conclusion.[262]

Yet there was another side to Blessing in the Third Reich. It later emerged that he was linked to the *Kreisauer Kreis*, or Kreisau Circle, an opposition group comprised of conservatives disillusioned with Hitler.[263] During this time, too, Blessing became associated with members of the '20 July' group, named after the date in 1944 during which an assassination attempt failed to kill Hitler. At his testimony at Nuremberg, Blessing claimed to have links to the group that dated from November 1943.[264] Both the Kreisau Circle and the '20 July' group were brutally crushed in the aftermath of the failed coup. Blessing's name was found on at least two lists of provisional cabinet members should the '20 July' coup attempt have succeeded.[265] How did he escape punishment, however? According to Blessing, Walther Funk, the man who replaced Schacht as Reichsbank president in 1939, vouchsafed for his credentials, persuading the SS that Blessing knew nothing of the plot on the Führer's life.[266]

Blessing's career during the inter-war period, then, was full of contradictions. 'It is surprising that a man with this past could be the first president of the Bundesbank', noted one astonished Bundesbank official in 1998, after learning of Blessing's history.[267] The Reichsbanker was an active member of Himmler's *Freundeskreis*. But his name could be found on the Reichsbank memorandum sent to Hitler in 1939. Blessing participated in a meeting that persecuted Germany's Jewish population. Yet he was linked to a group of army officials who sought to kill Hitler. While it is likely that Blessing's relationship with the Third Reich was never based on conviction – rather, the evidence suggests it was one was founded upon opportunism – the purpose of this section is not to pass judgment on Blessing's character. Instead it seeks to highlight the

---

[262] 'Militaergerichtshof Nr. IV, Fall V, Nuernberg, Deutschland 18. August 1947. Sitzung von 9.30 – 12.30 Uhr (Karl Blessing's testimony)', p. 5557.

[263] Lindenlaub, 'Karl Blessing', p. 15.

[264] 'Militaergerichtshof Nr. IV, Fall V, Nuernberg, Deutschland 18. August 1947. Sitzung von 9.30 – 12.30 Uhr (Karl Blessing's testimony)', pp. 5578–9.

[265] Blessing's name appeared in the following two lists: Ernst Kaltenbrunner to Martin Bormann, 27 Jul. 1944, DBHA, B330/3506; and Ernst Kaltenbrunner to Martin Bormann, 10 Aug. 1944, DBHA, B330/3506. His name also appeared in an account found in Ernst Kaltenbrunner to Martin Bormann, 6 Sep. 1944, DBHA, B330/3506.

[266] 'Militaergerichtshof Nr. IV, Fall V, Nuernberg, Deutschland 18. August 1947. Sitzung von 9.30 – 12.30 Uhr (Karl Blessing's testimony)', pp. 5578–9.

[267] The comment is found in an internal memorandum. See Jochen Plassmann, 'OMGUS-Akten Political background of Karl Blessing', 1 Oct. 1998, DBHA, BSG 1/12.

different ways in which Blessing's career *could* have been interpreted in the post-war era.

And what of Schacht? After being sacked from the Reichsbank, Schacht remained a minister without portfolio in Hitler's cabinet – in reality, a sinecure.[268] But Schacht, too, had become linked to resistance circles. In the end, even the resistance found him too unreliable a character to be of any genuine value. Once the coup failed, though, this association landed Schacht in a number of concentration camps, where he escaped death and saw out the final days of the war.[269]

Nuremberg

It is here, then, that we return to the military officer's report, 'In search of the Reichsbank'. He had been assigned to compile as much information about the Reichsbank as possible. It was during this period, too, that the Allied military authorities set about discerning the events that transpired for purposes of trying leading officials of the Third Reich. But in contrast to his erstwhile colleagues, Schacht, for his part, was not accused of crimes against humanity. He was charged with 'conspiring to bring about the war' and 'participating in the preparation of war'.[270]

Schacht, along with his lawyer, Rudolf Dix, 'a man of distinguished diplomacy and a gifted speaker' in the eyes of Schacht, set about organising the former Reichsbank president's defence.[271] Among the defence witnesses called by Dix were Vocke and Hülse, the two former Reichsbank directors.[272] In justifying his selection of these men, Schacht's lawyer stated, 'Vocke and Huelse were Schacht's closest collaborators at the Reichsbank and at the International Bank at Basel. They know of events and developments which Schacht may not be able to recall in detail.'[273] The Allied military government sent both Vocke and Hülse to Nuremberg. They were lodged in a guesthouse specifically set aside for witnesses; Vocke would remain at Nuremberg for six weeks, waiting for

---

[268] 'Intelligence report no. EF-FB-2. Interrogation of Hjalmar Horace Greeley Schacht, July 11, 1945, 1050 hours', 25 Jul. 1945, p. 11.
[269] Kopper, *Hjalmar Schacht*, pp. 355–8.   [270] Schacht, *76 Jahre meines Lebens*, p. 574.
[271] Ibid., p. 581.
[272] See *Trials of the major war criminals before the International Military Tribunal, vol. VIII* (Nuremberg, 1947), p. 541.
[273] Due to circumstances unexplained, Hülse never stepped into the courtroom in Nuremberg. Instead, Dix would use a written version of his testimony. Vocke later hinted that Hülse's absence in the courtroom was due to his nervous and angst-ridden disposition while at Nuremberg. For the testimony, see *Trials of the major war criminals before the International Military Tribunal, vol. XLI*, pp. 290–1. See also Vocke, *Memoiren*, p. 144.

his appearance in court.[274] It was during this time that Vocke conferred with Dix about the strategy to be used at Schacht's trial.[275]

In the lead-up to Schacht's appearance at Nuremberg, his lawyer Dix set about crafting a narrative of past events, buttressed by an array of documentary evidence, amid efforts to sanitise the record of the former central banker. In this respect, Dix saw Vocke's testimony as instrumental. Above all, the lawyer sought to portray Schacht as one of the few men who attempted to resist Hitler, a man who tried to do his best to rein in the government's spending and hinder rearmament, and one whose expulsion from the Reichsbank in 1939 effectively meant the end of the central bank's independence, turning the central bank into a tool of the state.

The Reichsbank memorandum of January 1939 was one of the leading documents, if not the most important one, relied upon by Dix and Schacht.[276] It demonstrated that Hitler dismissed Schacht because of the latter's objections to the further financing of rearmament. At Nuremberg, the memorandum was, for the first time, fused with a moral tone, one that was laced with condemnation of the Third Reich. According to Dix, Schacht and the Reichsbank directorate were men who said 'no' to the dictator and paid their price for such intransigence: they became martyrs to the ideals of sound currency. In other words, monetary martyrs.

And yet, such an interpretation of the 1939 memorandum could be contested. Indeed, it was contested. The prosecution team listed the Reichsbank memorandum as evidence *against* Schacht.[277] The prosecution claimed that the memorandum limited itself to technical considerations of the currency; it had made no mention of a moral objection to Hitler's rearmament, merely a financial one – in other words, all the directorate wanted to do was evade financial responsibility and jump ship.[278] The fact that the prosecution team used the memorandum as a prosecution document highlights the extent to which the monetary past of the Reichsbank was fair game at Nuremberg. Different historical narratives competed against each other. Nothing was certain as to which ones would win the day.

---

[274] Vocke, *Memoiren*, pp. 143–4.   [275] Ibid., p. 144.

[276] It was listed as a document for the defence. See *Trials of the major war criminals before the International Military Tribunal, vol. XII*, p. 526.

[277] For the prosecution's document listing, see *Trials of the major war criminals before the International Military Tribunal, vol. XXIV* (Nuremberg, 1949), p. 147. This fact was mentioned in the courtroom, too. See also *Trials of the major war criminals before the International Military Tribunal, vol. XII*, p. 525.

[278] *Trials of the major war criminals before the International Military Tribunal, vol. XII*, pp. 533–5.

It was Schacht's defence, however, that emerged triumphant at the expense of the United States chief prosecutor, Robert Jackson. The prosecutor proved no match for the former central banker. 'Schacht is too smart for him', admitted one judge, somewhat ruefully.[279] The memorandum, Schacht argued,

indicates clearly that we [the directorate] opposed every further increase of state expenditure and would not assume responsibility for it. From that, Hitler gathered that he would in no event be able to use the Reichsbank with its present directorate and president for any future financial purposes. Therefore, there remained only one alternative; to change the directorate, because without the Reichsbank he could not go on.[280]

Dix argued that the directorate's decision to send the memorandum sparked the elimination of the Reichsbank's independence from government instruction. This was an important point for Dix, and Schacht's lawyer returned to this point more than once throughout the trials.[281] By focusing on the central bank legislation passed in the wake of Schacht's sacking, Dix attempted to portray Schacht as an independent man, and the Reichsbank as a proud, independent institution. It meant that, in Schacht's own words, 'an end had to be put to the independence of the Reichsbank' if Hitler wanted to continue pursuing inflationary policies.[282] It was only when Schacht was sacked, Dix claimed, that the Reichsbank was transformed into a cog of Hitler's war machine and the currency descended into ruin. The rise and fall of central bank independence, according to this account, was linked to the ascent and descent of Schacht.

At Nuremberg, Schacht claimed that Hitler reacted in fury upon reading the Reichsbank memorandum, shouting, 'This is mutiny!' When pressed on the origins of this statement, the former Reichsbanker said it came from his old colleague, Vocke.[283] Days later, sitting in the courtroom as a defence witness, Vocke confirmed this statement, noting he

---

[279] Schacht also had the benefit of being fluent in English, allowing him some additional time to carefully prepare the formulation of his answers while the court officials translated Jackson's questions into German. See Kopper, *Hjalmar Schacht*, p. 366.

[280] *Trials of the major war criminals before the International Military Tribunal, vol. XII*, p. 534.

[281] For example, during the court appearance of Hans Lammers, the head of the Hitler's Reich chancellery, Dix intervened from the side lines and directed the discussion to a point concerning Schacht's departure and the elimination of central bank independence, and explicitly returned to it again when he deemed Lammers's answer unsatisfactory. See *Trials of the major war criminals before the International Military Tribunal, vol. XI* (Nuremberg, 1947), p. 90.

[282] *Trials of the major war criminals before the International Military Tribunal, vol. XII*, p. 534.

[283] Ibid., p. 536.

had heard it from an official in the finance ministry.[284] In the 1950s, Hitler's exclamation of mutiny would later be included often in post-war articles and essays about the BdL's leadership, in turn boosting Vocke's credibility as a central banker who stood up to profligate governments. And yet its origins in the post-war public sphere actually came from Vocke himself. Schacht's lawyer, for his part, referred to Hitler's mutiny comment a number of times in his concluding defence of Schacht at Nuremberg.[285]

Vocke's testimony proved important for Schacht. The directorate member delivered a strong performance, eloquently defending his former boss, and arguing Schacht was a fierce opponent of war.[286] This was not unexpected. Prior to Vocke's appearance at Nuremberg, he was asked by Allied military authorities to write a statement about Schacht. It was to be used for the trial at Nuremberg, Vocke was told. After doing so, however, the central banker was greeted with a curt response. 'This is a eulogy', the military official said, holding the statement in his hand.[287] It was at Nuremberg that Vocke also defended the legality of the 'Mefo' bills, though he admitted that they were dreadful instruments and designed from the start to be abused.[288]

But there were slight discrepancies between Schacht and Vocke's statements. Schacht spoke of how the resignations of Vocke and Blessing were 'granted', while Vocke claimed he had been 'dismissed' by Hitler.[289] Both men were describing the same event: the resignations of Vocke and Blessing had to be accepted by Hitler.[290] But they chose to present this same event in different lights. Vocke, for his part, explicitly linked his dismissal to his refusal to have anything to do with the new law

---

[284] Vocke's exact words concerning the origins of Hitler's comment 'This is mutiny!': 'I cannot remember that anymore. I believe it was Herr Berger of the finance ministry. But I cannot say exactly.' See *Trials of the major war criminals before the International Military Tribunal, vol. XIII*, p. 62.

[285] *Trials of the major war criminals before the International Military Tribunal, vol. XVIII* (Nuremberg, 1948), pp. 297–300.

[286] *Trials of the major war criminals before the International Military Tribunal, vol. XIII*, pp. 59–60; and Viktor von der Lippe, *Nürnberger Tagebuchnotizen: November 1945 bis Oktober 1946* (Frankfurt, 1951), p. 254.

[287] The military official was quoted in English. See Vocke, *Memoiren*, p. 143. Indeed, a fragment of this testimony may have survived, though it is not certain. See Wilhelm Vocke, 'Handwritten account [English]', no date, DBHA, B330/6305/2.

[288] *Trials of the major war criminals before the International Military Tribunal, vol. XIII*, p. 60.

[289] For Schacht's statement, see *Trials of the major war criminals before the International Military Tribunal, vol. XII*, p. 534; for Vocke's numerous remarks, see *Trials of the major war criminals before the International Military Tribunal, vol. XIII*, pp. 49, 59–60, 62.

[290] A copy of Vocke's dismissal, complete with Hitler's signature, can be found in Deutsche Bundesbank, *Geheimrat Wilhelm Vocke*, p. 88.

that eliminated the Reichsbank's remaining independence.[291] His was a moral defiance: Vocke portrayed himself as a monetary martyr.

The Reichsbank memorandum proved crucial in the acquittal of Schacht of all charges at Nuremberg. Indeed, among the reasons behind the acquittal, the tribunal explicitly centred on the memorandum in that it 'urged a drastic curtailment of armament expenditures and a balanced budget as the only method of preventing inflation'.[292] Schacht, the tribunal decided, was a free man.

And Blessing? Blessing never appeared at Schacht's trial. Instead, he was a witness at the trial of Friedrich Flick, which occurred in 1947, examining the relationship between industrialists and the National Socialist party.[293] At Nuremberg, too, Blessing referred to his expulsion from the Reichsbank in 1939 in light of protesting against Hitler's inflationary spending amid efforts to defend his record.[294] It was here that his membership of Himmler's 'circle of friends', his board membership of Continental Oil and his links to German resistance groups were first discussed in post-war Germany.[295] Eventually, the tribunal at Nuremberg ruled that 'as a group (it can hardly be labelled an organisation) the Circle [of Friends] played no role in the implementation of politics in the Third Reich'.[296] Blessing would later fall back on this ruling – as well as various other Nuremberg documents, such as the Reichsbank memorandum – when news reports in the media emerged during the 1960s that he was a member of Himmler's 'circle of friends'.

Nuremberg set out to determine whether leading Third Reich officials and personalities were guilty of crimes. At Schacht's trial, competing narratives, both positive and negative, emerged in the courtroom. The record of both the man and the Reichsbank were placed under serious scrutiny for the first time in a post-war setting, and in the public eye to boot. After all, the Nuremberg trials were a media sensation, reported upon by both German and foreign journalists alike. By acquitting Schacht of all charges, the tribunal acknowledged the documentary evidence in support of his case. And by the trial's end, the Reichsbank

---

[291] *Trials of the major war criminals before the International Military Tribunal, vol. XIII*, pp. 59–60.

[292] *Trials of the major war criminals before the International Military Tribunal, vol. XXII* (Nuremberg, 1949), pp. 554, 556.

[293] Blessing's name can be found in a list of witnesses in *Trials of war criminals before the Nuernberg Military Tribunal under Control Council Law No. 10, vol. VI*, p. 1238.

[294] 'Militaergerichtshof Nr. IV, Fall V, Nuernberg, Deutschland 18. August 1947. Sitzung von 9.30 – 12.30 Uhr (Karl Blessing's testimony)', p. 5564.

[295] Ibid.

[296] See '22 Dez. Militärgerichtshof Nr. IV, Fall V. Anklagepunkte Vier und Fünf', DBHA, B330/3506, p. 5.

memorandum was not a cowardly document, one that sought to excul-
pate the central bank directorate of blame, as the prosecution had
claimed. Rather, it had become a powerful and defiant 'no' to a dictator
intent on bringing war to the European continent.

The Nuremberg trials played a crucial role for two reasons. First, they
helped to determine some of the parameters of what later emerged to be
the West German central bank's monetary mythology. And second, the
Bundesbank would go on to use selected Nuremberg documents, testimonies and judgments as ammunition amid efforts to discredit damaging
allegations in the public sphere, particularly during the 1960s. The trials,
then, provided both the foundation and building blocks of monetary
mythology.

Conclusion

By examining the emergence and record of central bank independence
during the inter-war era, we have seen that it was a mixed one. The
Reichsbank was independent of government instruction at the height of
the hyperinflation and depths of deflation. Moreover, the central bank
was made independent at the behest of foreign powers. Though today we
often see central bank independence as a quintessentially 'German' institution, this was not the case back in the era of the Weimar Republic. In
the words of Helfferich in 1922, the Autonomy Law was a 'dictate' forced
upon Germany by the Allies. The play of events during the hyperinflation
and deflation damaged the credibility of central bank independence
during the inter-war era. But this chapter has in no way argued that the
institution of central bank independence was solely *responsible* for both
the hyperinflation and deflation. Far from it; the causes of the hyperinflation, for instance, lie at the government's door. This chapter merely
contends the following: the fact that the monetary authority was independent of political instruction during these two key periods would go on
to offer useful ammunition for opponents of the West German central
bank's autonomy in the post-war period. That is the key point here.

Schacht transformed the Reichsbank into a political actor during the
1920s. It is here we recall the contemporary's remark back in 1930:
nobody knew or even cared what Havenstein looked like, but Schacht
attracted front-page headlines. The Reichsbank now had a face, voice
and personality. Much of this development can be attributed to the
central bank's independence and the manner in which the publicity-
savvy Schacht wielded it. One caricature, depicted in the chapter, demonstrated how Schacht – like Vocke and Blessing later – embodied both
the central bank and its independence in the public sphere. Decisions

may have been jointly made by a number of men behind the scenes, but in the public sphere, the Reichsbank was a one-man show.

Vocke and Blessing were children of the Reichsbank. By the time of Vocke's resignation, he was by far the longest-serving member of the directorate. He was known as the 'foreign minister' of the central bank. Blessing, though younger, was known as Schacht's protégé. After January 1939, Blessing joined Himmler's 'circle of friends' and later became a board member of Continental Oil, an organisation established to exploit the oil reserves of occupied south-east Europe. After the Second World War, there were a variety of ways in which one could view Blessing's career. Was he a Nazi sympathiser who socialised with SS officials? Or was he a monetary martyr who later became linked to resistance groups? These were questions that remained to be determined in the post-war public sphere. As will be seen in later chapters, the records of Vocke and Blessing were tied to that of the inter-war Reichsbank.

However, if we must go 'in search of the Reichsbank' – like that American official back in 1945 – to determine the origins of monetary mythology, it is not 1876, the year in which the Reichsbank was established, to which we must return. Rather, all roads lead back to Nuremberg. It was in Nuremberg that the history of the Reichsbank was first scrutinised and vetted in the post-war public sphere. And it was in Nuremberg that monetary mythology was first applied – and indeed, in defence of Schacht's person. By acquitting Schacht, and noting the importance of the Reichsbank memorandum of 1939 in his acquittal, the tribunal at Nuremberg effectively gave the green light for the latter's use as a document of moral meaning in the post-war era. In doing so, the tribunal laid a crucial foundation stone towards the future image of the BdL, and later, the Bundesbank. The Reichsbank memorandum assumed a new, moral importance at Nuremberg, and Vocke played an active, formative role in helping to determine this outcome.

As it happens, the Nuremberg trials were important for an entirely different reason, too. It was here that Vocke met his future press chief, Viktor von der Lippe, for the first time. The two men were stationed in the same guesthouse and soon befriended each other. At the time, von der Lippe was a defence attorney for Erich Raeder, an admiral, as well as other defendants at Nuremberg.[297] Von der Lippe would later go on to dominate the press department of the BdL, and later the Bundesbank, for a quarter of a century. If Vocke played a crucial role in the formation

---

[297] 'Biographical section: Viktor von der Lippe', *The International Year Book and Statemen's Who's Who*, 1974, DBHA, B330/8144. Von der Lippe would later document his time at Nuremberg in von der Lippe, *Nürnberger Tagebuchnotizen*.

of monetary mythology, von der Lippe would certainly play an important role in maintaining it.

But all that remained ahead of the two men. Back in 1946, neither had any idea of what the future held in store for them. At Nuremberg, the relationship between Vocke and von der Lippe was simply one of friendship in uncertain times.[298] Thirty years later, von der Lippe would recall how the two men often met in Nuremberg's zoo – or, at least, what was left of the zoo after it had been bombed. Sitting on a bench before an aviary of wide-eyed owls that had survived the war, they would discuss the events of the day, all the while staring at the winged creatures. 'Together we observed them', von der Lippe recalled.[299] It was the beginning of a fruitful partnership. Before them lay a destroyed landscape. It would be up to them to rebuild it.

---

[298] And it was a friendship that would grow stronger over time. Shortly before Vocke's death, he described von der Lippe as 'my best friend'. The comment can be found in an earlier draft of Vocke's memoirs, in a section that was removed from the finished book. See 'Die heutige Lage', extract from an earlier draft of Wilhelm Vocke's *Memoiren*, DBHA, BSG 1/389, p. 176.

[299] This anecdote can be found in von der Lippe's retirement speech, delivered in late January 1977. See Viktor von der Lippe, 'Abschiedsworte', 31 Jan. 1977, DBPA, no. 717, pp. 2–4.

2   The Bank deutscher Länder and the Foundation of West Germany, 1948–1951

Introduction

An unusual conference took place in Munich on 12 June 1950. Twenty-five West German experts, hailing from the realms of private banking, central banking, politics, academia and the media, sat around a discussion table. The participants were in Munich to discuss ideas and proposals for the upcoming Bundesbank Law, a crucial piece of legislation that would establish the institutions and structure of a federal central bank. This new monetary authority, it was acknowledged, would replace West Germany's existing central bank, the Bank deutscher Länder (BdL), which had been created by the Allied military powers back in 1948 and made independent of German political instruction.

Carl Schaefer, a private banker, and the chair of the conference, opened the discussion by outlining the current public controversies surrounding the Bundesbank Law.[1] There were two main points of contention, he said. First, should this new federal central bank retain the BdL's decentralised structure, or revert to a more centralised organisation, akin to the inter-war Reichsbank? And second, how should the Bundesbank Law outline the central bank's relationship vis-à-vis the federal and state governments? Schaefer supported the idea of an independent monetary authority. While discussing it, however, the banker touched upon the tricky legacy of the inter-war era, as well as current trends evident elsewhere in the world of central banking. '*Tempora mutantur et nos mutamur in illis*', he remarked – 'Times are changing and we are changing with them.'

It would be tempting, especially today, to demand the political independence of the central bank, since our currency is dependent upon the central bank

---

[1] The transcript of the conference was published as a small book in 1950. See Adolf Weber (ed.), *Die Bundesbank. Aufbau und Aufgaben. Bericht über eine Aussprache führender Sachverständiger mit dem Entwurf eines Bundesgesetzes über die Errichtung einer Bundesbank* (Frankfurt am Main, 1950).

leadership, and not upon the iron law of free convertibility, which had constrained the role of the government. But in light of the fact that, of the 57 central banks in the world today, some 36 are already nationalised (among them the Bank of England and the Bank of France) and only 12 remain in private hands, and in light of the additional fact that, previously, the independence of the German central bank had always been brought about at the request or order of a foreign power (the 1922 reparation commission, the 1924 Dawes Plan and the military government in 1948), it is inconceivable that the [lower] parliament – the Bundestag – as a representative of a state fighting for its sovereignty, would declare the Bundesbank as independent of the federal government, thereby doing away with federal influence, especially when, in the end, it is the government that carries responsibility for the currency. The total independence of the Bundesbank can therefore be rejected. Likewise, though, the unconditional dependence of the central bank in the manner of the Reichsbank Law of 16 June 1939 is also out of the question.[2]

The banker's comments were telling. By discussing the contemporary need for central bank independence, Schaefer, almost inadvertently, fell back upon the experiences of Germany's inter-war era to give some grounding, context and additional weight to his points. He was not alone. The public debate that centred on the Bundesbank Law – a dispute that lasted from 1949–57 – saw West German elites discussing their troubled monetary past in detail. They did so amid efforts to create a new central bank, one that incorporated the lessons of recent history, which could provide for a brighter and more stable future.

Note, however, that Schaefer referred to the examples of other central banks, such as the Bank of England and Bank of France. Contemporary examples, especially the Federal Reserve System of America, were important ones during the Bundesbank Law debate. But the major reference point during this period was the record of the Reichsbank. Where did the inter-war central bank go wrong? What did it get right? These questions forced West German elites to look back on the inter-war era and discern from it lessons that could be applied to the legislation establishing the Bundesbank. These questions, however, often gave rise to different answers depending on who was being asked. And as Schaefer's observation reveals, the very lessons stemming from Germany's inter-war era could be diffuse. As we will see, during the years 1948–51, various competing historical narratives circulated throughout the discussion pertaining to the establishment of the new central bank.

But why exactly was this conference in June 1950 an unusual one? After all, in depth monetary discussions, though somewhat abstract affairs, are hardly peculiar by their own nature. No, the conference was

---

[2] Ibid., p. 22.

unusual because the shadow of the BdL lay behind its organisation.[3] The central bank, with the help of its ally and proxy, the established economics journalist Volkmar Muthesius, organised a furtive media campaign aimed at influencing the elite debate concerning the Bundesbank Law in the lead-up to 1951. The Munich gathering was just one example of a wider operation; newspaper articles, pamphlets, books, public speeches, and private lobbying efforts were other aspects of it. Historical lessons of Germany's two inflations lay at the heart of the BdL's argument for central bank independence. While Muthesius's relationship with the monetary authority was a remunerative one, it was also based on conviction. These men believed that central bank independence should form a core tenet of any legal rulebook that aimed to bring about economic stability.

Yet the BdL was not the only player to revert to historical lessons. A variety of elites – West German politicians and interest group officials, among others – often framed their ideas and policies with reference to the country's monetary history. If the BdL chose to point to the dizzy heights of Germany's two inflations as a warning against potential government influence over the future central bank, others chose to single out the independent Reichsbank's alleged role in helping to turn an inter-war recession into a depression. But why were these West German elites looking to the past in the first place? Was this a simple case of these men going out of their way to employ cynical public relations strategies in the effort to secure their interests?

Well, no, not exactly. There was a more fundamental dynamic at work here, one that independently propelled these elites to make sense of Germany's history. The dynamic in question was the institutional divide in West Germany's legislative fabric, a divide left behind by the Allied military authorities. There are two points to note here. First, the Allies created a central bank that pre-dated the foundation of the West German state. And second, the military powers ensured that this central bank would remain independent of West German federal government influence, until the moment when the Allies chose to return monetary sovereignty back to the Germans. In doing so, however, the Allies in effect set in place the conditions for a domestic power struggle that followed in their wake, once they decided to pull out of the realm of West German monetary affairs. This power struggle was a three-way affair: at its heart lay the central bank, the federal government, and the

---

[3] The conference's organisation, and its subsequent publication as a pamphlet, is documented in Volkmar Muthesius to Victor Wrede, 26 Jun. 1950, Deutsche Bundesbank Historisches Archiv [DBHA], B330/3345.

various *Länder*, or West German state governments.[4] They all responded to the same underlying incentive: that is, they all vied for influence over the new Bundesbank Law. And in doing so, Germany's monetary history became a political football.

'*Tempora mutantur et nos mutamur in illis.*' Schaefer's observation was only partly correct. Times were indeed changing in the world of central banking; but it remained to be seen whether West Germans would change with them. This chapter examines how various, contradictory lessons of Germany's inter-war period came to the fore during the Bundesbank Law debate in the years 1948–51 – the latter being the crucial year in which the Allies ended up returning monetary sovereignty to the West Germans. In doing so, the chapter fuses together two separate literatures. The first literature is that of economic and banking history, which has focused primarily on the contemporary political discussion concerning the Bundesbank Law. The other literature is more cultural, however. It examines how West Germans came to interpret and frame their recent, turbulent past in the 1950s. Both literatures offer valuable insights. But they have yet to incorporate each other's perspectives. This chapter seeks to do just that, while examining the central bank from an institutional angle.[5] Moreover, it approaches the Bundesbank Law debate from the perspective of the BdL. In doing so, the chapter shows how a certain narrative of inter-war events – first applied in defence of Hjalmar Schacht, the former Reichsbank president, at the Nuremberg trials in 1946 – competed with others that portrayed the Reichsbank's record in a more negative light.

The discussion concerning the Bundesbank Law was ostensibly an abstract, legal one. And it was a debate complicated by two other factors.

---

[4] Jörg Bibow is the first to acknowledge the three-way power struggle in detail. But he overlooks the impact that this debate had upon how German elites viewed their monetary history. See Jörg Bibow, 'Zur (Re-)Etablierung zentralbankpolitischer Institutionen und Traditionen in Westdeutschland: Theoretische Grundlagen und politisches Kalkül (1946–1967)', in Christian Scheer (ed.), *Die deutschsprachige Wirtschaftswissenschaft in den ersten Jahrzehnten nach 1945: Studien zur Entwicklung der Ökonomischen Theorie, Band XXV* (Berlin, 2010), p. 493.

[5] See John B. Goodman, *The politics of central banking in Western Europe* (London, 1992); Carl-Ludwig Holtfrerich, 'Monetary policy under fixed exchange rates (1948–70)', in Deutsche Bundesbank (ed.), *Fifty years of the Deutsche Mark: central bank and the currency in Germany since 1948* (Oxford, 1999); and, more recently, Carl-Ludwig Holtfrerich, 'Monetary policy in Germany since 1948: national tradition, international best practice or ideology?', in Jean Philippe Touffut (ed.), *Central banks as economic institutions* (Cheltenham, 2008), pp. 36–46. See also the perspective of Helge Berger, *Konjunkturpolitik im Wirtschaftswunder: Handlungsspielräume und Verhaltensmuster von Bundesbank und Regierung in den 1950er Jahren* (Tübingen, 1997); and Helge Berger and Jakob de Haan, 'A state within the state? An event study on the Bundesbank (1948–1973)', *Scottish Journal of Political Economy*, Vol. 46, No. 1 (1999).

First, West Germany already had a central bank in the form of the Frankfurt-based BdL. Decisions taken in Frankfurt, occasionally unpopular, could at times polarise the political discussion in Bonn, where the federal government was based, angering key participants and reinforcing prejudices. Moreover, given that there was no legal resolution mechanism by which one could formally solve disputes between the federal government and the BdL, conflicts were often 'dramatised', spilling into the public sphere and creating controversies that centred on the monetary authority's independence.[6] And second, the Bundesbank Law debate was also influenced by the business cycle. This point is important. The state of the economy mattered. For example, if the BdL tightened credit at a time of high unemployment, politicians and media commentators could compare the decision of the central bank to the restrictive policies of the Reichsbank during the Great Depression – an assertion without grounding, of course, but an explosive one all the same.

The first section of the chapter will discuss the debates concerning the idea of a German central bank prior to the establishment of the BdL in 1948. These debates offer telling insights into the views of German elites before the foundation of the Federal Republic. The second section looks at the BdL, its leadership and how the central bank's uncertain legal position in 1948 and 1949 incentivised the monetary authority to undertake efforts in arguing its case and try and influence the debate surrounding both itself and the future Bundesbank. This was crucial, given how controversies relating to its monetary policy decisions were likely to influence the parameters of the Bundesbank Law debate. Third, the chapter analyses the emergence of the Federal Republic and the struggle that followed between Frankfurt, Bonn and state governments. The chapter concludes with the crucial moment during which the Allied powers returned monetary sovereignty to West German hands. This resulted in the somewhat unexpected form of the Transition Law of 1951, which preserved the BdL's independence for years to come.

---

[6] A number of studies have highlighted the role played by 'dramatisation' in the nature of the relationship between the central bank and government. See Bertold Wahlig, 'Relations between the Bundesbank and the Federal Government', in Stephen F. Frowen and Robert Pringle (eds.), *Inside the Bundesbank* (Basingstoke, 1998), p. 52; Bibow, 'Zur (Re-)Etablierung zentralbankpolitischer Institutionen und Traditionen in Westdeutschland', p. 569; and Dieter Lindenlaub, 'Deutsches Stabilitätsbewußtsein: Wie kann man es fassen, Wie kann man es erklären, welche Bedeutung hat es für die Geldpolitik', in Bernhard Löffler (ed.), *Die kulturelle Seite der Währung. Europäische Währungskulturen, Geldwerterfahrungen und Notenbanksysteme im 20. Jahrhundert* (Munich, 2010), pp. 82–3.

Before the Bank deutscher Länder

The BdL was a by-product of its era. Established in 1948, it pre-dated the foundation of the West German state by well over a year. The Allied military authorities – more precisely, the American and British ones – created the central bank, tasking it with overseeing the new deutschmark, itself another 'child of the occupation'.[7] The BdL was the first trizonal institution in what later emerged to be West Germany. Since no centralised form of government existed at the time, the central bank's counterpart in the political sphere was the Frankfurt-based Economic Council, or Wirtschaftsrat, which, in the words of Christian Glossner, was 'Germany's first post-war legislative parliament and progenitor of the German Bundestag'.[8]

But the central bank's establishment arrived almost three years after Germany's defeat in the Second World War. That was a long time. In the intervening period, both the Allies and German elites had various ideas about the ideal central bank for Germany's economic difficulties. Yet the Allies were themselves divided. Prior to the unification of all three western zones – that is, during the years 1945, 1946 and 1947 – the British were intent on a centralised central bank, one akin to the interwar Reichsbank, which they believed could grapple with the sheer enormity of the challenges afoot in the British zone of occupation.[9] The Americans, by contrast, were adamant that the central banking system in their zone be decentralised and largely independent from German governmental authorities.[10] Part of this attitude can be attributed to the example of the Federal Reserve System of America, itself decentralised and independent. But it also spoke to concerns on the part

---

[7] See the title of Hans Roeper, *Die D-Mark: Vom Besatzungskind zum Weltstar* (Frankfurt, 1978); the term is also used in Otmar Emminger, *D-Mark, Dollar, Währungskrisen: Erinnerungen eines ehemaligen Bundesbankpräsidenten* (Stuttgart, 1986), p. 20. The tussle between American and British ambitions surrounding what emerged to become the BdL is documented in Theo Horstmann, 'Kontinuität und Wandel im deutschen Notenbanksystem. Die Bank deutscher Länder als Ergebnis alliierter Besatzungspolitik nach dem Zweiten Weltkrieg', in Theo Pirker (ed.), *Autonomie und Kontrolle. Beiträge zur Soziologie des Finanz- und Steuerstaats* (Berlin, 1989).

[8] Christian L. Glossner, *The making of the German post-war economy: political communication and public reception of the social market economy after World War Two* (London, 2010), p. 1.

[9] Eckhard Wandel, *Die Entstehung der Bank deutscher Länder und die deutsche Währungsreform 1948* (Frankfurt, 1980), pp. 65–6.

[10] Christoph Buchheim, 'The establishment of the Bank deutscher Länder and the West German currency reform', in Deutsche Bundesbank (ed.), *Fifty years of the Deutsche Mark: central bank and the currency in Germany since 1948* (Oxford, 1999), p. 67; and Christoph Buchheim, 'Die Unabhängigkeit der Bundesbank. Folge eines amerikanischen Oktrois?', *Vierteljahrshefte für Zeitgeschichte*, Vol. 49, No. 1 (2001), p. 29.

of the United States that Germany should be prevented from centralising power structures again. These worries stemmed from the experience of the Third Reich.

The result that eventually emerged, the Bank deutscher Länder Law, was ultimately a compromise between the Americans and British in March 1948.[11] The French zone joined a few weeks after the central bank's establishment.[12] The BdL was a two-tier central bank. Its centre lay in Frankfurt but the real power was dispersed across the states in the Western Bloc. Each state could appoint a president of its Landeszentralbank, or state central bank, who in turn visited Frankfurt every fortnight to attend the central bank council. The council in question was the decision-making body of the BdL, which made decisions by majority vote. The central bank council elected both its own chairman as well as the chairman of the directorate, which was essentially a board of managers who ran the BdL's day-to-day operations.[13] The Allied military authorities decided that the BdL was to be independent of German political instruction, but that its decisions be subject to the instructions and potential veto of the Allied Banking Commission (ABC), a small Allied body housed in the same building as the BdL.[14] The idea behind the ABC was to ensure that the central bank did not pursue policies that were deemed against the interests of the military occupiers.[15]

A more detailed discussion about the BdL follows later in this chapter. It has been necessary, however, to detail the final provisions of the central bank law to make an initial point of contrast – one which centres on the German proposals concerning the establishment of central banking in the occupied zones prior to the BdL's foundation. Several economic and banking historians have examined the debates in early post-war years, highlighting how many German elites were against the idea of an independent central bank – though they differ markedly as to the prevalence and degree of such opinions.[16] What can be ascertained, however, is that

---

[11] For the American law, see Law No. 60, 'Establishment of the Bank deutscher Länder', Military government gazette, 1946–1949, No. 805; for the law in the British zone, see 'Military government – Germany – British zone of control. Ordinance No. 129. Establishment of a Bank deutscher Länder', Mar. 1948, DBHA, B330/8599.

[12] Dieter Lindenlaub, 'Die Errichtung der Bank deutscher Länder und die Währungsreform von 1948: Die Begründung einer stabilitätsorientierten Geldpolitik', in Dieter Lindenlaub, Carsten Burhop and Joachim Scholtyseck (eds.), Schlüsselereignisse der deutschen Bankengeschichte (Stuttgart, 2013), p. 298.

[13] Law No. 60, 'Establishment of the Bank deutscher Länder', p. 13.   [14] Ibid., p. 10.

[15] For more on the ABC, see Monika Dickhaus, 'Fostering "The bank that rules Europe": the Bank of England, the Allied Banking Commission, and the Bank deutscher Länder, 1948–51', Contemporary European History, Vol. 7, No. 2 (1998).

[16] Lindenlaub differs from Buchheim, challenging the latter's assertion that central bank independence emerged in West Germany primarily as the result of an American Oktroi,

at least a large minority of German experts were against the idea of an independent central bank.[17] In other words, it was a subject of controversy and debate.

The historian Christoph Buchheim has documented how German bank experts in the American zone, among them future members of the BdL's central bank council and directorate, explicitly opposed the principle of central bank independence during the year 1946, when the United States pushed ahead with plans to establish state central banks in its own zone of occupation.[18] The American authorities rejected two German drafts of a law concerning the establishment of state central banks in their zone. Following the rejection of the second draft, one American official remarked '[t]here seems to be a very deliberate attempt on the part of the German authorities, in an indirect way, to give complete power over the banks to the government'.[19] Eventually the Americans accepted a third draft written by the Germans, which envisaged largely independent state central banks – but only after the Americans explicitly stated that such institutions should be 'as independent as possible from political influences'.[20]

As plans progressed towards a gradual unification of the western zones, two German expert bodies were given the opportunity to put forward suggestions and ideas with respect to the monetary make-up of the western zone. These two committees offer telling examples of German elite opinion prior to the establishment of the BdL. As the economist Jörg Bibow notes, both bodies revealed a marked scepticism with respect to the independence of a central bank, instead proposing a

or decree, one imposed 'against the almost unanimous resistance of German experts, including Ludwig Erhard'. In his 2013 essay, Lindenlaub himself notes that, while sources concerning German views on central bank independence are admittedly 'thin and confusing', 'a majority agreement' nonetheless existed with respect to the idea of a monetary authority independent of German political influence. Both Buchheim and Lindenlaub are quoted in Lindenlaub, 'Die Errichtung der Bank deutscher Länder und die Währungsreform von 1948', p. 299. For Buchheim's original argument, see Buchheim, 'Die Unabhängigkeit der Bundesbank', p. 6. Lindenlaub's thoughts on the subject can also be found in Lindenlaub, 'Deutsches Stabilitätsbewußtsein', p. 86 (footnote).

[17] See, for instance, Bibow, 'Zur (Re-)Etablierung zentralbankpolitischer Institutionen und Traditionen in Westdeutschland', pp. 541–3.

[18] These men were Wilhelm Könneker, Heinrich Hartlieb and Otto Pfleiderer. Könneker would later become vice chairman of the directorate; Hartlieb would also join the directorate; and Pfleiderer became a member of the central bank council. See Buchheim, 'Die Unabhängigkeit der Bundesbank', pp. 3–6.

[19] Ibid., p. 7.   [20] Ibid., p. 8.

form of close co-operation between the monetary authority and state, whereby the latter would have the last say on policy decisions.[21]

The Sonderstelle für Geld und Kredit, or Special Committee for Money and Credit, was one such forum. The German political body in Frankfurt commissioned the committee, with the consent of the Allies, and tasked it with formulating a suitable currency reform.[22] Among the members was Ludwig Erhard, the future economics minister of West Germany and father of the so-called 'economic miracle'. The Sonderstelle's working remit, however, considerably overlapped with the sphere of central banking. The committee was divided on the subject. Some members, such as Hans Möller and Günter Keiser, were explicitly opposed to an independent central bank, while others, such as Erhard, were in favour of an autonomous central bank, but one that had a constrained independence, which in turn would allow the government to have the last word on policy in times of economic distress.[23]

The Sonderstelle proposed the establishment an unusual body, a Currency Office, or Währungsamt, which would operate alongside the central bank. Technically, this Currency Office could not issue instructions to the monetary authority. But it could issue wide-ranging laws in times of emergency.[24] The wording was left suitably vague. What is intriguing is that one of the men who espoused this idea of a Currency Office was Victor Wrede, an economist and member of the Social Democratic Party (SPD). The BdL's central bank council later appointed Wrede to spearhead the economics department of the central bank, where he emerged to become a powerful advocate of an independent central bank. Prior to his arrival at the central bank, however, Wrede's opinion concerning an independent monetary authority was one of suspicion.[25] In the end, the Allied military authorities rejected almost all the Sonderstelle's proposals, which were submitted in April 1948 and came to be known as the 'Homburg Plan'.[26]

---

[21] Bibow, 'Zur (Re-)Etablierung zentralbankpolitischer Institutionen und Traditionen in Westdeutschland', pp. 541–2.

[22] For more on the *Sonderstelle*, see Anthony J. Nicholls, *Freedom with responsibility. The social market economy in Germany, 1918–1963* (Oxford, 1994), pp. 156–7; and James C. van Hook, *Rebuilding Germany. The creation of the social market economy, 1945–1957* (Cambridge, 2004), pp. 156–61. See also, Karl Häuser, 'Gründung der Bank deutscher Länder und Währungsreform', in Hans Pohl (ed.), *Geschichte der deutschen Kreditwirtschaft seit 1945* (Frankfurt am Main, 1998), pp. 35–7. The most detailed account, however, is offered in Arne Weick, *Homburger Plan und Währungsreform: kritische Analyse des Währungsreformplans der Sonderstelle Geld und Kredit und seiner Bedeutung für die westdeutsche Währungsreform von 1948* (St. Katharinen, 1998).

[23] 'The central bank council fifty years ago', *Monthly Report of the Deutsche Bundesbank*, Mar. 1998, p. 25; and Buchheim, 'Die Unabhängigkeit der Bundesbank', p. 11.

[24] Ibid., p. 16.   [25] Ibid.   [26] See Weick, *Homburger Plan und Währungsreform*.

The second body of experts, somewhat cumbersomely called the Expert Commission 'Länder Union Bank', or Sachverständigen-Kommission 'Länder Union Bank', coalesced around the same time as the Sonderstelle. In early 1948, this committee was tasked with suggesting proposals or changes to some fundamental principles that had been already ironed out by the British and American authorities with respect to the impending central bank law. By now, West German experts had become accustomed to American demands for an independent central bank, an awareness that may have biased their eventual proposals.

The German commission proposed that a strict credit limit should constrain the relations between the central bank and government considering Germany's history with inflation.[27] But there was a strong scepticism as to the federal aspect of the proposed central bank: the commission was concerned that state central bank presidents, coming together at council meetings in Frankfurt, would factor only regional considerations into the policy decisions. To counter this perceived danger, the commission proposed to expand the central bank council, to include representatives from industry, agriculture and other interest groups.[28] The idea behind this dilution of the central bank council was to weld ostensibly regional state interests together with wider macroeconomic ones. The commission also argued for a removal of the ABC's ability to give the central bank instructions. In the end, the Allied military authorities rejected both the expansion of the central bank council and the removal of the ABC. But they did accept other, smaller changes – such as altering the name of the central bank. It was here that the term 'Bank deutscher Länder' first emerged – the 'Bank of German States'.

Why were German elites so cautious with respect to central bank independence? There are two broad reasons. First, as Schaefer, the private banker, hinted in Munich, a new monetary paradigm was afoot – that of Keynesianism. Proponents of Keynesianism argued for a close, co-operative relationship between the central bank and government with the goal of forming a cohesive economic policy. Abroad, several central banks, such as the Bank of England and Bank of France, were nationalised. The events of the Second World War brought the Federal Reserve System of America closer to the government too. These developments

---

[27] 'The central bank council fifty years ago', *Monthly Report of the Deutsche Bundesbank*, p. 24; Lindenlaub, 'Die Errichtung der Bank deutscher Länder und die Währungsreform von 1948', p. 300.

[28] Christoph Buchheim, *Die Wiedereingliederung Westdeutschlands in die Weltwirtschaft, 1945–1958* (Munich, 1990), p. 13.

were indicative of an international trend in the late 1940s, one of greater co-operation between the government and central bank.[29]

As Leopold Baranyai, the former governor of the Bank of Hungary, noted around this time, there were now 'two worlds of monetary policy'.[30] A closer relationship between central bank and state was often seen as a modern, forward-looking idea during the early post-war years – and indeed, for some time yet to come. That was one world, at least. What was the other? In short, it was known as monetary 'orthodoxy'; that is, the use of conventional monetary instruments, such as use of the discount rate. Monetary orthodoxy, often implemented by the independent central banks of old, was seen in many circles as out of date and discredited by the experiences of the inter-war period. Even the German ordoliberal school of economics, which flourished after the Second World War, did not provide a theoretical underpinning for central bank independence; instead ordoliberal economists envisaged a co-operative framework between the central bank and state, stressing the importance of pursuing an economic policy that was a unified whole.[31] There is no mention of central bank independence, for instance, in Walter Eucken's *The foundations of economics*, one of the seminal works of ordoliberal thought.[32]

The second reason stemmed from Germany's inter-war history. The lessons were conflicting. Germans had endured two inflations and one deflation within a single generation. But the experience of the independent Reichsbank under Schacht, and later, under Hans Luther, was still fresh in the minds of some experts. They recalled how deflationary policies of the Weimar era led to mass unemployment and subsequent political radicalisation. 'If unemployment figures increase again, I think it's out of the question that the central bank mounts its high horse once more and shows indifference', remarked Erhard during a Sonderstelle meeting in January 1948. 'That is not going to happen. Politicians will

---

[29] For contemporary views, see Miroslav A. Kritz, 'Central banks and the state today', *The American Economic Review*, Vol. 38, No. 4 (1948); and 'Who should control the central bank?', *The Statist*, 25 Feb. 1950. For an historical account of what John Singleton describes as the 'first revolution' in the realm of central banking, see John Singleton, *Central banking in the twentieth century* (Cambridge, 2011), pp. 113–14, 127.

[30] See Leopold Baranyai, 'Zwei Welten der Geldpolitik', *Die Zeitschrift für das gesamte Kreditwesen*, 15 Jan. 1951.

[31] Jörg Bibow, 'On the origin and rise of central bank independence in West Germany', *The European Journal of the History of Economic Thought*, Vol. 16, No. 1 (2009), pp. 168–74, 184; and Bibow, 'Zur (Re-)Etablierung zentralbankpolitischer Institutionen und Traditionen in Westdeutschland', pp. 522–41, 549.

[32] See Walter Eucken, *The foundations of economics*, trans. T. W. Hutchison (London, 1950).

always have the last word, but an institution that is there solely to protect the currency must be given a large measure of independence.'[33]

In the early post-war years, then, the debate surrounding central bank independence represented a fault line between the two experiences of hyperinflation and deflation. Should West Germans factor the lessons of the hyperinflation, which, at first glance at least, stressed an independent central bank, one that could say 'no' to government demands for financing? Or should West Germans remain wary, lest another 'Schacht' get his hands on the central bank, and use it as a political tool to increase his own power at the expense of democratically elected governments? These were questions that provoked a fiery debate in the early years of the Federal Republic. And they either directly or indirectly touched on the tainted record of the Reichsbank.

Before we set our sights on the political climate in the new Federal Republic, however, let us first examine the BdL and its internal debates in the lead-up to the foundation of the new state.

The Bank deutscher Länder

The BdL was seen as a provisional institution, one created by means of occupation law. A foreign creature, it did not fit into the vision of the new republic in the eyes of many German elites. In 1948, however, the BdL could operate without serious consideration of German political interests. Yet the central bank, for its part, was not a monolithic entity. Quite the opposite. It was a federal organisation, one made up of several different elements. Who were the personalities that populated the halls of Frankfurt? The historians Monika Dickhaus and Theo Horstmann argue convincingly in their respective studies that the first appointment of such men – and they were always men – was a defining moment for the monetary authority. The various traditions, experiences and working styles these characters brought with them would define how the central bank operated and responded to challenges.[34]

The Allied military authorities ensured that only candidates of respectable political vintage would be accepted on the central bank council. But each Western power had its own preferences and priorities. In the

---

[33] 'The central bank council fifty years ago', *Monthly Report of the Deutsche Bundesbank*, p. 25. For the original German version of the article, from which the author has translated Erhard's quote, see 'Der Zentralbankrat vor fünfzig Jahren', *Monatsbericht der Deutschen Bundesbank*, Mar. 1998, p. 25.

[34] Monika Dickhaus, *Die Bundesbank im westeuropäischen Wiederaufbau: die internationale Währungspolitik der Bundesrepublik Deutschland 1948 bis 1958* (Munich, 1996), p. 60; Horstmann, 'Kontinuität und Wandel im deutschen Notenbanksystem', pp. 148, 151.

American zone, the *Land* central bank presidents were neither Reichsbank officials nor former Nationalist Socialist party members. Max Grasmann (Bavaria), Hermann Tepe (Bremen), Otto Veit (Hesse) and Otto Pfleiderer (Baden-Württemberg) were, for the most part, lawyers and economists involved in industry, science and banking.[35] Indeed, Pfleiderer and Veit were known to be Keynesians.[36]

There was more of a Reichsbank presence in the French zone, where Wilhelm Boden (Rhineland-Palatinate), Eugen Christian Hinckel (Baden) and Karl Mürdel (Württemberg) were appointed to the *Land* central bank presidencies. Hinckel and Mürdel were former Reichsbank officials, while Boden was a former politician who had later gone into business.[37] In the British zone, the Reichsbank tradition was again pronounced – in part keeping with the British argument that maintaining a centralised banking system in post-war Germany was both sensible and necessary, as well as the fact that British officials held a favourable attitude towards former Reichsbank officials given the latter's strong inter-war ties with the Bank of England.[38] Karl Klasen (Hamburg) – a member of the SPD and a man would later go on to assume the presidency of the Bundesbank in 1970 – Max Sentz (Lower Saxony), Otto Burkhardt (Schleswig-Holstein), who was another member of the SPD, and Ernst Hülse (North Rhine-Westphalia) were appointed in the zone.[39] Sentz and Hülse were former Reichsbank men. Indeed, Hülse was a member of the Reichsbank directorate from 1935 onwards and his written testimony played a minor role in securing the acquittal of Schacht at Nuremberg.[40] He was also a contemporary of Wilhelm Vocke.[41]

It fell before these appointees, who together formed the central bank council, to select the chairman of the council and the directorate respectively. But the affair turned out badly. The ABC rejected outright their first choice for the chairman of the central bank council, Otto Schniewind, because of his inter-war record.[42] Thus, the Allies vetoed

---

[35] This is not to say that they were outright opponents of the Third Reich. In the 1930s, Veit and Pfleiderer published work praising the 'primacy of the state'. By 1943 Pfleiderer was exalting the 'total organisational penetration of the economy'. See Dickhaus, *Die Bundesbank im westeuropäischen Wiederaufbau*, pp. 61–2.

[36] As noted in 'Ein Jahr D-Mark', *Vereinigte Wirtschaftsdienste*, 16 Jun. 1949, DBHA, B330/ 6305/2, p. 2.

[37] See Dickhaus, *Die Bundesbank im westeuropäischen Wiederaufbau*, p. 61.

[38] Horstmann, 'Kontinuität und Wandel im deutschen Notenbanksystem', p. 142.

[39] Dickhaus, *Die Bundesbank im westeuropäischen Wiederaufbau*, p. 61.

[40] See Chapter 1 for more details about Hülse's role at Nuremberg.

[41] Wilhelm Vocke, *Memoiren* (Stuttgart, 1973), pp. 110, 134, 141.

[42] David Marsh, *The Bundesbank: the bank that rules Europe* (London, 1992), pp. 150–2.

the very first decision made by the central bank council on political grounds. After some delay, Karl Bernard was voted in to take his place. Bernard had worked in the economics ministry before being dismissed by the Nazi regime and had later entered private banking.[43]

The Reichsbank tradition was more pronounced in the directorate. The members of this body were Wrede (who, as mentioned above, headed the economics department), Erich Zachau (organisation and human resources), Fritz Paersch and Hans Treue (foreign), Karl-Friedrich Wilhelm (currency) and, from 1950 onwards, Bernard Benning (banking and credit).[44] Wilhelm Könneker was appointed vice president of the directorate. Wilhelm, Treue and Könneker were former Reichsbank men.[45] Yet it was perhaps Vocke, appointed chairman of the directorate, who above all embodied the continuity with the Reichsbank. Shortly after the end of the Second World War, Vocke had been deputy chairman of the Reichsbankleitstelle, or the Reichsbank control centre, in the British zone of occupation.[46] As noted in Chapter 1, Vocke had been a member of the Reichsbank directorate for some twenty years. Originally, the private banker Hermann Josef Abs had been elected chairman of the directorate, but again, the ABC rejected his appointment on the grounds of his past involvement with Deutsche Bank during the Third Reich.[47] In light of all this confusion, which lasted some weeks, Bernard was only appointed on 5 May 1948, and Vocke on 1 June of that year.[48]

To use the phrase of the writer David Marsh, found in his popular history of the Bundesbank, did these men represent 'the return of the old guard' of the Reichsbank?[49] Numerically speaking, when Vocke, who, in addition to his chairmanship of the directorate, was the vice chairman of the central bank council, is included in the tally, former Reichsbankers constituted five votes out of a total of eleven. That was not enough for a majority. Indeed, Dieter Lindenlaub, a banking historian and former head of the Bundesbank historical archive, has challenged Marsh's

---

[43] 'Lebenslauf von Dr. h. c. Karl Bernard', Deutsche Bundesbank Pressearchiv [DBPA], no. 1361.

[44] Dickhaus, *Die Bundesbank im westeuropäischen Wiederaufbau*, p. 62.

[45] 'Personaldaten: Wilhelm Könneker', no date, DBPA, no. 591.

[46] Vocke, *Memoiren*, pp. 140–1; Theo Horstmann, *Die Alliierten und die deutschen Großbanken. Bankenpolitik nach dem Zweiten Weltkrieg in Deutschland* (Bonn, 1991), pp. 72–3.

[47] The record of Deutsche Bank during the Third Reich was a troubled one. See Harold James, *The Deutsche Bank and the Nazi economic war against the Jews: the expropriation of Jewish-owned property* (Cambridge, 2001).

[48] See Wandel, *Die Entstehung der Bank deutscher Länder und die deutsche Währungsreform 1948*, pp. 74, 76.

[49] See Marsh, *The Bundesbank*, p. 159.

'continuity thesis' as lacking in evidence.[50] Leaving aside the question of personnel, as well as the preference for price stability over full employment concerns with respect to the central bank's goals, Lindenlaub contends there was little continuity between the BdL and the Reichsbank.[51] That the BdL was not the legal successor of the Reichsbank stands to Lindenlaub's argument. Throughout the decades, both the BdL and its successor, the Bundesbank, stressed this fact.[52]

Nevertheless, as will be shown later in this chapter, the BdL was closely identified with the Reichsbank – and Reichsbankers – in the public sphere. If there was little institutional continuity, there was nevertheless a sizeable degree of continuity when it came to the post-war central bank's image in the media. This development had important implications for the debate surrounding the Bundesbank Law, and it can be attributed in large part to the person of Vocke and the BdL's press department.

The division of power within the central bank was still fluid in these early years.[53] And though Vocke's directorate was technically subordinate to Bernard's central bank council, a power struggle ensued between the two chairmen. Each man attempted to mould the BdL in his own image. Vocke was a dominant, authoritarian character. The central bank's economics director, Wrede, came to complain about Vocke's 'dictatorial disposition' and the '*Führer* system' with which he clamped down on independent thought in the directorate.[54] Vocke's ideal of a future Bundesbank was a centralised monetary authority that was completely independent of government interference. Bibow is arguably correct when he describes how Vocke saw the relationship between the government and central bank as an antagonistic one by dint of its very nature.[55] This is an attitude that likely stemmed from his inter-war experience with the Reichsbank. By contrast, Bernard was the quiet,

[50] See Dieter Lindenlaub, 'Review: "Die Bundesbank: Geschäfte mit der Macht" by David Marsh', *Vierteljahrschrift für Sozial- und Wirtschaftsgeschichte*, Vol. 81, No. 3 (1994), p. 440.

[51] Ibid.; and Lindenlaub, 'Die Errichtung der Bank deutscher Länder und die Währungsreform von 1948', p. 304.

[52] See, for instance, 'Präsident Dr. Klasen, Vizepräsident Dr. Emminger und die Mitglieder des Direktoriums Dr. Irmler und Dr. Schlesinger vor der Presse am 5. Januar 1976 (nach Bandaufnahme)', 5 Jan. 1976, DBHA, B330/7896.

[53] Horstmann, 'Kontinuität und Wandel im deutschen Notenbanksystem', pp. 148, 151.

[54] Victor Wrede to Karl Bernard, 4 Jul. 1949, DBHA, PERS 101/20924, p. 8. See also the opinion of Otmar Emminger, another directorate member, in Emminger, *D-Mark, Dollar, Währungskrisen*, pp. 69, 90–1.

[55] Bibow, 'Zur (Re-)Etablierung zentralbankpolitischer Institutionen und Traditionen in Westdeutschland, p. 574; and Bibow, 'On the origin and rise of central bank independence in West Germany', pp. 167, 183.

unassuming type, who pushed for the maintenance of independence and the decentralised structure.

Vocke quickly emerged in the ascendant. By the spring of 1950, a Bank of England official, who dealt with the BdL, commented that, 'in practice, the president of the board of managers [Vocke] does all the work and takes all the decisions, while the president of the board of directors [Bernard] does not cut much ice'.[56] This dominance would filter through to the central bank's interaction with government officials and other West German elites during the Bundesbank Law debates. By 1950, Bernard felt compelled to complain to the federal chancellor's office that it was often Vocke who was invited to crucial meetings, despite Bernard being chairman of the central bank council, the key forum where decisions were taken.[57]

Due to the confusion surrounding the appointment of the central bank council and directorate, the first *full* sitting of the central bank's decision-making body only took place in early June 1948, some three months after the BdL's establishment (Figure 2.1). Tellingly, it was Vocke who delivered the opening address. It is from here that we can discern both his and the central bank's priorities. 'Because of its responsibility for the purely technical management of monetary policy, the independence of the bank and its leadership is an absolute necessity', Vocke declared, pointing out that the existing occupation legislation protected the bank from all political influences. 'It is only when bank's independence is respected on all sides that the central bank achieves the asset that is more important than popularity and acclaim, and even more important than gold and foreign exchange: confidence at home and abroad.'[58] Central bank independence, then, was a means towards a greater end: confidence in the young deutschmark. The media reported Vocke's speech some days later, despite the minutes of the central bank council meeting being confidential.[59]

Of course, the chairman's voice was just one among many at the central bank council, which was essentially a platform for debate and one that operated by majority vote. Occasionally Vocke found himself in the minority. This was especially the case concerning the central bank's

[56] Dickhaus, 'Fostering "The bank that rules Europe"', pp. 167–8.
[57] Joseph Rust to Konrad Adenauer, 21 Aug. 1950, Bundesarchiv, Koblenz [BAK], B136/1198.
[58] BdL central bank council minutes, 1 Jun. 1948, DBHA, B330/2/3.
[59] Indeed, the chairman's remarks are extensively detailed in 'Dr. Vocke über die Aufgaben der Notenbank', *Die Neue Zeitung*, 6 Jun. 1948. It is likely that either Vocke's speech or the minutes of the meeting were handed to the journalist in question.

Figure 2.1 The Bank deutscher Länder building in Frankfurt in 1950.
(DBHA, BSG 3/306 – © Deutsche Bundesbank – Historisches Archiv)

structure.[60] The *Land* central bank presidents, more often than not, were in support of a decentralised organisation, one to which they owed their very appointments. By contrast, Vocke was a fierce supporter of a centralised monetary authority, on the grounds that a centralised control of the monetary lever would be better adept and quicker at tackling crises.

However, the members of the central bank council were inclined, with varying degrees, to support an independent central bank. Intriguingly, this included erstwhile opponents of central banking, such as Pfleiderer and Wrede, who emerged to be supporters of central bank independence in the public sphere. While no sources exist that explicitly explain the change in their mindsets, three potential reasons can be discerned. First, the removal of the central bank's autonomy would have weakened their new-found power and influence over economic policy. Second, the BdL's independence allowed the central bank council to embark on what it believed to be the correct path of monetary policy – one that quickly proved to be fruitful in defending the value of the deutschmark. And

---

[60] As Vocke himself noted in a letter to the Christian Democratic Union politician Hugo Scharnberg. See Wilhelm Vocke to Hugo Scharnberg, 23 Jan. 1953, DBHA, B330/2042.

third, historians have written of the 'Becket' effect in the central bank council, named after Thomas Becket, the former chancellor of the English king, Henry II, who went on to turn against his former master after being appointed Archbishop of Canterbury.[61] Like Becket, who became an effective representative of the Catholic Church's interests, members of central bank council came to support the interests of the BdL. Debates were of a technical nature and restricted to questions of the currency, with political viewpoints fading into the background. This fostered a common identity of purpose.

The months that followed the BdL's establishment in 1948 were turbulent ones. After the currency reform and the gradual, select removal of price controls on the part of Erhard, pent up demand in the economy led to a sharp inflation.[62] Consumer prices shot up by 30 per cent.[63] In addition, the currency reform, though successful, also had meant a steep cut in the money supply. This generated a lot of anger among the population at the time, a point often overlooked in subsequent decades. Even Bernard, chairman of the central bank council, was at first reluctant to be associated with the deutschmark. In the immediate days following the currency reform, Bernard scolded a member of the Hamburg senate who wrote in *Die Welt* of the need to place trust in 'our creation', the deutschmark.[64] The deutschmark was not the Germans' currency, Bernard corrected him; it was the currency of the occupation authorities.[65] The central bank's economics director, Wrede, was more forthright to the politician: 'In no way can [the deutschmark] be said to be the work of German experts.'[66]

This reluctance to assume responsibility reflected the dire prospects for the currency at the time. The BdL had no currency reserves to support the deutschmark. An English central banker told Vocke that the German currency was something akin to 'a bad joke'.[67] Schacht was blunter and told his former colleague that the deutschmark had six

---

[61] Marsh, *The Bundesbank*, pp. 22–3; Buchheim, 'Die Unabhängigkeit der Bundesbank', p. 15; and Lindenlaub, 'Die Errichtung der Bank deutscher Länder und die Währungsreform von 1948', p. 310.

[62] Nicholls, *Freedom with responsibility*, pp. 216–18; see also van Hook, *Rebuilding Germany*, p. 166.

[63] Lindenlaub, 'Die Errichtung der Bank deutscher Länder und die Währungsreform von 1948', pp. 300–1.

[64] Karl Bernard to Walter Dudek, 21 Jun. 1948, DBHA, B330/3356.   [65] Ibid.

[66] Victor Wrede et al. to Walter Dudek, 21 Jun. 1948, DBHA, B330/3356.

[67] As recalled by Vocke years later. See 'Interview von Präsident Dr. W. Vocke in Sendung: "Bleibt unser Geld stabil?" im Zweiten Deutschen Fernsehen, Mainz', 21 Jun. 1963, DBPA, no. 1244, p. 1.

weeks before it would bite the dust.[68] The price level was on the verge of becoming erratic. And yet unemployment remained stubbornly high. Writing in August 1948, Vocke lamented, with some justification, that '[t]he German economy feels an oppressing concern and fear from both inflation and deflation'.[69] This was a revealing point. Rising prices could evoke fears of 1922–3 and Germany's second inflation. But deflation could remind the population of the twilight era of Weimar. In the years 1948, 1949 and 1950, the condition of what emerged to be the West German economy would play an important role in influencing the parameters of the Bundesbank Law debate.

Take the year 1948, for example. The difficulties prevalent in the economy, predominantly of a structural nature, led the BdL to become the subject of political attacks.[70] In late September 1948, two leading German political figures in Frankfurt launched public outbursts against the central bank. Erich Köhler, a Christian Democratic Union (CDU) politician and the president of the Economic Council, the German parliamentary body, stated that, 'the time will come, one of these days, with the gradual consolidation of our legal relations, when the Bank deutscher Länder will be subject to the direct influence of a German government' in the interests of 'an absolute co-ordination of policy' between the central bank and future state.[71]

These comments followed those of another senior official, the CDU politician Hermann Pünder, who declared that 'it was intolerable in the long run' that the bizonal government in Frankfurt could not exert influence upon the BdL. Pünder called on the Allies for a change in the law to allow such a development to take effect.[72] Both comments were quickly spotted by the BdL's press department and reported to the leadership – an act that suggests both an awareness of, and sensitivity to, the central bank's awkward legal position.[73] Vocke had the internal

---

[68] This observation was noted some twenty-five years later in a retrospective article. See Wilhelm Vocke, 'Schwieriger Start der neuen Zentralbank', *Die Zeitschrift für das gesamte Kreditwesen*, 15 Jun. 1973.

[69] Original quote in English. See Wilhelm Vocke to Otto Niemeyer, 23 Aug. 1948, DBHA, B330/2036, p. 2.

[70] For a detailed account of the West German economy during this turbulent era, see Werner Abelshauser, *Deutsche Wirtschaftsgeschichte seit 1945* (Bonn, 2004), pp. 120–74; see also Alan Kramer, *The West German economy, 1945–1955* (Oxford, 1991), pp. 134–48.

[71] See 'Aus der Rede des Abg. Dr. Köhler im Namen der CDU/CSU zur 3. Lesung des Haushaltes 1948', 27 Sep. 1948, DBHA, B330/6201, p. 1.

[72] 'Auszug aus der Rede des Oberdirektors Dr. Hermann Pünder vor dem Wirtschaftsrat am 27. September 1948', 27 Sep. 1948, DBHA, B330/6201.

[73] See Werner Nehlsen, 'Aktennotiz', 29 Sep. 1948, DBHA, B330/6201.

report forwarded to a representative of the ABC, keen to keep the Allied body in the loop about the hostile political climate.[74]

The central bank's relative silence in the public sphere helped to foster this negative sentiment. Bernard gave a radio interview in the days following the currency reform in July 1948.[75] The central bank released a statement the following month, declaring the free market to be an essential precondition for a sound currency.[76] But there was little else. This silence can be attributed in part to internal disagreements behind the scenes.[77] Press policy was the preserve of the economics department, whose head, Wrede, was a member of the directorate.[78] However, in contrast to the central bank council, which was a collegiate body, the directorate was a presidial one. Vocke exerted an iron grip over proceedings.

Wrede was an enthusiastic advocate of engaging the media.[79] In his own words, he was concerned about the 'poor state' of the central bank's 'public relations'.[80] But in late 1948 Wrede met the strong scepticism of his boss Vocke, as well as others in the directorate, concerning inter-action with the press.[81] The chairman of the directorate issued an order to all departments within the central bank that any statement to the media had first to be signed off by him.[82] Vocke's authority did not extend to the central bank council – a fact that allowed members of that body, if they so wished, to communicate with the press, though very few did during the years 1949–51. But it nevertheless demonstrated the surprising extent to which the BdL, a decentralised, federal body, had a centralised communication channel.[83]

Internal disagreements were not the only stumbling block, however. As Wrede noted, the BdL's 'tactical position' vis-à-vis the German administration in Frankfurt, on the one hand, and the ABC on the other,

---

[74] Ibid. A note in English was scribbled on the BdL report: 'For Mr. Ingrams [of the ABC]'s attention. Return to Dr. Vocke with thanks.'

[75] 'Ein Monat neuer Währung: Interview mit dem Vorsitzenden des Zentralbankrats der Bank deutscher Länder Karl Bernard', *Bank deutscher Länder Auszüge aus Presseartikeln*, No. 10, 20 Jul. 1948, DBPA, no. 75.

[76] 'Pressenotiz', 18 Aug. 1948, DBHA, B330/4967.

[77] Victor Wrede to Wilhelm Vocke, 20 Dec. 1948, DBHA, B330/3356.

[78] 'Vorläufiger Geschäftsplan der Bank deutscher Länder', 1 Oct. 1948, DBHA, B330/DRS. 113, p. 16.

[79] Victor Wrede, 'Verhältnis der Bank deutscher Länder zur Presse', 6 Oct. 1948, DBHA, B330/3356; and Wrede to Vocke, 20 Dec. 1948; for his membership of the SPD, see 'Das Porträt des Tages: Dr. Viktor [*sic*] Wrede', *Hamburger Abendblatt*, 18 Dec. 1948.

[80] Wrede, 'Verhältnis der Bank deutscher Länder zur Presse'.

[81] See Victor Wrede, 'Veröffentlichung von Berichten', 7 Oct. 1948, B330/3356; and, in particular, Wrede to Bernard, 4 Jul. 1949, p. 7.

[82] See Wilhelm Vocke to all departments in the Bank deutscher Länder, 2 Aug. 1948 and 4 Aug. 1948, DBHA, B330/3356.

[83] Emminger, *D-Mark, Dollar, Währungskrisen*, p. 69.

had been an 'extraordinarily difficult' one to balance.[84] As a result, the central bank had sought to tread lightly. But already by the end of 1948, it was explicitly acknowledged that the BdL's silence in the public sphere was breeding mistrust among German elites and leading to political attacks. Although he increasingly came to hold his economics director in low esteem, Vocke grudgingly came around to Wrede's arguments: the central bank, with Vocke's assent, began to take steps towards influencing the public debate surrounding it.[85]

Thus, around this time, the press department was overhauled with the purpose of clearly outlining its duties as well as an expansion of its activities.[86] The central bank began publishing monthly reports concerning the economic situation in the western zone. The first report was published for the month of January 1949.[87] Wrede began to enter the public sphere on behalf of the central bank by means of articles and speeches. These contributions focused on discussing in detail the Western Bloc's economic difficulties while giving the central bank's take on the situation.[88]

The BdL also set about establishing tentative relationships with journalists. In June 1948, the economics journalist Muthesius approached the central bank with the idea of using his new publication, *Die Zeitschrift für das gesamte Kreditwesen*, an elite journal for banking, academic and political circles, 'as an opportunity to influence public opinion'.[89] As the cultural historian S. Jonathan Wiesen notes, Muthesius 'was one of the most prolific business publicists in West Germany, devoting a multi-decade career to scores of company biographies, economic primers, and popular/scholarly books'.[90]

---

[84] Wrede, 'Verhältnis der Bank deutscher Länder zur Presse', 6 Oct. 1948; and Victor Wrede to Fritz Sänger, 16 Mar. 1949, DBHA, B330/3356, p. 1.

[85] That Vocke agreed with Wrede can be discerned from a penciled addition, written by Wrede, found at the bottom of the following letter: see Wrede to Vocke, 20 Dec. 1948, p. 2. For Vocke's low opinion of Wrede, refer to the emotional letter written by Wrede to Bernard, the chairman of the central bank council. See Wrede to Bernard, 4 Jul. 1949, pp. 1–4.

[86] Hans Möller, 'Bericht über Aufgaben und Organisation des Referats 941 "Pressestelle"', 27 Dec. 1948, DBHA, B330/3355; Willy Tomberg, 'Bericht mit Vorschlägen zur Frage: "Presseumlaufmappen, Presserundschau und täglicher Pressebericht"', 10 Jan. 1949, DBHA, B330/3355; and Erich Zachau, 'Betr.: Bericht über Aufgaben und Organisation des Referats 941 "Pressestelle" von Herrn. Dr. Möller vom 27.12.1948', 13 Jan. 1949, DBHA, B330/3355.

[87] *Monatsberichte der Bank deutscher Länder, Jan. 1949*. See www.bundesbank.de/resource/ blob/690212/b5599f84e7dd2b584f283e793e9293bd/mL/1949-01-monatsbericht-data.pdf. Last accessed on 20 December 2018.

[88] Victor Wrede, 'Wendepunkt der Kreditpolitik', *Die Welt*, 16 Nov. 1948, DBHA, B330/ 3356; and 'Geldreform und Preisentwicklung', *Frankfurter Rundschau*, 23 Nov. 1948.

[89] Volkmar Muthesius to Victor Wrede, 12 Jun. 1948, DBHA, B330/3356.

[90] S. Jonathan Wiesen, *West German industry and the challenge of the Nazi past, 1945–1955* (London, 2001), p. 150.

The BdL did not take up Muthesius's offer at the time. By late 1948, however, possibly owing to the negative political climate, the central bank had a change of heart. The directorate set about establishing plans for the financial support of Muthesius's newspaper by asking the state central banks to take out sizeable subscriptions of the publication.[91] During the same meeting, too, it was agreed that the BdL would offer funding for 'support of economic establishments', with Muthesius's newspaper specified as one such example.[92] The central bank council reaffirmed this decision some days later.[93]

The end of 1948 proved to be a crucial moment: stung by political attacks, the BdL was beginning to adopt a more open-minded and co-operative relationship with the wider public sphere. Already, then, it can be seen how an institutional divide – a divide that separated the control of monetary policy from political influence – was already bringing the BdL around to the idea of engaging with the media. At the same time, however, the central bank remained cautious. Why was this the case? In short, its 'legal structure', as Wrede admitted months later, still placed the BdL in a 'downright difficult situation'.[94]

But co-operation with the media in 1948 could only be effective up to a point. Vocke saw the political climate as highly unfavourable. Confiding to an old friend at the Bank of England, the central banker reaffirmed his conviction that '[p]olitical influences must continue being kept away from the Bank deutscher Länder'.[95] Vocke turned to the one body that stood between the central bank and domestic political pressure. He looked towards the ABC.

On paper, the ABC could issue instructions to the central bank council and veto its decisions. However, leaving aside the bumpy start to their relationship, this rarely happened. Instead, a fruitful working relationship developed between the directorate, central bank council and the BdL's oversight body.[96] Vocke and Bernard quickly came to see the benefit of having an external committee, one that was not beholden to any demo-cratic pressure, bolstering the autonomy of the central bank vis-à-vis

---

[91] BdL directorate meeting minutes, 23 Sep. 1948, DBHA, B330/2054.   [92] Ibid.

[93] Bibow has already discovered the central bank council's decision to support Muthesius's publication financially. But, as seen above, the origins of the decision can be traced to Vocke's directorate some days prior. The directorate was the real driver in press policy at the central bank. Refer to BdL central bank council minutes, 28 Sep. 1948, DBHA, B330/5/2. See also Bibow, 'Zur (Re-)Etablierung zentralbankpolitischer Institutionen und Traditionen in Westdeutschland', pp. 549–50 (footnote).

[94] Wrede to Sänger, 16 Mar. 1949.

[95] Wilhelm Vocke to Otto Niemeyer, 20 Aug. 1948, DBHA, B330/4967, p. 8.

[96] As later noted by Vocke. See Wilhelm Vocke to Konrad Adenauer, 31 Oct. 1949, DBHA, B330/2011, p. 8.

German politicians in Frankfurt. Within the walls of the directorate chairman's office, the Allies had come to be treated as, well, allies.

By November 1948, there was significant political pressure placed on Erhard to abandon the path to liberalisation and return to price controls.[97] The BdL's independence would be tied to its record defending inflation. But this in turn depended on the success of Erhard's model of the social market economy: price decontrol, market competition and the gradual liberalisation of the economy. The central bank's fight for independence, then, was linked inextricably to the development of the social market economy. A setback for Erhard's budding political project was a setback for the central bank.

Vocke maintained a steady correspondence with the ABC throughout this period. In late November 1948, he lobbied the Allied representatives to maintain their supervision over the BdL. Vocke began with a quote. "'Let the Germans assume exclusive responsibility for their own problems!'" he wrote, before continuing:

This slogan is increasingly voiced by the very Germans. There is, however, no position more short-sighted and more dangerous with respect to the supply of food, of raw material, and especially to the currency itself ... Entrusting the responsibility for the currency to German agencies alone would mean to renounce completely the attainment of the purposes for which the Allied powers have been striving through this currency reform and also by the Marshall Plan. The only outcome would be the chaos of an inflation connected with controlled economy, as it prevailed prior to the currency reform.[98]

Vocke repeated these warnings a few months later in a separate letter to Henry Conrad, a member of the ABC.[99]

The central bank's credit restrictions soon corrected the inflationary spike. In doing so, the BdL won strong praise for its handling of the currency. Indeed, the monetary authority had won credibility both at home and abroad. At the same time, however, these measures meant that the economy soon reversed into a recession. After overcoming the inflationary crisis of 1948, prices fell and unemployment rose from 3.2 to 8 per cent by early 1949.[100] By early 1950, some two million workers were out of work.[101] Vocke saw this dire situation as being compounded

[97] An episode described in gripping detail in van Hook, *Rebuilding Germany*, pp. 167–86.
[98] The English is in the original. See Wilhelm Vocke to Allied Banking Commission, 26 Nov. 1948, DBHA, B330/2012, pp. 4–5.
[99] Wilhelm Vocke to Henry C. Conrad, 7 Mar. 1949, DBHA, B330/2012.
[100] Dickhaus, 'Fostering "The bank that rules Europe"', p. 173.
[101] Werner Abelshauser, *Die langen Fünfziger Jahre: Wirtschaft und Gesellschaft der Bundesrepublik Deutschland 1949–1966* (Düsseldorf, 1987), p. 19.

by 'the constant influx of refugees from the east', fleeing territory occupied by the Russians.[102]

Where inflation had once threatened, deflation now reared its head. The BdL entered the year 1949 with fears of sinking prices prevalent in the economy. 'Charges are being made to an ever increasing extent against the credit policy as practiced [sic] by the central bank system, which is said to be about if not provoking but at least permitting a serious deflation crisis of [the] West German economy', wrote Eduard Wolf, a leading BdL official, in somewhat stilted English. '[T]he increase of unemployment fills the minds of critics with apprehension.'[103] And indeed, it was doing so just as events gathered pace concerning the establishment of the West German state.

If a new republic was being born, then it was being born into crisis – at least in the minds of contemporaries. The newspaper headlines that announced the foundation of the Federal Republic often ran alongside those detailing the extent of unemployment and the 'fear of a deflation crisis'.[104] '1.2 million jobless' screamed one headline, just two days after the establishment of West Germany.[105] These economic difficulties provoked an outcry in the media, particularly among publications on the left, such as the SPD newspaper *Neuer Vorwärts*.[106] During the summer of 1949, the central bank leadership itself was subject to 'multiple attacks' in the media.[107] The events provided a seemingly clear parallel with the latter years of the Weimar Republic, when an independent Reichsbank presided over ballooning unemployment levels with apparent indifference.[108] As a result, Bernard and other central bank officials felt forced to enter the public sphere and refute allegations that the BdL was pursuing a deflationary policy; West Germany's economic problems, they argued, were structural ones, and the fall in prices only temporary.[109]

---

[102] 'German financial problems. Dr Wilhelm Vocke, president of the BdL', 29 Nov. 1949, Institut für Zeitgeschichte [IfZ], FIN/17/18 BICO FIN Gp, p. 1.

[103] See Eduard Wolf, 'Sidelights on the currency policy situation early in March 1949: Is a deflation imminent?', 6 Mar. 1949, DBHA, B330/2012, p. 1.

[104] Quoted in 'Der Rückschlag', *Allgemeine Zeitung*, 10 May 1949; see also 'Herrscht heute Deflation?', *Wirtschaftsdienst*, 3 Heft, Mar. 1950; and 'Teuere Deflationspolitik', *Der Telegraf*, 1 Oct. 1949.

[105] '1,2 Millionen Arbeitslose kosten 10 Milliarden DM', *Wiesbadener Kurier*, 25 Aug. 1949.

[106] For instance, see 'Arbeitslosigkeit und Kreditpolitik', *Neuer Vorwärts*, 26 Mar. 1949.

[107] This was explicitly noted in 'Diskussion über das Zentralbanksystem in Westdeutschland', *Neue Zürcher Zeitung*, 3 Dec. 1949.

[108] See, for instance, 'Vorgefecht um Bundesbank', *Die Welt*, 4 Oct. 1949.

[109] See 'Keine Deflationspolitik in Westdeutschland', *Neue Zürcher Zeitung*, 8 May 1949. Another example is Karl Bernard, 'Ansprache von Herrn Karl Bernard', Mitteilungen

But the Western Bloc's economic woes were not the only reason why the shadow of the inter-war Reichsbank loomed heavily in the public sphere. Another reason was its leadership. As one newspaper noted in March 1949,

Vocke has survived them all; the great German currency blunders of 1919/1923 (inflation), 1929/33 (deflation), 1934/39 (laying the foundation for the new inflation) and 1945/48 (the ruination of the German saver) ... The *Geheimrat* [privy councillor, Vocke's title] was already once involved in the 'successful' so-called 'safeguarding of the currency'. That was during 1929/33 and we ended up with seven million unemployed and Nazism. Does he now want to lead us to similar 'successes' again?[110]

Vocke, the article contended, was of the 'old Reichsbank school' whose 'master' was Schacht. The central banker, it continued, likely saw the current economic recession as a purifying one, wringing out the inefficiencies prevalent in the western zone. 'More than a million "purified" unemployed will certainly know to thank him.'[111] Certainly, the article was an angry polemic. But the point here is that the writer sought to make sense of West Germany's current troubles by weighing it against the record of the country's monetary past.

Other newspapers, too, highlighted that Vocke was a 'Reichsbanker'.[112] The article detailed above was just one of many that portrayed the current leadership of the BdL as one being dominated by a 'group' of Reichsbankers.[113] This development can be attributed to not only the central bank's pursuit of a liberal, ostensibly orthodox monetary policy, but also Vocke's public profile in the West German media sphere. He quickly came to personify the monetary authority, with Bernard, the other chairman, fading into the background. Vocke was noted for his 'unusual vigour and willingness to take on responsibility', said the *Frankfurter Allgemeine Zeitung*.[114] According to *Die Zeit*, his name had become 'bound' with the

der Bank deutscher Länder, No. 49, 1 Oct. 1949, DBPA, no. 75. See also the riposte to such comparisons in Rolf Lüke, 'Falsche Parallelen', *Frankfurter Rundschau*, 8 May 1950.

[110] The name of the publication is not known, but it is likely a left-wing newspaper. The article is published in a commemorative book published by the Bundesbank. For the article, see 'Wer ist Vocke?' [outlet unknown], in Deutsche Bundesbank (ed.), *Geheimrat Wilhelm Vocke, Hüter der Währung, Zum hundertsten Geburtstag am 9. Februar 1986* (Frankfurt am Main, 1986), p. 120.

[111] Ibid.   [112] 'Vocke', *Wirtschaftszeitung*, 2 Mar. 1949.

[113] See, for example, 'Ein Jahr D-Mark', *Vereinigte Wirtschaftsdienste*, 16 Jun. 1949, p. 2. The Reichsbank group was portrayed as being pitted against the more Keynesian members of the central bank council, such as Otto Veit and Otto Pfleiderer.

[114] 'Vocke', *Frankfurter Allgemeine Zeitung*, 9 Feb. 1951.

fortunes and fate of the new currency, the deutschmark.[115] By the mid-1950s, both SPD and CDU politicians used 'Vocke' as a byword for the BdL during parliamentary debates, suggesting the sizeable degree to which his name came to dominate the central bank's image.[116]

Vocke was closely associated with Schacht during these years. When Köhler, the president of the Economic Council, spoke before the German assembly in September 1948, he expressed his concern that Schacht was reported in the media as having visited Vocke at the BdL.[117] This was the same speech during which Köhler called for more government influence over the central bank. Some years later, too, Vocke stood for the second time as a defence witness for the former Reichsbank president in a courtroom. In 1952, the Hamburg state senate had refused to grant Schacht permission to establish a private bank.[118] Vocke testified to Schacht's good character, and was subsequently depicted in a regional newspaper's cartoon as having helped Schacht sneak away from a fight.[119]

Why was Vocke so closely associated with the Reichsbank in the early post-war years? One reason was that the BdL's press department *embraced* his inter-war record, and indeed, used it as a source of credibility. In an economy wracked by disruption, sources of information remained minimal. Journalists of the day relied heavily on the career résumés sent out by businesses and organisations. This was no different with respect to coverage concerning the central bank. The events surrounding Vocke's departure from the Reichsbank in early 1939 were explicitly marked out as career experience on his curriculum vitae. The central banker was 'dismissed by Hitler' because of the 1939 memorandum.[120] Thus, Vocke was not an accomplice to monetary disasters; rather, he was one of the few men who said 'no' to the dictator. The 1939 memorandum often featured in newspaper profile pieces about

---

[115] See 'Der Unbequeme', *Die Zeit*, 8 Feb. 1951.

[116] Indeed, the SPD politician in question was one Helmut Schmidt, the future chancellor. '2. Deutscher Bundestag. 118. Sitzung. Bonn, den Freitag 9. Dezember 1955', p. 6279. See http://dipbt.bundestag.de/doc/btp/02/02118.pdf. Last accessed on 18 January 2016; and '2. Deutscher Bundestag. 180. Sitzung. Bonn, Donnerstag, den 13. Dezember 1956', p. 9958. See http://dipbt.bundestag.de/doc/btp/02/02180.pdf. Last accessed on 18 January 2016.

[117] 'Aus der Rede des Abg. Dr. Köhler im Namen der CDU/CSU zur 3. Lesung des Haushaltes 1948', 27 Sep. 1948, pp. 1–2.

[118] Hjalmar Schacht, *The magic of money*, trans. Paul Erskine (London, 1967), p. 119. See also, 'Vocke: Mefo-Wechsel zulässig', *Frankfurter Allgemeine Zeitung*, 22 Nov. 1952. The newspaper article is found in Deutsche Bundesbank, *Geheimrat Wilhelm Vocke*, p. 95.

[119] The newspaper was the *Hamburger Anzeiger*. Ibid., p. 97.

[120] See 'Personal – Daten (Wilhelm Vocke)', no date, DBHA, BSG 1/56. See also the résumé published in Deutsche Bundesbank, *Geheimrat Wilhelm Vocke*, p. 6.

Vocke, implicitly portraying the man in a moral light amid the BdL's struggles with contemporary German governments.[121] Indeed, in his memoirs, the central banker portrayed his stint at the Reichsbank as an edifying experience from which he learned the importance of sound monetary principles that should be applied in the post-war era.[122]

At the same time, however, Vocke tended to shy away from the limelight. 'In general, I strictly confine myself to expressing my opinion in public only when I see a specific need for it', he once wrote.[123] The central banker rarely spoke in public. And when asked in 1951 by Leo Brawand of *Der Spiegel* if he would like to appear on the front page of the magazine, he declined.[124] This stance should not be construed as suggesting an indifference to the public sphere. Rather, Vocke knew he was a controversial character. As such, he preferred an alternative route.

The central banker exerted influence from behind the scenes. A key moment came in 1949 when the chairman appointed Viktor von der Lippe as his personal advisor, a man whom he had met back in Nuremberg three years earlier.[125] To date, von der Lippe has been overlooked in the historiography of the West German central bank. He came from a Westphalian family but grew up in Austria.[126] His name rarely appeared in the official minutes of directorate meetings, but he exerted a significant influence behind closed doors. Indeed, he was actually present at directorate meetings in his official capacity as minute taker, and would participate in the informal discussions that were never recorded in the minutes.[127] Von der Lippe possessed a sharp, calculating mind.

---

[121] Examples can be found in 'Der Unbequeme', *Die Zeit*, 8 Feb. 1951; 'Hüter der D-Mark', *Hamburger Abendblatt*, 9 Feb. 1951; 'Vocke', *Frankfurter Allgemeine Zeitung*, 9 Feb. 1951; 'Präsident Vocke 65 Jahre', *Die Welt*, 9 Feb. 1951; and 'In Schäffers Kompetenzsack', *Der Spiegel*, 30 Jan. 1952.

[122] Vocke, *Memoiren*, p. 73.

[123] Wilhelm Vocke to Volkmar Muthesius, 21 Oct. 1954, DBHA, B330/2035.

[124] Vocke grounded his polite refusal with the point that he had recently made two speeches in public and it would be 'not opportune' to appear on the magazine cover. See Leo Brawand to 'Pressestelle der Bank deutscher Länder', 23 May 1951, DBHA, B330/2045; and Viktor von der Lippe to 'Wirtschaftsredaktion des SPIEGEL', 28 May 1951, DBHA, B330/2045.

[125] This episode is recounted in von der Lippe's retirement speech. See Viktor von der Lippe, 'Abschiedsworte', 31 Jan. 1977, DBPA, no. 717.

[126] 'Persönliche Daten von Viktor von der Lippe', no date, DBPA, no. 1498.

[127] There is evidence of this in the 1960s. One such informal discussion, relating to the central bank's interaction with the press, took place in a directorate meeting on 19 October 1965. Von der Lippe actively participated in it and summarised the results of the conversation in a letter to Blessing the following day. The discussion, however, was not recorded in the minutes of the meeting. See Viktor von der Lippe to Karl Blessing, 20 Oct. 1965, DBHA, B330/280. Contrast with the Bundesbank directorate meeting minutes, 19 Oct. 1965, DBHA, B330/2067.

He quickly became Vocke's confidant at the central bank. Von der Lippe advised Vocke on matters pertaining to the media; he drafted the chairman's speeches; and he would often answer letters that were addressed to Vocke on the latter's behalf. He may not have been a member of the directorate, but the man's influence clearly outranked his station.

For now, however, let us return to Vocke's perception of the press during the early years of the BdL. Soon after his appointment as personal advisor, von der Lippe was also assigned to direct the press department.[128] Von der Lippe, then, held a dual role in the central bank. His two positions highlighted the close link between Vocke's office, on the one hand, and the central bank's press department, on the other. Upon his arrival at the press office, von der Lippe explicitly noted that 'Vocke wishes to continue, as before, to receive as many journalists in person as possible'.[129] This is clear evidence that, while the chairman was shy of the public spotlight, he was keen to maintain close contact with journalists on the ground. A profile piece on Vocke summed up the man nicely. 'Dr. Vocke is one of the most mentioned, but also one of the most frequently attacked personalities in Germany. He steps into the limelight only seldom. He refers to remain in the background and let others do the talking.'[130]

But hold on a second: why exactly should we care that Vocke was treated in public as a former Reichsbanker? Taking a step back, we can begin to see how this reputation might complicate the early Bundesbank Law debates. Vocke increasingly personified the BdL, and yet he was also closely associated with the inter-war Reichsbank. Both his person and past reinforced existing prejudices on the part of political opponents: was he just another stubborn Schacht who, if given the chance, would cause havoc for a new, democratic government?

The Federal Republic

The BdL entered the Federal Republic as an unpopular institution. It had earned the respect of the markets, and surprised many by its ability to defend the deutschmark.[131] But such policies came at a price. They had left a sour taste in the mouth of the wider population, suffering from unemployment. Press reports in late 1949 documented the apparent

---

[128] BdL directorate meeting minutes, 6 Apr. 1950, DBHA, B330/2054.

[129] Viktor von der Lippe, 'Entwurf für meine Tätigkeit als Pressereferent', 14 Apr. 1950, DBHA, B330/3357.

[130] 'Porträts der Wirtschaft: Wilhelm Vocke', *Echo der Woche*, 9 Feb. 1951.

[131] See, for example, 'Stabilität', *Hamburger Freie Presse*, 22–3 Apr. 1950; and 'Ein Erfolg orthodoxer Bankpolitik', *Die Neue Zeitung*, 28 Oct. 1949.

inevitability of the federal government's influence over the new central bank once the monetary authority was established.[132] 'In all countries, the non-political central bank belongs to the past', wrote *Die Welt* in early October 1949. 'It came to awful experiences in 1931 with the Reichsbank that was independent from the state.'[133] As one journalist put it in a letter to Bernard, on the day after Konrad Adenauer had been elected chancellor, 'Do you believe that it is correct to hold on to the complete autonomy of the central bank now that a democratically formed and parliamentary controlled government could assume the responsibility of monetary and credit policy?'[134]

This mood filtered into the political sphere too. As the historian Volker Hentschel notes, '[p]oliticians of all parties were of the view that the complete independence of the Bank deutscher Länder was a mistake of occupation policy in need of correcting'.[135] Even Erhard, the new economics minister and key ally of the central bank in its fight for independence, acknowledged the primacy of the state in the formation of economy policy. While he opposed the idea of a central bank being subject to government instruction, Erhard advocated close co-operation between an independent monetary authority and government authorities as a means of avoiding conflicts.[136] Where politicians and interest groups differed was over the manner in which, and the extent to which, the federal government, and state governments, should be able to influence monetary policy.

The constitution of West Germany, the *Grundgesetz*, or Basic Law, stated, 'the federal government establishes a bank of currency and issue as a federal central bank'.[137] It would be left to politicians, then, to decide the institutions and structure of the new central bank. But the arrival of the federal government in Bonn created a new power struggle.

[132] See, for example, 'Wer die Notenbankpolitik bestimmt', *Wiesbadener Kurier*, 29 Aug. 1949; 'Bundesregierung und Bundesbank', *Industriekurier*, 18 Oct. 1949; and 'Föderative Bundesbank', *Deutsche Zeitung und Wirtschaftszeitung*, 26 Oct. 1949; and 'Kooperative Bundesbank in Sicht', *Deutsche Zeitung und Wirtschaftszeitung*, 25 Dec. 1949.
[133] 'Vorgefecht um Bundesbank', *Die Welt*, 4 Oct. 1949.
[134] Bernard politely declined to answer the question. See Eckhard Budewig to Karl Bernard, 16 Sep. 1949, DBHA, B330/358. For Bernard's response, see Karl Bernard to Eckhard Budewig, 23 Sep. 1949, DBHA, B330/358.
[135] Volker Hentschel, 'Die Entstehung des Bundesbankgesetzes 1949–1957. Politische Kontroversen und Konflikte: Teil I', *Bankhistorisches Archiv*, Vol. 14 (1988), p. 10.
[136] Ludwig Erhard to Fritz Schäffer, 12 Oct. 1950, BAK, B102/5706, pp. 3–4; see also Volker Hentschel, *Ludwig Erhard. Ein Politikerleben* (Munich, 1996), pp. 122–3.
[137] Deutsche Bundesbank (ed.), *30 Jahre Deutsche Bundesbank. Die Entstehung des Bundesbankgesetzes vom 26. Juli 1957* (Frankfurt am Main, 1988), p. 19.

Before, there had been the central bank and the various *Länder*, or states. Now there was a new kid on the block. The federal government had absolutely no influence with respect to the BdL's policy decisions, or indeed the appointment procedures for members of the central bank council and directorate. The Bundesbank Law was seen by some German politicians as an opportunity to rectify this status quo. As Bibow argues, the central bank, the federal government and the state governments all vied for influence over the new Bundesbank Law.[138] The public debate surrounding the Bundesbank Law was not a tale of two cities, Frankfurt and Bonn; rather, it was one of many cities.

The platforms through which the Bundesbank Law would pass were diffuse. Ultimately, the lower parliament – that is, the Bundestag – would pass the final version of the law. But the cabinet, the second parliament (Bundesrat), and the political parties within the Bundestag could all put forward their own drafts. As a result, what was expected to be a quick procedure soon turned into a slow, drawn out process that lasted years. Indeed, it was often the case that more than one draft was in discussion; a confusing development that led to what Hentschel has termed the 'dualism of drafts'.[139] 'Still no Bundesbank', complained the *Stuttgarter Zeitung* in October 1949.[140] For that, the newspaper would have to wait for almost eight more years. Between 1949 and 1957, there were twenty-five drafts in total of the Bundesbank Law.[141]

Two central issues came to the fore during the Bundesbank Law debates: the central bank's relationship to the government; and the organisational structure of the monetary authority. These two questions divided the cabinet, they divided political parties and they even, albeit to a lesser degree, divided the central bank council itself. These divisions in turn gave rise to the public debate.

The BdL was keenly aware that the political landscape had changed because of the Federal Republic's establishment. The central bank's legal department worried about the implications of the Basic Law for its future relationship with the federal and state governments. 'There is no doubt that the Bank deutscher Länder is not what the drafters of the Basic Law have envisioned for the Bundesbank', wrote Friedrich Wilhelm von

---

[138] Bibow, 'Zur (Re-)Etablierung zentralbankpolitischer Institutionen und Traditionen in Westdeutschland', pp. 505–6
[139] Hentschel, 'Die Entstehung des Bundesbankgesetzes 1949–1957. Politische Kontroversen und Konflikte: Teil I', p. 22.
[140] 'Noch keine Bundesnotenbank', *Stuttgarter Zeitung*, 29 Oct. 1949.
[141] Hentschel, 'Die Entstehung des Bundesbankgesetzes 1949–1957. Politische Kontroversen und Konflikte: Teil I', p. 10.

Schelling, head of the central bank's legal department.[142] The Basic Law, he felt, left the federal government in a very strong position to overhaul the central bank. Tellingly, in providing context for his points, von Schelling referred not to contemporary legal examples from abroad, but rather the constitutions of the Second Reich and Weimar Republic and their respective provisions on monetary matters.[143] He used German monetary history and precedents to inform his viewpoints. While von Schelling was an influential and respected figure in the central bank, this was the opinion of just one man. What did the central bank think at an institutional level?

In late August 1949, shortly before Adenauer's ascent to the chancellorship, the central bank council decided to create a task force to observe the public debate and prepare its own position concerning the 'fundamental questions' of the Bundesbank Law.[144] The initiative, originally proposed by Wolf, the official in the economics department and a close confidant of Vocke, was a direct reaction to some bad news stemming from one of the German committees established to organise the transition from zonal governance to that of the Federal Republic.[145] The committee in question was the finance committee. It had recommended that the BdL's remit concerning the formation of economic policy be transferred to the government, and that the government be given a direct influence over the creation of credit.[146] Wolf saw the finance committee's views as indicative of a wider trend in the political sphere – and the central bank needed to counter them.[147]

The task force was composed of the two chairmen – Vocke and Bernard – and four *Land* central bank presidents: Boden, Burkhardt, Klasen and Veit.[148] This committee met on 26 September 1949 to begin discussions on its position, and reported its findings at the next central bank council meeting.[149] What did the task force conclude? It argued

[142] Friedrich Wilhelm von Schelling, 'Vermerk. Betr: Errichtung einer Währungs- und Notenbank', 6 Sep. 1949, DBHA, B330/358, p. 2.
[143] Ibid., p. 1.
[144] BdL central bank council minutes, 30–31 Aug. 1949, DBHA, B330/17/1.
[145] Eduard Wolf to Wilhelm Vocke, 15 Aug. 1949, DBHA, B330/6458/14; see also Eduard Wolf, 'Stellungnahme zu den Vorschlägen Dr. Weissers über das Verhältnis von Notenbank und Bundesregierung', 15 Aug. 1949, DBHA, B330/6458/14.
[146] For more on the finance committee, see Buchheim, 'Die Unabhängigkeit der Bundesbank', pp. 18–19.
[147] Wolf to Vocke, 15 Aug. 1949; and Wolf, 'Stellungnahme zu den Vorschlägen Dr. Weissers über das Verhältnis von Notenbank und Bundesregierung', 15 Aug. 1949.
[148] Grasmann, another central bank council member, was added two weeks later. See BdL central bank council minutes, 30–31 Aug. 1949; and BdL central bank council minutes, 13–14 Sep. 1949, DBHA, B330/17/2.
[149] BdL central bank council minutes, 27–28 Sep. 1949, DBHA, B330/18/2.

that the new Bundesbank should be a replica of the current central bank, its independence and decentralised structure left intact. There were two changes proposed, however. First, the federal president should confirm the appointment of the central bank's two chairmen. And second, a small committee should be formed with the aim of ensuring co-operation between Bonn and Frankfurt. The committee would include the central bank's two chairmen, the chancellor, finance minister and the economics minister. Its role was purely advisory; the committee could not issue instructions or veto decisions.[150] An internal report of the task force's meeting also noted that its members felt that, in the interests of the currency's stability, the ABC's veto powers should remain in place for the time being.[151]

The task force's suggestions, two weeks after the election of Adenauer, put forward an extreme version of independence vis-à-vis the federal government. Vocke wrote to the chancellor soon afterwards, detailing these proposals – and lobbying, too, for the maintenance of the ABC's remit over the BdL.[152] The ABC, the central banker argued, somewhat implausibly, was the 'embodiment of international co-operation', and one whose oversight had by now effectively stopped, allowing the central bank the freedom it needed to safeguard the deutschmark.[153]

At Vocke's request, von Schelling of the legal department – a former Reichsbank man himself – outlined the central bank's legal footing with respect to the federal government in late October.[154] In short, it was weak. Von Schelling stressed that it was likely the federal government would change the wording of the BdL occupation law had it the chance to do so.

The central bank's concerns were justified. In defiance of the German tradition, it was Fritz Schäffer, the finance minister, and not the economics minister Erhard, who was responsible for the Bundesbank Law.[155] In late 1949, Schäffer, a Christian Social Union (CSU) politician and federalist, stated publicly at two CSU committees that he was a supporter of central bank independence.[156] Schäffer was simply paying lip service

---

[150] Hentschel, 'Die Entstehung des Bundesbankgesetzes 1949–1957. Politische Kontroversen und Konflikte: Teil I', pp. 8–9.

[151] Willi Schmidt, 'Vermerk über die Sitzung des Arbeitsstabes für die Vorbereitung einer Stellungnahme zu dem nach dem Bonner Grundgesetz zu erwartenden Entwurf eines Bundesnotenbankgesetzes', 29 Sep. 1949, DBHA, B330/358, p. 5.

[152] Vocke to Adenauer, 31 Oct. 1949, pp. 5–7.   [153] Ibid., p. 8.

[154] Friedrich Wilhelm von Schelling to Wilhelm Vocke, 24 Oct. 1949, DBHA, B330/2011, p. 1.

[155] Bibow, 'On the origin and rise of central bank independence in West Germany', p. 161.

[156] As recorded in Max Grasmann to Karl Bernard, 22 Dec. 1949, DBHA, B330/358. See also Max Grasmann to Fritz Schäffer, 5 Nov. 1949, DBHA, B330/358, in addition to Max Grasmann to Karl Bernard, 17 Nov. 1949, DBHA, B330/358.

here; for, in private, the finance minister had already emerged as a fierce opponent. The early, internal drafts of the Bundesbank Law that circulated within the finance ministry echoed, in part at least, the Reichsbank of old. In late 1949, for example, the establishment of a *Kuratorium* – historically, a governmental oversight body for the Reichsbank – was suggested, though its exact powers and relationship remained undefined.[157] Schäffer's views on central bank independence were known in elite circles. Vocke found them 'extraordinarily worrisome'.[158] And indeed, in a letter to Adenauer in early November, Schäffer suggested that, when the time came, the chancellor should replace the functions of the ABC.[159] Such a move would have allowed Adenauer to issue instructions to the central bank.

On what basis did Schäffer ground his views? It was out of the question that an independent central bank should be equipped with the ability to carry out unpopular policies, Schäffer argued, when it was the government that was left to bear the political consequences.[160] An independent central bank was desirable, he continued – but only one within the constraints of a wider co-operation between monetary and government policy.[161]

Public opinion data, commissioned by the government, confirmed the finance minister's fears. The government came first place in a survey that asked West Germans who was to blame for the state's swelling unemployment figures. Though the BdL was not explicitly named as an option to select in the survey, the entry 'monetary and credit shortage' came in fifth place.[162] Indeed, as observed Elisabeth Noelle-Neumann, whose company Institut für Demoskopie conducted the survey, the public opinion data demonstrated that West Germany's current travails were seen as 'a parallel to the developments in the years 1930/1', whereby the government was being blamed for the economy's troubles.[163]

---

[157] Paul Hahn, 'Entwurf eines Gesetzes über die Deutsche Bundesbank', 3 Dec. 1949, BAK, B136/1199, p. 1; see also Kremer, 'Betr: Errichtung einer Bundesbank', 5 Dec. 1949, BAK, B136/1199.

[158] This phrase is found in the first draft of Vocke's letter to Adenauer on 31 October 1949. But it was later omitted in the second and final draft. See Wilhelm Vocke to Konrad Adenauer, 31 Oct. 1949 (draft), DBHA, B330/2011, p. 7.

[159] Fritz Schäffer to Konrad Adenauer, 14 Nov. 1949, BAK, B136/1199, p. 2.

[160] Ibid., pp. 2–3; see also Hentschel, *Ludwig Erhard*, pp. 121–2.

[161] Schäffer to Adenauer, 14 Nov. 1949, p. 3.

[162] Accurate percentiles cannot be given, as many respondents ticked more than one option. This resulted in numbers that exceeded 100. 'Das Politische Klima. Ein Bericht über die Stimmung im Bundesgebiet 1951', *Institut für Demoskopie*, Jan. 1952, BAK, B145/4221, p. 27.

[163] Elisabeth Noelle-Neumann to Konrad Adenauer, 1 Jun. 1950, BAK, B145/1566, p. 5.

Schäffer's stance clashed with Erhard's opinion, however. The economics minister argued that the 'independence of the central bank should not be touched' – at least in the manner that Schäffer proposed.[164] Instead of exerting a direct government influence over the new central bank, Erhard suggested that the Bundesbank Law should allow for an independent monetary authority. The economics minister pushed for a close co-operative relationship between Frankfurt and Bonn: government officials should attend central bank council meetings, which in turn were to be comprised of members that the government itself had carefully appointed. If the Bundesbank Law was to equip the government with a veto, then it was merely a veto that required the central bank council to vote a second time.[165]

This 'Erhardian' solution was one preconditioned on trust and close co-operation: crucially, however, it proposed no formal process through which disagreements between the central bank and federal government concerning monetary policy could be solved. And in contrast to Schäffer, who pushed for the maintenance of a decentralised central bank system, Erhard would soon emerge to become a powerful advocate of a centralised Bundesbank.[166]

Already tensions had been running high when, in late 1949, the finance minister and the ABC sidestepped the BdL, and together agreed to revise the occupation law so as to relax the strict borrowing terms constraining the federal government at the time. This move provoked the fury of the central bank council and directorate.[167] Schäffer, for his part, had already been chafing at the central bank's intransigence. Writing to Vocke, he snapped: 'It's not like every finance minister just sees a central bank as a printing press.'[168]

The first draft of a new Bundesbank Law, spearheaded by officials in the finance ministry, emerged in February and assumed full form by March 1950.[169] The organisation, tasks and authorities of the new Bundesbank would resemble the decentralised BdL. The question of independence was not addressed, but Schäffer suggested that a federal committee would oversee policy decisions in instances when there were

---

[164] Ludwig Erhard to Konrad Adenauer, 7 Nov. 1949, BAK, B136/1199, pp. 1–2.
[165] Erhard to Schäffer, 12 Oct. 1950, pp. 3–4.   [166] Ibid., pp. 1–2.
[167] Karl Bernard to Allied Banking Commission, 23 Nov. 1949, DBHA, B330/2030; Wilhelm Könneker to Wilhelm Vocke, 24 Nov. 1949, DBHA, B330/2030; and 'German financial problems. Dr Wilhelm Vocke, president of the BdL', 29 Nov. 1949.
[168] Fritz Schäffer to Wilhelm Vocke, 14 Nov. 1949, DBHA, B330/2043, p. 2.
[169] Hentschel, 'Die Entstehung des Bundesbankgesetzes 1949–1957. Politische Kontroversen und Konflikte: Teil I', pp. 10 (footnote), 11.

disputes between the central bank and the government. In early March, the exact nature of this federal committee was left unspecified.[170] But it was enough to scare the BdL of what was to come.

Prior to the final version of Schäffer's draft, Vocke sent a letter of protest on behalf of the central bank.[171] In doing so, he explicitly linked the justification of the central bank's independence to Germany's troubled monetary history – that is, the two inflationary episodes. 'A certain mistrust of the central bank leadership runs like a red thread through your newly added provisions', Vocke wrote, referring to Schäffer's concern that an independent central bank could bring down the government.[172] 'The cardinal question or, phrased better, the essential question of the currency is that of the independence of the central bank', the chairman argued.

The existing [Bank deutscher Länder] law makes the bank independent of instructions from political bodies. This provision, and thus one of the essential safeguards for the protection of the currency, is simply left out in this draft. Every reader with a critical eye, both at home and abroad, will see this straight away.[173]

In support of his argument, Vocke turned to the example of the German people. 'After two inflations the people are distrustful when it comes to money', he wrote. 'The mere possibility that [government control of the central bank] could happen can damage confidence.'[174] Vocke once again defended the ABC's oversight with respect to the BdL's policy, arguing that it proved a convenient safeguard from democratic pressures. To underline his point, Vocke sent copies of this letter to Adenauer and Erhard.[175]

Historical narratives, or lessons, concerning the two inflations were thus explicitly linked to the institutional struggle in which both the government and central bank found themselves. But Vocke's letter also highlighted the fact that the BdL was in a weak position. A letter of protest was all well and good. But it would be politicians, and not unelected central bankers, who decided the nature of the future central bank.

This weakness was demonstrated when the finance minister's draft was revised later and a copy sent to the BdL. Vocke's protest amounted to nothing. According to article 4 outlined in the draft, the Bundesbank's new tasks were to 'guard the currency while giving consideration to

---

[170] A neat chronology of this draft's emergence is detailed in Deutsche Bundesbank, *30 Jahre Deutsche Bundesbank*, p. 25.
[171] Wilhelm Vocke to Fritz Schäffer, 7 Mar. 1950, DBHA, B330/2043, p. 2.
[172] Ibid., p. 1.   [173] Ibid., p. 2.   [174] Ibid., p. 3.
[175] As noted in Wilhelm Vocke to Karl Bernard, 23 Mar. 1950, DBHA, B330/2014.

economic necessities' and regulate the flow of credit in the economy.[176] Article 20 stated that the president of the republic was to confirm the appointment of the central bank's two chairmen. These chairmen could be dismissed by the federal president in cases of gross misconduct.[177]

The Bundesbank would retain the same credit instruments as the BdL, but it would no longer be independent in decisions pertaining to them. According to articles 21 and 22, two ministers or government representatives could attend the council meetings. These two officials would have the right to receive information, they could put forward motions and, crucially, raise objections to decisions taken by the council. If an objection were raised, the implementation of the central bank's decision would be suspended.[178]

In the case of such an objection, Schäffer proposed a resolution mechanism: a federal arbitration committee would be established to decide on the disagreements between Frankfurt and Bonn. Five representatives would be appointed by the government, and five representatives would be appointed by the central bank council – the latter representatives including the two central bank chairmen. A final person, the committee chairman, was appointed by the federal president. In a vote that was tied, the chairman called the decision.[179] Moreover, a *Beirat*, or advisory board, would be established, one comprised of interest group representatives, from industry, trade, agriculture, the trade unions, among others.[180]

Adenauer, for his part, supported the proposals. Writing to Schäffer in mid-1950, the chancellor noted, 'we need to find a solution which provides the government with the option to give instructions to the central bank in case the bank refuses to undertake a measure that is required to support the implementation of government policy'.[181] Noting that other countries had enacted similar measures, the chancellor justified his concerns by referring to the West German constitution: the chancellor was ultimately responsible for policy, not the central bank.[182]

The finance ministry's draft, then, conflicted directly with the BdL's independence vis-à-vis Bonn. In response, the central bank council

---

[176] 'Anlage I: Ministerialentwurf eines Bundesgesetzes über die Errichtung einer Bundesbank', BAK, B136/1199, p. 1.

[177] Ibid., p. 7.

[178] Ibid., pp. 8–9. There was an exception, however. Decisions relating to the discount and Lombard rates, as well as ones concerning minimum reserve levels, would not be postponed. They could take effect immediately despite the use of the veto. But they would then be subject to the review of the federal committee.

[179] Ibid., p. 9.   [180] Ibid.

[181] Konrad Adenauer to Fritz Schäffer, 26 Jul. 1950, BAK, B102/5706, p. 2.

[182] Ibid., pp. 1, 2.

formulated a counterproposal to the ministerial draft.[183] It was drafted over the course of three days.[184] While the BdL agreed with much in the finance ministry's outline, the central bank council said, the 'core problem' remained in scenarios when the federal government disagreed with the central bank.[185] The central bank council wished to keep its independence – and at the heart of its argument lay Germany's terrible past with inflation:

> The central bank council strongly believes that the independence of the central bank system, which centres on a manipulated currency, is indeed the most essential element behind the safeguarding of the currency and the maintenance of trust in the currency. The validity of this view is particularly appropriate in present day Germany, whose population has become particularly suspicious of state influences on the central bank leadership in light of two inflations triggered by the state occurring within a single generation.[186]

Central bank independence, in other words, was justified by Germany's troubled history with inflation. According to the central bank's counterproposals, two government representatives could attend the council meetings. These two representatives were allowed to object to a decision if it did not correspond to the general economic policy pursued by the government. In such a scenario, the council would postpone the implementation of the decision, convene for a second time, discuss the government's objection and vote again.[187] The government's proposal of an 'arbitration committee will – once it has been established as a permanent institution – undermine and weaken the authority of the central bank council in the long run', the council protested.[188]

Tensions between the BdL and the government were running high. The central bank had sought to lobby Bonn behind the scenes. And these efforts found little, if any success.

Turning to the Public Sphere

With little prospect of resolution, the BdL took to the public sphere amid efforts to influence the debate surrounding the Bundesbank Law. Prior to the chancellor's falling-out with the BdL in 1956, the 'problem of central bank independence', to use the words of one of the chancellor's

---

[183] 'Anlage II: "Bankentwurf." Bundesgesetz über die Währung und Notenbank', BAK, B136/1199.
[184] BdL central bank council minutes, 31 Mar. and 4–5 Apr., 1950, DBHA, B330/25/1.
[185] Ibid.   [186] Ibid.
[187] 'Anlage II: "Bankentwurf." Bundesgesetz über die Währung und Notenbank', p. 11.
[188] BdL central bank council minutes, 31 Mar. and 4–5 Apr. 1950.

advisors, remained restricted to a rarefied sphere of elites.[189] During this period, for example, the government did not commission any public opinion polls to ascertain the attitude of the average West German concerning central bank independence. Instead, more often than not, such surveys focused on Adenauer's foreign policy, West German attitudes to Hitler and opinions about the communist east.[190] The lack of such polling about central bank independence is revealing in itself. The Bundesbank Law was a matter for the experts.

The evidence suggests that, during the 1950s, the central bank also viewed the Bundesbank Law debate as an elite one; the central bank's press chief, von der Lippe, would equate 'public opinion' with the 'press' – in other words, journalists.[191] Not that the average West German read what the journalists had to say, however. Public opinion data during this period suggest that a large majority, some 64 per cent, of adult Germans read a newspaper 'on a regular basis'.[192] But another poll, conducted in March 1955, highlighted the extent to which West Germans avoided the business section. It was the least-read newspaper section out of fifteen categories.[193] West Germans, it seems, were far more enthused about the serialised fiction section (which came in eleventh place) than matters concerning the central bank.

In 1950, the BdL did not set out to win the masses. Rather, the central bank set its sights on those elite groups that could be influenced. After all, these were the groups that mattered with respect to the passage of the Bundesbank Law. However, because of its tentative legal situation, the central bank had to be cautious. An aggressive press policy could backfire, strengthening the resolve of its political opponents, such as Schäffer, who held the better hand of cards.

The groundwork for the central bank's media campaign was laid out at a directorate meeting in late 1949, some weeks after the Federal Republic came into existence.[194] The directorate, not the central bank council, launched these efforts. The economics journalist Muthesius had become

---

[189] Joseph Rust to Konrad Adenauer, 7 Nov. 1950, BAK, B136/1200.

[190] The federal archives in Koblenz contain a wealth of such polls, all of which were commissioned by Adenauer's government.

[191] Viktor von der Lippe to Wilhelm Vocke, 15 Feb. 1956, DBHA, B330/2032 I, p. 2.

[192] The survey, conducted in January 1953, had a sample base of 2,000 people, all of whom were aged over 17. 'Zeitungen und Zeitschriften. Die statistische Struktur der Lesenschaft', Institut für Demoskopie, Apr. 1953, BAK, B145/4223, pp. 1–2.

[193] Local news ranked as the most-read section of the newspaper, followed by advertisements and political news reports. See Elisabeth Noelle and Erich P. Neumann (eds.), Jahrbuch der öffentlichen Meinung, 1947–1955 (Allensbach, 1956), p. 56.

[194] BdL directorate meeting minutes, 21 Oct. 1949, DBHA, B330/2054.

a close confidant of Vocke. The chairman had already asked Muthesius to take on an advisory position at the central bank for its public relations activity. But as Muthesius recounted in his memoirs, after long discussions both men decided 'that it would be better for both parties if I remained as editor of the journal [*Die Zeitschrift für das gesamte Kreditwesen*] and, in my own publishing activity, supported the intellectual world of sound money and a stable currency in the public sphere without a direct connection to the central bank'.[195]

This proved to be a fruitful strategy. In January 1950, the directorate's Wrede and Muthesius reached 'agreements concerning the cultivation of public opinion'.[196] A working relationship had been in progress before. But it was now agreed to take it to a new level. In internal correspondence, Wrede linked Muthesius's campaign on behalf of the central bank to the BdL's expansion of financial support for *Die Zeitschrift für das gesamte Kreditwesen*.[197] This campaign did not just restrict itself to the question of independence, however; it also tackled the debates surrounding deficit financing and the work creation programmes propounded by the government.[198] Nevertheless, the theme of central bank independence took centre stage.

What did Muthesius's efforts actually entail, however? There are four aspects to note here. First, the journalist penned a number of articles in support of central bank independence in a variety of publications.[199] He also published a popular book on the 'future of the D-Mark'.[200] Second, he ensured that *Die Zeitschrift für das gesamte Kreditwesen* became a mouthpiece for the BdL and its cause of autonomy – the journal, he noted to Wrede, made for 'good propaganda'.[201] The third aspect of Muthesius's campaign was the organisation of conferences, which allowed the BdL's leadership to step onto the public platform and deliver speeches.[202]

---

[195] Volkmar Muthesius, *Augenzeuge von drei Inflationen. Erinnerungen und Gedanken eines Wirtschaftspublizisten* (Frankfurt am Main, 1973), p. 128.

[196] Volkmar Muthesius to Victor Wrede, 9 Mar. 1950, DBHA, B330/3357.

[197] Victor Wrede, 'Vermerk', 11 Jan. 1950, DBHA, B330/3345. See also Wilhelm Vocke and Wilhelm Könneker to Verlag Fritz Knapp, 13 Jan. 1950, DBHA, B330/3345.

[198] As noted in Muthesius to Wrede, 9 Mar. 1950, p. 2.

[199] For examples of Muthesius's articles, see Volkmar Muthesius, 'Notenbank muß unabhängig bleiben', *Die Neue Zeitung*, 11 Mar. 1950, DBHA, B330/2035; and Volkmar Muthesius, 'Die Unabhängigkeit der Notenbank', *Wirtschaftspolitische Gesellschaft von 1947*, 15 Apr. 1950, DBHA, B330/3345. For more on the *Wirtschaftspolitische Gesellschaft von 1947*, see Mark E. Spicka, *Selling the economic miracle: economic reconstruction and politics in West Germany, 1949–1957* (Oxford, 2007), p. 109.

[200] Volkmar Muthesius, *Die Zukunft der D-Mark* (Frankfurt, 1950).

[201] This was explicitly noted in Muthesius to Wrede, 9 Mar. 1950, p. 2.

[202] Here are two examples. For a September 1950 conference attended by Bernard, see 'Probleme des Kreditwesens', *Frankfurter Rundschau*, 29 Sep. 1950, DBPA, no. 75; see 'Unabhängige Notenbank', *Frankfurter Allgemeine Zeitung*, 30 Sep. 1950. For the May

But it was the fourth element that was perhaps the most crucial. Muthesius set about covertly winning the editorial support of leading newspapers across West Germany. But there was a problem: in the early 1950s, the media sphere was largely still a fractured, regional one.[203] Muthesius addressed this issue by arranging meetings to take place in Düsseldorf, Stuttgart, Munich, Hamburg and Frankfurt – in other words, West Germany's major cities.[204] A member of the central bank council attended the meetings in Düsseldorf and Stuttgart.[205] What went on during these discussions, however? Documents relating to the Frankfurt meeting still survive today. Von der Lippe, Vocke's personal advisor, was present. The need for central bank independence was stressed to the general agreement of the journalists present.[206] According to the agenda points, this need for independence was explicitly tied to the consequences of Germany's history of inflations and the fragile state of the currency.[207] During the meeting, it was agreed by the attendees, with minor nuances, that the newspapers in question would support the central bank's cause.[208]

It is difficult to measure the exact impact of these meetings. Certainly, Muthesius was convinced of their worth. 'Considering the short period in which our agreement has been made', he wrote to Wrede, 'I think I am able to say that a relatively satisfactory starting position has been won.'[209] The journalist noted how newspapers in Düsseldorf began publishing pro-BdL articles after his meeting with editors there. Another example stands out, too. Among the participants lined up for the Frankfurt meeting was the editor of the *Frankfurter Rundshau*.[210] Two weeks after

---

1951 conference attended by Vocke, see Wilhelm Vocke, 'Address at the Conference on Credit Policy organised by *Die Zeitschrift für das gesamte Kreditwesen*', 17 May 1951, DBHA, B330/6305/1.

[203] Christina von Hodenberg, *Konsens und Krise: eine Geschichte der westdeutschen Medienöffentlichkeit 1945–1973* (Göttingen, 2006), p. 88.

[204] Muthesius to Wrede, 9 Mar. 1950, pp. 1–2; and Muthesius to Wrede, 26 Jun. 1950, p. 1.

[205] Erich Leist, then vice president of the *Land* central bank of North Rhine-Westphalia, attended the meeting in Düsseldorf. Pfleiderer, the president of the *Land* central bank of Baden-Württemberg, was present at the discussion in Stuttgart. See Muthesius to Wrede, 9 Mar. 1950, pp. 1–2.

[206] Viktor von der Lippe to Victor Wrede, 12 Apr. 1950, DBHA, B330/3357.

[207] 'Diskussionsthesen für die Aussprache am 11. April 1950', 11 Apr. 1950, DBHA, B330/3357; see also Volkmar Muthesius to Jürgen Eick, 4 Apr. 1950, DBHA, B330/3357; and von der Lippe to Wrede, 12 Apr. 1950.

[208] The existence of these minor nuances was merely noted, not specified. See von der Lippe to Wrede, 12 Apr. 1950.

[209] Muthesius to Wrede, 9 Mar. 1950, p. 2.

[210] The editor was listed as among those who were invited to the meeting. See Volkmar Muthesius to Victor Wrede, 4 Apr. 1950, DBHA, B330/3357.

the discussion was held, von der Lippe observed that the newspaper, 'up to now Social Democratic oriented', had 'in the last weeks' begun to publish 'a whole row' of positive articles about the BdL.[211] Indeed, by September 1950, the *Frankfurter Rundshau* was publishing articles entitled, 'Independence of the central bank – precondition for sound currency'.[212] Of course, this is just a single example. It does not prove that the central bank altered the parameters of debate surrounding the Bundesbank Law. But these two examples do suggest that, at the very least, these meetings had some traction in swinging the press to the side of the monetary authority. None of Muthesius's efforts were recorded explicitly in directorate or central bank council meetings. They were conducted behind the scenes.[213]

But why this sustained effort to enter the public sphere? The drive to influence the Bundesbank Law was reinforced by the realisation that, if the BdL did not, its political opponents certainly would regardless. And one reason why the central bank needed to court the favour of journalists was because the very legacy of central bank independence remained in dispute. For instance, in an article entitled 'The central bank – a state within a state?' published in *Die Welt*, the economics journalist Wilhelm Grotkopp argued that the independent Reichsbank actively contributed to mass unemployment in the late Weimar years.[214] '[Government] proposals to revive the economy by credit expansion and job creation were rejected by [Reichsbank president] Schacht and his successor Luther, because they threatened the stability of the currency. At that time Schacht and Luther, as presidents of the Reichsbank, were more powerful than the government.'[215] If it had happened once already, Grotkopp argued, it could happen again: the Allied-imposed independence of the BdL needed to be changed.

Muthesius, for his part, was incensed by Grotkopp's article. Writing to the central bank's head of the press department – that is, Vocke's personal advisor, von der Lippe – he recommended that the directorate chairman write a piece in response to Grotkopp's publication. Muthesius advised Vocke to not write *directly* about the Bundesbank Law. No, he

---

Viktor von der Lippe to Wilhelm Vocke, 26 Apr. 1950, DBHA, B330/6305/1.

'Unabhängigkeit der Notenbank – Voraussetzung für gesunde Währung', *Frankfurter Rundschau*, 30 Sep. 1950.

Muthesius's name was recorded only once at a directorate meeting. It was in relation to press policy, but no other details about the discussion were given. See BdL directorate meeting minutes, 21 Oct. 1949.

Wilhelm Grotkopp, 'Die Notenbank – ein Staat im Staate?', *Die Welt*, 15 Apr. 1950, DBHA, B330/2042.

Ibid.

had a better idea. Vocke should write a 'portrayal of the past', one that nipped Grotkopp's misuse of history in the bud.[216] An article penned by Vocke tackling Grotkopp's claims directly could 'generate some successful publicity and make a good impact'.[217] Muthesius offered *Die Zeitschrift für das gesamte Kreditwesen* as a natural home for such a piece. Both the chairman and his advisor, however, were hesitant of such a step – at least, immediately.[218] Nevertheless, Vocke and von der Lippe did begin working on material that would result in the chairman's first podium speech in May 1950, and later be published in Muthesius's journal.

Interestingly, however, Muthesius also stressed that Vocke should seek out Grotkopp himself. Vocke's personal advisor requested a meeting with the economics journalist to discuss 'the historical remarks found in the article'.[219] But when Grotkopp replied by inviting the chairman to a group table discussion about the upcoming Bundesbank Law with leading journalists, Vocke declined.[220] The chairman wished to speak with the journalist directly and privately. Vocke, for his part, wished to run the BdL's communication channel on his own terms. He wanted to remain behind the scenes.

The journalists Muthesius and Grotkopp were just two examples. These men diverged markedly on the question of independence. Yet there was a wide spectrum of opinion and debate. Other journalists referred to the central bank's mixed record during the inter-war period. 'We have all lived through disruptive circumstances that lead to inflation', wrote Hans Baumgarten, a journalist at the *Frankfurter Allgemeine Zeitung*.

But we have also experienced something else. In the year 1931 the deflationary policies of the independent central bank, with their imperative nature and rigidity, led the German economy and society to ruin, resulting in the domination of National Socialism with all its manifestations. Therefore we know – or should know – that insufficient use of monetary policy can result in just as much misfortune as its abuse.[221]

Certainly, Hermann Höpker-Aschoff, a leading figure in the Free Democratic Party (FDP), leant heavily on the dire experiences of the latter Weimar era in an article published in the *Industriekurier*. Höpker-Aschoff drew a direct lesson from the 1931 banking crisis, during which

---

[216] Volkmar Muthesius to Viktor von der Lippe, 18 Apr. 1950, DBHA, B330/2035.
[217] Ibid.
[218] Viktor von der Lippe to Volkmar Muthesius, 21 Apr. 1950, DBHA, B330/2035.
[219] Viktor von der Lippe to Wilhelm Grotkopp, 21 Apr. 1950, DBHA, B330/2024.
[220] Wilhelm Grotkopp to Wilhelm Vocke, 27 Apr. 1950, DBHA, B330/2024; and Wilhelm Vocke to Wilhelm Grotkopp, 2 May 1950, DBHA, B330/2024.
[221] Hans Baumgarten, 'Die Währung geht jeden an', *Frankfurter Allgemeine Zeitung*, 9 May 1950.

the independent Reichsbank, under Luther, refused to help the nation's banks. The central bank, the politician continued, even forced a deflationary policy upon the government of Heinrich Brüning, one that was 'grist to the mill of National Socialism'.[222] And the lesson for West Germany? The government needed to exert a direct influence over the monetary authority.[223]

During the early post-war years, the lessons of the inter-war period were still up for grabs. As such, the central bank leadership fought hard to make the concept of central bank independence synonymous with economic stability. In the 2010s, this might sound like a relatively easy sell. In 1949, the year in which West Germany was established, it was not. After all, the inter-war record of central bank independence was a very different thing to the post-war one.

This is not to say, however, that the Reichsbank was the sole reference point during these debates. Far from it. Recall the comments of Schaefer, the private banker, at the start of this chapter. Sitting at the conference table in June 1950, he discussed his country's recent monetary past and the implications it had for West Germany's present. But the banker also touched on contemporary examples, such as the Bank of France and the Bank of England.[224] Banking historians have correctly documented the influence that foreign central bank models exerted upon the structure and institutions of West Germany's first monetary authority.[225] This was most apparent in the case of the Federal Reserve System: American occupation officials pushed for a decentralised central bank in the Western Bloc, one that was independent of domestic political influence. The British, for their part, lobbied for a more centralised model, akin to their Bank of England back home. The compromise that resulted, of course, was the two-tiered structure of the BdL.

But how did the example of foreign central banks influence the Bundesbank Law debate in the Federal Republic? After the Reichsbank, the Federal Reserve System was the most common point of reference for

---

[222] Hermann Höpker-Aschoff, 'Die künftige Bundesnotenbank', *Industriekurier*, 6 May 1950, BAK, B102/5704 I.

[223] Höpker-Aschoff, however, would later change his opinion concerning central bank independence due to the BdL's successful defence of the deutschmark during the Korean crisis, the outbreak of which is discussed in greater detail later in this chapter.

[224] Weber, *Die Bundesbank. Aufbau und Aufgaben*, p. 22.

[225] Among others, see Wandel, *Die Entstehung der Bank deutscher Länder und die deutsche Währungsreform 1948*; Horstmann, 'Kontinuität und Wandel im deutschen Notenbanksystem'; Buchheim, 'Die Unabhängigkeit der Bundesbank'; and Lindenlaub, 'Die Errichtung der Bank deutscher Länder und die Währungsreform von 1948'.

West German elites.[226] The model of the American monetary authority, however, meant different things to different people. Schäffer, the finance minister and a marked federalist from Bavaria, evoked its decentralised structure as something to which the new Bundesbank should aspire. Yet he had little taste for the Federal Reserve System's independence. Erhard and Vocke, on the other hand, saw the American central bank's relative autonomy from political instruction as laudatory, but were disdainful of its decentralised structure. They argued that the Bundesbank should adopt a more centralised model. Other central banks were discussed by politicians and government officials alike, but, more often than not, to stress the exceptional nature of West Germany's monetary conditions.[227] 'Since its nationalisation, the Bank of England is formally dependent to the government', noted Hans Henckel, an influential official in the economics ministry. He continued:

The Bank of France is autonomous. The board of governors is a forum of seven personalities appointed by the president, who are not bound by government instruction. The circumstances in Germany, which already has two inflations behind it, are not easily comparable to those of other countries. One should leave the question of dependence or independence entirely to the Germans.[228]

It was often the case that examples of foreign central banks, carefully selected and worded, played into the hands of political arguments concerning the Bundesbank Law. In this regard, they were no different to how West German elites used narratives of the Reichsbank. If monetary history became a political football, so too did contemporary reference points.

A decisive, more aggressive shift with respect to the BdL's press interaction occurred in May 1950. At the start of that month, Vocke took to the podium for the first time in Hamburg before a meeting at the Association of German Savings Banks and Giro Institutions, or Arbeitsgemeinschaft Deutscher Sparkassen- und Giroverbändes und Girozentralen – nearly two years after he assumed the chairmanship of

---

[226] See, for instance, 'Änderung des Währungsgesetzes?', *Frankfurter Neue Presse*, 19 Nov. 1949; 'Staat und Notenbank. Die "Unabhängigkeit der Federal Reserve Banken"', *Die Zeitschrift für das gesamte Kreditwesen*, 15 Nov. 1949; and 'USA: Um die Unabhängigkeit des Federal Reserves Systems', *Die Zeitschrift für das gesamte Kreditwesen*, 1 Apr. 1951.

[227] For example, see the note drawn up by the finance ministry in 1950. Dürre, 'Vermerk. Betr: Bundesbankgesetz – Kritische Punkte des Entwurfs', 21 Nov. 1950, pp. 4–5, BAK, B102/5706; and Wilhelm Vocke to Ludwig Erhard et al., 25 Aug. 1950, DBHA, B330/2021 I, p. 3.

[228] See Hans Henckel, 'Vermerk. BdL – und LZB-Gesetz. Notiz für eine Besprechung auf dem Petersberg am 12.1.1951', 12 Jan. 1951, BAK, B102/28119 I, p. 3.

the directorate. Vocke's speech was explosive. It clearly outlined his world view, denoting the dilemmas that the currency faced in terms of fostering confidence and, consequently, the necessity of central bank independence.

Indeed, the address would go on to establish a rhetorical blueprint for later years. Three themes emerged. First, the stability of the currency should constitute the government's top economic priority – 'an inflationary currency … harms and corrupts the economic system, as we in Germany have twice learned in painful fashion', Vocke said.[229] Second, central bank independence was crucial for the maintenance of such stability. And third, the BdL represented the interests of the West German people against a spendthrift government and lobby groups. The monetary authority was, in other words, the government's antagonist. 'Now I come to the position of the central bank', Vocke remarked, in closing:

> But first let me state a fact. An independent central bank, one free from politics, is the best guarantee of the currency, especially here in Germany, where the currency stands or falls with the central bank and its management. An independent central bank is therefore of even greater importance, both for the working and saving population and for the government itself. That is in fact clearly recognised within the government. The time when you have to destroy the independence of the central bank is when you wish, as Hitler did, to start an inflation. No sensible person wants to do that now.[230]

The speech is remarkable for its clarity and defiant tone. It was an overtly political argument. Vocke, for the first time, referenced the two inflationary episodes of Germany's history on a public platform and explicitly linked them to the warning that the government was not to be trusted with the printing press. The chairman's speech made the headlines. And it did so far more than any public utterance the BdL had hitherto made.[231]

But why May 1950? In a confidential letter to an acquaintance at the Federal Reserve, Vocke outlined the reasons why he pushed himself into the limelight. They centred on the currency. Three factors had culminated towards a recent fall in the deutschmark in international markets, he explained. One reason was the recently increased credit ceiling for the federal government, which had given cause for worry. The next factor

---

[229] Wilhelm Vocke, 'Sound money for savers', 12 May 1950, DBPA, no. 1242, pp. 3–5.
[230] Ibid., pp. 5–6.
[231] See, for example, 'Ein Lob dem deutschen Sparer', *Hamburger Abendblatt*, 13 May 1950; and 'Die Notenbank kann nicht zaubern', *Frankfurter Allgemeine Zeitung*, 13 May 1950.

was the government's work creation programmes designed to combat unemployment. These had shaken confidence in the currency. And the reason listed as number one? The increasing uncertainty surrounding the Bundesbank Law.[232]

The Korean Crisis

The Bundesbank Law debate, however, was blindsided by two major events during the course of 1950 and 1951. The first was West Germany's balance of payments crisis, sparked by the Korean War. The second event was the decision of the Allied authorities to transfer monetary sovereignty to the West German state.

In early 1950, the economy experienced an upturn in business activity and the price level started to rise. The threat of deflation, and with it references to the Great Depression, was passing. Yet the Korean War, starting in June of that year, transformed West Germany's fragile economic condition into the state's first balance of payments emergency. Cold War tensions ran high. As the historian Volker Berghahn observes, it is 'important to appreciate fully the feeling of panic which the Korean events unleashed in Washington and in Western Europe. Was it not quite possible that divided Germany would soon become a "second Korea"?'[233] With these fears in mind, the conflict sparked panic buying and hoarding among segments of the population. Flows of imports surged as a result.[234] This development was amplified by West Germany's recent accession to the European Payments Union (EPU), an organisation inspired by the Marshall Plan and one that liberalised trade between member countries.[235] Companies were thus allowed to import large quantities of raw materials amid efforts to replace their depleted stock after the war.

The result was a substantial deficit in the balance of payments. The central bank found it difficult to withstand this strain. The West German crisis assumed international dimensions given the state's importance to the fortunes of Western Europe at the time. Both Erhard and the BdL began to face sustained pressure both at home and abroad to abandon

---

[232] Wilhelm Vocke to Stephen Szymczak, 24 May 1950, DBHA, B330/2045, p. 1.

[233] Volker Berghahn, *The Americanisation of West German industry, 1945–1973* (Leamington Spa, 1986), p. 135. See also the detailed account – in a subsection entitled 'Germany – a second Korea?' in Schwarz, *Die Ära Adenauer. Gründerjahre der Republik. 1949–1957*, pp. 104–19.

[234] Emminger, *D-Mark, Dollar, Währungskrisen*, pp. 48–50.

[235] Monika Dickhaus, 'The West German central bank and the construction of an international monetary system during the 1950s', *Financial History Review*, Vol. 5, No. 2 (1998), pp. 167–8.

the road to liberalisation and re-establish price controls and import quotas.[236] These external pressures created a politically charged atmosphere. They made it even more difficult for the monetary authority to defend its independence. West Germany secured a credit line from the EPU that allowed to it survive financially, if still somewhat precariously.[237]

All the while, the Bundesbank Law debate was underway. These international difficulties, coupled with Schäffer's drive to boost employment in the economy by means of work creation schemes, placed enormous political pressure on the BdL. Its independence vis-à-vis Bonn was still safe under Allied jurisdiction. But for how long? West German elites knew the Allies would withdraw from the monetary sphere at some point in time. The only question was when.

Lobbying efforts resumed on the part of the BdL. Vocke sent another report to several cabinet ministers and Bundesrat officials, calling for central bank independence. The chairman admitted, though, that 'political changes in most countries have led to an elimination of central bank independence: in totalitarian countries, the central bank is an instrument of the state's will; in democratic countries, the measures of war and their consequences have led to a curtailment of independence'.[238] Sharing his observations in private, one central bank council member confided to Vocke, 'the facts do not lie in our favour'.[239]

And so the BdL's efforts found little success. Both Adenauer and Schäffer were determined to place the central bank under the government's aegis. A second proposal was drawn up by the finance ministry and completed on 5 September 1950.[240] The draft adopted an even harder stance against the central bank's independence in comparison to the first one earlier in the year. Tellingly, this time, the finance ministry reverted to lessons from the inter-war era to ground the legal provisions

---

[236] The Korean crisis is best outlined in the series of essays published in 1986 by the Ludwig-Erhard-Stiftung. See Ludwig-Erhard-Stiftung, *Die Korea-Krise als ordnungspolitische Herausforderung der deutschen Wirtschaftspolitik. Texte und Dokumente* (Stuttgart, 1986). For shorter accounts, see Abelshauser, *Die langen Fünfziger Jahre*, pp. 19–21; van Hook, *Rebuilding Germany*, pp. 213–20; and Nicholls, *Freedom with responsibility*, pp. 270–99.

[237] Emminger, *D-Mark, Dollar, Währungskrisen*, pp. 50–1; see also Erin E. Jacobsson, *A life for sound money. Per Jacobsson. His Biography* (Oxford, 1979), pp. 236–45.

[238] Vocke to Erhard et al., 25 Aug. 1950.

[239] Otto Veit was responding to a draft of the report that was later sent. He was referring to the independence of the Federal Reserve System in America, where, upon closer look, even the American central bank was not as independent as it appeared on paper. See Otto Veit to Wilhelm Vocke, 3 Aug. 1950, DBHA, B330/2049.

[240] 'Entwurf eines Gesetzes über die Währungs- und Notenbank des Bundes' (Bundesbankgesetz)', 5 Sep. 1950, BAK, B136/1199.

outlined in the draft. It did so in the *Begründung*, a statement of grounds that preceded the legal provisions. Ultimately, it was the federal government and parliament that bore responsibility for economic policy, the *Begründung* argued. 'A central bank, one that is autonomous with respect to its currency- and credit policy, is no guarantee for a unified economic policy on occasions when the opinions of the government and central bank diverge.'

> The government must therefore be allowed a sphere of influence over the central bank, as the adherence of central bank policy to the general economic policy is required. The experience of the past, in particular that of the Reichsbank, does not speak against this point. Germany has indeed experienced two episodes in which the central bank was dependent on the state and in which the currency collapsed. In both cases, however, the destruction of the currency came about because the government abused its influence with respect to the Reichsbank as a result of war and, concomitantly, its cash requirements in the form of unlimited borrowing.
>
> But this does not mean that any form of state influence – including that of a democratic state with parliamentary oversight – poses a danger for the stability of the currency … It should not be overlooked that Germany, before 1933, when the Reichsbank was independent of government influence, had been led into a difficult economic crisis, not least because of the lack of agreement between central bank and state policy.[241]

What's more, the finance ministry's new draft proposed that the federal government, in conjunction with the Bundesrat, would be able to determine the location of the new Bundesbank.[242] Both Schäffer and Adenauer had in mind Cologne, a city that neighboured the capital Bonn.[243] Furthermore, the new federal bank would be required to comply with the economic policy of the government in the completion of its task, and that guidelines for monetary and credit policy would be determined by the federal government.[244] The proposal of a *Beirat*, the interest group advisory body, remained.[245]

The idea of a federal arbitration committee stayed put, too. But it was now altered, giving the government a decidedly stronger say. The committee was to be formed with six members: the chancellor, the finance minister, the economics minister, the two central bank chairmen and a

---

[241] 'Begründung – Entwurf. Gesetz über die Währungs- und Notenbank des Bundes (Bundesbankgesetz)', Sep. 1950, BAK, B102/5648 II, pp. 3–5.

[242] 'Entwurf eines Gesetzes über die Währungs- und Notenbank des Bundes' (Bundesbankgesetz)', p. 1.

[243] Karl Bernard to Fritz Schäffer, 23 Sep. 1950, BAK, B136/1199, p. 3.

[244] 'Entwurf eines Gesetzes über die Währungs- und Notenbank des Bundes' (Bundesbankgesetz)', pp. 1–2.

[245] Ibid., pp. 11–12.

Beirat official. The committee would decide by majority voting and, in cases of a tied decision, the chancellor, as chair of the committee, would have the final decision.[246] The federal president was to confirm the appointments of the two central bank chairmen and could dismiss them.[247] In short, the provisions outlined in the September 1950 were intended to eliminate the Bundesbank's independence. In cases of disagreement, the monetary authority would be compelled to follow the direction of the state.

Bernard, acting in his capacity as chairman of the council, wrote a letter of protest to Schäffer. Basing his comments heavily on the BdL's first counterproposal back in April, Bernard saw fit to mention that the central bank council spoke out 'unanimously' against the government's proposal of an arbitration committee.[248] Less than a week after penning this letter, Bernard took to the public sphere to state his case. In late September 1950, the chairman stepped on to the podium and, among other items, spoke about the 'problem of independence', stressing the need for central bank independence as a brake for government profligacy.[249] The text of the speech does not survive. But it is quite probable that his comments were inspired by the implications of the finance ministry's latest draft of the Bundesbank Law.

Bernard was not the only one unhappy with the new draft. Schäffer had divided the cabinet with it. His vision of the central bank was a federalised one. On this point, he could be assured to receive the support of the Bundesrat, which represented *Länder* interests. But now both Erhard and Thomas Dehler, the justice minister, came out strongly for an independent, centralised monetary authority.[250] The division in the cabinet resulted in Adenauer commissioning an inter-coalition committee, chaired by CDU politician Hugo Scharnberg. The committee was assigned to iron out differences between the coalition partners in the cabinet. Vocke and Bernard were invited to attend one of the sessions to express their views.[251] Both men were united in their support of central bank independence, but differed as to the structure of the new Bundesbank. Vocke pushed for a centralised structure.[252] By contrast, Bernard

[246] Ibid., pp. 10–11.   [247] Ibid., pp. 8–9.   [248] Bernard to Schäffer, 23 Sep. 1950.

[249] 'Probleme des Kreditwesens', *Frankfurter Rundschau*, 29 Sep. 1950. See also 'Unabhängige Notenbank', *Frankfurter Allgemeine Zeitung*, 30 Sep. 1950.

[250] Hentschel, 'Die Entstehung des Bundesbankgesetzes 1949–1957. Politische Kontroversen und Konflikte: Teil I', p. 13.

[251] Dürre, 'Vermerk über die Sitzung des interfraktionellen Ausschusses der Regierungsparteien für die Beratung des Entwurfs zum Bundesbankgesetz am 23.11.50', 25 Nov. 1950, BAK, B102/5706.

[252] As noted in Vocke to Scharnberg, 23 Jan. 1953.

argued for the maintenance of the decentralised system, which, he stressed, had proved its worth in recent years.

Intriguingly, Bernard argued that a decentralised central bank could act as a bulwark against future governments dominated by the SPD, should that political party ever take the reins of federal power in Bonn.[253] In this sense, Bernard pitched the idea of an independent central bank, one reinforced with a decentralised structure, as a force to keep leftist trends at bay. A ballast against populist, democratic pressures.

Certainly, Bernard had cause for worry. Since 1948, the SPD had continually attacked the policies of the BdL. Articles condemning both the BdL's independence and its monetary 'orthodoxy', still stained with the apparent mistakes of the inter-war era, featured often in the party's newspaper, *Neuer Vorwärts*.[254] In the Bundestag, Kurt Schumacher, the SPD leader, made no secret of his dislike of the BdL's orthodoxy – a point that chimed with the opinions of some CDU politicians, too.[255] While he never expressed a clear position on central bank independence, the idea of an independent monetary authority clearly did not fit with the SPD leader's conception of 'economic democracy'.[256]

But where Schumacher was silent, others stepped forward. One SPD politician, Hellmut Kalbitzer, went so far as to accuse the central bank of being a 'shadow government' during a parliamentary debate.[257] The central bank, in the words of Erik Nölting, an SPD economics expert, sat happily upon its autonomy while snubbing its nose at politicians.[258] This anger found its manifestation in internal policy positions too.

---

[253] Dürre, 'Vermerk über die Sitzung des interfraktionellen Ausschusses der Regierungsparteien für die Beratung des Entwurfs zum Bundesbankgesetz am 23.11.50', p. 3.

[254] See, for example, 'Demokratisch kontrollierte oder autoritäre Bundesbank?', *Neuer Vorwärts*, 1 May 1950; 'Wirtschaftspolitische Forderungen der SPD', *Neuer Vorwärts*, 6 Apr. 1951; and 'Der Bundesnotenbank-Gesetzentwurf', *Neuer Vorwärts*, 5 Oct. 1951.

[255] For Kurt Schumacher's remarks, see 'Deutscher Bundestag. 6. Sitzung. Bonn, Mittwoch, den 21. September 1949', p. 39. See http://dipbt.bundestag.de/doc/btp/01/01006.pdf. Last accessed on 20 December 2018. For the remarks of Franz Etzel, a CDU politician, see 'Deutscher Bundestag – 8. Sitzung. Bonn, Dienstag, den 27. September 1949', p. 141. See http://dipbt.bundestag.de/doc/btp/01/01008.pdf. Last accessed on 20 December 2018.

[256] Willy Albrecht, *Kurt Schumacher: Ein Leben für den demokratischen Sozialismus* (Bonn, 1985), pp. 47–54; for more on the SPD's 'economic democracy' in the early years of the Federal Republic, see van Hook, *Rebuilding Germany*, pp. 95–6, 255–68.

[257] 'Deutscher Bundestag – 108. Sitzung. Bonn, Freitag, den 15. Dezember 1950', p. 4062. See http://dipbt.bundestag.de/doc/btp/01/01108.pdf. Last accessed on 20 December 2018.

[258] 'Deutscher Bundestag – 75. Und 76. Sitzung. Bonn, Freitag, den 14. Juli 1950', p. 2703. See http://dipbt.bundestag.de/doc/btp/01/01075.pdf. Last accessed on 20 December 2018.

During this period, the economics committee of the SPD met to discuss its position vis-à-vis the Bundesbank Law. The discussion was to remain confidential. But the minutes clearly indicate that the SPD, though itself divided by moderates and hardliners, was against the idea of an independent central bank.[259] The government's economic policy had to come before the concerns of central bank policy, the committee contended, evoking the lesson learned from the Weimar chancellor Heinrich Brüning, 'who sacrificed the economy to the currency'.[260]

Although the SPD would not enter the federal government until 1966, and even then only as a junior coalition partner, this policy stance was an important one. The SPD was the major opposition party in the Bundestag throughout the 1950s.[261] And it was largely seen as an economically credible one, too: according to public opinion data in 1952, a clear majority of West Germans thought that economic development since 1949 would have either been the same, or better, had the SPD won the election instead of Adenauer's coalition.[262]

So much for the political opposition. What was the position of leading interest groups with respect to central bank independence? The sources for the early years of the Federal Republic are sparse. Although the Bundesverband der Deutschen Industrie (BDI), the influential peak organisation for industrial interests, largely praised the actions of the BdL in the years following 1948, it maintained a cautious position with respect to the idea of an independent monetary authority. Commenting on the Bundesbank Law discussion, its annual report for 1950–1 stated that the BDI's position was: 'independence [of the central bank] so far as possible; but not to the extent that it thwarts the economic policy of the authorities put in place by the constitution'.[263] This point was not elaborated upon in the report. There is no evidence, however, that the BDI directly intervened in the Bundesbank Law debate during this time;

---

[259] The members were divided on the question of organisation. See Harold Koch and Rudolf Pass, 'Protokoll zur Tagung des Wirtschaftspolitischen Ausschusses beim Parteivorstand der SPD am 1. und 2. Juni 1951', no date, Archiv der sozialen Demokratie, Friedrich-Ebert-Stiftung [AdsD], 2/PVBF000003.

[260] Ibid., p. 2.

[261] For more on the SPD acting as a 'constructive opposition' during the Adenauer era, see Heinrich Potthoff and Susanne Miller, *Kleine Geschichte der SPD 1848–2002* (Bonn, 2002), pp. 199–222.

[262] More precisely, 18 per cent believed the SPD would have done a better job, and 36 per cent thought there would have been no difference. See 'Die Stimmung im Bundesgebiet. Eine SPD-Regierung?: Umfrage 44', *Institut für Demoskopie*, Jul. 1952, BAK, B145/4222, p. 1.

[263] 'Geschäftsbericht des Bundesverbandes der Deutschen Industrie, 1 April 1950–31 Mai 1951, vorgelegt der 2. ordentlichen Mitgliederversammlung in München am 26. Juni 1951', *Bundesverband der Deutschen Industrie*, 26 Jun. 1951, p. 30.

this is likely because industrial interests were embroiled in other, more immediate matters, such as the Co-determination Law, a piece of legislation that sought to ease labour tensions, as well as early discussions surrounding Erhard's anti-cartel legislation.[264]

And the trade unions? Again, the sources are somewhat thin. But a report on the central bank, published in 1951 by the Wissenschaftliches Institut der Gewerkschaften, or Academic Institute of the Trade Unions, is revealing.[265] The think tank was linked to the Deutscher Gewerkschaftsbund, or German Trade Union Confederation, an umbrella organisation for several unions. In a section entitled 'Comparison of the central bank system with the earlier Reichsbank system', the institute called not only for the elimination of foreign influence on the central bank, but also 'the restoration of state influence on the central bank'.[266] Yet the pamphlet is rather vague on this point. It called for a 'a position of limited independence with respect to the government', but stressed that the central bank should be obliged to follow the direction of the government's economic policy.[267]

What is interesting, though, is that the authors of the trade union report used *Die Bundesbank: Aufbau und Aufgaben* as one of their sources, a pamphlet whose origins can be traced back to the economics journalist Muthesius who worked on behalf of the BdL's press department (indeed, the pamphlet was quoted at length at the start of this chapter).[268] Though the publication was used by the trade union think tank to make a point related to the Reichsbank in the time of the gold standard, its very use suggests that Muthesius's publication was influential in so far as that other elites, even those on the left of the political spectrum, used it to ground their opinions concerning the wider Bundesbank Law debate.

And indeed, back to the debate at hand. The Korean crisis resulted in a test for the BdL's policies and priorities. Yet Vocke came to realise that the Korean crisis was also an opportunity for the central bank. Writing to Adenauer, the chairman argued that, given that the West German state was in 'dangerous and stormy waters', the federal government should work towards fostering confidence in the central bank. If the state felt it necessary to put the Bundesbank Law on the agenda, then this legislation should be written in a manner that increased confidence in the central

---

[264] For more on the Co determination Law and the early anti-cartel debate, see Berghahn, *The Americanisation of West German industry*, pp. 204–30 and pp. 155–72 respectively; and Wiesen, *West German industry and the challenge of the Nazi past*, pp. 180–8.

[265] See Wirtschaftswissenschaftliches Institut der Gewerkschaften, *Notenbank im Umbau: Föderal oder Zentral?* (Cologne, 1951).

[266] Ibid., pp. 41, 42.   [267] Ibid., pp. 45–6.   [268] Ibid., p. 43.

bank and its ability to protect the currency.[269] In short, Vocke implied, the Bundesbank Law should ensure central bank independence.

Nevertheless, at a time of economic trouble, political pressure and legal uncertainty, the BdL was forced to walk a tightrope. The central bank decided in September 1950 to increase the minimum reserve requirements for banks, a move that tightened credit in the economy.[270] Shortly afterwards, the central bank council intended to follow this decision by increasing the discount rate from 4 to 6 per cent, and the Lombard rate 5 to 7 per cent. Adenauer was infuriated by the BdL's intention. In an unprecedented move, the chancellor called the BdL's decision-making body to convene in Bonn in October 1950.[271] The statesman forcefully argued against the hike in interest rates. But Bernard and Vocke rebuffed the chancellor's arguments. The central bank council held steady in its decision and increased the interest rates.[272]

It was the first direct clash between the central bank and the federal government. In the words of Otmar Emminger, later president of the Bundesbank, it 'was undoubtedly a historic milestone in the relations between the central bank and the federal government – a highly visible signal of the independence of the German central bank'.[273] Whether it was seen as such at the time was another matter. With a draft of the Bundesbank Law in flux, the incident merely reaffirmed Adenauer and Schäffer's drive to place the central bank under the thumb of the federal government. Personal animosities also played a role. The chancellor had little taste for Vocke, reportedly describing him as 'an over-cooled icebox'.[274] Newspaper reports suggested that Adenauer was eager to pass through legislation as quickly as possible.[275]

On 7 November 1950, Vocke wrote to Erhard confidentially asking for his support. Once again, the chairman outlined the logic behind allowing the central bank to remain independent. Vocke highlighted his concerns about the timing of the legislation and the danger of having such a debate in heated circumstances. The legislation should be kicked down the road, the central banker argued, to allow some breathing space for

---

[269] Wilhelm Vocke to Konrad Adenauer, 14 Oct. 1950, DBHA, B330/2011, pp. 5–6.
[270] BdL central bank council minutes, 20–21 Sep. 1950, DBHA, B330/31/1.
[271] Karl Bernard to members of *Land* central banks and the president on the Berlin central bank, 24 Oct. 1950, DBHA, B330/2014. See also Emminger, *D-Mark, Dollar, Währungskrisen*, pp. 13–14.
[272] BdL central bank council minutes (Bonn), 26 Oct. 1950, DBHA, B330/32/2.
[273] Emminger, *D-Mark, Dollar, Währungskrisen*, p. 14.
[274] Ibid., p. 463 (footnote). For more on the relationship between Vocke and Adenauer, see Marsh, *The Bundesbank*, pp. 179–80.
[275] See, for instance, 'Notenbankgesetz vor Verabschiedung', *Frankfurter Allgemeine Zeitung*, 1 Nov. 1950.

policymakers.[276] During this period, von der Lippe also provided the economics minister with news articles favourable to the central bank's position amid efforts to keep Erhard informed and updated.[277]

All the while, it was politically expedient for Schäffer to play along with the narratives of the two inflations. In his budget speech, the first budget speech of the Federal Republic, Schäffer declared that, '[t]he legislature of the Basic Law, with regard to the guidelines of fiscal policy, has taken to heart the lessons stemming from the inflationary experiences of 1918–23 and the currency reform of 1948. It wanted to protect the German people and savers from similar disappointments for ever more.'[278]

Schäffer was eager to be seen as fiscally prudent. The finance minister was particularly sensitive to bad publicity. When one journalist accused Schäffer, following the latter's budget speech, of starting yet another repressed inflation, the finance minister protested to the publication's editor. Moreover, Schäffer requested Vocke to use whatever influence he had to make sure such comments did not appear again in that particular publication, a comment that hints that the finance minister was aware that the chairman played the media.[279] Vocke quickly disassociated himself from the journalist's remarks.[280]

On another occasion, Schäffer took the BdL to task for its December 1950 report, which contained critical remarks about the federal budget. The central bank monthly report in question proved to be the source material for a news article that challenged Schäffer's budget, arguing that 'the great inflations have never been sparked by the banks, rather always by the finance ministers'.[281] It was with 'astonishment', Schäffer wrote to Vocke, that he found the central bank's monthly report encouraging such overtly political views.[282] At the very least, these two incidents demonstrate that the BdL faced pressure behind the scenes.

[276] Wilhelm Vocke to Ludwig Erhard, 7 Nov. 1950, DBHA, B330/2021 I, pp. 4–5.
[277] Viktor von der Lippe to Ludwig Erhard, 8 Nov. 1950, DBHA, B330/2021 I; see also Viktor von der Lippe to Ludwig Erhard, 20 Nov. 1950, DBHA, B330/2021 I.
[278] Fritz Schäffer, 'Erster Jahreshaushaltsplan: Mitteilung an die Presse', 10 Nov. 1950, DBHA, B330/2043, p. 1.
[279] See the commentary piece in question 'Soziale Marktwirtschaft in Gefahr', *Wirtschaftspolitische Gesellschaft von 1947*, no. 94, 25 Nov. 1950, DBHA, B330/2043; see also Fritz Schäffer to Herbert Gross, 5 Dec. 1950, DBHA, B330/2043; and Fritz Schäffer to Wilhelm Vocke, 8 Jan. 1951, DBHA, B330/2043.
[280] Wilhelm Vocke to Fritz Schäffer, 13 Jan. 1951, DBHA, B330/2043.
[281] 'Fehlbetrag im Bundessäckel trotz hoher Steuereinnahmen', *Wiesbadener Kurier*, 7 Feb. 1951.
[282] Fritz Schäffer to Wilhelm Vocke, 10 Feb. 1951, DBHA, B330/2043.

By February 1951, given the sustained controversy surrounding Schäffer's Bundesbank Law drafts, the finance minister gave way and opted to lose the idea of an arbitration committee in cases of disagreement between Bonn and Frankfurt. Instead, during that month, the finance ministry published a new draft, one that sought to accommodate cases of disputes in a more co-operative manner.[283] This time, the central bank council would be forced to vote a second time in instances when the government objected to policy decisions. This second vote, however, would require a qualified majority to pass. According to the draft, both the finance minister and economics minister could both attend and vote at this second meeting. Indeed, the two cabinet members would, alongside the two chairmen, form a small subsection of the vote, whereby each of their votes counted as two votes. So, these four men would have eight votes in total, allowing for a sizeable government influence on the central bank council.[284] This draft, which continued to propose a decentralised central bank, failed to establish a consensus surrounding the Bundesbank Law. The battle lines, aided by the lobbying efforts of the BdL, had become hardened. Nevertheless, it was during this time that an opportunity presented itself to Schäffer. That opportunity came in the form of the Allied powers.

The Transition Law

On 6 March 1951, the Allied High Commission, the Allied governing body for West Germany, informed Adenauer of its intention to withdraw from the 'administrative responsibilities conferred upon it by military government legislation as regards internal banking and currency management'.[285] In other words, they were withdrawing from the monetary sphere. There was a catch, however. The Allies expected the West German state to enact legislation as soon as possible to allow this transfer to happen.[286] As Bibow convincingly argues, it was the intention of the Allies that the West German government assume responsibility for monetary policy; their goal was not to create a vacuum of power in which the central bank would remain independent.[287]

---

[283] 'Entwurf eines Bundesgesetzes über die Errichtung einer Bundesbank', 21 Feb. 1951, BAK, B136/1200.
[284] Ibid., pp. 10–11.
[285] André François-Poncet to Konrad Adenauer, 6 Mar. 1951, DBHA, B330/6305/1.
[286] Ibid.
[287] Bibow, 'Zur (Re-)Etablierung zentralbankpolitischer Institutionen und Traditionen in Westdeutschland', pp. 514–16.

Both Adenauer and Schäffer kept this information secret. The evidence suggests that the BdL leadership discovered its existence only at the end of March.[288] The cabinet was informed some days earlier, on 20 March 1950, and, because of the polarised debate surrounding the Bundesbank Law, it opted to go for a temporary law. The cabinet expected that this stop-gap solution would be replaced by the actual Bundesbank Law over the coming year.[289] Schäffer saw an opportunity and proposed a simple change to the Allied military law. Referring to the ABC's oversight with respect to the BdL, Schäffer proposed switching the term 'Allied Banking Commission' with the words 'federal government'.[290] This would have imposed government control over the central bank.

The central bank, furious, submitted a counter-response arguing that 'a right to give instructions in the hand of the federal government can in no way be compared with the existing right of instruction held by the Allied Banking Commission, since [this alteration] amounts to making the most important borrower of the central bank system the master of that very central bank'.[291] In supporting this economic argument, the central bank council once again turned to Germany's turbulent monetary history. 'The central bank has already detailed earlier the crucial importance of the principle of the central bank's independence with a manipulated currency – especially in Germany, whose currency has been completely shattered within a generation twice through inflations caused by the state. It is in this context that the council argues a government veto is something completely different to the previous right of instruction of the Allied Banking Commission.'[292]

The following days were crucial. Schäffer and the BdL leadership met the day prior to the key cabinet meeting in which Adenauer sought an agreement.[293] On 3 April 1950, Bernard and the vice president of the directorate, Wilhelm Könneker, represented the BdL at the cabinet.[294]

---

[288] Wilhelm Vocke to Karl Bernard, 28 Mar. 1951, DBHA, B330/2016.

[289] Ursala Hüllbüsch (ed.), *Die Kabinettsprotokolle der Bundesregierung, Band 4: 1951* (Boppard am Rhein, 1988), p. 259.

[290] 'Entwurf Gesetz über die Bestimmung der Bank deutscher Länder zur Währungs- und Notenbank des Bundes', Mar. 1951, DBHA, B330/2016.

[291] 'Entwurf einer Entschliessung des Zentralbankrats zu dem Entwurf eines Übergangsgesetzes über die Bestimmung der Bank deutscher Länder zur Währungs- und Notenbank des Bundes vom 20. März 1951', 28 Mar. 1951, DBHA, B330/2016; see also 'Stellungnahme des Zentralbankrats der Bank deutscher Länder', 29 Mar. 1951, DBHA, B330/2016, p. 3.

[292] BdL central bank council minutes, 29 Mar. 1951, DBHA, B330/41/1.

[293] 'Entwurf entspricht inhaltlich der am 2. April 1951 zwischen Schäffer, Könneker und Bernard erzielten Verständigung', 2 Apr. 1951, DBHA, B330/2016.

[294] Hüllbüsch, *Die Kabinettsprotokolle der Bundesregierung, Band 4: 1951*, pp. 280–1.

Bernard argued forcefully against Schäffer's existing draft that sought to replace the ABC with the federal government. In doing so, he stressed the harmful impact that this would have on 'public opinion' and the deutschmark, a currency whose value that central bank had worked so hard to defend.[295]

A compromise, however, was reached by the afternoon, outside of the cabinet meeting.[296] Schäffer withdrew his demand for a government veto. By 18 April 1951, the cabinet approved the wording of the new Transition Law.[297] As a concession to Schäffer, the BdL agreed to become 'obliged to support the general economic policy of the federal government and support it within the remit of the central bank's duties'.[298] Yet such wording was vague. And in effect, it allowed the central bank to remain independent of government instruction. Bonn officials were now allowed to attend central bank meetings. But their veto powers were restricted to delaying the council's decisions by up to eight days.[299] The Transition Law, then, provided no resolution mechanism by which disputes between Bonn and Frankfurt would be resolved by formal process.

During a parliamentary debate concerning the Transition Law, Schäffer declared that the legislation should suffice until 31 December 1951, by which time the Bundesbank Law will have likely passed.[300] What the federal government did not know, however, was that it would take until 1957 to pass the Bundesbank Law, leaving a period of six years for the BdL to assert its independence in the minds of the West German people. Yet even the parliamentary debate concerning the Transition Law was revealing. The discussion surrounding central bank independence compelled one politician – a member of the small Bavaria Party – to evoke the experiences of Germany's history of inflation, and the subsequent need to safeguard the central bank's autonomy. 'We have not yet forgotten the time of the Reichsbank and its president [Rudolf] Havenstein', he cried, before continuing to detail the consequences of the second inflation too.[301] The law passed through parliament in August 1951.[302]

[295] Ibid., p. 280.   [296] Ibid., p. 281.   [297] Ibid., p. 313.
[298] As stated in the Transition Law. For a copy of the legislation, see 'Übergangsgesetz zur Änderung des Gesetzes über die Errichtung der Bank deutscher Länder', Deutsche Bundesbank, *30 Jahre Deutsche Bundesbank*, p. 108.
[299] Ibid.
[300] 'Deutscher Bundestag – 147. Sitzung. Bonn, Mittwoch, den 6. Juni 1951', p. 5878. See http://dipbt.bundestag.de/doc/btp/01/01147.pdf. Last accessed on 20 December 2018.
[301] Ibid., p. 5879.
[302] 'Übergangsgesetz zur Änderung des Gesetzes über die Errichtung der Bank deutscher Länder', Deutsche Bundesbank, *30 Jahre Deutsche Bundesbank*, p. 108.

A month after the Transition Law was agreed upon, both Bernard and Vocke took to the stage. Bernard, for his part, delivered a speech defending the BdL's policy decisions and overall performance in the previous years. For instance, when focusing on the dire economic situation of 1949, Bernard stressed that the references to the dire years of 1931–2 were completely unjustified.[303] And Vocke, for his part, delivered a speech at a credit conference organised by Muthesius's *Die Zeitschrift für das gesamte Kreditwesen*. The fight to maintain the central bank's independence had been won – for now – but there was more time to promulgate the central bank's message. Vocke appealed directly to the saver, a German constituent that transcended all social and religious divides.

The central banker's appeal to the saver was all the more resonant in a state that eventually became home to 3.6 million refugees fleeing Germany's former eastern territories.[304] These people had left behind their homes, alongside much of their assets, and had a vested interest in the maintenance of the currency's stability amid efforts to rebuild their wealth.[305] The expellees from Germany's former east were not alone; much of the population in the west had also lost property and wealth amid the Allied bombing and ground campaigns. They were keen to rebuild their lives, homes and savings. Everyone, Vocke argued, had an interest in a stable future. 'It is always the mass of workers, clerks and small savers who pay for an inflation', he said. 'That is a thing which we have thoroughly learnt twice in our lifetime.'[306] Stability was becoming synonymous with an independent central bank.

Conclusion

An institutional divide in West Germany, one left behind by the Allied authorities, created a power struggle over the future of the state's central bank. This clash of interests centred on the Bundesbank Law, and created a public debate in which West German elites discerned lessons from their monetary past amid efforts to ground their political arguments with historical weight and context.

[303] Karl Bernard, 'Währungspolitik und Außenhandel', *Bank deutscher Länder Auszüge aus Presseartikeln*, No. 52, 4 May 1951, DBPA, no. 75, p. 1. See also 'Wieder Bernard', *Die Zeit*, 17 May 1951.
[304] See Kramer, *The West German economy*, p. 213.
[305] For a more detailed discussion concerning expellees from the former German east, see Abelshauser, *Die langen Fünfziger Jahre*, pp. 33–42, esp. pp. 35–6.
[306] Vocke, 'Address at the Conference on Credit Policy organised by *Die Zeitschrift für das gesamte Kreditwesen*', p. 6.

A variety of contradictory historical narratives circulated and competed during these early years. The power struggle acted as the underlying dynamic propelling the use of these narratives. The BdL, and its allies, propounded the lessons of Germany's two inflations. Its political opponents stressed the troubled record of the Reichsbank during the Great Depression. Both sides presented a skewed version of events, one suited to their political interests. And at the dawn of the new republic, it remained to be seen which history would emerge triumphant.

Vocke came to gradually personify the BdL in the public sphere. In parliament, his surname would eventually become a byword for the monetary authority. And yet Vocke was also closely identified with the inter-war Reichsbank. A 'Reichsbank group', according to one media report, dominated the central bank council. Certainly, there was no *legal* continuity between the inter-war central bank and post-war monetary authority. But this was not the case for the BdL's reputation in the media. Vocke did not shy away from his past, controversial though it was. Rather, he embraced it with full force. The 1939 Reichsbank memorandum, having acquired its moral sheen at Nuremberg, was put to work and used as evidence that Vocke had the courage to say 'no' to profligate governments. Vocke derived part of his credibility as a central banker from his inter-war record.

As Hentschel and Bibow note, the Transition Law would prove to be a crucial step in prejudicing what eventually emerged to be the Bundesbank's independence vis-à-vis the federal government.[307] The lack of an adequate resolution mechanism in the legislation – one that forced the central bank and federal government to sit down at a table and reach agreement by means of formal process – meant that conflicts between Bonn and Frankfurt were likely to spill into the public sphere. The Transition Law, then, enshrined the institutional clash between the central bank and government in German law. It failed to address the divide left behind by the Allies in a satisfactory manner. And in failing to do so, it reaffirmed the underlying dynamic propelling the use of inter-war historical narratives.

It would only be a matter of time, then, before the differences between the BdL and the government would erupt again. The central bank did not have to wait long. In 1956, it was faced with a challenge laid down by Adenauer.

---

[307] Hentschel, 'Die Entstehung des Bundesbankgesetzes 1949–1957. Politische Kontroversen und Konflikte: Teil I', p. 18; and Bibow, 'On the origin and rise of central bank independence in West Germany', p. 167.

3 Adenauer's Challenge: The 'Gürzenich Affair' and the Bank deutscher Länder, 1956–1957

Introduction

In March 1958, Wilhelm Vocke stood before a monetary conference held at Arden House, a grand manor some 48 miles north of New York City.[1] 'Publicity is one of the sharpest weapons in the arsenal of a central bank', declared the former directorate chairman of the Bank deutscher Länder (BdL).

It should not be restricted to statistics which only interest experts and scientists … Publicity of the central bank means not only full sincerity but also wisdom, tact and sometimes courage. A warning by the monetary authority in the right moment, showing plainly the consequences, will have a salutary and beneficial effect.[2]

With almost ten years at the helm of West Germany's central bank behind him, Vocke could look back on a successful tenure. He had been the chairman of its executive body. The monetary authority, forged by the Allies in the aftermath of the Second World War, played a crucial role in overseeing the economic reconstruction of a shattered nation. By 1958, West Germany had been reaccepted into the international community and woven into the very fabric of European economic life. The nation's exports were booming, unemployment was minimal, and the deutschmark, not even a decade old, had already assumed the status of one of Europe's 'hard' currencies.

This was a far cry from the spring of 1948, the year in which the BdL was established in Frankfurt. Back then, several cities were still in ruins. The German economy was still paralysed by price controls and rationing. There were shortages of the most basic of goods. The reichsmark was worthless. And Germany was still under occupation too. The Allied

---

[1] See 'Transportation Guide. Arden House. Harriman Campus of Columbia University', 1958, Deutsche Bundesbank Historisches Archiv [DBHA], B330/6307.
[2] Wilhelm Vocke, 'Address before the monetary conference at Arden House on 27 March 1958', 27 Mar. 1958, Deutsche Bundesbank Pressearchiv [DBPA], no. 1242, p. 4.

military authorities – Britain, France, the United States of America and the Soviet Union – bickered amongst themselves over how to proceed with the 'German question'. Uncertainty reigned and the future looked bleak. Yet West Germany experienced a transformation in those ten years. A lot had changed – but not everything. After all, the country's central bank remained independent vis-à-vis the federal government in Bonn.

Vocke, though recently retired, stood triumphant before his audience. Not long before, the BdL had successfully defended itself from a public attack by the chancellor, Konrad Adenauer. Speaking at an annual gathering of industrialists in 1956, the statesman took issue with the central bank's restrictive monetary policy and described its recent interest rate hikes as a 'guillotine' falling upon the German people.[3] 'The central bank council, gentlemen, is completely sovereign from the federal government', Adenauer said. 'It is of course accountable to itself, but here we have an institution that is responsible to no one, not to parliament, not even to a government.'[4] The audience was shocked. One observer present recalled the comments as being the 'sensation of the evening'.[5] But they were more than that.

Adenauer's remarks caused a media scandal. The question of central bank independence had seemingly been settled for years. The provisions of the Transition Law of 1951, originally seen as a temporary stepping stone to the Bundesbank Law – a piece of legislation that would establish a new central bank to replace the BdL – soon came to represent the status quo. The Transition Law meant that West Germany's central bank was effectively independent from government instruction. Moreover, the years prior to Adenauer's speech had been witness to an economic boom over which the independent monetary authority presided. The BdL's autonomy basked in the warm glow of economic growth. Now, however, the central bank's independence, and implicitly the future Bundesbank's autonomy, was back on the political agenda.

In the public uproar that followed, the media sided decisively with the central bank. It was one of Adenauer's few political mistakes. The clash occurred at a sensitive time, when the Bundesbank Law debate was entering its final stages, and another federal election on the horizon. Several historians have already examined what came to be called the

---

[3] Konrad Adenauer, 'Rede von Bundeskanzler Dr. Adenauer am 23. Mai 1956 in Köln', *Bank deutscher Länder Auszüge aus Presseartikeln*, No. 58, 28 May 1956, DBHA, N3/173, p. 1.
[4] Ibid.
[5] Daniel Koerfer, *Kampf ums Kanzleramt: Adenauer und Erhard* (Stuttgart, 1987), p. 117.

'Gürzenich affair' – named after the Cologne venue in which Adenauer launched his attack on the BdL – as well as its political consequences.[6] After all, it is well known that Adenauer, by now an isolated critic of central bank independence, was eventually forced to back down. The Bundesbank Law that passed the next year provided for a largely independent central bank.

But no historian has yet documented the extent to which the 'Gürzenich affair' was important in narrowing – and indeed ossifying – the parameters through which West Germans would interpret their monetary history. Chapter 2 demonstrated the variety of competing historical narratives concerning the inter-war era swirling around the public sphere in the late 1940s and early 1950s. This chapter, however, documents how, in 1956, one version of events triumphed over the others, eventually finding its manifestation in the very provisions of the Bundesbank Law itself.

This is important. Why? Given that the Bundesbank Law provided for no resolution mechanism through which Frankfurt and Bonn could solve disagreements on policy by formal process, it crystallised a power struggle between the two centres. In doing so, the piece of legislation ensured that the institutional divide left behind by the Allied military authorities essentially remained. We have already seen in Chapter 2 how this cleft created an underlying dynamic through which historical narratives of the inter-war era prospered. The provisions in the Bundesbank Law allowed for future public debates concerning the central bank's independence to erupt, in turn providing further instances in which it only seemed natural for West Germans to revert to their country's traumatic history of inflation.

The chapter puts forward four points. First, it contends that the BdL became increasingly confident and assertive as the years progressed. Its reputation had grown steadily since 1951. If Vocke and Karl Bernard, the chairman of the central bank council, were not household names during the early years of the Federal Republic, they were certainly well known

[6] Ibid., pp. 84–127; Hans-Peter Schwarz, *Die Ära Adenauer. Gründerjahre der Republik. 1949–1957 (Geschichte der Bundesrepublik Deutschland, Band 2)* (Stuttgart, 1981), pp. 319–27; Helge Berger, *Konjunkturpolitik im Wirtschaftswunder: Handlungsspielräume und Verhaltensmuster von Bundesbank und Regierung in den 1950er Jahren* (Tübingen, 1997), pp. 217–28; Christian N. Wolz, *Konflikte zwischen der Notenbank und der Regierung in der Bundesrepublik Deutschland 1956–1961* (Stuttgart, 2009), pp. 17–22; Manfred J. M. Neumann, 'Monetary stability: threat and proven response', in Deutsche Bundesbank (ed.), *Fifty years of the Deutsche Mark: central bank and the currency in Germany since 1948* (Oxford, 1999), pp. 289–92; and Helge Berger and Jakob de Haan, 'A state within the state? An event study on the Bundesbank (1948–1973)', *Scottish Journal of Political Economy*, Vol. 46, No. 1 (1999), pp. 25–7.

personalities by 1957. Slowly, the central bank began to shed its image of being a foreign creation. This newfound confidence in part stemmed from its legal status. With the Transition Law of 1951, the Bundestag now enshrined the BdL's independence, albeit by means of altering an Allied occupation law.

A combination of time and economic success lent the monetary authority a sense of legitimacy. The BdL played an important, positive role in the economic boom that characterised the 1950s. And it oversaw the deutschmark, a currency whose success became a symbol of pride in a state where political nationalism remained taboo. The confidence of the central bank's leadership grew alongside the burgeoning economy. When the Federal Republic was established, the BdL stressed in public its co-operative relationship and goodwill to the government. By the mid-1950s, however, Vocke and Bernard regularly took to criticising government policy in the public sphere.

Second, the ongoing political debate concerning the Bundesbank Law continued to incentivise West German elites to confront the country's monetary past and discern from it lessons for political gain. After the Transition Law had, inadvertently, prejudiced the eventual emergence of the Bundesbank's independence from political instruction, the debate quickly shifted to the (still somewhat related) question of the new central bank's structure, and the appointment procedures for its leadership. This was one of the last real avenues through which government authorities could exert influence upon the future Bundesbank.

Who exactly should appoint the members of the monetary authority's decision-making body? This question provoked a power struggle between the federal government and the various state governments, ultimately delaying the emergence of the Bundesbank Law until 1957. Some members of the federal cabinet, such as the economics minister Ludwig Erhard, preferred a centralised Bundesbank, where its leadership could be appointed by the powers that be in Bonn. The state governments, of course, gunned for the maintenance of the hitherto successful structure of the BdL – a decentralised, federal central bank similar to the organisation of the Federal Reserve System in America. Like the question of independence, the question of structure impelled elites to look to the past. Wasn't the inter-war Reichsbank a centralised monetary authority? And was it not the case that the centralised structure of the Reichsbank allowed it to be quickly politicised by a ruthless government? *Länder* government elites continually underlined these points.

The third aspect of the chapter shows how the 'Gürzenich affair' demonstrated the triumph of a certain version of the inter-war past, one that stressed the lessons of Germany's two inflations. In part, this development was a function of the business cycle, in which rising prices, as opposed to a rising unemployment rate, became the main economic concern in the heady days of the West German 'economic miracle'. As a result, the few elites still highlighting the mixed record of the independent Reichsbank under its presidents Hjalmar Schacht and Hans Luther, such as the Bundesverband der Deutschen Industrie (BDI), the industrialist interest group, found themselves in the small minority by 1956. Crucially, the Social Democratic Party (SPD) – the workers' party and major oppositional force in the Bundestag – came out in full support of central bank independence in the aftermath of the 'Gürzenich affair' amid efforts to capitalise on Adenauer's discomfort. And with that pivot, the SPD's references to the actions of the independent Reichsbank during the Great Depression fell by the wayside – at least among the leadership. The parameters of debate, and the references used, had become narrowed to such an extent that few challenged those who propounded the lessons of inflation. In other words, the West German central bank's version of monetary mythology had become the dominant historical narrative in the public sphere. And the provisions outlined in the Bundesbank Law spoke to that mythology.

Finally, the chapter closes with a fourth point. The Bundesbank Law was 'Erhardian' in nature when it came to the relationship between the central bank and federal state. It allowed for a largely independent central bank, but one whose directorate, which sat at the central bank council, was appointed by Bonn. Erhard stressed a close co-operation above all, whereby the state exerted its influence via personal relationships. But this eventual outcome of the Bundesbank Law did not provide for a formal process whereby instances of disagreement could be solved behind closed doors. As a result, spats between Bonn and Frankfurt were likely to spill out into the public sphere from the very start – just as they had done in the years 1950 and 1956. These elite disputes turned into public debates, in which historical narratives of the inter-war era rallied to the Bundesbank's cause. Over time, the Bundesbank Law helped turn an elite debate into a popular one.

Unfinished History: Centralisation or Decentralisation?

After the passage of the Transition Law, the focus of the Bundesbank Law debate switched to the question of the future Bundesbank's structure and organisation. This development occurred, in part, because Fritz Schäffer, the finance minister, used the wording found in the crucial passage of the Transition Law for subsequent drafts of the Bundesbank

Law.[7] This is not to suggest, however, that the issue of independence vis-à-vis state authorities subsided. Far from it. The issue merely assumed another form. As the historian Volker Hentschel observes, if Bonn could not issue the central bank with instructions, or be in a position to veto its decisions, then the question of who appointed the monetary authority's decision-making body assumed an added, crucial importance.[8]

Recall that the BdL predated the establishment of the West German state. When the federal government formed in late 1949, it had no influence whatsoever with respect to who led the central bank. Instead, it was the *Länder* that exerted influence – albeit in an indirect fashion. Each state could appoint one president to lead its state central bank. This official would then attend the central bank council meeting every two weeks at the BdL's building in Frankfurt. It was the central bank council that elected the two chairmen of the monetary authority, Vocke and Bernard. Votes were made by majority decision. The Bundesbank Law, then, was seen by some politicians in Bonn as an opportunity to redress this perceived imbalance between the state and federal levels of government.

To describe this struggle in such simple terms, however, would be misleading. The question of the Bundesbank's structure divided opinion across several levels of government. First, it split the cabinet. Schäffer, a Bavarian and a member of the Christian Social Union (CSU), pushed heavily for a decentralised monetary authority. Erhard, on the other hand, gradually hardened his opposition to the finance minister's plans and lobbied for a centralised Bundesbank akin to the inter-war Reichsbank.[9] Erhard pointed to the Basic Law, or constitution, of West Germany, and argued that a decentralised solution would be unconstitutional.[10] In this respect, the economics minister had the powerful support of the justice minister, Thomas Dehler.[11] The difference in opinion between Erhard and Schäffer took on an added importance in light of the fact that both the finance and economics ministries were pitted against each other, fighting over the control of sphere of money and credit, an area that included responsibility for the Bundesbank Law. Schäffer would eventually lose the remit over the Bundesbank Law to Erhard in March 1952.[12]

---

[7] Christoph Buchheim, 'Die Unabhängigkeit der Bundesbank. Folge eines amerikanischen Oktrois?', *Vierteljahrshefte für Zeitgeschichte*, Vol. 49, No. 1 (2001), p. 24.

[8] Volker Hentschel, 'Die Entstehung des Bundesbankgesetzes 1949–1957. Politische Kontroversen und Konflikte: Teil I', *Bankhistorisches Archiv*, Vol. 14 (1988), pp. 18–19.

[9] Ludwig Erhard to Fritz Schäffer, 12 Oct. 1950, Bundesarchiv, Koblenz [BAK], B102/5706.

[10] Ibid.

[11] Thomas Dehler to Fritz Schäffer, 5 Oct. 1950, BAK, B102/28119 I, pp. 1–3.

[12] Ludwig Erhard to Wilhelm Vocke, 19 Mar. 1952, DBHA, B330/2021 I.

Second, the question divided Adenauer's governing coalition. In late 1950, an inter-coalition committee was established to find a consensus that suited all parties present at the cabinet table. The Free Democratic Party (FDP) were strong advocates of a centralised Bundesbank 'in the manner of the old Reichsbank', as the committee's chairman, the Christian Democratic Union (CDU) politician Hugo Scharnberg, noted. But the Union parties were divided: the CSU fought for a decentralised monetary authority, while some in the CDU were in favour of a centralised one.[13] Even the opposition, the SPD – or at least its economics committee, comprised of experts – was split on the question during this period.[14]

Third, the central bank council was itself divided on the future Bundesbank's structure. Indeed, there was only one voice on the central bank council that was a strong proponent of centralisation: Vocke, the former Reichsbanker.[15] Bernard and other members of the central bank council often spoke in support of maintaining the decentralised structure of the BdL, referring to its strong success record to date.[16] And finally, any draft of the Bundesbank Law that advocated a centralised solution would, at some stage, have to run the gauntlet of the Bundesrat, or second parliament. The Bundesrat formed a stronghold of *Länder* interests and had little time for legislation that reduced the influence of the states.

The debate concerning the Bundesbank's structure, then, was a highly divisive one. But it was further complicated by the fact that the cabinet, the Bundesrat, and individual political parties within the Bundestag, too, could all propose their own drafts of the Bundesbank Law, and submit them for debate, leading to occasions when more than one draft was in discussion. As the economist Jörg Bibow contends, it was a power struggle between the federal government and states that primarily caused the delay in the Bundesbank Law's passage into legislation – a power struggle from which the BdL benefited. Other legislative debates, such as those surrounding the Credit Law and the Anti-cartel Law, also influenced the nature and pace of the Bundesbank Law discussion.[17]

---

[13] Hugo Scharnberg to Konrad Adenauer, 10 Apr. 1951, BAK, B136/1200, p. 1.

[14] Hans Henckel to Ludwig Erhard, 26 Sep. 1951, BAK, B102/5691, p. 2.

[15] Wilhelm Vocke to Hugo Scharnberg, 23 Jan. 1953, DBHA, B330/2042.

[16] See, for instance, 'Niederschrift über in der Sitzung des Ausschusses Nr. 12. Ausschuss für Geld und Kredit', 12 Jan. 1950, *1. Bundestag (12.) Ausschuss für Geld und Kredit Protokolle 1.-55. Sitzung 1949–51*, Deutscher Bundestag Parlamentsarchiv [DBP], pp. 27–8.

[17] For a recent discussion of the Credit Law of 1961, see Niels F. Krieghoff, 'Banking regulation in a federal system: lessons from American and German banking history', doctoral thesis, The London School of Economics and Political Science (2013), esp. pp. 119–38, 123, 191–3. Volker Berghahn, for his part, addresses the Anti-cartel Law

All the while, as the parliaments debated, the central bank and its independence gradually assumed more and more credibility on the economic front, presiding over a prosperous economy.

Often overlooked, however, is how the Bundesbank Law debates once again encouraged West German elites to revert to their monetary past. Monetary history became a rhetorical device through which both federal and state level governments expressed their political interests. Scharnberg's observation concerning the FDP and their push for a Bundesbank structure 'in the manner of the old Reichsbank' was a telling one. Indeed, the legacy of the Reichsbank cast a long shadow over the debate concerning the structure of the Bundesbank. When Erhard lobbied Schäffer for a centralised Bundesbank in October 1950, for example, he did so with explicit, repeated references and comparisons to the Reichsbank.[18] Centralisation, too, fit with his and Dehler's conception of central bank independence: the future Bundesbank would be free to decide what policy it might, but the federal government could pick its leadership.

When it came to the idea of centralisation, various *Land* central bank presidents spoke out against it. Interestingly, they did so evoking the Reichsbank's inter-war record. For instance, Hermann Tepe, *Land* central bank president of Bremen, drafted a short memo for use in a cabinet meeting detailing his '[t]houghts on the Bundesbank problem'.[19] Tepe contended that a decentralised bank of issue could help deter the concentration of power in the West German political sphere; moreover, the very term 'Reichsbank', Tepe argued, was intricately linked to two inflations, the banking crisis of 1931 and the turbulent era that followed Adolf Hitler's ascension to power.[20] And was it not the case, too, that socialist and communist governments alike were centralising power structures in their respective states? Better to have a decentralised monetary authority that could act as a bulwark against such socialist tendencies. Why should West German politicians forego a decentralised central bank system that had proved so successful since 1948?[21]

Similarly, Otto Pfleiderer, the *Land* central bank president of Baden-Württemberg, also stressed the mixed record of the 'old Reichsbank'

---

discussions in his work examining the relationship between industrialists and politics in the Federal Republic. See Volker Berghahn, *The Americanisation of West German industry, 1945–1973* (Leamington Spa, 1986), pp. 155–81.

[18] Erhard to Schäffer, 12 Oct. 1950.

[19] Hermann Tepe, 'Gedanken zum Problem Bundesbank', 25 Feb. 1952, DBHA, B330/2047.

[20] On the copy of the report that Tepe had sent to Vocke, a question mark was scribbled beside these remarks by its recipient. Vocke, it appears, was not impressed. Ibid., p. 2.

[21] Ibid., p. 3.

amid efforts to lobby for a decentralised Bundesbank.[22] Pfleiderer was more nuanced in his argument than Tepe, however. In normal times, the Reichsbank had executed its duties with precision and care, he contended. It was not responsible for the two inflations, like some had claimed in a recent Bundestag debate. Rather, these episodes were the price paid for defeat in war. Moreover, one could not blame a centralised central bank system for the abuses of war financing during the Third Reich; a decentralised monetary authority would have been inconceivable under a totalitarian government anyway. All the same, Pfleiderer noted, 'one cannot spare the Reichsbank system from the charge that, in the years around 1930, it committed a mistake so disastrous to our fortunes by forgoing a constructive policy of reviving the economy and pushing for Germany's increased involvement in world trade in favour of its deflation policy and holding an unrealistic exchange rate for so long in a world of devaluation'.[23]

What Bundestag debate was Pfleiderer referring to, however? The central banker was speaking three months after the event in question, during which the finance ministry's state secretary used the record of the inter-war Reichsbank as ammunition against the proponents of a centralised Bundesbank – in this case, FDP representatives in the Bundestag, who had proposed a draft of their own. 'Our people have experienced the collapse of a currency twice within a single generation, and the legislation must therefore be carried out thoroughly and conscientiously', the finance ministry official declared.[24] Those proposing a centralised Bundesbank argued that such a monetary authority would be 'more powerful' than a decentralised one, he contended; and yet, the 'lessons' of the inter-war do not support the argument for a centralised monetary authority. 'The Reichsbank system was not able to stop two currency collapses, while the [current] central bank system has significantly contributed to the stability of our currency.'[25]

Tepe and Pfleiderer, for their part, were not alone. *Land* central bank presidents continually entered the public sphere to push for a decentralised central bank throughout the years.[26] As such, the record of the

[22] Otto Pfleiderer, 'Einstufige oder zweistufige Notenbank?', *Industrie- und Handelsblatt, Nachrichtenblatt der Industrie- und Handelskammer Stuttgart*, 15 May 1953, DBPA, no. 836, p. 1.
[23] Ibid., p. 3.
[24] 'Deutscher Bundestag – 249. Sitzung. Bonn, Mittwoch, den 4. Februar 1953', 4 Feb. 1953, DBHA, B330/66630, p. 11872.
[25] Ibid., p. 11873.
[26] In early 1956, for instance, a new *Land* central bank president, Carl Wagenhöfer, called for a decentralised, independent central bank. See 'Sicherung der Währung', *Süddeutsche Zeitung*, 1 Feb. 1956.

Reichsbank offered different lessons to different men behind the walls of the central bank. This debate surrounding the Bundesbank's structure highlights two points. First, it shows the extent to which Vocke did not exert a monopoly controlling what the central bank officials could say in public. He could control what the directorate said, but not members of the central bank council. Instead, the chairman resorted to using his press chief and personal advisor, Viktor von der Lippe, to quietly lobby journalists behind the scenes for a centralised Bundesbank.[27]

Second, however, it illustrates how this divergence of opinion on the point of structure did not interfere with the BdL's more general push for central bank independence. For instance, during his remarks in which he lobbied for a decentralised Bundesbank, Pfleiderer also reverted to the edifying canon of 'central bank history' and how it 'teaches that a currency collapse occurs only when – and one is tempted to add: always when – the central bank falls into a state of dependency to the government. It is therefore an essential requirement to make the central bank as independent as possible'.[28] The two tiers of the central banking system, then, were united for in their drive for monetary autonomy. They just had different ideas as to whether this independence should manifest itself in a centralised or decentralised fashion.

Rearmament

The Bundesbank Law debates took place amid a backdrop of increased international tensions. Following the establishment of the Federal Republic, the Cold War escalated. Germany had long ceased to be the enemy. Instead, the Soviet Union presented the paramount threat. The Americans argued that West Germany, now a democratic republic, should be rearmed due to the danger at hand. The French, however, were strongly against the idea. An international debate ensued. In West Germany, too, a domestic discussion took place – particularly after the outbreak of hostilities in divided Korea.[29] Adenauer was eager to restore his state's influence on the European continent, and the idea of a West German army played an important part in his vision.[30] But the German currency had been destroyed twice through the financing of war.

---

[27] See, for example, von der Lippe's letter to Rolf Lüke, an influential journalist, in 1952. Viktor von der Lippe to Rolf Lüke, 25 Nov. 1952, DBHA, B330/2032 II.

[28] Pfleiderer, 'Einstufige oder zweistufige Notenbank?', pp. 7–8.

[29] Berghahn, *The Americanisation of West German industry*, p. 135.

[30] See Charles Williams, *Adenauer: the father of the new Germany* (London, 2000), pp. 365–79; Schwarz, *Die Ära Adenauer*, pp. 109–18.

Did the push for rearmament mean that West Germany was once again heading for the abyss?

Like the discussions concerning centralisation, the legacy of the Reichsbank played an important role in these debates. Historical narratives of the two inflationary episodes – particularly the latter one, the repressed inflation that occurred during the fascist era – began to be used against Adenauer's government. In these incidences, such narratives were not explicitly linked to calls for the maintenance of the central bank's independence. Rather, they sufficed in reminding journalists and citizens of West Germany that twice before the German nation had armed itself, and twice before these efforts led directly to the destruction of the currency. They worked towards creating an image of a spendthrift government that was not to be trusted.

Perhaps an example will suffice to demonstrate this point. The BdL enjoyed close links with *Der Spiegel*, a magazine that took a general line in support of the central bank.[31] It is quite possible that, in *Der Spiegel*'s eyes, central bank independence acted as a bulwark against the development of what the magazine saw as Adenauer's authoritarian *Kanzlerdemokratie*, a democratic system dominated by the office of the chancellor.[32] Tapping into the debate surrounding West Germany's rearmament, *Der Spiegel* released a critical piece heavily reliant on internal central bank sources – most likely Vocke himself. 'West Germany's rearmament debate reminds old bankers uncannily of those weeks in January 1939, which led to the destruction of the reichsmark', the magazine wrote.[33] *Der Spiegel* then referred to the memorandum, drafted by Vocke and signed by the Reichsbank directorate, which protested against Hitler's war financing – leading instantly to their dismissal and, consequently, an alleged martyrdom for the ideals of a sound currency.[34] Today, *Der Spiegel* continued, that spirit lived on in the form of Vocke who embodied the lessons of the inter-war era. The government is thinking of conducting monetary experiments? Vocke had already said no once. 'He would say no again.'[35] In other words, the experiences of the inter-war era, which *Der Spiegel* saw as being embodied in the leadership of the BdL, provided powerful arguments against the contemporary government's spending ambitions. (In reality, of course, Vocke had just

[31] See, for example, the evidence of editorial support found in Leo Brawand to 'Pressestelle der Bank deutscher Länder', 23 May 1951, DBHA, B330/2045.
[32] Christina von Hodenberg, *Konsens und Krise: eine Geschichte der westdeutschen Medienöffentlichkeit 1945–1973* (Göttingen, 2006), pp. 152, 219–20, 293–5.
[33] 'In Schäffers Kompetenzsack', *Der Spiegel*, 30 Jan. 1952.
[34] Reichsbank directorate to Adolf Hitler, 7 Jan. 1939, BAK, B122/5008.
[35] 'In Schäffers Kompetenzsack', *Der Spiegel*, 30 Jan. 1952.

one vote on the central bank council, which made decisions by majority vote.) Nevertheless, articles such as this one tapped into the BdL's wider critique of government spending. Vocke and Bernard directly criticised Bonn's expenditure plans as early as 1952.[36]

Chapter 2 has already detailed the occasion in which Vocke acted as a defence witness for Schacht at a Hamburg courtroom in 1952. The state senate had denied Schacht the right to establish a private bank.[37] But Vocke's appearance was interesting for another reason too. While Vocke had praised Schacht as the 'predominant expert in our field and a man of irreproachable character', the chairman also defended the legality of the 'Mefo' bills. In the 1930s, Schacht created these financial instruments, which allowed Hitler to finance his armaments programme covertly. The Hamburg state senate used this fact when grounding its case against the former Reichsbank president. Vocke was unrepentant, however. 'We had six million unemployed and were faced with the necessity of expanding the money supply for the purposes of job creation', the BdL chairman was reported as saying. 'Any central bank facing a similar scenario would not just sit there with hands in its lap.'[38]

It can be seen here that Vocke's presence in Schacht's Reichsbank directorate meant that the chairman's credibility was also in the court-room dock. At the same time, however, Vocke turned a negative example into an edifying lesson. The chairman informed the court that similar threats to stability still existed: Vocke, 'the former Reichsbank director and current president of the Bank deutscher Länder', alleged that a 'high-ranking personality' had told him back in 1950 of their intention to 'create Mefo bills again'.[39] Predictably, the press was outraged to learn of such things.[40] No names were mentioned, and Vocke never raised this incident again. But the episode shows how the BdL leadership continually used the inter-war period to create populist resentment against government spending.[41] And it did so despite Vocke's own seat at the very Reichsbank directorate that had pushed ahead with the passage of

---

[36] Wilhelm Vocke, 'Ansprache von Präsident Geheimrat Dr. Vocke', *Bank deutscher Länder Auszüge aus Presseartikeln*, No. 143, 12 Dec. 1952, DBPA, no. 1244, p. 1. See also 'Vocke warnt vor Aufblähung der Staatswirtschaft', *Stuttgarter Zeitung*, 15 Dec. 1952.

[37] Hjalmar Schacht, *The magic of money*, trans. Paul Erskine (London, 1967), p. 119.

[38] 'Vocke: Mefo-Wechsel zulässig', *Frankfurter Allgemeine Zeitung*, 22 Nov. 1952; see also Deutsche Bundesbank, *Geheimrat Wilhelm Vocke*, p. 95.

[39] 'Geheimrat Vocke plaudert aus', *Deutsche Woche*, 3 Dec. 1952, DBPA, no. 1242.

[40] Ibid.

[41] See, for example, Wilhelm Vocke, 'Topical questions of central bank policy. An address before the Übersee-Club in Hamburg on the 7 November 1955', *Bank deutscher Länder Auszüge aus Presseartikeln, Sonderdruck*, No. 125, 9 Nov. 1955, DBPA, no. 1244, p. 5.

the 'Mefo' bills in the first place.[42] 'No German armament with the help of the printing press' ran one newspaper headline.[43] This headline was only significant in the fact that it resembled many others during the 1950s.

Confidence and the Bank deutscher Länder

The BdL began to enjoy an increased public profile as time went on. Although some elites, even as late as 1953, were still calling the BdL 'an institution dictated by the occupation authorities, an improvisation of the military government', their opinions were in the distinct minority.[44] Gradually, the central bank began to shed its image in the West German media as a product of Allied occupation law. Instead, it began to be seen as a German institution. In part, this was because the Bundestag now acknowledged its independence by means of the Transition Law.

However, strong economic growth, and the deutschmark's ascension to one of the most trusted currencies on the continent, also strengthened the legitimacy of the monetary authority's structure and institutions. The deutschmark had come to assume a position of pride in a state where political nationalism remained off limits.[45] This success inspired confidence in, and indeed *within*, the central bank. The population, too, became increasingly accustomed to the idea of an unelected council body that decided the state's monetary policy.

As the 1950s progressed, too, public awareness of the BdL grew substantially. More column inches and importance were attached to media coverage on the central bank. In 1951, a speech by Bernard would have been relegated to the back of the business section, itself barely read by the West German population. By 1956, however, the central bank leadership would appear on the front page of weekly magazines (as will be shown in greater detail later in this chapter). As ever, the person of Vocke

[42] Vocke claimed to have been against the creation of the 'Mefo' bills. See Wilhelm Vocke to Hjalmar Schacht, 6 Apr. 1966, DBHA, B330/294, pp. 1–2.
[43] 'Keine deutsche Rüstung mit Hilfe der Notenpresse', *Hamburger Anzeiger*, 25 Mar. 1955. The article can be found in Deutsche Bundesbank, *Geheimrat Wilhelm Vocke*, p. 204.
[44] As noted by Pfleiderer with frustration. The *Land* central bank president did not name these people in his article. But he noted they were high-ranking officials whose opinions, however misguided, could not be dismissed out of hand. See Pfleiderer, 'Einstufige oder zweistufige Notenbank?', p. 2.
[45] See, for instance, the chapter 'A return to national history? The master narrative and beyond' in the co-written work of Konrad H. Jarausch and Michael Geyer, *Shattered past: reconstructing German histories* (Princeton, 2003), pp. 37–60. See also Jürgen Habermas, 'Der DM-Nationalismus', *Die Zeit*, 30 Mar. 1990.

still dominated the face of the BdL. For example, SPD officials, during internal party discussions concerning the Bundesbank Law, referred to the BdL as 'Vocke's tower'.[46] The former Reichsbanker had come to personify the decisions taken by the monetary authority's decision-making body, the central bank council.

The BdL also refined its interaction with the press during this period. Under von der Lippe, the press department developed a network of contacts in journalistic and government circles. Sympathetic journalists would often inform von der Lippe of any important information they came across.[47] Indeed, on at least one occasion, the press chief organised for financial support to be sent to a pro-BdL journalist in support of the latter's work.[48] The central bank's cultivation of contacts provided it with a crucial and confidential communication channel, which allowed it to judge the political atmosphere in Bonn in a more lucid manner. The central bank's monthly and annual reports also helped form the parameters of monetary debate in that they were respected and used by politicians and economic think tanks for reports and speeches.[49]

The BdL, then, was becoming increasingly 'German' and accepted. But its foreign origins remained. In a confidential speech, not intended for public consumption, the vice president of the directorate, the former Reichsbanker Wilhem Könneker, admitted as much. 'Legally speaking, in its current form, the German central bank system holds a special position among the central banks of the world', he said to an audience of young, up-and-coming bankers. 'It is still based upon occupation law and is therefore created by foreign powers. The central bank existed before our state was even established.'[50] All the same, central bank

---

[46] Minutes of Social Democratic Party meeting (Wirtschaftspolitischer Außschuss), 5 Nov. 1956, Archiv der sozialen Demokratie, Friedrich-Ebert-Stiftung [AdsD], 1/ HSAA008629, p. 9.

[47] See, for instance, the following letters: Viktor von der Lippe to Wilhelm Vocke, 16 Jun. 1951, DBHA, B330/2032 I; Viktor von der Lippe to Wilhelm Vocke, 10 Nov. 1955, DBHA, B330/6306/2; Viktor von der Lippe to Wilhelm Vocke, 15 Feb. 1956, B330/2032 I; Viktor von der Lippe to Wilhelm Vocke, 17 Jul. 1956, DBHA, B330/2032 I; Friedrich Lemmer to Viktor von der Lippe, 25 Jun. 1957, DBHA, B330/6307; and Viktor von der Lippe to Wilhelm Vocke, 28 Jun. 1957, DBHA, B330/6307.

[48] See Rolf Lüke to Viktor von der Lippe, 9 Aug. 1954, DBHA, B330/2032 II; and the note confirming the transfer of money, Hildegard Langenberg to Rolf Lüke, 12 Aug. 1954, DBHA, B330/2032 II. See also Rolf Lüke to Wilhelm Vocke, 21 Jan. 1951, DBHA, B330/2032 II.

[49] When the term 'Bank deutscher Länder Monatsbericht' (the central bank's monthly report) is typed into the Bundestag online search engine, 20 instances of it appear during parliamentary debates in the first two parliament sessions, 1949–53 and 1953–7. See http://pdok.bundestag.de. Last accessed on 20 December 2018.

[50] The speech was marked 'Only for internal use! Not intended for publication!' The vice chairman was speaking to students who were to sit an advanced bank examination. See

independence was certainly becoming more and more popular in the media. A newspaper article, published in early 1955, captured the shifting sentiment perfectly. It recalled the troubled times of 1949 and 1950, when unemployment was high. 'A few years ago one would occasionally hear the following advice: "Write something against the Bank deutscher Länder whose restrictive credit policy makes our lives so difficult!"' the *Handelsblatt* opined.

This has changed substantially. Today the Bank deutscher Länder is often praised as 'having had the courage to implement unpopular measures'. Among those who say such things today were the critics at the time. Rightly, therefore, Vocke can declare: 'our success has made our measures, though initially unpopular, subsequently very popular'.[51]

The article referred to Vocke's recent speech in Zürich in March 1955.[52] Standing on the podium, Vocke focused on two concerns. The first was inflation: given the recent upswing in the economy, the price level began to increase markedly once more; the economy was approaching full employment, too. The second point related to the government's accumulation of funds for the armament of a West German army. Since 1953, the finance ministry had been collecting revenues that now amounted to four billion deutschmarks – worth some 20 per cent of federal spending in 1955 – to spend on armaments.[53] This enormous sum had come to be called Schäffer's *Juliusturm*, named after the tower in which French reparations payments were stored following the Franco-Prussian War in the 1870s.[54] By law, such savings were required to be stored at the central bank. This allowed the ever-mounting *Juliusturm* to act in counter-cyclical manner with respect to the business cycle. But with an election on the horizon, pressure began to mount in Bonn for these funds to be splashed out on fiscal transfer programmes with the aim of buttering up the electorate. Schäffer increasingly found himself fending off the unwelcome advances of ministerial colleagues.

In his speech, Vocke warned against making sensational statements about how armament spending inevitably leads to another inflation. But he noted 'it is hardly to be wondered at, in light of Germany's

Wilhelm Könneker, 'Aktuelle Notenbankprobleme', May 1955, DBPA, no. 591, pp. 3–4.

[51] 'Klare Notenbank-Politik', *Handelsblatt*, 13 Apr. 1955.
[52] Wilhelm Vocke, 'Remarks on Germany's present policy in the field of credit and currency', *Bank deutscher Länder Auszüge aus Presseartikeln, Sonderdruck*, No. 33, 23 Mar. 1955, DBPA, no. 1244.
[53] Berger, 'The Bundesbank's path to independence: evidence from the 1950s', p. 440.
[54] Anthony J. Nicholls, *Freedom with responsibility: the social market economy in Germany, 1918–1963* (Oxford, 1994), p. 353.

experiences with inflations, that people there should be vigilant and suspicious' of such spending ambitions.[55] In the same speech, Vocke attacked those 'people who, on the grounds of some misunderstood Keynesian theories, believe that for political reasons one simply cannot afford for a few months to impose a high discount rate on a country. Is it preferable, I ask, to expose the country to the protracted suffering and finally the distress and catastrophe of an inflation?' Inherently tied to this statement was the rectification of classical instruments of monetary policy, so maligned in light of the experiences of the inter-war era. Instruments such as the discount rate had successfully combatted the threat posed by the Korean crisis some years before, Vocke reminded this audience.[56]

Moreover, the central banker continued, Keynesian measures were reminiscent of economic policy during the era of the Third Reich. 'As the horrors of the Nationalist Socialist "welfare state," the war and the inflation are receding into the past, we tend to forget that a free economy, liberalised trade and a stable currency are not a matter of course or a windfall, but that great sacrifices had to be made and pains taken to obtain them, and that they must be defended in the same way', stressed the chairman of the directorate.

Nor must we forget that, in Germany at least, the stability of the currency was only achieved and maintained, and can only be secured in the future, by the central bank remaining independent and unhampered by political influences in the administration of its business and in its currency and credit policies.[57]

The monetary authority's autonomy, in other words, was part of a carefully forged identity that incorporated lessons from National Socialism and the war economy. Central bank independence acted as a bulwark against retreats into what the chairman once termed as 'National Socialist trains of thought' – what Vocke defined as lines of reasoning that promoted artificial incursions into the natural laws of economic life.[58] Indeed, Vocke was not the only West German elite to compare Keynesian economic theory to the practices of the Third Reich. The historian Mark Spicka has shown convincingly how, during the 1953 and 1957 elections, Adenauer and his government successfully portrayed the SPD's vision of an 'economic democracy' as an inherently totalitarian one – to the detriment of the SPD's electoral fortunes throughout the

---

[55] Vocke, 'Remarks on Germany's present policy in the field of credit and currency', p. 2.
[56] Ibid., p. 4.   [57] Ibid., p. 5.
[58] Wilhelm Vocke, 'Das Erste Jahr der neuen Währung', *Die Zeitschrift für das gesamte Kreditwesen*, Jun. 1949, DBPA, no. 1244, p. 273.

1950s.[59] The West German press received Vocke's speech enthusiastically; the chairman's arguments and references were picked up by the media and echoed in print.[60]

The Hamburg Speech

The rhetoric of the Zürich speech foretold things to come. The economy had entered a boom, sparking off labour unrest. Miners and engineering unions, among other groups, pushed for higher wages.[61] With a federal election scheduled for 1957, and dire poll ratings to dampen its spirit, Adenauer's administration sought to boost its popularity through fiscal measures. By increasing government spending during the economic boom, however, Bonn would only aggravate inflationary forces. In August 1955, the BdL increased the discount rate from 3 to 3.5 per cent. Minimum reserve requirements were raised too.[62] The monetary authority hit the credit brakes because it found the current economic situation to be 'alarming', according to its monthly report for August 1955.[63]

This was a big moment. 'For the first time since 1952', *The Economist* observed, 'the Bank deutscher Länder took steps last week to tighten credit'.[64] And there was something else, too. This time, the central bank combined the restrictive measures with a public critique of the federal government's spending policies. As Vocke later stated, the decision was to serve as a 'warning which is meant seriously', implicitly with reference to the federal government.[65] The move was indicative of a central bank

---

[59] See the argument outlined in Mark E. Spicka, *Selling the economic miracle: economic reconstruction and politics in West Germany, 1949–1957* (Oxford, 2007). For a general discussion of Keynesianism and its 'underdevelopment' in West Germany, see the influential essay of Christopher S. Allen, 'The underdevelopment of Keynesianism in the Federal Republic of Germany', in Peter A. Hall (ed.), *The political power of economic ideas: Keynesianism across nations* (Princeton, 1989).

[60] See, for instance, 'Die Währung ist und bleibt stabil', *Frankfurter Allgemeine Zeitung*, 25 Mar. 1955; 'Notenbank wird die Rüstung nicht finanzieren', *Süddeutsche Zeitung*, 25 Mar. 1955. The fact this was so, was commented upon in a letter by Max Grasmann, president of the Bavarian *Land* central bank, in a letter to Vocke. The chairman's speech, Grasmann said, found 'a good reception and a lively echo'. See Max Grasmann to Wilhelm Vocke, 28 Mar. 1955, DBHA, B330/2024.

[61] 'Germany's boom', *The Economist*, 13 Aug. 1955; 'Ueber Preissenkungen einig', *Frankfurter Allgemeine Zeitung*, 9 Sep. 1955; and 'Averting labour unrest', *Manchester Guardian*, 10 Sep. 1955.

[62] BdL central bank council minutes, 3 Aug. 1955, DBHA, B330/87/1.

[63] *Monatsbericht der Bank deutscher Länder*, Aug. 1955, p. 4.

[64] 'Germany's boom', *The Economist*, 13 Aug. 1955.

[65] Vocke, 'Topical questions of central bank policy. An address before the Übersee-Club in Hamburg on the 7 November 1955', p. 2.

that had become confident in its ability to assert its independence on its own terms.

The BdL was not the only one concerned by the economic climate. By October 1955, both the finance minister and economics minister, erstwhile opponents, found themselves in agreement that the economic boom needed to be slowed down. Erhard was fearful of inflation. Schäffer was worried that his much-guarded *Juliusturm* would be splashed out on pre-election initiatives for voters. During that month, the two men set about pushing through a package of counter-cyclical measures aimed at taking the government's foot off the gas pedal.[66] These measures ultimately proved ineffective. But it was during this time that Vocke got word of some 'tendencies' within ministerial circles to 'trim the monetary freedom' of the central bank – a mindset no doubt reinforced by the BdL's recent monetary restrictions.[67] Within a matter of weeks, the BdL found itself the natural ally of the two embattled ministers, Erhard and Schäffer.[68]

The central bank had come under heavy pressure from the BDI, the industry lobby group headed by Fritz Berg, a close confidant and ally of the chancellor. The industrialist Berg was no friend to the more liberal Erhard.[69] By tightening credit in the economy, the BdL jeopardised the economic boom that was so beneficial to industry, Berg contended. In early November 1955, the central bank and representatives of industry met for informal discussions.[70] Industry officials argued that BdL policy should give special consideration to the concerns of industry due to the latter's dominant position in the economy. On the table was the suggestion of a central bank advisory council that, implicitly, would reflect the interests of industry.

The following Monday, Adenauer applied additional pressure, sending Vocke a short, cold letter simply stating that, 'The economic and political situation requires the co-operation of all responsible bodies. I would therefore be grateful if the Bank deutscher Länder would make no drastic measures in the field of credit policy without prior consultation with government having taken place.'[71] On the same day, however,

---

[66] Ludwig Erhard and Fritz Schäffer, 'Gemeinsames Exposé über die konjunkturpolitische Situation und die Mittel zur Aufrechterhaltung der Stabilität unserer Wirtschaft und Währung', 3 Oct. 1955, BAK, B102/12595; see also Berger, *Konjunkturpolitik im Wirtschaftswunder*, p. 211.

[67] BdL directorate meeting minutes, 11 Oct. 1955, DBHA, B330/2057; see also Berger, 'The Bundesbank's path to independence: evidence from the 1950s', p. 441.

[68] 'Der Kanzler auf dem Block', *Der Spiegel*, 12 Oct. 1955.

[69] Berghahn, *The Americanisation of West German industry*, p. 177.

[70] 'Kabinett berät Währungsfragen', *Süddeutsche Zeitung*, 7 Nov. 1955.

[71] To which Vocke replied that such decisions belonged to the central bank council as a whole. See Konrad Adenauer to Wilhelm Vocke, 7 Nov. 1955, DBHA, B330/2011; and Wilhelm Vocke to Konrad Adenauer, 8 Nov. 1955, DBHA, B330/2011.

Vocke stepped once more onto the stage. This time it was before the Übersee Club in Hamburg, founded by the banker Max Warburg.[72] The Übersee Club served as an elite forum for political and economic issues.

Vocke opened fire on those who challenged the concept of an independent central bank as well as those policymakers whose minds were embedded in the Keynesian school of analysis. Underlining the central bank's commitment to the West German people, Vocke stressed that it was the saver, the man on the street, who was set to lose the most with the onset of an inflation. The speech, written by his personal advisor von der Lippe, is worth quoting at length, given its clarity.

We do not serve the industry, nor do we serve the workers, or agriculture, or any other group, however important it may be. Even the largest groups are minorities as compared with the grand total of our nation, whom we serve undividedly; this total includes the housewives who are entitled to see that they can make both ends meet until the last day of the month. It also includes the officials, the pensioners and, last but not least, the savers. As heretofore they can rely upon us; we shall not hesitate to take action if danger should be imminent. Let me add in this connection a few words on the independence of the central bank, which happily we possess today and which must remain intact under all circumstances.[73]

The chairman listed a string of politicians who expressed their support for an independent central bank. Vocke included Adenauer among them. The chancellor had been careful not to oppose central bank independence in public and, years before, had expressed lukewarm support for it. Vocke preferred to attack the government in indirect terms. Whenever specific names were mentioned, he rarely had a bad word to say about them in public.[74] Nevertheless, the passage that followed directly after made Vocke's message perfectly clear.

If the management of the central bank were to be subordinated to politics, to the government, then it would have to be expected that the government office in charge possess[es] a greater measure of technical expert knowledge and practical experience in monetary and credit matters than the central bank management, the government then clearly being the actual authority directing the bank. Nobody desires such an arrangement and the government itself is interested in seeing that an institution which occasionally must not shrink from unpopular

---

[72] Before doing so, Vocke sent a copy of his speech to Bernard for his comments. The speech was met with broad approval by the other chairman. This suggests that the two chairmen were united in their stand. See Karl Bernard to Wilhelm Vocke, 4 Nov. 1955, DBHA, B330/6306/2.

[73] Vocke, 'Topical questions of central bank policy. An address before the Übersee-Club in Hamburg on the 7 November 1955', pp. 2–3.

[74] Vocke's actual take the chancellor was more sobering. See Wilhelm Vocke, *Memoiren* (Stuttgart, 1973), pp. 147–54. See also Wilhelm Vocke, 'Adenauer und die Wirtschaft', no date, DBPA, no. 1243.

measures is not directed according to political conceptions or according to considerations based on elections or changes in party tendencies, but is genuinely objective with the sole aim of maintaining a stable currency.

This system has stood the test in Germany. Should a tendency arise in any quarter to curtail or impair the independence of the central bank, the people would have every reason to show distrust. Action in the interest of the currency will be taken by the central bank on its own. Any compulsion on the part of the government could only take effect where it is a case of imposing or forcing other points of view on the central bank, such as obliging it to act in a way which it considers dangerous for the currency. Only if this effect is desired should its independence be discontinued or restricted. In actual fact the abuses of which governments have been guilty in respect of the central banks have been instrumental in bringing about currency decay in many cases throughout the world.

Why should we forget the lessons which a terrible record of inflations has taught us? Why should we relinquish the safeguards and guarantees which we have today and which have proved their worth? I am not saying this because I believe in a change of opinion in this direction within responsible government quarters but because, when the new central bank law, sooner or later, comes up for discussion the independence of the central bank must be regarded as the indestructible foundation and basis for the future as well. Why is this so? Because we need independence as a guarantee against the danger of inflation which, despite all progress in the monetary field, is at all times ready to rear its head everywhere in the world.[75]

Let us take a moment here: Vocke directly linked the 'terrible record' of Germany's two inflations to the need for an independent central bank – itself portrayed as an 'indestructible foundation' for future prosperity. Within the space of a breath, too, the central banker stressed the need to maintain this independence in the upcoming Bundesbank Law. Historical narratives were thus explicitly linked by the chairman to a political, legislative argument concerning the future monetary authority.

Vocke was not finished, however. 'People may have forgotten all about this a little – and indeed fortunately so – but we are determined to remind them of these things, in particular those who are not keen on hearing such a reminder', he said. 'I am recalling these facts because there are people whose memory appears to be short. Their attitude is this: certainly let us have a sound currency – but not at the expense of full employment, nor at the expense of the capital market, nor yet at the expense of present wage or profit prospects!'[76]

---

[75] Vocke, 'Topical questions of central bank policy. An address before the Übersee-Club in Hamburg on the 7 November 1955', pp. 2–3.

[76] Ibid., p. 4.

In particular, Vocke targeted the idea of an advisory council – and, more implicitly, the industrialists' lobby group, the BDI. 'It creates a strange impression that one powerful economic group should demand that it be granted practical influence on monetary policy by being represented in an advisory council to be attached to the central bank', he said. 'This notion appears to me somewhat grotesque.' Vocke continued: 'The impartiality and independence of the bank of issue is an inestimable asset, without which Germany would not have a stable currency. And if independence it is to be, let us first of all be independent of sectional interests! And likewise of politics!'[77] Vocke concluded with a declaration, addressed 'to the whole nation, which for its life relies upon a sound and stable currency and which includes the housewives, the man in the street, the pensioners and the savers: be without fear, we are on guard!'[78]

The Hamburg speech was aimed directly at Adenauer's government and the BDI. Certainly, both the chancellor and publications such as *Der Spiegel* interpreted it as such.[79] The speech received extensive and favourable coverage. The central banker's language, references and analogies found a sizeable echo in the media. 'Vocke fights for the stability of the currency', declared one headline. 'Bank deutscher Länder: "Halt! No further!"' was another.[80] The lessons of Germany's two inflationary episodes, a spendthrift government, interest groups that wished to sacrifice the stability of the currency for their own short-term benefit, and an independent central bank fighting on behalf of the West German people in light of the country's tragic past – these points had now become mainstays of the BdL's rhetoric. The speech reinforced Vocke's image as a stern, vigilant guard of the deutschmark, an image that was quite reminiscent of various depictions of Schacht as Reichsbank president during the Weimar Republic.[81] In both democracies, regardless whether it was Weimar or Bonn, central bank leaders were portrayed as opponents of narrow-minded sectoral group interests.

Between the years 1951 and 1955, then, the central bank's public image had flowered. The BdL was already seen as strong, independent and outspoken – and on the side of the average West German citizen.

---

[77] Ibid., p. 3.   [78] Ibid., p. 5.
[79] See, for example, 'Die Weiche wird gestellt', *Der Spiegel*, pp. 15–16.
[80] 'Vocke kämpft um die Stabilität der Währung', *Frankfurter Allgemeine Zeitung*, 8 Nov. 1955; 'Eine bitterernste Warnung', *Westfälische Nachrichten*, 9 Nov. 1955; 'Bank deutscher Länder warnt: "Haltet Maß"', *Nürnberger Nachrichten*, 8 Nov. 1955; 'Scharfe Warnungen des Notenbank-Präsidenten', *Süddeutsche Zeitung*, 8 Nov. 1955; and 'Die Inflation ist eine schleichende Pest', *Westfalen-Blatt*, 12 Nov. 1955.
[81] See Reichsbank, *Schacht in der Karikatur: Im Auftrage des Reichsbankdirektoriums zusammengestellt in der Volkswirtschaftlichen und Statistischen Abt. der Reichsbank. Zum 22 Januar 1937* (Berlin, 1937).

Its two chairmen, Vocke and Bernard, carried weight in the media. '*Geheimrat* Vocke enjoys tremendous respect at home and abroad', one newspaper noted in early 1956. 'But he was never actually popular. Only in recent times has he become more prominent in the public sphere.'[82] Citizens wrote to Vocke in support of his comments, a fact that suggests his arguments were effectively transferred through the press. 'I would like to take this opportunity to thank you on behalf of thousands of others for your words relating to the currency', wrote one admirer following Vocke's Hamburg speech. 'In my circle of friends one hears the following sentence: "Only now do I finally believe in a stable currency after Vocke spoke. His words are more valuable to me than all the ministers in Bonn."'[83]

Leading up to the 'Gürzenich Affair'

Relations between Frankfurt and the chancellery had become increasingly tense. But the central bank had found allies in Schäffer and Erhard. Indeed, the finance minister Schäffer now wrote to Vocke expressing his support for central bank independence, seeing the chairman's Hamburg speech as 'support of the policy, which I and the economics minister together represent'.[84] Implicitly, Schäffer had his eye on the *Juliusturm*. Erhard, for his part, had his own worries. By early 1956, his relationship with Adenauer had become quite strained. *Der Alte*, or the Old Man, was becoming increasingly irate with his economics minister, whom he saw as a long-winded professor.[85] Adenauer much preferred to listen to the BDI's Berg, a man with whom he shared a capacity for straight, to-the-point discussions.[86] Adenauer, too, was heavily reliant on the BDI for campaign spending in the upcoming election, and knew the group wielded some influence in the Bundestag.[87] The BDI's support was important to the chancellor. Erhard found himself increasingly ostracised.

And so it came to be that Vocke, Erhard and Schäffer established an informal triumvirate called the *Konjunkturrat*, or economic council, in which they sought to put forward a common economic policy and

---

[82] 'Wilhelm Vocke', *Frankfurter Allgemeine Zeitung*, 9 Feb. 1956.
[83] F. Petz to Wilhelm Vocke, 14 Nov. 1955, DBHA, B330/6306/2.
[84] Fritz Schäffer to Wilhelm Vocke, 10 Nov. 1955, DBHA, B330/2043.
[85] Koerfer, *Kampf ums Kanzleramt*, pp. 86, 96–101; for more on the tumultuous relationship between Adenauer and Erhard, see Volker Hentschel, *Ludwig Erhard. Ein Politikerleben* (Munich, 1996), pp. 93–6, 417–25.
[86] For Adenauer's attitude to Berg, see Koerfer, *Kampf ums Kanzleramt*, p. 86.
[87] Berger, *Konjunkturpolitik im Wirtschaftswunder*, p. 213.

redirect the public debate.[88] But already months before, the BdL knew it needed allies. Within days of Vocke's speech delivered on the platform in Hamburg, von der Lippe received word that 'Herr Berg will apparently give an answer to your Hamburg speech'.[89] That answer arrived in December 1955, when the BDI president attacked the central bank's credit tightening as 'a massive blow against the boom'.[90] In doing so, Berg evoked the experiences of the Great Depression. 'The monetary and credit-tightening measures were overdone and they were harmful to the boom', the BDI president was reported to have said. 'In the years 1930 to 1933, Germany had already experienced all too drastically where a monetary policy detached from reality could lead. Deflationary measures were no less disastrous than inflationary ones.'[91]

Berg was not the only industrialist to evoke the record of the Reichsbank. Some two months later, the 'Money, Credit and Currency Committee' of the BDI came together to discuss 'problems of the future Bundesbank Law'.[92] Both an official from the BdL and Hans Henckel from the economics ministry were invited to the talks. The central bank official, however, found himself having to fend off one industrialist's points comparing the BdL's actions to those of the Reichsbank back in the 1930s. The industrialist in question went by the name of Herr Stock, a representative of the food industry. There were some who wanted a 'completely independent' central bank, Stock remarked, but 'one still has bad memories of the former Reichsbank's autonomous monetary policy'.[93] He continued:

In the years of the great crisis, the supposed independence [of the Reichsbank] had been paid for with victims comparable to the losses of a lost war. The experiences with the mistaken measures and missed opportunities of the former Reichsbank's leadership back then should have led to the realisation that a central bank can no longer go about its business independently, but rather should be appointed to steer the most important part of economic policy. One should therefore incorporate representatives of those who primarily must bear the

---

[88] Koerfer, *Kampf ums Kanzleramt*, pp. 109–10.
[89] Von der Lippe to Vocke, 10 Nov. 1955.
[90] For the speech, see 'Die deutsche Industrie im Rahmen der Weltwirtschaft. Von Präsident Berg. 19. Dezember 1955', 26 Dec. 1955, Historische Archiv des Bundesverbandes der Deutschen Industrie [BDI-Archiv], S7IW   P 6660. See also 'Ein massiver Schlag gegen die Konjunktur', *Frankfurter Allgemeine Zeitung*, 20 Dec. 1955.
[91] Ibid.
[92] 'Niederschrift über die Sitzung des Geld-, Kredit- und Währungsausschuss des BDI vom 16.2.1956 in Köln', 16 Feb. 1956, BAK, B102/5707.
[93] Ibid., p. 10.

consequences of central bank policies into the circle of the central bank leadership.[94]

The point, though indirect, could not have been lost among the participants. After all, in the public sphere, Vocke was still strongly linked to the inter-war Reichsbank. The 'mistaken measures' and 'missed opportunities' of the Reichsbank's leadership, paid for with countless 'victims', meant the central bankers of the inter-war era had monetary blood on their hands. Stock fused this historical narrative with the demand that the interests of industry should be represented by an advisory board, one that had direct access to the ears of the central bank leadership. This was the apparent lesson that the industrialist took from the past. Taking a step back, then, we can see again how a clash of interests, one stemming from the institutional divide left behind by the Allies, was pushing elites to discern lessons of monetary history along lines of argument that suited their political goals.

As it happens, the BdL official present at the committee was one Friedrich Wilhelm von Schelling, a former Reichsbanker and trusted confidant of Vocke.[95] The period following 1929 was 'not a good example' of central bank independence, von Schelling responded to the industrialist. But was it not also the case that 'the government had pursued a deflationary policy just as much as the Reichsbank'?[96] Von Schelling was correct, of course: the Reichsbank's restrictive monetary policy was broadly in line with that of the chancellor, Heinrich Brüning, at the time. But his argument fell on deaf ears. The meeting resulted in little agreement. The BDI was still adamant that it be allowed to exert an influence upon central bank policy.

The battle lines had formed. In the same month, von der Lippe detailed the political divide surrounding the central bank's credit tightening. 'Our side', von der Lippe told Vocke, was comprised of the central bank, the economics ministry, the finance ministry, some ministers in the cabinet and 'public opinion'. Indeed, von der Lippe equated 'public opinion' with 'the press', suggesting again the elite nature of this conflict, at least from the perspective of the BdL.[97] The business editor of the *Frankfurter Allgemeine Zeitung*, he continued, had assured von der

---

[94] Ibid., pp. 10–11.
[95] Von Schelling's record with the Reichsbank was noted in 'The Reichsbank and its relations with other institutions. Appendix: – personalities', Aug. 1944, Institut für Zeitgeschichte [IfZ], 2/206/4 FINAD, p. x.
[96] 'Niederschrift über die Sitzung des Geld-, Kredit- und Währungsausschuss des BDI vom 16.2.1956 in Köln', p. 12.
[97] His exact words were 'public opinion (the press clearly stand on the side of the [central] bank)'. See von der Lippe to Vocke, 15 Feb. 1956, p. 2.

Lippe of the 'loyalty of the FAZ to the central bank and its independence'.[98] The 'other side' of the conflict, however, was made up of parliamentary representatives, particularly from the governing coalition parties, Adenauer, his influential state secretary Hans Globke, and various interest groups.[99]

The BdL's press chief fielded the opinions of four political journalists in February 1956, asking for advice about the central bank's position concerning 'the Bonn–Frankfurt problem'.[100] The reporters replied, stressing that the monetary authority did not realise how strong 'currents of an inflationary sort' actually were in Bonn.[101] Asked how the central bank should respond, the journalists advised the BdL to remain strong and search for allies in the economics ministry, finance ministry, key ministers in the cabinet, 'as well as public opinion'.[102] Von der Lippe's advice to Vocke, then, was to seek out the support of Bonn and the media for what may well be a turbulent few months ahead.

Amid efforts to safeguard the success of the economic boom, Vocke, Schäffer and Erhard had now come to meet regularly to discuss economic matters and work together to provide a counterweight to those forces wishing for a prolongation of the boom.[103] This triumvirate was eventually dubbed the 'three wise men' by the press. Such reports caused tremendous irritation in Palais Schaumburg, the residence of the chancellor.[104] And the cabinet, for its part, was still dominated by the presence of *Der Alte*.

Adenauer's Challenge

The central bank council, in response to sustained inflationary pressures, decided to increase the discount rate from 3.5 to 4.5 per cent in early March 1956.[105] The move sparked off anger in Bonn. Adenauer knew the decision was coming. As such, the chancellor sent Erhard and Schäffer to Frankfurt to apply the government's suspensive veto at the meeting in question – a move that would temporarily postpone the

---

[98] Indeed, just days prior, the *Frankfurter Allgemeine Zeitung* had published a hagiographic profile on Vocke, documenting his dramatic departure from the Reichsbank in 1939 in protest to Hitler's armament financing. Ibid., p. 2; and 'Wilhelm Vocke', *Frankfurter Allgemeine Zeitung*, 9 Feb. 1956.

[99] Von der Lippe to Vocke, 15 Feb. 1956, p. 2.   [100] Ibid., pp. 1, 2.   [101] Ibid., p. 3.

[102] Ibid., pp. 2–3.

[103] Fritz Schäffer to Wilhelm Vocke, 11 Apr. 1956, DBHA, B330/2043; and Wilhelm Vocke to Fritz Schäffer, 13 Apr. 1956, DBHA, B330/2043.

[104] Ursala Hüllbüsch (ed.), *Die Kabinettsprotokolle der Bundesregierung, Band 9: 1956* (Munich, 1998), pp. 279–80.

[105] BdL central bank council minutes, 7–8 Mar. 1956, DBHA, B330/92/2.

central bank council's decision for a period of eight days.[106] Both Schäffer and Erhard, however, actually colluded with the central bank council, ensuring that such a veto did not take place. It was argued that the veto had already been implicitly issued by means of two phone calls in late February and thus had already expired.[107]

Adenauer was furious. The chancellor called Bernard and Vocke to Bonn. He wanted the two chairmen to explain the BdL's decision.[108] The discussion was strained at best. When told by Adenauer that it was the central bank's 'duty to observe and support the [government's] economic policy', Bernard countered by noting that the central bank was not obliged to do so when it saw the stability of the currency as being endangered. The chancellor was stunned.

FEDERAL CHANCELLOR : Are you then of the opinion that you stand on equal ground with the federal government?
BERNARD : Yes.
FEDERAL CHANCELLOR : That is not the way I see it.[109]

The two chairmen remained firm. Bernard defended such measures in a radio interview soon afterwards – and fought off the journalist's assertion that the 'problem of central bank independence' had been the central topic of discussion in Bonn.[110] A week later, the chairman of the central bank council also stressed the benefits and necessity of central bank independence in an interview with an American broadcaster.[111]

The media knew that Adenauer dragged both men to Bonn to explain themselves. Once again, the lack of a formal resolution mechanism governing the relations between Frankfurt and Bonn meant that the conflict spilled into the public sphere, allowing the press to interpret the institutional divide in historical terms. 'The principle of central bank independence appears to be in no way as fixed as previously claimed by those in high places', opined *Die Zeit*.

---

[106] Ibid. This was a concession to the federal government outlined in the Transition Law of 1951. See Chapter 2.
[107] This discussion was not detailed in the official minutes but recorded in the actual transcript of the meeting. See Berger, *Konjunkturpolitik im Wirtschaftswunder*, pp. 218, 220.
[108] 'Die Diskontsatzerhöhung in Westdeutschland', *Bank deutscher Länder Auszüge aus Presseartikeln* , No. 34, 20 Mar. 1956, DBPA, no. 75, p. 2.
[109] Hüllbüsch, *Die Kabinettsprotokolle der Bundesregierung, Band 9: 1956*, p. 249.
[110] 'Rundfunkgespräch des Herrn Peter Antes mit dem Präsidenten des Zentralbankrats der Bank deutscher Länder Dr. h. c. Karl Bernard am 19. März 1956', *Bank deutscher Länder Auszüge aus Presseartikeln*, No. 34, 20 Mar. 1956, DBPA, no. 75, p. 2.
[111] Karl Bernard, 'Die währungspolitische Situation in Westdeutschland', 29 Mar. 1956, DBHA, B330/3311, p. 2.

That would indeed be dangerous, not only for the currency, but also for politics in general. In the public, there exists agreement that the central bank council must be protected against political influences in all its guises, because otherwise a clear and expert central bank policy would not be possible. Finally, everyone knows that, in Germany, with two currency catastrophes behind us, the floodgates of inflation were opened up at a time when the government still possessed the trust of the population. From the first inflation, we know that is was not because of ill intent or insufficient morality, but rather a lack of technical competence.[112]

Not that such an argument swayed the chancellor in the slightest. 'These men haven't a clue about politics', he later said of the BdL leadership.[113] Adenauer was not alone in his opposition, either. Just two days after the chancellor's clash with Bernard in March 1956, the SPD's economics committee convened to discuss its latest position on the Bundesbank Law – indeed, for the first time since back in 1952.[114] The SPD committee members still remained divided on the question of the Bundesbank's structure and independence. As the committee chairman, Hermann Veit, noted during his concluding remarks:

With respect to the question of autonomy, it has to be noted that we are now living in the 'blue sky of the economic miracle', but it could also be that clouds are on the horizon. It remains to be settled whether we should allow the safety of the currency to the [central] bank alone, in any case, leaving it solely to the bank would be for us not acceptable.[115]

These discussions were kept confidential. But all the same, in early 1956, despite years of living under a 'blue sky' of prosperity, West Germany's major opposition party *still* expressed reservations with respect to the future Bundesbank's independence from government influence. There was still hesitance on the part of those SPD politicians who, back in the early years of the Federal Republic, had pointed to the mixed record of the inter-war Reichsbank to justify their arguments that the new central bank's autonomy should be reined in. This was a principled stand. Their discomfort centred on the need for democratic accountability over the sphere of monetary policy. This is an important point – particularly so, when we examine how the upcoming public controversy with Adenauer was to have a decisive impact on the

---

[112] 'Sachliches Gespräch im Palais Schaumburg', *Die Zeit*, 22 Mar. 1956.
[113] The chancellor's remarks were, on this occasion, in specific reference to Vocke. See Hüllbüsch, *Die Kabinettsprotokolle der Bundesregierung, Band 9: 1956*, p. 380.
[114] Rudolf Pass, 'Protokoll der Sitzung des Wirtschaftspolitischen Ausschuss beim Parteivorstand der SPD', 19 Mar. 1956, AdsD, 2/PVBF000007.
[115] Ibid., pp. 7–8.

SPD leadership's position regarding central bank independence from 1956 onwards.

The BdL increased the discount rate from 4.5 to 5.5 per cent in May 1956, as well as other measures.[116] This meant credit in the economy would now become even more expensive. But that was not all. It had soon become clear that the central bank co-ordinated its move with Erhard and Schäffer in Bonn. Just the day prior to the central bank council meeting in question, the two ministers submitted a 'second stabilisation programme' to the cabinet. And they did so out of the blue, catching the chancellor by surprise.[117] In fact, the informal *Konjunkturrat* of Vocke, Erhard and Schäffer had been working on the proposals for weeks.[118] They contained several measures aimed at slowing down the economic boom. Among them was a 30 per cent decrease in the tariff rate – a move that would have allowed cheaper imports to flow into the country, pushing down prices and, in turn, dampening the inflationary threat. This proposal, however, clashed with the interests of industrialists who catered to the domestic market. The higher domestic prices were, the better for industrialists.

On the day of the central bank council meeting, the economic and finance ministers gave an interview to the press. The two men stressed that the BdL and the two ministries were in 'complete agreement'.[119] Their goal was to place Adenauer on the back foot. The chancellor was, understandably, seething. Days after the ministers' interview, Adenauer delivered a speech at the annual convention of the BDI at the Gürzenich hall in Cologne. The chancellor stood before an audience of five hundred industrialists and journalists in Cologne and attacked the actions of the two ministers, as well as the central bank's credit tightening.

'The central bank council, gentlemen, is completely sovereign from the federal government', Adenauer stated. 'It is of course accountable to itself, but here we have an institution that is responsible to no one, not to parliament, not even to a government.'[120] The discount rate hike, Adenauer famously said, was like a 'guillotine' falling down on the West

---

[116] See BdL central bank council minutes, 18 May 1956, DBHA, B330/94/1.

[117] Helge Berger, 'The Bundesbank's path to independence: evidence from the 1950s', *Public Choice*, Vol. 93, No. 3–4 (1997), p. 442.

[118] Berger, *Konjunkturpolitik im Wirtschaftswunde*, pp. 221–6.

[119] 'Interview mit Bundeswirtschaftsminister Prof. Erhard und Bundesfinanzminister Schäffer über aktuelle wirtschaftspolitische Probleme', 18 May 1956, DBHA, B330/2025 II, p. 2.

[120] 'Rede von Bundeskanzler Dr. Konrad Adenauer am 23. Mai 1956 vor dem Bundesverband der Deutschen Industrie in Köln ("Gürzenich-Rede")', in Deutsche Bundesbank (ed.), *Geheimrat Wilhelm Vocke, Hüter der Währung, Zum hundertsten Geburtstag am 9. Februar 1986* (Frankfurt am Main, 1986), p. 154.

German people. And, in a phrase eerily similar to that used by his confidant, the BDI's Berg, back in December 1955, the central bank's actions constituted 'a heavy blow against the German boom'.[121] One journalist in the audience later commented how 'unusually slow' and deliberate these words came from Adenauer's mouth, almost if he was 'chanting every syllable'.[122]

The Aftermath

Adenauer slipped up. The remarks, the chancellor soon found out, were a grave mistake. By attacking the BdL's independence in such terms, it appeared that the chancellor openly wished to remove it. A media sensation ensued, with news articles and commentary pieces flowing in support of the monetary authority's policies and autonomy.[123] 'In praise of independence' was just one newspaper headline among many.[124] But not only domestic newspapers, international ones too. Vocke, described by the *Financial Times* as the 'boy wonder of the old Reichsbank', was now also the 'guardian of the D-Mark'.[125] 'In a country where inflation has wiped out savings twice within 25 years', the *Financial Times* continued, 'the position of the central bank is bound to be a strong one'. It was a direct result from these experiences that its wary chairman 'defends the independence of the bank tooth and nail'.[126]

Two weeks after Adenauer's speech at the Gürzenich hall, *Der Spiegel* depicted Vocke on the front page with the title 'chancellor of the deutschmark' (see Figure 3.1).[127] Recall that, when Vocke was asked to appear on the magazine's front cover back in 1951, he was hesitant to do so and rejected the offer. Now, in the heady aftermath of the 'Gürzenich affair', such caution fell by the wayside. Inside the cover, the current affairs magazine featured a thirteen-page spread detailing the clash between the statesman and the central bank. It offered a blow-by-blow account of the scandal. Indeed, it described some of the scenes with intimate detail. The article even noted what meal Erhard had ordered his housekeeper to make, having returned for an impromptu lunch at 1.30 p.m. on the dot following a tense meeting with the chancellor: fried eggs, sunny

---

[121] Ibid.   [122] Ibid., p. 157.
[123] See, for instance, 'Ein Lob der Unabhängigkeit', *Die Zeit*, 5 Jul. 1956; and 'Die Weiche wird gestellt', *Der Spiegel*, 6 Jun. 1956; 'Vocke – "Guardian of the D-Mark"', *Financial Times*, 19 Jun. 1956.
[124] 'Ein Lob der Unabhängigkeit', *Die Zeit*, 5 Jul. 1956.
[125] 'Vocke – "Guardian of the D-Mark"', *Financial Times*, 19 Jun. 1956.   [126] Ibid.
[127] Ibid.

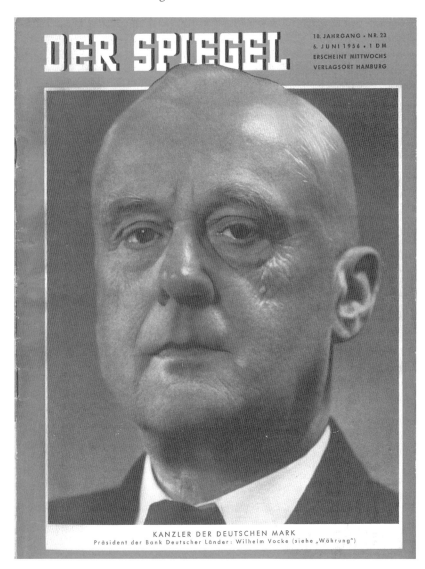

KANZLER DER DEUTSCHEN MARK
Präsident der Bank Deutscher Länder: Wilhelm Vocke (siehe „Währung")

Figure 3.1 Like Schacht and the Reichsbank during the inter-war era, the Bank deutscher Länder is portrayed as a one-man show. Vocke as the 'chancellor of the deutschmark', according to the title heading of *Der Spiegel*, 6 June 1956.
(© DER SPIEGEL 23/1956)

side up, with spinach on the side.[128] It is likely that Erhard and Vocke provided much of the information relating to the Gürzenich speech fallout.

The article offered readers an extensive account of the BdL's record since its establishment in 1948. The news piece fused historical narratives of the two inflations with the contemporary political debate in 1956, framing the BdL's current struggle in terms of the 1939 episode, during which the Reichsbank sent the memorandum protesting against Hitler's spendthrift government. 'Hitler raged that was mutiny', *Der Spiegel* noted – using the very term Vocke himself had established for public record at the Nuremberg courtroom back in 1946.[129] The BdL chairman was among those the dictator had sacked in 1939, the magazine continued. After detailing the moral importance of the Reichsbank memorandum that had led to his dismissal all those years ago, *Der Spiegel* ended the thirteen-page exposé with the following remark: 'Wilhelm Vocke wrote the memorandum'.[130]

Der Spiegel published a few images to go along with the article. The magazine, for example, printed two pictures on the same page. The first, placed at the top of the page, was of several men pushing a large wheelbarrow full of cash across the street at the height of the Weimar hyperinflation. *Der Spiegel* then directly linked this picture to one positioned at the bottom of the page, of Allied troops unloading boxes of newly printed deutschmark banknotes from a truck in 1948. 'Through two German inflations…', the caption under the first picture began, '… painful experiences are accumulated', the caption under the second photograph finished.[131] *Der Spiegel*, in other words, portrayed the experiences of the hyperinflation as providing a direct lesson, one that explained the success of the West Germany's young currency. A picture of Schacht, too, in his prime, was published with a caption mentioning Vocke had written the famous Reichsbank memorandum.[132] Vocke's record with the Reichsbank was explicitly used as a source of credibility, to demonstrate his moral superiority over Adenauer, a man in whom *Der Spiegel* had little faith.

Vocke was now popular in West Germany. Just *how* popular, though, can be discerned from the way in which the BdL chairman became the subject of tabloid media interest. *Bild Zeitung*, established in 1952 and already emerging as a dominant force in the country, published an interview with Vocke in early June 1956. The central banker now occupied the same sentence as a Hollywood superstar. 'An autograph from

[128] Ibid., p. 15.   [129] Ibid.   [130] Ibid., p. 27.   [131] Ibid., p. 20.   [132] Ibid., p. 23.

Greta Garbo – exciting', the interview began. 'An autograph from Vocke – reassuring.'

The more one has of them, the better. Please, just have a look in your wallets. Perhaps there is still one of those magic notes within. We've just had our paycheques arrive on the first of the month. Look: on the back, to the left, one can see 'Vocke'. It is the signature of ... Wilhelm Vocke, president of the directorate of the Bank deutscher Länder.[133]

Documenting the central bank's apparent bravery during the 'Gürzenich affair', the journalist noted 'it was not the first time Vocke showed his teeth'. Indeed, the first time was in 1939 when the central banker rebelled against Hitler and the latter's armament financing. Hitler 'raged' and removed him from the Reichsbank.[134]

Capitalising on the central bank's publicity triumph, a collection of Vocke's speeches was published in late 1956 under the title *Gesundes Geld*, or *Sound Money*.[135] Preparations for the book began less than a month after Adenauer's 'guillotine' speech in Cologne.[136] Fritz Knapp Verlag, the publishing house attached to Volkmar Muthesius, the economics journalist and central bank ally in the push to maintain central bank independence, published the book. The alliance between Vocke and Muthesius, then, forged back in 1949, had culminated with a selection of published speeches – and only a matter of months before the election year of 1957.

Muthesius even wrote the forward for the edition. 'The purpose of this volume', the journalist wrote, was to put the 'personal perspective of one of the most prominent central bankers of our time' before the eyes of the general reader.[137] The economics journalist portrayed Vocke's sound principles as having stemmed from his inter-war experience with the Reichsbank. Inevitably, the Reichsbank memorandum of 1939 featured heavily throughout. 'This document', Muthesius wrote, 'played an important role in the Nuremberg trial 1945/46 against the leaders of the Third Reich'.[138] The publicist, of course, did not mention that its use at Nuremberg was primarily towards vindicating the controversial record of Schacht; nor the fact that the prosecution had listed the memorandum as evidence *against* Schacht.[139]

---

[133] 'Er hält die Mark an der Kette', *Bild-Zeitung*, 4 Jun. 1956, DBHA, BSG 1/387.
[134] Ibid.   [135] Wilhelm Vocke, *Gesundes Geld* (Frankfurt, 1956).
[136] Viktor von der Lippe to Volkmar Muthesius, 18 Jun. 1956, DBHA, B330/2035.
[137] Volkmar Muthesius, 'Wilhelm Vocke', in Wilhelm Vocke, *Gesundes Geld* (Frankfurt am Main, 1956), p. 9.
[138] Ibid., p. 11.   [139] See Chapter 1.

Leaving aside the memorandum's appearance in the thick legal volumes of documents concerning the Nuremberg trials, Muthesius wrote, it had not yet been published in the West German public sphere – until now. West German readers could see for themselves the memorandum printed in the appendix of the book, published in its entirety.[140] Muthesius's introduction was careful to note that Vocke was the memorandum's main drafter. But it failed to mention that at least several other directorate members had a hand to play in its wording. As Figure 3.2 shows, the 1939 memorandum featured in an advertisement for *Gesundes Geld* in 1956, once again demonstrating the importance of the document for the central banker's image in the media.

In *Gesundes Geld*, the final speech was an edited version of Vocke's 1956 Hamburg address, which will be discussed in greater detail further below. This version, however, was heavily shortened and titled 'The independence of the central bank', though the original speech also touched on other topics.[141] The message was simple: only under an independent central bank, one that was run by apolitical experts, could the currency remain stable. The book was well received by the media. 'In view of the fact that the work and the name of the German central bank president is so closely linked to the development of the new German currency, you will be thankful today to have at hand his collected speeches and essays in book form', read one glowing review, 'all the more so, as a means to document the history of the German mark, which has been enriched since the currency reform by a competent and responsible monetary policymaker'.[142]

A Game Changer

Why was the 'Gürzenich affair' important? Well, there are two points to note here. First, the central bank emerged triumphant at the expense of the chancellor's standing. As *Der Spiegel* put it, '[w]hat suddenly became apparent through Adenauer's tactical blunder was the classic case of a conflict of interests between the government and the independent central bank, the latter fulfilling its statutory duty to guard the currency regardless of the politics of the day'.[143] Adenauer had attacked two of his most popular ministers in public, too. Erhard threatened to resign from his

---

[140] Muthesius, 'Wilhelm Vocke', *Gesundes Geld*, pp. 11–12.
[141] Vocke, *Gesundes Geld*, pp. 135–7.
[142] 'Gesundes Geld, Gesammelte Reden und Aufsätze von Geheimrat Dr. W. Vocke', *Neue Zürcher Zeitung*, 21 Nov. 1956.
[143] 'Die Weiche wird gestellt', *Der Spiegel*, 6 Jun. 1956, pp. 15–27.

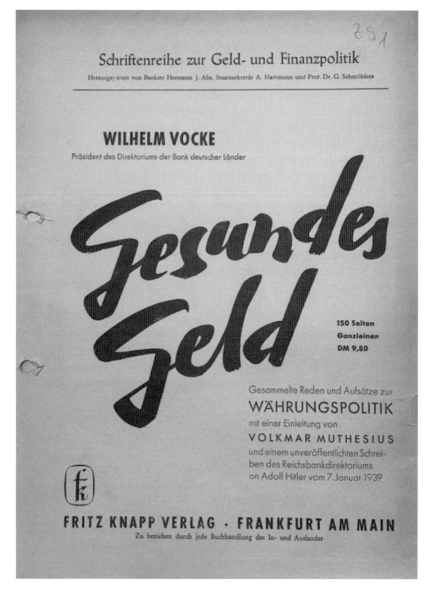

Figure 3.2 An advertisement for *Gesundes Geld*, or *Sound Money*, a collection of Vocke's speeches featuring 'an unpublished letter from the Reichsbank directorate to Adolf Hitler on 7 January 1939'.
Note: *Gesundes Geld*, DBHA, BSG 1/387.
(© Knapp Verlag GmbH)

post unless Adenauer retracted his comments. The chancellor subsequently did so. Soon after, the cabinet passed the two ministers' erstwhile controversial 'second stabilisation programme'. Nevertheless, the chancellor had still damaged the solidarity of his cabinet just a year before the next election.

'Dr Adenauer's enemies will make plenty of capital out of this affair', noted the foreign correspondent for the *Manchester Guardian*.[144] And so they did. It is here that we arrive at our second point. In short, Adenauer's difficulty was the SPD's opportunity. The opposition party swung in full support of the BdL's policies after the controversy erupted.[145] 'As the guardian of the currency, bank president Vocke could hardly have acted differently', opined *Vorwärts*, the party's newspaper.[146] On 22 June 1956, some weeks after Adenauer's speech in Cologne, Bundestag representatives of the SPD came out in strong support of central bank independence, noting how 'public opinion' was strongly in favour of it. All the while, they accused Adenauer of being in cahoots with the industrialists.[147] In November 1956, when the SPD economics committee convened to discuss the Bundesbank Law – the first time since the 'Gürzenich affair' – it accepted a largely independent Bundesbank.[148]

This is not to say that the SPD was a monolithic entity, however. The workers' party was split between moderates, such as Karl Schiller, and hardliners, who tended to be of the older generation.[149] The 'Gürzenich affair' give rise to circumstances in which the moderates prevailed, pushing the more sceptical hardliners on the back foot on the question of central bank autonomy. Moreover, it is important to view this development in the wider, more gradual shift in the SPD's position to the social market economy. Once hostile to Erhard's political programme, the SPD gradually came to slowly moderate its stance over the course of the 1950s, culminating in the centrist 'Godesberger Programme' of 1959.[150]

---

[144] 'German boom splits cabinet', *The Manchester Guardian*, 26 May 1956.
[145] See, for example, the following articles: 'Adenauers Kniefall vor der Industrie', *Vorwärts*, 1 Jun. 1956; and 'Die BdL antwortet', *Vorwärts*, 8 Jun. 1956.
[146] 'Die Konzeptionslosigkeit ist schuld', *Vorwärts*, 1 Jun. 1956.
[147] '2. Deutscher Bundestag – 152. Sitzung. Bonn, Freitag, den 22. Juni 1956', p. 8158. See http://dipbt.bundestag.de/doc/btp/02/02152.pdf. Last accessed on 20 December 2018.
[148] Minutes of Social Democratic Party meeting (Wirtschaftspolitischer Außschuss), 5 Nov. 1956, p. 10.
[149] Nicholls, *Freedom with responsibility*, pp. 248, 367–89.
[150] See Werner Abelshauser, *Die langen Fünfziger Jahre: Wirtschaft und Gesellschaft der Bundesrepublik Deutschland 1949–1966* (Düsseldorf, 1987), pp. 72–3; Spicka, *Selling the economic miracle*, pp. 241–2.

But back to 1956. For the SPD, the public controversy surrounding the 'Gürzenich affair' was a game changer. Any hesitation to embrace the cause of the BdL's independence – as evident in March 1956, just months prior – was now swept to the side. In doing so, however, the opposition party's leadership willingly narrowed the parameters within which it interpreted Germany's monetary past. In supporting the future Bundesbank's autonomy, the left-wing opposition effectively prioritised the lessons of the two inflations over other historical narratives. It brushed aside the experience of the independent Reichsbank during the Great Depression. Back in 1951, the SPD economics committee grounded its reservations concerning the monetary authority's independence with reference to the experience of mass unemployment.[151] The BdL was a 'shadow government', according to one angry SPD politician in parliament in 1950.[152] After the events of May 1956, however, especially in the lead-up to the Bundesbank Law's passage through parliament, there was no such talk. The 'Gürzenich affair' asserted the dominance of the BdL's version of monetary history.

Although Adenauer backed down in public, he did not give up entirely just yet. The chancellor demanded that the question of the Bundesbank's autonomy be returned to the cabinet table.[153] 'The current location of the central bank has led to it having a separate existence', he said on 11 July 1956.[154] That had to change. The chancellor had in mind Bonn or neighbouring Cologne as possible locations for the new monetary authority. Despite the recent public uproar sparked by Adenauer, too, central bank independence was still on the agenda. At least as far as the chancellor was concerned. 'The Bundesbank cannot pursue a policy against the government', he continued. 'That is not possible.'[155] Adenauer faced resistance among his ministers, however. Nevertheless, at his behest, a new draft of the Bundesbank Law was formulated, one in which the future central bank's independence was heavily watered down.

By this time, however, Adenauer was an isolated figure. Support for the BdL's independence had become so pervasive, and its interpretation of monetary history so dominant in the public sphere, that

---

[151] Harald Koch and Rudolf Pass, 'Protokoll zur Tagung des Wirtschaftspolitischen Ausschusses beim Parteivorstand der SPD am 1. und 2. Juni 1951', no date, AdsD, 2/PVBF000003, p. 2.

[152] 'Deutscher Bundestag – 108. Sitzung. Bonn, Freitag, den 15. Dezember 1950', p. 4062. See http://dipbt.bundestag.de/doc/btp/01/01108.pdf. Last accessed on 20 December 2018.

[153] Von der Lippe to Vocke, 17 Jul. 1956; 'Das Notenbankgesetz erneut zurückgestellt', *Frankfurter Allgemeine Zeitung*, 12 Jul. 1956.

[154] Hüllbüsch, *Die Kabinettsprotokolle der Bundesregierung, Band 9: 1956*, p. 474.

[155] Ibid., p. 477.

Erhard could feel able to reduce the debate to a simple equation. Writing to the CDU's Scharnberg, who still expressed reservations about the Bundesbank's independence, Erhard countered with the following remark: 'The formula "dependent central bank = inflation" is valid at all times and everywhere. Historical experience proves that to us with crystal clarity.'[156]

Vocke, too, emerged from the 'guillotine' affair stronger and more confident. Speaking before an audience of bankers and local notables in Hamburg, Vocke discussed the indispensability of central bank independence for the economy's health. What followed was the most explicit reference towards maintaining the central bank's independence when the Bundesbank was to replace the BdL. If the law had but one goal, Vocke declared, it was to maintain that level of independence without any alteration:

We appear to live in a somewhat nervous and excitable period, and currency matters are among those which exercise people's minds. The Bank deutscher Länder has seen no cause for excitement but has pursued a calm, steady and consistent course. It is true that the bank saw fit to act, and did so in good time. There has been no lack of criticism directed at us. Thus we were told by industrialists that we had dealt the German economy a crushing blow […].

Developments in the world are in constant movement and fluctuation, and in this up and down we wish to preserve a stable currency retaining its value, such as we have built up for the benefit of our country. In this context I once before declared – and I now repeat it – that the essential prerequisite for this is the independence of the central bank, as it exists today under the terms of a law enacted by the federation itself. This independence must remain unassailable; nothing must be detracted from it nor must it be toned down or hollowed out […].

Nobody after all can be interested in once more depriving the German people of this guarantee of a stable currency, or in the curtailing such a guarantee, now that on this basis we have built up a stable currency which is indeed to all intents and purposes de facto a convertible one. The central bank requires no political influences in order to do what is necessary to maintain stability. To this end there is no need for political supervision or intervention but merely for expert knowledge and practical experience. Why, then, should there be any need to exert political pressure on the central bank? Would it be in order to force upon the central bank something which it deems to be dangerous or unbearable for the stability of the currency? Or possibly in order to stop the bank from doing something which it might deem essential to the defence of the currency?

All this has happened before, but the remembrance of the experiences which the German nation has passed through in the currency field has been terrible and is still alive in our memories. If it is desired to produce a new bank law, then such

---

[156] Ludwig Erhard to Hugo Scharnberg, 20 Jul. 1956, BAK, B102/12595, p. 3.

a law must have only one aim, viz. the preservation of what we have achieved in the currency field, the reinforcement and maintenance of confidence in the currency and of confidence in the central bank. It is only a clear line that will inspire confidence.[157]

Once again, the press faithfully reported Vocke's words and arguments.[158] In the election of 1957, the economy took on an unprecedented level of importance in the public debate given that the economy was grappling with full employment.[159] At the heart of the argument was the increasing price level.[160] 'Prices will decide the election', wrote *Der Volkswirt*, an economics magazine.[161] The two chairmen of the central bank took to the public sphere in the lead-up to the election to push once more for the central bank's independence.[162]

In the *Frankfurter Allgemeine Zeitung*, Vocke, in particular, once again returned to the topic of central bank independence and Germany's two inflationary episodes, welding the BdL's success record to the experiences of the West German past: 'It is necessary, of course, that the central bank, which has to defend the currency, should not be hindered in its duty by political influences. If things are better in Germany than other countries in this respect, it depends not least on the fact that the German people have two terrible inflations behind them and the memory of which still cuts to the bone.'[163] Bernard's speech, which spoke out in defence of the monetary authority's autonomy, was heavily reported upon too.[164]

---

[157] Wilhelm Vocke, 'Address on the occasion of the hundredth anniversary of the Vereinsbank at Hamburg', 11 Aug. 1956, DBPA, no. 1244, pp. 1, 4–5.

[158] 'Die Notenbank soll unabhängig bleiben', *Frankfurter Allgemeine Zeitung*, 13 Aug. 1956; 'Geheimrat Dr. Vocke verteidigt die Währungspolitik der Bank deutscher Länder', *Industrie- und Handels-Kurier*, 9 Sep. 1956; 'Bundesbank ohne Aufsicht?', *Die Zeit*, 16 Aug. 1956; and 'Ist die Unabhängigkeit der Notenbank bedroht?', *Stader Tageblatt*, 16 Aug. 1956.

[159] See the insightful commentary of Koerfer, *Kampf ums Kanzleramt*, pp. 84–5.

[160] For example, refer to 'Preisauftrieb ohne Ende', *Der Volkswirt*, 23 Feb. 1957.

[161] Ibid.

[162] Wilhelm Vocke, 'Härte Währung', *Bank deutscher Länder Auszüge aus Presseartikeln*, No. 14, 4 Feb. 1957, DBPA, no. 1244; Karl Bernard, 'Gedanken zur Kreditpolitik', *Bank deutscher Länder Auszüge aus Presseartikeln*, No. 18, 18 Feb. 1957, DBPA, no. 75, p. 3.

[163] Vocke, 'Härte Währung', p. 1.

[164] 'Die Vormögensteuer überprüfen', *Frankfurter Allgemeine Zeitung*, 16 Feb. 1957; 'Stabile Währung ist Lebensbasis', *Frankfurter Rundschau*, 16 Feb. 1957; 'Die Unabhängigkeit der Notenbank ist kein Selbstzweck', *Frankfurter Rundschau*, 16 Feb. 1957. See also 'Auf einen Blick...', *Die Zeit*, 21 Feb. 1957; and 'Die Grenzen der Notenbankpolitik', *Finanznachrichten: Fachschrift für das gesamte Finanz- und Kreditwesen*, 30 Mar. 1957.

Vocke's memoirs are surprisingly reticent about his time at the BdL. Fewer than thirty pages out of a total of over 220 are devoted to his chairmanship of the West German central bank.[165] However, in an essay that was later published in 1965, Vocke gave his thoughts on the affair.[166] 'Adenauer was certainly no expert in the field of economics, finance and the currency', he wrote. 'Although he gave wide-ranging freedom to Erhard in his economic policy and Schäffer in his budget and tax policy, he could be tempted to intervene in monetary policy and establish guidelines that could only be resisted with difficulty. And so it came to differences with the central bank, which was not a glorious chapter in Adenauer's book. Of course, nothing happened. But only because the law of the central bank acknowledged the essential necessity of independence and because the leadership of the central bank defended its independence with success.'[167]

The Bundesbank Law of 1957

After almost eight years of ongoing debate, the Bundesbank Law was finally passed on 26 July 1957.[168] The result, one that was conditioned in the public sphere as well as the West German parliament, was a more centralised monetary authority, the Bundesbank. That the law took so long to pass through the legislature can be attributed to the power struggle between the federal and state levels of government concerning the central bank's organisational structure. But its delay of passage can also be put down to the fact that other debates, such as the Credit Law and Anti-cartel Law, were entwined with the fortunes of the Bundesbank Law.[169] According to articles 1 and 2 of the new law, the state central banks had become subsidiaries of the federal central bank.[170] This shift towards centralisation had an impact on the structure of the leadership, too. The two chairmen positions were now consolidated into one

---

[165] Vocke, *Memoiren*, pp. 145–71.
[166] Wilhelm Vocke, 'Adenauer und die Wirtschaft', in Hans-Joachim Netzer (ed.), *Adenauer und die Folgen: Siebzehn Vorträge über Probleme unseres Staates* (Munich, 1965); see also the copy of Vocke, 'Adenauer und die Wirtschaft' in the DBHA.
[167] Vocke, 'Adenauer und die Wirtschaft', p. 4.
[168] 'Gesetz über die Deutsche Bundesbank. Vom 26. Juli 1957', *Bundesgesetzblatt, Teil I, Ausgegeben zu Bonn am 30. Juli 1957*, Nr. 33, 1957, p. 745. See www.bgbl.de/xaver/bgbl/start.xav?startbk=Bundesanzeiger_BGBl#__bgbl__%2F%2F*%5B%40attr_id%3D%27bgbl157s0745.pdf%27%5D__1473433479381. Last accessed on 20 December 2018. See also Wilhelm Könneker, *Die Deutsche Bundesbank*, 2nd ed. (Frankfurt, 1973), p. 9.
[169] Krieghoff, 'Banking regulation in a federal system', p. 123.
[170] 'Gesetz über die Deutsche Bundesbank. Vom 26. Juli 1957', p. 745.

role: the president of the Bundesbank. The president led both the directorate and central bank council.[171]

Nevertheless, the new central bank's autonomy was somewhat diluted in comparison to the independence once enjoyed by the BdL. This suggests that the experiences of the Reichsbank during the late 1920s and early 1930s were also in part reflected in the Bundesbank Law.[172] As a compromise, the government could now appoint the directorate. This included the president of the directorate, its vice president, and up to eight more members. In the days of the BdL, only one member of the directorate had voting rights at the central bank council. This person was either the directorate's chairman or, in his absence, his deputy, the vice chairman. Now, according to the Bundesbank Law, *all* members of the directorate were entitled to vote on the central bank council.[173] Numerically, the directorate members constituted a maximum of ten seats on the central bank council. The remainder of the forum was to be made up of the presidents of the ten *Länder* central banks.[174] The federal government, in other words, could appoint up to 50 per cent of the central bank council.[175] Bonn saw this change in the appointment procedure as a dramatic improvement, given that the federal government had zero input on who had sat at the BdL's central bank council. The federal cabinet could now exert a sizeable, if somewhat indirect influence on the monetary authority's decision-making body, should it select the 'right' candidates for the directorate.

The duty of the new central bank was to 'guard the currency', as outlined in article 3.[176] And according to article 12 of the legislation, '[t]he Deutsche Bundesbank is obliged, within the remit of its duties, to support the general economic policy of the federal government'.[177] Such wording was vague, however. In effect, it left the Bundesbank in a position to define what that 'support' actually entailed.

Government representatives could attend central bank council meetings. But they were not given voting rights. However, if they wished, they could issue a suspensive veto with respect to decisions taken by the

---

[171] More specifically, the federal government nominated directorate members, after which the federal president confirmed their appointment. Ibid., pp. 745–6.

[172] I am grateful to the banking historian Dieter Lindenlaub who highlighted this point to me.

[173] 'Gesetz über die Deutsche Bundesbank. Vom 26. Juli 1957', p. 746.

[174] See articles 7 and 8 of the Bundesbank Law. The presidents of the *Länder* central banks were to be nominated by the Bundesrat and confirmed in their appointment by the federal president. Ibid., p. 746.

[175] This point is noted in Krieghoff, 'Banking regulation in a federal system', p. 191.

[176] 'Gesetz über die Deutsche Bundesbank. Vom 26. Juli 1957', p. 745.

[177] Ibid., p. 747.

central bank council. This veto would delay the implementation of the central bank council's decision for a period of two weeks.[178] Thus, despite strong opposition from certain figures within the federal government over the years – among them, Adenauer and Schäffer – the central bank managed to maintain a strong degree of policy independence. The Bundesbank, later renowned as one of the world's most independent and successful monetary institutions, had arrived.

Crucially, however, the Bundesbank Law did not provide for any comprehensive resolution mechanism through which conflicts between Bonn and Frankfurt could be solved by formal process. The government's permanent veto and the federal arbitration committee, ideas once proposed by Schäffer back in 1950, had long since disappeared from the negotiating table. Instead, the Bundesbank Law embraced an 'Erhardian' vision of relations between the central bank and government. Bonn could not issue instructions to Frankfurt, nor could it veto the Bundesbank's decisions on a permanent basis. But it did exert a sizeable influence as to who was running the central bank. Erhard had always stressed a close co-operation between Frankfurt and Bonn.

Nevertheless, this lack of a formal mechanism by which one could solve disputes, essentially reaffirmed the institutional divide created back in 1948 by the Allied military authorities. The overall task of running the economy remained divided between Bonn and Frankfurt. As such, the provisions in the Bundesbank Law meant that, on occasion, a power struggle could emerge over the direction of monetary policy. By allowing the central bank to pursue its own policy, one largely independent of the government's considerations, the Bundesbank Law thus allowed for the creation of circumstances through which future Bonn–Frankfurt disputes could emerge.

Indeed, some politicians were aware at the time that the Bundesbank Law's provisions would lead to a 'dramatisation' of conflicts, which in turn would be played out in the public arena, and influenced by public opinion.[179] But here lies the key point: it would be in these 'dramatised'

---

[178] Ibid.

[179] For instance, refer to the comments of the SPD politician Walter Seuffert. '2. Deutscher Bundestag – 175 Sitzung. Bonn, Freitag, den 30. November 1956', p. 9716. See http://dipbt.bundestag.de/doc/btp/02/02175.pdf. Last accessed on 20 December 2018. This point is also clearly outlined in a report concerning a meeting in 1957 of the Committee for Money and Credit, a forum in which various levels of government and the central bank could reach consensus on the Bundesbank Law. See 'Schriftlicher Bericht des Ausschusses für Geld und Kredit (22. Ausschuss) über den Entwurf eines Gesetzes über die Deutsche Bundesbank', BDI-Archiv, S8IWB – NB 252 1957, p. 9. And finally, see the comments of the CDU's Scharnberg in 1957 in Deutsche Bundesbank (ed.), *30 Jahre Deutsche Bundesbank.*

conflicts that historical narratives, or lessons, of the two inflations would naturally flourish again – just as they had done in the early years of the Federal Republic. The origins of a German 'trauma' of inflation might well have been psychological and derived from the experiences of the 1920s and 1940s. But the Bundesbank Law ensured that a cultural preoccupation with the inflationary past would remain, fuelled by an underlying institutional struggle between Bonn and Frankfurt, one that centred on the direction of monetary policy.

Conclusion

It is here that we return to Arden House in the United States in 1958. Vocke, though recently retired, stood with pride before his audience. Publicity, the former Reichsbanker declared, was 'one of the sharpest weapons in the arsenal of a central bank', not to be restricted to statistics and numbers alone. 'Central banks cannot take their course according to theories or books of science. Common sense must guide them. They should not look only to the actual figures of today, but sense the dynamic tendencies and estimate the dangers threatening from this or that angle, and adjust their policies according to the conditions of the day, always having in mind the fundamental weight of confidence.'[180]

Following the passage of the Transition Law in 1951, a piece of legislation that settled the question of independence – at least temporarily – the debate surrounding the future Bundesbank's structure and organisation continued to incentivise West German elites to return to their inter-war monetary past, discerning from it lessons with which they could ground their political arguments. We have seen how the shadow of the Reichsbank loomed over the efforts of the federal and state governments fighting each other for influence with respect to the decision-making body of the Bundesbank. The BdL's reputation and confidence grew over the years. The business cycle played an important role in this respect. Presiding over economic prosperity, the central bank gradually shed its image as a creature of the occupation. By 1955, the Bank deutscher Länder's confidence was such that it could even issue self-styled 'warnings' to the government.

In the early 1950s, a variety of historical narratives concerning the inter-war period competed against each other. By 1957, however, a single

---

Die Entstehung des Bundesbankgesetzes vom 26. Juli 1957 (Frankfurt am Main, 1988), p. 148.

[180] Vocke, 'Address before the monetary conference at Arden House on 27 March 1958', p. 5.

version had become dominant. The 'Gürzenich affair' played an important role in this development. The circumstances surrounding the episode highlight how an ongoing institutional divide incentivised West German elites to frame a contemporary political debate in historical terms. True, industrialists did evoke the experiences of the Reichsbank's independence during the Great Depression, an independence 'paid for with victims comparable to the losses of a lost war'. But by the mid-1950s the BDI and its president Berg were among the very few elites who still referred to the experiences of the Great Depression. Under the 'blue sky of the economic miracle', it became increasingly difficult to challenge the institution of central bank independence on the grounds of unemployment figures. Even the left-wing SPD, still floundering in opposition in 1956, failed to challenge the historical narratives propounded by the central bank and its allies in the media.

Instead, the BdL's version of history had become dominant. Vocke actively drew on his own past and experiences. The Reichsbank memorandum, first emerging at the Nuremberg trials in 1946 as a moral document, had come to assume a big importance in the image of the post-war central bank. The BdL acted in the manner that it did, Vocke argued, because it was painfully aware of the lessons of Germany's history. Indeed, by 1956, the entire record of inter-war monetary history could be reduced to a simple equation. In the words of Erhard, 'The formula "dependent central bank = inflation" is valid at all times and everywhere. Historical experience proves that to us with crystal clarity.' The 'Gürzenich affair' helped narrow and ossify the parameters of monetary debate.

The Erhardian vision of the Bundesbank Law set on much firmer ground an institutional power struggle that was so evident in the years prior to 1957. By leaving conflicts without a means of being solved behind closed doors (by means of an arbitration committee, for example), the Bundesbank Law increased the likelihood that such disputes would spill into the public sphere. Taken together, Chapters 2 and 3 have shown how contemporary disputes created circumstances in which West Germans were incentivised to understand an institutional divide in historical terms. The Bundesbank Law, for its part, would play a crucial role in influencing how future generations of West Germans understood their past. The BdL's monetary mythology helped to forge the Bundesbank Law. And after 1957, the Bundesbank Law helped maintain the central bank's monetary mythology.

4 The Shadow of National Socialism: Karl Blessing and the Bundesbank in 1965

Introduction

It is the scene of a cabaret show. Two men in tattered army uniforms are standing on the stage. The audience has come from in and around Frankfurt to see the performance. The date is Wednesday, 13 October 1965.[1] One of performers is holding a book, *Deutschland Report*, in his hand. 'You know, I read something recently about Himmler's circle of friends', the man says to his acquaintance. 'Himmler had friends?' The man raises the book to the audience and replies, '[o]h yes, a whole bunch of benefactors, really rich ones'. Indeed, some of these men were still around today, he continued. The audience might happen to know them. There was the industrialist Friedrich Flick, of course – one of the wealthiest men in West Germany. And Heinrich Bütefisch of IG Farben notoriety, too. 'Are there any more?' The man stands before the audience. Why yes, he replied. There was Karl Blessing, who happens to be the current president of the Bundesbank.[2]

During the Third Reich, Blessing had been a member of the *Schutzstaffel* (SS) Reichsführer's *Freundeskreis*, or 'circle of friends'.[3] The group of elite industrialists and SS officials met on a regular basis to discuss matters of economic importance, while providing a steady stream of funding for the SS.[4] The Bundesbank press department learned of the cabaret's impending performance in Frankfurt just a week

---

[1] The cabaret show was advertised in the local Frankfurt press. See 'Newspaper advertisement', 6 Oct. 1965, Deutsche Bundesbank Historisches Archiv [DBHA], B330/3506.

[2] An internal Bundesbank memo, written some months earlier by the press department, describes the scene in detail. See 'Notiz vom 30. Mai 1965', 30 May 1965, DBHA, B330/3506.

[3] Blessing's relationship with the *Freundeskreis* is documented in Christopher Kopper, *Bankiers unterm Hakenkreuz* (Munich, 2008), pp. 194–5.

[4] For more on Himmler's *Freundeskreis*, see 'Relations with government leaders, various political parties, the SS, and the "Circle of Friends" of Himmler', in *Trials of war criminals before the Nuernberg Military Tribunal under Control Council Law No. 10, vol. VI*, pp. 226–87.

before the show's arrival. Viktor von der Lippe, the central bank's press chief, and personal advisor to Blessing, was livid. He was well aware of the cabaret's notoriety. 'Apparently this damned Munich cabaret is now coming to Frankfurt!' von der Lippe wrote to Blessing.[5]

The cabaret to which von der Lippe was referring was the Münchner Lach- und Schiessgesellschaft, one of the most influential cabaret outfits in the history of the Federal Republic.[6] On this particular occasion, the name of the show was 'The unloading of guilt is forbidden'.[7] An irreverent, political display, the performers on stage sought to highlight what they saw as the hypocrisy of the West German state. In addition to singing the line '*Ja, Flick und Kameraden, die kamen nie zu schaden*', the cabaret accompanied the burial of the deutschmark 'at the tender age of seventeen' by means of song.[8] The cause of the currency's untimely death? The free market.[9] There were other scenes as well, of course. But it was the accusation that Blessing was a confidant of Himmler that infuriated the Bundesbank's press chief. Before the show arrived in Frankfurt, von der Lippe asked a contact in Munich, the vice president of the state central bank in Bavaria, whether the latter could exert his influence and get the scene omitted from the show.[10] 'Here at the headquarters of the Bundesbank, one can only really await this performance with very mixed feelings', he noted. 'A repeat of the attacks on our president here would be particularly nasty.'[11] Von der Lippe's efforts did not succeed.

Blessing's membership of Himmler's *Freundeskreis* was not breaking news. The fact had been clearly established at the Nuremberg trials that followed the Second World War. In 1947 Blessing was a witness at the Flick trial, which examined the links between big industry and National

[5] Von der Lippe's message was typed below the newspaper clipping that had advertised the show. The clipping was sent to Blessing. See 'Newspaper advertisement', 6 Oct. 1965.
[6] Axel Schildt and Detlef Siegfried, *Deutsche Kulturgeschichte. Die Bundesrepublik von 1945 bis zur Gegenwart* (Munich, 2009), p. 169. A recent exhibition in Leipzig has documented the history of political cabaret in Germany. See Stiftung Haus der Geschichte der Bundesrepublik Deutschland (ed.), *Spass beiseite. Humor und Politik in Deutschland* (Leipzig, 2010), esp. pp. 41–51. For a personal account of the *Münchner Lach- und Schiessgesellschaft*, see Dieter Hildebrandt, *Was bleibt mir übrig. Anmerkungen zu (meinen) 30 Jahren Kabarett* (Munich, 1987).
[7] '"Schuld abladen verboten." Das zwölfte Programm der Münchner Lach- und Schießgesellschaft', *Die Andere Zeitung*, 10 Jun. 1965, DBHA, B330/3506.
[8] The lyric can be translated as: 'Flick and his comrades, they never came to harm.' A transcript of the scene in question can be found in Dieter Hildebrandt, *Ich mußte immer lachen. Dieter Hildebrandt erzählt sein Leben* (Cologne, 2006), pp. 131–3. See also 'Notiz vom 30. Mai 1965'.
[9] See again 'Notiz vom 30. Mai 1965'.
[10] Viktor von der Lippe to Fritz Oechsner, 6 Oct. 1965, DBHA, B330/3506. [11] Ibid.

Socialism. Following the Nuremberg trials, however, the Bundesbank's president's chequered past was broadly overlooked by the West German mainstream press. With the exception of a marginal, left-wing publication called *Das Dossier*, no other newspaper or magazine detailed Blessing's troubled history.

Instead, the media depicted Blessing as having followed in the footsteps of Wilhelm Vocke, one of the former chairmen of the Bank deutscher Länder (BdL), the Bundesbank's predecessor. As such, Blessing was the *Hüter*, or guardian, of the currency. A former Reichsbanker, Blessing's signature could also be found on the memorandum sent to Adolf Hitler in 1939, which had protested against the inflationary policies of the Third Reich. In the Federal Republic, press reports continually reminded West Germans that the memorandum led to the sacking of Vocke and Blessing. Like Vocke, then, Blessing's image was that of a martyr to the ideals of sound currency. The signature written on that Reichsbank memorandum could now be found on the deutschmark banknotes that West Germans carried in their pockets.

By mid-1960s, however, the complacency found in some sectors of the media began to fade. An East German propaganda campaign, spearheaded by the Ministerium für Staatssicherheit – more commonly known as the Stasi – targeted the elites of West Germany. Newspapers in the Eastern Bloc began to publish articles that highlighted the Nazi pasts of leading officials in the Federal Republic, with the general aim of tarnishing the country's reputation. That the East German state employed propaganda against its Western counterpart was nothing new.[12] But something else was. By the early 1960s, certain parts of the West German media, conditioned by generational change, had become more assertive, more critical. The 'consensus' journalism so evident during the early 1950s was eroding.[13]

In West Germany, journalists and mainstream publications began to pick up on the East German allegations. In 1965 *Deutschland Report*, a book that traced the continuities between the Third Reich and the Federal Republic, detailed Blessing's link to the Himmler circle.[14] In doing so, the book used a plethora of documents from the Nuremberg

---

[12] See Michael Lemke, 'Kampagnen gegen Bonn. Die Systemkrise der DDR und die West-Propaganda der SED 1960–1963', *Vierteljahrshefte für Zeitgeschichte*, 41. Jahrg. 2. H. (Apr., 1993); and Christina von Hodenberg, *Konsens und Krise: eine Geschichte der westdeutschen Medienöffentlichkeit 1945–1973* (Göttingen, 2006), pp. 386–9.
[13] Christina von Hodenberg, 'Mass media and the generation of conflict: West Germany's long sixties and the formation of a critical public sphere', *Contemporary European History*, Vol. 15, No. 3 (2006).
[14] Bernt Engelmann, *Deutschland Report* (Berlin, 1965), p. 76.

trials to back up its explosive claims. The appearance of *Deutschland Report* helped to provide the inspiration for the aforementioned cabaret show, which itself was broadcast on national television in May 1965.[15] Mainstream publications, too, such as *Der Spiegel*, the *Frankfurter Rundschau* and *Zeitung* magazine, started to pick up on the *Freundeskreis* story. These news stories called into question the credibility of the Bundesbank's president. As such, the central bank felt forced to respond. But how? The damaging claims could not be left unanswered. Yet an official statement on the matter would only fuel the media's interest about Blessing's history. For von der Lippe, the priority was to kill the story as quickly, and as quietly, as possible.

As will be detailed later in this chapter, the press department countered these allegations with its own competing version of history. Von der Lippe, with the personal help of Blessing, formulated a sanitised past, outlined in a document entitled the 'short comprehensive summary'.[16] This document depicted the Bundesbank president's record in the finest light possible, given the revelations at hand. The 'short comprehensive summary' – as well as documents from the Nuremberg trials, such as the 1939 Reichsbank memorandum and Blessing's and Vocke's testimonies – was sent directly to the journalists who had written the negative articles. The central bank took the caution of using proxies to send these documents, lest it be seen as directly interfering in the controversy. Von der Lippe's proxies also contacted editors of the publications in question and encouraged them to read the documents, seeking redress to the allegations made. In this web of correspondence, the Bundesbank remained in the shadows. The news story, after several months of sporadic recurrence, faded away by the end of 1965. The media moved on to other news items. Von der Lippe continued with the press department's usual business. And Blessing, though somewhat tarnished by the affair, remained a martyr.

The incident highlighted the existence of two competing identities of the Bundesbank in the public sphere, both of which could trace their origins to the courtrooms of Nuremberg in the late 1940s. The first identity embodied the ideals so carefully crafted by Blessing's predecessor, Vocke. It emphasised the importance of the 1939 Reichsbank memorandum as a moral document. The second one, however, was murkier. It implied a lack of morality, which in turn could invite

---

[15] The date of the television premiere, 29 May 1965, is noted in 'Programme der Münchner Lach- und Schießgesellschaft' in Hildebrandt, *Was bleibt mir übrig*, p. 317.
[16] Karl Blessing and Viktor von der Lippe, 'Kürze zusammenfassende Darstellung', May 1965, DBHA, B330/3506.

scepticism on the part of the West German population. As a result, at moments when it was challenged by the record of the past, the Bundesbank sought to influence the parameters of debate amid efforts to create a sanitised image of itself, one suited to fostering confidence in the deutschmark.

The argument underlying this chapter is threefold. The first strand of argument stresses the element of continuity – in the public sphere – between the BdL and its successor, the Bundesbank. In doing so, it places a specific emphasis on the reputations of the two institutions. In short, they were broadly the same. The aura of a strong, independent central bank was firmly in place before the Bundesbank was established. This reputation merely continued with the Bundesbank. In tracing this continuity, the chapter stresses the role of the central bank's leadership. This is because Blessing personified both the Bundesbank and the deutschmark in the public sphere, a trend that the press department itself actively promoted. This continuity, however, brought with it occasional challenges. Like the BdL, the Bundesbank was not the legal successor of the Reichsbank. But it was linked to the record of the Reichsbank due to the men who walked along its corridors. The West German media both recognised and noted this continuity.

This is where the second layer of argument comes in. Given the emphasis placed on the central bank's leadership by the media, the mixed record of the Reichsbank during the inter-war period continued to burden the Bundesbank in the post-war era. The challenges of the past remained. As a result, the monetary authority actively sought to shape historical narratives in the media when these challenges emerged. But which challenges, exactly?

In making its argument, the chapter focuses on three case studies, all of which occur in and around the year 1965. First, it examines the public accusation made by Hjalmar Schacht, the former Reichsbank president, that Blessing actively supported the second inflation, which had occurred during the Third Reich and eventually ended with the destruction of the reichsmark.[17] Second, it tackles the emergence of the Himmler *Freundeskreis* news story and documents the efforts of the Bundesbank's

---

[17] Dieter Lindenlaub was the first to note this episode in his 2008 essay on Blessing. However, he does so only in passing, devoting a single sentence to Schacht's accusation. See Dieter Lindenlaub, 'Karl Blessing', in Hans Pohl (ed.), *Deutsche Bankiers des 20. Jahrhunderts* (Stuttgart, 2008), p. 13.

press department to stifle it. And third, the chapter analyses the Bundesbank's endeavours to discredit the term 'third inflation'.[18]

The 'third inflation' was an expression used by some West German commentators, politicians and citizens to describe West Germany's struggle with 'imported inflation'; a slow, creeping inflation that ate away at the value of the deutschmark. Its appearance in public discourse was treated with concern in Frankfurt. Before, the BdL had linked historical narratives of the two inflations to the need for legal independence from political influence. But the emergence of the 'third inflation' as a term of reference was an example of how such narratives could also be turned *against* the central bank itself. Instead of being seen as preventing an inflation, the Bundesbank was now accused of *presiding* over one. In this respect, the 'third inflation' was a subversive narrative. And as Blessing himself noted, it could be easily misunderstood by the average man on the street. Could the 'third inflation' turn out just as bad as the first two? The very term itself invited historical parallels – which the Bundesbank saw as most unwelcome and unjustified.

But who lent currency to this term in the 1960s West German public sphere? The Bundesbank president knew the person in question quite well. It was Blessing's old mentor, Schacht. The former Reichsbank president was now an old man, and somewhat isolated from respected society. But he was determined as ever to have his voice heard – even if it meant appearing in disreputable illustrated magazines with front covers featuring images of scantily clad women. At certain moments, then, the Bundesbank was forced to face the legacy of the inter-war past. And the central bank was determined to do so on its own terms.

Chapters 2 and 3 argued that the BdL used historical narratives of Germany's two inflationary episodes amid efforts to influence the Bundesbank Law, a piece of legislation that established the future central bank. More specifically, Vocke and other leading central bankers used the lessons of the two inflations to defend the monetary authority's independence from the West German government. This chapter's third layer of argument contends that historical narratives were still of crucial importance for the Bundesbank. With the Bundesbank Law already passed, however, they were simply used for a different purpose.

---

[18] The term 'third inflation' has rarely ever been discussed in the literature. Lindenlaub, though, briefly notes that the 'third inflation' was a point of discussion in 1960s West Germany. See Dieter Lindenlaub, 'Deutsches Stabilitätsbewußtsein: Wie kann man es fassen, Wie kann man es erklären, welche Bedeutung hat es für die Geldpolitik', in Bernhard Löffler (ed.), *Die kulturelle Seite der Währung. Europäische Währungskulturen, Geldwerterfahrungen und Notenbanksysteme im 20. Jahrhundert* (Munich, 2010), p. 77.

This purpose was what Blessing termed 'moral persuasion', a concept closely related to the uses of public opinion. The Bundesbank pursued an active press policy to influence monetary attitudes among the West German population. Historical narratives stemming from the inter-war provided the key reference points and examples with which the central bank conditioned its arguments. The Bundesbank's goals were to augment the effectiveness of its policies and provide a historical legitimacy for central bank independence.

The use of 'moral persuasion' was further motivated by a generational change that was taking place in the 1960s. A whole new generation of West Germans had grown up without any experience of the two inflations. The central bank, for its part, was determined to impart the lessons of such events to the young. In illustrating its points, the chapter highlights two narratives in particular: the necessity of central bank independence in light of the absence of a gold standard; and the consequences of government control of the printing press. The Bundesbank wielded these narratives in the public sphere to defend its interests.

Karl Blessing and the Bundesbank: Reputation and Continuity

Blessing arrived at the Bundesbank in 1958 and left at the end of 1969. As such, the Bundesbank president entered office when Konrad Adenauer was at the height of his power. Blessing's tenure outlasted two subsequent coalition governments, the first led by the father of the 'economic miracle', Ludwig Erhard, the latter by Kurt Georg Kiesinger, a Christian Democratic Union (CDU) politician. He left the Bundesbank shortly after Willy Brandt became chancellor of the first Social Democrat-led coalition government. His twelve years at the helm of the central bank oversaw two currency revaluations and several international monetary crises. By the time he left office, Blessing had become one of the most influential monetary figures in Europe.

Chapter 1 has already documented Blessing's inter-war record. In short, it was full of contradictions. Blessing was an active member of Himmler's *Freundeskreis*, but his name could be found on the Reichsbank memorandum sent to Hitler in 1939. The central banker participated in meetings that persecuted Germany's Jewish population, yet he was linked to a clandestine group that sought to kill Hitler. Blessing's relationship with the Third Reich was never one based on conviction – rather, the evidence suggests it was one was founded upon opportunism. His career could have been interpreted in several ways in the post-war era. Was Blessing a martyr to sound currency? Or was he an 'ambitious Nazi technocrat', as described by the writer David Marsh?[19] In the late 1950s, these questions remained outstanding. Their answers would be determined in the public sphere. Newspapers, magazines, radio shows and television programmes would play a decisive role in how West Germans saw Blessing, the Bundesbank and the deutschmark.

The image and reputation of the Bundesbank president mattered. The media, for its part, closely identified the fortunes of the deutschmark with this one man – as demonstrated by the front cover of *Der Spiegel* in Figure 4.1: Blessing was the 'president of the deutschmark'. Image did not always correspond to reality, of course. After all, Blessing held only one vote on the central bank council, itself comprised of a newly empowered directorate as well as presidents of the state central banks. The central bank council, like that of the BdL, decided policy by majority vote. But when it came to communicating the central bank's goals and objectives to the government and West German public, Blessing was the central figure of the Bundesbank's communication efforts. Indeed, the Bundesbank was more centralised than the BdL in this regard. Where the BdL had two chairmen – who held different views on crucial questions, such as the ideal structure of the monetary authority – the Bundesbank Law of 1957 centralised the top echelon into one position.

Blessing entered the central bank on the back of overwhelmingly positive press coverage. Yet these reports are also interesting in how they viewed the newly established Bundesbank. Under Vocke and Karl Bernard, the other chairman of the monetary authority, the BdL had firmly established the idea of a strong, independent and even rebellious central bank that fought for a stable currency. As noted in Chapter 3, the 'Gürzenich affair' back in 1956 was a key moment in this respect. Adenauer might have been the chancellor of the West German state, but Vocke was the 'chancellor of the deutschmark'.[20]

The Bundesbank, from its inception, was treated in the same terms. In the eyes of the media, the credibility hard won by the BdL was simply carried over to the Bundesbank. Journalists and commentators highlighted those aspects of Blessing's career that fit best with the image of an independent central bank. Blessing was 'an independent man', according to the *Frankfurter Rundschau*.[21] After all, the newspaper continued, Blessing was among those men who were dismissed by Hitler in 1939 after the Reichsbank directorate had sent a 'virulent memorandum' warning that the currency was threatened by the dictator's profligacy.

---

[19] David Marsh, *The Bundesbank: the bank that rules Europe* (London, 1992), p. 21.
[20] See the title page of *Der Spiegel*, 6 Jun. 1956.
[21] 'Der neue Hüter der Deutschen Mark', *Frankfurter Rundschau*, 12 Jul. 1957.

Figure 4.1 The Bundesbank as a one-man show. Karl Blessing, president of the Bundesbank, and 'president of the deutschmark', on the front cover of *Der Spiegel*, smoking an Erhardian cigar, 17 August 1960.
Note: Contrast this picture with images of Ludwig Erhard, the economics minister and later chancellor, who was rarely photographed without a cigar at hand. For a similar image of Erhard, see Mark E. Spicka, *Selling the economic miracle: economic reconstruction and politics in West Germany, 1949–1957* (Oxford, 2007), p. 180.
(© DER SPIEGEL 34/1960)

'The result was not only a cleansing of the uncompromising Reichsbank leadership, but also the passage of a secret law that eliminated the independence of the Reichsbank.'[22] Blessing was thus a martyr for his ideals – another one of the few men who said 'no' to the dictator during the Third Reich. Other publications went so far as to stress a direct link between Blessing and Vocke. 'Karl Blessing', wrote *Der Spiegel*, 'like Vocke before him, is a prisoner of a deeply-rooted collective trauma of the Germans: after two devastating inflations within a generation, federal citizens respond to any increase of prices with panic.'[23]

As these quotes suggest, there was indeed a pronounced Reichsbank narrative to be found in these articles. Blessing was publicly identified as having been under the tutelage of the old Reichsbank president Schacht – something that would emerge to become quite problematic in 1965. The Württemberger 'came from the old Reichsbank administration and out of the Schachtian school', according to *Die Welt* in 1959.[24] A current affairs magazine, *Aktuell*, went somewhat further. In a detailed profile piece on the Bundesbank president, the publication printed a picture of Schacht with the subheading 'Blessing's first "master."'[25]

The Bundesbank was not the legal successor to the Reichsbank. But in the media's eye, there was clearly a perceived line of continuity between the Reichsbank, the BdL and the Bundesbank. This link was perceived because of the men who staffed the halls of these central banks. The media portrayed these men as being imbued with the lessons of the history. And it was from these very lessons, the media repeatedly claimed, that Vocke and Blessing drew their ideals, convictions – and credibility. Thus, from the moment it was established, the Bundesbank benefitted from the strong image established by the BdL. But it was an image that was based upon a certain historical narrative of the inter-war past. This left the central bank vulnerable to political attacks should one choose to portray the inter-war era in a different perspective.

Why were the media so favourable to Blessing upon his arrival? When he became Bundesbank president, one newspaper noted the distinct lack of information surrounding his past.[26] There was simply too little to go on. This suggests that the Bundesbank – or more specifically, its press department – had an opportunity to mould the parameters within which the new Bundesbank president would be portrayed.

---

[22] Ibid.   [23] 'Das D-Mark-Karussell', *Der Spiegel*, 17 Aug. 1960, p. 18.
[24] 'Die goldenen Fünfziger', *Die Welt*, 29. Apr. 1959, DBHA, BSG 1/12.
[25] 'Karl Blessing. Ein unbequemer Mann zwar – aber ein ehrlicher Makler', *Aktuell*, 5 May 1962, DBHA, BSG 1/12, p. 14.
[26] 'Der neue Hüter der Deutschen Mark', *Frankfurter Rundschau*, 12 Jul. 1957.

Von der Lippe and the Press Department

There were other aspects of continuity that marked the arrival of the Bundesbank. Like other departments at the central bank, the press department remained in its entirety. Von der Lippe continued in his dual capacity as head of the press department and personal advisor to the president. He was Vocke's confidant and played a key role in how the BdL interacted with the press. The former Nuremberg defence attorney arrived at the BdL in 1949 and remained with the Bundesbank until January 1977.[27]

As with his time at the BdL, von der Lippe continued to exert an important influence in the background. He remained present at directorate meetings in his capacity as minute taker, and would participate in the informal discussions that were never recorded in the minutes.[28] Von der Lippe quickly became Blessing's confidant at the central bank. He advised Blessing on media matters; he drafted the president's speeches; and, as with Vocke, he would often answer letters addressed to Blessing on the latter's behalf. Not many documents pertaining to the press department survive. However, the files that do offer an insight into how it operated. Furthermore, these files are important if we wish to gain a deeper understanding of how the press department responded to the challenges documented later in this chapter.

The Bundesbank press department was originally placed under the jurisdiction of Eduard Wolf, a directorate member who was responsible for economics and statistical matters.[29] It was under Wolf, too, that the central bank's monthly and annual reports were compiled. In practice, Wolf devoted himself to the central bank's reports and left von der Lippe to his own devices. The press department, for its part, had no input in the drafting of the monthly and annual reports. Rather, Wolf, aided by several officials in the economics department, undertook the arduous task of compiling them. When Wolf died in 1964, the press department was placed under the jurisdiction of the president, Blessing.[30] This

---

[27] See von der Lippe's retirement speech, delivered on 31 January 1977. Viktor von der Lippe, 'Abschiedsworte', 31 Jan. 1977, Deutsche Bundesbank Pressearchiv [DBPA], no. 717.

[28] Some of these occasions are noted when von der Lippe is first discussed in Chapter 2 (footnote 127).

[29] See, for instance, 'Geschäftsverteilung im Direktorium der Deutschen Bundesbank', 1959, DBHA, B330/58602.

[30] More specifically, press matters were now marked as the reserve of Blessing. The economics and statistics department continued to compile the monthly and annual reports, however. This shift is documented in 'Geschäftsverteilung im Direktorium der Deutschen Bundesbank', 1966, DBHA, B330/58602.

formal transfer of jurisdiction merely reflected existing practice, however: the press department was controlled by von der Lippe, who worked closely alongside Blessing as his personal advisor.

The Bundesbank's interaction with the press followed the same structure as the BdL. The first tier was comprised of statistical reports and information. The second tier, however, was the press department's interaction with the media – speeches, press conferences and newspaper interviews – a tier that was instrumental in building the Bundesbank's reputation. As under the BdL, the official name of the press department was 'Press and information, library and archive, and foreign language service'. Von der Lippe, then, dealt with matters relating to the central bank's library, archive and foreign translations of the Bundesbank's monthly and annual reports.[31] In 1957, leaving the number of archive and library staff aside, the press department was staffed by seven people, including von der Lippe.[32] The number was broadly the same by the end of Blessing's tenure.

What were von der Lippe's official duties at the new central bank? A telling incident occurred in April 1959, with the publication of the Bundesbank's annual rules of procedure, the *Geschäftsordnung*. The document detailed the duties of each leading official at the central bank. 'The head of the press department is to keep in touch with members of the directorate and provide them with important information', the document read. 'He is available to the president with regard to the Bundesbank's external communications and participates in directorate meetings insofar as to record the minutes of the decisions made, unless special confidentiality is required.'[33] But this description angered von der Lippe. It underestimated his role at the central bank, he claimed. 'This sounds as if I do a little bit of work for the president and, among other things, record the minutes', he wrote. 'In actual fact, I am the personal advisor of the president and, so to speak, the leader of the press department, in addition to being entrusted with the recording of the directorate minutes.'[34]

---

[31] See, for example, 'Bank deutscher Länder Schematische Übersicht zum Geschäftsverteilungsplan (chart)', Apr. 1956, DBHA, B330/DRS. 113; 'Presse und Information, Bücherei und Archiv, Fremdsprachendienst'.
[32] Refer to 'Geschäftsverteilungsplan der Bank deutscher Länder', 15 Feb. 1957, DBHA, B330/DRS. 113.
[33] 'Geschäftsordnung für das Direktorium der Deutschen Bundesbank', 22 Apr. 1959, DBHA, B330/8140, p. 4.
[34] See Viktor von der Lippe to Heinrich Hartlieb, 19 Jun. 1959, DBHA, B330/8140.

A document clearly outlining the Bundesbank's principles of *Pressepolitik*, or press policy, does not survive.[35] But von der Lippe's press strategy can be gleaned indirectly from his correspondence with members of the directorate – often at moments when the policies of the Bundesbank were being attacked in the public sphere. In these scenarios, von der Lippe would write a short memorandum outlining the press department's current approach to the media. These memorandums were effectively von der Lippe's opinions – and they did not always reflect the views of directorate members. Nevertheless, given the extent to which he dominated the press department for over a quarter of a century, and given how he acted as the confidant of Blessing, von der Lippe's personal views were important. They remain the clearest indication historians have of the rationale behind the Bundesbank's interaction with the press, and, to date, they have been overlooked by the literature on the central bank.

For von der Lippe, it was only natural that the Bundesbank did not have an official spokesperson – a point that explains his anonymity in the wider public sphere. 'The legitimate spokespersons are the leading men of the central bank with their speeches, press conferences, interviews and talks', he once argued. In this sense, '[t]he monthly reports of the Bundesbank are also "spokespersons"'.[36] The personalities who led the monetary authority inspired the central bank's credibility with the markets. As a result, it was important that no barrier, or third party, interfere with this link, which to date had fostered such confidence in the currency. Here von der Lippe was speaking to a personification of both the Bundesbank and the deutschmark. And it is important to remember such words when we see images of Blessing on the front page of leading newspapers and magazines, such as the one depicted in Figure 4.1.

Nor should the monetary authority forget what it was: 'A central bank should not think in terms of "public relations," for it is not a commercial enterprise that engages in advertising', von der Lippe contended. 'Nor should it practise "political propaganda," because otherwise it would fall into the daily trappings of politics which would do more harm than good.'[37] What the Bundesbank should do, however, is engage in the spread of comprehensive information 'through speeches, interviews, press conferences and conversations with central bank's leading men,

---

[35] The directorate first discussed the 'principles' of the central bank's press policy back in 1948. These principles, however, were never recorded in detail in the minutes. See BdL directorate meeting minutes, 23 Sep. 1948, DBHA, B330/2054.

[36] Viktor von der Lippe to Otmar Emminger, 19 Mar. 1974, DBHA, B330/6181/5, p. 2.

[37] Ibid., p. 3.

and through monthly reports and press announcements'. These efforts have been 'in general, quite adequate and in no way unsuccessful'.[38]

At the same time, though, von der Lippe's conception of a press policy, one rarefied from the daily political tussle in Bonn, did not always fit with his arguments. When discussing the Bundesbank's continual release of press excerpts, or *Presseauszüge*, for instance, they were compiled in such a manner 'that one can indeed talk of "politics" or "psychological warfare"'. Indeed, '[t]he reaction with respect to the public is, as noted, in general quite positive and helpful', von der Lippe noted.[39] 'Hardly any other central bank in the world is manifested in speech and writing so often and so thoroughly about its aspirations and concerns as the Bundesbank.'[40]

That is not to say that von der Lippe overestimated the Bundesbank's immediate sphere of influence. Monetary policy was a complicated topic. It was difficult to talk about. As such, the press chief was acutely aware of the difficulties when it came to spreading the central bank's message. The Bundesbank needed help. This is where the press came in. In late 1964, the press chief elaborated on the role of the modern media. 'The ignorance of the great majority of the population with regard to the monetary system is quite extensive', von der Lippe wrote. 'It is because of this ignorance that the "mass media" have an open field in which to do good or bad.'[41] And for von der Lippe (Figure 4.2), there was a clear distinction between matters relating to monetary matters as a whole, on the one hand, and the Bundesbank specifically, on the other. Banking and savings associations played crucial roles in explaining monetary issues to the wider population. So too did a number of publications, such as the BdL's old ally, *Die Zeitschrift für das gesamte Kreditwesen*.[42] But the central bank, von der Lippe continued, should restrict itself to those issues that directly concerned it. Even then, the Bundesbank's task was complicated by the sheer technicality of its functions. 'There is simply no Philosopher's Stone through which one can influence uneducated or biased people within a short space of time.'[43]

---

[38] Ibid.
[39] In using the English expression 'psychological warfare', von der Lippe was actually quoting the state central bank president Fritz Schiettinger. The latter complained in 1974 to the Bundesbank president, Karl Klasen, that the central bank needed to pursue 'psychological warfare' to defend itself from political attacks. Ibid., p. 2.
[40] Ibid.
[41] Viktor von der Lippe, 'Bemerkung zu den Vorschlägen von Herrn H. zur "Erweiterung der Öffentlichkeitsarbeit der Bundesbank"', 24 Dec. 1964, DBHA, B330/8142, p. 1.
[42] Ibid., p. 2.   [43] Ibid., pp. 2–3.

Figure 4.2 Viktor von der Lippe
(DBHA, BSG 3/7562 – © Deutsche Bundesbank – Historisches Archiv)

This sober view was tempered with some optimism. For those matters that directly concerned the Bundesbank, von der Lippe argued that the monetary authority had a better chance of influencing people through existing media channels – for instance, newspapers, magazines and radio.[44] This is where the central bank's relationship with journalists was important. And indeed, the Bundesbank press department made a point of actively fostering relationships with journalists. 'We have long had good relationships with individual journalists', von der Lippe wrote. 'The better the quality of the journalist, the more one usually gets from him, and vice versa. A lot more can be achieved with a good relationship. This is something we have done repeatedly.'[45] The press department was to execute requests for information on a technical level – that is, it was to act as an information mediator of sorts – but 'political' questions as such were normally passed on to those were in a position to answer them; for example, to members of the directorate.

The press department continued to develop its network of journalists and media contacts. And it carefully monitored the press, too. It scoured newspapers on a daily basis for coverage on the Bundesbank. Articles relating to the Bundesbank were photocopied and filed in the central bank's press archive. Negative articles were flagged and misleading paragraphs underlined. If an article made claims that were deemed to be particularly egregious, exclamation marks were placed beside the offending passages. In these cases, the journalists who penned the articles were often contacted directly.[46] Von der Lippe was not afraid of being blunt, and occasionally hinted at the implications of such negative pieces. 'I called Herr Salchow [a journalist] and said to him that his article in the *Hamburger Abendblatt* was absolutely awful and not worthy of a serious journalist', von der Lippe once reported. Furthermore, the journalist was told he had 'disgraced' von der Lippe, who had originally vouched for the journalist's work. The offending journalist was informed, somewhat ominously, that 'he had damaged his reputation at the central bank'.[47]

Von der Lippe's relationships were not restricted to the newspapers alone. The central bank's long-lasting association with the publicist Volkmar Muthesius continued as ever. As in the era of the BdL, Muthesius went on to write favourable articles about the Bundesbank.[48] But there was another sphere in which the journalist aided the central bank. Muthesius was linked to a local publisher in Frankfurt, Fritz Knapp Verlag. In 1956, shortly after a public clash with the chancellor, the

---

[44] Ibid., p. 3.   [45] Von der Lippe to Emminger, 19 Mar. 1974, p. 2.

[46] See, for example, one particular incident in 1969. Von der Lippe was unhappy with claims made in the Swiss *Neue Zürcher Zeitung*, an influential newspaper in West Germany. See Viktor von der Lippe to Hans Zimmerman, 21 Feb. 1969, DBHA, B330/8142.

[47] Viktor von der Lippe to Anon., 27 Mar. 1973, DBHA, B330/8143.

[48] For example, see Volkmar Muthesius, 'Hände weg vom Bundesbankgesetz', *Die Zeitschrift für das gesamte Kreditwesen*, 1 Dec. 1965.

BdL's Vocke released a collection of speeches, under the title *Gesundes Geld*, or *Sound Money*, through the publisher.[49] In 1960 Blessing noted 'the many years of excellent co-operation' between the publisher and central bank.[50] This relationship would only prosper during the era of Blessing. A collection of the Bundesbank president's speeches, *Die Verteidigung des Geldwertes*, was released in 1960, when the central bank faced heavy criticism in light of its credit policies.[51] And in the years 1966–7, the period in which the Bundesbank was accused of 'toppling' Erhard's coalition government, the Bundesbank published three additional books with Fritz Knapp Verlag amid efforts to increase its presence and message in the public sphere.[52] Von der Lippe acted as the point of contact between both parties.[53]

Von der Lippe's press strategy enjoyed the full confidence of the Bundesbank president. 'With regard to informing the public, the Bundesbank, I believe, does far more than other central banks', wrote Blessing in 1969 in a private letter. 'It publishes a comprehensive annual report, it publishes monthly reports, moreover the central bank publishes an overview of relevant press articles, and the leading men of the bank often give public speeches, which are again published by the bank.' Blessing, for his part, was satisfied with the Bundesbank's outreach. 'One can hardly do more.'[54]

Indeed, the press department benefited from Blessing's more open attitude to the media – a mentality conditioned, perhaps, by almost a decade of experience in post-war industry. The BdL always displayed caution with the press, choosing to intervene in the public sphere only when it had to; Vocke frequently declined requests for interviews, and instead directed journalists to his latest speech. Blessing, by contrast, was far more media friendly.[55] From 1958 onwards the number of speeches and interviews given by Blessing and members of the directorate

[49] See Chapter 3 for more details. In 1951, von der Lippe published his account of the Nuremberg trials with the publisher, see Viktor von der Lippe, *Nürnberger Tagebuchnotizen: November 1945 bis Oktober 1946* (Frankfurt, 1951).
[50] Karl Blessing to Fritz Knapp, 2 Dec. 1960, DBHA, B330/277.
[51] Karl Blessing, *Die Verteidigung des Geldwertes* (Frankfurt am Main, 1960).
[52] Karl Blessing, *Im Kampf um gutes Geld* (Frankfurt, 1966); also Wilhelm Könneker, *Die Deutsche Bundesbank*, 2nd ed. (Frankfurt, 1973); and Otmar Emminger, *Währungspolitik im Wandel der Zeit* (Frankfurt, 1966).
[53] A point noted in Volkmar Muthesius to Karl Blessing, 5 Jul. 1966, DBHA, B330/284/II.
[54] Karl Blessing to Erich Wolf, 14 May 1969, DBHA, B330/305 IV.
[55] Lindenlaub has already noted Blessing's more media-friendly attitude at the helm of the Bundesbank in comparison to the more cautious Vocke at the BdL. See Lindenlaub, 'Karl Blessing', pp. 27–9.

increased markedly.[56] Vocke's initial caution – in his early years at the BdL, at least – had given way to Blessing's subsequent enthusiasm.

Moreover, Blessing recognised the importance of the Bundesbank presidency in the public sphere. 'The experience of the past twelve years has clearly demonstrated that the president of the Deutsche Bundesbank plays a significantly more important role than that envisaged in the provisions of the Bundesbank Law', Blessing contended in 1970, in a report co-written with Heinrich Troeger, the former vice-president, shortly after their retirement from the Bundesbank. 'Time and time again, the president is seen in the public eye as the representative who is responsible for the Bundesbank.'[57] In other words, Blessing realised the importance of the Bundesbank president's reputation. And he explicitly stated that it was an importance that could not be explained in legal terms alone.

Taking a step back, then, we can discern how the press department's strategy in terms of the media was comprised of proactive and reactive measures. It realised the importance of central bank credibility – a credibility that was tied to the leadership of the Bundesbank. As press chief and personal advisor to Blessing, von der Lippe embodied the close link between the central bank's leadership and its interaction in the public sphere. Speeches and interviews, coupled with the central bank's monthly and annual reports, formed the main pillars of the Bundesbank's press output. Von der Lippe continually pressured journalists behind the scenes. For example, negative articles were countered with, at times, stinging criticism directed at the journalists who wrote them. All these points suggest that von der Lippe and his press department actively sought to influence contemporary debates.

So far, however, much of the detail outlined has concerned itself with press policy and efforts to influence contemporary affairs. What happened when questions relating to the past arose? The next section examines three challenges of the past, and the key role played by the Bundesbank in trying to influence the way in which they were reported.

Challenges of the Past

The Bundesbank sought to foster the image of a strong, independent monetary institution. Yet the legacy of the inter-war era was not far

---

[56] See, for example, a detailed speech schedule for the year 1959, Viktor von der Lippe to Karl Blessing, 28 Jan. 1959, DBHA, B330/280.

[57] This powerful image clashed with the reality, Blessing and Troeger noted: the Bundesbank president had but one vote at the central bank council. See Karl Blessing and Heinrich Troeger, '12 Jahre Bundesbank', 14 Jan. 1970, DBHA, B330/6425/4, p. 4.

Table 4.1 *Nazi party membership of leading West German central bank officials*

	Total	Number of whom, ex-Nazis	
1948			
Bank deutscher Länder			
Central bank council	13	1	(8%)
Central bank council and directorate	18	3	(17%)
1958			
Bundesbank			
Central bank council	19	5	(26%)
Central bank council and *Land* boards	34	13	(38%)
1968			
Bundesbank			
Central bank council	20	8	(40%)
Central bank council and *Land* boards	34	18	(53%)
1978			
Bundesbank			
Central bank council	19	2	(11%)
Central bank council and *Land* boards	34	6	(18%)
1948–80 (cumulative)			
Bank deutscher Länder and Bundesbank			
Council, directorate and *Land* boards	126	49	(39%)

Note: The table requires two points of clarification. First, following the establishment of the Bundesbank in 1958, the directorate was incorporated into the central bank council. Thus the directorate does not appear explicitly in the table after that year. And second, the table includes '*Land* boards', boards that formed the managerial crux at the state central bank level. Marsh provides a detailed breakdown of this table in the appendix of his book. See Marsh, *The Bundesbank*, pp. 20, 338–44.

behind. Where the BdL struggled with the memory of mass unemployment during the period 1949–51, the Bundesbank struggled with the past of National Socialism in the mid-1960s. Blessing's involvement with the Third Reich was not unusual. As time progressed, the number of former Nazi party members increased at the central bank. Table 4.1 illustrates this shift. The era of Blessing was the period in which the number of former Nazis peaked at the monetary authority.

This trend created some obvious difficulties. Could one preach prudence in the present while having supported questionable policies in the past? There was a credibility issue here. Previous sections of this chapter have outlined the extent to which the confidence in the deutschmark centred on the leadership of the central bank. Blessing recognised this, the Bundesbank directorate recognised this, and von der Lippe certainly recognised it. This section of the chapter outlines three different case studies. The first incident examines the public fight that occurred between Blessing and Schacht. In 1965, the former Reichsbank president openly accused Blessing of playing an active part in fostering the second inflation. The incident serves to demonstrate the sensitive position in which the Bundesbank could occasionally find itself in the post-war period. The second case study charts the emergence in 1965 of Blessing's links to National Socialism – particularly his membership of Himmler's *Freundeskreis*. The chapter then shows how the central bank, led by von der Lippe, created a rival history through which it could try to suffocate the questionable one. And third, the chapter examines the discourse surrounding the 'third inflation', and how the Bundesbank fought to hinder the establishment of such a concept in the minds of West Germans.

Schacht

Schacht was a tarnished figure in the post-war era.[58] The former Reichsbank president oversaw the early rearmament of the Third Reich; he participated in Hitler's cabinet as a commissary economics minister; and, despite his removal from the Reichsbank in 1939, he remained as minister without portfolio for a period of years. Schacht was acquitted of all charges at Nuremberg, however. With the help of Vocke, along with other defence witnesses – and of course the 1939 Reichsbank memorandum, which made its first public appearance at Nuremberg – 'Hitler's magician' persuaded the court that he was innocent of the charges placed against him.[59]

But the finance man still commanded the attention of the press in the Federal Republic.[60] In 1953, for instance, Schacht published his memoirs, *76 Jahre meines Lebens*, or *My first seventy-six years*, as its English translation was titled.[61] A commercial success, its appearance

---

[58] As noted in Christopher Kopper, *Hjalmar Schacht. Aufstieg und Fall von Hitlers mächtigstem Bankier* (Munich, 2010), pp. 383–5.

[59] The sobriquet, still quite common in the post-war period, was taken from a work published during the years of the Third Reich. See Norbert Mühlen, *Hitler's magician: Schacht. The life and loans of Dr. Hjalmar Schacht*, trans. E. W. Dickes (London, 1938).

[60] For instance, refer to 'Mehr Geld – mehr Kapital – mehr Arbeit', *Die Zeit*, 22 Sep. 1949.

[61] See Hjalmar Schacht, *76 Jahre meines Lebens* (Bad Wörishofen, 1953). For the English translation, which appeared two years later, see Hjalmar Schacht, *My first seventy-six years*, trans. Diana Pyke (London, 1955).

in book shops was complemented by a series of extracts published in the West German glossy magazine *Revue*.[62] The reader stumbled upon the extracts of Schacht's memoirs while flicking through stories of the British royal family and consumer advertisements.

Instead of playing a part in history, Schacht now took to writing it.[63] He was not alone. It was in this period that the first history of the inter-war Reichsbank was recorded. For instance, the recollections of Hans Luther, the Reichsbank president during the years of deflation, were published a few years later.[64] Schacht, then, remained active in the public sphere. He took care, though, to send Blessing a note should the Bundesbank president have had any concerns about this. 'As you know, I have always avoided polemicising against the Bundesbank and will continue to do avoid doing so in the future, so you as long are leading the central bank', Schacht wrote.[65]

But the former Reichsbank president had a knack for attracting headlines all the same. 'Blessing is unable to say "no"' ran the title of one such interview with Schacht in the same year – published in the respected *Industriekurier*, no less. Schacht would use these opportunities to propound his own remedies for West Germany's monetary malaise. For Blessing, these articles were troublesome. In the media, the Bundesbank president was linked to the inter-war Reichsbank and, in particular, his role as Schacht's protégé.

Schacht's crusade continued. Though he was approached for comment by credible publications in the early years of the Federal Republic, such as *Der Spiegel* and *Die Zeit*, such attention began to wane by the 1960s. Schacht felt increasingly snubbed by West German elites. His advice was being ignored. So the former Reichsbank president did something novel. He took to the more populist press. 'I knew I had to express myself in a manner which could not be ignored or suppressed', he later wrote.[66] In an unusual move, Schacht wrote polemical essays in the glossy magazine *Quick*, a popular publication. *Quick* boasted one of the largest

[62] See 'Hjalmar Schacht: 76 Jahre meines Lebens. Die Memoiren des grossen Finanzmannes', *Revue*, 19 Sep. 1953, DBHA, B330/9686, pp. 12, 22–9; 'Hjalmar Schacht: 76 Jahre meines Lebens. Die Memoiren des grossen Finanzmannes', *Revue*, 10 Oct. 1953, DBHA, B330/9686, pp. 16–21; and 'Hjalmar Schacht: 76 Jahre meines Lebens. Die Memoiren des grossen Finanzmannes', *Revue*, 17 Oct. 1953, DBHA, B330/9686, pp. 12, 36.

[63] Indeed, he had already begun to do so shortly after the Second World War. See Hjalmar Schacht, *Abrechnung mit Hitler* (Hamburg, 1948).

[64] Hans Luther, *Vor dem Abgrund, 1930–33. Reichsbankpräsident in Krisenzeiten* (Berlin, 1964).

[65] Hjalmar Schacht to Karl Blessing, 8 Nov. 1962, DBHA, B330/294.

[66] Hjalmar Schacht, *The magic of money*, trans. Paul Erskine (London, 1967), p. 149.

circulations in West Germany. By 1970, for example, one-fifth of the West German population read the magazine.[67] Schacht appeared in two issues. Both of their front covers featured racy photos of attractive women. The first magazine sported a front-page story that was titled 'Men are no longer chivalrous'. The second magazine invited readers to discover more about the 'marriage market' in West Germany. 'I'm looking for a man', ran the headline. Well, *Quick*'s editors had already found *their* man. According to them, Schacht, 'whose reputation as a financial expert is legendary around the world', combined 'revolutionary ideas with a conservative frame-work'.[68] The magazine was delighted to have the former Reichsbank president to write two 'exclusive reports' on the state of the currency.[69]

Schacht's prose was succinct and clear. It was, for the most part, tailored for a broadly uneducated audience. 'I have maintained a public silence for years', he began. 'But I have watched the development of our currency with growing concern during this time. Now the moment has come – for I can remain silent no longer. My responsibility as a citizen of the state forces the pen into my hand.'[70] The deutschmark had lost half its value within just half a generation, Schacht exclaimed. And who was to blame? The state. It was the state who 'cheated the German people out of their money' by means of its reckless spending programmes.[71] It was the state that was bringing monetary ruin upon West Germans. 'It is a scandal.'[72] Where was the Bundesbank in all this? The monetary authority's policy, Schacht contended, was in effect no different to those pursued by the American and British central banks: 'Betrayal of the people as the official line of monetary policy!'[73] Schacht also dragged the record of Vocke and the BdL into his firing line. As per usual, the former Reichsbank president used the opportunity to expound his own, *dirigiste* recommendations for West Germany's monetary problems.[74]

Schacht's articles, and the manner in which they appeared, came as a shock in Frankfurt. As the media noted at the time, the Bundesbank was considering whether to respond to these allegations.[75] The Bundesbank,

---

[67] Von Hodenberg, *Konsens und Krise*, p. 90.
[68] Hjalmar Schacht, 'Der Staat betrügt uns um unser Geld: Ein Bericht von Reichsbankpräsident a. D. Hjalmar Schacht', *Quick*, 29 Nov. 1964, p. 16, DBHA, B330/9686.
[69] Ibid., p. 12.   [70] Ibid., p. 16.
[71] See Hjalmar Schacht, 'So kann unser Geld gerettet werden! Ein Bericht von Reichsbankpräsident a. D. Dr. Hjalmar Schacht', *Quick*, 6 Dec. 1964, DBHA, B330/9686, p. 112.
[72] Schacht, 'Der Staat betrügt uns um unser Geld', p. 16.   [73] Ibid., p. 104.
[74] See Schacht, 'So kann unser Geld gerettet werden!', pp. 116–19.
[75] These reports appeared before the actual publication of Schacht's articles. In order to achieve maximum publicity, *Quick* sent preprints to various newspapers so as to build

behind the scenes, recognised that Schacht's reputation in the public sphere was dire – indeed, the very appearance of 'Hitler's magician' in *Quick* suggested a degree of desperation – but the former Reichsbank president still commanded attention. For von der Lippe, Schacht's articles had 'without a doubt a large impact' in the public sphere.[76] At the same time, however, the Bundesbank was constrained in terms of how it could respond. 'Unfortunately, in the case of Schacht, it comes that he is a personality in the public's eye. To go on the counter-attack would be impossible', von der Lippe wrote. 'Were Vocke and Blessing to attempt to do so, it would be self-defeating; for they would have to defend themselves with logic and reason, while demagogic attacks are far easier. Furthermore, they could not lower themselves to the level of *Quick*, and an "answer" via radio or television would only serve to dignify Schacht's attacks.'[77] Thus, the Bundesbank was 'largely helpless' in this scenario.[78] The central bank gave no official reply to Schacht's comments. Nor did the government offer an official comment, for that matter.[79]

But they didn't have to. A crucial factor that conditioned von der Lippe's reasoning was the reaction of the press itself. Schacht was exposed to ridicule. For satirists, the sight of the former Reichsbank president in the midst of bikini-clad models and crime fiction was too good an opportunity on which to pass. 'I'm sitting at the hairdressers and flicking through *Quick* (where else do you come across it?)', opined one writer. 'Who else did I see but our dear and venerable doyen Schacht, former Reichsbank president, sitting alongside tearjerkers, crime and sex starlets.' He continued: 'Herr Schacht, I read to my amusement, is against inflation.'[80]

Other commentators were blunter. 'Schacht of all people!' ran one headline in the *Süddeutsche Zeitung*.[81] 'Hitler's magician' was now resorting to 'quackery', as journalist Hans Roeper put it in the *Frankfurter Allgemeine Zeitung*.[82] Due to these articles, the Bundesbank did not need

hype. See, for instance, 'Schacht greift an', *Frankfurter Neue Presse*, 24 Nov. 1964, DBHA, B330/9686.

[76] Von der Lippe, 'Bemerkung zu den Vorschlägen von Herrn H. zur "Erweiterung der Öffentlichkeitsarbeit der Bundesbank"', p. 1.

[77] Ibid.   [78] Ibid.

[79] A point noted in 'Ohne Kommentar', *Die Zeit*, 1 Jan. 1965. When asked about Schacht's comments in *Quick*, a government representative dodged an official response, choosing to answer the question in a personal capacity.

[80] Paul Ecré-Visse [pseudonym for Paul Krebs, a director at Deutsche Bank], 'Schach(t) der Inflation', *Handelsblatt*, 18–19 Dec. 1964, DBHA, B330/278; see also Paul Krebs to Dankmar Seibt, 23 Dec. 1964, DBHA, B330/278.

[81] Walter Slotosch, 'Ausgerechnet Herr Schacht!', *Süddeutsche Zeitung*, 25 Nov. 1964.

[82] Hans Roeper, 'Die Rezepte des Herrn Schacht', *Frankfurter Allgemeine Zeitung*, 12 Jan. 1965.

to respond to Schacht's attacks. The former Reichsbank's president's public discrediting was enough. Schacht, looking back on the affair, was bruised but still standing. 'The response [in the media] was amusing, and yet at the same time shaming', wrote the finance man. 'But at all events my serious aim had been achieved – the battle against inflation moved into the centre of the political arena. Now I was to be the victim of ignorance and political narrow-mindedness.' All the same, Schacht mused, 'there was no gainsaying the fact that the million-odd readership of *Quick* expressed its lively agreement with my article'.[83]

Schacht was not finished, however. On 15 July 1965, Blessing received a note from his press chief. A 'pretty nasty and once again thoroughly confused essay by Schacht' had just been published, 'in which the Bundesbank and you personally are attacked'.[84] The article in question accused Blessing of actively supporting the second inflation that destroyed the reichsmark. This time, the article could be found in the reputable *Deutsche Hochschullehrer-Zeitung*.[85] Was there any truth to the claim? Following Hitler's removal of the Reichsbank's independence in 1939, an executive board was formed to support the central bank's directorate in an advisory capacity.[86] Blessing, Schacht noted, was a member of this executive board that participated in supporting the inflation.[87] 'He participated in supporting the inflation for six years until the end of the war.'[88]

Blessing was furious. Upon learning of the article's publication, the Bundesbank president took to drafting a letter to be sent directly to Schacht. 'I would not like to take a position to your remarks in the *Deutsche Hochschullehrer-Zeitung*', Blessing began, 'but I must reject in the strongest terms, however, your claim that I had "participated in supporting" the inflation for six years until the war's end'.[89] Schacht was well aware, the Bundesbank president countered, that the advisory council had little to no influence over the directorate. Moreover, it had rarely convened during the period in question. 'At the very least', Blessing concluded, 'one by rights could level at you the same accusation of which you have accused me – that you "participated" in Hitler's war policies'.[90]

[83] Schacht, *The magic of money*, p. 149.
[84] Viktor von der Lippe to Karl Blessing, 15 Jul. 1965, DBHA, B330/294.
[85] Hjalmar Schacht, 'Zur Währungspolitik', *Deutsche Hochschullehrer-Zeitung*, Jul. 1965, DBHA, B330/294.
[86] For evidence of Blessing's membership, see 'Beirat der Deutschen Reichsbank [list of members]', 1939, Bundesarchiv, Berlin-Lichterfelde [BAB], R2501/6861, p. 1.
[87] Schacht, 'Zur Währungspolitik', *Deutsche Hochschullehrer-Zeitung*, p. 14.   [88] Ibid.
[89] Karl Blessing to Hjalmar Schacht (draft two), 16 Jul. 1965, DBHA, B330/294, p. 1.
[90] Ibid., p. 2.

Schacht never received the letter. Because it was never sent. Von der Lippe circulated a draft of Blessing's message to the directorate for feedback. Two directorate members, Erich Zachau and Heinrich Hartlieb, advised against it. They also cautioned Blessing against responding in the public sphere.[91] Their reasons were not stated. But it was likely that a letter sent to *Deutsche Hochschullehrer-Zeitung*, or an article published in a newspaper, would only serve to heighten media interest in the affair. But the accusation levelled at Blessing in the *Deutsche Hochschullehrer-Zeitung* was not a one-off incident. Schacht repeated the claims in his new 1966 memoir, *Magie des Geldes*, or *The magic of money*, appearing in 1967 in English.[92]

Indeed, Schacht used *The magic of money*'s publication as another opportunity to attack the leadership of the post-war central bank. This time he set his sights on both Blessing and his predecessor, Vocke. Time and time again, Schacht argued, his reputation had been dragged through the mud in the post-war era because of the 'Mefo' bills, those covert financial instruments that allowed Hitler to finance the armament of the Third Reich. Yet the 'Mefo' bills had been passed 'unanimously' by the Reichsbank directorate, according to Schacht.[93] 'All this did not prevent two of these members, the Privy Councillor Vocke, and later Herr Blessing, from being chosen to manage the Bundesbank.'[94] This was plainly unfair and reeked of double standards on the part of the West German governing authorities, the former Reichsbank president contended.

This earned Schacht a fiery, personal letter from Vocke, who was stung by this accusation. 'With this historical portrayal, you appear to have fallen victim to a mistake of your own memory.' Schacht failed to mention that Vocke expressed serious reservations about the 'Mefo' bills during the crucial meeting.

> But you did not listen to my remarks – as you should now still remember! You speak of a unanimous decision. You did not allow it to come to a vote in this session nor otherwise in principle. The colleagues were of your opinion, that was good enough for you.[95]

Vocke went on to list fifteen other mistakes that he found in *The magic of money*. The former BdL chairman vented his frustration to Blessing. Understandably, Vocke found a sympathetic ear. 'I have also asked

---

[91] Viktor von der Lippe to Karl Blessing, 19 Jul. 1965, DBHA, B330/294.
[92] See Hjalmar Schacht, *Magie des Geldes: Schwund oder Bestand der Mark* (Düsseldorf, 1966); for the English version, see Schacht, *The magic of money*.
[93] Schacht, *The magic of money*, p. 119.   [94] Ibid.
[95] Wilhelm Vocke to Hjalmar Schacht, 6 Apr. 1966, DBHA, B330/294, p. 1.

myself what Schacht is actually trying to do with this book, so full of inaccuracies and half-truths', the Bundesbank president consoled Vocke. 'It is a shame the vehemence with which Schacht is destroying his halo.'[96]

Once again, the Bundesbank decided not to respond to Schacht's publication. In April 1966, around the time of the book's appearance, the directorate discarded a suggestion to respond in an active manner.[97] The central bank did not need to, though. A pattern was emerging: the mainstream press treated Schacht's new publication with disdain. As one title of a commentary piece in the *Frankfurter Allgemeine Zeitung* put it: 'From magician to quack.'[98] Blessing, for his part, cut off his relationship with Schacht. Shortly afterwards, when a mutual friend asked whether Blessing was planning on attending Schacht's birthday celebrations in 1966, Blessing replied in the negative. Schacht, the Bundesbank president said, had called him a 'pushover when it comes to inflation' and accused him of 'support[ing] the inflation during the war. I can only describe that as infamy and I can see no possibility in having contact with him'.[99]

Leaving personal animosities aside, what does this episode reveal? For starters, it highlights that the legacy of the inter-war Reichsbank was never that far behind. There was a link between the two institutions. This link could be found in Blessing's past. Lingering controversies of the inter-war period could erupt once more during the post-war period. Second, the episode demonstrated that the Bundesbank could be placed in a remarkably sensitive position. Upon learning of Schacht's attacks, von der Lippe was immediately cautious. He sought to distance the central bank from the story. To have responded in an official manner would have only served to pour oil onto the fire. Given Schacht's tempestuous character, a spat in the public sphere would have engendered yet more articles from 'Hitler's magician', who thrived on publicity just as he had done in the 1920s and 1930s. And third, the incident revealed the extent to which the press supported the Bundesbank's cause. Schacht was lambasted in the public sphere. As such, this removed the immediate need for an official response.

---

[96] Karl Blessing to Wilhelm Vocke, 12 Apr. 1966, DBHA, B330/304, p. 1.
[97] Bundesbank directorate meeting minutes, 26 Apr. 1966, DBHA, B330/2068. A day before this decision was taken, however, Heinrich Irmler delivered a speech that touched briefly on Schacht's ideas – only to include them among the 'monetary mistakes' he was discussing. See Heinrich Irmler, 'Währungspolitischer Irrtümer', 25 Apr. 1966, DBHA, B330/9686.
[98] Klaus Dohrn, 'Vom Magier zum Wunderdoktor', *Frankfurter Allgemeine Zeitung*, 7 May 1966.
[99] See Karl Blessing to Franz Reuter, 4 Oct. 1966, DBHA, B330/290.

But what happened when other, more unfavourable historical narratives emerged in the public sphere? What happened when Blessing's ties with National Socialism emerged as a point of press discussion? As the next case study reveals, the Bundesbank could not always rely on the goodwill of the media. And it was in these scenarios that the central bank fought to control the parameters of debate.

Himmler

The *Freundeskreis* story makes for an intriguing case study. It is one of the few instances where documents from the press department survive. Almost every letter, internal memorandum, and news article related to the emergence of the story was documented and compiled into a single, thick folder to be found in the Bundesbank's historical archive.[100] As a result, it is possible to trace the intricate course of events as seen from within the walls of the Bundesbank. Recall that Blessing's links to Himmler's *Freundeskreis* had been established at the Nuremberg trials: the future Bundesbank president acted as a defence witness during the Flick trial and elaborated on his involvement with the group.[101] This testimony was soon published among countless other Nuremberg documents and had become available to the public in the post-war years. Few journalists sought it out, however. Up until 1965, no mainstream publication mentioned Blessing's links with the *Freundeskreis*. If a profile piece on Blessing mentioned the inter-war period, it was with reference to the Reichsbank memorandum of 1939.

The sole exception was a marginal, left-wing publication called *Das Dossier*. The newsletter, devoted to exposing the links between the Third Reich and Federal Republic, was a subscription-based, amateurish affair. This suggests that the publication enjoyed very little circulation. *Das Dossier* began to publish allegations about Blessing's past from 1960 onwards.[102] Von der Lippe soon became aware of the publication. But given that *Das Dossier* was a marginal force within the public sphere, one that was driven by ideological considerations, von der Lippe chose simply to ignore it. Nevertheless, the publication continued to highlight Blessing's links with National Socialism, this time with a 1963 article about

---

[100] The folder, otherwise nondescript, is marked 'personal'. See DBHA, B330/3506.
[101] 'Militaergerichtshof Nr. IV, Fall V, Nuernberg, Deutschland 18. August 1947. Sitzung von 9.30–12.30 Uhr (Karl Blessing's testimony)', 18 Aug. 1947, DBHA, B330/3506.
[102] See *Das Dossier*, 9 Jan. 1960; *Das Dossier*, 9 Nov. 1960; and *Das Dossier*, 2 Jan. 1962. All three issues can be found in DBHA, B330/3506.

Blessing's participation in the 1938 conference that placed the fine of one billion reichsmarks on Germany's Jewish population.[103]

Das Dossier did not just target Blessing. It took aim at other leading elites in the Federal Republic. As such, it came to the attention of the government news office, the Presse- und Informationsamt der Bundesregierung. In an exchange with an official based there, von der Lippe stated that *Das Dossier* contained the 'crudest and most unprofessional attacks' on the character of the Bundesbank president.[104] But von der Lippe sent more than just a letter. In a move that anticipated his strategy in 1965, the press chief included three additional documents. The first was Blessing's testimony at Nuremberg. Second, von der Lippe sent the Nuremberg judgment on the Flick process, which found the group to be of little genuine significance. And third, von der Lippe sent the official an SS report, written in 1944 in the aftermath of the '20 July' assassination attempt on Hitler's life, which implicated Blessing in the conspiracy. These documents, von der Lippe suggested, were to be used 'as material to refute the attacks made then [in 1960] and now'.[105] It remains unclear whether the government press official, one Herr P. M. Weber, made any use of these documents. And in the same letter, von der Lippe requested their eventual return. Yet *Das Dossier* was the exception to the rule. No other publication highlighted Blessing's involvement with the Third Reich.

This complacency began to change in 1965. The primary factor for the appearance of the *Freundeskreis* news story in the West German press can be traced to the other side of the Iron Curtain. The East German government sought any opportunity to expose what it saw as the clear link between fascism and capitalism so evident in its Western counterpart. The Stasi played a crucial role in this regard. In and around 1962–3, the Stasi – more specifically, Hauptverwaltung A of the Stasi, led by the notorious Markus Wolf – established a new, secret branch called 'Division X'. This section was to devote itself, among other goals, to 'black propaganda', exposing and discomforting elite figures in West Germany by highlighting their Nazi pasts.[106]

In February of 1965, chancellor Erhard awarded Blessing the *Großkreuz des Verdienstordens*, or Grand Cross of the Order of Merit, in

---

[103] 'Die Kristallnacht und ihre Folgen. Die Rolle der Krosigk, Hilgard und Blessing', *Das Dossier*, 29 Oct. 1963, DBHA, B330/3506.

[104] Viktor von der Lippe to P. M. Weber, 29 Jun. 1964, DBHA, B330/3506; and P. M. Weber to Viktor von der Lippe, 8 Jul. 1964, DBHA, B330/3506.

[105] See von der Lippe to Weber, 29 Jun. 1964.

[106] von Hodenberg, *Konsens und Krise*, pp. 386–9.

recognition of the latter's services as Bundesbank president.[107] And with that moment, whether the central bank liked it or not, the Bundesbank became embroiled in the politics of Cold War Europe. Blessing, as president of the renowned central bank, and as the personification of West Germany's proudest export, the deutschmark, became a prime target for the East German state.[108]

The event received favourable coverage in the Federal Republic. But the East German media seized on the news story. 'Erhard decorates friend of the SS', ran one headline.[109] 'Nazi financier is today Bundesbank president', another.[110] These headlines were complemented by the emergence of the *Braunbuch: Kriegs- und Naziverbrecher in der Bundesrepublik*, or *Brown book: War and Nazi criminals in the Federal Republic*, an East German publication that detailed the questionable pasts of high-profile West Germans.[111] The publication used documents from the Nuremberg trials to give grounding to its various damning claims, some of which were true, others not. Like the West German central bank, then, the East German state reverted to the Nuremberg trials to bolster its own version of the past, one suited to its political interests.

Blessing's history was detailed extensively – though the account contained several mistakes, and it overlooked the more positive aspects of Blessing's record, such as his association with the '20 July' group.[112] Nevertheless, *Braunbuch* documented Blessing's attachment to the *Freundeskreis*. He 'participated decisively in the financing, preparation and completion of the armament and war preparations'.[113] Furthermore, the *Braunbuch* highlighted IG Farben's high opinion of the man: 'Due to the high position Blessing had at the time, he had close ties with IG Farben. IG Farben wrote about Blessing to a South African firm: "He is a leading personality in the economics ministry and one of the Schacht's

---

[107] 'Bundesverdienstorden für Freund Himmlers', *National-Zeitung*, 12 Feb. 1965, DBHA, B330/3506.

[108] According to von der Lippe in May 1965, '[t]he trigger for the current agitation took place a few months ago in the Soviet zone with the honouring of Herr Blessing on his 65th birthday. The Soviet press published numerous articles, most of which were primitive and stupid.' See Viktor von der Lippe to Fritz Oechsner, 28 May 1965, DBHA, B330/3506.

[109] 'Erhard dekorierte SS-Freund', *Berliner Zeitung*, 12 Feb. 1965, DBHA, B330/3506.

[110] 'Nazifinanzier ist heute Bundesbankpräsident', *Neues Deutschland*, 16 Feb. 1965, DBHA, B330/3506. See also 'Blessing und die Arisierung', *National-Zeitung*, 16 Feb. 1965, DBHA, B330/3506.

[111] See Nationalrat der Nationalen Front des Demokratischen Deutschland (ed.) *Braunbuch: Kriegs- und Naziverbrecher in der Bundesrepublik* (Berlin, 1965).

[112] 'Bundesbank extract of "Braunbuch Kriegs- und Nazi-verbrecher in der Bundesrepublik, Berlin 1965"', 1965, DBHA, B330/3506.

[113] Ibid.

closest collaborators" with which they pointed out what an important role Blessing played in the Nazi state.'[114] The book continued: 'Blessing not only actively participated in the pillaging and enslaving of occupied countries, he also helped to prepare planned acts of aggression against neutral countries.'[115] The East German campaign, it appeared, was met with little success. These stories filtered through to the margins of the West German press. As per usual, the left-wing *Das Dossier* published a detailed report of Blessing's ties to Himmler, Göring and Goebbels.[116] But, on the whole, the mainstream press did not pick up on the Himmler story.

This changed, however, with the publication in West Germany of *Deutschland Report* on 26 May 1965.[117] Written by Bernt Engelmann, a former journalist with *Der Spiegel* and producer of *Panorama*, an investigative news show, the book traced what it saw as the links between the Third Reich and Adenauer's Federal Republic.[118] Like the East German state authorities, Engelmann fell back on the findings exposed during the Nuremberg trials. Among other targets, such as Heinrich Lübke, the president of the Federal Republic, Engelmann attacked Blessing and his ties to the Himmler circle.[119] The author did not mention the 1939 Reichsbank memorandum, nor did he mention Blessing's link to the '20 July' group.[120] Amid the lines documenting Blessing's apparent enthusiasm for the *Freundeskreis*, Engelmann took care to add that '[b]anknotes of the Federal Republic carry his signature', a point further reinforced by a graphical representation of a deutschmark banknote.[121] In doing so, the journalist was implicitly linking what he saw as Blessing's morally bankrupt past with the moral bankruptcy of the West German capitalist state.

In 1992, following the collapse of East Germany and the opening of the state's archives, it emerged that the Stasi sent Engelmann material for his books several times over the years.[122] This relationship dated back until at least 1982, when Engelmann became an unofficial employee

---

[114] Ibid.   [115] Ibid.
[116] 'Karl Blessing. Eine Schwindel erregende Karriere', *Das Dossier*, 9 Feb. 1965, B330/3506.
[117] Von der Lippe noted the exact date that the book appeared. 'The day before yesterday the book *Deutschland Report* by Herr Berndt [*sic*] Engelmann, Exlibris Verlag, Berlin, was published.' See von der Lippe to Oechsner, 28 May 1965, p. 1.
[118] For a contemporary report on Engelmann's journalistic background, see 'Bilanz der Bundesrepublik', *Die Zeit*, 18 Jun. 1965.
[119] Engelmann, *Deutschland Report*, p. 76.
[120] An observation bitterly noted by von der Lippe. See von der Lippe to Oechsner, 28 May 1965.
[121] Emphasis in original. Engelmann, *Deutschland Report*, p. 76.
[122] For the revelations, see 'Schlimmste Schreier', *Der Spiegel*, 10 Feb. 1992.

(*Inoffizieller Mitarbeiter*) with the Stasi, operating under the code name 'Albers'.[123] Engelmann was just one of several West German journalists and media figures who colluded with the East German state security ministry during the Cold War.[124] It remains unclear, however, the exact nature of his relationship with the Stasi in the year 1965.

Reading the accusations levelled against Blessing in *Deutschland Report*, von der Lippe became 'physically nauseous'; the book was a 'thinly disguised communist concoction of clearly malicious intent'.[125] Nevertheless, it was the first proper publication in West Germany to level these charges against the Bundesbank president. The press department scrambled for information relating to both the author and the publishing house, with detailed reports quickly drawn up.[126] It was discovered that Engelmann's book was rejected by its original publisher due to its controversial contents. But a new, left-wing publishing house in Berlin took on the job. Von der Lippe, for his part, worried that the *Deutschland Report* would find a large audience. He was right.

As these internal reports were being drafted, it came to light that an influential Munich-based cabaret group – the Münchner Lach- und Schiessgesellschaft, led by Dieter Hildebrandt – was using *Deutschland Report* as material for the group's new show. It was on stage in Munich six days a week.[127] And what's more, it was beginning to receive media attention. A recording of the show was broadcast on Frankfurt radio on 27 May 1965.[128] Von der Lippe began assembling as much information as possible related to the show and its performers. Another internal report was drafted. Written by a member of von der Lippe's staff, it was marked 'strictly confidential!' and its contents suggest that von der Lippe had the staff member travel down to Munich to visit the show to document exactly what was said on stage.[129] Indeed, the internal report

[123] 'Stasi führte Bernt Engelmann als IM "Albers"', *Die Welt*, 19 Jun. 2004.
[124] Von Hodenberg, *Konsens und Krise*, pp. 389–96.
[125] See von der Lippe to Oechsner, 28 May 1965, p. 1. A transcript of the book's passage relating to Blessing was typed up for the press department's use. See 'Aus Bernt Engelmann "Deutschlandreport" 1965 Exlibris Buchhandlung GmbH-Verlag, Berlin', DBHA, B330/3506.
[126] For the internal report on the two publishing houses, see 'Information note about Verlag Gustav Lübbe and Verlag Exlibris', 27 May 1965, DBHA, B330/3506; for the internal report on the book *Deutschland Report* specifically, see 'Notiz vom 1. Juni 1965', 1 Jun. 1965, DBHA, B330/3506; and, finally, for the internal report on its author, Engelmann, see 'Notiz vom 3. Juni 1965', 3 Jun. 1965, DBHA, B330/3506.
[127] Loesch, 'Vermerk: Lach- und Schießgesellschaft', 26 May 1965, DBHA, B330/3506.
[128] This was according to von der Lippe, who noted the upcoming broadcast in a letter. See von der Lippe to Fritz Oechsner, 28 May 1965, p. 1.
[129] See Loesch, 'Vermerk: Lach- und Schießgesellschaft', 26 May 1965, DBHA, B330/3506.

took care to note how the controversial scene was received by those who saw it: 'At the close of the scene, small applause, but evident surprise among the audience.'[130]

The head of the press department also contacted an ally in Munich – Fritz Oechsner, the vice president of the Bavarian Landeszentralbank – to glean his views on the local cabaret group.[131] Furthermore, von der Lippe sent Oechsner copies of Blessing's Nuremberg testimony, the Nuremberg report of the Flick trial, and the 1944 SS report that implicated Blessing in the '20 July' group. He requested that Oechsner use his influence – in a strictly private capacity – to have these documents placed in the hands of the cabaret performers. Oechsner had a contact who close to the group: 'Hopefully, [these documents] will shame them to have attacked such an honourable man in public.'[132] When the cabaret show arrived in Frankfurt some months later, in October 1965, von der Lippe went as far as asking Oechsner if he could exert his influence to have the performers omit the scene in which Blessing was attacked and the deutschmark buried.[133]

But where was Blessing in all this? The Bundesbank president, visibly shaken by the play of events, was kept continually informed by his press chief.[134] An official response to these allegations would only inflame the interest of the media. A public statement on the issue was out of the question. It was only a matter of time before mainstream newspapers began to pick up on the story. Indeed, the Bundesbank press department learned that a performance of the cabaret show would be broadcast on national television on Saturday 29 May – just two days after the Frankfurt radio broadcast.[135] It was obvious that such a broadcast would have a sizeable impact in the media. The Bundesbank press department entered crisis mode.

As such, the Bundesbank president and von der Lippe sought to preempt and counter any stories that would be published. On the day of the national broadcast of the cabaret show, the two men began work on drafting a counter version of Blessing's past – a competing historical

---

[130] Ibid.   [131] Von der Lippe to Fritz Oechsner, 28 May 1965.   [132] Ibid.
[133] Indeed, in this episode, it appears that Sammy Drechsel, the producer and director of the cabaret show, was Oechsel's contact in Munich. See von der Lippe to Oechsner, 6 Oct. 1965. Drechsel's name also appears in the same context in a scribbled note found in Viktor von der Lippe to Fritz Oechsner, 15 Jul. 1965, DBHA, B330/3506.
[134] Blessing's reaction was later recounted by von der Lippe. See Viktor von der Lippe to Maximilian Bernhuber, 14 Oct. 1965, DBHA, B330/236.
[135] This show was referenced in two letters. The memoirs of Dieter Hildebrandt also confirm the date 29 May 1965. See Karl Blessing to Viktor von der Lippe, 29 May 1965, DBHA, B330/3506; and von der Lippe to Oechsner, 28 May 1965. And finally, for the date of the show, see Hildebrandt, *Was bleibt mir übrig*, p. 317.

narrative to the one expounded in the *Deutschland Report* and the Münchner Lach- und Schiessgesellschaft's cabaret scene. The document went through at least five drafts, the original of which was hand-written by Blessing. It came to be called the 'short comprehensive summary'.[136] Its purpose? Blessing stated that it should only be used if 'serious newspapers' and other media channels picked up on the *Freundeskreis* story following the television broadcast.[137] Blessing restated this point in the same letter: 'It should only be published if the situation leaves us with no other choice.'[138] The document was to be left anonymous. There were no signatures. There was no Bundesbank heading.

An earlier draft of the 'short comprehensive summary' began by couching the emergence of the Himmler story in a Cold War context: 'Herr Blessing was recently the target of distorting and confounding journalistic attacks on his conduct during the Nazi period, which had their origins in the eastern zone.'[139] This wording survived the final draft largely intact. For von der Lippe, then, the claims made against Blessing were primarily ones motivated by ideological interests and not based on objective research. The document then went on to portray Blessing's involvement in the Third Reich in the best possible light, given the revelations at hand. The first half of the essay concerned itself with the favourable side of Blessing's history; the second part delved into the more questionable aspects of his résumé. The 'short comprehensive summary' was short and sweet, amounting to two pages. And amid efforts to make the summary as clear and precise as possible – no doubt with an eye to helping journalists race to meet their article deadlines – the two men highlighted five simple points and numbered them accordingly.

First, Blessing had signed the 'famous' 1939 Reichsbank memorandum. 'This memorandum, which Hitler labelled as a mutiny, was directed with clarity and openness against the financing of excessive armament and, as such, represented one of the most important acts of resistance of its time.'[140] An earlier draft of the 'short comprehensive summary' described the memorandum as 'one of the fiercest acts of resistance' of its time.[141] But this rhetoric was watered down in later refinements. As Chapter 1 has shown, we know that this claim of

---

[136] All the drafts of the 'short comprehensive summary' can be found in the same folder, DBHA, B330/3506. For the finished version, see Blessing and von der Lippe, 'Kürze zusammenfassende Darstellung', May 1965.

[137] Karl Blessing to Viktor von der Lippe, 29 May 1965, DBHA, B330/3506.   [138] Ibid.

[139] Karl Blessing and Viktor von der Lippe, early draft of 'Kürze zusammenfassende Darstellung', May 1965, DBHA, B330/3506.

[140] Blessing and von der Lippe, 'Kürze zusammenfassende Darstellung', May 1965, p. 1.

[141] See the earlier draft in DBHA, B330/3506.

'mutiny' can be linked back to Vocke at Nuremberg in 1946. Blessing was further portrayed in the 'short comprehensive summary' as having been sacked by Hitler as a direct consequence of signing the memorandum. We know that it was the slightly more nuanced case of Blessing choosing to resign after being overlooked by the dictator.

Second, after being forced to leave the Reichsbank in 1939, Blessing 'entered the Unilever Concern, which at the time was decried by National Socialists as a "Jewish capitalist" enterprise'.[142] The document continued: Blessing was forced to leave his position because of pressure stemming from leading Nazi officials Reinhard Heydrich and Hermann Göring. Unilever had become a target of Göring's Four Year Plan, and Blessing had to go. For the second time, then, Blessing was removed because of political machinations. The 'short comprehensive summary' took the caution of noting the particular date and newspaper in which the announcement could be found – the *Deutscher Reichsanzeiger und Preussischer Staatsanzeiger* on 30 June 1941.

Then, moving onto its third point, the 'short comprehensive summary' detailed Blessing's link to the '20 July' group. The Bundesbank president had bravely collaborated with men who sought to overthrow Hitler. 'With regard to these points, of course, the opponents of Herr Blessing are silent', an earlier draft noted. 'By contrast, they billow grotesquely about his participation in the Keppler- or Himmler circle.'[143]

Indeed – just what about Blessing's involvement with the Himmler *Freundeskreis*? There is where the second half of the document began. The fourth point of the 'short comprehensive summary' pleaded for some context to be allowed. 'As like anyone else who had a public profile in the "Third Reich," Blessing had to make concessions in outward appearances. Whoever wants to accuse him today, either had the fortune of standing in the shadows back then, or not knowing what it was like to live in those circumstances, because he was too young.'[144] Implicitly, this point hinted at the generational change afoot in the West German media industry during the 1960s.

Moreover, as the document's fifth and final point made clear, the 'current alleged revelations come eighteen years too late'.[145] Blessing's involvement with the Himmler *Freundeskreis* had been well documented in the military tribunals at Nuremberg. There was no sinister cover up.

---

[142] Blessing and von der Lippe, 'Kürze zusammenfassende Darstellung', May 1965, p. 1.
[143] The Himmler *Freundeskreis* was originally known as the 'Keppler circle', named after a leading SS official, Wilhelm Keppler. See an earlier draft of Blessing and von der Lippe, 'Kürze zusammenfassende Darstellung', May 1965, pp. 1–2.
[144] Blessing and von der Lippe, 'Kürze zusammenfassende Darstellung', May 1965, p. 2.
[145] Ibid.

All the documents and transcripts from the Nuremberg trials had been publicly published. They could even be found in public libraries. That went for Blessing's testimony, as it did for the court's judgement of the Flick trial, which judged 'that the "Keppler- or Himmler circle" in practice exerted little political or economic influence'.[146] Taken as a whole, the document continued, the book *Deutschland Report* used the documents and minutes of the Nuremberg trials in a 'very one-sided' manner, with no mention of the Reichsbank memorandum of 1939, nor Blessing's connection to the '20 July' group.[147]

There, the 'short comprehensive summary' ended.[148] But it was merely a summary. Von der Lippe also took the caution of compiling documents, which he later termed as 'counter-material', to be sent along with the 'short comprehensive summary' if and when the need arose.[149] In the Bundesbank archive, it is unclear as to which documents were sent.[150] But a complete set of the counter-material remains in the federal archives in Koblenz, given that Blessing sent the 'short comprehensive summary' and its complements to the federal president Lübke.[151] The Bundesbank president also dispatched the material to the chancellor's office.[152] Von der Lippe's counter-material was as follows:

- Blessing's testimony at Nuremberg in August 1947.
- The Nuremberg military court's judgment concerning the Flick trial in December 1947, which argued that the political importance of Himmler's *Freundeskreis* was minimal.
- Extract of Schacht's testimony at Nuremberg in 1946, stressing the impact of the Reichsbank memorandum of 1939.
- The Reichsbank memorandum sent to Hitler in 1939.
- Extract of Vocke's testimony at Nuremberg in 1946, detailing the consequences of the 1939 memorandum.
- Statement under oath of Karl Lindemann, a former member of the *Freundeskreis*, in 1947. Lindemann's statement suggested that Blessing

---

[146] Ibid.   [147] Ibid.
[148] Blessing's original draft had actually ended with seething anger; von der Lippe wisely removed these words. See Karl Blessing, 'Statement', 29 May 1965, DBHA, B330/3506.
[149] Von der Lippe to Bernhuber, 14 Oct. 1965.
[150] Though all of the relevant files, and more, can be found in the folder, von der Lippe never did write out an explicit list detailing exactly what counted as 'counter-material'.
[151] See Karl Blessing to Heinrich Lübke, 13 Oct. 1965, DBHA, B330/3506. The complete set of counter-material can be found in Bundesarchiv, Koblenz [BAK], B122/5008. See also Sehrbrock, 'Vermerk: Betr: Angriffe gegen den Präsidenten der Deutschen Bundesbank, Herrn Karl Blessing', 26 Oct. 1965, BAK, B122/5008.
[152] Karl Blessing to Ludger Westrick, 4 Jun. 1965, DBHA, B330/3506.

was more of an expert whose opinions were sought after by SS officials, and who had little interest in the *Freundeskreis*.

- A copy of an article, published in the *Deutscher Reichsanzeiger und Preussischer Staatsanzeiger* on 30 June 1941, which announced the establishment of a 'Reich commissar' to lead the Unilever concern.
- Three letters written by SS officials in 1944, listing Blessing's name as a member of the provisional cabinet should the '20 July' group have succeeded in its coup against Hitler.[153]

Thus a small army of detailed documents, many of which dated back to the Nuremberg trials, backed up the 'short comprehensive summary'. These files were essentially the building blocks of the Bundesbank's monetary mythology; and the 'short comprehensive summary', its distillation. As a result, at the end of May 1965 – less than a week after *Deutschland Report*'s publication, and on the very weekend of the national broadcast of the Münchner Lach- und Schiessgesellschaft's cabaret show – the Bundesbank was prepared for the worst.

Over the coming weeks and months, some mainstream newspapers picked up on the story.[154] In late June 1965, the Stuttgart-based weekly magazine, *Zeitung*, published a piece about the *Deutschland Report*, and highlighted Blessing's murky history in particular.[155] The left-wing *Konkret* magazine – which had received financial support from the East German Stasi up until 1964 – published a lengthy excerpt of Engelmann's book in August – again, featuring the material on the *Freundeskreis*.[156] *Der Spiegel*, too, a magazine that often devoted favourable coverage to Blessing, picked up on the story and wrote a piece about it in October 1965.[157] Indeed, the current affairs magazine even published a photograph of Himmler addressing the *Freundeskreis*, and marked out Blessing in the picture.[158] Readers saw Himmler and Blessing in the same room together. The *Frankfurter Rundschau* also published an editorial article, following the staging of the cabaret in Frankfurt in the same month.[159]

---

[153] See BAK, B122/5008. All of the documents can also be found in DBHA, B330/3506.
[154] See, for instance, '"Schuld abladen verboten." Das zwölfte Programm der Münchner Lach- und Schießgesellschaft', *Die Andere Zeitung*, 10 Jun. 1965.
[155] 'Ein Verlag bekam kalte Füsse', *Zeitung*, 21 Jun. 1965, DBHA, B330/3506.
[156] Bernt Engelmann, 'Freundeskreis Himmler', *Konkret*, Aug. 1965, DBHA, B330/3506. For *Konkret*'s relationship with the Stasi, see von Hodenberg, *Konsens und Krise*, p. 389.
[157] 'Himmler-Kreis: Treue im Choir', *Der Spiegel*, 13 Oct. 1965, DBHA, B330/3506.
[158] This article caused particular irritation on Blessing's part; for he noted that *Der Spiegel* had been kind to him in the past. See 'Himmler-Kreis: Treue im Choir', *Der Spiegel*, 13 Oct. 1965, p. 74. See also Karl Blessing to Heinrich Lübke (draft), 13 Oct. 1965, DBHA, B330/3506.
[159] 'Schuld abladen verboten', *Frankfurter Rundschau*, 15 Oct. 1965.

How did the Bundesbank respond in each of these cases? As von der Lippe reflected on his strategy to a colleague, 'On our side, nothing has been done in a personal or official capacity, because we have come to the conclusion that, with such a matter, one can only make it worse with official or half-official interventions.'[160] Instead, von der Lippe sought to use third parties who were instructed to act in a strictly personal capacity.[161] Von der Lippe stood at the centre of this web of correspondence. The Bundesbank's name was not to be mentioned. It was to remain in the shadows. With regard to *Zeitung* magazine in Stuttgart, the head of the Bundesbank press department first assembled information about the publication's staff.[162] The contact details of one Karin Mönkemeyer, the offending journalist, were pinned down.

Von der Lippe asked Oechsner, his contact in Munich, to contact Mönkemeyer using the counter-material provided – and to do so in a strictly personal capacity.[163] The goal was to seek redress where possible. Oechsner contacted the *Zeitung* journalist and, when his letter remained unanswered, followed it up with another message.[164] The Munich proxy eventually received a meek response, with Mönkemeyer, somewhat half-heartedly, admitting that she was unaware of the other aspects of Blessing's role in the Third Reich. Oechsner kept von der Lippe up to date.

It was a similar story with regard to the article found in *Der Spiegel*. This time, von der Lippe availed of the services of Gerhard Riedel, director of the economics department of the Berliner Handels-Gesellschaft, a private bank. Armed with von der Lippe's counter-material, Riedel contacted *Der Spiegel*'s editorial team.[165] Seven days after the magazine's article appeared, von der Lippe confidently reported to Blessing that *Der Spiegel* was in possession of the counter-material.[166] 'The "short comprehensive summary" is performing well.'[167] Von der Lippe thanked Riedel for his efforts. 'Your intervention was very useful!'[168]

---

[160] Viktor von der Lippe to Otto Kranzbühler, 23 Jun. 1965, DBHA, B330/3506.
[161] Ibid.
[162] See 'ZEITUNG EIN DEUTSCHES MAGAZIN STUTTGART', no date, DBHA, B330/3506.
[163] Viktor von der Lippe to Fritz Oechsner, 24 Jun. 1965, DBHA, B330/3506.
[164] Fritz Oechsner to Karin Mönkemeyer, 6 Jul. 1965, DBHA, B330/3506; Fritz Oechsner to Karin Mönkemeyer, 2 Aug. 1965, DBHA, B330/3506; and Karin Mönkemeyer to Fritz Oechsner, 4 Aug. 1965, DBHA, B330/3506.
[165] Gerhard Riedel to Ferdinand Simoneit, 18 Oct. 1965, DBHA, B330/3506.
[166] Viktor von der Lippe to Karl Blessing, 20 Oct. 1965, DBHA, B330/280.
[167] Viktor von der Lippe to Karl Blessing, 15 Oct. 1965, DBHA, B330/280.
[168] Viktor von der Lippe to Gerhard Riedel, 22 Nov. 1965, DBHA, B330/3506.

Von der Lippe also noted in a letter to Blessing that he had sent the counter-material to other people who had enquired with him about the *Der Spiegel* news story.[169] But these men or women were not named. The press chief did send the counter-material to Maximilian Bernhuber, however, who was a contact at the Bavarian state bank.[170] Von der Lippe requested that he should have the counter-material at hand to be used in an informal manner should the occasion arise. It was likely, then, that von der Lippe asked the same favour of the other men. Blessing, for his part, sent the 'short comprehensive summary' to contacts whenever the occasion called for it.[171]

A sense of the sheer extent to which the Bundesbank sought to suppress the *Freundeskreis* story can be gleaned from the curious case of *Die Penne*, a school newspaper of the Lessing Gymnasium, an elite school in Frankfurt. It came to the attention of the Bundesbank press department that an article, 'Auschwitz trial', was published in the school newspaper in late 1965.[172] The school article referred to Engelmann's *Deutschland Report* and the fact that Blessing, an erstwhile confidant of Himmler, was now president of West Germany's central bank. This school article was discussed among other offending pieces, such as the *Der Spiegel* and the *Frankfurter Rundschau* articles, at a Bundesbank directorate meeting on 19 October 1965. Although he was officially just the minute taker, and not a member of the directorate, von der Lippe actively participated in this discussion and reported it to Blessing in a letter the following day.[173] The minutes of the meeting do not record the discussion, suggesting it was deemed to be a sensitive matter.[174] The directorate resolved to pursue the same strategy as before: it was time to implement the Bundesbank's counter-material.

As a result, the central bank contacted the school's principal and the student editor of *Die Penne*.[175] The student editor was sent the 'short comprehensive summary' and, duly humbled by the attention of the Bundesbank and his school principal, the young boy saw fit to publish

---

[169] Von der Lippe to Blessing, 20 Oct. 1965.

[170] Von der Lippe to Bernhuber, 14 Oct. 1965.

[171] When an American friend of Blessing stumbled across an English translation of the *Braunbuch* when he was in East Berlin, Blessing quickly dispatched the document. See Karl Blessing to Erwin Adams, 9 Dec. 1965, DBHA, B330/3506.

[172] Excerpt of 'Auschwitz-Prozess', *Die Penne*, No. 3, 1965, DBHA, B330/280.

[173] Von der Lippe to Blessing, 20 Oct. 1965.

[174] See Bundesbank directorate meeting minutes, 19 Oct. 1965, DBHA, B330/2067.

[175] For the letter to the principal, see Deutsche Bundesbank to Karl Ringshausen, 2 Nov. 1965, DBHA, B330/280; for the letter sent to the student, see Deutsche Bundesbank to Michael Wolf, 2 Nov. 1965, DBHA, B330/280.

a lengthy excerpt of it in the letter section of the school newspaper as a form of retraction.[176] The excerpt itself is quite interesting, for student editor chose to include the following passage:

> As like anyone else who had public profile in the 'Third Reich', Blessing had to make concessions in outward appearances. Whoever wants to accuse him today, either had the fortune of standing in the shadows back then, or not knowing what it was like to live in those circumstances, because he was too young.[177]

The Himmler narrative remained in the press, sporadically, for some months until late 1965. And then it largely disappeared. Only once, it appears, was Blessing's past used for political gain in West Germany. In October 1967, the Social Democratic Party (SPD) mentioned the Bundesbank president's membership of Himmler's *Freundeskreis* in a press release while lobbying for a person affiliated with the SPD to be Blessing's successor at the helm of the central bank.[178]

For a brief period in 1965, then, two competing historical narratives floated in the public sphere. At heart, both narratives served interests. The East German government had a sizeable interest in blackening Blessing's name; and the Bundesbank, for its part, had a strong incentive in safeguarding the central bank's image as much as possible. The Bundesbank press department exerted pressure behind the scenes, leaving no evidence or mark that could be traced back to it; and, in a sense, so too did the East German Stasi. Proxies provided von der Lippe with a cover.

Both the Schacht and Himmler affairs related to the legacy of the inter-war period. But the Bundesbank responded in a very different manner for each case. What was the reason? In short, it was the media's reaction. With Schacht, the Bundesbank could take comfort in the fact that the claims of 'Hitler's magician' were treated with scorn. But with the emergence of the *Freundeskreis* story, the Bundesbank could not afford to adopt that attitude. Both the Schacht and *Freundeskreis* stories emerged at the same time, but were greeted by rather different responses on the part of Blessing and von der Lippe. References to the past were not always specifically related to individuals, however. The inter-war period offered an abundance of parallels – and some were more unfavourable than others. How did the Bundesbank respond when cries of a 'third inflation' were heard?

---

[176] 'Leserbriefe', *Die Penne*, Nr. 4, 1965, DBHA, B330/280.   [177] Ibid.
[178] See 'Interessenten und Parteibuchbeamte', *Sozialdemokratischer Pressedienst*, 9 Oct. 1967, B330/3506.

The 'Third Inflation'

In January 1965, Blessing stood before an audience at the Berlin stock exchange. Lately, the Bundesbank president acknowledged, there had been much talk of inflationary developments in West Germany. These trends, however, had to be put in context. It was important not to exaggerate the dangers facing the nation, Blessing declared.

This may also be said in relation to those who speak an irresponsible manner of an alleged 'third inflation'. Our first two inflations, both resulting from the world wars, are known to have resulted from government deficits financed by the Reichsbank – that is, by setting the printing presses in motion. Today neither the state nor the Bundesbank have any intention of undertaking such an act. Whoever speaks of a third inflation, then, is guilty of demagogy. What has happened in recent years in West Germany is something different altogether from the two world war inflations.[179]

'Guilty of demagogy'. These were strong words. And though they were expressed in a general manner, the remarks were directed at one individual in particular: Schacht.[180] For, in addition to accusing Blessing of partaking in the second inflation, the former Reichsbank president also contended that his erstwhile student was creating yet another monetary disaster – a 'third inflation' that would result in the destruction of the deutschmark.[181] Schacht did not coin the term 'third inflation'. The expression could be found sporadically in the media from the early 1950s onwards.[182] As the years progressed, it was used to describe the slow, creeping inflation that ate away at the value of the deutschmark. Nor was Schacht alone in his reference to the idea. Even respectable figures in the media referred to it.[183] Vocke would later speak of the 'third inflation' on at least two occasions.[184] When the economics journalist Muthesius took to writing his memoirs during this period, he

[179] Karl Blessing, 'Ansprache des Präsidenten der Deutschen Bundesbank Karl Blessing', 22 Jan. 1965, DBHA, B330/578, pp. 11–12.

[180] Indeed, the media interpreted Blessing's remarks as such. See 'Mefo-Stopheles', *Die Zeit*, 29 Jan. 1965. So too did Schacht, who mentioned Blessing's speech in his 1966 book, *Magie des Geldes*. See the English translation, Schacht, *The magic of money*, p. 150.

[181] 'Mefo-Stopheles', *Die Zeit*, 29 Jan. 1965; see also Schacht, 'Zur Währungspolitik', *Deutsche Hochschullehrer-Zeitung*, p. 14.

[182] See, for instance, 'Konstruktive Arbeitsbeschaffung notwendig', *Neuer Vorwärts*, 9 Jun. 1950; and 'Kein Kampf gegen die Wirtschaft', *Frankfurter Allgemeine Zeitung*, 26 Aug. 1954.

[183] Hartwig Meyer, 'Die Erosion hat begonnen', *Die Zeit*, 16 Jan. 1970.

[184] See Wilhelm Vocke, 'Währungsstabilität als Grundlage der Vermögensbildung – Mahnung: In der Inflationsbekämpfung nicht nachlassen', 22 Mar. 1972, DBPA, no. 1244; and Wilhelm Vocke, 'Die Bundesbank und die dritte Inflation', *Manager Magazin*, Aug. 1972, DBPA, no. 1243.

decided to call them *Augenzeuge von drei Inflationen*, or *Witness of three inflations*.[185]

But it was Schacht who gave the 'third inflation' a new life in 1965. The finance man talked openly of a 'third inflation' before an audience at the Rhein Ruhr Club in January of that year.[186] The former Reichsbank president also devoted an entire chapter to 'the third inflation' in his book, *The magic of money*.[187] Schacht used his notoriety to transform the concept into a point of public discussion, calling the population to arms, while at the same time calling into question the Bundesbank's ability to deal with the problem. It would not be the last time that Blessing felt compelled to downplay the idea of a 'third inflation'; *Frankfurter Allgemeine Zeitung* published a headline 'Do not worry about a "third inflation"' on the back of a speech by the Bundesbank president before the *Arbeitskreis*, or working committee, of the CDU at its 1965 party convention.[188]

But why did Blessing feel the need to go on the offensive? After all, when Schacht had accused Blessing of participating in the second inflation, the Bundesbank simply remained silent. There was no official response. Even the idea of a private letter to Schacht was rejected. The reason had little to do with the media's response to Schacht's use of the term, either. After Schacht delivered his January speech, *Die Zeit* ridiculed the 'much maligned' and 'notorious inventor of the Mefo-bill system'.[189] The press, once again, took to mocking 'Hitler's magician'. The idea of a 'third inflation', however, could not be discredited by means of deriding one man. Schacht was merely describing an existing phenomenon – the sustained and noticeable increase of prices in the West German economy; albeit he was doing so in wholly exaggerated terms. The danger of the 'third inflation', then, was bigger than the danger posed by Schacht. It was for this reason that the Bundesbank took to the public sphere.

The emergence of the 'third inflation' as a point of public discussion created a number of difficulties for the Bundesbank. Its predecessor, the BdL, was content to frame historical narratives in a manner that helped defend the central bank's policies, on the one hand, as well as influence the provisions of the Bundesbank Law, on the other. More specifically,

---

[185] Volkmar Muthesius, *Augenzeuge von drei Inflationen. Erinnerungen und Gedanken eines Wirtschaftspublizisten* (Frankfurt am Main, 1973).
[186] The speech was reported in the opinion piece 'Mefo-Stopheles', *Die Zeit*, 29 Jan. 1965.
[187] Schacht, *The magic of money*, pp. 142–59.
[188] Karl Blessing, 'Eine "dritte Inflation" ist nicht zu befürchten', *Frankfurter Allgemeine Zeitung*, 7 Apr. 1965.
[189] 'Mefo-Stopheles', *Die Zeit*, 29 Jan. 1965.

Vocke used the lessons of 1922–3 and the second inflation to defend the BdL's independence. But the BdL did so at a time of low inflation. Vocke's lessons were used in an abstract, almost counterfactual fashion to demonstrate to the West German people the consequences of a Bundesbank Law *if* it had allowed for government interference in the central bank's decisions. That 'if' is important here.

By contrast, Blessing was forced to reckon with actual inflationary pressures. The term 'third inflation' was being used to describe a contemporary development, not a counterfactual outcome. There was no longer an 'if'. The Bundesbank realised that such an expression invited unwelcome historical parallels of 1922–3. Wheelbarrows full of money, children along the pavement building small fortresses out of thick wads of banknotes. West Germans had seen these pictures, bandied about in the media. The expression 'third inflation', then, had the potential to create exaggerated inflation expectations. In his publications, Schacht was careful to make the distinction that the 'third inflation' was a slow, creeping one – altogether distinct from the episode that marked the Weimar Republic. For the man on the street, however, such distinctions would have seemed academic. The 'third inflation' could be misinterpreted by the 'man on the street' – and that was Blessing's explicit worry, as he expressed it himself in January 1965.[190]

This concern was justified. Fears surrounding a 'third inflation', for instance, could be discerned from the activities of one Oscar Blessing – no relation to the Bundesbank president – who took it upon himself to preach the lessons of inflation. Described in private by von der Lippe as probably a 'madman', Oscar Blessing distributed pamphlets warning citizens of the Federal Republic about the lessons of Germany's 'three inflations'.[191] One such leaflet sported the title '3 inflations do (not) fall from the sky – they were "made."'[192]

The example of Oscar Blessing, who continued to produce these pamphlets for a number of years, is no doubt an extreme one. But it demonstrates that the idea of a 'third inflation', whatever its actual merits, had, well, currency. The idea struck a nerve with West Germans. Letters, particularly from worried pensioners, arrived at the Bundesbank, pleading with Blessing, asking him to stop the inflationary tide. 'You write that the deutschmark is the hardest currency in the world', wrote an

---

[190] Blessing, 'Ansprache des Präsidenten der Deutschen Bundesbank Karl Blessing', p. 13.
[191] Viktor von der Lippe to Karl Blessing, 28 Apr. 1965, DBHA, B330/237; see also Oscar Blessing to Karl Blessing, 15 Apr. 1965, DBHA, B330/237.
[192] Oscar Blessing, '3 Inflationen fallen (nicht) vom Himmel. Sie werden gemacht', *Geldspiegel*, Jul. 1973, DBHA, B330/7419.

exasperated citizen, one Karl Otto Flemming, in 1968, 'but you have done away with the fifty per cent of our savings' purchasing power ... It is a crime against savers'.[193] Note here, too, that Flemming was personally blaming Blessing, not the central bank council, nor the Bundesbank in general. For the average citizen, Blessing personified both the central bank and the currency itself.

Politicians also got in on the act. One of the discussion points of the Christian Social Union (CSU) annual conference in 1970 was 'Are we threatened by a third inflation?'[194] And the danger of a 'third inflation' was thrown about in parliamentary debates during the same year, too.[195] Anxious readers wrote to newspapers referring to the prospect of a 'third inflation'.[196] Other public officials, too, received letters from anxious savers.[197] 'My generation is now being raped by the third inflation', one man wrote to Brandt, the chancellor from 1969 to 1974. 'Are these mass tragedies already forgotten by the government?'[198] According to numerous confidential surveys conducted for government use by the Institut für Demoskopie, a public opinion centre, inflation fears consistently trumped unemployment concerns as the number one worry of West Germans in the early 1970s.[199] Indeed, with regard to one confidential survey, 30 per cent of the West German population believed in January 1971 'that it would come to an inflation', a concern that the

[193] Quoted in Karl Otto Flemming to Karl Blessing, 4 Sep. 1968, DBHA, B330/7417. For other examples, see Anon. to Karl Blessing, 5 May 1965, DBHA, B330/284/I; and Blessing to Wolf, 14 May 1969.
[194] 'Nichts als Einverständnis in München. Kein Widerspruch der Delegierten auf dem CSU-Parteitag', *Frankfurter Allgemeine Zeitung*, 13 Apr. 1970.
[195] See 'Weiter Streit um Möllers Inflations-Äußerung', *Frankfurter Allgemeine Zeitung*, 9 Oct. 1970; and 'Vom Beckmessern im Hohen Haus', *Frankfurter Allgemeine Zeitung*, 9 Oct. 1970.
[196] 'Briefe an die Herausgeber: die dritte Inflation', *Frankfurter Allgemeine Zeitung*, 1 Oct. 1970; and 'Briefe an die Herausgeber: Zu spät?', *Frankfurter Allgemeine Zeitung*, 6 Apr. 1971.
[197] See, among other examples, G. Toelle to Karl Klasen, 28 Feb. 1970, DBHA, B330/7417; Margarete Schaller to Karl Klasen, 1 May 1970, DBHA, B330/7417, pp. 1–2; Richard Finster to Karl Klasen, 12 Mar. 1971, DBHA, B330/7417; Willi Jonas to Karl Klasen, 28 Mar. 1972, DBHA, B330/7418; and Hans Kruse to Karl Klasen, 27 Jul. 1972, DBHA, B330/7418.
[198] Hanns Steiner to Willy Brandt, 5 Aug. 1972, DBHA, B330/7418.
[199] According to the *Institut für Demoskopie Allensbach*, these surveys were statistically representative of the West German population. A survey of 2,000 people was considered standard practice by the institute. See Conrad Ahlers, 'Note concerning *Institut für Demoskopie* May 1970 report "Wirtschaftspolitische Wünsche"', 26 May 1970, BAK, B145/4260, Tabelle 1; Conrad Ahlers, 'Note concerning *Institut für Demoskopie* May 1971 report "Die wichtigste Forderung im Bereiche der Wirtschaftspolitik"', 14 May 1971, BAK, B145/6884; and Klaus Bölling, 'Note concerning *Institut für Demoskopie* September 1974 report "Aktuelle wirtschaftspolitische Lage"', 27 Sep. 1974, BAK, B145/11784, p. 1.

Table 4.2 *Public opinion survey: 'Fears of daily life' in January 1971*

Survey section: economic and monetary concerns

	'At the moment I am very concerned...'
	%
That prices are always rising	57
That it will come to an inflation	30
That one cannot get by with his income	21
That our economy is going downhill	15

Note: The total percentage exceeds 100 due to the fact that some of those surveyed selected two or more boxes. The survey was published in April 1971, but it was conducted in January of that year. See 'Lebensangst: Umfrage 1778', Institut für Demoskopie, Apr. 1971, BAK, ZSg. 132/1778/I, p. 3.

survey had made *distinct* from another category, 'that prices are always rising'. This survey is illustrated in Table 4.2.

Given that three out of every ten West Germans believed that the country was on the verge of another inflation, it is interesting to see how this figure itself breaks down according to age, educational background and location. This breakdown is depicted in Table 4.3. Those aged 60 and above were far more concerned about a 'third inflation' than younger West Germans, suggesting that there was a generational divide. Respondents with just a primary school education were more fearful of a 'third inflation' than those who had the benefit of secondary schooling. And, in terms of geography, people living in villages were more worried than those living in cities.

Thus far, however, this chapter has treated the expression 'third inflation' in abstract terms. Granted, it described a slow, gradual inflation of the deutschmark. But what was causing this development? Indeed, was there any truth behind Schacht's claim that the Bundesbank was helpless to fight its encroachment? Broadly speaking, the term 'third inflation' was associated with what came to be known as 'imported inflation' – that is, inflationary developments imported from abroad by dint of West Germany's trading partners and the framework of the post-war international monetary system.

In describing the genesis of 'imported inflation', it is important to note three conditioning factors. First, the deutschmark became convertible in the 1950s.[200] Exchange controls, for the most part, no longer hindered

---

[200] For more on this, see Christoph Buchheim, *Die Wiedereingliederung Westdeutschlands in die Weltwirtschaft, 1945–1958* (Munich, 1990), pp. 109–70.

Table 4.3 Breakdown of those surveyed in the 'Fears of daily life' poll, depicted in Table 4.2, who believed 'that it will come to an inflation' in January 1971

	Very worried	Frequent concerns	Sometimes worried	No worries overall	Cannot decide	Sample size
Base	283	246	232	124	52	937
Total	30.2	26.3	24.8	13.2	5.5	100.0
Sex						
Men	28.4	26.6	26.1	13.9	5.1	100.0
Women	31.5	26.0	23.8	12.7	5.9	100.0
Age						
16–29 years old	23.1	22.7	28.1	19.4	6.6	100.0
30–44 years old	28.7	24.1	27.8	13.5	5.9	100.0
45–59 years old	29.0	32.1	22.3	11.2	5.4	100.0
60 years and older	39.8	26.7	20.8	8.5	4.2	100.0
School Qualifications						
Primary school	32.5	26.3	24.1	11.2	5.8	100.0
Secondary school	22.3	26.0	27.0	20.0	4.7	100.0
Occupational Group						
Skilled labour	31.5	25.7	26.1	12.0	4.6	100.0
Semi-skilled labour	33.8	25.5	19.6	12.7	8.3	100.0
Senior officials and civil servants	30.8	28.6	23.1	14.3	3.3	100.0
Mid- and low- employees / civil servants	21.1	27.3	30.4	14.1	7.0	100.0
Independent	29.5	22.9	25.7	19.0	2.9	100.0
Farmers	43.7	29.6	18.3	5.6	2.8	100.0

	Party Preference					
SPD supporters	22.1	24.7	29.4	18.6	5.2	100.0
CDU/CSU supporters	36.5	27.9	22.3	8.7	4.6	100.0
FDP supporters	21.4	31.0	26.2	14.3	7.1	100.0
City and Country						
Villages	36.0	28.0	22.3	8.0	5.7	100.0
Small cities	36.6	25.1	24.1	9.9	4.3	100.0
Mid-size cities	23.4	29.9	26.6	16.8	3.3	100.0
Big cities	24.1	24.1	25.9	17.9	8.0	100.0

Source: 'Lebensangst: Umfrage 1778', Institut für Demoskopie, Apr. 1971, Tabellen.

trade and investment decisions, though capital controls remained. Second, the deutschmark operated in the Bretton Woods international monetary system. Like other currencies, it had a fixed exchange rate against the American dollar. The greenback was convertible into gold. The federal government in Bonn decided the deutschmark's exchange rate. As such, the Bundesbank was obliged to support this exchange rate. The third crucial factor: the West German economy had been experiencing a sustained economic boom since the 1950s.

These three factors – convertibility, Bretton Woods and strong economic growth – created the conditions for 'imported inflation'. There were two manners in which 'imported inflation' arose. First, in a system of fixed exchange rates, countries with lower rates of inflation ('Group A', let's say) still continue to import goods and services from countries with higher rates of inflation ('Group B'). The inflation rates of 'Group B', then, can impact the inflation rates of 'Group A' by means of trade. The second manner was less obvious. According to the Bundesbank Law, the central bank was obliged 'to safeguard the currency'.[201] In the Bretton Woods system of fixed exchange rates, this could be interpreted in two ways; on the one hand, keeping the domestic rate of inflation low; and, on the other, maintaining the external parity to the dollar. These two goals were not necessarily complementary. Indeed, in the case of West Germany, they often clashed.

Why was this? In short, the country was becoming a victim of its own success. Buoyed by signs of strong economic performance, foreign investors began pouring capital into West Germany.[202] Often such investors speculated that a revaluation of the deutschmark was in the offing. By purchasing deutschmarks today, these investors could 'cash in their chips', so to speak, by selling stronger deutschmarks tomorrow after a revaluation had taken place. But in doing so, investors were selling dollars to purchase West German currency. These capital inflows, then, placed downward pressure on the dollar and upward pressure on the deutschmark. Under the Bretton Woods system, the Bundesbank was obliged to maintain the external parities. As such, it was forced to create deutschmarks to sell, in order to purchase dollars amid efforts to

---

[201] 'Gesetz über die Deutsche Bundesbank. Vom 26. Juli 1957', *Bundesgesetzblatt, Teil I, Ausgegeben zu Bonn am 30. Juli 1957*, Nr. 33, 1957, p. 745. See www.bgbl.de/xaver/bgbl/start.xav?startbk=Bundesanzeiger_BGBl#__bgbl__%2F%2F*%5B%40attr_id%3D%27bgbl157s0745.pdf%27%5D__1473433479381. Last accessed on 20 December 2018.

[202] Ellen Kennedy, *The Bundesbank: Germany's central bank in the international monetary system* (London, 1991), pp. 58–60. For a more detailed discussion on this issue, and the difficulties stemming from it, see Otmar Emminger, *D-Mark, Dollar, Währungskrisen: Erinnerungen eines ehemaligen Bundesbankpräsidenten* (Stuttgart, 1986), pp. 33–41.

maintain the status quo. This obligation, however, increased the West Germany money supply and endangered the domestic rate of inflation.

Of course, the orthodox response to increases in the domestic price level would be for the central bank to raise the interest rate. The idea being that an increase in the interest rate would make borrowing more expensive and push down the price level in the economy. However, by increasing the interest rate, the Bundesbank would simply encourage even larger capital inflows from abroad – after all, a higher interest rate in West Germany, relative to elsewhere, would yield a larger return for a foreign investor. Such capital inflows, however, could place pressure on the deutschmark's external parity with the dollar.

The Bundesbank, then, was constrained in its room for manoeuvre on both sides. To use the language of economists, the Bundesbank was effectively trapped within a 'trilemma'.[203] The concept of 'imported inflation', for its part, was not a new one – it had been identified back in the mid-1950s. Indeed, among the first to discover the problem was the BdL's Otmar Emminger, then a member of the directorate, and later Bundesbank president during the 1970s.[204]

Schacht's remarks in January 1965 highlighted an existing problem for the Bundesbank. The monetary authority was constrained by the obligations imposed by the Bretton Woods system. Yet the emergence of the 'third inflation' in the public sphere discourse highlighted the urgent need to control inflation expectations among the public. The policy decisions undertaken by the Bundesbank to combat these inflationary pressures have already been well documented in the literature.[205] As a result, they will not be documented in detail here. What the literature overlooks, however, is how the Bundesbank used its interaction with the press amid efforts to influence attitudes among the West German people. These endeavours are addressed in the next section.

[203] For more on the trilemma, see Maurice Obstfeld and Alan M. Taylor, *Global capital markets: integration, crisis, and growth* (Cambridge, 2004), pp. 29–41.
[204] See Emminger, *D-Mark, Dollar, Währungskrisen*; and Otmar Emminger, *The D-Mark in the conflict between internal and external equilibrium, 1948–75* (Princeton, 1977).
[205] See, among others, Carl-Ludwig Holtfrerich, 'Monetary policy under fixed exchange rates (1948–70)', in Deutsche Bundesbank (ed.), *Fifty years of the Deutsche Mark: central bank and the currency in Germany since 1948* (Oxford, 1999), pp. 323–90; Rolf Caesar, *Der Handlungsspielraum von Notenbanken: Theoretische Analyse und internationaler Vergleich* (Baden-Baden, 1981), pp. 188–94; Christian N. Wolz, *Konflikte zwischen der Notenbank und der Regierung in der Bundesrepublik Deutschland 1956–1961* (Stuttgart, 2009); and Helge Berger and Jakob de Haan, 'A state within the state? An event study on the Bundesbank (1948–1973)', *Scottish Journal of Political Economy*, Vol. 46, No. 1 (1999), pp. 29–35.

Historical Narratives: 'Moral Persuasion' and the Two Inflations

Like the BdL, the Bundesbank availed of historical narratives stemming from the inter-war period. But the use of such historical narratives became more nuanced with the passage of the Bundesbank Law in 1957. Vocke used historical narratives predominantly to influence the *make-up* of institutions – that is, the Bundesbank Law. Blessing and the Bundesbank, however, used lessons arising from the inter-war era to influence attitudes *within* the constraints imposed by the Bundesbank Law. The use of such historical narratives, in other words, adapted to different uses.

What were these narratives? And what were the purposes of such lessons? For the sake of clarity, this section will be divided into different parts. First, it will examine how Blessing envisioned the use of these narratives, in what he described in public as 'moral persuasion'. Second, the section will focus on how the example of the gold standard was used to justify the necessity of central bank independence in the post-war era. And third, the section will close with how the central bank used lessons of the two inflations during moments of conflict with the federal government during this period.

'Moral Persuasion'

Bundesbank officials intervened in the public sphere for a variety of reasons. In doing so they used a multitude of arguments, references and examples, all tailored to a given moment or situation. One speech, then, could differ markedly to the next. Yet there is a guiding reference point through which they can all be analysed. That concept was 'moral persuasion', an idea explicitly tied to the uses of public opinion.[206]

In March 1960, the Bundesbank president elaborated on what he meant by the expression: the Bundesbank and the state were not alone in carrying responsibility for economic development; there were other important actors, too. Specifically, these were employers, trade unions and the man on the street. 'In boom times, such as those we have today', said Blessing, 'entrepreneurs have more favourable market opportunities as a result of the easing of competitive pressures, and unions a better bargaining position for the enforcement of wage increases. If both exploit

---

[206] The English term was first used by Blessing in March 1960. See Karl Blessing, 'Aktuelle Konjunktur- und Währungsfragen in der Bundesrepublik Deutschland', 9 Mar. 1960, DBHA, B330/576, p. 7.

their opportunities in a ruthless fashion, an increase in the general price level is inevitable.'[207] Should this happen, the Bundesbank president continued, the central bank would have no choice but to step in, dampening aggregate demand by means of tightening credit policy. However, were employers and unions to exercise restraint, they could achieve a higher living standard for all concerned – and without such negative effects as an increase in the price level. With restraint, a wage–price spiral could be avoided.

'Discipline pays for itself', declared Blessing. 'Man is neither an angel nor a devil – rather, the truth lies in between.'[208] A sustained, high aggregate demand would sooner or later lead to wage and price increases. It was therefore imperative that aggregate demand be kept within reasonable limits.

Beyond that, one should not discount what it nowadays referred to as 'moral persuasion' – we call it somewhat ironically as '*Seelenmassage*', or the 'massaging of the soul'. Ultimately, moral persuasion means something like the mobilisation of public opinion with the aim of bringing entrepreneurs and trade unions within the realm of reason – or, expressed differently: to mobilise public opinion so that the ruthless exploitation of temporary market conditions by entrepreneurs and trade unions is to be seen as 'indecent'.[209]

His speech in March 1960 would not be the last time that Blessing linked morals with public opinion. There were other occasions, too.[210] For instance, the Bundesbank president reaffirmed this idea in a letter to the private banker Robert Pferdmenges, two years later. With reference to the upcoming wage negotiations, it was imperative that social partners should be 'influenced by the moral pressure of public opinion'.[211] Moral pressure and public opinion, then, were two sides of the same coin.

Of course, the Bundesbank president was not the only central banker to refer to the use of moral persuasion. Indeed, as the historian John Singleton notes, '[m]oral suasion, the western equivalent of administrative guidance, was part of every central banker's toolbox, especially in states with highly concentrated banking sectors'.[212] The International Monetary Fund, for its part, viewed the Bundesbank's 'moral suasion' strictly as something exerted in the relationship between the central bank,

---

[207] Ibid., p. 6.   [208] Ibid.   [209] Ibid., pp. 6–7.

[210] See, among other examples, Karl Blessing, 'Ansprache des Präsidenten der Deutschen Bundesbank Karl Blessing', 28 Apr. 1967, DBHA, B330/580, p. 2; Karl Blessing, 'Ansprache des Präsidenten der Deutschen Bundesbank Karl Blessing', 25 Jul. 1967, DBHA, B330/580, p. 11; and Karl Blessing, 'Ansprache des Präsidenten der Deutschen Bundesbank Karl Blessing', 23 Apr. 1969, DBHA, B330/582, p. 4.

[211] Karl Blessing to Robert Pferdmenges, 13 Jul. 1962, DBHA, B330/288.

[212] John Singleton, *Central banking in the twentieth century* (Cambridge, 2011), p. 133.

on the one hand, and the private banking sector, on the other.[213] The argument underlying this chapter, however, contends that Blessing's 'moral persuasion' was also aimed at the population as a whole, and encapsulated a wider, more fundamental consideration of West Germany's monetary history amid efforts to give its policies some moral grounding. The central bank sought to influence attitudes of the population, for it was attitudes that in turn influenced price and wage decisions.

'The response from the public can be very significant for the success of some measures, because ... the psychological factor in monetary matters plays an important role', Blessing declared shortly after arriving at the Bundesbank in 1958.[214] This conviction would remain throughout his tenure in Frankfurt. Thus far, however, the section has only outlined the *purpose* of central bank's press efforts. What arguments, examples and references did the Bundesbank use in its speeches to achieve this objective? In a similar manner to the BdL, Blessing reverted to the lessons of the inter-war period. A central bank independent of political instruction, operating within a popular democracy, was to be given historical legitimacy because of Germany's recent, troubled history.

However, before delving into the historical narratives used, it is perhaps best to elaborate on how history, as a subject matter, was seen by Blessing. What were his personal views on the subject? The Bundesbank president elaborated his thoughts on history in a remarkable speech in 1969, towards the end of his tenure at the Bundesbank. 'I have had an interest in history since my youth, and in the course of my life I have seen how important history is as determining factor for our existence', the Bundesbank president said.

History outlines the streams of human thought and behaviour, as well as the results they have brought about. It describes, or it attempts to describe, the relationships and motivations, hopes fulfilled and disappointed, the deeds and misdeeds, the positive and negative features of important actors. 'Fruitful and ample is the realm of history; in its circle lies the whole moral world', wrote Schiller, who was a historian of distinction. And here, in the attempt of acquiring morality, the morality of events, and the morality of man, lies the most important moment. Seen in this manner, history is a masterful teacher par excellence.[215]

For Blessing, history was instructive and laced with a moral undercurrent. Indeed, the subject was very important for the younger generation.

---

[213] I. S. McCarthy, 'Instruments of Monetary Policy: Germany', Central Banking Service, International Monetary Fund, Aug. 1970, BAK, B126/55866, pp. 18–19.

[214] Karl Blessing, 'Die hohe Kunst der Währungspolitik', 17 Feb. 1958, DBHA, B330/574, p. 9.

[215] Karl Blessing, 'Gedanken zum Thema "Geschichte"', 25 Jul. 1969, DBHA, B330/582, p. 1.

The Bundesbank president concluded his speech: 'There are certain matters that every young person should learn, if that person wants to be a thoughtful and active citizen, and the area of history without question has its place in these matters.'[216] These concluding remarks touched on a deeper worry within the Bundesbank. By 1969, an entire generation of West Germans had grown up without any experience of the two inflations. Their grandparents experienced the dizzying excess of the 1922–3 hyperinflation; their parents, the muted destruction of the reichsmark. But this new generation had experienced nothing but economic growth and rising living standards.

'Our people have fifteen years of uninterrupted prosperity behind them', Blessing said in 1965.[217] Would this lack of hardship influence the younger generation's attitude to the deutschmark? This generational shift of monetary values was a point of public discussion. In 1970, for instance, *Die Zeit* published an article called 'The erosion has begun'. 'As the inflations in the first half of our century recede into the distance, the tolerance to price rises is increasing', the author wrote. 'Boys are not as squeamish as their fathers when it comes to the value of money. The erosion of the world-famous German stability-consciousness has already begun.'[218] What is interesting is that the article in part linked this generational change to the increasing acceptance of what it described as 'a third inflation'.[219]

Blessing was quite aware of the generational problem. At several events throughout the 1960s – particularly at birthday celebrations or retirement affairs – he highlighted the fact that the number of bankers who had experienced the depths of the inter-war period was dwindling fast.[220] And with their departure went a wealth of invaluable, crisis-worn experience. In 1970, Blessing, shortly before his death, gave one of his last interviews to *Euromoney*, an English publication. The 'trauma' of inflation was discussed. 'Presumably Germany's unfortunate experiences of inflation in the early 1920s have been psychologically a great help in maintaining such a stable economy?' the magazine asked. 'That's true',

[216] Ibid., p. 3.
[217] Karl Blessing, 'Zur währungs- und wirtschaftspolitischen Lage', Dec. 1965, DBHA, B330/579, p. 3.
[218] Meyer, 'Die Erosion hat begonnen', *Die Zeit*, 16 Jan. 1970.   [219] Ibid.
[220] Blessing stated the same observation on repeated occasions   often at more so informal, celebratory affairs. See Karl Blessing, 'Rede des Präsidenten der Deutschen Bundesbank Karl Blessing', 11 May 1962, DBHA, B330/7528, pp. 2–3; Karl Blessing, 'Zweite Tischrede am 21.4.1965', 21 Apr. 1965, DBHA, B330/578, p. 2; Karl Blessing, 'Ansprache des Präsidenten der Deutschen Bundesbank Karl Blessing', 6 Nov. 1964, DBHA, B330/578, p. 2; and Karl Blessing, 'Die heutige währungspolitische Lage', 3 Jun. 1966, DBHA, B330/579, p. 5.

Blessing responded. But did he think the memory was now fading? 'The younger generation does not understand or remember', Blessing replied. 'As time goes on that disciplinary factor is slowly fading away.'[221] Other Bundesbankers, such as Emminger, also talked of the 'contempt' of some segments of the younger generation with regard to the Bundesbank's *Stabilitätspolitik* and its economic achievements.[222]

How did the Bundesbank respond to this worrying shift? From the start, there were limits to its ambitions. In 1964, von der Lippe recognised the importance of imparting the value of *Stabilitätspolitik* upon the younger generation. But he was also rather sceptical of some strategies. For instance, he ruled out the idea of sending instructive pamphlets to schools. 'Given that teachers have a lack of knowledge about such things, I do not have big hopes', von der Lippe wrote. 'Many [pamphlets] would simply end up in the waste paper baskets.'[223] Instead, the Bundesbank would be better served by focusing its efforts on speeches and articles through existing media channels – newspapers, radio and the like.[224] Blessing would address several young audiences during his twelve-year tenure as Bundesbank president – each time delving into the lessons of the inter-war period.[225]

'Moral persuasion', then, was a concept linked to uses of public opinion – and one that was geared towards ensuring price stability. It was grounded with lessons of the inter-war period, and motivated by a growing worry of a generational shift in monetary values. With this in mind, let us turn to the following historical narratives.

Central Bank Independence in the Absence of the Gold Standard

'The greatest and perhaps the best international monetary system that the world has known was the gold standard, as it existed before 1914', Blessing once declared, for '[i]n large part it functioned independently

[221] 'The wages price spiral – Germany joins the crowd', *Euromoney*, Oct. 1970, DBHA, B330/582, p. 6.
[222] Otmar Emminger, 'Zwanzig Jahre deutsche Geldpolitik – Rückblick und Ausblick', 4 Mar. 1968, DBHA, N2/9, p. 6.
[223] Von der Lippe, 'Bemerkung zu den Vorschlägen von Herrn H. zur "Erweiterung der Öffentlichkeitsarbeit der Bundesbank"', 24 Dec. 1964, p. 2.
[224] Ibid., p. 3.
[225] Among other examples, see Karl Blessing, 'Vortrag des Präsidenten der Deutschen Bundesbank Karl Blessing', 10 Nov. 1961, DBHA, B330/7528, pp. 1–5; Karl Blessing, 'Empfang von Lehrlingen am 30. Mai 1962', 30 May 1962, DBHA, B330/577, pp. 1–2; and Blessing, 'Ansprache des Präsidenten der Deutschen Bundesbank Karl Blessing', 25 Jul. 1967, pp. 1–4.

from the decisions of man'.[226] The Bundesbank president often spoke of his nostalgia for the gold standard. Indeed, it was his central reference point with regard to the inter-war era. Blessing noted that life was simpler for the central banker back in the days of the gold standard. '[I]n the years before 1914, no one would have had the idea of wishing to influence economic development and price outcomes by means of central bank policy', he said in 1958.[227] 'Today's circumstances – unfortunately, it has to be said – are completely different to the situation under the rule of the gold standard'.[228] In the post-war era, central banks were expected to intervene in the economy, stimulating economic growth in the effort to attain a level of full employment in the economy. The stability of the currency – a sacrosanct thing during the era of the gold standard – was in danger of becoming a thing of the past, Blessing warned.[229] Central bank policy was in danger of becoming politicised in the post-war era, a mere tool of politicians to be used to stimulate economic growth amid efforts to win the next election, and to the detriment of the country's long-term interests.

'You might interpret from my comments something of a silent longing for the gold standard', Blessing said on one occasion. 'I do not deny that this is the case to some degree.'[230] But the Bundesbank president always took the caution of stressing that he did not envision a return to the gold standard. In his own words, he was too much of a 'realist' for such schemes.[231] A return to the gold standard would have entailed sacrifices on the part of the West German population that were no longer possible in a post-war welfare state. 'Two world wars and profound changes of every kind' meant that such a monetary system was never coming back.[232] But in the past, a country's commitment to the gold standard served as an important sign of its credibility. And it was credibility, Blessing argued, which West Germany needed above all after two disastrous inflations. It was imperative, then, that the West German central bank should remain independent in light of the gold standard's absence. 'Central banks should be as independent as possible, so that they cannot

---

[226] Blessing, 'Vortrag des Präsidenten der Deutschen Bundesbank Karl Blessing', 10 Nov. 1961, p. 1.

[227] Karl Blessing, 'Aktuelle Währungsfragen', 30 Apr. 1958, DBHA, B330/574, p. 1.

[228] Blessing, 'Die hohe Kunst der Währungspolitik', 17 Feb. 1958, p. 5.

[229] Ibid., pp. 2–3.

[230] Karl Blessing, 'Vortrag des Präsidenten der Deutschen Bundesbank, Herrn Karl Blessing', 22 Feb. 1959, DBHA, B330/575, pp. 11–12.

[231] Ibid., p. 12.

[232] Blessing, 'Die hohe Kunst der Währungspolitik', 17 Feb. 1958, p. 2.

be misused by governments, allowing them to guarantee the inviolability of the currency.'[233]

The Bundesbank president would go on to repeat this argument throughout his tenure at the helm of the monetary authority. Central bank independence was not a direct substitute for the stability of the gold standard – but it was certainly the clearest safeguard for the stability of the currency in a democratic society where politicians, responding to democratic pressures, were incentivised to espouse irresponsible economic policy goals. Given that the deutschmark was a *fiat* currency – in other words, one not directly backed by a physical commodity, such as gold – it was imperative that the central bank be placed in a position that allowed it to foster confidence in West Germany's legal tender. In short, that meant central bank independence. Implicit in Blessing's rhetoric was a certain weariness about the implications of democracy.

The Lessons of the Two Inflations – Conflicts with the Government

'On the grounds of its experience the German nation is more sensitive to inflation than any other nation in the world', Blessing declared in his first speech as central bank president. 'It would be as well if those who suggest that we give up our supposed island life did not forget this.'[234] In a similar manner to the BdL, the Bundesbank propounded the lessons of Germany's two inflations during the era of Blessing. The narratives were presented in a simple, direct fashion: the monetary chaos that characterised the events of 1922–3 and the fall of the reichsmark during 1936–45 was directly attributable to government control of the printing press. As such, it was essential that the central bank remained independent of political instruction from Bonn to safeguard the stability of the currency. The use of such narratives had become more complicated as time progressed, however. Where Vocke felt free to roam, Blessing was now restricted to a careful balancing act. The Bundesbank president used the lessons of the two inflations, but often noted that contemporary inflationary trends were a different creature altogether.

Historical narratives of the two inflations served two purposes for the Bundesbank. The first purpose was somewhat related to the uses of the gold standard narrative: the lessons of the two inflations were used in the post-war era to affirm the historical necessity of central bank

---

[233] Karl Blessing, 'Das monetäre Gleichgewicht und die ökonomischen Probleme', 13 May 1952, DBHA, B330/6895, p. 8.
[234] See Karl Blessing, 'Address by Karl Blessing', 7 Jan. 1958, DBHA, B330/574, p. 2.

independence. The second purpose, however, was to justify to the West German public the occasionally unpopular policies undertaken by the Bundesbank. When implementing restrictive policies, the Bundesbank occasionally referred to the lessons of the inter-war era, and how West Germans, in Blessing's words, were 'allergic' to inflation.[235] This metaphor suggested that the Bundesbank's policies, though unpopular, were justified in light of what Blessing described as the 'trauma' created by recent history.[236]

Thus far, nothing has been said of *when* such narratives were used. The inflation narratives were particularly useful during moments of conflict with the federal government. Indeed, there were several public spats between the Bundesbank and Bonn during the Blessing era: they quarrelled in the lead-up to the revaluation of the deutschmark in 1961; they clashed during the period 1966–7 when the Bundesbank tightened monetary policy; and they fell out over the deutschmark's second revaluation, which took place towards the end of 1969. For the sake of clarity, and in the interests of space, this section only addresses the most serious conflict.

This occurred during 1966–7. Given the high aggregate demand and sustained inflationary pressures evident at the time, Blessing delivered several speeches warning of the consequences of irresponsible government spending.[237] Indeed, at one point, Blessing hinted to Erhard that he would have no choice but to resign from his post unless there was a substantial change of government policy.[238] The central bank resorted to tightening credit policy amid efforts to dampen demand. The government, industrialists and unions protested alike.[239] A recession followed, and unemployment rose, sparking the events that led to the fall of Erhard's government in late 1966. It was West Germany's first recession

---

[235] This word was often used by the Bundesbank to describe West Germans attitudes to inflation. See, for example, Karl Blessing, 'Referat des Präsidenten der Deutschen Bundesbank Karl Blessing über die währungspolitische Lage', 30 Mar. 1965, DBHA, B330/578, p. 1.

[236] 'Trauma' was another word often used by Blessing. See Karl Blessing, 'Rede des Präsidenten der Deutschen Bundesbank Karl Blessing', 27 Jan. 1967, DBHA, B330/580, p. 2.

[237] Two good examples are Blessing, 'Zur währungs- und wirtschaftspolitischen Lage', pp. 1–8; and Karl Blessing, 'Zwischen Euphorie und Realität', 24 Feb. 1966, DBHA, B330/579, pp. 5–7.

[238] Karl Blessing to Ludwig Erhard, 16 Jun. 1966, DBHA, B330/242, p. 2.

[239] For an example of government protest, see the letter sent by economics minister Kurt Schmücker in November 1966, during the final weeks of the embattled government coalition's existence. Kurt Schmücker to Karl Blessing, 14 Nov. 1966, DBHA, B330/246. The attitude of the unions was noted in Ludger Westrick to Karl Blessing, 8 Aug. 1966, DBHA, B330/242.

since the advent of the 'economic miracle'. And it served as a moment of reflection. The Bundesbank had 'toppled' Erhard's government, according to Karl Schiller, a leading SPD politician and the subsequent economics minister. Schiller declared this quite openly in parliament. A cry was heard from the benches – 'Unfortunately he is right!' It was Kurt Schmücker, the economics minister of the government that had been 'toppled'.[240]

As a result of its policies, the Bundesbank was placed under intense scrutiny in the media. Was it right for an independent institution to have the power to help bring down an elected government? The events of 1966–7 sparked questions about the central bank's independence. The public debate surrounding its independence had lain dormant since the passage of the Bundesbank Law in 1957. But now it had become a heated topic of public discussion. Blessing was forced to downplay the central bank's independence on several occasions, stressing instead the Bundesbank's commitment to co-operating with the government as far as possible.[241] The central bank, he argued, was not a 'state within a state'.[242] Indeed, throughout his tenure at the Bundesbank, Blessing stressed the importance of a healthy, active co-operation between Frankfurt and Bonn.

In the midst of the 1966–7 recession, however, the central bank president felt obliged to bat away references to the deflation of the Great Depression.[243] It was irresponsible government spending, not monetary policy, which was at the root of the current recession, he argued.[244] And besides, '[a] central bank that does not fight, in an era of mass democracy, industrial society and the welfare state, is synonymous with bad money'.[245] But Blessing also used the inflation narratives to support the Bundesbank's arguments. Its job, after all, was to ensure the stability of the deutschmark. In January 1967, towards the tail-end of the recession, Blessing remarked in a telling moment that, while 'the acute danger of

---

[240] See 'Deutscher Bundestag – 5. Wahlperiode – 241. Sitzung. Bonn, Donnerstag, den 19. Juni 1969', 19 June. 1969, DBHA, N3/173, p. 13448.

[241] See, for instance, Karl Blessing, 'Vortrag des Präsidenten der Deutschen Bundesbank Karl Blessing vor der Technischen Universität, Berlin', 16 Dec. 1966, DBHA, B330/580, p. 2.

[242] Karl Blessing, 'Ansprache des Präsidenten der Deutschen Bundesbank Karl Blessing', 10 Nov. 1967, DBHA, B330/580, pp. 5–6.

[243] See, for example, Karl Blessing, 'Ansprache des Präsidenten der Deutschen Bundesbank Karl Blessing', 23 Nov. 1966, DBHA, B330/580, p. 5; Blessing, 'Rede des Präsidenten der Deutschen Bundesbank Karl Blessing', 27 Jan. 1967, p. 7.

[244] Karl Blessing, 'B.B.C. Interview', 10 Jan. 1967, DBHA, B330/580, pp. 1–2, 4.

[245] Blessing, 'Vortrag des Präsidenten der Deutschen Bundesbank Karl Blessing vor der Technischen Universität, Berlin', 16 Dec. 1966, p. 2.

inflation has passed, one should not believe that the trauma of inflation no longer exists'.[246] When it came to defending itself in the public sphere, the central bank had every reason to ensure that such a 'trauma' continued to exist.

It is also interesting to note how the Bundesbank responded to the recession in a more general sense. The central bank increased markedly its presence in the public sphere. The Bundesbank – including the directorate and central bank council – delivered ninety-five speeches, articles and interviews in the year 1966 alone.[247] All the while, von der Lippe kept Blessing up to date on journalistic gossip and the tone of the daily press.[248] The central bank complemented these efforts with the release of three books amid the turbulence of 1966–7, all published with Fritz Knapp Verlag. Blessing released a second collection of his speeches – *Im Kampf um gutes Geld* in 1966; Emminger published a collection of speeches in the same year; and Wilhelm Könneker, a member of the directorate, released a book about the Bundesbank in 1967.[249] The media received Blessing's publication positively. 'At no better time could the book of the Deutsche Bundesbank president appear than now', wrote one reviewer, 'where the *Kampf um gutes Geld*, or fight for good money, has culminated in an open conflict between the Bonn government, which lusts for expansion, and the cautious monetary guardians of Frankfurt'.[250] The timing of these publications suggests that the Bundesbank pushed to increase its presence in the public sphere amid efforts to influence the parameters of political debate.

Yet, unlike the era of Adenauer – a period in which politicians had yet to become used to the idea of a powerful, independent central bank – no heavyweight politician came out in public support of removing the Bundesbank's independence. Why was this? The reason centred on public opinion. 'I do not believe that anyone seriously has the intention of restricting the autonomy of the Bundesbank', said Blessing in 1969, looking back on his twelve-year tenure. 'Indeed, I do not believe that

---

[246] Blessing, 'Rede des Präsidenten der Deutschen Bundesbank Karl Blessing', 27 Jan. 1967, p. 2.

[247] Sixty-nine speeches, articles and interviews were given by members of the directorate; twenty-six were given by members of the central bank council. Blessing delivered the most (twenty-two), followed by the directorate's Otmar Emminger (nineteen). See 'Verzeichnis der Veröffentlichungen von Mitgliedern des Zentralbankrates im Jahre 1966', 27 Jan. 1967, DBHA, B330/18224, pp. 1–5.

[248] See, for instance, Viktor von der Lippe to Karl Blessing, 29 Apr. 1966, DBHA, B330/280.

[249] Blessing, *Im Kampf um gutes Geld*; Emminger, *Währungspolitik im Wandel der Zeit*; and Könneker, *Die Deutsche Bundesbank*.

[250] 'Karl Blessing: Im Kampf um gutes Geld', *Finanz und Wirtschaft*, 28 Jan. 1967.

public opinion would tolerate a restriction of the Bundesbank's autonomy.'[251] The idea of an independent central bank, conditioned by the
Bundesbank's 'moral persuasion', remained a popular one with the
electorate.

Conclusion

It is here that we revisit that 'damned' cabaret show in Frankfurt in
October 1965. 'Himmler had friends?' one of the performers asked.
'Oh yes, a whole bunch of benefactors, really rich ones', came the
answer. Why, didn't the audience know that Blessing was a member of
Himmler's infamous *Freundeskreis*? According to the Bundesbank's
'short comprehensive summary', however, Blessing was a man who
signed the Reichsbank memorandum of 1939. The document described
this memorandum as 'one of most famous acts of resistance of its time'.
Moreover, the 'short comprehensive summary' stressed, the Bundesbank
president was linked to the '20 July' group that plotted to kill Hitler.

For a brief period in 1965, then, there existed two competing identities
that sought to define Blessing. The reputation of both Blessing and the
Bundesbank had been shoved to the very fault line of a divided Europe,
with the central bank president's past becoming a political football in the
Cold War. Within days of the *Freundeskreis* story's emergence, the
Bundesbank went to great lengths to stifle the story as quickly and as
quietly as possible. The central bank's directorate even took to scolding a
young schoolboy in local Frankfurt. The purpose of this chapter has not
been to pass judgment on Blessing's past, however. Rather, it sought to
highlight the different ways in which the record of the inter-war period
could be used in the West German public sphere – and how interests,
ideological or otherwise, could determine the survival of one historical
narrative over another.

Unlike other central banks in Europe, the Bundesbank was continually
forced to shape the contours of its past; for if the central bank did not, it
knew others certainly would, as in the case of Engelmann's *Deutschland
Report*. In 1965, there was no guarantee that the *Freundeskreis* story would
disappear. There was every risk that it might become subject to a media
scandal. The Bundesbank, led by von der Lippe, took efforts to ensure
that one historical narrative remained dominant over another. When
Blessing retired, he did so as a monetary martyr, not as a former member
of Himmler's *Freundeskreis*.

---

[251] Karl Blessing, '2 Dt. Fernsehen [Balkhausen, Schröder]', 15 Jul. 1969, DBHA, B330/
582, p. 3.

There was a pronounced element of continuity between the BdL and the Bundesbank. The image of a strong, independent central bank was firmly in place by the time of Blessing's arrival. And in the public eye, at least, the Bundesbank was also linked with the inter-war Reichsbank. At times this link brought with it a troubled past – and it was a troubled past that had to be defended. We saw this during the Schacht–Blessing affair, the *Freundeskreis* news story and the Bundesbank's rejection of the 'third inflation'.

In particular, the central bank saw the emergence of the 'third inflation' as a point of discussion in the mid-1960s as a cause for worry. Tied down by the constraints imposed by the international monetary system, the central bank used press policy to augment the effectiveness of its policies. We have seen how the Bundesbank used historical narratives, conditioned by Blessing's 'moral persuasion', a concept closely related to the uses of public opinion. The lessons of the inter-war period were stylised in such a fashion that reminded West Germans of the apparent historical necessity of central bank independence, while supporting the Bundesbank's public image and protecting the central bank from political attacks. The recession of 1966–7 was used as a short example to elaborate on these points. The Bundesbank's use of 'moral persuasion' was further motivated by generational concerns. By the late 1960s, a whole generation of West Germans had grown up without any experience of a serious inflation. The central bank, for its part, was determined to inform them about Germany's inflationary episodes, if not via the classroom then through the media.

In 1969, Blessing was in the final year of his tenure at the Bundesbank. It was an election year, too – one in which the revaluation of the deutschmark had become a point of debate. In August of that year, von der Lippe recorded in his work diary that Blessing expressed the 'greatest concern' should the SPD win the coming election. 'We have three weeks of rest, then the storm breaks loose', Blessing remarked.[252] The Bundesbank president was referring to the expected revaluation of the deutschmark were the SPD to win the election. But he could have said the same thing about the 1970s, the decade in which the SPD came to dominate federal politics in West Germany. After all, the 1970s became known as the era of the 'Great Inflation'. And it is to the era of social democracy that this book now turns.

---

[252] Viktor von der Lippe, 'Tagebuchähnliche Aufzeichnungen – 29.8.1969', 29 Aug. 1969, DBHA, B330/6915-1.

5 The Bundesbank, Social Democracy and the Era of the 'Great Inflation', 1970–1978

Introduction

Karl Klasen stood on the podium. Before him sat a range of West German dignitaries. 'One speaks often, and rightly so, of the German people's psychological aversion to the dangers of inflation, of their fear of currency depreciation, and of the experience of two inflations induced by war', Klasen declared. The date was Tuesday, 13 January 1970, and it was the new Bundesbank president's first official speech at the helm of the monetary authority. He was speaking at a ceremony that marked the retirement of his predecessor, Karl Blessing.

This was not the first time that a president of the central bank had evoked the memories of Germany's two inflationary episodes in the public sphere. In this regard, Klasen was merely echoing a line of rhetoric carefully carved out by Blessing and Wilhelm Vocke, the defiant chairman of the Bank deutscher Länder (BdL), the Bundesbank's forerunner. His audience had heard such references before. But then something strange happened – something unprecedented. Klasen wasn't finished. He began to qualify the 'psychological aversion to inflation':

But a greater part of our population also had to endure mass unemployment during the Great Depression. This led to the collapse of the Weimar Republic, it brought us the regime of Hitler, and thus contributed to the emergence of the Second World War. The last recession [of 1966–7], however short-lived, has demonstrated the sensitivity to which our people react to fluctuations in employment. The recession had a considerable impact on political events in the Federal Republic and proved that unemployment can endanger our social structure. Inflation and unemployment, both are a trauma of our population.[1]

Klasen had equated the inter-war lessons of inflation and mass unemployment. This was a first for the central bank. Before, the

---

[1] Karl Klasen, 'Ansprache des Präsidenten der Deutschen Bundesbank Dr Karl Klasen', *Deutsche Bundesbank Auszüge aus Presseartikeln*, No. 4, 16 Jan. 1970, Deutsche Bundesbank Pressearchiv [DBPA], no. 575, pp. 6–7.

monetary authority always stressed the primacy of *Stabilitätspolitik* – in other words, policies supporting the stability of the currency. This preference often meant using lessons stemming from Germany's two inflations to underline the historical legitimacy of such policies. Klasen did not stop there, though. There was another distinct shift in rhetoric – as one man in the audience knew all too well. Viktor von der Lippe, the personal advisor to Blessing and Vocke, as well as press chief of the Bundesbank, looked on as Klasen, his new boss, spoke of the central bank's 'autonomy' vis-à-vis the federal government in Bonn.[2] Von der Lippe had written the first draft of Klasen's speech.[3] But the press chief's references to the central bank's 'independence', or *Unabhängigkeit*, in the original draft were simply overlooked by the new president. Klasen, who sought a more accommodating attitude to Bonn, did not mention the word 'independence' even once. The Bundesbank, in Klasen's eyes, was 'autonomous'. It was a word that signalled a certain freedom of manoeuvre with respect to the federal government, but not outright independence.

Von der Lippe was not the only person who noticed the change of rhetoric. Klasen's 'new tones' were much remarked upon in the media.[4] They were 'unmistakable', according to the *Neue Zürcher Zeitung*, and signalled more of a willingness to work closely with the federal government in Bonn.[5] 'Two weeks is not enough time to gauge the views and intentions of a central bank president', observed *Der Volkswirt*, an influential economics magazine. 'But even in this short time period, the new man at the top of the central bank has let it be known that his politico-economic world view differs quite clearly from his predecessor.'[6] Klasen's pointed references to the recent recession of 1966–7, and the subsequent rise in unemployment, were instructive in this regard. Under Blessing, the Bundesbank had been accused in the media as having intentionally created an economic downturn and, in turn, inadvertently helped to topple a democratically elected government. If Blessing prized the stability of the currency over considerations of full employment, Klasen sought to demonstrate that he at least offered a more nuanced view of economic priorities.

---

[2] Ibid., p. 7.
[3] Von der Lippe's draft did not make any reference to the 'trauma' of mass unemployment. See Viktor von der Lippe, 'Ansprache des Präsidenten der Deutschen Bundesbank Dr. Karl Klasen (Entwurf von Lippe für Rede am 13.1.1970)', no date, Deutsche Bundesbank Historisches Archiv [DBHA], B330/6987.
[4] 'Neue Töne im deutschen Notenbankpräsidium', *Neue Zürcher Zeitung*, 16 Jan. 1970.
[5] Ibid.   [6] 'Klasens Einstand', *Der Volkswirt*, 16 Jan. 1970.

The end of the 1960s marked the start of a new era. The conservative Blessing, after twelve years as president of the Bundesbank, had stepped into retirement. In his wake, the federal government appointed a new man. Klasen was a banker. But he was also a card-carrying member of the Social Democratic Party (SPD). He had joined the political party in 1931, two years before the National Socialists assumed power.[7] Klasen brought with him a different past from those of Blessing and Vocke, two men who were schooled in the inter-war Reichsbank. And his appointment to the Bundesbank reflected wider changes in the political sphere of West Germany. In late 1969, the Grand Coalition, led by Kurt Georg Kiesinger, gave way to the SPD-led coalition government of Willy Brandt. For the first time since the Weimar Republic, the country's federal government was led by the Social Democrats – albeit in a coalition with the more market-orientated Free Democratic Party (FDP). The rise of the people's party brought with it Klasen to the Bundesbank.

The words of the new Bundesbank president, then, caused something of a stir in the West German public sphere. But were they indicative of a politicised central bank, one that would be more willing to factor considerations of full employment into its policy decisions? And what did Klasen's arrival in Frankfurt mean for the monetary authority's independence, as outlined in the Bundesbank Law of 1957? The 1970s were years littered with economic crises, both of an international and domestic nature. Labour strikes, inflation and ever-lengthening dole queues dominated the news headlines in West Germany. Politicians in Bonn grappled to maintain control of the situation. And faced with unprecedented inflationary pressures, the Bundesbank felt obliged to tighten monetary policy substantially in the early 1970s. Such decisions caused considerable headaches in the political capital. Some voices called for more control over the Bundesbank, noting that the central bank's independence could be overturned by a simple majority vote in the West German parliament. As such, the 1970s were years that saw the first blatant attempt since the era of Konrad Adenauer, the former chancellor, to limit the independence of the Bundesbank. And none other than Klasen's own political party spearheaded these attempts. How did the Bundesbank cope with the challenge of social democracy in the era of the 'Great Inflation'?[8]

---

[7] Anon., 'Zur Erinnerung an Karl Klasen. Bank und Geschichte: Historische Rundschau', *Historische Gesellschaft der Deutschen Bank*, No. 19, Apr. 2009, p. 1.

[8] Otmar Emminger, the vice president of the Bundesbank between 1970 and 1977, later to become president during the years 1977–9, often referred to the 'Great Inflation' throughout the 1970s. See, for instance, Otmar Emminger, 'The role of the central banker', 10 Dec. 1975, DBHA, N2/19, pp. 9–10.

There are three strands of argument underlying this chapter. The first layer contends that, with a new generation of leadership in power, the Bundesbank began to shed its link to the Reichsbank in the public sphere. Of course, the Bundesbank, and its predecessor, the BdL, were not the legal successors to the Reichsbank. But Blessing and Vocke, newspapers often noted, were former Reichsbankers. And they were men who actively transformed their inter-war experiences into edifying lessons for *Stabilitätspolitik* in the post-war public sphere. Klasen had a different background though. So too did Otmar Emminger, the new vice president, and a long-time member of the central bank directorate since the days of the BdL. These two men used the media to distance the Bundesbank from the legacy of the past.

The second strand of argument centres on the relationship between social democracy and the central bank. Unlike other mainstream parties during the 1970s, sizeable segments within the SPD were still ill at ease with the implications of central bank independence. These concerns, once isolated cries in the lower ranks of the party, became more pronounced after the recession of 1966–7. Left-wing critics and trade unions accused the Bundesbank of intentionally causing the 1966–7 downturn and, in turn, questioned the idea of allowing an independent institution to control such a powerful lever of economic policy. This debate was compounded further by, on the one hand, the economic difficulties of the early 1970s, and the spectacular falling-out between the so-called super-minister Karl Schiller and the Bundesbank president, on the other. In 1973, the finance ministry, led by the Social Democrat Helmut Schmidt, embarked on a legislative initiative to change the Bundesbank Law, one that sought to limit the independence of the Bundesbank in a nuanced manner.

Schmidt's proposals sparked a fiery debate, one in which politicians, interest groups and trade unions fought to get their views heard. Suddenly, the Bundesbank Law was open to question again. It was no longer untouchable. And in a manner reminiscent of the 1950s debates, historical narratives of Germany's two inflations, as well as the mixed record of the independent Reichsbank during the inter-war era, were used for political gain amid efforts to influence the proposed *Novellierung*, or amendment, to the Bundesbank Law. The legislative effort, however, was quickly shelved due to two factors: the uproar in the media and coalition infighting.

In the end, the debate was quickly forgotten. But it was a telling one all the same. Within six months of the affair, a somewhat stung Schmidt, who had since become chancellor, submitted a confidential report to the SPD's leadership. It stated, '[w]e are not able to make use of any public conflict with the Bundesbank: public opinion would not stand on our side'.[9] From this moment onwards, in a decade riven by economic crises that prompted commentators to call into question the independence of the Bundesbank, the leadership of the SPD actively sought to play down debates concerning the Bundesbank's independence. It did so for fear of public backlash. This chapter argues that this development was indicative of a 'paradox' in West German democracy: in short, public opinion played a crucial role in protecting an institution – one that was not beholden to democratic pressure – from democratic accountability itself. And this, too, during an era in which West Germans were called on by the SPD's election campaign slogan to 'dare more democracy'.[10]

Here is where the third layer of argument comes in. The central bank did not play a passive role in the development of this West German 'paradox'. Given the Bundesbank's sensitive position in the democratic makeup of the country – the scrutiny of which only heightened by economic troubles and generational change – the monetary authority pursued an active press policy to influence public opinion. In this regard, historical narratives of the inter-war period continued to play a formative role in how the Bundesbank responded to challenges, both of a political and economic sort. They were used quite blatantly in moments of political crisis, such as during the media storm following the resignation of Schiller. And they were employed to sell harsh (but often necessary) policies undertaken by the central bank to the West German public before and after the first oil crisis in 1973.

But even these narratives themselves changed in nature as the 1970s progressed. There are two points to note here. First, as the legacy of the Reichsbank receded into the past, certain reference points in the public sphere fell by the wayside. The Reichsbank memorandum of 1939, for instance, was no longer referenced in the 1970s – albeit with one notable exception. Second, historical narratives adapted to a new monetarist environment, one characterised by a floating exchange rate. The predecessors of Klasen and Emminger – namely, Vocke and Blessing – often thought in what would later be called monetarist terms. For example, Vocke sought to balance the supply of money with the level of goods and services in the economy. But these were also central bankers conditioned by the example of the classical gold standard. To these men, the concept

---

[9] Helmut Schmidt, 'Bericht – Persönlich – Vertraulich', 7 May 1974, Archiv der sozialen Demokratie, Friedrich-Ebert-Stiftung [AdsD], 1/HSAA008631, p. 57.

[10] See Daniela Münkel, 'Politiker-Image und Wahlkampf. Das Beispiel Willy Brandt: Vom deutschen Kennedy zum deutschen Helden', in Bernd Weisbrod (ed.), *Die Politik der Öffentlichkeit – die Öffentlichkeit der Politik: politische Medialisierung in der Geschichte der Bundesrepublik* (Göttingen, 2003), p. 73.

of *Stabilitätspolitik* had an important external connotation. The fixed exchange rate was, as Blessing once declared, a 'sacrosanct' thing, 'to be altered only if all other means fail'.[11] After 1973, in light of floating exchange rates, the Bundesbank had an interest in reframing what *Stabilitätspolitik* meant. Emminger, in particular, sought to focus that sacrosanctity on questions of internal purchasing power, with the external commitment fading into memory.

The 1970s were replete with monetary anniversaries too. And these occasions, coupled with the economic crises at hand, served as moments of reflection. They allowed the Bundesbank to bolster its image with historical narratives. For example, the year 1973 marked the twenty-fifth anniversary of the deutschmark, as well as the fiftieth anniversary of the hyperinflation during the Weimar Republic. The year 1976 marked the centenary of German central banking, prompting the Bundesbank to publish a collection of essays spanning the early days of the Reichsbank to the troubled 1970s. And in 1978, a grand ceremony was held in Frankfurt to celebrate thirty years of the deutschmark. Achievements were acknowledged. And contemporary dangers threatening such accomplishments were underlined. These anniversaries allowed the Bundesbank to crystallise and commemorate the historical narratives it had so carefully tailored over the past three decades.

The first section of the chapter examines the new leadership of the Bundesbank – Klasen and Emminger – and how the public image of the Bundesbank changed in light of its new governors. It looks at von der Lippe's fading role in the central bank too. Second, the chapter turns to West German attitudes concerning inflation at the start of the decade. It notes that the narratives of the two inflations had become firmly entrenched in the public sphere by this time.

The third part of the chapter details the relationship between social democracy, as embodied by the SPD, and the Bundesbank. Primarily, this section serves to offer context for the two case studies that follow. It details how the SPD's attitude to the central bank's independence evolved over time; and it contrasts the party's stance in the 1970s to those of other mainstream parties, such as the FDP and the Christian Democratic Union (CDU). Keeping with this theme, the chapter then examines two public controversies and their outcomes: the Schiller–Klasen affair, which sparked off in 1972; and Schmidt's *Novellierung* debate concerning the Bundesbank Law in 1973. The Schiller–Klasen crisis is used to demonstrate the fact that the Bundesbank resorted to

---

[11] Karl Blessing, 'Statement by Karl Blessing, president of the Deutsche Bundesbank, at a press conference in Bonn', 5 Mar. 1961, DBHA, B330/576, p. 1.

historical narratives at moments in which it was politically challenged. The *Novellierung* example is used to highlight how closely entwined the inflation narratives were with the Bundesbank Law itself, reinforcing the arguments found in Chapters 2 and 3. And finally, the chapter addresses the way numerous anniversaries were treated during this era.

Klasen and Emminger

Between 1970 and 1979 two men dominated the Bundesbank's interaction with the public sphere. The first man was Klasen, the president of the central bank; the second, Emminger, its vice president until 1977, and then president for two years thereafter. Bundesbank policy decisions were undertaken by majority vote on the central bank council. Each member had one vote. But it was left to Klasen, Emminger and a small number of members of the Bundesbank directorate – the body that ran the central bank's day-to-day operations – to communicate these decisions to government officials, interest group representatives, the media and the West German population as a whole. As such, despite the size of the central bank council, the communication channel remained a concentrated one, offering these men the opportunity to impart their own thoughts and opinions when elaborating on the actions undertaken by the Bundesbank's decision-making body.

Klasen was born in Hamburg in 1909. Joining the SPD in 1931, he also became a member of the Reichsbanner and the paramilitary Eiserne Front, two left-wing organisations that opposed monarchism and National Socialism.[12] 'It was clear that Hitler meant war', Klasen later told a journalist, on eve of becoming Bundesbank president. 'Only the SPD appeared to me to be able to engage in effective resistance against this man.'[13] He studied law at Hamburg University with the original intention of becoming a judge.[14] In newly fascist Germany, however, the young man was now burdened with a questionable political past. A career in the courts was ill advised. As a result, Klasen found refuge in private banking. He worked for Deutsche Bank between 1935 and 1943, becoming general counsel of the legal department of the bank's branch in Hamburg.[15] He was then drafted into the German army for the remaining two years of war.

[12] 'Der Mann, der über unser aller Geld zu wachen hat', *Kölner Stadt-Anzeiger*, 13–14 Dec. 1969.
[13] Ibid.
[14] Anon., 'Zur Erinnerung an Karl Klasen. Bank und Geschichte: Historische Rundschau', p. 1.
[15] 'Personal data [Klasen's CV]', no date, DBHA, BSG 1/33.

Following the cessation of hostilities – and a stint of internment in an American prisoner of war camp – Klasen re-entered the sphere of private banking, becoming deputy director at Deutsche Bank's Hamburg branch in July 1945. He became director in 1948. But shortly afterwards, Klasen was appointed as the president of the state central bank of Hamburg in April of that year. For the next four years, Klasen was a member of the BdL's central bank council. Given that he was a member of the SPD, the conservative Vocke at times treated him with suspicion.[16] A relatively young man, Klasen's influence in the central bank council was not a sizeable one, as one colleague lamented at the time.[17] He left the realm of central banking in 1952 to become a board member of Norddeutsche Bank, one of the successor institutions to the Deutsche Bank after the latter had been broken up by the Allied authorities. This breakup proved temporary, however. By 1957, Klasen (Figure 5.1) had returned to a newly remerged Deutsche Bank to become a board member there for the next twelve years. Between 1967 and 1969, he was joint chief executive officer of Deutsche Bank alongside Franz Heinrich Ulrich.[18]

In 1970, then, a man who spent the vast majority of his career in private banking led the Bundesbank. He cut a commanding, even 'auto-cratic' figure in the central bank council.[19] 'He had a tactic which he learned from Hermann Josef Abs [the private banker]', recalled one contemporary. 'He could make people who spoke too pompously look silly. There is nothing worse than to have a serious speech met with laughter.'[20] Nevertheless, Klasen's background brought with it its own troubles. He sought to distance himself from the SPD upon his appoint-ment, for instance. He 'never attended party meetings', as he took care to mention to *The New York Times* just before assuming the reins of the Bundesbank.[21] This claim was not entirely accurate. In 1951, when Klasen was still president of the state central bank in Hamburg, he attended an economics committee meeting of the SPD, one in which the upcoming Bundesbank Law lay at the centre of the discussion.[22] The committee was broadly hostile to the idea of an independent central

[16] See, for example, Wilhelm Vocke to Karl Klasen, 22 May 1951, DBHA, B330/2029.

[17] 'I am convinced, however, that your [Klasen's] influence on the decisions of the central bank council will in future be greater as has been to date.' See Otto Pfleiderer to Karl Klasen, 21 Apr. 1949, DBHA, N1/214.

[18] Anon., 'Zur Erinnerung an Karl Klasen. Bank und Geschichte: Historische Rundschau', pp. 1–5.

[19] David Marsh, *The Bundesbank: the bank that rules Europe* (London, 1992), p. 189.

[20] Ibid., p. 77.

[21] 'Bundesbank: "Crown" to Klasen', *The New York Times*, 25 Dec. 1969.

[22] 'Anwesenheitsliste. Sitzung des Wirtschaftspolitischen Ausschusses beim Parteivorstand am Freitag, den 1.6.1951 in Bonn, Bundeshaus', 1 Jun. 1951, AdsD, 2/PVBF000003.

Figure 5.1 Karl Klasen, president of the Bundesbank, 1970–7.
(DBHA, BSG 3/268 – © Deutsche Bundesbank – Historisches Archiv)

bank. And its conclusions stated that the central bank should not be placed in a position that would allow it to work against the policies of a democratically elected government.[23] The minutes did not record Klasen's personal opinion on this issue, however. All that is known is that he attended and participated in the discussion. It is likely, though, given Klasen's role in helping to draft the BdL's original stance on the Bundesbank Law in late 1949 (he was a member of the task force set up by the central bank), that Klasen pushed for independence.

But what was Klasen's stance on the central bank's independence twenty years on? Were commentators in 1970 correct in interpreting Klasen's opening speech as one indicative of a more politicised central bank? Surprisingly, not many personal documents relating to Klasen's stint in the Bundesbank survive today. But the question above can be answered by examining Klasen's statements in the media, as well as his personal thoughts recorded in discussions with colleagues in Frankfurt. Across the years, Klasen used the terms 'autonomous' and 'independent' almost interchangeably. From the outset, Klasen vowed to newspapers to do all that was in his power to protect the independence of West Germany's monetary authority.[24] And he meant it. During crisis-stricken moments, such as when the Bundesbank learned of Schmidt's efforts to limit central bank independence in the early 1970s, Klasen confided to von der Lippe that 'his [Klasen's] line' was 'to reject everything that endangered the central bank's autonomy'.[25] This primarily meant fending off attempts to limit the central bank's independence via changes in the Bundesbank Law.

This raises another question, however. What exactly did Klasen mean by 'autonomy'? The Bundesbank president accepted the implications of the Bundesbank Law: the central bank was independent of government instruction. And so it should remain, he argued.[26] But his use of the term 'autonomy' hinted at the acknowledgement that, while the Bundesbank was independent, it was nevertheless obliged by the Bundesbank Law to support the economic policies of the government, so long as they did not

---

[23] Harold Koch and Rudolf Pass, 'Protokoll zur Tagung des Wirtschaftspolitischen Ausschusses beim Parteivorstand der SPD am 1. und 2. Juni 1951', no date, AdsD, 2/PVBF000003.

[24] See, for instance, his interview in 'Bundesbank: "Crown" to Klasen', *The New York Times*, 25 Dec. 1969.

[25] Viktor von der Lippe, 'Tagebuchähnliche Aufzeichnungen – 18.9.1973', 18 Sep. 1973, DBHA, B330/6917-1.

[26] '"Acht plus X Prozent": Peter Sweerts-Sporck sprach mit Bundesbank-Präsident Karl Klasen', *Wirtschaftswoche*, 25 Apr. 1974.

endanger the stability of the currency. 'Autonomy' for Klasen, then, was an attitude. It was a mindset.

During his tenure, the Bundesbank president worked closely with the top echelon in Bonn. Indeed, Klasen was a close *Duzfreund* of heavy-weight politicians such as Schmidt and Schiller – that is, he addressed them both with the familiar form of the second person pronoun, *du*.[27] It signalled a close friendship. All three were old-time acquaintances, having encountered each other in Hamburg during the early post-war years. And there was a level of intimacy, too. As chancellor, Schmidt was an honorary guest at the wedding of Klasen's son, a Porsche-driving private banker.[28] During their stints at the top, Schmidt and Klasen often met up during the weekend for private discussions centring on economic policy and current affairs.[29] The Bundesbank president would then arrive back in Frankfurt to update the central bank council on the latest developments. It was a relationship of mutual respect; Schmidt often sought out Klasen for advice on the economy.[30] 'Probably there has never been so close and fruitful a teamwork between a Bundesbank president and chancellor in the history of the Federal Republic, as had been the case with Klasen and me', Schmidt later recalled.[31] Vocke had fallen out with chancellor Adenauer; Blessing had kicked up a ruckus with chancellor Kiesinger. But, Schmidt observed, 'Karl Klasen, as president of the Bundesbank, fell out neither with chancellor Brandt nor with me.'[32]

Did this close co-operation endanger the independence of the Bundesbank? At first glance, yes. That Klasen allowed himself to be influenced by politicians such as Schmidt and Schiller certainly suggests that the *personnel* independence of the Bundesbank was compromised. Upon closer inspection, however, this argument is not entirely fair. Klasen arguably did a service to central bank independence during a potentially explosive era. There are two points to note here. First, the close working

---

[27] 'Per du', *Der Spiegel*, 24 Nov. 1969; and 'Knallhart zu werden – das geht ihm ab', *Wirtschaftswoche*, 25 Apr. 1974.
[28] 'Sohn des Bundesbankchefs Klasen heiratet junge Ärztin', *Bild*, 14 Jun. 1974.
[29] As briefly documented in numerous entries in the professional working diary of von der Lippe. See, for example, the following entries, which in themselves span a number of years: Viktor von der Lippe, 'Tagebuchähnliche Aufzeichnungen – 3.10.1973', 3 Oct. 1973, DBHA, B330/6917-1; Viktor von der Lippe, 'Tagebuchähnliche Aufzeichnungen – 17.12.1975', 17 Dec. 1975, DBHA, B330/6918/1; Viktor von der Lippe, 'Tagebuchähnliche Aufzeichnungen – 22.3.1976', 22 Mar. 1976, DBHA, B330/6918/2; and Viktor von der Lippe, 'Tagebuchähnliche Aufzeichnungen – 28.8.1976', 28 Aug. 1976, DBHA, B330/6918/2.
[30] Helmut Schmidt, *Men and powers: a political retrospective*, trans. Ruth Hein (New York, 1989), p. xv.
[31] Helmut Schmidt, 'Dank an einen Hanseaten', *Die Zeit*, 20 Apr. 1984.   [32] Ibid.

relationship between Klasen and Schmidt embodied the original vision of central bank independence as outlined by Ludwig Erhard, the father of West Germany's so-called 'economic miracle', and a powerful defender of the BdL's independence back in the early years of the Federal Republic. In late 1950, in a letter addressed to Fritz Schäffer – then the finance minister, who was charged with drafting the Bundesbank Law at the time – Erhard rejected the idea of establishing an arbitration committee as a means of solving disputes between Bonn and Frankfurt. Such an arbitration committee, weighted in favour of the government, would have effectively eliminated the central bank's independence. Instead, Erhard countered, the government should appoint suitable men who, though independent of political instruction, should ideally set about working closely as possible with government officials to avoid conflicts wherever possible.[33] This accurately summarises Klasen's own behaviour during his time as Bundesbank president.

The second point can be demonstrated by means of comparison, and perhaps even a counterfactual scenario, with respect to Klasen's predecessors: Blessing and Vocke. During the 1960s, under the presidency of Blessing, the relationship between Frankfurt and Bonn was quite antagonistic at times (though it should be noted that Blessing, to his credit, sought co-operation wherever he thought possible). This was particularly case during the recession of 1966–7, when unemployment increased markedly. Open disputes between government ministers and the Bundesbank spilled into the public sphere. In 1969, for instance, Schiller stood in the West German parliament and publicly accused the central bank of having toppled the previous government, as Chapter 4 has noted.[34] There were private clashes between Bonn and Frankfurt during the tenure of Klasen, of course. But such *public* disputes were quite rare. Surprisingly, the Bundesbank and the federal government did not clash amid the unemployment crisis of 1974–5. This was despite the fact that unemployment figures – rising above a million – were far worse than those occurring in the 1966–7 recession.[35] The relatively peaceful relations between Bonn and Frankfurt can be traced in large part to the accommodating attitude of Klasen, who understood political realities and proved an adept communicator at times of crisis.

---

[33] Ludwig Erhard to Fritz Schäffer, 12 Oct. 1950, Bundesarchiv, Koblenz [BAK], B102/5706.

[34] 'Deutscher Bundestag – 5. Wahlperiode – 241. Sitzung. Bonn, Donnerstag, den 19. Juni 1969', 19 June. 1969, DBHA, N3/173, p. 13448.

[35] 'Arbeitslose: Stürzt knappes Geld die SPD?', *Der Spiegel*, 17 Feb. 1975.

By co-operating and communicating with the federal government as clearly and as much as possible, Klasen headed off the likelihood of a fight with Bonn. In doing so, Klasen ensured that discontent with central bank independence, so evident in the lower rungs of the SPD, did not filter up into the higher reaches of key ministerial posts – albeit with one notable exception (as discussed later in this chapter). Co-operation between Frankfurt and Bonn helped to ensure that calls to limit the Bundesbank's independence were restricted – for the most part, at least – to the relative fringes of the party, and to trade unions. Klasen's goodwill, then, contributed to the maintenance of the Bundesbank Law's independence in the crucial decade of the 1970s. Such an outcome might have been unlikely if, say, Vocke – often described as 'cold', even 'misanthropic' – had been in Klasen's place during this period.[36] Personalities matter in politics, and above all in moments of crisis.

In his capacity as Bundesbank president, Klasen delivered speeches, gave interviews to journalists, and penned articles when the occasion required. On the whole, however, when it came to the public sphere, Klasen was not as active as his predecessor Blessing. This can perhaps be attributed to personal inclination. Klasen preferred to solve issues behind the scenes. But it could also be linked to the rise of Emminger as vice president.

Born in Augsburg in 1911, Emminger studied jurisprudence and economics at the Berlin-based Frederick William University – later to become Humboldt University – as well as Ludwig Maximilian University of Munich. He followed this in 1932 with brief stints of study at Edinburgh University and, later, the London School of Economics, where he encountered the economist and philosopher Friedrich Hayek in seminar discussions.[37] The conclusion outlined in Emminger's doctoral thesis praised the inter-war British government for its decision to take the pound sterling off the gold standard and float the currency.[38] During the inter-war period, Emminger became a member of the National

---

[36] As von der Lippe confided to a friend in 1960, when looking back on Vocke's stint in the central bank: 'Many people found him [Vocke] somewhat "cold," and in actual fact he did have a bit of misanthropy in him.' See Viktor von der Lippe to R. von Fieandt, 12 Aug. 1960, DBHA, B330/8140, p. 2.

[37] Deutsche Bundesbank (ed.), *Währung und Wirtschaft in Deutschland 1876–1975* (Frankfurt am Main, 1976), p. 790; and Otmar Emminger, *D-Mark, Dollar, Währungskrisen: Erinnerungen eines ehemaligen Bundesbankpräsidenten* (Stuttgart, 1986), p. 41.

[38] 'Kein Sancho Pansa [*sic*] von Don Klasen', *Welt am Sonntag*, 12 Jun. 1977; Emminger, *D-Mark, Dollar, Währungskrisen*, pp. 17, 279.

Socialist party – though this fact would only emerge in 1990, years after his death.[39]

Emminger entered the BdL in 1950 and quickly assumed the leadership of the economics and statistics department. He joined the directorate in 1953 and remained there until his departure from the Bundesbank as president in 1979. Emminger was a close friend of Kiesinger, the chancellor from late 1966 to 1969, and was tipped to become the next Bundesbank president should Kiesinger have won the election in 1969.[40] Instead, the Social Democrats emerged triumphant and Emminger became vice president as part of a political compromise. Upon Klasen's retirement in 1977, however, Emminger became president, with Karl Otto Pöhl, a Social Democrat, assuming the vice presidency. It was a rule of thumb that the top two positions in Frankfurt were divided out to the right and left of the political spectrum, the priority of which dependent on which political party came out the better in the last election.

Emminger had a first-rate mind, but he also had a habit of antagonising his colleagues in Frankfurt. At central bank council meetings, he had an 'awe-inspiring capacity for long-windedness', as the writer David Marsh puts it. Short questions were often answered with fifteen-minute lectures. Emminger 'was incapable of diplomacy', recalled one Bundesbank official. 'He always wanted to be right.'[41] Nevertheless, the Augsburger demonstrated a keen awareness of the media's importance from the start.[42] Already during the era of Blessing, he rivalled the old Bundesbank president as one of the most prolific public speakers of the central bank.[43]

By the time he assumed the vice presidency in 1970, Emminger was already recognised as a leading authority on monetary matters. He made himself readily accessible to journalists; interview requests were rarely declined. Emminger (Figure 5.2) was a great speaker, and a regular on the international monetary conference circuit. He actively cultivated a profile in the public sphere. And his reputation only increased as the

---

[39] The *Financial Times* journalist David Marsh, who would later write a book on the Bundesbank, made this discovery. See 'Germany's durable elites keep a hold on levers of power', *Financial Times*, 12 Jul. 1990.
[40] Marsh, *The Bundesbank*, p. 189; Viktor von der Lippe, 'Tagebuchähnliche Aufzeichnungen – 29.8.1969', 29 Aug. 1969, DBHA, B330/6915-1; 'Per du', *Der Spiegel*, 24 Nov. 1969.
[41] Both quotes can be found in Marsh, *The Bundesbank*, p. 78.
[42] Emminger, *D-Mark, Dollar, Währungskrisen*, pp. 26–8.
[43] In the year 1966, for example, Blessing delivered a total of twenty-two speeches, interviews and articles. Emminger came in second place in the central bank council with a total of nineteen. See 'Verzeichnis der Veröffentlichungen von Mitgliedern des Zentralbankrates im Jahre 1966', 27 Jan. 1967, DBHA, B330/18224.

Figure 5.2 Otmar Emminger, vice president of the Bundesbank, 1970–7, and later president 1977–9.
(DBHA, BSG 3/134 – © Deutsche Bundesbank – Historisches Archiv)

years went by. By 1969 newspapers were describing Emminger as the 'foreign minister' of the Bundesbank.[44] In 1974, he was described by *Time* magazine as 'one of the continent's most respected monetary authorities'.[45] By 1977, the year in which he assumed the Bundesbank presidency, Emminger was described as the 'monetary Kissinger', with one Bank of England official opining that he was 'the best ambassador Germany has ever had'.[46] In terms of constituting the public voice of the Bundesbank, then, it was arguably Emminger as much as Klasen who helped to shape the public image of the central bank.

How did Emminger himself view the importance of the press for the Bundesbank's cause? 'From the outset, the German central bank undertook strenuous efforts to promote the understanding and support of stability policy among the population', Emminger recounted in his memoirs. 'At the same time these efforts were also required in order to fix the *independence of the central bank* on a firm foundation ... Formally, the independence of the Bundesbank is only secured by the Bundesbank Law – that is, a simple law – not by the constitution.' He continued:

When I entered the Bank deutscher Länder, as it was known back then, in 1950, I often discussed this problem with my friend Eduard Wolf, the long-term chief economist of the central bank. We agreed that the independence of the Bundesbank would only be secure if it had the overwhelming support of the people; only then would it be immune against political interference. If the Bundesbank was not held responsible to the government or parliament, in a democratic society it must nevertheless account for its actions to the people. So, in order to win this support and understanding, we decided to promote the measures of the central bank through a lively publishing activity.[47]

As a member of the BdL's directorate, Emminger wrote essays on international monetary problems of the day. Vocke, however, exerted an iron grip on what directorate members were allowed to say in public. Speeches and articles, for example, had to be signed off by Vocke before their publication.[48] Emminger, an early and convinced monetarist, chafed at such control and earned the anger of Vocke on several occasions.[49] On one such occasion, in a preliminary draft of a speech,

---

[44] See, for example, 'Der neue Bundesbankpräsident hat große Erfahrungen', *Frankfurter Allgemeine Zeitung*, 21 Nov. 1969; and 'Zuviel Macht für die Bundesbank?', *Wirtschaftswoche*, 16 Feb. 1973, pp. 50–1.

[45] 'Monetary reforms in cold storage', *Time*, 10 Jun. 1974.

[46] 'The bankers' banker heads for the top', *Sunday Times*, 13 Mar. 1977.

[47] The emphasis is found in the original text. See Emminger, *D-Mark, Dollar, Währungskrisen*, pp. 26–8.

[48] See Wilhelm Vocke to all departments in the Bank deutscher Länder, 2 Aug. 1948, DBHA, B330/3356.

[49] Emminger, *D-Mark, Dollar, Währungskrisen*, p. 69.

Emminger had identified the problem of 'imported inflation' – that is, inflationary developments imported from abroad by dint of West Germany's trade relations and the framework of the international monetary system. This was an economic phenomenon that Vocke refused to recognise.[50] As a result, Emminger was forced to change the speech before delivering it. It was only with the establishment of the Bundesbank that officials on the directorate became independent members of the central bank council. And, as such, they were only then given the freedom to say what they wanted to in public.[51] Emminger took that freedom to heart, and would play an important role in determining the public image of the central bank during the 1970s.

Cutting the Cord with the Reichsbank

It was during the two presidencies of Klasen (1970–7) and Emminger (1977–9) that the Bundesbank began to shed its link to the Reichsbank in the public sphere. The BdL and the Bundesbank were not the legal successors to the Reichsbank.[52] But for over twenty years, the BdL and the Bundesbank were closely identified with the inter-war central bank in press reports and interviews. This was because Vocke and Blessing were former Reichsbankers. As Chapters 2, 3 and 4 have demonstrated, these men used their negative experiences from the inter-war period, and turned them into edifying lessons for *Stabilitätspolitik* in the public sphere. Indeed, Vocke and Blessing derived some of their credibility from the inter-war era. Their signatures could be found on the 1939 Reichsbank memorandum that was sent to Adolf Hitler, and which protested against the inflationary armaments financing of the Third Reich.[53]

With Klasen and Emminger, however, newspapers documented a different past. Klasen's history was one associated with social democracy and private banking. Emminger was a young man during the Third Reich and, though a member of the National Socialist party, he did not assume national prominence until well after the end of the Second World War. Unlike Blessing, he lacked a public profile during the Third Reich. Instead, almost the entirety of Emminger's professional career was associated with the rise of the deutschmark, which, as the title of one

---

[50] Ibid., p. 38.   [51] Ibid., p. 69.

[52] 'Präsident Dr. Klasen, Vizepräsident Dr. Emminger und die Mitglieder des Direktoriums Dr. Irmler und Dr. Schlesinger vor der Presse am 5. Januar 1976 (nach Bandaufnahme)', 5 Jan. 1976, DBHA, B330/7896.

[53] Reichsbank directorate to Adolf Hitler, 7 Jan. 1939, BAK, B122/5008.

1978 book put it, went from being a 'child of the occupation to world star'.[54]

Furthermore, Emminger actively distanced the Bundesbank from the record and legacy of the Reichsbank. 'The Bundesbank, which is not the legal successor of the liquidated Reichsbank, has cut the cord with the Reichsbank', Emminger was once quoted as saying when he was Bundesbank president.

> When I arrived in the central bank in 1950, I had no role model for my next steps. Indeed we had a unique task for which there hardly was any model: to build a strong and stable currency out of a weak one with no currency reserves and a broken economy![55]

Emminger's words were bolstered by another distinct break in this history of the Bundesbank. In March 1973, the deutschmark went from a currency with a fixed parity vis-à-vis the dollar to one that floated via market forces – though within the constraints of the 'snake', the first attempt at European monetary co-operation. This came after the slow implosion of the Bretton Woods international monetary system that began in late 1971. The 1920s and 1930s were characterised by economic nationalism and currency devaluations. These events had a formative impact on the minds of Vocke and Blessing, as well as other elites in government circles. For Vocke, in particular, the stability of the deutschmark had first and foremost external considerations – that is, not the domestic purchasing power of the currency, but rather the deutschmark's parity against other currencies. At its inception, West Germany's legal tender had to win international confidence if it was to survive.

The same went for Blessing. As the historian Dieter Lindenlaub argues, the main lesson that Blessing took from the inter-war period concerned exchange rate policy; a fixed exchange rate, coupled with convertibility, should be maintained wherever possible.[56] 'For a central bank the parity of the currency is, after all, sacrosanct and a thing to be altered only if all other means fail', Blessing declared in 1961.[57] His position was to change on this as the 1960s progressed, however. By 1969, he came out in favour of a revaluation. Nevertheless, for two

---

[54] Hans Roeper, *Die D-Mark: Vom Besatzungskind zum Weltstar* (Frankfurt, 1978).
[55] 'Der Währungshuter tritt ab', *Deutsche Zeitung*, 21 Dec. 1979.
[56] Lindenlaub goes on to note that Blessing would change his opinion in the late 1960s. See Dieter Lindenlaub, 'Karl Blessing', in Hans Pohl (ed.), *Deutsche Bankiers des 20. Jahrhunderts* (Stuttgart, 2008), p. 16.
[57] See Blessing, 'Statement by Karl Blessing, president of the Deutsche Bundesbank, at a press conference in Bonn', p. 1.

decades, the Bundesbank's message of *Stabilitätspolitik* took on external as well as internal considerations. West Germans were repeatedly told of the importance of the deutschmark's stability vis-à-vis other leading international currencies.

The central bank from which Klasen retired in 1977, then, was a rather different creature to the one that he had entered. What consequences did this transition have for the Bundesbank's message to the West German people? After 1973, the Bundesbank sought to portray its primary goal in terms of domestic price stability. With Emminger in particular, the central bank extrapolated that objective back into the past. The external commitment – that is, the obligation to maintain a fixed exchange rate – faded quickly into memory.[58] This was an important change in rhetoric. After all, Blessing once stated that 'flexible exchange rates are an element of disintegration, not of integration'.[59] To remind West Germans that the external commitment was an important part of *Stabilitätspolitik* was to underline the anomaly of having a floating exchange rate. Now that the deutschmark floated, considerations of price stability took on predominantly domestic connotations. From within the walls of the Bundesbank, then, the concept of *Stabilitätspolitik* changed fundamentally in March 1973. It had to. Even in retrospective pieces about the 1957 Bundesbank Law, for instance, the central bank would frame the objective of the central bank in monetarist terms. In part, it was able to do this because of the vagueness of the Bundesbank Law: the Bundesbank was merely required 'to safeguard' (*zu sichern*) the deutschmark. Now, what did that mean exactly? Well, after 1973, the central bank asserted that it meant domestic price stability.

In the 1970s, the shadow of the Reichsbank began to fade. Unlike Vocke and Blessing, Emminger and Klasen were not burdened by the mixed legacy of central banking during the inter-war period. And as time progressed, the central bank's history became increasingly myopic. The inter-war period began to be used less and less as a reference point. Instead, a new, more recent and positive history began to emerge, one that emphasised personal histories and events following the currency reform of 1948.

Press Department

What did the arrival of the new leadership mean for the press department? Following Blessing's retirement, control of the media division was

---

[58] Emminger, *D-Mark, Dollar, Währungskrisen*, p. 25.
[59] Karl Blessing, 'Notenbankpolitik in der heutigen Zeit', 8 Dec. 1964, DBHA, B330/578, p. 7.

formally transferred to Emminger, reflecting his strong interest in media matters.[60] Klasen, due to his position as president, was still entrusted with 'important affairs of the press and various duties concerning journalism'.[61] The directorate, for its part, continued to exert complete control over the central bank's press policy. A curious incident occurred in early 1974, when a new state central bank president, Fritz Schiettinger, requested documents concerning the central bank's press policy and efforts. Klasen rebuffed Schiettinger, stating that such material was too sensitive to be shared with central bank council members. The Bundesbank president informed Schiettinger that he would have to wait thirty years until the documents were opened to the public.[62]

Von der Lippe, the personal advisor to Vocke and Blessing, remained as head of the press department until his retirement in January 1977.[63] This meant that the man spent over a quarter of a century representing the central bank in the public sphere. He exerted a powerful influence, working effectively and 'silently', as one journalist observed, behind the scenes.[64] But his position was not always secure. As von der Lippe himself noted on the day of his retirement, the security of his 'dual role' as personal advisor to the president was somewhat precarious during moments of presidential transition.[65] This was an indirect reference to Klasen. With the new Bundesbank president's arrival in 1970, von der Lippe's influence within the Bundesbank began to wane. Klasen and von der Lippe developed differences, though the nature of these differences – whether they were political, personal or professional – remains unclear. Another man, Peter Titzhoff, gradually assumed von der Lippe's duties. Titzhoff eventually became Klasen's personal advisor; he drafted the president's speeches and assumed control of the press department following von der Lippe's retirement.

In the meantime, however, von der Lippe continued to play an important role at the Bundesbank. His professional working diary, carefully maintained, demonstrates this point. Starting in 1968 and wrapping up on the day of his departure, the diary offers a revealing insider's account

---

[60] 'Geschäftsverteilung im Direktorium der Deutschen Bundesbank', 1970, DBHA, B330/58602.

[61] 'Geschäftsverteilung im Direktorium der Deutschen Bundesbank', 1975, DBHA, B330/58602.

[62] Karl Klasen to Fritz Schiettinger, 19 Feb. 1974, DBHA, B330/8392.

[63] Viktor von der Lippe, 'Tagebuchähnliche Aufzeichnungen – 31.1.1977', 31 Jan. 1977, DBHA, B330/6918/2.

[64] This was acknowledged by the long-time economics journalist Robert Platow. See 'Personalwechsel bei der Bundesbank', Der Platow Brief, 4 Nov. 1976, DBPA, no. 1498.

[65] Viktor von der Lippe, 'Abschiedsworte', 31 Jan. 1977, DBPA, no. 717, p. 4.

behind the walls of Bundesbank during a period of continual economic crisis, paying close attention to media reports about the central bank as well as any public attacks on its independence.[66] It was written for von der Lippe's own personal reference. The diary demonstrates that Klasen still confided in von der Lippe. In moments of crisis, the Bundesbank president would ask for his opinion on how the monetary authority should react.[67] Von der Lippe, for his part, continued to keep Klasen up to date on media affairs.[68] After decades in his role as press chief, he had developed a large array of contacts with the economics and business media.[69] Many of these relationships had been built upon long, fruitful years of working together.[70] As such, when it came to the Bundesbank's interaction in the public sphere in the 1970, von der Lippe continued to exert a sizeable, if somewhat diminished influence.

Entrenchment of the Inflation Narratives

By the early 1970s, the narratives surrounding Germany's two inflationary episodes had become firmly entrenched in the public sphere. In articles and profile pieces about the Bundesbank, journalists, domestic and foreign alike, would make reference to Germany's 'trauma' of inflation.[71] The hyperinflation of the Weimar Republic had become a bit of 'colour', a journalistic term used to describe a line that spices up the text of an article. Here is just one example: 'Stability is a cardinal virtue here', wrote the West German correspondent for *The Wall Street Journal* in 1977.

To Germans who have lived through – or endlessly heard about – the disastrous inflation of the 1920s, the ensuing Nazi era and the devastation of war, a stable economy is more highly cherished than any marginal increase in living standards achieved through risky government meddling.[72]

---

[66] Von der Lippe's professional working diary comprises eight thick archive folders' worth of material. This book is the first time that such material has been researched. See folders DBHA, B330/6915-1 to DBHA, B330/6918/2.

[67] For evidence of this claim, see Viktor von der Lippe, 'Meinung zum Thema "Erklärung"', 27 Jul. 1972, DBHA, B330/6987; and Viktor von der Lippe, 'Vermerk vom 2.8.1972', 2 Aug. 1972, DBHA, B330/6987.

[68] See, among others, Viktor von der Lippe to Karl Klasen, 6 Sep. 1972, DBPA, no. 570; Viktor von der Lippe to Karl Klasen and Otmar Emminger, 4 Oct. 1972, DBHA, B330/8141; and Viktor von der Lippe to Karl Klasen, 28 Mar. 1973, DBHA, B330/8143.

[69] 'List of journalists, newspapers and addresses', 1 Aug. 1971, DBHA, B330/8140.

[70] As noted, for example, in Viktor von der Lippe to Walter Slotosch, 22 Apr. 1971, DBHA, B330/8143.

[71] See, for instance, 'Germany: long memories and the need to ease the credit policy', *The Times*, 17 Nov. 1970.

[72] 'Drawing the line: West Germany resists U.S. pleas to increase outlays to aid growth', *The Wall Street Journal*, 9 Feb. 1977.

This passage is remarkable only in the fact that it resembles countless other journalistic pieces published during the 1970s. How did Bundesbank officials view this development? It is difficult to say. But a telling episode occurred in 1977 when *National Geographic* wrote a piece about the Bundesbank's tough policies in the earlier years of the decade. The magazine's journalist interviewed Emminger while researching for the article. Once the initial draft had been written, the editor of *National Geographic* sent a copy back to Emminger so as to allow the central banker to verify each and every fact found in the draft – even down to the number of floors in the Bundesbank building – prior to the article's publication in the magazine. What follows is a passage from the original, uncorrected draft that arrived at Emminger's desk:

The Bundesbank had slammed the brakes on West German inflation [in early 1973]. But not without cost. Interest rates soared; money grew tight; the German real estate boom burst. There were 20,000 bankruptcies. 'It was painful, very harsh,' Dr. Emminger said. But West Germans accepted the 'correction.' Burned into their national memory was the inflation of the 1920s when money presses ran round the clock and the reichsmark tumbled from 10 to the dollar to 1.5 billion to the dollar. The price of a restaurant meal went up, literally, while customers ate. Family savings vanished, nightmarish depression set in.[73]

Emminger, in correcting the passage above, crossed out the word 'reichsmark', replacing it with 'mark'. The central banker also changed the exchange rate from 10 to 4.2 to the dollar. But the sensational references to a national memory scarred by inflation remained untouched.[74] Emminger, for his part, would also occasionally talk about the Weimar hyperinflation in interviews. 'The next president of the Bundesbank does not hide the influence that recent German political history has also had on his economic thinking', wrote one journalist for *The New York Times* in 1977.

'I was a student in Berlin and my father was a member of the Reichstag while Hitler was coming to power,' Dr. Emminger recalls. 'So I met many of the politicians of the time and I saw how the inflation of the Weimar Republic made Germans believe they couldn't be democratic.' Dr. Emminger recounts other memories of those difficult years. 'My family comes from Augsburg, where I was born. And I remember how, when my father was posted away from home, the money he sent back to us lost a quarter of its value in the mail,' he says. Such memories may have made Dr. Emminger a conservative economist.[75]

---

[73] Marcia Butler to Otmar Emminger, 20 Apr. 1977, DBHA, N2/24; and 'National Geographic text copy', 20 Apr. 1977, DBHA, N2/24, pp. 7–8.
[74] 'National Geographic text copy', 20 Apr. 1977, pp. 7–8.
[75] 'Atop the Bundesbank', *The New York Times*, 1 May 1977.

According to Emminger's logic, the fight against inflation was the fight for West German democracy. An independent central bank had an important role to play in this regard. Inflation wasn't the result of social conflict; inflation was one of its primary causes.[76] By fighting inflation, then, the independent Bundesbank was doing its service to democracy. By 1977, the year in which *The New York Times* article was published, central bank independence had long since become synonymous with economic stability in West Germany – an association that was not necessarily evident in 1949, the turbulent year in which the state was established. On several occasions throughout the 1970s, Emminger compared the economic phenomenon of inflation to a form of totalitarian government. Speaking in 1975, for example, Emminger declared, 'One important point we have learned in the past two years is that you have no chance of conquering inflation if you do not begin early. Inflation is like dictatorship. If you do not resist dictatorship before it has become established, then you are lost, because it is very difficult to get rid of.'[77] This was a rather subtle reference to the second, 'repressed' inflation, one that occurred during the Third Reich. In the post-war era, various journalists and elites referred to it as 'Hitler's inflation'.[78]

What emerged in the media was a dialectic of sorts, with the inflation narratives being continually propounded back and forth between the Bundesbank and journalists. Indeed, by the 1970s, it would often be the latter who raised the topic of Germany's history of inflation in interviews. 'The public attitude played a very big role in helping the government', Emminger said in one such discussion.

As you [the journalist] suggest, in Germany perhaps more than in most other countries there is a sensitivity to inflation due to memories of the terrible inflation we suffered in the 1920s. This special sensibility is sometimes criticized as abnormal and psychopathic. But I consider it a major asset, since if people are not sensitive to inflation, you can't ask sacrifices.[79]

---

[76] This argument is best outlined in 'Geld ist geprägte Freiheit: DZ-Gespräch mit Bundesbankpräsident Otmar Emminger', *Deutsche Zeitung*, 10 Jun. 1977.

[77] See 'Keeping inflation under control', *The Guardian*, 5 Mar. 1975. For another example, see Otmar Emminger, 'Ausführungen von Otmar Emminger', 26 Mar. 1979, DBPA, no. 287, p. 4.

[78] See, for instance, Volkmar Muthesius, *Augenzeuge von drei Inflationen. Erinnerungen und Gedanken eines Wirtschaftspublizisten* (Frankfurt am Main, 1973), p. 162. See also Gerhard Weisser, 'Verhandlung mit Sir Eric Coates, dem Finanzberater General Robertsons, über die Finanz- und Geldpolitik Westdeutschlands am 8.10.49 in Düsseldorf', 10 Oct. 1949, DBHA, B330/358, p. 2.

[79] 'How Germany beat inflation', *Dun's Review*, Nov. 1974, DBHA, N2/17.

Sacrifices, of course, meant lower economic growth in the short term, and, in some cases, increased unemployment. This was particularly evident during the Bundesbank's highly restrictive monetary policy in 1973, launched amid efforts to stem the inflationary tide. And it wasn't just Emminger. Klasen often referred to the inflationary experiences of the West German people, too. 'Germany has lived through ruinous inflations in 1923 and another in 1948', Klasen told an American audience, shortly after becoming president of the Bundesbank. 'Germans are therefore allergic to the slightest sign of an inflation. That is why Germans are prepared to make substantial sacrifices in the interest of price stability.'[80]

Nevertheless, the Bundesbank was not alone in its references to Germany's two inflations. The narratives had come to be used by various institutional actors whenever it happened to suit them. The Deutscher Industrie- und Handelskammertag, or German Chamber of Commerce and Industry, spoke of West Germany's sensitivity to inflationary policies in 1977 while expressing its strong scepticism of American president Jimmy Carter's efforts to co-ordinate a global reflation with the help of German spending.[81] Although personal memory of the Weimar inflation was fading, the use of such narratives continued to experience a strong life, often by people who were too young to have experienced the event. This was because the narratives remained in large part useful reference points for contemporary political debates.

There are two main points that should be taken from this section. First, the narratives concerning Germany's two inflations were firmly embedded in the public sphere, both domestic and international. And second, inflationary fears among the West German population were firmly entrenched long before the first oil crisis in late 1973, an event that sparked double-digit inflation among several of the world's leading industrial economies.

Two 'Traumas' and an Independent Central Bank

Inflation was not the only threat endangering the stability of the West German economy in the 1970s, however. The other was unemployment – and this time it appeared in a new, uncertain environment. The 'Phillips curve', a tenet of Keynesian thought that demonstrated the inverse relationship between rates of inflation and unemployment, no longer

[80] See Karl Klasen, 'Remarks on our common efforts to curb inflation', 27 Jan. 1971, DBPA, no. 572, pp. 2–3.
[81] 'West German business opposed to Carter plan', *The Journal of Commerce*, 10 Feb. 1977.

appeared to work in much of the Western hemisphere. In its wake, a new economic phenomenon emerged: 'stagflation'. Characterised by high rates of inflation and unemployment coupled together, stagflation meant that politicians spent much of the decade simultaneously grappling with rising prices and lengthening dole queues. The coalition government, comprised of the SPD and the FDP, faced a choice. Should it place more emphasis on tackling inflation or unemployment?

Left-wing circles argued that government spending should be primed to alleviate the problem of unemployment. In other words, the government should step in where the private sector stepped back, stimulating aggregate demand via a more active fiscal policy. Others, often found on the political right, countered that the stability of the currency had to come first. This stance called for tight monetary policy to rein in the credit that was flushing around the economy. Such a move would help dampen demand, in turn pushing down prices, and allowing West Germany to increase its competitiveness vis-à-vis its trading partners. This development, so the argument went, would provide a stimulus to the domestic labour market, increasing job opportunities for the unemployed.

Trade union leaders knew on which side of the debate they stood. In 1972 Heinz Oskar Vetter, the chairman of the Deutscher Gewerkschaftsbund, or German Trade Union Confederation, lambasted what he termed the 'fetish' of stability consciousness, or *Stabilitätsgedanken*, in West German public life.[82] Similarly, IG Metall, a large industrial trade union, called for the end of the 'taboo-isation' of inflation in 1977.[83] These trade unions warned of the dangers that unemployment posed to society at large.

The Bundesbank, too, knew on which side of the fence it sat. Klasen and Emminger argued forcefully for a *Stabilitätspolitik*-orientated solution to West Germany's economic problems: government spending should be cut and credit in the economy reduced sharply. It was no surprise, then, that the Bundesbank pursued a tight monetary policy in the early years of the 1970s. That it was able to do so was in large part due to the central bank's policy independence. As the economy's troubles increased, however, intense scrutiny began to be placed on its autonomy in a democratic society. Of course, these fears were always voiced whenever the central bank had tightened monetary policy in the past.

---

[82] As noted in Volkmar Muthesius, 'Der Bund und seine Bank', *Die Zeitschrift für das gesamte Kreditwesen*, 1 Sep. 1972, p. 2.
[83] 'IG Metall: Inflation ist nicht so schlimm', *Handelsblatt*, 23 Mar. 1977.

But this time it was different. There were two reasons. First, the Bundesbank faced heavy criticism for its restrictive monetary policy in the lead-up to the 1966–7 recession. Prior to this event, West Germans had known only prosperity since the days of the so-called 'economic miracle'. During the short-lived recession, several media observers and academics were disgruntled by what they saw as the Bundesbank acting in an overtly political fashion, evoking memories of the controversial behaviour of Hjalmar Schacht, the Reichsbank president during the late 1920s.[84] The central bank's alleged role in the events of 1966–7 helped to increase support and awareness for the idea of a more democratically accountable monetary authority.[85] Second, the West German government, under Kiesinger and his economics minister Schiller, embarked on its first dalliance with Keynesian demand management with the passage of the 1967 Stability and Growth Law.

This piece of legislation set forth a 'magic square' of economic policy priorities to be pursued by the government: i) price stability, ii) full employment, iii) economic growth and iv) balanced trade.[86] The law afforded the government new instruments that allowed it to embark on a more interventionist approach in economic affairs.[87] Its passage marked the brief highpoint of Keynesian economics in West Germany.[88] But a question remained. To what extent was the Bundesbank obliged to cater for all four angles of the square? A debate raged in legal circles in subsequent years, centring on the Stability and Growth Law, on the one hand, and the Bundesbank Law, on the other.[89] The Bundesbank, for its part, had always insisted that its duty, first and foremost, and as outlined in the Bundesbank Law, was to 'safeguard the currency'.[90] This stubborn viewpoint, the central bank's critics argued, ignored the

---

[84] Rüdiger Robert, *Die Unabhängigkeit der Bundesbank: Analyse und Materialien* (Kronberg im Taunus, 1978), pp. 36–40.

[85] Dieter Duwendag (ed.), *Macht und Ohnmacht der Bundesbank* (Frankfurt, 1973), p. 6.

[86] Christopher S. Allen, 'The underdevelopment of Keynesianism in the Federal Republic of Germany', in Peter A. Hall (ed.), *The political power of economic ideas: Keynesianism across nations* (Princeton, 1989), p. 276.

[87] Wolfgang Kitterer, 'Public finance and the central bank', in Deutsche Bundesbank (ed.), *Fifty years of the Deutsche Mark: central bank and the currency in Germany since 1948* (Oxford, 1999), pp. 180–2.

[88] Jörg Bibow, 'On the origin and rise of central bank independence in West Germany', *The European Journal of the History of Economic Thought*, Vol. 16, No. 1 (2009), p. 182.

[89] This debate is neatly summarised in Rolf H. Kaiser, *Bundesbankautonomie Möglichkeiten und Grenzen einer unabhängigen Politik* (Frankfurt, 1980), pp. 6–20.

[90] A representative view of the Bundesbank's position can be found in Friedrich-Wilhelm von Schelling to Karl Klasen, 1 Jun. 1970, DBHA, B330/42138. Von Schelling supported the arguments outlined in Joachim von Spindler, Willy Becker and Otto-Ernst Starke, *Die Deutsche Bundesbank: Grundzüge des Notenbankwesens und Kommentar zum Gesetz über die Deutsche Bundesbank* (Stuttgart, 1969).

premises outlined in the Stability and Growth Law. It was the latter piece of legislation that would provide the key reference point for most of the attacks on the Bundesbank's independence during the 1970s.

Social Democracy and the Bundesbank

The battle lines concerning the central bank's independence were drawn. Both the CDU and the FDP were in full support of the Bundesbank's autonomy during the 1970s.[91] But where did the SPD stand on the issue? Historically, the SPD had always demonstrated a mixed attitude about the autonomy of the central bank. Chapter 1 has noted how politicians from the SPD spoke out in support of the Autonomy Law back in May 1922.[92] The Autonomy Law saw the emergence of an independent Reichsbank for the first time. But disillusionment quickly set in among the left after the Reichsbank became an increasingly political player under Schacht. By the late 1920s, Social Democrats began to call into question the legitimacy of an independent monetary authority in a democratic republic.[93]

In the early years of the Federal Republic that was established after the Second World War, the SPD remained uncomfortable with the idea of an independent central bank. The memories of the 1920s and 1930s were still fresh. Internal party discussions in 1951, for instance, decided against a monetary authority that would be outright independent vis-à-vis the federal government.[94] Yet the party failed to take a public stance on the question of independence in these post-war early years. Any criticism was delivered indirectly: for example, in articles that appeared in *Neuer Vorwärts*, the party newspaper, attacking the restrictive policies of the BdL.[95] On occasion, these articles took direct issue with the 'authoritarian' personality of Vocke.[96] Though the chairman had but one vote on the central bank council, he soon came to embody the policies of the BdL, at least in the eyes of the SPD.

---

[91] Kaiser details the stance of each mainstream party towards central bank independence during the 1970s. See Kaiser, *Bundesbankautonomie*, pp. 50–4.

[92] Statistische Abteilung der Reichsbank, 'Stellung der Sozialdemokratie zur Autonomie der Reichsbank', 11 Jan. 1928, Bundesarchiv, Berlin-Lichterfelde [BAB], R2501/6405, pp. 1–2.

[93] Ibid., p. 5.

[94] Koch and Pass, 'Protokoll zur Tagung des Wirtschaftspolitischen Ausschusses beim Parteivorstand der SPD am 1. und 2. Juni 1951'.

[95] See, for instance, 'Demokratisch kontrollierte oder autoritäre Bundesbank?', *Neuer Vorwärts*, 1 May 1950; and 'Wirtschaftspolitische Forderungen der SPD', *Neuer Vorwärts*, 6 Apr. 1951.

[96] 'Demokratisch kontrollierte oder autoritäre Bundesbank?', *Neuer Vorwärts*, 1 May 1950.

The feeling was mutual, though. A conservative at heart, Vocke had little taste for social democracy.[97] He made numerous speeches attacking the idea of placing full employment on the pedestal of economic policy priorities. Karl Bernard, the other chairman of the BdL, also evoked the ghost of social democracy during coalition government discussions concerning the Bundesbank Law. Only a decentralised central bank, Bernard argued, with power dispersed across the states, was the best means of defending the monetary authority's independence should the Social Democrats ever become the leading power in Bonn.[98]

In early November 1956, however, the SPD came out in full support of an outright independent central bank.[99] As Walter Seuffert, one of the party's economic experts, declared later that month in the West German parliament:

It is also the viewpoint of the social democratic opposition that the central bank should be independent in any circumstance, independent from any political influence, independent from the government – I should say: from any government, independent from regional policies and regional interests, independent in all its parts and in all its institutions, and in this totality it should also be independent from the private sector.[100]

Within earshot stood a journalist and BdL ally, who kept the central bank abreast of the latest Bonn gossip. He noted that Seuffert laid particular stress on the word 'any' when remarking that the future Bundesbank should be independent of 'any government'.[101] If Seuffert wanted to make a point, he made it – and then some. But what caused this change of heart on the part of the SPD? Seuffert's determined words on the parliament floor actually hid much hand-wringing behind the scenes. Internal party debates concerning the Bundesbank Law took place across the span of 1956. Some party figures, such as Heinrich Troeger, a man who later became vice president of the Bundesbank, argued forcefully for an independent central bank.[102] Others, however,

---

[97] For example, refer to the letter sent from Vocke to the leader of the SPD, Kurt Schumacher in 1951. Wilhelm Vocke to Kurt Schumacher, 22 May 1951, DBHA, B330/2044.

[98] Dürre, 'Vermerk über die Sitzung des interfraktionellen Ausschusses der Regierungsparteien für die Beratung des Entwurfs zum Bundesbankgesetz am 23.11.50', 25 Nov. 1950, BAK, B102/5706.

[99] Minutes of Social Democratic Party meeting (Wirtschaftspolitischer Außschuss), 5 Nov. 1956, AdsD, 1/HSAA008629, p. 10.

[100] Quoted in Robert, *Die Unabhängigkeit der Bundesbank*, p. 29.

[101] The man in question was Friedrich Lemmer. See Friedrich Lemmer to Viktor von der Lippe, 30 Nov. 1956, DBHA, B330/66630.

[102] Rudolf Pass, 'Protokoll der Sitzung des Wirtschaftspolitischen Ausschuss beim Parteivorstand der SPD', 19 Mar. 1956, AdsD, 2/PVBF000007, pp. 2–3.

were scornful of the deflationary policies that 'Vocke's tower' had embarked upon in the past.[103] Such a deflationary scenario might happen again if the future Bundesbank retained as much independence as the BdL had enjoyed, it was suggested.

Even as late as 1956, then, the party was divided on the issue. But two factors pushed the party to take a position in support of independence. First, it was grudgingly acknowledged that central banking autonomy remained popular in a country 'living under the blue sky of the economic miracle' – as one Social Democrat put it during a confidential meeting.[104] The other important factor was the 'Gürzenich affair' that kicked off in mid-1956. Adenauer, no friend of the BdL, miscalculated and delivered a speech comparing the central bank's restrictive monetary policy to a 'guillotine' falling on the little people.[105] A media storm ensued and the mainstream press sided overwhelmingly with the central bank.

Adenauer's difficulty, then, was the Social Democrats' opportunity – especially with the 1957 election on the horizon. The party hoped to win political plaudits by siding with the cause of the deutschmark's guardian. As a result, the party's leadership was in support of independence ever since 1956.[106] This was a crucial moment in the emerging dominance of the West German central bank's monetary mythology in the public sphere. But as one SPD member pointed out in an internal discussion at the time, 'the clouds might well return' and cast a shadow over the economy.[107] If this were to happen, would central bank independence retain the popularity it had enjoyed in the mid-1950s?

Those clouds did return. They came in the form of the 1966–7 recession and the economic troubles of the early 1970s. These events challenged the political consensus surrounding *Stabilitätspolitik* in West Germany and, in turn, questioned the independence of the central bank – a potential 'additional government', as one critic called it in 1969.[108] How did the SPD react to the change in the economic climate? To

---

[103] Minutes of Social Democratic Party meeting (Wirtschaftspolitischer Außschuss), 5 Nov. 1956, p. 9.

[104] Pass, 'Protokoll der Sitzung des Wirtschaftspolitischen Ausschuss beim Parteivorstand der SPD, stattgefunden am 16. März 1956', pp. 7–8.

[105] Konrad Adenauer, 'Rede von Bundeskanzler Dr. Adenauer am 23. Mai 1956 in Köln', *Bank deutscher Länder Auszüge aus Presseartikeln*, No. 58, 28 May 1956, DBHA, N3/173.

[106] See Kaiser, *Bundesbankautonomie*, pp. 50–4.

[107] Pass, 'Protokoll der Sitzung des Wirtschaftspolitischen Ausschuss beim Parteivorstand der SPD, stattgefunden am 16. März 1956', p. 8.

[108] Friedrich-Wilhelm Dörge, 'Die Bundesbank – eine Nebenregierung?', *Die Zeit*, 31 Oct. 1969.

answer this question, the chapter will turn to two debates surrounding the central bank in the early 1970s: the Schiller–Klasen affair in 1972; and the *Novellierung* debate sparked by Schmidt's finance ministry in late 1973.

Schiller's Downfall

'For the first time, we have an economics minister and president of the Bundesbank addressing each other with "*du*"', Schiller remarked in late 1969, after the government announced that Klasen would be appointed the next Bundesbank president.[109] It was a proud moment. But while Schiller and Klasen enjoyed a close friendship, it was not to last. In 1972, the Bundesbank toppled one of the most influential ministers of the post-war era. Or at least – that is how the West German media saw it. The reality was somewhat different. In July of that year, Schiller resigned from his cabinet position as minister for economics and finance, in a move that would end his career in front-bench politics.[110] He did so after a dispute in cabinet concerning the best method to overcome a flood of foreign capital flowing into West Germany. International investors sought a safe haven after the British pound had crashed out of the monetary 'snake'. Alongside Switzerland, West Germany was one such safe haven, and the inflow of international money placed intense pressure on the deutschmark, creating the potential for inflation.

In a cabinet meeting in Bonn on 28 and 29 June 1972, Schiller pushed for two measures. First, a higher cash reserve requirement, or *Bardepot*, should be put in place for foreign currency deposits in the West German economy. In short, domestic borrowers would be required to deposit more of their foreign currency borrowings with the Bundesbank at a non-interest bearing rate.[111] The goal of this measure was to soak up much of the liquidity in the economy, reducing the risk of inflation. And second, Schiller advocated a temporary float of the currency – one co-ordinated with other Europcan countries, in particular France – vis-à-vis the American greenback as the best solution for the monetary crisis. Given the strong international confidence in the deutschmark, it was expected that such a float would allow the currency to revalue via market forces, alleviating speculative pressures.[112]

---

[109] 'Per du', *Der Spiegel*, 24 Nov. 1969.
[110] Originally just the economics minister, Schiller also assumed the finance portfolio in May 1971 becoming, as the media dubbed it, a 'super-minister'.
[111] 'Karl, billiger werden wir dich nicht los', *Der Spiegel*, 3 Jul. 1972.
[112] 'Schiller und Klasen: Wie eine Freundschaft zerbrach: Scheidung nach Paragraph 23', *Die Zeit*, 7 Jul. 1972.

But the minister's arguments were pitted against those of Klasen. Horst Ehmke, a cabinet minister, invited the Bundesbank president to express the central bank's position at the cabinet meeting.[113] It was not unusual for the Bundesbank president to be invited to Bonn. Indeed, the Bundesbank Law stated that the central bank had the right to act in an advisory capacity with regard to government economic policy.[114] Klasen had no issue with the idea of introducing a higher cash reserve requirement for foreign currency deposits. He was in favour of it. But Klasen did oppose Schiller's suggestion of a co-ordinated float. The Bundesbank president felt that a co-ordinated float of major European currencies was not a viable option given the political realities abroad – especially in France. This was a position that Klasen had come around to after numerous discussions with other central bank presidents at international meetings.[115]

Instead, the Bundesbank president argued that the existing exchange parities should remain in place. Klasen put forward the proposal of making the sale of West German interest-bearing securities to non-residents (that is, those international investors seeking a safe haven) subject to prior authorisation, thereby allowing the authorities to stop the tide of capital flooding into the country.[116] This measure meant invoking a *dirigiste* – and therefore controversial – clause of the 1961 Foreign Trade Law, or *Außenwirtschaftsgesetz*. Klasen's suggestion was not new. The idea had been bandied about before in discussions between the central bank and the economics and finance ministries.[117] Such a proposal was 'no panacea' to West Germany's problems, the central banker admitted. But he pointed out that the cabinet had little choice, given the political realities in Europe at the time.[118] A co-ordinated float was hardly feasible. 'We have to act.'[119]

Klasen's proposal had the support of the Bundesbank directorate.[120] This included Emminger, who, though a monetarist at heart, agreed with his boss that a co-ordinated float was not workable given the opposition to be found in France to such an idea.[121] The *dirigiste* measure also found

---

[113] Viktor von der Lippe, 'Tagebuchähnliche Aufzeichnungen – 28.6.1972', 28 Jun. 1972, DBHA, B330/6916-2; Viktor von der Lippe, 'Tagebuchähnliche Aufzeichnungen – 29.6.1972', 29 Jun. 1972, DBHA, B330/6916-2.
[114] Karl Klasen, 'Erklärung von Bundesbankpräsident Klasen', *Die Zeit*, 4 Aug. 1972.
[115] Ibid.   [116] Emminger, *D-Mark, Dollar, Währungskrisen*, p. 218.
[117] Klasen, 'Erklärung von Bundesbankpräsident Klasen'.
[118] Viktor von der Lippe, 'Tagebuchähnliche Aufzeichnungen – 5.7.1972', 5 Jul. 1972, DBHA, B330/6916-2.
[119] 'Karl, billiger werden wir dich nicht los', *Der Spiegel*, 3 Jul. 1972.
[120] Bundesbank directorate meeting minutes, 26 Jun. 1972, DBHA, B330/4961.
[121] Emminger, *D-Mark, Dollar, Währungskrisen*, p. 220.

favour among other cabinet ministers. A federal election was only five months away. Were the cabinet to push ahead with Schiller's float, it was highly likely that the deutschmark would revalue vis-à-vis other currencies, making West German business more uncompetitive. Several ministers, among them heavy weight figures such as Schmidt and Walter Scheel, the foreign minister, were keen to avoid causing unnecessary controversies in the monetary realm before polling day.[122] When Klasen promised 'four or five months of peace on the monetary front', the point was not lost on the politicians at the cabinet table.[123] After all, they had votes to win.

But the Bundesbank president's objections in the cabinet meeting came as a complete surprise to Schiller. Both men had met in an informal setting some days before and, according to Schiller's later account, Klasen had intentionally chosen not to inform the minister of the Bundesbank's intentions.[124] A heated cabinet debate ensued. Though Schiller agreed in principle with Klasen's *dirigiste* proposal, the minister felt the moment inopportune; the *dirigiste* clause of the Foreign Trade Law should only be used as a last resort if a co-ordinated float did not come to pass.[125] It was later reported in the media that both men had threatened to resign if they did not get their own way.[126]

In the end, the cabinet meeting came to two separate votes. The first vote centred on the introduction of a higher cash reserve requirement for foreign currency deposits. This vote was passed with little drama.[127] The second vote, however, concerned Klasen's *dirigiste* proposal. The cabinet sided with Klasen almost unanimously. Only one minister voted against the measure. That man was Schiller.[128] It was a crushing blow for the 'super-minister'. Days later, Schiller submitted his resignation to chancellor Brandt.[129]

This resignation came as a surprise to the men in Frankfurt. Colleagues in the Bundesbank noted that Klasen was 'visibly shocked' at hearing the news of Schiller's resignation.[130] He had not expected this.

---

[122] 'Karl, billiger werden wir dich nicht los', *Der Spiegel*, 3 Jul. 1972.

[123] Arnulf Baring, *Machtwechsel: Die Ära Brandt-Scheel* (Stuttgart, 1982), p. 671.

[124] Karl Schiller, 'Was Klasen nicht sagte', *Die Zeit*, 18 Aug. 1972.

[125] 'Karl, billiger werden wir dich nicht los', *Der Spiegel*, 3 Jul. 1972.

[126] Viktor von der Lippe, 'Tagebuchähnliche Aufzeichnungen – 30.6.1972', 30 Jun. 1972, DBHA, B330/6916-2.

[127] 'Schiller und Klasen: Wie eine Freundschaft zerbrach: Scheidung nach Paragraph 23', *Die Zeit*, 7 Jul. 1972.

[128] Ibid.

[129] Viktor von der Lippe, 'Tagebuchähnliche Aufzeichnungen – 6.7.1972', 6 Jul. 1972, DBHA, B330/6916-2.

[130] Emminger, *D-Mark, Dollar, Währungskrisen*, p. 221.

'With Schiller, it's like you're always dealing with a hyper-intelligent loon!' Klasen confided to von der Lippe in exasperation.[131] The immediate news of the resignation had consequences in the public sphere too. 'Does the government reside in Frankfurt?' ran one headline in *Welt am Sonntag*.[132] The Bundesbank was portrayed in the media as having toppled Schiller.[133] It was unwelcome attention. Such claims could only heighten the tension surrounding the central bank's independence. As a result, Klasen spent the days following the cabinet meeting embarking on a media blitz, stressing that he had acted in accordance with the Bundesbank Law.[134] There, the affair should have died down. Yet it refused to go away. Why?

The controversy took centre stage in the public spotlight for 'weeks on end', recalled Emminger wearily, years later.[135] The main reason for this was Schiller's resignation letter to the chancellor. Someone leaked it to the press. *Quick*, the illustrated weekly magazine, published the letter in mid-July.[136] In his letter, Schiller attacked the actions of Klasen: the Bundesbank president's conduct was unacceptable. By remaining silent in the days leading up to the cabinet meeting, he allowed his erstwhile friend to be ambushed by others in the cabinet. That Klasen had deliberately chosen not to inform the minister responsible for finance and economics was 'simply absurd'.[137] The actions of the Bundesbank president called into question the future relationship between the central bank and government, Schiller argued.[138]

The publication of the resignation letter meant that the crisis entered a new phase. The Bundesbank was subjected to negative media coverage – in some quarters of the press, at least – for its apparent role in Schiller's downfall.[139] 'A really skewed, hostile "Balance" television show tonight against Klasen and his "monetary dirigisme"', noted von der Lippe on 20 July 1972.[140] One of the presenters claimed that Klasen had abused

[131] Viktor von der Lippe, 'Tagebuchähnliche Aufzeichnungen – 13.7.1972', 13 Jul. 1972, DBHA, B330/6916-2.
[132] 'Sitzt die Regierung in Frankfurt?', *Welt am Sonntag*, 2 Jul. 1972.
[133] See, for example, 'Scheidung nach Paragraph 23', *Die Zeit*, 7 Jul. 1972.
[134] Viktor von der Lippe, 'Tagebuchähnliche Aufzeichnungen – 4.7.1972', 4 Jul. 1972, DBHA, B330/6916-2; Viktor von der Lippe, 'Tagebuchähnliche Aufzeichnungen – 5.7.1972', 5 Jul. 1972; and Viktor von der Lippe, 'Tagebuchähnliche Aufzeichnungen – 13.7.1972'.
[135] Emminger, *D-Mark, Dollar, Währungskrisen*, p. 221.
[136] Viktor von der Lippe, 'Tagebuchähnliche Aufzeichnungen – 18.7.1972', 18 Jul. 1972, DBHA, B330/6916-2.
[137] Ibid.   [138] Schiller, 'Was Klasen nicht sagte'.
[139] Viktor von der Lippe to Karl Klasen, 21 Jul. 1972, DBHA, B330/6987; and 'Wirtschaftsberichte: Hessischer Rundfunk', 1 Sep. 1972, DBPA, no. 570.
[140] Viktor von der Lippe, 'Tagebuchähnliche Aufzeichnungen – 20.7.1972', 20 Jul. 1972, DBHA, B330/6916-2.

the position of his office, in a move that would have implications for the future independence of the central bank.[141] Opposition politicians, such as the CSU's Franz Josef Strauß, accused the Bundesbank president actively participating in a coup against Schiller, who was 'the victim of a conspiracy', one inspired by rival figures in the SPD.[142]

Initially, Klasen was against the idea of publishing a response to the claims found in Schiller's resignation letter.[143] Certainly, von der Lippe had mixed views about such a move; the press chief feared it would only serve to fan the flames of the controversy.[144] But with such negative media coverage the Bundesbank president felt forced to respond. The central bank, Klasen acknowledged, could not allow Schiller to frame the parameters of the controversy. Whatever came next, 'you are not to blame', the Bundesbank president told von der Lippe. 'You have warned me!'[145] At the next directorate meeting, three steps were decided upon. First, Klasen would publish a counter-attack to Schiller's claims in *Die Zeit*. Second, this article would find its way into the Bundesbank's *Presseauszüge aus Presseartikeln* – the central bank's newsletter press release. And third, it was decided that the central bank would publish a 'special article about the relationship between the federal government and the Bundesbank' in its monthly report for August 1972.[146]

Klasen devoted his *Die Zeit* article to rebutting Schiller's claims 'about the role of the Bundesbank and my personal conduct' in the political fallout.[147] The Bundesbank president stressed he acted in accordance with the Bundesbank Law, in that he was invited by the cabinet to discuss monetary issues. This right was firmly outlined article 13 of the Bundesbank Law, Klasen continued. The Bundesbank president also stated that he had informed Schiller prior to the cabinet meeting that he, Klasen, was indeed invited. Furthermore, he continued, Schiller was well aware of the central bank's stance from previous discussions when it came to the application of *dirigiste* measures in the event of an emergency. Klasen denied threatening to resign during the cabinet meeting.[148] As von der Lippe suspected, however, the temperamental Schiller soon launched a

[141] Ibid.
[142] Viktor von der Lippe, 'Tagebuchähnliche Aufzeichnungen – 15.7.1972', 15 Jul. 1972, DBHA, B330/6916-2.
[143] Viktor von der Lippe, 'Tagebuchähnliche Aufzeichnungen – 26.7.1972', 26 Jul. 1972, DBHA, B330/6916-2.
[144] Von der Lippe, 'Meinung zum Thema "Erklärung"'.
[145] Von der Lippe, 'Vermerk vom 2.8.1972'.
[146] Bundesbank directorate meeting minutes, 28 Jul. 1972, DBHA, B330/4961.
[147] Klasen, 'Erklärung von Bundesbankpräsident Klasen'.   [148] Ibid.

counter-attack, questioning Klasen's interpretation of events – an action that prolonged the dispute in the media.[149]

Perhaps even more crucial when it came to the public sphere, however, was the 'special article' published in the monthly report for August 1972. Heinrich Irmler, a directorate member and former Reichsbanker, was entrusted to write the essay.[150] The article was an unprecedented move: the Bundesbank had never used the monthly report in such an overtly political fashion before. The monthly reports were usually dense, statistical affairs, occasionally helping to shape economic debate in the country. What did the article say, however? 'In recent times, the relationship between the federal government and the Bundesbank has been of particular interest to the public', the monthly report read.[151] It echoed the arguments outlined in Klasen's rebuttal in *Die Zeit*. But the article added a new dimension. It centred on the legal relationship between Frankfurt and Bonn. Stressing that the central bank had acted in accordance with the Bundesbank Law, the monthly report reverted to historical narratives of Germany's two inflations amid efforts to justify the Bundesbank's independent position in the Federal Republic. 'The Bundesbank Law has entrusted to the Bundesbank a high degree of independence – not least on the ground of historical experience, which has seen two world wars and two subsequent inflations linked to a central bank that was subjected to government instruction – allowing the Bundesbank to give its monetary and credit policies sufficient firepower.'[152] This passage simply ignored the fact that the Reichsbank was independent of government instruction during the 1922–3 hyperinflation.

Nevertheless, the media immediately picked up on the monthly report's publication. Several newspapers echoed the historical line detailed in the special article and swung in favour of the central bank. One such article, though sceptical of Klasen's actions, was published in the *Deutsches Allgemeines Sonntagsblatt*. 'The fathers of the Bundesbank Law, promulgated in 1957, were still stung from the shock of the two German inflations', it noted. 'The runaway inflation of 1921/3 and the repressed inflation of 1940/1948 had been caused by central banks beholden to government instruction, which, at best, could put up a fight by its leadership resigning *en masse* – as happened in 1939 – but not by means of the law.'[153]

---

[149] Schiller, 'Was Klasen nicht sagte'.
[150] Viktor von der Lippe, 'Tagebuchähnliche Aufzeichnungen – 28.7.1972', 28 Jul. 1972, DBHA, B330/6916-2.
[151] *Monatsbericht der Deutschen Bundesbank*, Aug. 1972, p. 15.   [152] Ibid.
[153] 'Ein Gralshüter zeigt Schwächen', *Deutsches Allgemeines Sonntagsblatt*, 27 Aug. 1972.

Emminger, looking back on the crisis, cited the appearance of the 'special article' as evidence of how seriously the Bundesbank treated the potential consequences stemming from the fallout with Schiller.[154] In government circles, too, its arrival was later treated as a key moment. Some years afterwards, in 1979, a confidential report concerning the Bundesbank's legal and political position in the Federal Republic was drawn up by Schmidt's chancellery.[155] A variety of accompanying documents were attached to the study. Among them, the 'special article' in the August 1972 monthly report was included for the purpose of summarising the Bundesbank's perspective on the relationship between Bonn and Frankfurt.

After the dust settled, the controversy surrounding the fall of Schiller – 'an endless drama in 27 acts', as Schmidt put it at the time – only heightened the perception of the Bundesbank's independence from Bonn.[156] The central bank, for its part, felt obliged to use historical narratives of the two inflations amid efforts to defend its independence from attacks in the media. The August 1972 report was a key moment in this regard, pushing the media over to the side of the central bank at a crucial moment. But as the writer Rolf Kaiser rightly notes, the actual events of the affair had little to do with the central bank's independence.[157] By imparting his advice to the cabinet, Klasen was acting in accordance with the statutes of the Bundesbank Law. The central banker's presence at the cabinet table was an example of co-operation, not conflict. Indeed, the vast majority of the cabinet voted to support the Bundesbank president's proposals. Though Klasen's participation in the cabinet debate provided the immediate trigger for Schiller's resignation, there were other factors at work that explain the outplay of events. The economics and finance minister, a dominant force in government debates, had become estranged from his colleagues for some time.[158] He was seen as overbearing in his conduct, and had already fallen out with fellow ministers in light of the upcoming budget for 1973.[159] A 'weariness of Schiller', or *Schillermüdigkeit*, had played a key role in the cabinet vote.[160] Schiller saw the decision as a vote against his person and acted accordingly.[161]

---

[154] Emminger, *D-Mark, Dollar, Währungskrisen*, p. 468.
[155] The purpose of this report is unknown. See Gamerdinger and Müller-Uri, 'Rechtliche und politische Position der Deutschen Bundesbank', 11 Jan. 1979, BAK, B136/11551.
[156] The quote is taken from Baring, *Machtwechsel*, p. 664.
[157] Kaiser, *Bundesbankautonomie*, pp. 60–1.
[158] Robert, *Die Unabhängigkeit der Bundesbank*, p. 23.
[159] Emminger, *D-Mark, Dollar, Währungskrisen*, p. 223.
[160] Baring, *Machtwechsel*, p. 672.   [161] Ibid.

In the end, then, the affair strengthened the image of a powerful, independent monetary authority. The scenario was initially not a welcome one for the Bundesbank, given the scrutiny placed upon it by the media. But, forced into a situation, the central bank intervened in the public sphere amid efforts to align the debate to parameters that suited it best. Even if Schiller never seriously questioned central bank independence as an institution, it still stood to reason that the Bundesbank used the episode to solidify the historical necessity of its autonomy. That such an episode could be sparked by the actions of Klasen, a Bundesbank president who above all sought to foster a close working relationship between central bank and government, was particularly ironic.

The *Novellierung* Debate

'It is no secret that there are people who do not like our autonomy', Irmler was reported to have said in August 1973.[162] The Bundesbank directorate member was right. During that month, a debate concerning the Bundesbank Law and the central bank's independence erupted in the West German public sphere. The dispute gave anyone who had an issue with the autonomy of the Bundesbank the opportunity to stand up and speak out. And so they did. At the centre of the debate lay a draft proposal, written by Schmidt's finance ministry, to change the Bundesbank Law. The draft law proposed strengthening the monetary tool kit at the disposal of the central bank, allowing it to tackle the country's economic difficulties more effectively. In particular, there were two tools that lay at the heart of the matter. First, it was proposed that the Bundesbank should be granted the ability to introduce *Aktivzuwachsreserve* at a time of emergency. In this scenario, banks would be obliged to not only deposit a portion of their assets in non-interest-bearing accounts at the Bundesbank – as was the case before – but also a portion of their loans that had already been lent out.[163] The second measure proposed was the ability to impose a quantitative credit ceiling, or *Kreditplafondierung*, upon banks in moments of crisis.

But there was a catch. The draft proposal stated that the Bundesbank could avail of these additional tools only when it had the green light from the federal government. This was known as the 'two-key theory'. One key in Frankfurt, the other in Bonn; both to be turned at the same time.[164]

---

[162] 'Tüchtig verschaukelt', *Der Spiegel*, 20 Aug. 1973.   [163] Ibid.
[164] The appearance of the 'two-key theory' was not entirely unprecedented. In December 1971, a temporary addendum was added to the Foreign Trade Law – and not, it is important to note, the Bundesbank Law – which made the Bundesbank's use of the *Bardepot* conditional on a green light given by Bonn. The addendum remained in force

The draft law, then, proposed a very subtle change in the relationship between Frankfurt and Bonn. The Bundesbank could have more powers to tackle economic emergencies. But it could only use these additional powers on the condition that the government said 'yes' at the given moment.

Within a few months, however, the draft law was shelved for good because of uproar in the media and disputes it triggered within the coalition government. West Germans, preoccupied with the implications of a growing oil crisis, quickly forgot about it by the year's end. The debate concerning this *Novellierung*, or amendment, of the Bundesbank Law, can be seen as storm in a teacup – one that was dwarfed by far greater challenges facing the country. Nevertheless, it was a telling one. The *Novellierung* called the Bundesbank Law into question; or, more specifically, the relationship between Frankfurt and Bonn. In doing so, it broke a taboo. The idea of changing the Bundesbank Law became open to debate. Suddenly, politicians of all stripes, as well as interest groups, started to debate the relationship between Frankfurt and Bonn, with an eye to adding their own twists to the proposed amendment. Narratives of Germany's two inflationary episodes were used to justify political arguments on both sides of the fence.

The origins of the *Novellierung* debate actually date back to the mid-1960s – in other words, the era of Blessing. During that period, the Bundesbank directorate and central bank council discussed the idea of widening the set of monetary instruments through which Frankfurt could exert a greater influence on the amount of credit flushing around in the economy.[165] These internal discussions never amounted to much, however, and eventually dissipated.[166] The idea of a quantitative credit ceiling was also raised during discussions between the central bank and federal government concerning the 1967 Stability and Growth Law. Given that it was seen as a *dirigiste* tool of sorts, it was treated as an extreme measure, to be used only in times of economic emergency. But the central bank quickly lost interest in the idea after the government proposed an early version of the 'two-key theory' as a precondition of the Bundesbank using the instrument. The discussions floundered.[167]

---

until September 1974. See Rolf Caesar, *Der Handlungsspielraum von Notenbanken: Theoretische Analyse und internationaler Vergleich* (Baden-Baden, 1981), p. 176.

[165] Eichhorn to Karl Otto Pöhl, 6 Aug. 1982, DBHA, B330/42138.

[166] Eichhorn, 'Betreff Novellierung des Bundesbankgesetz (BbankG) in Jahren 1972/73, hier: Chronologie des Novellierungsverfahrens in seinen wichtigsten Zügen', 5 Aug. 1982, DBHA, B330/42138, p. 1.

[167] Anon., 'Betr: Kreditplafondierung', 22 Jun. 1970, BAK, B126/37719, p. 1.

At the turn of the 1970s, the economy faced increasing economic difficulties. Under the constraints of the Bretton Woods monetary system, the Bundesbank was finding it difficult to control inflation given the amount of foreign capital flooding into the country. As such, it was acknowledged in both Frankfurt and Bonn that the Bundesbank's existing set of tools – for instance, its discount rate policy, and minimum reserves policy – were increasingly becoming inadequate when it came to influencing the amount of credit in West Germany.[168] The authorities faced a choice. On the one hand, they could revaluate the deutschmark, either through a government-determined revaluation or a float of the currency. This would alleviate speculative pressures on the deutschmark. Or, on the other hand, they could introduce capital controls to stifle the inflow of capital, allowing the exchange rate parity to be maintained.

As the early 1970s progressed, the pressure towards more capital controls became evident. West Germany went from a country with minimal controls in the late 1960s to a state with sizable ones by 1973. Indeed, the events leading to the downfall of Schiller, the erstwhile 'super-minister' who, where possible, favoured market solutions, should be seen in this wider context.[169] When it came to the execution of *Stabilitätspolitik*, *dirigiste* arguments increasingly trumped market-orientated ones. Nevertheless, Klasen's measures implemented after the departure of Schiller in July 1972 were quickly deemed to be insufficient. Loopholes were found. Credit entered the economy through circumventions of these new restrictions.[170]

In the autumn of 1972, then, Klasen called on Bonn to grant the central bank additional powers.[171] At the heart of the discussion lay the establishment of the *Aktivzuwachsreserve* and the ability to impose quantitative credit controls. Klasen later came to regret this decision. By requesting the government's help and input, the Bundesbank president set in a train of events that quickly slipped out of the central bank's control, culminating in a fiery public debate months later. Schmidt was later reported to have said at the time: 'There is no way that the Bundesbank, which is politically responsible to no one, is going to get more powers' – at least without some form on control on the part of Bonn.[172]

---

[168] Albrecht and Schloenbach, 'Geld- und Kreditpolitik im Rahmen einer Stabilitätsstrategie zur Bekämpfung des Preisauftriebs', 24 Jan. 1973, BAK, B126/43353.

[169] Baring, *Machtwechsel*, p. 671.

[170] Age Bakker, *The liberalization of capital movements in Europe: the monetary committee and financial integration, 1958–1994* (Dordrecht, 1996), p. 122.

[171] Eichhorn, 'Betreff Novellierung des Bundesbankgesetz (BbankG) in Jahren 1972/73', p. 3.

[172] 'Tüchtig verschaukelt', *Der Spiegel*, 20 Aug. 1973.

This viewpoint was reinforced by the fact that the political independence of the Bundesbank had increased markedly earlier that year, when the deutschmark began to float. Before, it was the federal government who decided the fixed exchange rate and the timing of each revaluation. After the float, however, the Bundesbank's room for manoeuvre increased substantially.

Klasen and Schmidt were friends. But politics was politics. In response to Klasen's request, the economic and finance ministries, both of which were still under the temporary 'super-minister' Schmidt, drew up a set of framework proposals for the new *Novellierung* in November 1972.[173] Once again the Bundesbank found itself rejecting the suggestion of the 'two-key theory', pointedly referring to the central bank's same refusal some years earlier.[174] Frankfurt began to worry about what it had started. Realising his miscalculation, Klasen confided to von der Lippe, 'I am wondering if Schmidt wants a confrontation – a confrontation with me!'[175]

Events came to a head in the autumn of 1973. On 2 August of that year, Bundesbank and government officials met in Bonn to discuss a new draft composed by Schmidt's finance ministry.[176] According to the latest version, a newly empowered Bundesbank could avail of the *Aktivzuwachsreserve* as well as the ability to impose quantitative credit ceilings – but only with the government's assent. It was the 'two-key theory' yet again. The central bank council discussed the implications of this new draft some days later.[177] Emminger raised significant concerns over the 'two-key theory', remarking 'it would be treated in the public sphere as an upheaval of the Bundesbank's autonomy'.[178]

Emminger was right. News of Schmidt's *Novellierung* first appeared in the press on 13 August 1973.[179] While the implications of the *Novellierung* concerned only the use of the additional instruments – in other words, not the Bundesbank's existing set of tools – much of the mainstream media jumped on the *Novellierung* as a blatant attempt by Schmidt

---

[173] Eichhorn, 'Betreff Novellierung des Bundesbankgesetz (BbankG) in Jahren 1972/73', p. 3.
[174] Dick, 'Verbesserung des notenbankpolitischen Instrumentariums', 4 Dec. 1972, BAK, B136/7346.
[175] Viktor von der Lippe, 'Tagebuchähnliche Aufzeichnungen – 22.8.1973', 22 Aug. 1973, DBIIΛ, B330/6917 1.
[176] Eichhorn, 'Betreff Novellierung des Bundesbankgesetz (BbankG) in Jahren 1972/73', p. 5.
[177] Bundesbank directorate meeting minutes, 9 Aug. 1973, DBHA, B330/6708/2, p. 21.
[178] Ibid.
[179] Viktor von der Lippe, 'Tagebuchähnliche Aufzeichnungen – 13.8.1973', 13 Aug. 1973, DBHA, B330/6917-1.

to hammer a wedge into the relationship between Bonn and Frankfurt, through which he could create a precedent and eventually curtail the Bundesbank's independence.[180] Opposition politicians had a field day. 'The politically explosive nature of this draft law is the restriction of the autonomy of the Bundesbank', declared Hermann Höcherl, a CSU politician. 'Obviously this amendment, which Schmidt so desires, comes down to the expansion of his own position of power, and not a better technical solution. In a roundabout way, he wants to expand his super-ministry further, gaining even more power.'[181]

The Bundesbank took a lesson in damage control. It was leaked to the media that the central bank was no longer interested in being granted additional powers.[182] Klasen, however, urged caution when it came to the Bundesbank's comments in the public sphere, believing the best way to overcome the crisis was to talk to Bonn behind closed doors.[183] The Bundesbank president's 'line', he told von der Lippe, was to protect the central bank's independence at all costs.[184]

And those costs were mounting. The *Novellierung* broke a taboo by raising the idea of legally changing the relationship between Bonn and Frankfurt. In doing so, the draft law opened the gate for others to make similar calls. Within days of the *Novellierung* entering the public sphere, for instance, the leadership of the Deutscher Gewerkschaftsbund called on Schmidt to 'use the opportunity of a change in the Bundesbank Law ... to solve the problem of the "autonomy of the Bundesbank" once and for all'.[185]

The trade union argued that two measures should be implemented. First, the Bundesbank should be required to support all four objectives of economic policy as outlined in the Stability and Growth Law. In other words, the central bank should be obliged to factor into its policy decisions considerations of price stability – *and* full employment, economic growth and balanced trade. Of course, in this respect, the trade union's eye was very much on full employment, which would strengthen its

[180] Viktor von der Lippe, 'Tagebuchähnliche Aufzeichnungen – 17.8.1973', 17 Aug. 1973, DBHA, B330/6917-1.
[181] 'Zur Vorlage der Novelle des Bundesbankgesetzes erklärt Hermann Höcherl, MdB, Vorsitzender des Arbeitskreises für Haushalt, Steuern, Geld und Kredit der CDU/CSU-Fraktion', *Pressereferat CDU/CSU-Fraktion des Deutschen Bundestages*, 13 Aug. 1973, AdsD, 2/BTFG002672.
[182] Von der Lippe, 'Tagebuchähnliche Aufzeichnungen – 13.8.1973'.
[183] Von der Lippe, 'Tagebuchähnliche Aufzeichnungen – 22.8.1973'.
[184] Von der Lippe, 'Tagebuchähnliche Aufzeichnungen – 18.9.1973'.
[185] This letter soon emerged in the press. See George Neeman to Helmut Schmidt, 23 Aug. 1973, BAK, B136/7346, p. 1; Viktor von der Lippe, 'Tagebuchähnliche Aufzeichnungen – 8.9.1973', 8 Sep. 1973, DBHA, B330/6917-1.

bargaining power during wage negotiations. And second, the government's temporary veto should be extended to a period of twelve weeks – not just fourteen days, as outlined in the original Bundesbank Law.[186] The trade union, then, did not call for the elimination of central bank independence. Rather, it merely pushed for a revised Bundesbank Law that gave the federal government a slightly better hand of cards with which to play when it came to serious conflicts between Frankfurt and Bonn.

In this regard, the trade union was not alone in its opinion. Schmidt's *Novellierung* also stirred up debate within the SPD. Alex Möller, a former finance minister, was against Schmidt's 'two-key theory'.[187] But, like the Deutscher Gewerkschaftsbund, the party heavyweight did call for a change in the Bundesbank's policy objectives. The Bundesbank Law, Möller argued, should factor in all four angles of the Stability and Growth Law's 'magic square'. Other party figures went further, however. One such man was Herbert Ehrenberg, a SPD politician who stood on the left of the party. Ehrenberg was a former state secretary in the labour ministry, and later became labour minister in 1976.[188] Within a day of the *Novellierung*'s appearance in the public sphere, Ehrenberg launched the first of what would be several attacks on the Bundesbank's independence.[189] 'If we are going to expand the number of instruments at the Bundesbank's disposal, then that should only happen with a concomitant restriction of its independence', the politician told *Handelsblatt*, a business newspaper.[190] Like Möller, Ehrenberg contended that the central bank should be obliged to support all four corners of the 'magic square', not just price stability. In this sense, his criticisms again highlight the extent to which the Stability and Growth Law served as a reference point for criticisms against the Bundesbank.

But Ehrenberg did not stop there. A key weakness of the Bundesbank Law, he claimed, was that it failed to provide a formal resolution

---

[186] Neeman to Schmidt, 23 Aug. 1973, p. 2.
[187] 'Bundesbank an der Regierungsleine?', *Frankfurter Allgemeine Zeitung*, 6 Sep. 1973; 'Der CSU-Abgeordnete Dr. Reinhold Kreile erklärt zur Stellungnahme des stellvertretenden Vorsitzenden der SPD-Bundestagsfraktion, Prof. Dr. Alex Möller, zum Bundesbankgesetz folgendes', *Pressereferat CDU/CSU-Fraktion des Deutschen Bundestages*, 5 Sep. 1973, AdsD, 2/BTFG002672; see also Viktor von der Lippe, 'Tagebuchähnliche Aufzeichnungen – 31.8.1973', 31 Aug. 1973, DBHA, B330/6917-1.
[188] Holtfrerich, 'Monetary policy in Germany since 1948: national tradition, international best practice or ideology?', in Jean-Philippe Touffut (ed.), *Central banks as economic institutions* (Cheltenham, 2008), p. 32.
[189] 'Autonomie der Bundesbank soll eingeschränkt werden', *Handelsblatt*, 14 Aug. 1973.
[190] Ibid.

mechanism for instances in which the central bank and federal government clashed over monetary policy. The lack of such a formal resolution mechanism allowed the Bundesbank a tremendous degree of independence. 'In the worst-case scenario, a board of officials can cripple the policy of a parliamentary-elected government', Ehrenberg declared.[191] As such, he called for the establishment of an 'arbitration committee' to handle 'serious disputes' between Bonn and Frankfurt.[192] This arbitration committee, he continued, should be comprised of politicians, formed either from the economics committee in the lower house of parliament, the Bundestag, or a selection of politicians from both parliamentary houses. In other words, the central bank would not be represented on the arbitration committee. Ehrenberg's proposal, in this regard, was more extreme than the original arbitration committee outlined in the 1950 draft of the Bundesbank Law, spearheaded by Schäffer, the finance minister back in the days of the BdL. Schäffer's arbitration panel, though weighted in favour of Bonn, contained a sizeable presence of central bank officials.

For Ehrenberg, the *Novellierung* debate was an opportunity. He kept up his attacks in the media, calling for more democratic accountability in the monetary sphere.[193] The figure of the Bundesbank president resembled some sort of 'economic pseudo-Kaiser', he contended.[194] Ehrenberg had an entrepreneurial spark, too. His controversial arguments came off the back of his new book, *Zwischen Marx und Markt* (*Between Marx and the market*), which appeared on bookshop shelves in late 1973.[195] *Zwischen Marx und Markt*, fired by the recent experience of the 1966–7 recession, launched a number of assaults on the central bank. And it used a certain version of Germany's monetary history to back up its arguments. The politician referred in detail to the record of inter-war central bank independence to argue against the continuation of the Bundesbank's independence. 'There exists (temporarily at least) little understanding among the German public with regard to the critical questioning of the Deutsche Bundesbank's autonomy', he argued.

The belief in the wisdom and independence of senior officials [of the Bundesbank] seems to be far greater in Germany than belief in the parliamentary system. The bad experiences with two (initially repressed) inflations apparently speak for this vote of confidence for an independent

---

[191] Ibid.   [192] Ibid.
[193] 'Wir müssen jetzt differenziert lockern: Spiegel-Interview mit dem SPD-Konjunkturexperten Herbert Ehrenberg', *Der Spiegel*, 5 Sep. 1973, p. 37.
[194] Herbert Ehrenberg, 'Zwischen Marx und Markt', *Wirtschaftswoche*, 12 Oct. 1973.
[195] Herbert Ehrenberg, *Zwischen Marx und Markt: Konturen einer infrastrukturorientierten und verteilungswirksamen Wirtschaftspolitik* (Frankfurt, 1973).

central bank. But the person who makes this argument knows regrettably little of German monetary history: both the inflation in 1923 and the Great Depression in 1929 took place with the powerful help of a Reichsbank whose autonomy was nothing less than that currently granted to the Bundesbank.[196]

Ehrenberg then went on to examine both inflationary episodes. He accused the independent Reichsbank of actively working towards a hyperinflation back in 1922–3.[197] And under Hans Luther, the Reichsbank, in its 'autonomous grandeur', participated in the 'execution' of the Weimar Republic by insisting on a restrictive monetary policy that defied economic logic.[198] An autonomous Reichsbank between 1933 and 1938 also actively supported the second inflation that occurred during the Third Reich, Ehrenberg argued.[199] 'The study of German history is rarely encouraging; the monetary history of the autonomous Reichsbank is no different', the SPD man concluded.[200] 'At the very least, it suggests that a small (autonomous) group of officials should not inspire more confidence than parliamentary political authorities.'[201] Ehrenberg continued to launch several attacks on the Bundesbank's independence during this crucial period, some of which availed of the historical arguments listed in *Zwischen Marx und Markt*.[202]

If Ehrenberg wanted controversy, he found it. In early November 1973, the FDP's Otto Graf Lambsdorff took direct aim at the left-winger's interventions in the media.[203] The politician highlighted two points. First, Ehrenberg's suggestion of an arbitration committee was simply unconstitutional, he argued. Such an arbitration committee blurred what was supposed to be a clear divide between the executive and legislative bodies of government; the Bundesbank was created by a legislative act, after all. And second, the SPD man was also misguided in

[196] The quote is taken from the second edition, but it can be found in the first edition too. See Herbert Ehrenberg, *Zwischen Marx und Markt: Konturen einer infrastrukturorientierten und verteilungswirksamen Wirtschaftspolitik*, 2nd ed. (Munich, 1976), p. 174.

[197] Ibid., pp. 174–5. [198] Ibid., p. 175. [199] Ibid. [200] Ibid. [201] Ibid.

[202] See the following articles: 'Wir müssen jetzt differenziert lockern: Spiegel-Interview mit dem SPD-Konjunkturexperten Herbert Ehrenberg', *Der Spiegel*, 5 Sep. 1973; Ehrenberg, 'Zwischen Marx und Markt', *Wirtschaftswoche*, 12 Oct. 1973; 'Ein Sündenregister der Deutschen Bundesbank', *Handelsblatt*, 18 Oct. 1973; Herbert Ehrenberg, 'Für ein neues Bundesbank-Gesetz', no publication listed, no date, AdsD, 2/BTFG002672; Viktor von der Lippe, 'Tagebuchähnliche Aufzeichnungen – 5.11.1973', 5 Nov. 1973, DBHA, B330/6917-1; Herbert Ehrenberg, 'Deutsche Bundesbank mit Schlagseite', *Vorwärts*, 7 Mar. 1974; and Herbert Ehrenberg, 'Soll die Bundesbank auch weiterhin ihre autonome Position behalten?', *General-Anzeiger*, 11 Mar. 1974.

[203] 'Graf Lambsdorff im "Vorwärts". Warum die Autonomie der Bundesbank gewahrt blieben muss', *fdk tagesdienst (Pressedienst der Bundestragsfraktion der F.D.P.)*, 7 Nov. 1973, AdsD, 2/BTFG002671, p. 2.

how he used the central bank's history. 'The experiences of the past speak for the upholding of the present system of checks and balances in the economic and monetary spheres', Lambsdorff declared.[204] Just look at the example of the second inflation. 'The "repressed" financing of war preparations from 1933 to 1938 was not, as Ehrenberg contends, implemented by an autonomous Reichsbank, but rather a Reichsbank whose autonomy had already been effectively eliminated by 1933 via the Enabling Act', a piece of legislation that gave Hitler dictatorial powers.[205] Lambsdorff did not address Ehrenberg's provocative claims concerning the behaviour of the independent Reichsbank during the 1920s.

A proposed minor amendment to the Bundesbank Law in 1973, then, sparked a wide debate concerning the Bundesbank's present position in democratic society, and, indeed, the history of the inter-war Reichsbank. In a similar manner to the Bundesbank Law debates back in the 1950s, narratives of the two inflations were used for political gain. The debate between Ehrenberg and Lambsdorff, however, reflected a wider rift between the two parties in the coalition government: the SPD and the FDP. They remained uncomfortable bedfellows since the election of 1969, and the troubled partnership was reaffirmed again in the 1972 election. Soon after news of the *Novellierung* appeared in the public sphere, government ministers from the FDP voiced their opposition towards any restriction of the Bundesbank's independence. This included Hans Friderichs, the economics minister, who assumed his portfolio following the 1972 election, leaving the erstwhile 'super-minister' Schmidt to be content with just the finance ministry.[206] But Schmidt had still pulled off a coup of sorts; he succeeded in transferring the division for money and credit from the economics ministry to that of finance. Schmidt's finance ministry was now responsible for relations with the Bundesbank.[207]

The SPD had its man in the finance ministry; the FDP had its man in the economics ministry. Schmidt, then, risked a bout of 'religious wars' should the *Novellierung* be pushed ahead under his sponsorship.[208] The finance minister also faced the hostility of much of the mainstream press. As the *Frankfurter Allgemeine Zeitung* put it, 'any attempt to weaken the position of the central bank will be met with the sharpest resistance in the

---

[204] Ibid., p. 3.   [205] Ibid., p. 4.

[206] 'Tüchtig verschaukelt', *Der Spiegel*, 20 Aug. 1973; and Viktor von der Lippe, 'Tagebuchähnliche Aufzeichnungen – 15.8.1973', 15 Aug. 1973, DBHA, B330/6917-1.

[207] Kenneth Dyson and Kevin Featherstone, *The road to Maastricht: negotiating economic and monetary union* (Oxford, 1999), p. 295.

[208] 'Tüchtig verschaukelt', *Der Spiegel*, 20 Aug. 1973.

German public'.[209] In light of these two considerations – that is, the media uproar, on the one hand, and coalition infighting, on the other – pushing ahead with the *Novellierung* was a risk Schmidt was not willing to take.[210] A third factor was the floating of the deutschmark earlier in 1973, which eventually allowed the Bundesbank's traditional monetary toolkit to gain traction once again, removing the urgent need for an amendment to the Bundesbank Law.

Schmidt decided to retreat. In late August 1973, Klasen returned to Frankfurt with relief. He had just arrived back from confidential discussions with Schmidt and Friderichs in Bonn. There would be 'no crash' between the Bundesbank and the federal government concerning the *Novellierung*, Klasen said.[211] By October 1973, reports began to emerge that the draft law was to be 'put on ice', to be considered at a future point in time.[212] It was, as one reporter quipped at the time, a somewhat 'silent funeral' for the amendment to the Bundesbank Law.[213]

Yet it was a rather bruising experience for the finance minister. Schmidt took a lesson from the whole affair. In early 1974, the SPD was stung by an electoral defeat in the state of Hamburg, suggesting voters were becoming fed up with the party's apparent indecision on the economy. Unemployment was rising fast, hurting the electoral base of the SPD.[214] Schmidt was among those who attributed the Hamburg defeat in part to the government's failure in the realm of public relations.[215] It was not doing enough to sell its policies and ideas to the public. The SPD desperately needed to revitalise its communication channel with the wider population, and win the support of the West German electorate, he argued.

At this crucial moment, it was arguably the *Novellierung* affair that impelled the SPD leadership to re-evaluate its stance towards the Bundesbank – at least in the public sphere. Schmidt had come to realise that the population would side with the Bundesbank should a direct, public conflict emerge between the central bank and the Social Democrat-led federal government. This conclusion was outlined quite clearly in a confidential party report addressed to the party's leadership in

---

[209] 'Bundesbank an der Regierungsleine?', *Frankfurter Allgemeine Zeitung*, 6 Sep. 1973.

[210] Indeed, these two factors were singled out in an internal Bundesbank report years later. See Eichhorn to Pöhl, 6 Aug. 1982.

[211] Viktor von der Lippe, 'Tagebuchähnliche Aufzeichnungen – 30.8.1973', 30 Aug. 1973, DBHA, B330/6917-1.

[212] 'Währungshüter auf der Hut', *Mannheimer Morgen*, 19 Oct. 1973.

[213] 'Bonner Kulisse', *Die Zeit*, 12 Oct. 1973.

[214] 'Arbeitslose: Stürzt knappes Geld die SPD?', *Der Spiegel*, 17 Feb. 1975; and 'Kampf um die Bundesbank', *Wirtschaftswoche*, 25 Apr. 1975.

[215] Baring, *Machtwechsel*, p. 702.

May 1974.[216] 'We are not able to make use of any public conflict with the Bundesbank: public opinion would not stand on our side', it declared.[217] Its author was none other than Schmidt. Less than a year after the first oil crisis, then, the SPD sought a strategy of non-confrontation with the Bundesbank in the domestic political sphere.

Schmidt's confidential report was leaked to the media the day after he became chancellor in May 1974.[218] Behind closed doors, this report was an important moment for the central bank. Von der Lippe's diary noted the public appearance of Schmidt's study with glee.[219] Years later, when detailing the important role played by the Bundesbank's publicity efforts in safeguarding the independence of the central bank from political attacks, Emminger singled out the emergence of Schmidt's document in May 1974 as a crucial moment for Frankfurt.[220] Indeed, Emminger treated the report as the proud and direct result of the Bundesbank's successful efforts at influencing public opinion.[221] The implications of public opinion, then, helped to protect an institution, which was directly accountable to no one, from democratic accountability itself.

This was the 'paradox' of West German democracy. The development that can trace its roots back to the early years of the post-war state. In Chapter 3, for instance, we saw how inflation narratives were mobilised against Adenauer and the interests of his *Kanzlerdemokratie*. They helped to establish a clear limit of democratic accountability in the West German political sphere. Subsequent chancellors, including Schmidt, faced the same problem.

Yet Adenauer and Schmidt had another thing in common. Both chancellors are known to have attended a central bank council meeting. In 1950, an irate Adenauer demanded that the BdL's decision-making body travel to Bonn and convene in his presence. The chancellor then berated the central bank for tightening monetary policy and demanded that it ease credit conditions. Adenauer, as Chapter 2 noted, was rebuffed. By contrast, when Schmidt travelled to Frankfurt in November 1978 to deliver a secret speech before the central bank council, his mind was not on domestic monetary matters, but European ones. 'I am in a

---

[216] Schmidt, 'Bericht – Persönlich – Vertraulich'.   [217] Ibid., p. 57.

[218] Helmut Schmidt, 'Helmut Schmidt: "Was wir nicht tun dürfen, damit wir Inflation, Inflationserwartung und 'Angstlücke' nicht vergrößern"', *Die Zeit*, 17 May 1974; see also the opinion piece published by *Die Zeit* in the same issue: 'Unsicherheit ist gift', *Die Zeit*, 17 May 1974.

[219] Viktor von der Lippe, 'Tagebuchähnliche Aufzeichnungen – 16.5.1974', 16 May 1974, DBHA, B330/6917-2.

[220] Emminger, *D-Mark, Dollar, Währungskrisen*, p. 28.   [221] Ibid.

different situation to Adenauer 28 years ago', Schmidt told his curious audience. 'I have no demands on you.'[222]

Except, of course, when it came to Europe. Schmidt was in Frankfurt to convince the central bank council of the merits of the European Monetary System (EMS), the brainchild of the West German chancellor and his counterpart across the Rhine, the French president Valéry Giscard d'Estaing. Both men wanted monetary stability in Europe; and in their mind, the EMS could achieve it. Envisioned as a successor to the monetary 'snake', the EMS sought to create a 'zone of monetary stability' in Europe via a system of fixed exchange rates, albeit a flexible one that allowed for realignments and, taking heed of the troubled experiences with the dollar under the Bretton Woods monetary system, eschewed the idea of an anchor currency.[223] Flexibility was key here. Under the EMS, currencies could fluctuate within a margin of +2.25 per cent and −2.25 per cent around a central rate.[224] This meant that central banks played an important role; for it would be central banks that had to intervene in markets to ensure that currencies remained within this tight band.

The Bundesbank was not convinced. The central bank council worried that it would be forced to support weaker currencies at the expense of ensuring price stability at home. Yet, for Schmidt, West Germany's future was intricately tied to the European project – for West Germany's own benefit, and the benefit of its neighbours. The EMS was more than just about money; it would be a way of embedding the lessons of his state's troubled past into a European structure. As Marsh notes, Schmidt saw the EMS as a crucial 'stepping stone' towards economic and monetary union in Europe.[225] The chancellor was deeply conscious of German history, and the weaknesses that stemmed from it. For the EMS to be '[a] purely German initiative would have been completely out of the question', the chancellor told the central bank council.[226] 'Any attempt by Germany to go it alone in this field would trigger visceral fears in other countries of being steamrollered, and so provoke instant and widespread opposition.'[227] Instead, the EMS had to be a Franco-German project that enjoyed the support of other countries, a project that would also

[222] Transcript of the speech delivered by Helmut Schmidt to the central bank council, 30 Nov. 1978, DBHA, N2/269, p. 2.
[223] Horst Tomann, *Monetary integration in Europe* (Basingstoke, 2007), p. 12.
[224] The Italian lira was an exception, however; it availed of a wider band. See Ellen Kennedy, *The Bundesbank: Germany's central bank in the international monetary system* (London, 1991), p. 80.
[225] David Marsh, *The euro: the battle for the new global currency* (Southampton, 2011), p. 75.
[226] Transcript of the speech delivered by Helmut Schmidt to the central bank council, pp. 14, 15.
[227] Ibid., p. 15.

prevent West Germany, for the benefit of everyone, assuming too strong a position in Europe.

Concerns of West German foreign policy were never too far away from Schmidt's mind. The country's foreign policy rested on 'two key pillars', he told the central bankers before him: the European Community and the North Atlantic Treaty Organization.[228] West Germany's foreign policy strategy of the last decade revolved around them. With this in mind, the chancellor then went on to say something remarkable:

> We are vulnerable on two fronts and will remain so until well into the next century. We are vulnerable, first, because of Berlin and because of the open flank in the east, because of the division of our nation, symbolised by Berlin's insular position. And we are vulnerable, second, because of Auschwitz. The more successful we are in the fields of foreign, economic, social and defence policy, the longer it will take for Auschwitz to fade from the fore of collective consciousness.[229]

The legacy of the Holocaust had now become fused with the history and role of West Germany's currency. And in the forum of the central bank council to boot. The deutschmark had long since been a success story, something that West Germans could be proud about in a country where political forms of nationalism had once led to the attempted extermination of a people. But with the deutschmark assuming ever more European and international significance, it could no longer escape the shadow of the Second World War. The currency had a role to play. West Germany's future was a European one, Schmidt believed; the same went for that of the deutschmark.

Schmidt left Frankfurt with the Bundesbank's reluctant support of the EMS. Years later, after his fall from power, Schmidt stated publicly that, in order to win the central bank's acquiescence to the EMS, he threatened the central bank council at the meeting that he would amend the Bundesbank Law and remove its independence.[230] Such a statement, however, doesn't quite gel with the turbulent events of 1973, following which Schmidt explicitly said that the SPD could not make any use of a conflict with the central bank; 'public opinion would not stand on our side'.

The secret transcript of the meeting, released thirty years later, bears this out. Schmidt did not threaten the Bundesbank's independence at the meeting. Far from it. 'For me, [altering] the independent position of the German central bank is out of the discussion', he assured the central

---

[228] Ibid.   [229] Ibid.
[230] Marsh, *The euro*, p. 90; Kennedy, *The Bundesbank*, pp. 80–1, 122 (footnote).

bank council.[231] The chancellor actually went on to praise the role of the monetary authority's autonomy in recent weeks and months.[232] Instead, Schmidt won the Bundesbank's assent to the EMS by offering it key concessions and assurances.[233]

Schmidt's proposed *Novellierung* in 1973, then, was the only legal attempt to change the relationship between Bonn and Frankfurt during the 1970s. It did not propose an overhaul of central bank independence. The draft law suggested that the Bundesbank could avail of additional powers, but only with the explicit consent of the government. The proposed 'two-key theory' was a minor change – though its critics were right in that it might well have created an unwelcome precedent for further changes to the Bundesbank Law, had it been implemented.

The *Novellierung* to the Bundesbank Law pushed the central bank into crisis mode. This was never the case with Ehrenberg's far more radical suggestions. The SPD politician did not come up as a topic of discussion at directorate or central bank council meetings during the early 1970s. This suggests that he was not seen as a credible threat. And when journalists raised the politician's ideas in interviews with the Bundesbank president, Klasen just brushed them off.[234] Schmidt's threat was more serious though. And it dominated discussions behind the scenes. After the *Novellierung* debate, however, leading figures from the SPD never again sought to change the relationship between Bonn and Frankfurt in such a blatant fashion.

This was despite sizeable pressure from the ranks below in the SPD.[235] In 1975, for example, the *Orientierungsrahmen '85* programme, which sought to map out the people's party's vision for West Germany for the coming ten years, stated that the Bundesbank should be autonomous within the confines of the Stability and Growth Law.[236] And trade unions continued to attack the degree of independence enjoyed by the Bundesbank.[237] In 1975, the leadership of IG Metall accused Frankfurt of

---

[231] Transcript of the speech delivered by Helmut Schmidt to the central bank council, p. 3.

[232] Ibid., pp. 65–6.

[233] Ibid., pp. 18–22; for the letter referenced in this discussion, see Otmar Emminger to Helmut Schmidt, 16 Nov. 1978, DBHA, N2/269.

[234] Karl Klasen, 'Interview des Bayerischen Fernsehens (Herr Weiß) mit Präsidenten Klasen nach der Zentralbankratssitzung', 18 Apr. 1974, DBPA, no. 567, p. 1.

[235] Rolf H. Kaiser, 'Deutsche Bundesbank: Stärkung der personellen Autonomie', *Die Zeitschrift für das gesamte Kreditwesen*, 15 Apr. 1980.

[236] Heick, 'Kurze vorläufige Stellungnahme zum Orientierungsrahmen 85', 13 Jan. 1975, BAK, B145/13963; Viktor von der Lippe, 'Tagebuchähnliche Aufzeichnungen – 16.11.1975', 16 Nov. 1975, DBHA, B330/6918/1.

[237] See, for example, Viktor von der Lippe, 'Tagebuchähnliche Aufzeichnungen – 19.7.1974', 19 Jul. 1974, DBHA, B330/6917-2; and Viktor von der Lippe, 'Tagebuchähnliche Aufzeichnungen – 21.11.1975', 21 Nov. 1975, DBHA, B330/6918/1.

pursuing 'a one-sided partisan policy in favour of the employer'.[238] These attacks were in large part due to the unemployment crisis unfolding in West Germany at the time, with more than one million workers out of a job in February of that year.[239]

Nevertheless, during this awkward period, senior Social Democrat ministers reaffirmed the independence of the central bank.[240] As chancellor, Schmidt spoke out in explicit support of central bank independence in May 1977:

Seen from the viewpoint of the federal government, co-operation with the Bundesbank and with you, dear president Klasen, worked quite well, and it did so not despite the fact that the Bundesbank is autonomous, but rather – and I do mean what I say here – it worked really well precisely because the Bundesbank is autonomous.[241]

Schmidt was speaking at a ceremony marking the retirement of Klasen. Ceremonies such as these often served as important moments, allowing government figures and central bankers to frame the present in terms of the past. It is at this point, then, that the chapter turns to how anniversaries helped structure the manner in which the monetary past was perceived by West Germans.

Anniversaries amid Crises

The 1970s were replete with anniversaries pertaining to German monetary history. And contemporary economic crises, for their part, served to compound the importance of such occasions. West Germany was a young country – and in more senses than one. As Knut Borchardt, an economic historian, noted in 1972, not more than 13 per cent of the population at that time was above the age of 65, and thus able to remember consciously the experiences of the 1922–3 hyperinflation.[242] The Weimar generation was dying away. A younger generation was

[238] '"Loderer: Bundesbank 'unterstützt' Interessen der Arbeitgeber"', *Vereinigte Wirtschaftsdienste*, 13 Feb. 1975', in *Deutsche Bundesbank Auszüge aus Presseartikeln*, No. 14, 19 Feb. 1975. See also Viktor von der Lippe, 'Tagebuchähnliche Aufzeichnungen – 20.2.1975', 20 Feb. 1975, DBHA, B330/6918/1.
[239] 'Arbeitslose: Stürzt knappes Geld die SPD?', *Der Spiegel*, 17 Feb. 1975.
[240] Viktor von der Lippe, 'Tagebuchähnliche Aufzeichnungen – 23.11.1975', 23 Nov. 1975, DBHA, B330/6918/1.
[241] 'Auszug aus: Ansprache des Bundeskanzlers anläßlich eines Abendessens für den scheidenden Präsidenten der Deutschen Bundesbank Dr. Karl Klasen am 11. Mai 1977', 11 May 1977, BAK, B136/11551.
[242] Knut Borchardt, 'Die Erfahrung mit Inflationen in Deutschland', in Johannes Schlemmer (ed.), *Enteignung durch Inflation? Fragen der Geldwertstabilität* (Munich 1972), p. 9.

replacing it. It was during the 1970s that the two inflationary episodes began to shift from the sphere of personal experience to the realm of historical narrative.

In 1973, West Germans could look back on twenty-five years of the deutschmark, a currency that had come to assume a curious element of national pride in a country where political nationalism remained forbidden. The year also marked a half-century since the hyperinflation of Weimar Republic. In 1976, there was the centenary of central banking, marking 100 years since the foundation of the Reichsbank. The twentieth anniversary of the Bundesbank's establishment arrived twelve months later. And, in 1978, the thirtieth anniversary of the deutschmark took place. These anniversaries served as moments of reflection, grounding the currency's development along historical lines while allowing West German elites to acknowledge the feats achieved – and the challenges that remained.

There was no official ceremony to mark a quarter of a century of the deutschmark's creation in June 1973. This was largely because of the sheer economic uncertainty and concern prevalent at the time. Instead, commemoration took place in the public sphere of newspapers and journals. To mark the anniversary, Klasen gave an interview to the newswire *Deutsche Presse-Agentur* amid efforts to stress the importance of a return to *Stabilitätspolitik*.[243] The deutschmark's twenty-fifth birthday should not be treated as an occasion for mourning, Klasen stressed. Rather, it should be a positive event. Despite its initially poor prospects back in 1948, he continued, West Germany's deutschmark was 'among the world's most respected currencies'.[244] The relative stability that marked the 1950s and 1960s was not necessarily lost. It could be achieved again. And it *had* to be achieved again, lest inflation disrupt West German society once more: 'A redistribution of wealth through such a high rate of inflation, such as we have at the moment, is the most unsocial method of which one could think', Klasen declared.[245]

Members of the directorate, such as Irmler, also marked the anniversary. But again, Irmler did so somewhat indirectly. Speaking at a ceremony to mark the fiftieth anniversary of the Deutsche Verkehrs-Kredit-Bank, an institution established in May 1923, Irmler delved into the troubled history of Germany's currency.[246] Irmler was a former Reichsbanker, joining the inter-war central bank in 1937 and remaining

---

[243] 'dpa-Interview mit Bundesbankpräsident Dr. Klasen', 18 Jun. 1973, DBPA, no. 569.
[244] Ibid.   [245] Ibid.
[246] Heinrich Irmler, 'Möglichkeiten und Grenzen der Kreditpolitik', 29 Jun. 1973, DBHA, B330/18224.

there until the end of the war.[247] According to Irmler, Germany's unfortunate path during the Great Depression should not only be attributed to events in America, but also Germany's experience of hyperinflation. During the twilight years of the Weimar Republic, '[t]he fear of inflation had so thoroughly cut to one's bone' that policies of reflation were eschewed in favour of a more restrictive course.[248]

The central banker acknowledged, however, that the Reichsbank committed some serious errors during this period. The record of the interwar period demonstrated 'the good and bad, and yes, even fatal side of credit policy'.[249] But these errors, Irmler took care to caution the audience, should be seen in the context of contemporary monetary thought at the time, in addition to the political conditions that were prevalent in the latter years of the Weimar Republic. These somewhat open remarks of Irmler, a senior figure in the Bundesbank directorate, were a novel occurrence. And they were indicative of a central bank that was now more willing to face the mistakes of the past.

The anniversary of the deutschmark was also observed in more unofficial quarters. 'No reason for celebration', ran the heading of an editorial piece in the anniversary issue of *Die Zeitschrift für das Gesamte Kreditwesen*, capturing the mood of the country.[250] The influential publication, founded in the year of the currency reform, maintained an editorial stance that, by and large, supported the West German central bank for a quarter of a century. In the debates leading up to the Transition Law of 1951, for instance, a crucial period in which the BdL's independence vis-à-vis Bonn was at stake, Volkmar Muthesius, one of its editors, used the publication as a platform for the central bank's voice in the public sphere.[251] Muthesius also organised confidential meetings between central bank officials and leading newspapers amid efforts to consolidate editorial support for central bank independence during this sensitive time.[252]

The journalist, though somewhat disillusioned by the economic data of recent years, remained a strong ally of the Bundesbank. And the anniversary edition, appearing in June 1973, featured contributions that looked back on the surprising success of deutschmark. Among the contributors were Vocke, who had long since retired, and Otto Pfleiderer, an influential member of the central bank council, who had recently stepped

[247] Deutsche Bundesbank, *Währung und Wirtschaft in Deutschland 1876–1975*, p. 793.
[248] Irmler, 'Möglichkeiten und Grenzen der Kreditpolitik', p. 4.   [249] Ibid.
[250] Volkmar Muthesius, 'Kein Grund zum Feiern', *Die Zeitschrift für das gesamte Kreditwesen*, 15 Jun. 1973, p. 1.
[251] Muthesius, *Augenzeuge von drei Inflationen*, p. 128.
[252] See Chapter 2 for more details.

into retirement as well. The former chancellor, Ludwig Erhard, who was the director of the German authorities that helped implement the currency reform in 1948, also contributed an essay to the publication.[253]

In his article, entitled 'Difficult start for the new central bank', Vocke recounted the sheer number of challenges facing the BdL in 1948.[254] The deutschmark had no currency reserves and the economy was shattered, with little prospect of recovery. West Germany's new currency, a colleague from the Bank of England told him at the time, was 'a bad joke'.[255] Schacht told Vocke that the deutschmark had six weeks to live. 'I did not let Schacht's pessimistic words discourage me', Vocke recalled.

> When I began my office as president of the directorate, I delivered some words to my new colleagues in the central bank council. I said that, in light of the almost insurmountable task of creating a permanently stable currency without gold or currency reserves at hand, we had little chance of laurelled successes. But there was just one asset that we alone could achieve: confidence. If we succeeded in acquiring confidence in the deutschmark, the rest would fall into place. And so it came to pass.[256]

Vocke did not note it in the article, but a central point of that speech he delivered back in 1948 centred on the crucial role of central bank independence in fostering such confidence.[257]

But it was perhaps Pfleiderer who penned the most interesting essay, '25 and 50 years ago: turning points of German monetary history'.[258] The recently retired president of the state central bank in Baden-Württemberg drew parallels and contrasts across half a century of turbulent monetary history. Yet it was a curiously selective essay. 'Twenty-five years have passed since the spectacular event through which the deutschmark came to life in 1948, and 50 years since the great inflation reached its climax in 1923', wrote Pfleiderer. 'Not only did a new chapter of monetary history begin, but also one of economic, even political life, with the introduction of a new currency on both occasions. So it is that the monetary system has played such a fateful role in our century.'[259]

---

[253] Ludwig Erhard, '20. Juni 1948 – Ende und Anfang', *Die Zeitschrift für das gesamte Kreditwesen*, 15 Jun. 1973.

[254] Wilhelm Vocke, 'Schwieriger Start der neuen Zentralbank', *Die Zeitschrift für das gesamte Kreditwesen*, 15 Jun. 1973.

[255] Ibid.   [256] Ibid.

[257] The original speech can be found in 'Vermerk: in der ersten Vollsitzung des Zentralbankrats der Bank deutscher Länder', 4 Jun. 1948, DBHA, B330/4967, pp. 1–2.

[258] Otto Pfleiderer, 'Vor 25 und vor 50 Jahren: Wendepunkt der deutschen Geldgeschichte', *Die Zeitschrift für das gesamte Kreditwesen*, 15 Jun. 1973.

[259] Ibid.

What were the parallels between the two inflations? Well, there was just one, according to Pfleiderer. Both inflations were the result of central banks that abused the printing press amid efforts to finance growing government deficits. Pfleiderer did not mention that the Reichsbank was autonomous from May 1922 onwards. There, the similarities stopped. The former central banker went on to document the differences between the galloping inflation that characterised the years of Weimar, and the repressed inflation, which followed in the Third Reich. These two experiences provided a crucial lesson when forming a new central banking system unburdened by the past, according to Pfleiderer. 'The new central bank system was without legal and – at least with regard to the composition of the central bank council, which decided monetary policy – without personnel continuity with the old Reichsbank.'[260] This remark only vaguely hinted at the strong element of continuity in the directorate. Vocke, the president, and Wilhelm Könneker, vice president, were both former Reichsbankers who played crucial roles concerning the BdL's interaction in the public sphere. For Pfleiderer, then, there was very little continuity between the inter-war central bank and post-war Bundesbank. This was a position reinforced by Emminger throughout the 1970s.

Muthesius contributed an extract taken from his recently published memoirs, *Augenzeuge von drei Inflationen*, or *Witness of three inflations*.[261] The article, entitled 'When the old reichsmark rotted', was a carefully chosen one.[262] Muthesius sought to give the deutschmark a moral underpinning by documenting his experiences with the black market in the years that preceded the introduction of the new currency. The former economics journalist detailed the painstaking efforts and time involved to track down mere standard household items. And he documented the dire quality of goods to be found on the black market. 'The concentration of the mind on how to find the most basic living necessities brought even the sane man down to his knees – a symptom of mental, one might even say moral damages inflicted by inflation', Muthesius remarked. 'He who has not experienced this himself – and indeed, about half of the current population is not of an age to appreciate the impact of such mental tortures that were prevalent during the years 1940–1947 – can hardly understand that such memories remain oppressive decades later.'[263]

---

[260] Ibid.　　[261] For his memoirs, see Muthesius, *Augenzeuge von drei Inflationen*.

[262] Volkmar Muthesius, 'Als die alte Reichsmark verfaulte', *Die Zeitschrift für das gesamte Kreditwesen*, 15 Jun. 1973.

[263] Ibid.

Taken as a whole, the 1973 anniversary was a troubled one. And despite the deutschmark's international success, uncertainty concerning the global economy meant that it was not a time for celebration. The oil crisis that shortly followed only compounded such worries. Nevertheless, whether it was the Bundesbank president or a former economics journalist, historical narratives were used amid efforts to take stock of existing achievements and emphasise the need for the maintenance of *Stabilitätspolitik* in West German political culture.

The centenary of central banking made for a more nuanced affair. The Reichsbank was founded in 1876. Discussions concerning the celebration of a centenary, however, were tentative. After all, an event or ceremony that marked 100 years of central banking would imply at least some form of continuity between the old Reichsbank and the Bundesbank. That was an unwelcome association. In the end, the directorate decided to rule out a formal ceremony, because it saw the centenary as an anniversary not specifically related to the Bundesbank.[264] Instead, it decided that a Festschrift, or commemorative book, would mark the occasion.

The monetarist Helmut Schlesinger, a member of the Bundesbank directorate (and the future central bank president), was given the task of spearheading the book. It was to be called *Währung und Wirtschaft in Deutschland 1876–1975* (*Currency and economy in Germany 1876–1975*).[265] Fritz Knapp Verlag, a publisher that enjoyed a long-time working relationship with the central bank, published the book. Academics and central bankers alike were enlisted to pen essays detailing the history of the Reichsbank, BdL and Bundesbank, from the days of the Second Reich through to the turbulent 1970s. Emminger, Irmler and Pfleiderer were among those representing the Bundesbank.[266] German academics such as Knut Borchardt, Rolf Caesar, Wilhelmine Dreißig and Hans Möller also featured.[267]

In the book's foreword, Klasen noted that the history of German central banking 'had some dark sides'.[268] As such, some of the more sensitive chapters – though not all – detailing the Reichsbank's record

---

[264] Bundesbank directorate meeting minutes, 18 Dec. 1974, DBHA, B330/6461.

[265] Deutsche Bundesbank, *Währung und Wirtschaft in Deutschland 1876–1975*.

[266] See, for instance, Otmar Emminger, 'Deutsche Geld- und Währungspolitik im Spannungsfeld zwischen innerem und äußerem Gleichgewicht (1948–1975)', in Deutsche Bundesbank (ed.), *Währung und Wirtschaft in Deutschland 1876–1975* (Frankfurt am Main, 1976).

[267] Among others, Borchardt, 'Währung und Wirtschaft'.

[268] Karl Klasen, 'Vorwort', in Deutsche Bundesbank (ed.), *Währung und Wirtschaft in Deutschland 1876–1975* (Frankfurt am Main, 1976).

were entrusted to independent academics.[269] When announcing the book to the press in January 1976, Klasen took caution to explicitly stress that the two post-war central banks were not the legal successors to the Reichsbank.[270] Yet the Festschrift was the first time that the Bundesbank published a work implying that a continuity existed, however indirect, between the Reichsbank and Bundesbank.

One example of this was the appearance of the 1939 Reichsbank memorandum in the book. The entire directorate had sent the letter to Hitler, protesting against the inflationary financing of the Third Reich. Pictures of the memorandum took up three full pages of the Festschrift, one of which centred on the signatures at the bottom of the memorandum.[271] Vocke and Blessing's signatures could be found among them. Newspapers in the post-war era often mentioned this memorandum when writing profile pieces of these two men. Indeed, the two men derived some of their credibility from the document, in that it allowed them to portray themselves as among the few men who said 'no' to Hitler. The very same Festschrift, however, provided images of deutschmark banknotes elsewhere in the volume. Blessing's signature can be found on them.[272] The signature of a man who was portrayed as a martyr for the ideals of sound money later vouchsafed the credibility of each and every deutschmark banknote. This was in marked contrast to the left-wing journalist, Bernt Engelmann, who had caused the Bundesbank such headaches in 1965 with the publication of his book *Deutschland Report*. As seen in Chapter 4, Engelmann used a picture of Blessing's signature on a deutschmark banknote to highlight the degree of continuity between elites in the Third Reich and Federal Republic.[273] The Bundesbank's Festschrift implied an altogether different continuity.

In their detailing of the Reichsbank memorandum – 'without a doubt the courage of the memorandum must be admired' – academics Karl-Heinrich Hansmeyer and Rolf Caesar claimed that the document led to the direct dismissal of Schacht, Vocke and Blessing.[274] As Chapter 1 has

[269] Ibid.
[270] 'Präsident Dr. Klasen, Vizepräsident Dr. Emminger und die Mitglieder des Direktoriums Dr. Irmler und Dr. Schlesinger vor der Presse am 5. Januar 1976 (nach Bandaufnahme)'.
[271] Karl-Heinrich Hansmeyer and Rolf Caesar, 'Kriegswirtschaft und Inflation (1936–1948)', in Deutsche Bundesbank (ed.), *Währung und Wirtschaft in Deutschland 1876–1975* (Frankfurt am Main, 1976), pp. 381–3.
[272] Wilhelmine Dreißig, 'Zur Entwicklung der öffentlichen Finanzwirtschaft seit dem Jahre 1950', in Deutsche Bundesbank (ed.), *Währung und Wirtschaft in Deutschland 1876–1975* (Frankfurt am Main, 1976), p. 691.
[273] Bernt Engelmann, *Deutschland Report* (Berlin, 1965), p. 77.
[274] Hansmeyer and Caesar, 'Kriegswirtschaft und Inflation (1936–1948)', pp. 384–5.

noted, this is not entirely accurate. Certainly, the events of January 1939 led to the departure of all three men. But the dismissal notice, sent from Hitler's office on 20 January 1939, did not include the names of Vocke and Blessing.[275] Rather, it mentioned Schacht and two other directorate members. Vocke and Blessing were not sacked. They left of their own accord, resigning voluntary in the weeks that followed.[276]

The year 1976 quickly passed and more anniversaries followed. The twentieth anniversary of the Bundesbank, marking the passage of the Bundesbank Law in 1957, also arrived. In July 1977, Klasen, by then recently retired, marked the occasion in an article published by the SPD's news service.[277] The former Bundesbank president stressed the close continuity between the BdL and the Bundesbank. He even played down the occasion. 'In a material sense it was not a particularly serious break in the history of the German central banking system after the Second World War, for there existed complete legal continuity, even identity, between the Bank deutscher Länder and Bundesbank', Klasen argued. 'There was also no caesura with regard to the policies of the bank.'[278] The Bundesbank, Klasen contended, picked up where the BdL left off.

The thirtieth anniversary of the deutschmark in 1978, however, set itself apart from the other occasions. The anniversary was commemorated with a formal ceremony in Frankfurt. Attended by roughly a thousand officials from political, banking and industrial circles, the ceremony was also broadcast live on television.[279] The occasion was complemented with a media blitz orchestrated by the Bundesbank. Central bank officials published a flurry of articles and delivered numerous speeches to audiences. There was a marked contrast here with the subdued tones of 1973. Why was this the case? In large part, it was because of favourable economic conditions. The threat to *Stabilitätspolitik*, though still somewhat sizeable, was now seen as a manageable one. The worst was over and the future looked brighter. Five years earlier, such an opinion would have been rarely expressed.

The anniversary offered an opportunity to explain the deutschmark's success. 'When abroad I'm often asked: what is the explanation for your relatively greater stability and the strength of your D-Mark?' remarked

[275] Chancellor's office to the Reichsbank directorate, 20 Jan. 1939, BAB, R43 II / 234.
[276] Marsh, *The Bundesbank*, p. 313; Lindenlaub, 'Karl Blessing', p. 15; Wilhelm Vocke, *Memoiren* (Stuttgart, 1973), p. 110.
[277] Karl Klasen, '20 Jahre Deutsche Bundesbank. Das Bundesbankgesetz hat sich bewährt. 28 Juli. 1977', *Deutsche Bundesbank Auszüge aus Presseartikeln*, No. 51, 17 Aug. 1977, DBPA, no. 564, p. 1.
[278] Ibid.   [279] 'Monetary memorial', *Time*, 3 Jul. 1978.

Emminger at the ceremony in Frankfurt. 'Are you luckier? Are you smarter? Is there something special about your economy or society that we lack?'[280] Certainly, there was some luck, Emminger admitted. In Erhard, Germany had the right man at the right time; and it was fortunate that the Allied military authorities established a resilient central banking system. 'So we had a good start, then.'[281]

But there were important factors that helped its strong progress. Moderate wage agreements and social partners played key roles in helping West Germany to avoid economic disaster. And in particular, Emminger noted, *Stabilitätspolitik* in West Germany, more than in any other country, was supported by a large majority of the population. 'That was – and remains – a decisive help for the *Stabilitätspolitik* of the Bundesbank', Emminger declared. 'I would like to use this opportunity to thank the support from the public, from the media and, last not least, the support of our governments down the years.'[282]

Foreign observers were somewhat puzzled by the gravitas and pomp of such a ceremony. 'It may have been the first time that any nation paid official homage to the strength and prestige of its own currency', reported *Time* magazine.[283] It was 'a very German thing', as the *Frankfurter Allgemeine Zeitung* put it, 'inventing a new form of memorial day'.[284] Articles appeared in the press, recounting the tales of West Germans and what they bought with their first deutschmarks. 'I bought food, food', chancellor Schmidt was reported to have said, rolling his eyes with pleasure.[285] Thirty years after the establishment of the deutschmark, the record of the Reichsbank was increasingly falling into the backdrop. West Germans had created a new reference point: the success of the deutschmark from 1948 onwards. Future achievements and failures were now to be set against the record of a currency that had gone from being a 'child of the occupation' to a 'world star', to quote again the title of a popular book by journalist Hans Roeper, published in 1978.[286] 'When a monetary event changes the history of a nation to such an extent, it is hardly surprising that it is commemorated', *Time* magazine remarked. 'Someday they may even build a monument to the deutsche mark.'[287]

---

[280] Otmar Emminger, '30 Jahre D-Mark', *Deutsche Bundesbank Auszüge aus Presseartikeln*, No. 46, 21 Jun. 1978, DBPA, no. 285.
[281] Ibid.   [282] Ibid.   [283] 'Monetary memorial', *Time*, 3 Jul. 1978.
[284] The *Frankfurter Allgemeine Zeitung* was quoted in 'Monetary memorial', *Time*, 3 Jul. 1978.
[285] Ibid.   [286] Roeper, *Die D-Mark: Vom Besatzungskind zum Weltstar*.
[287] 'Monetary memorial', *Time*, 3 Jul. 1978.

Conclusion

The West German state never did build a monument to the deutschmark. But the formal ceremony that marked the thirtieth anniversary of
the currency was an important, if curious milestone in the evolution of
the deutschmark's history. Speaking before hundreds of West German
elites, Emminger, then president of the Bundesbank, singled out the
support of public opinion when explaining the success of the monetary
authority's *Stabilitätspolitik*. As he would later note in his memoirs, this
support was actively cultivated by the central bank through the media
across three decades of post-war history, with the explicit aim of safeguarding the monetary authority's independence.[288]

Let us rewind to Klasen standing on the podium in 1970. By equating
the two 'traumas' of the inter-war period, the new Bundesbank president
signalled the start of a new era. But if commentators were fearful that his
arrival in Frankfurt compromised the independence of the Bundesbank,
they were mistaken. Klasen sought accommodation with Bonn, far more
so than his predecessor Blessing. This attitude was best exemplified in his
close relationship with Schmidt. The fruits of this teamwork were evident. Unlike the 1966–7 recession, there was no public fallout between
Frankfurt and Bonn during the unemployment crisis of 1974–5. And the
new Bundesbank president defended his interests when push came to
shove. Klasen stood by his 'line' in the face of political challenge: there
was to be no compromise of the Bundesbank's legal independence.

The continuity in the public sphere between the Reichsbank and post-
war central bank began to fade in the 1970s. Although the Bundesbank
had always stressed that there was no link between itself and the Reichsbank, Chapters 2, 3 and 4 have demonstrated that this was not the case
in the public sphere. With the departure of key Reichsbank figures, and a
new generation at the helm and in the spotlight, this continuity began to
fade however. A new history began to emerge in its place, one closely tied
to the success of the deutschmark. The Bundesbank's history was
becoming increasingly myopic. The recent successes documented by
Emminger replaced the old painful experiences recounted by Blessing.

By the mid-1970s, the SPD, arguably the only mainstream party that
could have challenged the independence of Frankfurt, actively sought to
play down conflicts with the Bundesbank – even at the height of an
unprecedented unemployment crisis. There are several factors that contributed towards this stance. Schmidt's *Novellierung* in 1973 caused a

---

[288] Emminger, *D-Mark, Dollar, Währungskrisen*, pp. 26–8.

media scandal after it called into question the relationship between the central bank and the federal government. And, troubled by rising unemployment and flagging electoral support, the new chancellor sought to avoid public conflicts with the Bundesbank. Any dissent among the lower ranks of the political party – or, indeed on its fringes, such as the trade unions – rarely filtered through to the leadership. This was primarily due to considerations of public opinion, as outlined in Schmidt's confidential report in May 1974. Any attempt to limit the independence of Frankfurt would have had to run the gauntlet of public opinion. In this sense, then, a 'paradox' of West Germany democracy was evident. Popular pressure kept democratically elected officials from making the Bundesbank more accountable to the people during an economically explosive decade.

The Bundesbank itself played an important role in this development. At moments when it was politically challenged, it reverted to the lessons of monetary history. This can be most clearly seen in the episode with Klasen and Schiller. Boxed into a corner, the central bank fought back, publishing an unprecedented article in its August 1972 monthly report. The article examined the relationship between Frankfurt and Bonn, and referred to Germany's two inflationary episodes to justify its independence.

But wait – haven't we been here before? A generation lay between the chancellorships of Adenauer and Schmidt. Yet the public debate concerning the Bundesbank Law that played out in late 1973 was eerily reminiscent of the debate that took place in the early 1950s. The same language and references were used. Taking a step back, we can see how the *Novellierung* affair itself demonstrated the extent to which historical narratives surrounding Germany's two inflations were intricately tied to the Bundesbank Law.

In 1957, this piece of legislation reaffirmed a power struggle between Bonn and Frankfurt, by allowing the central bank to maintain a sizeable degree of independence. At times, this independence caused headaches in the political capital, creating conflicts between the central bank and Bonn that spilled into the public sphere – and in turn giving rise to further instances in which the inflation narratives were used. We have seen how, in 1973, politicians almost inadvertently fell back upon inter-war German history to augment their political arguments. This was because the provisions in the Bundesbank Law could create circumstances in which Germany's monetary history suddenly *became* relevant again. Though the *Novellierung* debate was quickly forgotten, the larger, institutional power struggle that underpinned it remained. It was not the first clash between the central bank and government. And it would not be the last.

'The West German state never did build a monument to the deutschmark.' The opening sentence of this conclusion is not entirely accurate. There *was* a monument to the success of the deutschmark. But this monument did not assume the form of a memorial. Rather, it came to manifest itself in something much bigger and much more consequential. It assumed the form of the euro and that currency's monetary guardian. This book began its journey with the European Central Bank. And so it is only fitting that we now return to Mario Draghi and the *Pickelhaube*.

Conclusion

'The Germans had terrible experiences with inflation in the twentieth century', recalled Mario Draghi, the president of the European Central Bank (ECB) in March 2012. He was speaking to two journalists from the tabloid newspaper *Bild* at the ECB's headquarters, who had just given him a *Pickelhaube*. 'It does away with value and makes forecasting impossible. More still – inflation can downright destroy the society of a country.'[1] To be dead set against inflation, to be for a strong currency, and to be independent of politics – these were 'German virtues'. And they were virtues, Draghi said, that every European central banker should strive towards.[2]

Four months later, Draghi declared that the ECB was ready to do 'whatever it takes' to preserve the euro. 'And believe me, it will be enough.'[3] The ECB president's declaration came as a response to the unprecedented challenges facing the eurozone's economy. That meant straying beyond the conventional territory of monetary policy and sailing into uncharted waters. Draghi's speech was widely credited with alleviating market tensions surrounding the euro's future. It became a key moment in the eurozone crisis. A game-changer. And yet, at the time, it was a gamble. His comments caught all and sundry off guard – including other members of the governing council, the ECB's decision-making body.[4]

Not everyone was happy. Behind the scenes, *Reuters* later wrote, the ECB president scrambled to consolidate support on the governing

---

[1] 'Interview mit EZB-Chef Mario Draghi zur Euro-Krise: "Deutschland ist ein Vorbild"', *Bild*, 22 Mar. 2012. See www.bild.de/politik/ausland/mario-draghi/deutschland-ist-ein-vorbild-23270668.bild.html. Last accessed on 20 December 2018.

[2] Ibid.

[3] 'Speech by Mario Draghi, president of the European Central Bank, at the Global Investment Conference in London, 26 July 2012', www.ecb.europa.eu/press/key/date/2012/html/sp120726.en.html. Last accessed on 20 December 2018.

[4] As noted in 'Special report: Inside Mario Draghi's euro rescue plan', *Reuters*, 25 Sep. 2012. See www.reuters.com/article/us-ecb-draghi-plan-idUSBRE88O09A20120925. Last accessed on 20 December 2018.

council for his far-reaching statement. Four days after his speech, in his office, Draghi met for coffee with Jens Weidmann, the Bundesbank president and an influential member of the governing council. 'Displayed on a shelf behind Draghi's conference table was a black-and-gold spiked Prussian helmet from 1871', *Reuters* remarked.[5] As president of the Bundesbank, Weidmann had but one vote on the governing council, which usually made decisions by consensus. But his opinion carried considerable weight. According to *Reuters*, Weidmann informed Draghi that he would refuse to support any revival of the ECB's bond-buying, in a reference to the central bank's efforts back in 2010 and 2011 to purchase sovereign bonds on the secondary market. And so it came to pass that Draghi, at a press conference on 2 August 2012, stated that the governing council was 'unanimous with one reservation' that the ECB could soon embark on bond purchases. That one reservation, Draghi hinted, came from Weidmann.[6] But the proposal still remained somewhat vague, even skeletal. Only one month later, on 6 September 2012, did the ECB president put flesh on the bones of his previous statement and announced the creation of the Outright Monetary Transactions (OMT) programme.

Under strict, specific conditions, the OMT programme allowed the Eurosystem, itself comprised of the ECB and national central banks, to embark on unlimited purchases of sovereign bonds on the secondary market.[7] As Martin Wolf, a *Financial Times* columnist, put it years later, the emergence of the OMT programme allowed Draghi to turn his promise of 'whatever it takes' into official ECB policy.[8] At the press conference that announced the OMT, a journalist asked Draghi if the decision on the governing council had been unanimous. 'Well, it was not

---

[5] Ibid.

[6] Draghi's exact words were: the endorsement to do 'whatever it takes to preserve the euro as a stable currency has been unanimous. But, it's clear and it's known that Mr Weidmann and the Bundesbank – although we are here in a personal capacity and we should never forget that – have their reservations about programmes that envisage buying bonds [...].' See 'Introductory statement to the press conference (with Q&A), 2 August 2012'. www.ecb.europa.eu/press/pressconf/2012/html/is120802.en.html#qa. Last accessed on 20 December 2018.

[7] 'Introductory statement to the press conference (with Q&A), 6 September 2012', www.ecb.europa.eu/press/pressconf/2012/html/is120906.en.html. Last accessed on 20 December 2018. See also 'Technical features of Outright Monetary Transactions', www.ecb.europa.eu/press/pr/date/2012/html/pr120906_1.en.html, 6 Sep. 2012. Last accessed on 20 December 2018.

[8] Martin Wolf, 'Imaginative reform is vital for the eurozone to survive', *Financial Times*, 26 Sep. 2017. See www.ft.com/content/451d26e6-a264-11e7-b797-b61809486fe2. Last accessed on 20 December 2018.

unanimous', Draghi answered. 'There was one dissenting view. We do not disclose the details of our work. It is up to you to guess.'[9]

Weidmann was in the minority on the governing council. During the heady days of 2012, however, the Bundesbank president knew that he could rely on the support of the German media. 'Rebellion of the Bundesbank', ran the front cover of *Der Spiegel*.[10] Just two months prior, the weekly magazine depicted the euro shattering into pieces.[11] Nothing was sacred; even Draghi's recently acquired Prussian helmet got dragged into the uproar. 'Yet more ECB billions for indebted states?' asked an incredulous *Bild*. 'Then *Bild* wants the *Pickelhaube* back!'[12] Indeed, even at the press conference that saw the unveiling of the OMT, a journalist reminded Draghi that the *Frankfurter Allgemeine Zeitung* had recently warned of 'the "liraisation" of the euro, moving away from a deutschmark culture to a lira culture', in a reference to Italy's currency prior to the euro's introduction.[13]

There were times when Draghi felt the need to portray his own personal history in German terms. In an interview with *Die Zeit*, the ECB president talked of his experience with inflation when he had returned to Italy in the 1970s after a spell abroad. 'In Germany, some people say of me – ah, that Italian, he is sure to fuel inflation in the German economy!', he told the newspaper's editor. 'And I explain to them that their experience of inflation dates back to the 1920s, while mine is far more recent.'[14] At other times, however, the negative sensationalism so often found in German media outlets got to Draghi, who normally cut a suave and polished figure. In an interview with *Spiegel Online* in early 2014, after the journalist had harangued him with doom-laden questions concerning the euro's future, the ECB president curtly defended his policies: 'Each time it was said, for goodness' sake, this Italian is ruining Germany. There was this perverse angst that things were turning bad, but the opposite has happened: inflation is low and uncertainty reduced.'[15]

---

[9] 'Introductory statement to the press conference (with Q&A), 6 September 2012'.
[10] See the front cover of *Der Spiegel*, 27 Aug. 2012.
[11] Refer to the front cover of *Der Spiegel*, 25 Jun. 2012.
[12] 'Kein deutsches Geld mehr für Pleite-Staaten, Herr Draghi!', *Bild*, 24 Oct. 2012. See www.bild.de/politik/ausland/euro-krise/ezb-entscheidung-ueber-neue-milliarden-hilfen-esm-staatsanleihen-kauf-25453080.bild.html. Last accessed on 20 December 2018.
[13] 'Introductory statement to the press conference (with Q&A), 6 September 2012'.
[14] 'Wenn du deinen Mut verlierst, hast du alles verloren', *Die Zeit*, 15 Jan. 2015. See www.zeit.de/2015/03/mario-draghi-ezb/seite-2. Last accessed on 20 December 2018.
[15] 'Draghi defends euro rescue policies', *Spiegel Online*, 2 Jan. 2014. See www.spiegel.de/international/europe/spiegel-interview-with-ecb-president-mario-draghi-a-941489.html. Last accessed on 20 December 2018.

A 'perverse angst'. Draghi's comment was a telling one. Not that *Spiegel Online* was to be swayed in its opinion. Far from it; for the media outlet knew all too well the apparent lessons of Germany's monetary history. 'For the Bundesbank', the news website observed some years earlier, 'it has always been taboo to finance the state by purchasing its sovereign bonds.' It continued:

Behind this belief was the terrifying example of its predecessor, the Reichsbank, which had printed money with abandon in the 1920s in order to support the budget of the Weimar Republic. The result was a hyperinflation that has become deeply entrenched in the collective memory of Germans.[16]

The *Spiegel Online* article from which the passage is quoted – and which also appears in this book's introduction – was ostensibly meant to be about the ECB's response to the eurozone crisis. And yet, at the same time, it is a perfect example of monetary mythology. Today, the lessons of Germany's inter-war history seem almost obvious. But this was not the case in the early years of the Federal Republic. We have forgotten the 'openness of past moments', so eloquently described by the historian Jeffrey Herf, 'before choices congealed into seemingly inevitable structures'.[17] This book has shown how an underlying institutional struggle, its origins dating back to 1948, created a public debate in which West German elites felt compelled to look towards the past amid efforts to build a new central bank that could provide for a more stable future. The Allied military authorities, in this regard, played a crucial role. By establishing the Bank deutscher Länder (BdL) well over a year before the foundation of the Federal Republic, and by protecting the central bank from German political pressure until 1951, the Allies, somewhat inadvertently, laid the foundations for a clash of interests between the BdL, federal government and state governments.

The Bundesbank Law provided the stage for this three-way power struggle. And indeed, that much has already been documented by the existing literature. But what has been overlooked is the extent to which the debate was fused with historical narratives that, over time, came to harden. The record of the Reichsbank constituted the overwhelming reference point during the discussions concerning the Bundesbank Law, and with it, the monetary legacy of the inter-war era.

---

[16] 'Breaking taboos: concerns mount in Germany over ECB bond buys. Part 2: we cannot give way to panic', *Spiegel Online*, 15 Aug. 2011. See www.spiegel.de/international/spiegel/breaking-taboos-concerns-mount-in-germany-over-ecb-bond-buys-a-780258-2.html. Last accessed on 20 December 2018.

[17] Jeffrey Herf, *Divided memory: the Nazi past in the two Germanys* (Cambridge, MA, 1997), preface.

As Chapter 1 has shown, the record of the Reichsbank could be a complicated one. In 1949, West Germans looked back on three turbulent decades of monetary history, during much of which the central bank was independent. Legally speaking, the Reichsbank was free of government instruction from 1922 until well into the 1930s – a fact that could be, and was, used by political opponents of central bank independence in the post-war era. This time-frame, too, allowed the question of central bank independence to touch upon the fault line of two competing so-called traumas of the German inter-war era; those of inflation and mass unemployment. Should the West German state prioritise lessons stemming from the two inflations? Or should the young republic rather heed the lessons of mass unemployment? Of course, these lessons were not mutually exclusive. But players such as Wilhelm Vocke, the BdL's chairman of the directorate, saw them as such – at least in the long-run.

Chapter 2 documented the early years of the Bundesbank Law debate. It demonstrated the extent to which a number of competing historical narratives of the inter-war era gave ballast to proposals and counter-proposals pertaining to the new Bundesbank. If the BdL stressed the experience of Germany's two inflations, Fritz Schäffer, the finance minister in the early 1950s, pointed to the record of the Reichsbank during the depths of depression.

As such, the rise of the West German central bank's monetary mythology, first established in the courtrooms of Nuremberg in defence of Hjalmar Schacht, the former Reichsbank president, was by no means certain. Yet this book has been a story of institutions and what human agency can forge from them. When the Bundesbank published in February 2016 an article on its website that described Vocke as the 'pioneer of the Bundesbank's independence', it was quite justified in doing so.[18] We have seen how the Transition Law of 1951 played an important role in the gradual dominance of monetary mythology, both in terms of postponing and prejudicing the outcome of the Bundesbank Law, which emerged some six years later. With Vocke, the BdL's leadership took advantage of that opportunity. Driven by its tenuous legal position and uncertain future, we have seen how the central bank began a partly concealed media campaign, one with historical narratives concerning the two inflations at its heart, to influence the Bundesbank Law.

---

[18] The article was published in celebration of the 130th anniversary of Vocke's birth. See 'Vorkämpfer für die Unabhängigkeit der Bundesbank', www.bundesbank.de/de/aufgaben/themen/vorkaempfer-fuer-die-unab-haengigkeit-der-bundesbank-664786. Last accessed on 20 December 2018.

By the mid-1950s, the West German central bank had become a popular institution in the public sphere. This was in large part because it presided over rising living standards in the 'blue sky of the economic miracle'. The BdL's successful monetary policy had deservedly won the central bank, and its independence, plaudits. Gradually, the central bank began to lose its reputation as a creature of the Allied occupation. Chapter 3 demonstrated the importance of the 1956 'Gürzenich affair' in cementing the BdL's reputation. In doing so, the chapter also highlighted how the 'Gürzenich affair' proved crucial in narrowing and ossifying the parameters of monetary debate in the Federal Republic. Prior to the controversy, both industrialists and the Social Democratic Party (SPD) still expressed reservations concerning the BdL's independence, grounding their worries, in part, with reference to the inter-war era. After the controversy in May 1956, however, the left-wing opposition party came out in strong support of central bank independence in the lead-up to the Bundesbank Law's passage through parliament.

The workers' party did so to damage the political credibility of Konrad Adenauer, the chancellor. And in this respect, the 'Gürzenich affair' was a case in point of how narratives of the two inflations could be set against the ambitions of *Der Alte* within the *Kanzlerdemokratie* of 1950s West German society. After all, it was not Adenauer who was portrayed in 1956 as 'chancellor of the deutschmark' on the front cover of *Der Spiegel*. Rather, it was Vocke. If the period 1949–55 is to be described as one indicative of the 'recovery of economic sovereignty' on the part of the West German state, as Werner Abelshauser labels it, then we need to treat such an observation with a more nuanced viewpoint.[19] Adenauer was chancellor of the West Germans. But in the mindsets of many, he was not the chancellor of their currency. Sovereignty, as Adenauer would have understood it, stopped at the door of monetary policy. This is important when we acknowledge that the deutschmark itself would eventually become 'the very symbol of West Germany and her economic success', as Neil MacGregor notes in his critically acclaimed work on the German nation.[20]

We have seen, too, how the provisions of the Bundesbank Law of 1957 reaffirmed the institutional conflict first set in place by the Allies some nine years earlier. It allowed for a central bank that was independent of political instruction. By not providing for a formal process through which cases of disagreement between Frankfurt and Bonn concerning

---

[19] Werner Abelshauser, *Die langen Fünfziger Jahre: Wirtschaft und Gesellschaft der Bundesrepublik Deutschland 1949–1966* (Düsseldorf, 1987), p. 25.
[20] Neil MacGregor, *Germany: memories of a nation* (London, 2014), p. 504.

the central bank's monetary policy could be solved, the Bundesbank Law encouraged such conflicts to spill into the public sphere. These conflicts created media controversies surrounding the central bank's independence. As such, the Bundesbank Law allowed for the creation of circumstances in which the lessons of the two inflations could be applied in defence of the central bank.

In making this argument, however, the book is not suggesting that the preoccupation of Germany's political culture with inflation is entirely down to some cynical, successful public relations strategy on the part of the central bank. Far from it. As Chapter 2 has shown, the central bank was merely one of several players who reverted to the events of the inter-war era to ground their arguments with historical weight. What the book *is* arguing, however, is that an institutional struggle provided the underlying dynamic behind which West German elites felt it only natural to embrace lessons from the inter-war past to make their points. The Bundesbank Law allowed for the creation of public disputes between the central bank and government in which Germany's inter-war monetary history could continually *become* relevant.

Perhaps a counterfactual question can help demonstrate this point. Could these open clashes have occurred in the public sphere had Schäffer succeeded in 1950 in pushing through his finance ministry's idea of an arbitration committee dominated by government officials? Such disagreements would have likely remained behind closed doors, nipped in the bud by the federal government's arbitrary will.

To date, the reputation of the Bundesbank has defied trends in the field of cultural history, trends that have stripped away the thin veneer of the *Stunde Null* – the idea of a new, fresh start – that had once characterised the narrative of the Federal Republic's creation. One underlying theme of this study, however, has been to document the extent to which the BdL and – for the first ten years of its existence, at least – the Bundesbank, too, were strongly linked to the inter-war Reichsbank in the public sphere. There was an important element of continuity here, and that it existed was in large part due to the post-war central bank's leadership.

Even though Vocke and his successor, the president of the Bundesbank, Karl Blessing, had but one vote on the central bank council, these men nevertheless came to personify both the West German central bank and its currency in the media. The central bank as a one-man show. This image, of course, dates back to the days of the inter-war Reichsbank. Whether it was Schacht portrayed in 1930 as the sole pillar supporting the independence of the Reichsbank, or Vocke depicted as the 'chancellor of the deutschmark' in 1956, or Blessing as the 'president of the deutschmark' in 1960, these men came to dominate the public image of the monetary authority during their respective tenures. Viktor von der Lippe, the Bundesbank's press chief who remained with the central bank for a quarter of a century, actively fostered this development. The legitimate spokespersons of the central bank, von der Lippe declared, should be the very men who led the monetary authority. No third party or barrier should interfere with that link.

And so the BdL became 'Vocke's tower' in West German public life; and the same went for its central bank council, seen by some segments of the media to be dominated by a group of former Reichsbankers. Vocke's past brought with it problems, however. The central banker 'survived them all', wrote one newspaper in 1949: the first inflation, the deflation and the second inflation. Recall Vocke's signature co-guaranteeing the 'value' of a banknote worth 50 million marks issued in September 1923 at the height of the hyperinflation. The man had quite a history.

Yet the BdL embraced Vocke's record, framing it as an edifying experience. His very person embodied the lessons of the two disastrous inflations. This was a point that infuriated Schacht in the 1960s. The former Reichsbank president felt unfairly blamed for the record of the Reichsbank during the era of the Third Reich. Schacht cried double standards. After all, he claimed, was not Vocke a member of the very same directorate that passed the 'Mefo' bills? Schacht's question fell on deaf ears. We have seen how the BdL used Vocke's Reichsbank record as a means of establishing his credibility vis-à-vis Adenauer's coalition governments. The Reichsbank memorandum of 1939 was underlined in résumés sent out to journalists, and even published in its entirety alongside a collection of Vocke's post-war speeches. Vocke had once said 'no' to a profligate government. 'He would say no again', as *Der Spiegel* put it in 1952.

But these narratives could be challenged, as Chapter 4 demonstrated. In particular, a small number of case studies reveal how the West German central bank could be placed in an extremely awkward position. Schacht, Blessing's 'first master', to use the phrase of one magazine back in 1962, publicly accused his erstwhile protégé of actively partaking in the second inflation that had destroyed the reichsmark. This caused no end of frustration to Blessing. The Bundesbank could not respond to these allegations in the public sphere, lest it wish to dignify the claims of an attention-hungry Schacht, a man who thrived on publicity. And yet the central bank did not have to respond. The press set about ridiculing Schacht. Hitler's former magician had turned to 'quackery', according to the *Frankfurter Allgemeine Zeitung*, a strong ally of the West German central bank.

What happened, however, when more damaging allegations emerged in the public sphere? What happened when pictures of Blessing and Heinrich Himmler both present in the same room were published in mainstream publications? The emergence of the *Freundeskreis* news story forced the Bundesbank to intervene in the public sphere. Led by von der Lippe, the central bank created an alternative version of history, aided by an array of documents dating from the Nuremberg trials, with the goal of killing the news story as quickly as possible. In doing so, the Bundesbank used proxies and remained largely in the shadows. Among the documents sent were the testimonies of Vocke and Schacht at Nuremberg, both of which highlighted the devastating impact of the 1939 Reichsbank memorandum for the careers of those who signed the document. This point is crucial. The use of such evidence underlines the extent to which the West German central bank's mythology was forged in the courtrooms at Nuremberg.

Yet we have seen how the Bundesbank's leadership – already enjoying one of the most prestigious reputations in the world of central banking by the 1960s – felt itself compelled to send a stern letter to a local boy for publishing a story in his school newspaper about Blessing's inter-war history. The Bundesbank also sent the boy the 'short comprehensive summary' that read, '[w]hoever wants to accuse him [Blessing] today, either had the fortune of standing in the shadows back then, or not knowing what it was like to live in those circumstances, because he was too young'. This action alone suggests that the West German central bank had an awareness of a vulnerability that could not be brushed aside by success on the monetary front. And it demonstrates that the Bundesbank was not immune to the wider, more generational challenges afoot in West German society at the time.

The shadows of the Reichsbank and the inter-war period, then, loomed large in the public sphere. That began to change in the 1970s. With the arrival of Karl Klasen and Otmar Emminger, a new leadership took charge. It was during this decade that the link between the Reichsbank and the Bundesbank was cut in the public sphere. Klasen and Emminger spoke of a different past. The Bundesbank embraced fully a more recent history, one that began with the currency reform of 1948. The era of the Reichsbank fell by the wayside; and in its place, a phoenix rising from the ashes. Several monetary anniversaries allowed the Bundesbank to reaffirm its own monetary mythology during an era that was plagued by uncertainty and troubles.

The 1970s were years in which economic crises reigned. It was the decade of the 'Great Inflation'. Indeed, West Germans had already taken to calling it the 'third inflation' for some years, an expression that suggested historical narratives of the two inflations could also work *against* the interests of the Bundesbank. Back in the late 1940s and during the 1950s, Vocke spoke of counterfactual outcomes in the lead-up to the Bundesbank Law; think of what could happen *if* the Bundesbank Law allowed for a sizeable degree of political influence. But, with the Bundesbank Law now passed by parliament, Blessing had to deal with the reality of presiding over an actual sustained, creeping inflation. 'Three inflations do (not) fall from the sky – they were "made"' screamed one sensationalist pamphlet. The Bundesbank, for its part, was keen to stress that the era of great inflations belonged to the past. The monetary authority was an advocate of *Stabilitätspolitik*, one grounded by historical lessons, and the idea of an independent central bank lay at the heart of such policies.

Yet the 1970s were years of unemployment too – years in which the SPD assumed the reins of a coalition government and called on West Germans to 'dare more democracy'. Since the late 1920s, we have seen how much of the opposition to central bank independence stemmed from the left of the political spectrum. As such, at a time of economic crisis, the 1970s constituted the last serious chance for the Bundesbank's independence to be challenged. At the same time, though, Chapter 5 highlighted the extent to which lessons of the two inflations were intricately tied to public debates related to the Bundesbank Law, as shown in the case study of the 1973 *Novellierung* proposal. Figures from the SPD and its coalition partner, the Free Democratic Party (FDP), looked to the same inter-war past and took from it different lessons. The SPD's Herbert Ehrenberg pointed to the actions of an independent Reichsbank during the hyperinflation; while the FDP's Otto Graf Lambsdorff fell back on the lessons of the second inflation.

A generation separated the eras of Adenauer and Helmut Schmidt. And yet West German elites spoke the same language, appealed to the same examples, and grounded their arguments with the same references. The Bundesbank Law ensured that Germany's monetary past would remain a political football for years to come. Another underlying theme found in Chapter 5 was how the Bundesbank still fell back upon the lessons of the two inflations when politically challenged. During the controversy surrounding the fall of the so-called super-minister Karl Schiller, the Bundesbank published a special article on the relationship between Frankfurt and Bonn in its monthly report for August 1972 – an unprecedented act – and reverted to historical narratives of the two inflations to justify the provisions of the Bundesbank Law that allowed for central bank independence.

It would not be the last time the Bundesbank did so. Throughout the 1980s, West Germany struggled with unemployment. For much of this decade, the press output of the central bank omitted any such references to the lessons of the two inflations. The Bundesbank found itself often rejecting journalists' references to the Great Depression during these years. It almost appeared as if the inflation narratives had disappeared from use. But then something strange happened.

In the late 1980s and early 1990s, the Bundesbank once again began referring to the lessons of the two inflations. This time, however, these historical narratives were applied in a different manner, and towards a different goal: the West German central bank found itself caught up in a political current sweeping across the continent, one that pushed towards economic and monetary union.

To understand the establishment of the ECB, one must first understand the events and decisions that led to the Maastricht Treaty, signed in February 1992. Although the idea of European economic and monetary union went back decades, a few factors in the 1980s spurred policymakers towards the creation of a single currency area. First, as the historian Harold James puts it, the 'very unsatisfactory early experience' of the European Monetary System (EMS), scarred by recurrent realignments, made policymakers realise the potential benefits of deepening monetary integration.[21] Second, that realisation was underlined further with the signing of the Single European Act in early 1986. A battle-cry for liberalisation, the Single European Act would break down capital barriers and allow for cross-border flows that only served to increase pressure on the EMS.[22]

But there was also a third reason as to why numerous European Economic Community member states were contemplating about whether or not to give up their monetary sovereignty in the 1980s. In short, they did not really *have* any monetary sovereignty – at least in practice. The economic historian Barry Eichengreen writes how the EMS evolved into an asymmetric framework in which the Bundesbank more or less 'set the tone for monetary policy throughout Europe'.[23] West Germany had become the anchor of the EMS, a fact that other countries

---

[21] Harold James, 'Karl-Otto Pöhl: the pole position', in Kenneth Dyson and Ivo Maes (eds.), *Architects of the euro: intellectuals in the making of the European monetary union* (Oxford, 2016), pp. 177–8.

[22] Kenneth Dyson and Kevin Featherstone, *The road to Maastricht: negotiating economic and monetary union* (Oxford, 1999), p. 3.

[23] Barry Eichengreen, *The European economy since 1945: coordinated capitalism and beyond* (Princeton, 2007), p. 348. Refer also to Otmar Issing, *The birth of the euro* (Cambridge, 2008), pp. 234–5.

such as France and Italy found deeply frustrating.[24] Were a European monetary authority to be created, however, these countries could at least have a seat at the decision-making table. That was an attractive idea.

Some politicians in West Germany, such as Hans-Dietrich Genscher, the foreign minister at the time, worried that the status quo – which saw the Bundesbank often subject to a barrage of criticism from abroad – was detrimental to West Germany's long-term interests. Genscher made headlines in early 1988 when he penned a memorandum that called for the creation of a single currency area and an independent ECB. What is more, the foreign minister pushed for something entirely novel: the creation of a committee of wise men with 'professional and political authority' to develop a plan for economic and monetary union.[25] This committee should be appointed by the European Council at its summit in Hanover that summer, Genscher argued.

Enter Jacques Delors, the president of the European Commission, who was already riding high with the passage of the Single European Act during his tenure. Delors had to be careful; he knew that the Bundesbank would greet any move towards economic and monetary union with instinctive suspicion. Behind closed doors, Delors won the support of the West German chancellor, Helmut Kohl, not only for the formation of the committee of wise men, but that Delors himself should chair it.[26] And so it came to pass. In June 1988, the European Council agreed at Hanover to the establishment of a committee on economic and monetary union: the Delors Committee. It was made up of Delors, the cumbersomely titled committee of governors of the central banks of the European Economic Community (committee of central bank governors, for short), three independent experts and a European Commissioner by the name of Frans Andriessen. Each member was to act in a personal capacity, as opposed to representing the interests of his institution.[27]

One of those experts was Alexandre Lamfalussy, the general manager of the Bank for International Settlements and the future president of the European Monetary Institute (EMI), a forerunner to the ECB that was established in 1994. Lamfalussy was impressed by the grace with which Delors played his hand of cards. In 2013, looking back at events, Lamfalussy recalled that Delors 'had the European Council task a group dominated by central banks with preparing the way for the banks' own

---

[24] Eichengreen, *The European economy since 1945*, pp. 349–50.
[25] Dyson and Featherstone, *The road to Maastricht*, p. 331.   [26] Ibid., pp. 339–40.
[27] Harold James, *Making the European monetary union: the role of the committee of central bank governors and the origins of the European Central Bank* (Cambridge, MA, 2012), pp. 234–5.

suicide'. He added, not without a touch of humour: 'It was absolutely inspired.'[28]

Karl Otto Pöhl, the Bundesbank president, was furious upon learning the news. In his mind, it was absurd that Delors, a Brussels man, should chair a committee that dealt with monetary policy matters; such a committee might well give rise to 'Latin' views at the expense of the stability-orientated mindset of the West Germans.[29] Indignant about what he saw as a betrayal on the part of the West German chancellor, Pöhl was initially reluctant to join the Delors Committee. But his colleagues at the Bundesbank, in addition to the Dutch central bank president Wim Duisenberg, persuaded him to embrace it. After all, if Pöhl did not take part, 'the field would be left open to others'.[30] Better in than out. With Pöhl's participation, the Bundesbank could at least ensure that its views were forcefully put forward. This is exactly what Kohl had hoped for. By presenting the Bundesbank with a fait accompli at Hanover, the chancellor was able to 'bind in' the central bank, forcing it to take part in discussions and removing its ability to stand on the sidelines, where it could snipe away.[31] Moreover, the Delors Committee tasked Pöhl with drafting the 'ideal profile' of a future ECB. The Germans could hardly say no. And with that move, Lamfalussy recalled, Delors had 'rendered them captive'.[32]

The Bundesbank found itself on the back foot. The central bank was now caught up in a wider push towards economic and monetary union. But if this book has shown anything, it has demonstrated that the Bundesbank had the capacity to fight back – and to do so using a specific version of German history to frame the terms of debate. In the direct aftermath of Hanover, the Bundesbank took to the media to argue its line. One example was Pöhl's article in *The Wall Street Journal* in July 1988. 'Movement toward a European central bank cannot occur before some important questions are answered', he wrote. One such question concerned the task of the future ECB. It can only be price stability, Pöhl argued.

[The ECB's task] should agree with the aim of the Deutsche Bundesbank Act – 'safeguarding the currency' – which in practice means a policy ensuring stable prices [...] Most Germans, with traumatic memories of two hyperinflations,

---

[28] Christophe Lamfalussy, Ivo Maes and Sabine Péters, *Alexandre Lamfalussy: the wise man of the euro* (Leuven, 2013), p. 135.
[29] James, 'Karl-Otto Pöhl: the pole position', p. 181.
[30] Dyson and Featherstone, *The road to Maastricht*, p. 343.   [31] Ibid., pp. 336–7.
[32] Lamfalussy, Maes and Péters, *Alexandre Lamfalussy*, p. 136.

would not accept a central bank system that attributed this goal less significance than does the Bundesbank Act.[33]

His message was clear. If West Germany's support for an ECB was to be secured, then such an ECB would have to strongly resemble the Bundesbank. What other choice did West Germans have in light of their 'traumatic' history? Pöhl was not alone here. He could rely on support in Bonn, too. Just a day prior to the article's publication, the West German chancellor had visited the Bundesbank to win over the central bank council to the idea of the Delors Committee and the wider question of economic and monetary union. Kohl stressed at the meeting the 'great value of an independent central bank for the history of the Federal Republic'. And certainly, he said, so long as he was chancellor, nothing would happen to the Bundesbank's independence. In the negotiations to come, Kohl continued, West Germany will 'mark some fixed points that it considers indispensable'.

Among such points include all currency-related issues in view of the two major inflations in Germany in this century. This means that a future central bank system of the Community should correspond to the structure of the Bundesbank along with its independence from instructions from governments or the Commission.[34]

Kohl explicitly linked West Germany's position in the lead-up to economic and monetary union to his country's fateful history of inflation. And what is more, the chancellor – who happened to have a PhD in German history – did so unquestioningly. Almost forty years after the establishment of West Germany, politicians were once again discussing the lessons of their country's history amid efforts to discern the best structure of a central bank. This time, however, there was no debate about which lessons of the past to embrace. The Bundesbank's monetary mythology was the only game in town.

Pöhl expected little genuine results from the Delors Committee. Delors, for his part, knew that the Bundesbanker had been told by Bonn that he could not block an agreement. As Lamfalussy later put it, Kohl told Pöhl to 'keep quiet'.[35] In the lead-up to the committee's first meeting in September 1988, the Bundesbank set to work on a draft paper that Pöhl would present with the goal of framing the long-term discussion. The 'Pöhl paper' put forward an independent ECB and a price

---

[33] Karl Otto Pöhl, 'A vision of a European central bank', *The Wall Street Journal*, 15 Jul. 1988, Deutsche Bundesbank Pressearchiv [DBPA], no. 869.

[34] 'Protokoll der 754. Sitzung des Zentralbankrats der Deutschen Bundesbank in Frankfurt am Main am 14. Juli 1988', 14 Jul. 1988, DBHA, B330/17840, pp. 11–12.

[35] Lamfalussy, Maes and Péters, *Alexandre Lamfalussy*, p. 135.

stability mandate, among other points.[36] The Bundesbank was prepared for a fight. But already by February of the next year, Pöhl was observing 'a much greater degree of agreement on basic principles' than he thought would be the case.[37] Interestingly, however, as Kenneth Dyson and Kevin Featherstone note, this was not a 'hard-fought victory' for Pöhl and his men in Frankfurt. 'In effect, there had been no goalkeeper to block Pöhl's shots', they write.[38] The other committee members were, with varying degrees of emphasis, in agreement regarding an independent ECB and its price stability mandate. The Bundesbank central bank council, for its part, was very surprised that Pöhl's colleagues on the Delors Committee agreed with West Germany's stance.[39]

The Delors Report was presented in April 1989, just eight months after the committee first met. The European Council at its Madrid summit in June that year accepted the document as 'a sound basis for future work' and gave the green light to the Delors Report's follow-up procedures on achieving economic and monetary union.[40] Around two-thirds of the Delors Report eventually made it into the Maastricht Treaty, which laid out the roadmap for monetary union in Europe and the establishment of the ECB.[41] Nevertheless, a crucial stage came between the arrival of the Delors Report, on the one hand, and the signing of the Maastricht Treaty, on the other. The European Council established an inter-governmental conference to negotiate the details of economic and monetary union. Negotiators from across Europe would sit around the table to carve out a treaty that would redefine the continent. Significantly, a newly empowered committee of central bank governors was tasked with drafting a statute for the ECB in preparation for the inter-governmental conference.[42]

Pöhl rightly saw this committee of central bank governors as the 'decisive vehicle' through which the Bundesbank could shape the future European monetary authority.[43] The Bundesbank tabled a draft statute of the ECB at the start of discussions; the committee agreed to use this draft as '*the* draft for the negotiation'.[44] As James writes, the committee began to 'run with the ball' on designing the new ECB with an eye on the inter-governmental conference. And what is more, it was 'a very German

[36] Dyson and Featherstone, *The road to Maastricht*, p. 344.   [37] Ibid., p. 347.
[38] Ibid.   [39] James, 'Karl-Otto Pöhl: the pole position', p. 186.
[40] James, *Making the European monetary union*, p. 262.
[41] Lamfalussy, Maes and Péters, *Alexandre Lamfalussy*, p. 138.
[42] James, *Making the European monetary union*, p. 266.
[43] James, 'Karl-Otto Pöhl: the pole position', p. 187.
[44] Emphasis in original. Dyson and Featherstone, *The road to Maastricht*, p. 387.

ball'.[45] Though there were some disagreements that had to be ironed out among committee members, the Bundesbank dominated the outcome of the committee's draft of the ECB statute. Pöhl hammered the point home on central bank independence and the importance of price stability as the ECB's mandate. 'The future ECB thus came to look more and more like an internationalized version of the Bundesbank', notes James.[46] The committee finalised the ECB draft statute in November 1990. The following April, Pöhl gave it to the finance minister of Luxembourg in the latter's capacity of chair of the inter-governmental conference on economic and monetary union. When doing so, the Bundesbanker warned the politician not to tamper with the statute.[47]

The Delors Committee and the committee of central bank governors provided the key fora through which the Bundesbank shaped the future European monetary authority, and with it, Europe's own future. The committees' mark on the ECB statute that found its way into the Maastricht Treaty is unmistakable, particularly the latter committee.[48] Tipping its hat to the Delors Report, the Maastricht Treaty put forward three stages for monetary union. Stage I, beginning in 1990, called for the dismantling of remaining capital controls and for economic convergence of European economies on several fronts. Stage II saw the establishment of the EMI at start of 1994, an organisation tasked with co-ordinating economic policies and encouraging further convergence in preparation for Stage III: the transfer of monetary sovereignty by 1 January 1999 to a supranational central bank.[49]

Historians have often noted the extent to which the model of the Bundesbank exerted a powerful influence upon the establishment of the ECB. 'The Bundesbank's influence on the institutional shape of the ECB can hardly be overestimated', the historian Carl-Ludwig Holtfrerich has written. 'For all practical purposes, the two appear to be clones, or twin sisters.'[50] Christoph Buchheim, too, has wryly observed how central bank independence was twice imposed in Germany at the behest

---

[45] James, 'Karl-Otto Pöhl: the pole position', p. 190.
[46] James, *Making the European monetary union*, p. 267.
[47] Dyson and Featherstone, *The road to Maastricht*, p. 388.
[48] Harold James juxtaposes the ECB statute found in the Maastricht Treaty text alongside the draft ECB statute put forward by the committee of central bank governors. The similarities are striking. See Appendix B in James, *Making the European monetary union*, pp. 425–61.
[49] Kathleen R. McNamara, *The currency of ideas: monetary politics in the European Union* (Ithaca, 1998), pp. 163–4.
[50] Carl-Ludwig Holtfrerich, 'Monetary policy in Germany since 1948: national tradition, international best practice or ideology?', in Jean-Philippe Touffut (ed.), *Central banks as economic institutions* (Cheltenham, 2008), p. 40.

of foreign powers – only to be exported as a German product by means of the ECB's establishment.[51] Duisenberg, the Dutch central banker who became the first ECB president, once said that the euro spoke German.[52] His French successor, Jean-Claude Trichet, was seen by some media outlets as often trying to 'out-German the Germans', 'fighting inflation in the style of the Bundesbank'.[53] This mindset proved to be problematic at times. Eichengreen argues in his 2015 book on the global financial crisis that 'German fear now translated into European policy', with the ECB under Trichet increasing interest rates twice in 2011, pushing Europe's fragile recovery back into a recession.[54]

Overlooked in the literature, however, has been the extent to which a specific version of German *history* has been exported to the European continent via the provisions outlining the ECB. In the debate leading up to the passage of the Maastricht Treaty, the leadership of the Bundesbank, as well as German politicians, lobbied heavily for the future ECB to assume the form of the German central bank. Monetary mythology played an important role in defining the parameters of debate.

Just weeks before the Maastricht Treaty was signed, for example, Pöhl's successor as Bundesbank president, Helmut Schlesinger, delivered a lecture in the Netherlands. The title of the speech was 'German monetary history as a lesson for a European monetary union'. Schlesinger stood before his audience: 'German monetary history, the start of which I would equate with the foundation of the Second Reich, is a history of successes and failures.'[55] Understandably, Schlesinger began with charting its successes. The deutschmark ranked among the best currencies in the world. Throughout the post-war period, '[i]ts value increased considerably against the average of the major foreign currencies', he continued. 'Preceding this relative monetary and economic success, comes the destructive effects of the two inflations 1919–23 and 1936–48 chronologically.'[56] The negative experiences endured by the

---

[51] Christoph Buchheim, 'Von altem Geld zu neuem Geld. Währungsreformen im 20. Jahrhundert', in Reinhard Spree (ed.), *Geschichte der deutschen Wirtschaft im 20. Jahrhundert* (Munich, 2001), pp. 151–2.

[52] Carlo Tognato, *Central bank independence. Cultural codes and symbolic performance* (New York, 2012), p. 86.

[53] One former colleague added that Trichet was 'part of the generation of people whose job it was to make France more German'. Quoted in 'How Mario Draghi is reshaping Europe's central bank', *CNBC*, 9 Jan. 2013. See www.cnbc.com/id/100365250. Last accessed on 20 December 2018.

[54] Barry Eichengreen, *Hall of mirrors: the Great Depression, the Great Recession, and the uses – and misuses – of history* (New York, 2016), p. 8.

[55] Helmut Schlesinger, 'Deutsche Währungsgeschichte als Lehrstück für eine Europäische Währungsunion', 8 Nov. 1991, DBPA, no. 1053, p. 1.

[56] Ibid., p. 2.

German population, then, explained the success of the post-war deutsch-mark, in no small part due to that population's willingness to accept the occasionally harsh recipe of the Bundesbank's *Stabilitätspolitik*.

Schlesinger, however, went on to depict an accurate account of central bank independence in German history. It can be dated back to May 1922, he noted, with the passage of the Autonomy Law, and would remain in place until 1937. The central banker highlighted the positive role played by public opinion. He flagged the disputes over monetary policy back in 1950 and 1956, among others, as important events that fostered confidence in the central bank. But tellingly, too, he remarked that such public support was not a given – and that the central bank had to continually fight to win public opinion.[57] Schlesinger admitted that independence was 'no guarantee of stability', and pointed to the example of the independent Reichsbank during the hyperinflation of the Weimar Republic.[58]

These were surprisingly honest admissions on the part of the Bundes-bank's leadership; and this trend has become more pronounced under the more recent presidency of Weidmann.[59] But the key 'conclusion' to take from German history, Schlesinger said in his finishing remarks, was that a central bank should be free of political instruction and tied to maintaining price stability. 'The Bundesbank Law did this, and the draft of a European central bank provides for this too.'[60] In making this comment, Schlesinger linked German history to the importance of insti-tutions – or more accurately put, the important of establishing the *right* kind of institutions, as seen by the German central bank.

For Schlesinger, German monetary history began with the foundation of the Second Reich; the Bundesbank president explained the post-war success of the central bank in terms of historical events that predated the foundation of the Federal Republic. This was telling. For it is here we turn back to Draghi's *Pickelhaube*. A symbol of the Second Reich, the

---

[57] Ibid., p. 6.   [58] Ibid.

[59] In recent years, the German central bank has become more open about Germany's inter-war history. Its recently renovated *Geldmuseum*, or Money Museum, accurately traces the origins of German central bank independence to May 1922, during the hyperinflation. What is more, the Bundesbank announced in November 2017 that it was financing an independent, four-year research project that examines links between the Reichsbank, the BdL and the early years of the Bundesbank. For more details, see 'Bundesbank ermöglicht Forschungsprojekt zur Geschichte von Reichsbank, Bank deutscher Länder und früher Bundesbank', www.bundesbank.de/de/presse/pressenotizen/bundesbank-ermoeglicht-forschungsprojekt-zur-geschichte-von-reichsbank–bank-deutscher-laender-und-frueher-bundesbank-670114. Last accessed on 20 December 2018.

[60] Schlesinger, 'Deutsche Währungsgeschichte als Lehrstück für eine Europäische Währungsunion', p. 6.

Prussian military helmet too evoked experiences that took place prior the establishment of the West German central bank. Holding the *Pickelhaube* in his hand as he spoke to the two journalists in 2012, Draghi's language was fused with German history, just like Schlesinger's back in 1991.

Today, the lessons of Germany's inter-war history seem almost obvious. This is apparent when one drops by the ECB's visitor centre, situated in the lobby of the main building in Frankfurt. There, the visitor is greeted with 'some key economic events' that the ECB deems crucial to the understanding of its independence, mandate and evolution. The visitor centre lists the German hyperinflation among four important historical episodes – the others being the deflation during the Great Depression, the stagflation of the 1970s and the more recent global financial crisis. The hyperinflation of the Weimar Republic is the earliest historical event listed. If one visits the ECB, then, one leaves with an implicit message: in the beginning, there was hyperinflation.

And yet, the West German central bank's monetary mythology, so successful within the national sphere, is now playing out across the European continent. Can the eurozone as a whole, with nineteen different member states, develop a *Stabilitätskultur* in the manner that West Germany did? The ECB is imbued with a German history. Its president speaks with specific references. European central bankers, Draghi said, should strive towards German 'virtues'. But it remains to be seen whether this mythology, and the historical narratives that go along with it, can work well in a continent that includes so many different monetary cultures.

Draghi's 'whatever it takes' speech was a crucial moment in the ECB's history – and a positive one, too. The central bank stands at a crossroads. Yet it is unlikely that the spiked *Pickelhaube* will point Draghi, or his successor, in the right direction. We live in a new era with new monetary challenges. That has called for the use of new monetary instruments, such as the ones we have seen the ECB spearheading in recent years. But it also calls for a new history. Let us start writing one.

Bibliography

Archives

Archiv der sozialen Demokratie, Friedrich-Ebert-Stiftung, Bonn
Deutsche Bundesbank Historisches Archiv, Frankfurt
Deutscher Bundestag Parlamentsarchiv, Berlin
Deutsche Bundesbank Pressearchiv, Frankfurt
Historisches Archiv des Bundesverbandes der Deutschen Industrie e.V., Berlin
Bundesarchiv, Berlin-Lichterfelde
Bundesarchiv, Koblenz
Institut für Zeitgeschichte, Munich

Printed Primary Sources

'2. Deutscher Bundestag. 118. Sitzung. Bonn, den Freitag 9. Dezember 1955'.
'2. Deutscher Bundestag – 152. Sitzung. Bonn, Freitag, den 22. Juni 1956'.
'2. Deutscher Bundestag – 175 Sitzung. Bonn, Freitag, den 30. November 1956'.
'2. Deutscher Bundestag. 180. Sitzung. Bonn, Donnerstag, den 13. Dezember 1956'.
'5. Deutscher Bundestag. 241. Sitzung. Bonn, Donnerstag, den 19. Juni 1969'.
'Deutscher Bundestag. 6. Sitzung. Bonn, Mittwoch, den 21. September 1949'.
'Deutscher Bundestag – 8. Sitzung. Bonn, Dienstag, den 27. September 1949'.
'Deutscher Bundestag – 75. Und 76. Sitzung. Bonn, Freitag, den 14. Juli 1950'.
'Deutscher Bundestag – 108. Sitzung. Bonn, Freitag, den 15. Dezember 1950'.
'Deutscher Bundestag – 147. Sitzung. Bonn, Mittwoch, den 6. Juni 1951'.
'Deutscher Bundestag – 249. Sitzung. Bonn, Mittwoch, den 4. Februar 1953'.
Geschäftsbericht des Bundesverbandes der Deutschen Industrie, 1 Apr. 1950 – 31 May
    1951.
'Gesetz über die Deutsche Bundesbank. Vom 26. Juli 1957', *Bundesgesetzblatt,
    Teil I, Ausgegeben zu Bonn am 30. Juli 1957,* Nr. 33, 1957.
Hüllbüsch, U. (ed.), *Die Kabinettsprotokolle der Bundesregierung, Band 4: 1951*
    (Boppard am Rhein, 1988).
    (ed.), *Die Kabinettsprotokolle der Bundesregierung, Band 9: 1956* (Munich, 1998).
Law No. 60, 'Establishment of the Bank deutscher Länder', Military government
    gazette, 1946 – 1949, No. 805.
'Military government – Germany – British zone of control. Ordinance No. 129.
    Establishment of a Bank deutscher Länder', Mar. 1948.
Monthly Report of the Bank deutscher Länder, Jan. 1949. (English version.)

Monatsbericht der Bank deutscher Länder, Aug. 1955. (German version.)
Monatsbericht der Deutschen Bundesbank, Aug. 1972. (German version.)
Monatsbericht der Deutschen Bundesbank, Mar. 1998. (German version.)
Monthly Report of the Deutsche Bundesbank, Mar. 1998. (English version.)
Nationalrat der Nationalen Front des Demokratischen Deutschland (ed.) *Braun-buch: Kriegs- und Naziverbrecher in der Bundesrepublik* (Berlin, 1965).
Reichsbank, *Schacht in der Karikatur: Im Auftrage des Reichsbankdirektoriums zusammengestellt in der Volkswirtschaftlichen und Statistischen Abt. der Reich-sbank. Zum 22 Januar 1937* (Berlin, 1937).
Trials of the major war criminals before the International Military Tribunal, vol. VIII (Nuremberg, 1947).
Trials of the major war criminals before the International Military Tribunal, vol. XI (Nuremberg, 1947).
Trials of the major war criminals before the International Military Tribunal, vol. XII (Nuremberg, 1947).
Trials of the major war criminals before the International Military Tribunal, vol. XIII (Nuremberg, 1948).
Trials of the major war criminals before the International Military Tribunal, vol. XVIII (Nuremberg, 1948).
Trials of the major war criminals before the International Military Tribunal, vol. XXII (Nuremberg, 1949).
Trials of the major war criminals before the International Military Tribunal, vol. XXIV (Nuremberg, 1949).
Trials of the major war criminals before the International Military Tribunal, vol. XLI (Nuremberg, 1949).
Trials of war criminals before the Nuernberg Military Tribunal under Control Council Law No. 10, vol. VI (Washington, 1952).
Weber, A. (ed.), *Die Bundesbank. Aufbau und Aufgaben. Bericht über eine Aus-sprache führender Sachverständiger mit dem Entwurf eines Bundesgesetzes über die Errichtung einer Bundesbank* (Frankfurt am Main, 1950).
Wirtschaftswissenschaftliches Institut der Gewerkschaften, *Notenbank im Umbau: Föderal oder Zentral?* (Cologne, 1951).

Printed Secondary Sources

Abelshauser, W., *Wirtschaft in Westdeutschland 1945–1948: Rekonstruktion und Wach-stumsbedingungen in der amerikanischen und britischen Zone* (Stuttgart, 1975).
Die langen Fünfziger Jahre: Wirtschaft und Gesellschaft der Bundesrepublik Deutschland 1949–1966 (Düsseldorf, 1987).
Deutsche Wirtschaftsgeschichte seit 1945 (Bonn, 2004).
Acheson, K. and J. F. Chant, 'Mythology and central banking', *Kyklos*, Vol. 26, No. 2 (1973).
Ahamed, L., *Lords of finance: the bankers who broke the world* (New York, 2009).
Albrecht, W., *Kurt Schumacher: Ein Leben für den demokratischen Sozialismus* (Bonn, 1985).

Alesina, A. and L. H. Summers, 'Central bank independence and macroeconomic performance: some comparative evidence', *Journal of Money, Credit and Banking*, Vol. 25, No. 2 (1993).

Allen, C. S., 'The underdevelopment of Keynesianism in the Federal Republic of Germany', in Peter A. Hall (ed.), *The political power of economic ideas: Keynesianism across nations* (Princeton, 1989).

Anon., 'Zur Erinnerung an Karl Klasen. Bank und Geschichte: Historische Rundschau', *Historische Gesellschaft der Deutschen Bank*, No. 19, Apr. 2009.

Bakker, A., *The liberalization of capital movements in Europe: the monetary committee and financial integration, 1958–1994* (Dordrecht, 1996).

Balderston, T., *The origins and course of the German economic crisis: November 1923 to May 1932* (Berlin, 1993).

Economics and politics of the Weimar Republic (Cambridge, 2002).

Baring, A., *Machtwechsel: Die Ära Brandt-Scheel* (Stuttgart, 1982).

Im Anfang war Adenauer. Die Entstehung der Kanzlerdemokratie, 2nd edn (Munich, 1989).

Berger, H., *Konjunkturpolitik im Wirtschaftswunder: Handlungsspielräume und Verhaltensmuster von Bundesbank und Regierung in den 1950er Jahren* (Tübingen, 1997).

'The Bundesbank's path to independence: evidence from the 1950s', *Public Choice*, Vol. 93, No. 3–4 (1997).

Berger, H. and J. de Haan, 'A state within the state? An event study on the Bundesbank (1948–1973)', *Scottish Journal of Political Economy*, Vol. 46, No. 1 (1999).

Berghahn, V., *The Americanisation of West German industry, 1945–1973* (Leamington Spa, 1986).

Bessel, R. and D. Schumann (eds.), *Life after death: approaches to a cultural and social history of Europe during the 1940s and 1950s* (Cambridge, 2003).

Beyer, A., V. Gaspar, C. Gerberding and O. Issing, 'Opting out of the Great Inflation: German monetary policy after the break down of Bretton Woods', *European Central Bank: Working Paper Series*, No. 1020 (2009).

Bibow, J., 'On the origin and rise of central bank independence in West Germany', *The European Journal of the History of Economic Thought*, Vol. 16, No. 1 (2009).

'Zur (Re-)Etablierung zentralbankpolitischer Institutionen und Traditionen in Westdeutschland: Theoretische Grundlagen und politisches Kalkül (1946–1967)', in Christian Scheer (ed.), *Die deutschsprachige Wirtschaftswissenschaft in den ersten Jahrzehnten nach 1945: Studien zur Entwicklung der Ökonomischen Theorie, Band XXV* (Berlin, 2010).

Blessing, K., *Die Verteidigung des Geldwertes* (Frankfurt, 1960).

Im Kampf um gutes Geld (Frankfurt, 1966).

Blyth, M., *Austerity: the history of a dangerous idea* (Oxford, 2013).

Boelcke, W. A., 'Karl Blessing (1900–1971). Der Großbankier aus Enzweihingen', in Lothar Behr et al., eds., *Vaihinger Köpfe: Biographische Porträts aus fünf Jahrhunderten* (Vaihingen an der Enz, 1993).

Bofinger, P., K. Pfleger, and C. Hefeker, 'Stabilitätskultur in Europa', in Hans-Hermann Francke, Eberhart Ketzel and Hans-Helmut Kotz (eds.), *Europäische Währungsunion. Von der Konzeption zur Gestaltung* (Berlin, 1998).

Borchardt, K., 'Die Erfahrung mit Inflationen in Deutschland', in Johannes Schlemmer (ed.), *Enteignung durch Inflation? Fragen der Geldwertstabilität* (Munich, 1972).

'Währung und Wirtschaft', in Deutsche Bundesbank (ed.), *Währung und Wirtschaft in Deutschland 1876–1975* (Frankfurt am Main, 1976).

'Das Gewicht der Inflationsangst in den wirtschaftspolitischen Entscheidungsprozessen während der Weltwirtschaftskrise', in Gerald D. Feldman (ed.), *Die Nachwirkungen der Inflation auf die deutsche Geschichte 1924–1933* (Munich, 1985).

Borchardt, K. and C. Buchheim, 'The Marshall Plan and key economic sectors: a microeconomic perspective', in Charles S. Maier and Günter Bischof (eds.), *The Marshall Plan and Germany. West German development within the framework of the European Recovery Program* (New York, 1991).

Bordo, M. D., Ø. Eitrheim, M. Flandreau and J. F. Qvigstad (eds.), *Central banks at a crossroads: what can we learn from history?* (Cambridge, 2016).

Braun, H.-J., *The German economy in the twentieth century* (London, 1990).

Bresciani-Turroni, C., *The economics of inflation: a study of currency depreciation in post-war Germany* (London, 1937).

Brochhagen, U., *Nach Nürnberg: Vergangenheitsbewältigung und Westintegration in der Ära Adenauer* (Hamburg, 1994).

Brüning, H., *Memoiren 1918–1934* (Stuttgart, 1970).

Buchheim, C., *Die Wiedereingliederung Westdeutschlands in die Weltwirtschaft, 1945–1958* (Munich, 1990).

'The establishment of the Bank deutscher Länder and the West German currency reform', in Deutsche Bundesbank (ed.), *Fifty years of the Deutsche Mark: central bank and the currency in Germany since 1948* (Oxford, 1999).

'Von altem Geld zu neuem Geld. Währungsreformen im 20. Jahrhundert', in Reinhard Spree (ed.), *Geschichte der deutschen Wirtschaft im 20. Jahrhundert* (Munich, 2001).

'Die Unabhängigkeit der Bundesbank. Folge eines amerikanischen Oktrois?', *Vierteljahrshefte für Zeitgeschichte*, Vol. 49, No. 1 (2001).

Caesar, R., *Der Handlungsspielraum von Notenbanken: Theoretische Analyse und internationaler Vergleich* (Baden-Baden, 1981).

Chickering, R., *Imperial Germany and the Great War, 1914–1918*, 3rd ed. (Cambridge, 2014).

Clavin, P., 'Review: the Impact of inflation and depression on democracy. New writing on the inter-war economy', *The Historical Journal*, Vol. 38, No. 3 (1995).

The Great Depression in Europe, 1929–1939 (London, 2000).

'"Money talks." Competition and cooperation with the League of Nations, 1929–40', in Marc Flandreau (ed.), *Money doctors: the experience of international financial advising, 1850–2000* (London, 2003).

Securing the world economy: the reinvention of the League of Nations, 1920–1946 (Oxford, 2013).

Deutsche Bundesbank (ed.), *Währung und Wirtschaft in Deutschland 1876–1975* (Frankfurt am Main, 1976).

(ed.), *Geheimrat Wilhelm Vocke, Hüter der Währung, Zum hundertsten Geburtstag am 9. Februar 1986* (Frankfurt am Main, 1986).

(ed.), *30 Jahre Deutsche Bundesbank. Die Entstehung des Bundesbankgesetzes vom 26. Juli 1957* (Frankfurt am Main, 1988).

Dickhaus, M., *Die Bundesbank im westeuropäischen Wiederaufbau: die internationale Währungspolitik der Bundesrepublik Deutschland 1948 bis 1958* (Munich, 1996).

'The foster-mother of "The bank that rules Europe": the Bank deutscher Länder, the Bank of England and the Allied Banking Commission', in Alan Bance (ed.), *The cultural legacy of the British occupation in Germany* (Stuttgart, 1997).

'Fostering "The Bank that rules Europe": the Bank of England, the Allied Banking Commission, and the Bank deutscher Länder, 1948–51', *Contemporary European History*, Vol. 7, No. 2 (1998).

'The West German central bank and the construction of an international monetary system during the 1950s', *Financial History Review*, Vol. 5 No. 2 (1998).

Dreißig, W., 'Zur Entwicklung der öffentlichen Finanzwirtschaft seit dem Jahre 1950', in Deutsche Bundesbank (ed.), *Währung und Wirtschaft in Deutschland, 1876–1975* (Frankfurt am Main, 1976).

Dyson, K., 'Hans Tietmeyer, ethical ordo-liberalism, and the architecture of EMU: getting the fundamentals right', in Kenneth Dyson and Ivo Maes (eds.), *Architects of the euro: intellectuals in the making of the European monetary union* (Oxford, 2016).

Dyson, K. and K. Featherstone, *The road to Maastricht: negotiating economic and monetary union* (Oxford, 1999).

Duwendag, D. (ed.), *Macht und Ohnmacht der Bundesbank* (Frankfurt, 1973).

Ehrmann, M. and P. Tzamourani, 'Memories of high inflation', *European Journal of Political Economy*, Vol. 28 (2012).

Eichengreen, B., *Golden fetters: the gold standard and the Great Depression* (Oxford, 1992).

The European economy since 1945: coordinated capitalism and beyond (Princeton, 2007).

Hall of mirrors: the Great Depression, the Great Recession, and the uses – and misuses – of history (New York, 2016).

Ehrenberg, H., *Zwischen Marx und Markt: Konturen einer infrastrukturorientierten und verteilungswirksamen Wirtschaftspolitik* (Frankfurt, 1973).

Zwischen Marx und Markt: Konturen einer infrastrukturorientierten und verteilungswirksamen Wirtschaftspolitik, 2nd ed. (Munich, 1976).

Emminger, O., *Währungspolitik im Wandel der Zeit* (Frankfurt, 1966).

'Deutsche Geld- und Währungspolitik im Spannungsfeld zwischen innerem und äußerem Gleichgewicht (1948–1975)', in Deutsche Bundesbank (ed.), *Währung und Wirtschaft in Deutschland, 1876–1975* (Frankfurt am Main, 1976).

The D-Mark in the conflict between internal and external equilibrium, 1948–75 (Princeton, 1977).

D-Mark, Dollar, Währungskrisen: Erinnerungen eines ehemaligen Bundesbankprä-sidenten (Stuttgart, 1986).

Engelmann, B., *Deutschland Report* (Berlin, 1965).

Erhard, L., *Wohlstand für Alle* (Düsseldorf, 1957).

Eucken, W., *The foundations of economics*, trans. T. W. Hutchison (London, 1950).

Evans, R. J., 'Introduction: the experience of unemployment in the Weimar Republic' in Richard J. Evans, Dick Geary (eds.), *The German unemployed: experiences and consequences of mass unemployment from the Weimar Republic to the Third Reich* (London, 1987).

Evans, R. J. and D. Geary (eds.), *The German unemployed: experiences and conse-quences of mass unemployment from the Weimar Republic to the Third Reich* (London, 1987).

Feinstein, C. H., P. Temin and G. Toniolo, *The European economy between the wars* (Oxford, 1997).

Feldman, G. D., 'The historian and the German inflation', in Nathan Schmuk-ler, Edward Marcus (eds.), *Inflation through the ages: economic, social, psycho-logical, and historical aspects* (New York, 1983)

The great disorder: politics, economics, and society in the German inflation 1914–1924 (Oxford, 1996).

Allianz and the German Insurance Business, 1933–1945 (Cambridge, 2001).

Fergusson, A., *When money dies: the nightmare of the Weimar collapse* (London, 1975).

When money dies: the nightmare of deficit spending, devaluation, and hyperinflation in Weimar Germany (New York, 2010).

Fischer, A., 'Hans Luther [1879–1962]', in Hans Pohl (ed.), *Deutsche Bankiers des 20. Jahrhunderts* (Stuttgart, 2008).

Flandreau, M., 'The French crime of 1873: an essay on the emergence of the international gold standard, 1870–1880', *The Journal of Economic History*, Vol. 56, No. 4 (1996).

Flink, S., *The German Reichsbank and economic Germany* (New York, 1930).

Frei, N., *Vergangenheitspolitik: Die Anfänge der Bundesrepublik und die NS-Vergan-genheit* (Munich, 1996).

(ed.), *Karrieren im Zwielicht. Hitlers Eliten nach 1945* (Frankfurt, 2001).

Giersch, H. and H. Lehment, 'Monetary policy: does independence make a difference? – the German experience', *ORDO*, Vol. 32 (1981).

Glossner, C. L., *The making of the German post-war economy: political communi-cation and public reception of the social market economy after World War Two* (London, 2010).

Goodhart, C., D. Gabor, J. Vestergaard and I. Ertürk (eds.), *Central banking at a crossroads: Europe and beyond* (London, 2014).

Goodhart, C. and R. Lastra, 'Populism and central bank independence', *Open Economies Review*, Vol. 29, No. 1 (2018).

Goodman, J. B., 'Monetary politics in France, Italy, and Germany', in Paolo Guerrieri and Pier Carlo Padoan (eds.), *The political economy of European integration: states, markets and institutions* (London, 1989).

The politics of central banking in Western Europe (London, 1992).

Habermas, J., *The structural transformation of the public sphere: an inquiry into a category of bourgeois society*, trans. Thomas Burger and Frederick Lawrence (Cambridge, 1993).

Haffner, S., *Defying Hitler: a memoir* (London, 2002).

Halbwachs, M., *On collective memory*, trans. and ed. L. A. Coser (Chicago, 1992). *The collective memory*, trans. F. J. Ditter and V. Y. Ditter (New York, 1980).

Hansmeyer, K.-H. and R. Caesar, 'Kriegswirtschaft und Inflation (1936–1948)', in Deutsche Bundesbank (ed.), *Währung und Wirtschaft in Deutschland 1876–1975* (Frankfurt am Main, 1976).

Hardach, K., *The political economy of Germany in the twentieth century* (Berkeley, 1980).

Häuser, K., 'Gründung der Bank deutscher Länder und Währungsreform', in Hans Pohl (ed.), *Geschichte der deutschen Kreditwirtschaft seit 1945* (Frankfurt am Main, 1998).

Hayo, B., 'Inflation culture, central bank independence and price stability', *European Journal of Political Economy*, Vol. 14 (1998).

'Inflationseinstellungen, Zentralbankunabhängigkeit und Inflation', in Bernhard Löffler (ed.), *Die kulturelle Seite der Währung. Europäische Währungskulturen, Geldwerterfahrungen und Notenbanksysteme im 20. Jahrhundert* (Munich, 2010).

Hentschel, V., *Ludwig Erhard. Ein Politikerleben* (Munich, 1996).

'Die Entstehung des Bundesbankgesetzes 1949–1957. Politische Kontroversen und Konflikte: Teil I', *Bankhistorisches Archiv*, Vol. 14 (1988).

'Die Entstehung des Bundesbankgesetzes 1949–1957. Politische Kontroversen und Konflikte: Teil II', *Bankhistorisches Archiv*, Vol. 14 (1988).

Herf, J., *Divided memory: the Nazi past in the two Germanys* (Cambridge, 1997).

Hildebrandt, D., *Was bleibt mir übrig. Anmerkungen zu (meinen) 30 Jahren Kabarett* (Munich, 1987).

Ich mußte immer lachen. Dieter Hildebrandt erzählt sein Leben (Cologne, 2006).

Hockerts, H. G. and G. Schulz (eds.), *Der 'Rheinische Kapitalismus' in der Ära Adenauer* (Paderborn, 2016).

von Hodenberg, C., *Konsens und Krise: eine Geschichte der westdeutschen Medienöffentlichkeit 1945–1973* (Göttingen, 2006).

'Mass media and the generation of conflict: West Germany's long sixties and the formation of a critical public sphere', *Contemporary European History*, Vol. 15, No. 3 (2006).

Holtfrerich, C.-L., *The German inflation, 1914–1923: causes and effects in international perspective* (Berlin, 1986).

'Relations between monetary authorities and governmental institutions: the case of Germany from the 19th century to the present', in Gianni Toniolo (ed.), *Central banks' independence in historical perspective* (Berlin, 1988).

'Monetary policy under fixed exchange rates (1948–70)', in Deutsche Bundesbank (ed.), *Fifty years of the Deutsche Mark: central bank and the currency in Germany since 1948* (Oxford, 1999).

'Monetary policy in Germany since 1948: national tradition, international best practice or ideology?', in Jean-Philippe Touffut (ed.), *Central banks as economic institutions* (Cheltenham, 2008).

van Hook, J. C., *Rebuilding Germany. The creation of the social market economy, 1945–1957* (Cambridge, 2004).

Horstmann, T., 'Kontinuität und Wandel im deutschen Notenbanksystem. Die Bank deutscher Länder als Ergebnis alliierter Besatzungspolitik nach dem Zweiten Weltkrieg', in Theo Pirker (ed.), *Autonomie und Kontrolle. Beiträge zur Soziologie des Finanz- und Steuerstaats* (Berlin, 1989).

'Die Entstehung der Bank deutscher Länder als geldpolitische Lenkungsinstanz in der Bundesrepublik Deutschland', in Hajo Riese and Heinz-Peter Spahn (eds.), *Geldpolitik und ökonomische Entwicklung. Ein Symposion* (Regensburg, 1990).

Die Alliierten und die deutschen Großbanken. Bankenpolitik nach dem Zweiten Weltkrieg in Deutschland (Bonn, 1991).

Howarth, D. and C. Rommerskirchen, 'A panacea for all times? The German stability culture as strategic political resource', *West European Politics*, Vol. 36 (2013).

'Inflation aversion in the European Union: exploring the myth of a North–South divide', *Socio-Economic Review*, Vol. 15, No. 2 (2017).

Issing, O., 'Central bank independence and monetary stability', *Institute of Economic Affairs Occasional Paper*, No. 89 (1993).

The birth of the euro (Cambridge, 2008).

Jacobsson, E. E., *A life for sound money: Per Jacobsson: his Biography* (Oxford, 1979).

James, H., *The German slump: politics and economics 1924–1936* (Oxford, 1986).

'Economic reasons for the collapse of Weimar', in Ian Kershaw (ed.), *Weimar: why did German Democracy Fail?* (London, 1990).

'The Reichsbank 1876–1945', in Deutsche Bundesbank (ed.), *Fifty years of the Deutsche Mark: central bank and the currency in Germany since 1948* (Oxford, 1999).

The Deutsche Bank and the Nazi economic war against the Jews: the expropriation of Jewish-owned property (Cambridge, 2001).

'Die D-Mark', in Etienne François and Hagen Schulze (eds.), *Deutsche Erinnerungsorte, Band II* (Munich, 2001).

'Karl-Otto Pöhl: the pole position', in Kenneth Dyson and Ivo Maes (eds.), *Architects of the euro. Intellectuals in the making of the European monetary union* (Oxford, 2016).

Jarausch, K. H. and M. Geyer, *Shattered past: reconstructing German histories* (Princeton, 2003).

Johnson, P. A., *The government of money: monetarism in Germany and the United States* (Ithaca, 1998).

Kaiser, R. H., *Bundesbankautonomie – Möglichkeiten und Grenzen einer unabhängigen Politik* (Frankfurt, 1980).

Kennedy, E., *The Bundesbank: Germany's central bank in the international monetary system* (London, 1991).

'The Bundesbank', *German Issues*, Vol. 19 (1998).

Keynes, J. M., *The economic consequences of the peace* (London, 1919).

Kitterer, W., 'Public finance and the central bank', in Deutsche Bundesbank (ed.), *Fifty years of the Deutsche Mark: central bank and the currency in Germany since 1948* (Oxford, 1999).

Klasen, K., 'Vorwort', in Deutsche Bundesbank (ed.), *Währung und Wirtschaft in Deutschland, 1876–1975* (Frankfurt am Main, 1976).

Koerfer, D., *Kampf ums Kanzleramt: Adenauer und Erhard* (Stuttgart, 1987).

Kohut, T. A., *A German generation: an experiential history of the twentieth century* (London, 2012).

Kolb, E., *The Weimar republic* (London, 1988).

Könneker, W., *Die Deutsche Bundesbank* (Frankfurt, 1967).

Die Deutsche Bundesbank, 2nd ed. (Frankfurt, 1973).

Kopper, C., *Bankiers unterm Hakenkreuz* (Munich, 2008).

Hjalmar Schacht. Aufstieg und Fall von Hitlers mächtigstem Bankier (Munich, 2010).

Kramer, A., *The West German economy, 1945–1955* (Oxford 1991)

Krieghoff, N. F., 'Banking regulation in a federal system: lessons from American and German banking history', doctoral thesis, the London School of Economics and Political Science (2013).

Kritz, M. A., 'Central banks and the state today', *The American Economic Review*, Vol. 38, No. 4 (1948).

von Kruedener, J. F., 'Die Entstehung des Inflationstraumas. Zur Sozialpsychologie der deutschen Hyperinflation 1922/23', in Gerald D. Feldman (ed.), *Konsequenzen der Inflation* (Berlin, 1989).

Lamfalussy, C., I. Maes and S. Péters, *Alexandre Lamfalussy: the wise man of the euro* (Leuven, 2013).

Leaman, J., *The Bundesbank myth: towards a critique of central bank independence* (London, 2001).

Lemke, M., 'Kampagnen gegen Bonn. Die Systemkrise der DDR und die West-Propaganda der SED 1960–1963', *Vierteljahrshefte für Zeitgeschichte*, 41. Jahrg. 2. H. (Apr., 1993).

Lindenlaub, D., 'Review: "Die Bundesbank: Geschäfte mit der Macht" by David Marsh', *Vierteljahrschrift für Sozial-und Wirtschaftsgeschichte*, Vol. 81, No. 3 (1994).

'Karl Blessing', in Hans Pohl (ed.), *Deutsche Bankiers des 20. Jahrhunderts* (Stuttgart, 2008).

'Deutsches Stabilitätsbewußtsein: Wie kann man es fassen, Wie kann man es erklären, welche Bedeutung hat es für die Geldpolitik', in Bernhard Löffler (ed.), *Die kulturelle Seite der Währung. Europäische Währungskulturen, Geldwerterfahrungen und Notenbanksysteme im 20. Jahrhundert* (Munich, 2010).

'Die Errichtung der Bank deutscher Länder und die Währungsreform von 1948: Die Begründung einer stabilitätsorientierten Geldpolitik', in Dieter Lindenlaub, Carsten Burhop and Joachim Scholtyseck (eds.), *Schlüsselereignisse der deutschen Bankengeschichte* (Stuttgart, 2013).

von der Lippe, V., *Nürnberger Tagebuchnotizen: November 1945 bis Oktober 1946* (Frankfurt, 1951).

Löffler, B., 'Währungsrecht, Bundesbank und deutsche "Stabilitätskultur" nach 1945. Überlegungen zu mentalitätsgeschichtlichen Dimensionen normativ-institutioneller Regelungen', in Manfred Seifert and Winfried Helm (eds.), *Recht und Religion im Alltagsleben. Perspektiven der Kulturforschung. Festschrift für Walter Hartinger zum 65. Geburtstag* (Passau, 2005).

'Währungsgeschichte als Kulturgeschichte? Konzeptionelle Leitlinien und analytische Probleme kulturhistorischer Ansätze auf wirtschafts- und währungsgeschichtlichem Feld', in Bernhard Löffler (ed.), *Die kulturelle Seite der Währung. Europäische Währungskulturen, Geldwerterfahrungen und Notenbanksysteme im 20. Jahrhundert* (Munich, 2010).

(ed.), *Die kulturelle Seite der Währung. Europäische Währungskulturen, Geldwerterfahrungen und Notenbanksysteme im 20. Jahrhundert* (Munich, 2010).

Ludwig-Erhard-Stiftung, *Die Korea-Krise als ordnungspolitische Herausforderung der deutschen Wirtschaftspolitik. Texte und Dokumente* (Stuttgart, 1986).

Luther, H., *Vor dem Abgrund, 1930–33. Reichsbankpräsident in Krisenzeiten* (Berlin, 1964).

MacGregor, N., *Germany: memories of a nation* (London, 2014).

McNamara, K. R., *The currency of ideas: monetary politics in the European Union* (Ithaca, 1998).

Marsh, D., *The Bundesbank: the bank that rules Europe* (London, 1992).

The euro: the battle for the new global currency (Southampton, 2011).

Moeller, R., *Protecting motherhood: women and the family in the politics of postwar West Germany* (Berkeley, 1993).

War stories: the search for a usable past in the Federal Republic of Germany (Berkeley, 2001).

(ed.), *West Germany under construction: politics, society, and culture in the Adenauer era* (Ann Arbor, 1997).

Mombauer, A., *Helmuth von Moltke and the origins of the First World War* (Cambridge, 2001).

Mühlen, N., *Hitler's magician: Schacht: the life and loans of Dr. Hjalmar Schacht*, trans. E. W. Dickes (London, 1938).

Müller, H., *Die Zentralbank – eine Nebenregierung: Reichsbankpräsident Hjalmar Schacht als Politiker der Weimarer Republik* (Opladen, 1973).

Münkel, D., 'Politiker-Image und Wahlkampf. Das Beispiel Willy Brandt: Vom deutschen Kennedy zum deutschen Helden', in Bernd Weisbrod (ed.), *Die Politik der Öffentlichkeit – die Öffentlichkeit der Politik: politische Medialisierung in der Geschichte der Bundesrepublik* (Göttingen, 2003).

Muthesius, V., *Die Zukunft der D-Mark* (Frankfurt, 1950).

'Wilhelm Vocke', in Wilhelm Vocke, *Gesundes Geld* (Frankfurt am Main, 1956).

'Vorwort', in Karl Blessing, *Die Verteidigung des Geldwertes* (Frankfurt am Main, 1960).

Augenzeuge von drei Inflationen. Erinnerungen und Gedanken eines Wirtschaftspublizisten (Frankfurt am Main, 1973).

National Monetary Commission, United States Senate, *The Reichsbank, 1876–1900* (Washington, 1910).

Neumann, M. J. M., 'Monetary stability: threat and proven response', in Deutsche Bundesbank (ed.), *Fifty years of the Deutsche Mark: central bank and the currency in Germany since 1948* (Oxford, 1999).

Nicholls, A. J., *Freedom with responsibility: the social market economy in Germany, 1918–1963* (Oxford, 1994).

Noelle-Neumann, E., 'Geldwert und öffentliche Meinung: Anmerkungen zur "Psychologie der Inflation"', in Clemens-August Andreae, Karl-Heinrich Hansmeyer, Gerhard Scherhorn (eds.), *Geldtheorie und Geldpolitik: Günter Schmölders zum 65. Geburtstag* (Berlin, 1968).

Noelle, E. and E. P. Neumann (eds.), *Jahrbuch der öffentlichen Meinung, 1947–1955* (Allensbach, 1956).

Obstfeld, M. and A. M. Taylor, *Global capital markets: integration, crisis, and growth* (Cambridge, 2004).

Overy, R. J., *War and economy in the Third Reich* (Oxford, 1994).

Peterson, E. N., *Hjalmar Schacht for and against Hitler: a political–economic study of Germany 1923–1945* (Boston, 1954).

Pfleiderer, O., 'Die Reichsbank in der Zeit der großen Inflation, die Stabilisierung der Mark und die Aufwertung von Kapitalforderungen', in Deutsche Bundesbank (ed.), *Währung und Wirtschaft in Deutschland 1876–1975* (Frankfurt am Main, 1976).

'Die beiden großen Inflationen unseres Jahrhunderts und ihre Beendigung', in Peter Hampe (ed.), *Währungsreform und Soziale Marktwirtschaft: Rückblicke und Ausblicke* (Munich, 1989).

Poiger, U. G., *Jazz, rock, and rebels: cold war politics and American culture in a divided Germany* (London, 2000).

Potthoff, H. and S. Miller, *Kleine Geschichte der SPD 1848–2002* (Bonn, 2002).

Pöttker, H., 'Zwischen Politik und publizistischer Professionalität', in Jürgen Wilke (ed.), *Massenmedien und Zeitgeschichte* (Konstanz, 1999).

Reichsbank, *Schacht in seinen Äusserungen: Im Auftrage des Reichsbankdirektoriums zusammengestellt in der Volkswirtschaftlichen und Statistischen Abt. der Reichsbank. Zum Januar 1937* (Berlin, 1937).

Reinhardt, S., *Die Reichsbank in der Weimarer Republik. Eine Analyse der formalen und faktischen Unabhängigkeit* (Frankfurt am Main, 2000).

Richter, R., 'Stabilitätskultur als Problem der Institutionen-Ökonomik', in Helmut Hesse and Otmar Issing (eds.), *Geld und Moral* (Munich, 1994).

Robert, R., *Die Unabhängigkeit der Bundesbank: Analyse und Materialien* (Kronberg im Taunus, 1978).

Roeper, H., *Die D-Mark: Vom Besatzungskind zum Weltstar* (Frankfurt, 1978).

Rogoff, K., 'The optimal degree of commitment to an intermediate monetary target', *Quarterly Journal of Economics*, Vol. 100, No. 4 (1985).

Sargent, T. J., 'The demand for money during hyperinflations under rational expectations: 1', *International Economic Review*, Vol. 18, No. 1 (1977).

Sargent, T. J. and N. Wallace, 'Expectations and the dynamics of hyperinflation', *International Economic Review*, Vol. 14, No. 2 (1973).

Schacht, H., *Die Stabilisierung der Mark* (Stuttgart, 1926).

Das Ende der Reparationen (Oldenburg, 1931).

Abrechnung mit Hitler (Hamburg, 1948).

76 Jahre meines Lebens (Bad Wörishofen, 1953).

My first seventy-six years, trans. Diana Pyke (London, 1955).

The magic of money, trans. Paul Erskine (London, 1967).

Schildt, A., *Moderne Zeiten: Freizeit, Massenmedien und 'Zeitgeist' in der Bundesrepublik der 50er Jahre* (Hamburg, 1995).

Schildt, A. and A. Sywottek (eds.), *Modernisierung im Wiederaufbau: Die west-deutsche Gesellschaft der 50er Jahre* (Bonn, 1993).

Schildt, A. and D. Siegfried, *Deutsche Kulturgeschichte. Die Bundesrepublik von 1945 bis zur Gegenwart* (Munich, 2009).

Schissler, H. (ed.), *The miracle years: a cultural history of West Germany, 1949–1968* (Princeton, 2001).

Schmidt, H., *Men and powers: a political retrospective*, trans. Ruth Hein (New York, 1989).

Scholtyseck, J., 'Hjalmar Schacht', in Hans Pohl (ed.), *Deutsche Bankiers des 20. Jahrhunderts* (Stuttgart, 2008).

Schulz, G., 'Inflationstrauma, Finanzpolitik und Krisenbekämpfung in den Jahren der Wirtschaftskrise, 1930–33', in Gerald D. Feldman (ed.), *Die Nachwirkungen der Inflation auf die deutsche Geschichte 1924–1933* (Munich, 1985).

Schwarz, H.-P., *Die Ära Adenauer. Gründerjahre der Republik. 1949–1957 (Geschichte der Bundesrepublik Deutschland, Band 2)* (Stuttgart, 1981).

Singleton, J., *Central banking in the twentieth century* (Cambridge, 2011).

Spicka, M. E., *Selling the economic miracle: economic reconstruction and politics in West Germany, 1949–1957* (Oxford, 2007).

von Spindler, J., W. Becker and O. E. Starke, *Die Deutsche Bundesbank: Grund-züge des Notenbankwesens und Kommentar zum Gesetz über die Deutsche Bun-desbank* (Stuttgart, 1969).

Stiftung Haus der Geschichte der Bundesrepublik Deutschland (ed.), *Spass beiseite. Humor und Politik in Deutschland* (Leipzig, 2010).

Taylor, F., *The downfall of money: Germany's hyperinflation and the destruction of the middle class* (London, 2013).

Thelwall, W. F., *General report on the industrial and economic situation in Germany in December, 1920 (Department of Overseas Trade)* (London, 1921).

Tietmeyer, H., 'The role of an independent central bank in Europe', in Patrick Downes and Reza Vaez-Zadeh (eds.), *The evolving role of central banks*, International Monetary Fund (Washington, DC, 1991).

'The Bundesbank: committed to stability', in Stephen F. Frowen and Robert Pringle (eds.), *Inside the Bundesbank* (Basingstoke, 1998).

Tognato, C., *Central bank independence: cultural codes and symbolic performance* (New York, 2012).

Tomann, H., *Monetary integration in Europe* (Basingstoke, 2007).

Tooze, A. J., *The wages of destruction: the making and breaking of the Nazi economy* (London, 2007).

Tucker, P., *Unelected power: the quest for legitimacy in central banking and the regulatory state* (Princeton, 2018).

Vocke, W., *Gesundes Geld* (Frankfurt, 1956).

'Adenauer und die Wirtschaft', in Hans-Joachim Netzer (ed.), *Adenauer und die Folgen: Siebzehn Vorträge über Probleme unseres Staates* (Munich, 1965).

Memoiren (Stuttgart, 1973).

Vogel, J., 'Die Pickelhaube', in Etienne François and Hagen Schulze (eds.), *Deutsche Erinnerungsorte, Band II* (Munich, 2001).

Wahlig, B., 'Relations between the Bundesbank and the Federal Government', in Stephen F. Frowen and Robert Pringle (eds.), *Inside the Bundesbank* (Basingstoke, 1998).

Wallich, H. C., *Mainsprings of the German revival* (New Haven, 1955).

Wandel, E., *Die Entstehung der Bank deutscher Länder und die deutsche Währungsreform 1948* (Frankfurt, 1980).

Weick, A., *Homburger Plan und Währungsreform: kritische Analyse des Währungsreformplans der Sonderstelle Geld und Kredit und seiner Bedeutung für die westdeutsche Währungsreform von 1948* (St. Katharinen, 1998).

Weisbrod, B. (ed.), *Die Politik der Öffentlichkeit – die Öffentlichkeit der Politik: politische Medialisierung in der Geschichte der Bundesrepublik* (Göttingen, 2003).

Weiß, M., 'Journalisten: Worte als Taten', in Norbert Frei (ed.), *Karrieren im Zwielicht. Hitlers Eliten nach 1945* (Frankfurt, 2001).

Wiesen, S. J., *West German industry and the challenge of the Nazi past, 1945–1955* (London, 2001).

Williams, C., *Adenauer: the father of the new Germany* (London, 2000).

Wolz, C. N., *Konflikte zwischen der Notenbank und der Regierung in der Bundesrepublik Deutschland 1956–1961* (Stuttgart, 2009).

Zatlin, J. R., *The currency of socialism: money and political culture in East Germany* (New York, 2007).

Ziegler, D., 'Die Entstehung der Reichsbank 1875', in Dieter Lindenlaub, Carsten Burhop and Joachim Scholtyseck (eds.), *Schlüsselereignisse der deutschen Bankengeschichte* (Stuttgart, 2013).

Index

20 July group, 81, 219, 221, 223, 225–7, 250

Abs, Hermann Josef, 103, 259
Adenauer, Konrad, 16, 27, 118, 120–2, 124, 127, 137–8, 140–1, 144–5, 150, 155, 158–9, 164–5, 167, 169–70, 174–5, 183, 187, 198, 221, 249, 262, 312, 319, 321, 323
  criticism of the Bank deutscher Länder, 142, 150, 166, 173–4, 176, 184, 187, 298
  Gürzenich affair, 25, 30, 151, 153, 175–7, 179–81, 183–4, 199, 280, 319
  Kanzlerdemokratie, 16, 159, 298, 319
  opposition to central bank independence, 11, 16, 125, 136, 142, 148, 151, 167, 173, 177, 184, 189, 254
  sovereignty, 15–16, 319
  strained relations with Ludwig Erhard, 170, 181
Aktuell (magazine), 201
Allied Banking Commission (ABC), 96, 99, 102–3, 109, 111–12, 121–4, 145–6
  ability to veto central bank council decisions, 111
Allied High Commission, 144
Allied Reparation Commission (ARC), 47
Allies (First World War), 46–7, 52, 59, 61
Allies (Second World War), 33–4, 79, 82, 95, 147, 149
Allies (western), 11–12, 17, 28, 30, 90, 92, 95, 99, 101, 135–6, 148–9, 151, 172, 189, 259, 310, 317, 319
Andriessen, Frans, 325
anniversaries, monetary, 32, 257–8, 302–5, 307, 309, 322
Anti-cartel Law, 155, 187
Association of German Savings Banks and Giro Institutions (Arbeitsgemeinschaft Deutscher

Sparkassen- und Giroverbändes und Girozentralen), 133
Auschwitz, 229, 300
Austria, 45, 116

balance of payments, 46–7, 135
Bank deutscher Länder (BdL), 11–12, 14, 17–18, 25, *51*, 64, 77, 85, 88, 92, 94, 101, *106*, 110, 118, 169, 252, 267, 278, 317–18, 321
  and the 'Becket' effect, 107
  balance of payments crisis, 135
  Bank deutscher Länder Law of 1948, 96
  becoming obliged to support the general economic policy of the government, 146
  central bank council, 11, 96–7, 102, 105, 150, 154–5, 174–6, 278
  communication channel, 109, 131, 162
  continuity with the Bundesbank, 196, 199, 251
  continuity with the Reichsbank, 14, 103–4, 148, 196, 201, 255, 268, 306–8, 320
  counterproposal to Bundesbank Law draft of the finance ministry in early 1950, 125
  counterproposal to Bundesbank Law draft of the finance ministry in late 1950, 138
  criticism of government economic policy, 190
  discussions with the Bundesverband der Deutschen Industrie, 171
  embracing the inter-war record of Wilhelm Vocke, 15, 115, 148, 160, 179–80, 191, 268, 321
  establishment of, 10–11, 30, 46, 90, 94–5, 149, 154, 179, 305
  first emergence of its name, 99
  growing public profile of, 161, 169, 190
  Gürzenich affair, 25, 30

influencing the Bundesbank Law debate, 18, 92, 94, 126–8, 130, 148, 197, 318
Korean crisis, 141
legal uncertainty in the early post-war years, 94, 108–9, 111, 119, 121, 124, 127, 136, 162, 318
opinions of West German elites prior to the establishment of, 30, 96–7
political attacks on, 108, 113, 120, 130, 139, 150, 163, 171, 184
press department, 108, 110, 115, 141, 162, 173, 203
press policy, 30, 109, 111, 133, 162, 172
reports
annual, 162
monthly, 110, 143, 162, 165
subject to instructions by the Allies, 11, 96, 161
task force on the Bundesbank Law, 120
tightening monetary policy, 142, 165–6, 171, 173–4, 176, 278, 280, 298
Bank for International Settlements (BIS), 59, 61, 78, 325
Bank of England, 23, 39, 44, 52, 57, 59, 91, 99, 102, 105, 111, 132–3, 267, 305
Bank of France, 91, 99, 132–3
Bank of Hungary, 100
Baranyai, Leopold, 100
Bardepot, 281
Baumgarten, Hans, 131
Bavaria Party, 146
Becket effect, 107
Belgium, 48, 54
Benning, Bernard, 103
Berg, Fritz, 166, 170–1, 177, 191
Berliner Börsen Zeitung (newspaper), 56
Berliner Börsen-Courier (newspaper), 56
Berliner Handels-Gesellschaft, 228
Berliner Tageblatt (newspaper), 56
Bernard, Karl, 103–4, 107, 109, 111, 113–14, 118, 120, 138–9, 142, 145, 147, 151–2, 154–5, 160–1, 170, 174–5, 186, 199, 279
Bernhuber, Maximilian, 229
Bild (newspaper), 1, 316
interview with Mario Draghi, 1, 4, 7, 22, 314
interview with Wilhelm Vocke, 179
Blessing, Karl, 19, 21, 31, 35, 201, 214, 216–17, 219, 221, 249, 251–3, 256, 262–3, 269, 271, 289, 308, 311, 323
and 20 July group, 81, 198, 219, 221, 223, 225–7, 250
arrival at the Bundesbank, 198–9, 201, 251
attitude regarding the media, 57, 59, 199, 208–9, 249, 264
attitude towards National Socialism, 78–9, 81, 198
background, 44, 78, 254–5, 268, 270
Bundesbank press department coming under the jurisdiction of, 202
circle of friends (Freundeskreis), 20, 31, 79–80, 86, 88, 192–4, 196, 198, 218, 220–1, 223, 227–30, 250–1, 322
short comprehensive summary, 21, 195, 224–6, 228–9, 250, 322
concentration camps, 80
concern about the Social Democratic Party, 251
Continental Oil, 81
departure from the Bundesbank, 252, 254, 270
departure from the Reichsbank, 76, 79–80, 85–6, 225, 308–9
financial persecution of Jews in the Third Reich, 78
fixed exchange rate, 257, 269–70
and Fritz Knapp Verlag, 208
Gestapo interrogation, 80
gold standard, 39, 244–5
and Hjalmar Schacht, 19, 45, 57, 79, 88, 196, 201, 211–12, 215, 217, 220, 231, 321
Im Kampf um gutes Geld (book), 249
Kreisau Circle (Kreisauer Kreis), 81
and Ludwig Erhard, 247
Margarine-Union, 79
Nuremberg trials, 21, 80–1, 86, 193, 219, 223, 226
participation in the 1938 conference, 78, 81, 198, 218
portrayed as 'president of the deutschmark', 20, 200, 320
as the public face of the Bundesbank, 35, 194, 196, 199, 209, 234, 320
Reichsbank advisory council, 79, 215
Reichsbank memorandum, 19, 73, 74, 76, 81, 194–5, 198–9, 218, 224, 250
seeking co-operation with the government, 263
signature on banknotes, 221, 308
speeches, 208–9, 231, 240–8
third inflation, 231–3, 243
Verteidigung des Goldwertes, Die (book), 208
and Wilhelm Vocke, 267
Young Plan, 59
Blessing, Oscar, 233
Boden, Wilhelm, 102, 120
Brandt, Willy, 198, 234, 254, 262, 283

Braunbuch (book), 220
Brawand, Leo, 116
Bretton Woods, 238–9, 269, 290, 299
Brinkmann, Rudolf, 77
Brüning, Heinrich, 27, 65–7, 132, 140, 172
Bundesbank, 5, 9, 11, 19, 21–2, 29, 59, 64, 75, 81, 87–8, 102, 204, 220, 255, 273–4, 278, 281, 289, 315–16, 318, 322, 324, 326, 329–30
  accused of forcing Karl Schiller's resignation, 284–5
  accused of toppling Ludwig Erhard's government, 208, 248, 277
  Bundesbank Law of 1957, 5, 9–10, 12–13, 17–18, 24, 30–1, 150, 183–4, 191, 197, 199, 232, 238, 240, 248, 254–5, 259, 261, 270, 277, 279, 282, 284–7, 293, 297, 300, 309, 312, 317–19, 323, 326, 331
    advisory board (*Beirat*), 125, 137, 166, 169, 172
    arbitration committee, 125–6, 137, 144, 189, 191, 263, 294–5, 320
    debate as to whether it should be a decentralised or centralised institution, 10, 90, 152–5, 157, 175, 187
    debate influenced by the business cycle, 94, 108, 153
    entrenching a power struggle, 11, 26, 28, 30, 32, 93, 147, 151–2, 155, 189, 312, 317, 319
    first draft of, 123
    inflation narratives, 25, 31
    and Konrad Adenauer's *Kanzlerdemokratie*, 16
    ministerial responsibility over, 121, 154, 296
    Munich conference in 1950, 90
    Novellierung debate of 1973, 26, 255, 257, 281, 288–9, 291–4, 296–7, 300–1, 312, 323
    outline of, 187–9, 191
    passage through parliament, 187
    seen by politicians as a means of asserting federal influence over the central bank, 11, 119, 154, 188
    and the Social Democratic Party economics committee, 175
    as a subject of debate, 8, 11, 18, 35, 91, 93–4, 104–5, 117, 119, 123, 126, 130, 133, 135, 140–1, 144, 150, 155, 168, 171
    supporting the general economic policy of government, 53
  total number of drafts of, 119
  and the West German constitution, 9
  central bank council, 188, 199, 234, 298–9, 301, 327–8
  communication channel, 258, 271
  continuity with the Bank deutscher Länder, 196, 199, 201, 251, 309
  continuity with the Reichsbank, 14, 19, 31, 196, 201, 251, 255, 257, 268, 306–8, 311, 320
  engaging with the media, 32, 196, 209, 213, 239, 249, 256, 267, 287–8, 298, 309, 311–12, 323, 326, 331
  European Monetary System, 299–301
  headquarters as 'symbol of the stability culture', 24
  as a model for the European Central Bank, 2, 4, 327–31
  post-war success of, 2
  press department, 21, 192, 195–7, 201–3, 207, 209, 218, 223, 228–30, 249, 271
  press policy, 198, 204–5, 249
  reports
    annual, 202–3, 209
    monthly, 202–5, 208–9, 285–7, 312, 323
  sovereign bond purchases, 4
  Stunde Null, 14, 320
  tightening monetary policy, 247, 254, 275–7
  Transition Law of 1951, 94, 146–8, 150, 152–3, 161, 190, 304, 318
  Währung und Wirtschaft in Deutschland 1876-1975 (book), 307
Bundesrat, 36, 38, 119, 136–8, 155
Bundestag, 29, 91, 95, 119, 139–40, 152–3, 155, 157, 161, 170, 183, 294
Bundesverband der Deutschen Industrie (BDI), 29, 140, 153, 166, 169–72, 176, 191
Burkhardt, Otto, 102, 120
Bütefisch, Heinrich, 192

cabaret, 20, 192–3, 195, 223, 227, 250
Carter, Jimmy, 275
central bank independence, 7, 17–18, 21, 23, 30, 34, 45, 75, 84, 87, 132, 153, 181, 246, 248, 254, 257, 261, 274, 280, 287, 293–4, 302, 304, 318, 323, 329, 331
  consensus fracturing since global finance crisis, 22
  inflation narratives being used in support of, 8–9, 24–5, 92, 124, 126, 129, 134, 145–6, 158, 168–9, 177, 185–6, 191, 197, 233, 246–7, 251, 286, 320

League of Nations as an active supporter
    of, 45
popularity in the 1920s, 63
popularity in the 1980s and 1990s, 21
populist attacks on, 22
public opinion surveys on, 29, 127
West German elites split on the question
    of, 7, 30, 97, 99, 101, 154, 175
Christian Democratic Union (CDU), 108,
    115, 138–9, 155, 185, 198, 232, 237,
    257, 278
Christian Social Union (CSU), 121, 154–5,
    234, 237, 285, 292
Co-determination Law, 141
Cold War, 20, 135, 158, 220, 222, 224, 250
Committee of governors of the central
    banks of the European Economic
    Community, 325, 328–9
Conrad, Henry, 112
Continental Oil (Kontinentale Öl-
    Aktiengesellschaft), 80, 86, 88
Credit Law of 1961, 155, 187
Currency Office (*Währungsamt*),
    98
Czechoslovakia, 74

Darmstädter and National Bank, 54
Dawes Plan, 52, 59, 91
deflation, 6, 8, 13, 15, 67, 87, 101, 108,
    113–14, 135, 157, 171, 212, 332
Dehler, Thomas, 138, 154, 156
Delors Committee, 325–9
Delors, Jacques, 325–7
Delors Report, 328–9
Deutsche Bank, 36, 103, 258–9
Deutsche Demokratische Partei, 57
Deutsche Hochschullehrer-Zeitung (journal),
    215
Deutsche Presse-Agentur, 303
Deutsche Verkehrs-Kredit-Bank, 303
Deutsche Volkswirt, Der (magazine), 56
Deutscher Gewerkschaftsbund (German
    Trade Union Confederation), 141,
    276, 292–3
Deutscher Industrie- und
    Handelskammertag (German
    Chamber of Commerce and
    Industry), 275
*Deutscher Reichsanzeiger und Preussischer
    Staatsanzeiger* (publication), 225,
    227
Deutsches Allgemeines Sonntagsblatt
    (newspaper), 286
Deutschland Report (book), 20, 192, 194,
    221–2, 224, 226–7, 229, 250, 308

deutschmark (currency), 12, 14–17, 20–1,
    32, 95, 105–7, 115, 117, 121, 128,
    134, 146, 149, 152, 161, 163, 169,
    177, 179, 181, 193–4, 196–7, 199,
    204, 211, 213, 220–1, 223, 231, 233,
    235, 238, 243, 246–8, 251, 257,
    268–70, 280–1, 283, 290–1, 297,
    300, 303–6, 308–11, 313, 316,
    319–20, 330
Di Maio, Luigi, 22
Dix, Rudolf, 82–4
dollar (currency), 54, 238, 269, 273, 299
Dossier, Das (publication), 194, 218–19, 221
Draghi, Mario, 1–5, 22, 314–16, 331–2
Dresdner Bank, 54
Dreyse, Ernst, 75
Duisenberg, Wim, 326, 330
Economic Council (Wirtschaftsrat), 95,
    108, 115

Economist, The (magazine), 4, 165
Ehmke, Horst, 282
Ehrenberg, Herbert, 293–6, 301, 323
Eicke, Rudolf, 75
Eiserne Front, 258
Emminger, Otmar, 239, 244, 256–7, 265,
    266, 268, 270, 273–6, 282, 306–7,
    310
    arrival at the Bank deutscher Länder,
        265, 267, 269
    attitude regarding central bank
        independence, 142, 287, 291
    attitude regarding the media, 264–5, 267,
        271, 273
    background, 255, 264, 268, 270
    becoming president of the Bundesbank,
        265
    becoming vice president of the
        Bundesbank, 265
    distancing the Bundesbank from the
        Reichsbank, 269, 311, 322
    on Helmut Schmidt's party report of May
        1974, 298
    international reputation, 265
    on Karl Schiller, 284
    memoirs, 267, 311
    personality, 265
    as the public face of the Bundesbank,
        257–8, 267–8, 322
    speeches, 249, 265, 310 11
    and Wilhelm Vocke, 70, 115, 213, 216,
        305
employment, 10, 69, 72, 163, 168, 186,
    252, 277, 279, 292
Enabling Act of 1933, 296

Engelmann, Bernt, 221–2, 227, 229, 250, 308
Erhard, Ludwig, 17, 107, 112, 124, 141–2, 166, 170, 173, 183, 187, 198, 208, 219–20, 247, 305, 310
    attitude regarding central bank independence, 25, 98, 100, 118, 122, 153, 156, 185, 189, 191, 263
    balance of payments crisis, 135
    clash with Fritz Schäffer, 121–2, 154, 156, 263
    Gürzenich affair, 25, 177
    Konjunkturrat, 170, 173, 176
    Sonderstelle für Geld und Kredit (Special Committee for Money and Credit), 98, 100
    strained relations with Konrad Adenauer, 170, 181
    support for a centralised central bank, 123, 133, 138, 152, 154
    Wohlstand für Alle (book), 16
Eucken, Walter, 100
euro (currency), 22, 313–14, 316, 330
Euromoney (publication), 243
European Central Bank (ECB), 1–2, 4–5, 7, 313–17, 324–30, 332
European Commission, 22, 325
European Council, 325, 328
European Monetary Institute (EMI), 329
European Monetary System (EMS), 299–300, 324
European Payments Union (EPU), 135–6
Expert Commission 'Länder Union Bank' (Sachverständigen-Kommission 'Länder Union Bank'), 99

Federal Republic of Germany (West Germany), 7, 9, 11, 14, 18, 20, 26, 94, 101, 113, 117, 119–20, 127, 132, 140, 143, 151, 158, 175, 190, 193–4, 211–12, 218–21, 233, 252, 262–3, 278, 286–7, 308, 317, 319–20, 327, 331
Federal Reserve System, 9, 22, 57, 91, 95, 99, 132, 134, 152
Financial Times (newspaper), 23, 177, 315
First World War, 6, 40, 43–4, 54–5, 61
Flemming, Karl Otto, 234
Flick, Friedrich, 86, 192–3, 218–19, 223, 226
Foreign Trade Law of 1961, 282–3
Four Year Plan, 69, 225
France, 33, 36, 38, 48, 150, 281–2, 325
Franco-Prussian War, 1, 36, 40, 163

Frankfurter Allgemeine Zeitung (newspaper), 114, 131, 172, 186, 214, 217, 232, 296, 310, 316, 321
Frankfurter Rundschau (newspaper), 129, 195, 199, 227, 229
Free Democratic Party (FDP), 131, 155–7, 237, 254, 257, 276, 278, 295–6, 323
Friderichs, Hans, 296–7
Fritz Knapp Verlag, 180, 207–8, 249, 307
Funk, Walther, 81

Garbo, Greta, 180
Genscher, Hans-Dietrich, 325
German Democratic Republic (East Germany), 20, 194, 219–21, 224, 230
Germany, 1–2, 4–6, 8, 12–13, 16, 22, 24, 26–8, 33–8, 40–4, 46–50, 52–4, 59, 61, 63, 65–6, 69, 74, 77–8, 80–1, 86–7, 91–3, 95–6, 99–100, 102, 108, 124, 126, 129, 134, 137, 145, 147, 149, 157, 164, 168–9, 184, 186, 191, 197–8, 219, 233, 242, 251, 258, 272, 274, 294, 303–4, 310, 312, 316–18, 320, 323, 325, 332
    experience of two inflations, 3, 5, 7–9, 16, 18, 25–6, 31, 92, 100, 124, 126, 133–4, 143, 145, 147, 153, 156–9, 163, 168, 177, 179, 184, 190, 197, 201, 231, 240, 243, 246, 252–3, 255, 272, 274–5, 286, 289, 294, 296, 312, 326–7, 330
Gestapo (Geheime Staatspolizei), 80
Giscard d'Estaing, Valéry, 299
global financial crisis, 22, 330, 332
Globke, Hans, 173
Goebbels, Joseph, 78, 221
Gold Discount Bank, 50
gold standard, 6, 36–7, 39–40, 43, 45, 65, 141, 198, 240, 244–6, 256, 264
gold-exchange standard, 53
Göring, Hermann, 69, 80, 221, 225
Grasmann, Max, 102
Great Britain, 38, 40, 66, 150
Great Depression, 6, 10, 18, 34, 94, 135, 148, 153, 171, 184, 191, 248, 252, 295, 304, 324, 332
Grotkopp, Wilhelm, 130–1
Gürzenich affair, 25–6, 30, 151–2, 176–7, 181, 183–4, 191, 199, 280, 319

Haffner, Sebastian, 48–9
Hamburger Abendblatt (newspaper), 207
Handelsblatt (newspaper), 163, 293
Hartlieb, Heinrich, 216
Havenstein, Rudolf, 44, 47–9, 54–6, 65, 87, 146

Hayek, Friedrich, 264
Helfferich, Karl, 41, 46, 54, 87
Henckel, Hans, 133, 171
Henry II, 107
Heydrich, Reinhard, 78, 225
Hildebrandt, Dieter, 222
Hilferding, Rudolf, 62
Himmler, Heinrich, 20–1, 31, 79–81, 86,
    88, 192–4, 196, 198, 211, 218, 221,
    224–7, 229–30, 250, 322
Hinckel, Eugen Christian, 102
Hitler, Adolf, 4, 13, 15, 28, 34, 68–9, 72,
    76, 81–4, 127, 134, 211, 214–15,
    217, 230, 232, 258, 321
  20 July group assassination attempt, 81,
    198, 219, 225, 227, 250
  appointing Hjalmar Schacht as
    Reichsbank president, 68
  ascent to the chancellery, 6, 34, 68, 156,
    252, 273
  benefiting from Hjalmar Schacht's
    support during the Weimar
    Republic, 63
  confidence in Hjalmar Schacht, 69
  Enabling Act of 1933, 296
  Four Year Plan, 69
  Mefo bills, 15, 70, 160, 216
  Reichsbank memorandum, 14, 19, 72–6,
    81, 83–6, 115, 159, 179–80, 182,
    194, 198–9, 224–6, 268, 308
  removing Hjalmar Schacht from the
    Reichsbank, 34
  second inflation known as the 'Hitler
    inflation', 274
  Young Plan, 62
Höcherl, Hermann, 292
Holocaust, 300
Homburg Plan, 98
Höpker-Aschoff, Hermann, 131
Hülse, Ernst, 73, 75, 82, 102
Hungary, 45

IG Farben, 192, 220
IG Metall, 276, 301
Industriekurier (newspaper), 131,
    212
inflation, 2, 4–5, 12–14, 18, 21–2, 24, 27–9,
    31, 42–4, 47–50, 66–7, 86, 99,
    112–13, 126, 129, 131, 143, 146–7,
    151, 153, 163–4, 166–8, 175, 197,
    214–15, 217, 231, 233, 238–9,
    245–8, 251–2, 254, 257, 274–6, 281,
    290, 298, 303–6, 312, 314, 316, 320,
    322, 330
  1948 inflation, 107, 112

hyperinflation
  Austria, 27
  Germany, 3–6, 8–9, 15, 27, 34, 42,
    48–50, 52, 65, 67, 72, 87, 101, 108,
    114, 143, 175, 179, 233, 243, 246,
    257, 272–5, 286, 295, 302, 304, 317,
    321, 323, 326, 330–2
  Hungary, 28
  Poland, 27
  Russia, 27
imported inflation, 197, 235, 238–9, 268
second inflation, 4, 8, 20, 71, 79, 108,
    134, 146, 159, 196, 211, 215, 217,
    231–3, 246, 274, 286, 295–6, 306,
    321, 323, 330
third inflation, 20, 31, 197, 211, 230–5,
    239, 243, 251, 322
trauma, 4–5, 18, 27–8, 66–7, 151, 190,
    201, 243, 247, 249, 252, 272–5, 311,
    318, 326
Institut für Demoskopie, 122, 234
International Monetary Fund (IMF), 241
Irmler, Heinrich, 286, 288, 303–4, 307
Issing, Otmar, 5
Italy, 22, 24, 316, 325

Jackson, Robert, 84
Juliusturm, 163, 166, 170

Kaiser, 38, 42, 294
Kalbitzer, Hellmut, 139
Keiser, Günter, 98
Keppler, Wilhelm, 225–6
Keynesianism, 99, 102, 164, 167, 275, 277
Kiesinger, Kurt Georg, 198, 254, 262, 265,
    277
Kissinger, Henry, 267
Kladderadatsch (publication), 64
Klasen, Karl, 102, 253–4, 256, 260, 261,
    263–4, 276, 282–3, 303, 307, 309,
    322
  appointed as president of the Hamburg
    state central bank, 259
  arrival at the Bundesbank, 254, 281
  attitude regarding central bank
    independence, 253, 261–4, 284,
    288, 292, 297, 301, 311
  attitude regarding the media, 264, 271–2,
    285, 292
  background, 254–5, 258–9, 268, 270
  Bank deutscher Länder task force on the
    Bundesbank Law, 120, 261
  departure from the Bundesbank, 265, 270
  and Helmut Schmidt, 262–3, 291, 297,
    302

Klasen, Karl (cont.)
    and Karl Schiller, 257, 262, 281–7, 290, 312
    Novellierung debate of 1973, 290, 297
    as the public face of the Bundesbank, 257–8, 267–8, 322
    speeches, 252–3, 261, 264, 275, 311
    and Viktor von der Lippe, 271–2
Kohl, Helmut, 325–7
Köhler, Erich, 108, 115
Konjunkturrat (economic council), 170, 176
Konkret (magazine), 227
Könneker, Wilhelm, 103, 145, 162, 249, 306
Korean crisis, 17, 135, 141, 164
Korean War, 135, 158
Kreisau Circle (*Kreisauer Kreis*), 81
Kristallnacht, 78

Lambsdorff, Otto Graf, 295–6, 323
Lamfalussy, Alexandre, 325–7
League of Nations, 45
Lessing Gymnasium, 229, 250, 322
Lindemann, Karl, 226
lira (currency), 316
Lübke, Heinrich, 221
Luther, Hans, 63, 65–7, 100, 130, 132, 153, 212, 295
Luxembourg, 329

Maastricht Treaty, 324, 328–30
Manchester Guardian (newspaper), 183
Margarine-Union, 79
mark (currency), 35–6, 41, 43, 49, *51*, 273
Marshall Plan, 112, 135
Mefo bills, 15, 70–1, 85, 160–1, 216, 232, 321
Merkel, Angela, 24
miracle, economic (*Wirtschaftswunder*), 16, 98, 153, 175, 198, 248, 263, 280
Möller, Alex, 293
Möller, Hans, 98, 307
monetarism, 256, 267, 270, 282, 307
Mönkemeyer, Karin, 228
Münchau, Wolfgang, 23
Münchner Lach- und Schiessgesellschaft, 193, 222, 224, 227
Munich Agreement of 1938, 74
Mürdel, Karl, 102
Muthesius, Volkmar, 92, 110–11, 127–31, 141, 147, 180, 207, 231, 304, 306
mythology, monetary, 8, 13, 15, 21, 23, 29–30, 32, 34–5, 73, 87–9, 153, 191, 227, 280, 317–18, 322, 327, 330, 332

National Geographic (magazine), 273
National Socialism, 10, 28, 31, 62–3, 67, 69, 77, 131–2, 164, 194, 210–11, 218, 225, 254, 258, 264, 268
Netherlands, the, 42, 330
Neue Zürcher Zeitung (newspaper), 253
Neuer Vorwärts (SPD outlet), 113, 139, 278
New York Times, The (newspaper), 259, 273–4
Noelle-Neumann, Elisabeth, 122
Nölting, Erik, 139
Norddeutsche Bank, 259
Norman, Montagu, 44, 47, 57, 59
North Atlantic Treaty Organization (NATO), 300
Nuremberg trials, 13, 21, 30, 34–5, 70, 75, 80, 83, 86–8, 93, 148, 180, 191, 193–5, 218, 220–1, 225–7, 318, 322

Oechsner, Fritz, 223, 228
oil crisis of 1973, 256, 275, 289, 298, 307
ordoliberalism, 100
Orientierungsrahmen'85, 301
Outright Monetary Transactions (OMT), 315–16

Paersch, Fritz, 103
Panorama (show), 221
Penne, Die (school newspaper), 229
persuasion, moral, 198, 240–1, 244, 250–1
Pferdmenges, Robert, 241
Pfleiderer, Otto, 102, 106, 156–7, 304–5, 307
Phillips curve, 275
Pickelhaube, 1, 3–4, 313–16, 331–2
Pöhl, Karl Otto, 265, 326–8, 330
Poland, 61
Portugal, 24
pound sterling (currency), 264, 281
Presse- und Informationsamt der Bundesregierung (government news office), 219
Prussia, 37
Prussian Bank, 37
public sphere, 8, 19, 25–8, 31, 34, 44, 49, 55–7, 59, 63–5, 68, 70, 72–3, 79, 85, 87–8, 94, 104, 106, 109–11, 113, 116, 126, 128, 130, 138, 148, 151–3, 157, 170, 172, 174, 181, 184, 186–7, 191, 195–9, 204, 208–9, 212, 214, 216–18, 230, 232, 239–40, 249–50, 252, 254–7, 263–5, 268, 271–2, 275, 280, 284, 286, 288, 291–3, 296–7, 303–4, 306, 311–12, 319–22
    definition, 18–19
Pünder, Hermann, 108

Quick (magazine), 212, 214–15, 284

Raeder, Erich, 88
recession of 1966-7, 208, 247–9, 251–3,
    255, 263, 277, 280, 294, 311
refugees, 113, 147
Reichsbank, 6–7, 10, 14, 25, 29, 33,
    38–9, 61, 66, 92–5, 100, 102, 270,
    318
  1922–3 hyperinflation, 6, 9, 34, 50, 87
  advisory council, 79, 215
  Allied powers demanding that the
      Reichsbank be made autonomous,
      46
  Autonomy Law of 1922, 46–7, 49, 53,
      87, 278, 331
  Bank Act of 1924, 52–3, 66, 68
  Bank Law of 1875, 37–8, 52–3
  bank legislation of 1933, 68
  bank legislation of 1937, 76
  bank legislation of 1939, 76, 91, 201
  becoming independent in May 1922,
      45
  central bank reports during the Third
      Reich praising the close relationship
      with the state, 72
  central committee (*Zentralausschuß*), 38,
      46
  co-operating with government policy
      during the hyperinflation and
      deflation, 7, 65, 67, 172
  debates during the Second Reich about
      its nationalisation, 38
  deflation, 67, 87, 132
  establishment of, 29, 36–7, 88, 307
  general assembly (*Generalversammlung*),
      38
  general council (*Generalrat*), 52–3, 61, 68
  headquarters destroyed, 33
  Kuratorium, 38, 46, 53, 122
  left-wing support for central bank
      autonomy during the Second Reich,
      38
  legacy during the post-war era, 5, 9,
      13–14, 18–19, 31, 114, 130–1, 137,
      146, 153, 156–7, 171–2, 177, 180,
      184, 190, 196, 201, 231, 255–7,
      268–70, 277, 286, 295–6, 303–4,
      306–7, 310–11, 317–18, 320–2,
      331
  Mefo bills, 70
  memorandum of January 1939, 14–15,
      21, 34, 72–3, *74*, 75–6, 83, 159,
      179–80, 191, 194–5, 211, 218, 221,
      226, 256, 268, 308, 321–2

  note circulation requirements, 39, 41, 53,
      65
  operating alongside Rentenbank and
      Gold Discount Bank, 50
  as a political actor during the Weimar
      Republic, 6, 10, 54–5, 57, 62–3, 69,
      87, 278
  publishing Hjalmar Schacht's speeches,
      56
  as a reference point during the
      Bundesbank Law debate, 9–11, 35,
      91, 122, 132, 141, 152, 154, 156–7,
      171, 175, 317
  report regarding Social Democratic
      attitudes about central bank
      independence, 62
  and Rudolf Havenstein, 49
  warning the government about
      inflationary spending, 43, 73
Reichsbanner, 258
reichsmark (currency), 20, 52–4, 57, 61, 71,
    73, 78, 80, 149, 159, 196, 215, 219,
    243, 246, 273, 306, 321
Reichsrat, 46, 54
Reichstag, 36, 41, 62, 273
Rentenbank, 50
rentenmark (currency), 50, 54
reparations, 6, 36, 41, 43, 45–8, 52–3, 55,
    59, 61, 65–7, 70, 163
Reuters (news service), 314
Revue (magazine), 212
Rhein Ruhr Club, 232
Riedel, Gerhard, 228
Roeper, Hans, 214, 310
Romania, 80
Ruhr, 48
Russia, 80

Schacht, Hjalmar, 6, 10, 19, 31, 33, 35, *58*,
    100–2, 107, 130, 153, 201, 277–8
  and Adolf Hitler, 63, 68
  allegations of misconduct during the First
      World War, 54
  appointed as 'commissary' minister for
      the economy, 69
  appointed as general commissioner for
      the war economy, 69
  arrested, 33
  arrival at the Reichsbank, 54–5
  attitude regarding central bank
      independence, 68
  attitude regarding the media, 35, 55–7,
      87, 197, 212, 217, 321
  becoming a minister without portfolio, 69
  concentration camps, 82

Schacht, Hjalmar (cont.)
  demanding the return of the 'Polish
    corridor', 61
  departure from the Reichsbank in 1939,
    34, 70, 72, 81–4, 211, 308–9
  enjoying the confidence of Adolf Hitler,
    69
  evoking the 1922–3 hyperinflation, 72
  Hamburg state senate, 115, 160
  as 'Hitler's magician', 13, 70, 211, 214,
    217, 230, 232
  international respect, 57
  and Karl Blessing, 20, 79, 196, 211–12,
    215–17, 230–2, 321
  Lex Schacht, 62
  Magic of money, The (book), 216, 232
  Mefo bills, 15, 160, 216, 321
  memoirs, 211–12, 216
  Nuremberg trials, 13, 21, 30, 34–5, 74,
    83, 86, 93, 211, 226, 318, 322
  personifying central bank independence
    during the Weimar Republic, 63, 64
  political attacks on, 62
  portrayed as abusing the Reichsbank's
    independence, 62
  portrayed as the 'master' of Karl Blessing,
    201
  portrayed as the 'master' of Wilhelm
    Vocke, 114
  as the public face of the Reichsbank,
    56–7, 64, 169, 320
  Quick magazine, 213–14
  Reichsbank directorate's resistance to his
    appointment, 54
  Reichsbank memorandum, 14, 72–5, 74,
    83–4, 179–80
  Reichsbank speeches, 55–7
  resignation in 1930, 63, 78
  return as Reichsbank president in 1933,
    68
  second inflation, 72
  shift to right-wing politics, 57, 63
  support by Gustav Stresemann, 54
  tarnished reputation in the 1960s, 19,
    197, 211–12, 214, 217, 321
  third inflation, 197, 231–3, 239
  threatening to resign as Reichsbank
    president, 71
  and Wilhelm Vocke, 123
  Young Plan, 59, 61–2
Schaefer, Carl, 90–1, 93, 99, 132
Schäffer, Fritz, 136, 166, 170, 173
  attitude regarding central bank
    independence, 11, 121–4, 127, 136,
    142, 170, 189

budget, 143, 187
Bundesbank Law, 18, 121, 123, 125,
  137–8, 144, 154, 189, 263, 294, 318,
  320
clash with Ludwig Erhard, 123, 154, 156,
  263
Juliusturm, 163, 166, 170
Konjunkturrat, 170, 173, 176
and Konrad Adenauer, 122, 125
sensitivity to bad publicity, 143
support for a decentralised central bank,
  123, 133, 154
Transition Law, 145–6, 153
and Wilhelm Vocke, 149
Scharnberg, Hugo, 138, 155–6, 185
Schäuble, Wolfgang, 24
Scheel, Walter, 283
Schiettinger, Fritz, 271
Schiller, Friedrich, 242
Schiller, Karl, 183, 248, 263, 277, 288
  cabinet resignation, 256, 281, 283–5,
    287, 290, 323
  and Karl Klasen, 255, 257, 262, 281–5,
    287, 312
Schlesinger, Helmut, 307, 330–1
Schmidt, Helmut, 27, 283, 287, 296–8,
  310, 323
  ascent to the chancellery, 298
  attitude regarding central bank
    independence, 261, 287, 290,
    297–8, 300, 302, 312
  and Karl Klasen, 262–3, 291, 302, 311
  Novellierung debate of 1973, 255, 257,
    261, 281, 288, 291–3, 296–7, 301,
    311
  party report of May 1974, 298, 312
  speech before the central bank council in
    November 1978, 298–301
Schmücker, Kurt, 248
Schniewind, Otto, 102
Schumacher, Kurt, 139
Schutzstaffel (SS), 20, 79–81, 88, 192,
  219–20, 223, 227
Second Reich, 3, 35, 37, 77, 120, 307,
  330–1
Second World War, 3–4, 8, 12–13, 88, 95,
  99, 103, 149, 193, 252, 268, 278,
  300, 309
Sentz, Max, 102
Seuffert, Walter, 279
Single European Act of 1986, 324–5
snake, 269, 281, 299
Social Democratic Party (SPD), 29, 98,
  102, 113, 115, 139–40, 153, 162,
  164, 183, 191, 198, 230, 237, 248,

251, 254–5, 257–9, 265, 276, 278, 280, 285, 293, 296–7, 300–1, 309, 323
attacks on the Bank deutscher Länder, 139, 184
central bank independence, 31, 47, 62, 130, 140, 153, 175, 183, 255–7, 264, 278–9, 295, 297–8, 301, 311, 319, 323
economics committee, 140, 155, 175, 183–4, 259
Godesberger Programme, 183
'Gürzenich affair', 175, 183–4
Sonderstelle für Geld und Kredit (Special Committee for Money and Credit), 98
Soviet Union, 150, 158
Spain, 24
Spiegel, Der (magazine), 14–15, 20, 116, 159, 169, *177*, 179, 181, 195, *199*, 201, 212, 221, 227–9, 316, 319, 321
Spiegel affair of 1962, 19
Spiegel Online, 4, 316–17
Stabilitätskultur (stability culture), 23–4, 332
Stabilitätspolitik (politics of stability), 7, 244, 253, 255, 257, 268, 270, 276, 280, 290, 303, 307, 309–11, 323, 331
Stability and Growth Law of 1967, 277, 289, 292–3, 301
stagflation, 276, 332
Stalingrad, 81
Stasi (East German Ministry for State Security), 20–1, 194, 219, 221–2, 227, 230
Strauß, Franz Josef, 19, 285
Stresemann, Gustav, 49, 54
Strong, Benjamin Jr., 57
Stuttgarter Zeitung (newspaper), 119
Süddeutsche Zeitung (newspaper), 214
supervision, banking, 23
surveys, public opinion, 29, 122, 127, 140, 234
Switzerland, 281

Tepe, Hermann, 102, 156–7
Third Reich, 12–13, 15, 20, 34, 56, 59, 69–72, 77–8, 80–3, 86, 96, 103, 157, 164, 180, 192, 194, 196, 198, 201, 210–11, 216, 218–19, 221, 224–5, 228, 230, 268, 274, 295, 306, 308, 321
Tietmeyer, Hans, 22
Time (magazine), 32, 267, 310
Titzhoff, Peter, 271

Treue, Hans, 103
Trichet, Jean-Claude, 330
Troeger, Heinrich, 209, 279
Trump, Donald, 22
Tucker, Paul, 23

Übersee Club, 167
Ulrich, Franz Heinrich, 259
unemployment, 94, 100, 149, 275
  post-war, 108, 112–13, 117, 122, 135, 153, 163, 191, 210, 234, 247, 252–3, 263, 275–6, 297, 302, 311, 323–4
  trauma, 252, 311, 318
  Weimar Republic, 6, 10, 26, 28, 63, 66–7, 71, 100, 113–14, 130, 160, 184, 252, 318
Unilever, 79–80, 225, 227
United States, 66, 96–7, 150, 190

Veit, Hermann, 175
Veit, Otto, 102, 120
Versailles Treaty, 43
Vetter, Heinz Oskar, 276
Vocke, Wilhelm, 15, 19, 35, *60*, 88, 136, 158, 164, 166, 172, 174, 186, 197, 201, 214, 216, 233, 240, 252–3, 256, 263–4, 269, 271, 304, 318, 323
  activity during the Reichsbank years, 45, 59, 116
  appealing to the German saver, 147, 167, 169
  appointed as chairman of the Bank deutscher Länder directorate, 103, 305
  arguing that Keynesian policies were reminiscent of economic policy during the Third Reich, 164
  attitude regarding social democracy, 259, 279
  attitude regarding the central bank's relationship with the government, 104
  attitude regarding the media, 57, 59, 109–10, 116–17, 131, 133–4, 143, 208
  attitude towards National Socialism, 77
  attitude towards the Allied Banking Commission, 111
  background, 44, 254–5, 268, 270, 306
  Bank deutscher Länder task force on the Bundesbank Law, 120
  control of the Bank deutscher Länder directorate, 109, 267
  criticism of government economic policy, 160, 165, 167

Vocke, Wilhelm (cont.)
  departure from the Reichsbank, 76, 79,
    85, 115, 180, 308–9
  as deputy chairman of the
    Reichsbankleitstelle, 103
  and Ernst Hülse, 102
  financial persecution of Jews in the Third
    Reich, 77
  first address before the Bank deutscher
    Länder central bank council, 105, 305
  and Fritz Schäffer, 122–4, 170
  Gesundes Geld (book), 180–1, 208
  Gürzenich affair, 179–80
  and Hans Luther, 65
  and Hjalmar Schacht, 54, 68, 115, 160,
    216
  and imported inflation, 268
  international reputation, 170
  interview with *Bild*, 179
  and Karl Blessing, 216
  Konjunkturrat, 170, 173, 176
  and Konrad Adenauer, 121, 124, 141–2,
    166, 187, 262
  Mefo bills, 15, 70–1, 85, 160, 216, 321
  memoirs, 187
  Nuremberg trials, 14, 21, 75, 82, 84–5,
    88, 195, 211, 225–6, 322
  and Otmar Emminger, 267
  political attacks on, 15, 114, 117, 278,
    321
  portrayed as 'foreign minister of the
    Reichsbank', 15, 59, 88
  portrayed as 'guardian' of the
    deutschmark, 177, 183
  portrayed by *Der Spiegel* as 'chancellor of
    the deutschmark', 14, *177*, 199,
    319–20
  portrayed by the *Financial Times* as the
    'boy wonder of the old Reichsbank',
    177
  power struggle with Karl Bernard, 104
  as the public face of the Bank deutscher
    Länder, 14, 35, 104, 114, 117, 148,
    151, 159, 161, 169, 172, 194, 199,
    278, 280, 320–1
  reaching out to Ludwig Erhard for
    support, 142
  Reichsbank memorandum, 14–15, 73–6,
    74, 115, 148, 159, 179, 181, 194–5,
    308
  and Rudolf Havenstein, 49
  signature on banknotes, 14, *51*, 180, 321
  speeches, 15, 134, 147, 149, 163, 165,
    167, 169–71, 180–1, 185, 190, 246,
    321
    support for a centralised central bank,
      106, 133, 138, 155
    third inflation, 231
    as the vice chairman of the Bank
      deutscher Länder central bank
      council, 103
    and Volkmar Muthesius, 128, 180
    and Wilhelm Grotkopp, 131
    Young Plan, 59
Vögler, Albert, 59
Volkswirt, Der (magazine), 186, 253
Von Bismarck, Otto, 36, 39
Von der Lippe, Viktor, 117, 129–31, 143,
    162, 167, 172–3, 193, 195, 203–4,
    211, 216, 219, 230, 250
  appointed as personal advisor to Wilhelm
    Vocke, 116
  assigned to direct the Bank deutscher
    Länder press department, 117
  attitude regarding the media, 127, 158,
    172, 202, 204–5, 214, 217–18, 244,
    285, 321
  background and influence, 116
  circle of friends (*Freundeskreis*), 193, 195,
    211, 222–3, 228–30
    short comprehensive summary, 195,
      224, 226, 228–9, 250, 322
  contacts with journalists, 162, 171, 173,
    207, 209, 271–2
  correspondence with Volkmar
    Muthesius, 130, 207
  departure from the Bundesbank, 271
  diaries, 251, 271–2
  enjoying the confidence of Karl Blessing,
    208
  on Helmut Schmidt's party report of May
    1974, 298
  and Karl Klasen, 253, 257, 261, 271–2,
    284–5, 291–2
  Nuremberg trials, 88
  responsibilities at the Bank deutscher
    Länder, 117
  responsibilities at the Bundesbank,
    202–3, 209, 249, 271
  third inflation, 233
Von Schelling, Friedrich Wilhelm, 120–1,
    172
Vorwärts (SPD outlet), 63, 183
Vossische Zeitung (newspaper), 56

Wall Street Journal, The (newspaper), 272,
    326
Warburg, Max, 167
Warmbold, Hermann, 66
Weidmann, Jens, 315–16, 331

Weimar Republic, 3, 5–6, 13, 27–8, 43–4, 48,
    54–6, 65, 67, 69–70, 78, 87, 108, 113,
    120, 169, 233, 252, 254, 257, 272–3,
    295, 302, 304, 306, 317, 331–2
Welt am Sonntag (newspaper), 284
Welt, Die (newspaper), 107, 118, 130, 201
Wilhelm, Karl-Friedrich, 103
Wissenschaftliches Institut der
    Gewerkschaften (Academic Institute
    of the Trade Unions), 141
Wolf, Eduard, 113, 120, 202, 267
Wolf, Markus, 219
Wolf, Martin, 315

Wrede, Victor, 98, 103–4, 106–7, 109–10,
    128–9

Young Plan, 59, 61–2

Zachau, Erich, 103, 216
Zeit, Die (newspaper), 114, 174, 212, 232,
    243, 285–6, 316
Zeitschrift für das gesamte Kreditwesen, Die
    (journal), 110, 128, 131, 147, 205,
    304
Zeitung (magazine), 195, 227–8
Zwischen Marx und Markt (book), 294–5